Empathy and Ethics

Empathy and Ethics

Edited by
Magnus Englander and Susi Ferrarello

ROWMAN & LITTLEFIELD
Lanham • Boulder • New York • London

Published by Rowman & Littlefield
An imprint of The Rowman & Littlefield Publishing Group, Inc.
4501 Forbes Boulevard, Suite 200, Lanham, Maryland 20706
www.rowman.com

86-90 Paul Street, London EC2A 4NE, United Kingdom

British Library Cataloguing in Publication Information Available

Library of Congress Cataloging-in-Publication Data

Names: Englander, Magnus, editor. | Ferrarello, Susi, editor.
Title: Empathy and ethics / edited by Magnus Englander and Susi Ferrarello.
Description: Lanham : Rowman & Littlefield, 2023. | Includes bibliographical references and index.
Identifiers: LCCN 2022035771 (print) | LCCN 2022035772 (ebook) | ISBN 9781538154106 (cloth ; alk. paper) | ISBN 9781538154113 (electronic)
Subjects: LCSH: Empathy. | Caring. | Ethics.
Classification: LCC BJ1475 .E455 2023 (print) | LCC BJ1475 (ebook) | DDC 177/.7--dc23/eng/20220906
LC record available at https://lccn.loc.gov/2022035771
LC ebook record available at https://lccn.loc.gov/2022035772

∞™ The paper used in this publication meets the minimum requirements of American National Standard for Information Sciences—Permanence of Paper for Printed Library Materials, ANSI/NISO Z39.48-1992.

Contents

Introduction

Phenomenological Reflections on Empathy and Ethics

What is the relationship between empathy and ethics? Would such a question be helpful in guiding us toward answers about the human condition and how we take on matters such as science and society? Is the problem of empathy only a problem because the question that invoked it as being a problem was posed from the perspective of naturalism and relativism? In what way does our reflection on interpersonal understanding relate to acts such as sympathy and compassion? Is our contemporary understanding of empathy a type of unique or professional achievement separating us from each other and inflating the sense of modern individualism as the fundamental ground for our being with others? In this book, we have invited scholars from phenomenological philosophy and the human sciences to elucidate the relationship between empathy and ethics. As such, we were hoping to challenge the naiveté inherent in how such phenomena are currently being applied in philosophy, in the sciences, and in professional life.

Today we see professionals and researchers, mostly in psychology and the cognitive neurosciences, refer to empathy as mirror neurons, mentalization, simulation, theory of mind, and so on. All such attempts are examples of the naturalization of empathy, that is, attempts to explain empathy within the technologization of naturalism, rather than describe it as a phenomenon. The everyday use of the term is less scientific but portrays a conflation among empathy, sympathy, and compassion; suggesting that understanding and some type of caring for the other becomes one and the same act. In its most naïve, everyday sense, sympathy and compassion even becomes a prerequisite for interpersonal understanding. As such, the foundation of empathy as the perception of the meaning of lived bodily expression has now been mixed up with technology, morality, and even politics. Phenomenology could help us to sort these matters out, that is, by returning to the original meaning of empathy as a phenomenon and then see how it relates to ethics. The phenomenology of empathy might not provide us with the right kind of morals, but in a reflection of empathy, we could illuminate our reciprocal relation (or reversibility) with others, even if such a relation is purely imaginary. Perhaps then we are not just faced with the other as other but also faced with the other as the meaning of the other(s). In many ways, such a starting point will not automatically make us into a sympathetic or compassionate person; rather, it becomes a prerequisite for the possibility of understanding the relation between empathy and ethics.

Phenomenological ethics is a relatively new approach to ethics, in which emphasis is put on the description of the ethical phenomenon. Its origin can be traced back to Brentano's 1889 work, "The Origin of the Knowledge of Right and Wrong," however, it is with the development of Husserl's phenomenological ethics from 1908, 1914, and 1922 that its themes started to inspire a long line of thinkers, whose influence reached the fields of philosophy, psychology, theology, gender studies, bioethics, and political science. On the one hand, the main themes of phenomenological ethics focus on the epistemological understanding of the highest practical good and its ethical demand, as we see in the work of Husserl, Reiner, Pfänder, Sartre, Løgstrup, and Levinas. On the other hand, phenomenological ethicists are concerned with the description of what we do when we behave in a moral way, and highlighted by Scheler, Hildebrand, Hartmann, Beauvoir, and again by Levinas. In this book there is a focus on empathy as a *trait d'union* among these different themes to probe the question: In what way does empathy elucidate our sociality and moral stance?

The collection of essays will be loosely organized into three thematic sections: the main protagonists on the topic, the application of the results in psychology and health care, and further exploration of the topic in the arts. Each section will put an emphasis on one of the specific aspects of the interconnection between ethics and empathy.

In chapter 1, Drummond first shows us how the meaning of the English term *empathy* as referring to the identifying with, entering into, having an imaginative capacity to, and sharing the same feeling as the other is, in its literary sense of a translation of the term, similar to the German words *Einfühlung* and *Nachfühlen*. However, Drummond points out that the early phenomenologists did not refer to empathy as such. Instead, empathy is a recognition of the other as a minded being and has no practical significance. One could then say that empathy is a cognitive act and an abstraction, meaning that it has nothing to do with the practicalities of everyday life as it involves others. Nevertheless, to encounter others as minded beings also involves having affective responses to them. In this way, empathy becomes a prerequisite for ethics and serves to ground our fundamental moral emotions of sympathy and respect.

In chapter 2, Marín-Ávila takes on the question: How is it possible to live an ethical life in light of our dependency and vulnerability on others? This chapter provides us with an exploration into the context and intersection of violence, emotivity, vulnerability, and empathy. To guide such an inquiry, Marín-Ávila explores the relationship between trust and violence. Trust and being trusted is here seen as something that entails beliefs and feelings and constitutes as the prerequisite of taking part in any social relationships. Ethical reflection can help us to disclose the ethical issues relating to our own trust in others as well in their trust in us. In so doing, we can bring a sense of clarity to beliefs, values, and volitions that are present within our interpersonal relationships. Ethical reflection can thus shed some light on how we can make sense of our vulnerability and its relation to trust. Such a reflection should lead to a radical examination of problems related to empathy and trust.

In chapter 3, Derksen examines the paradox of fiction. In particular, he refers to the use that has been made of this paradox to study how emotions can relate to reality over an extended period of time. The paradox helps elucidating how empathy works in relation to others and how it can produce harm, especially because of other's conflicting perceptions.

In chapter 4, Wehrle presents Beauvoir's philosophy as a responsive ethics, in which freedom and vulnerability, mind and body, we and others, are necessarily intertwined. Wehrle argues that two insights are crucial for such an approach: existence is always embodied and situated (concretizing and complementing Husserl and Merleau-Ponty) and freedom can never be absolute but must be realized within concrete situations and in relation with others (arguing against Sartre).

In chapter 5, Moran takes a closer look into the similarities among Husserl's, Stein's, and Scheler's view of the concept of the person and its relation to ethics. Moran points to the shared view of these classical phenomenologists in understanding ethics as that which referred to a whole person, meaning that person refers to dimensions such as the affective, the rational, to volition, to the intellect, as well as the heart. In the context of the communal and historical lifeworld, persons are capable of a sense of responsible interaction, specifically pointing to their unique possibility of free agency and the capacity to recognize norms.

In chapter 6, Lobo is concerned with the relation between the reciprocal recognition as an ethical act (with its axiological and practical dimensions) and empathy as a transcendental (i.e., constitutive) performance. By recalling the analyses of the intentional articulations at the basis of this ethical phenomenon, Lobo comes back on Husserl's original approach of moral conscience, in its link with practical and axiological reason. From this perspective, the critical discussions of Hume and Kant are particularly enlightening and help us to understand what the main lines and achievements of Husserl's critique of practical and axiological reason are.

In chapter 7, Montes brings us to the convergence between Hildebrand's and Husserl's method of phenomenology, despite their known divergences of realism versus idealism. Montes shows us that Hildebrand's realist phenomenology leads to a proposal of reverence (*die Ehrfurcht*) as a fundamental moral attitude (*sittliche Grundhaltung*). which contains cognitive, volitional, and affective components. Montes argues that Hildebrand's sense of reverence can be seen as similar to Husserl's conception of phenomenology as embodying an ethical life.

In chapter 8, Brencio uses Heidegger's notion of intersubjectivity to clarify his critiques toward the concept of empathy. In doing so, the author reconstructs the hermeneutical shift introduced by Heidegger into phenomenology to clarify the understanding of Dasein in terms of facticity, subjectivity, and intersubjectivity. The author ultimately points out how Heidegger's account of intersubjectivity may contribute to enrich the dialogue between phenomenology and health care, a dialogue conceived in terms of a moral enterprise.

In chapter 9, Nörenberg, working from the insights by Løgstrup and Levinas, provides us with a phenomenological analysis of the relevant sense of the "excess phenomenon," in which he also outlines the ethical significance of this phenomenon. He discloses the most conspicuous traits of the excess phenomenon as constituted by the subjective sense of the irreducibility of a person to a set of categories and predictability of their reactions. In the course of his analysis, Nörenberg also provides an account of the bodily dimensions of the phenomenon. He points out that the excess phenomenon cannot ground ethical demands, although it can disclose the necessary condition to hold somebody responsible, simply because the other is recognized as a human being.

In chapter 10, Vincini and Staiti turn their attention to Tomasello's 2016 book, *A Natural History of Human Morality*, in which references appear to historical figures such as Rousseau, Hume, and Kant, as well as contemporary moral thinkers such as Darwall and Korsgaard. The authors provide an account of how Tomasello assigns an essential role to the cognitive foundations of morality (i.e., the constitution of the first-person-plural as a plural agent). Tomasello is aware of the complexity of the problem of clarifying the nature of the first-person plural and leaves it open for further philosophical debate. This chapter elucidates Husserl's contribution to this debate. They argue that Husserl's clarification of the "we" relies on a general theory concerning both individual and communal experiences. Like other early phenomenologists, Husserl's position is radically anti-Cartesian because it challenges the widespread assumption that a mental state can be had by only one individual subject.

In chapter 11, in the spirit of Frankfurt's seminal essay "the importance of what we care about," de Warren provides a Husserlian frame of analysis. He explores how Frankfurt's threefold distinction among knowing, ethical conduct, and caring is equally central to Husserl's phenomenology of reason. Here, de Warren points us to Husserl's phenomenological ethics of values and vocation in his Freiburg manuscripts from the 1920s and 1930s. He shows us how a phenomenological ethics of care and commitment stands under something that is worth valuing; yet, how this dimension of value has been largely ignored in much of the literature in "care ethics." However, such a grounding proves essential and defines phenomenological ethical thought. An ethics of care should provide a robust account of values, their ordering, mode of experiential givenness, and forms of uptake in our lives.

In chapter 12, Englander and Ferrarello seek to disclose how empathy and ethics have been constructed to idealized forms through the process of naturalization and relativization in science and professional practice. The chapter begins with a historical investigation of how the natural attitude continues into Galileo's technologization of nature. Following the basic structure of the natural attitude, we can also see how it shapes our interpretation of empathy. The authors disclose a paradox that seems to be unacceptable by the sciences related to modern psychology. This has resulted in the scientific community to explain empathy by sophisticated models (e.g., simulation, mirror neurons, etc.), in which the trace of the natural attitude continues, such as can be seen in the naturalization of empathy in the contemporary cognitive neurosciences. This idealization of empathy is then carried over from the sciences to professional practice resulting in a technological approach toward empathy. As a contrast, Englander and Ferrarello argue for a return to our fundamental relation to others as interpersonal understanding and a reflection of empathy that would open for the development of professional ethics as a reflective human activity, instead of a set of guidelines and principles that are, more often than not, sophisticated, bureaucratic processes thought to prevent unethical action and issues of liability. Only reflection of our being with others will lead us to *self-responsibility*.

In chapter 13, Taipale makes an inquiry into interpersonal understanding from the point of view of Daniel Stern's use of the term, "moments of meeting" (i.e., an experience by two individuals as "a shared private world.") Even though Stern's main interest was how this term applied to psychotherapy, Taipale sees its meaning in a nonclinical context. As such, Taipale's chapter explores how moments of meeting occur in everyday life, as in emotional sharing. Taipale discloses the phenomenon of moments of meeting as characterized by an asymmetric structure and that further complicates our understanding of the self-other relation.

In chapter 14, Boublil sketches the essentials of a response ethics of vulnerability based on the analysis of the notion of the heart (*Gemüt*) as it is meant in the anthropology of Kant, Husserl, and Stein. This response ethics, the author explains, is grounded in a conception of empathy based on the heart's disposition rather than on the sole cognitive or affective level of experience This chapter offers a phenomenological dynamic description of empathy that takes into consideration the way in which affectivity and vulnerability intersects with each other. Drawing also from contemporary phenomenological accounts of embodied cognition (Fuchs 2018) and affective intentionality (Steinbock 2021), the author emphasizes the interconnection between the affective disposition implied in empathy and the dynamics of resonance and resilience in the constitution of an ethical form of responsibility and mutual recognition.

In chapter 15, Camassa provides a "third path" for empathy that can transcend the unilateral portrayals of empathy made respectively by anti-empathists and pro-empathists. Camassa's claim is that empathy cannot constitute the cornerstone of morality; however, it plays a necessary role for it. To do so, he briefly sketches his conception of the term *empathy* and further examines how empathy can play an irreplaceable role for moral perception and, as such, is also closely related to moral judgment. Camassa concludes with the claim that empathy is an integral part of the fundamental characteristics of the virtuous person.

In chapter 16, Churchill suggests how we can transcend solipsism and move toward ethical and moral engagement. He explores the relation among embodiment, empathy, mutuality, and communality. In seeing the other's face, it calls us to action. Churchill shows us how such a principle holds true in all dimensions of otherness, such as "gender, race, species, even kingdom." Churchill illustrates his points by drawing from his experience within phenomenological ethology and phenomenological psychology.

In chapter 17, Vendrell Ferran explores the relationship between fictional characters and empathy. A fictional empathy can be valuable because it can aid empathizers in gaining insight into values. Specifically, it can help the empathizer to become acquainted with the values of others even if these values are distinctly different from one's own. Vendrell Ferran shows us how it is possible through fictional empathy to co-experience the other's values. Also included is a discussion about the epistemic challenges and in what situations fictional empathy could be seen as morally valuable.

In chapter 18, Hansen and Roald restore the empathy debate in the context of aesthetics, as it originated in Theodor Lipps's work. The authors make an investigation in how empathy allows for works of art to be experienced as revelatory of personal and moral value. Working from Lipps's description of "feeling of depth," the authors show how the feeling of depth is depicted by a "saturation of mood" and a "sense of 'living out.'" The authors discover that a feeling of depth is a relational type of feeling, which is enacted and felt by the person experiencing the work of art. The experience is characterized by "moments of evaluation and resonance' which 'unfolds through a dynamic fluctuation between alteration and self-identity." The conclusion reached is that aesthetic empathy entails an "epistemic modification," in which the work of art reveals a value specific to the aesthetic experience. As such there is an "empathic constitution of value" as in becoming of the person as an ethical person.

In chapter 19, Hansen, Høffding, and Krueger explore the meaning of empathy and ethics in music. After presenting a short overview of the use of empathy in the nineteenth century, they focus on two cases to show how music is conducive to open a space for empathic connectedness and introduce new experimental forms of social understanding and affective sharing. In both cases it becomes apparent how music is a means to share nonverbal communications and empathic understanding. Hence, they point out how the empathic spaces opened by music solicit the integration of both low-level affective and bodily resonance mechanisms as well as high-level acts of meta-reflection, imagination, and planning that contribute to different forms of empathic understanding.

In chapter 20, Schwarz raises questions concerning each other's understanding within the concrete plurality of subjects and the limits of our moral concern. The author challenges philosophical positions in relation to the ethical relevance of empathy, especially when interpreted through individualistic lenses. Her investigation starts from the analysis of the lived experience of subjects that are into each other's lives to develop a realistic understanding of empathy that is capable of explaining individuals as they live in complex interconnected situations. In particular, the author will sample a lived experience from policing and the other from nursing. The cases are discussed in light of de Beauvoir's idea of engagement and Arendt's concept of plurality. Ultimately, a notion of empathy will emerge from out of an ethics of engagement.

In chapter 21, Agostinelli explores the online community in our digital world and how it relates to empathy and ethics. Agostinelli guides us to the world of online gaming, a particular aspect of this digital world, and one that has become a giant in its own right. With its increasing popularity, Agostinelli points to the importance of understanding both empathy and ethics within this context of interaction as well as an attempt at explaining empathy within this online context. The chapter focuses on how to recognize the other's lived experience while playing online games and how an emphasis on empathy can help in advancing a viable work ethic for this particular community.

In chapter 22, Zahavi begins by discussing some contemporary critics of empathy. He then points to the ambiguity of the term and suggests that a clarification regarding its possible moral significance will require a closer look at how the term was originally used at the beginning of the twentieth century. Zahavi contrasts Lipps's proposal that empathy is matter of imitation and projection with a view defended by Husserl, Stein, and Scheler, according to whom, empathy is a form of perceptually based understanding of the other. The phenomenologists consequently defended a different view of empathy than the contemporary proposals that often take empathy to be either a matter of imaginative perspective taking or affective sharing. Zahavi ends the chapter by suggesting that although empathy is not sufficient for morality, it still remains relevant.

Let us return to the question opening this introduction: What is the relationship between empathy and ethics? The *and* in between the terms as marking the title of this collection of essays is far from coincidental. In fact, the *and* constitutes the essence of the relation between empathy and ethics. What this means for the human condition is a constant reminder: We can never assume that empathy and ethics go hand in hand without the effort of reflection.

Magnus Englander, Malmö University
Susi Ferrarello, California State University, East Bay
October 2021

Chapter 1

Why Empathy Means Nothing—and Everything—for Ethics

John J. Drummond

ABSTRACT

In folk psychology and the psychological literature, the English term *empathy* generally refers to the activity of or capacity for imaginatively understanding, identifying with, vicariously experiencing, or sharing the feelings of another from the other's perspective. The German terms *Einfühlung* and *Nachfühlen* used by the early phenomenologists similarly evoke the sense of entering into and vicariously sharing the same feeling as another. But this is not what the early phenomenologists mean by these terms. For them empathy is the cognitive recognition of another conscious being. It has in itself neither affective nor practical significance and, hence, is by itself insufficient to account for either our evaluations of things and situations in our emotional life or our choices regarding action. This is the sense in which empathy means nothing for ethics. Empathy in this sense, however, is, like all purely cognitive experiences, an abstraction from our everyday, ordinary, and original encounter of others as friends or foes, acquaintances or strangers, coworkers, partners, fellow citizens. These experiences are varied, complex, and multidimensional and do involve affective and practical significance. But they are what they are—affectively and practically significant encounters of other persons—only insofar as they empathically recognize others as persons. Empathy is an essential aspect—the base—of all interpersonal experience, including, and especially, sympathy and respect, which I take to be fundamental moral emotions, and which are fuller and richer levels of empathic recognition. This is the sense in which empathy means everything for ethics.

Keywords: empathy, respect, sympathy, compassion

In folk psychology and the psychological literature, the English term *empathy* generally refers to the activity of or capacity for imaginatively understanding, identifying with, vicariously experiencing, or sharing the feelings of another from the other's perspective. The German terms used by the early phenomenologists, *Einfühlung* (by, for example, Husserl [1970, 1973a, 1973b, 1973c, 1989] and Stein [1989]) and *Nachfühlen* (by Scheler [1973]) similarly evoke the sense of entering into and vicariously sharing the same feeling as another. But this is not what the early phenomenologists mean by these terms. For them empathy is the cognitive recognition of another conscious being. In itself it has neither affective nor practical significance and, hence, is of no significance for ethics. However, it is also the basis for the moral emotions of sympathy and respect and, therefore, has the utmost significance for ethics. This chapter will examine empathy, sympathy, and respect to disclose their importance for ethics.

NOTHING

Two long quotations from Husserl's characterization of what he calls "the natural attitude" provide the framework for my discussion:

> Every moment in waking consciousness, . . . I find myself in relation to the one and the same world, though it is constantly changing with respect to its make-up, its content. It is continuously "on hand" for me, and I am myself a member of it. This world is not thereby for me as a mere *world of things* [*Sachenwelt*]; instead, *with the same immediacy* [emphasis added], it is there *as a world of values, a world of goods, a practical world. Without further ado* [emphasis added], I find the things before me outfitted with the make-ups of things but just as much with valuable characteristics; I find them to be beautiful and ugly, pleasing and displeasing, agreeable and disagreeable, and the like. Things stand there immediately as objects of use, the "table" with its "books," the drinking glass," the "vase," the "piano," and so forth. These valuable characteristics and practical characteristics also belong *constitutively to the objects "on hand" as such*, whether or not I turn to those characteristics and to the objects in general. *The same holds naturally just as much for human beings and animals in my surroundings as for "mere things"* [emphasis added]. They are my "friends" or "foes," my "servants" or my "superior," a "stranger" or a "relative." (Husserl, 2014, pp. 49–50, translation modified)

> Everything that holds for me holds also . . . for all other human beings whom I find on hand in my environment. Encountering [*erfahrend*] them as human beings, I understand them and *take them as ego-subjects (just as I am one myself)* [emphasis added] and as related to their natural environment. But I do this in such a way that I construe their environment and my environment as *one and the same world, of which each of us becomes conscious merely in different ways* [emphasis added]. Each has his place from where he sees the things on hand, and, hence, things appear differently to each of us. The current fields of perception, of memory, and so forth are also different for each of us, apart from the fact that even matters of intersubjective and common consciousness enter into [each] consciousness in diverse ways, with diverse manners of construing them, diverse degrees of clarity, and so forth. In the course of all this, we make ourselves understood to our fellow human beings and commonly posit an objective, spatio-temporal actuality as *our environment, existing for all, to which we ourselves nonetheless belong*. (Husserl, 2014, p. 51, translation modified)

I have chosen these quotations (and I could have chosen many others) to counter the claim that Husserl thinks mere perception is the manner in which we first encounter things in the world in our everyday, straightforward experience of the world and that other experiences are built upon the mere perception to grasp the axiological and practical significance of what I perceive. The emphases added to the quotations are crucial to making this case. In the first place, Husserl insists that our original experience is not of a "mere world of things"; it is instead a "world of values," of "goods"—a practical world. Mere perception, Husserl tells us elsewhere, is an "abstraction";[1] it is an experiential possibility—we find it operative, for example, in the pure physical sciences with their abstraction from questions of value and praxis—but it is not the original experience of things. It is "with the same immediacy" and "without further ado" that I encounter the thing's valuable and practical features, which are objective features of the thing belonging "constitutively to the objects 'on hand,'" whether or not I attend to these features.

The upshot is that instead of thinking of the grasp of valuable and practical features as superimposed on the perception of the object's physical properties, we should think of the mere perception of these physical properties as a peeling away of the object's originally experienced axiological and practical features. There are distinguishable layers within the sense of the object—cognitive, axiological, and practical—that have a logical structure (see Drummond, 2013). So, for example, my choice, on seeing a tornado, to go immediately to a protected area in the house presupposes the axiological sense that the tornado is dangerous, which in turn presupposes the cognitive sense that the tornado is, say, wide, on the ground, and moving toward my location. Similarly, when I encounter "'friends' or 'foes,' my 'servants' or my 'superior,' a 'stranger' or a 'relative,'" I can strip away the evaluative and practical senses involved in these encounters and arrive at the "mere perception" of the "human beings and animals in my surroundings." This "perception" of other nonhuman and human animals is what Husserl calls "empathy."

Husserl indicates some of the special features of the empathic recognition of human beings in the second quotation. We grasp other humans as "ego-subjects" like me and as related to their natural environment such that I recognize that my environment and their environments make up "one and the same world." Although we see the world from different perspectives, in different aspects, and against the background of differing traditions, we recognize one another as subjects and posit a common shared world "existing for all, to which we ourselves nonetheless belong." I do not intend to explicate Husserl's specific sense of empathy, although I will use it as a basis for my discussion. The view of empathy I shall sketch also relies on the work of others beyond Husserl.[2]

Empathy, then, is the basic, face-to-face perceptual recognition of the bodily states, changes, and activities of another nonhuman or human animal and the accompanying apperceptive recognition of these bodily states, changes, and activities as expressive of another center of conscious experience. I might recognize someone's approach to a Seurat painting as an effort to gain a better sense of his pointillist technique; I might recognize physiological changes, physiognomic configurations, gestures, or movements as expressive of emotions or general moods (cf. Stein, 1989, p. 50); I might recognize someone's raising a hand as a request to ask a question; or I might hear acoustic bursts emitted from another's mouth as words expressing a belief or issuing a warning. I experience these bodily states, changes, and activities as expressive of a conscious agency controlling the body I perceptually encounter. I do not see mere changes of facial musculature; I see a smile expressing (depending on context) the agent's pleasure, joy, or amusement.

Because the concern in this chapter is the relation of empathy to ethics, I shall limit my discussion to the empathic experience of human animals. What distinguishes the empathic experience of human animals from that of nonhuman animals is that we encounter human animals as both rational and reflective agents. Such agents can (1) articulate in thought the ends they pursue—ends that are not limited to realizing the natural ends entailed by the constitutive features that make humans human—as well as the choices they make, (2) express their judgments regarding these ends and choices in both words and actions, and (3) most important, reflect on the choiceworthiness of the ends they pursue, the choices they make in the pursuit of those ends, and the practices and institutions they, along with others, establish in pursuing those ends.

The empathic perception of another human animal is, then, the perceptual recognition of an embodied being who is a practical, social, historical, and reflection-capable animal—in a word, a person. Central to the possibility of empathic perception is the unity of and interplay between interiority and exteriority in self-experience (Husserl, 1959, p. 62; 1973c, p. 457; Zahavi, 2014, p. 137). The sense of myself as an interiority is rooted in the proprioception of my body in somaesthetic and kinaesthetic sensations (Husserl, 1973c, p. 491). My body, however, is also available (at least in part) for exteroception; I am exteroceptively aware of my bodily activity as visually and tactually perceptible movements occurring in the world and as expressing my mental states and experiences. I encounter [*erfahre*] the bodily states, changes, and activities of another body as similar to those I proprioceptively and exteroceptively experience [*erlebe*] in the course of my own experience. In recognizing this similarity, I take the other's bodily states, changes, and activities to be the externalization and expression of another interiority. In brief, the other I encounter is a transcendent center of expressed conscious experience that is grasped as irreducibly different from me as far as the other's conscious experiences, expressed in her movements and actions, cannot be experienced in the way I experience my own motility, agency, and experiences. My second- and third-person encounters of others differ essentially from my first-personal awareness of my own experiences. Empathy, in short, involves both the similarity of self and other as well as their irreducible difference.

The empathic experience of the other is not an inference from the other's perceived body to the other as a center of conscious experience. I apperceive this center (Husserl, 1970, p. 108). I experience the other person in (not through) the perceptual presentation of the other's bodily changes and activities. Nor do I "feel myself into" the experience of the other or vicariously share her experience or stand in her shoes. I do not, for example, need to experience anger to recognize another person as angry (Zahavi, 2014, p. 113); I encounter the other's anger as expressed in her facial configurations, her bodily motions, the volume of her voice, and so on. Despite the asymmetry between experiencing my own body and the other person's body, and despite the irreducible difference between myself and the other person, the recognition of bodily states, motility, and actions as expressive of a conscious center of experience underlies the similarity central to empathic experience (Walsh, 2014, pp. 221–25).

Empathic recognition, then, grasps a special kind of object, one that is also a subject, a "subject-object," as Husserl calls it (1973c, p. 457)—an object who, like me, is a subject. Because the fundamental element in my self-awareness is the sense of myself not as an object but as an experiencing subject expressing itself in words and actions, my fundamental sense of the other subject-object is of another experiencing subject. I encounter this other subject as a co-subject sharing a world with me insofar as she is engaged with the objects with which I am engaged. Moreover, in recognizing the other, I recognize that the other person's experience includes her empathic experience of me as a subject-object in the world. She is an object in the world I intend, and I become an object in the world that she intends. To put the matter another way, when I experience another person, I experience her as a subject experiencing worldly objects, including myself as sharing a world with her (Husserl, 1973a, p. 427). Empathy is a reciprocated, mutual experience.

In this way, empathy both enriches my self-understanding as a being in the world with others (Zahavi, 2019) and establishes a community of persons capable of achieving a shared understanding of the world. This communalization is essential to objective knowledge (Husserl, 1970, p. 120; Mertens, 2000, pp. 10–14) and to the development of a set of practices and institutions that allows the community to realize shared goals. In short, empathic recognitions of other persons and the intersubjective relations grounded therein involve simultaneous identification (as persons), communalization (of persons), and, at the same time, irreducible differentiation, otherness, and individuation (as individuals) (see Drummond, 2002, 2006). The other person, although similar to me in some ways, is a unique individual.

Finally, this account of empathy in its basic form as the "perceptual" recognition of other persons is an abstraction. It is concerned to account for our experience of other subjects from, as it were, the ground up rather than to account for our everyday encounters of other persons in our joint dealings with one another and the surrounding world. Our straightforward, everyday, and original experiences of other persons are more complex and encompass affective and practical moments. Those everyday encounters include experiences such as the following: Janet sees someone she does not recognize across the room; Steve sees Walter approaching; Joe loves Ellen but, experiencing jealousy, sees Matt as a rival and fears losing Ellen's affection; Martha forms a business partnership with Janice; Beatrice joins a book group; Donald understands that Vladimir is a friend, but John sees a foe in Vladimir; and so forth. Nevertheless, the more abstract discussions are instructive because they disclose the fundamental structure universally present in the concrete experiences of other persons. This structure is similarity-in-irreducible-difference. It underlies all interpersonal encounters, whether they be friendship, a business partnership, membership (in, say, a union or professional organization), citizenship, and so on.

Empathy so understood is an experience that has no moral content. This is why it means nothing for ethics. By itself, it is insufficient to account either for our evaluations of things and situations in our emotional life or for our choices regarding moral action. Nevertheless, because empathy is essential to all interpersonal experience, it opens up the logical space in which we can situate our discussions of ethics and morality. It is the foundation on which our everyday, ordinary, and original encounters of others as friends or foes, acquaintances or strangers, coworkers, partners, fellow citizens are built. These experiences are varied, complex, and multidimensional and involve affective and practical significance. But they are what they are—affectively and practically significant encounters of other persons—only insofar as they empathically recognize others as persons. Empathy creates the space in which we locate the ethical and moral.

EVERYTHING

I turn now to a discussion of two affective complements to empathy, namely, respect and sympathy (along with compassion, a subspecies of sympathy).[3] I take these to be emotions that are fuller and richer levels of empathic recognition and that are fundamental to moral experience. This is the sense in which empathy means everything for ethics.

Respect

We do not—even in the encounter of the stranger—originally encounter persons merely as practical, social, historical, and reflection-capable animals. That said, however, these general, nonaxiological features reveal the crucial difference between nonhuman and human animals: Humans can reflect on their beliefs, attitudes, actions, and the ends at which they aim. We recognize nonhuman animals as perceiving things, pursuing goods, and acting in ways that realize those goods. They exhibit practical rationality, and empathy extends to the recognition of these animals as conscious, rational agents. Their ends, however, are rooted in their constitutively relevant animality. Persons, however, differ in the way they relate to truth. Higher nonhuman animals enact a nonlinguistic distinction between "truth" and "falsity" similar to the prelinguistic distinction humans make when, in a continuing perceptual experience, they correct their sense of an object. Nonhuman animals, however, do not have the capacity to fix their original or adjusted beliefs conceptually in a manner that gives rise to language and critical reflection. Persons, by contrast, having language and the capacity to reflect, are related to truth in an additional way. They are *concerned* with the truth, with the difference between the true and the false, the good and the apparent good, and the right and the wrong (MacIntyre, 1999, p. 37). The reflection-capable agent acts from reflectively chosen ends explicitly recognized as (apparently) choiceworthy ends.

The concern with the "truthfulness" of our cognitive, affective, and volitional experiences and judgments marks the teleological and eudaimonistic moment of the human as a rational agent. The *telos* of reason, and by extension of the person who experiences the world, is (1) to apprehend truthfully things and states of affairs, (2) to have appropriate affective and evaluative attitudes toward those things and states of affairs, that is, to value them correctly, and (3) to act rightly in response to and on the basis of our truthful cognitions and attitudes. When we do this "insightfully," that is, when we "decide" for ourselves in the light of evidence what is true, good, and right, we take responsibility for and ownership of our beliefs, attitudes, and actions. We are self-responsible persons, responsible for who we are. The end of a human person, in brief, is to be a self-responsible, truthful agent who rightly pursues insightfully grasped goods (Drummond, 2010).

Self-responsibility, then, is a second-order good superveniently realized in the insightfully justified, active pursuit of the first-order goods that are the targets of our everyday desires. Self-responsibility requires the correct grasp of the facts of our situation and its possibilities, the goods (for the agent and others) we seek to realize in that situation, and the actions to be undertaken to realize them. If, in other words, we grasp these things correctly and insightfully, then we also realize indirectly and superveniently the formal, second-order good of self-responsibility.

As mentioned, we do not—even in encountering strangers—originally encounter persons merely as the objects of a pure empathic recognition of humans as practical, social, historical, and reflection-capable animals. Instead, we originally encounter persons with particular characteristics and acting in particular ways. What is empathically encountered in the first instance is, in other words, the other's behaviors and actions as expressing her beliefs and attitudes about the (apparent) good and her beliefs and choices about the actions conducive to that good. When in encountering another person whose actions reveal a firm and habitual commitment to overarching first-order goods that give meaning to her life and order it to the greatest extent possible as a morally correct and coherent whole, our affective response is appraisal respect for the self-responsible rational agency intimated in that person's actions.[4] The valuation of another as appraisal respectable is rooted in the empathy-derived sense of the other as a radically transcendent subject, a subject who is irreducibly other and who is in this case responsible for her attitudes, choices, and actions. The empathic sense of the other as an agent, in other words, underlies and grounds appraisal respect for meritorious, self-responsible persons who pursue insightfully justified goods.

Recognition respect, by contrast, is more formal than appraisal respect, but is nevertheless grounded in particular experiences of appraisal respect. Encountering multiple self-responsible moral agents who elicit appraisal respect from us, we grasp that the common ground of our respect for them is that their lives realize insightfully chosen goods to the greatest degree possible given the circumstances in which their lives are lived. At the same time, however, we recognize the impossibility of anyone's meriting appraisal respect apart from the fact that their meritorious lives presuppose the rational, emotional, and volitional capacities whose exercise realizes those lives. The possession of these rational capacities is grasped both as a necessary condition for and conducive to the self-responsible life. The possession of these capacities constitutes the dignity of rational agents and makes them worthy of respect. Our empathic experience of a person having these capacities summons and demands the affective response that is recognition respect. Recognition respect grasps beings possessing these capacities, whether or not they are well exercised, as having a certain dignity just insofar as they are capable of self-responsible, truthful lives. Dignity, in Anthony Kenny's terms, is the "formal object" of recognition respect (Kenny, 1963, p. 132; see also Kriegel, 2017, p. 124). Given that we cannot recognize the capacities as necessary for and conducive to self-responsibility apart from experiencing their exercise in individual meritorious lives, appraisal respect is *phenomenologically* prior to recognition respect. However, recognition respect—as directed to the necessary conditions for the possibility of self-responsible lives—is *morally* prior to appraisal respect.

I have claimed that the intersubjectivity disclosed in and by empathy involves similarity and communalization in irreducible difference. The apprehension of the other as a conscious, free, responsible—and potentially self-responsible—rational agent grounds both recognition respect and appraisal respect. The two forms of respect presuppose and are affective complements of empathy just insofar as they apprehend the irreducible differences among subject-objects empathically perceived as agents having dignity and the freedom to decide matters for themselves. The two forms of respect, however, are not reducible to one another. Appraisal respect apprehends the other as a self-responsible center of experiences that are beyond my direct grasp, as a person who takes responsibility for and ownership of her beliefs, attitudes, and actions. Recognition respect, by contrast, apprehends the dignity of the other center of conscious experiences, as a person who is—insightfully or not—responsible for herself, but only potentially, reflectively self-responsible. There can be no appraisal respect without recognition respect, but there can be recognition respect without appraisal respect.

Sympathy

Whereas respect is the affective response to the empathic grasp of the other as irreducibly different, sympathy is the affective response to the similarity and communalization of empathically perceived subject-objects who share a world. When empathically experiencing another as grief-stricken, I am aware not only of the other's grieving but also of the intentional object of the grieving, say, a loss, such as the death of a spouse, and my engagement with the grieving person is a shared attending to the loss. Sympathy, by contrast, extends beyond the mere empathic recognition of the grieving and the loss; I undergo an affective response to that recognition. I experience sympathy for the grieving person out of a concern for her well-being. I need not grieve the other's loss to experience a sympathetic sorrow for the person suffering the loss. I do not, for example, grieve the death of a colleague's spouse when I do not know the spouse. I do, however, feel a sympathetic sorrow for my colleague who is grieving this loss. Sympathy complements empathy insofar as it directs its attention to the empathically grasped grieving subject as someone about whose well-being I care for her sake.

Even while grounding itself in empathy, sympathy differs from empathy insofar as it reveals a care, absent from empathy on its own, for the well-being of the other subject for the other's sake (Darwall, 1998, p. 261; Husserl, 2004, p. 194; Scheler, 1954, p. 8; Zahavi, 2008, p. 516). Sympathy involves an addition to empathy, and the addition is the affective response to the person whose experience—in this case, the experience of grief—is empathically grasped. While we often think of sympathy as coming into play in cases where the other's well-being has been threatened or harmed, we should not collapse it into pity, commiseration, or compassion. I can also sympathize with people experiencing positive emotions when their well-being has been advanced. Empathically perceiving another's joy, I sympathetically respond to that joy. I can savor, relish, or rejoice in it (Scheler, 1954, p. 42; Smith, 1976, p. 10; but cf. Darwall, 1998, 275). A father watching his daughter graduate from college will be independently joyful. But he will also, upon empathically seeing the joy in his daughter's face, rejoice in his daughter's joy. The intentional object of the father's joy is his daughter's graduating; the intentional object of his rejoicing is his daughter as joyful in having graduated.

In this example, both father and daughter experience joy (or rejoicing), but it is not a necessary feature of sympathy that the sympathizer experience the same emotion-type. Nor is the father's rejoicing an instance of emotional contagion. Emotional contagion occurs, for example, when I enter a room in which everyone is boisterously laughing. I "catch" the emotion. My amusement, despite the fact that it is the same emotion-type as experienced by those in the room, is a response to what I see in the room. My amusement does not have the same basis as the amusement of those in the room. Indeed, I do not know why they are laughing; I do not know what they find amusing. I respond to their amusement; I am caught up in the general amusement without being directed to anyone's particular amusement or to what they found amusing. Moreover, I am not experiencing an emotion that involves care for the well-being of those in the room for their sake. In sympathy, by contrast, it is your emotion that I experience. My sympathizing is directed at your grieving over a loss or your joy in graduating. We experience different emotions: sympathetic sorrow or rejoicing, on my side, directed to your grief or joy; on your side, grief at a loss or joy in graduating.

Sympathy can arise even when we think the other is mistaken in her beliefs or emotional responses. Consider Sarah and Patrick, friends who are also colleagues in an academic department. Patrick is denied tenure, and believing his record warrants tenure, he reacts angrily, feeling that he was wronged. Sarah, however, thinks that the scholarly quality of Patrick's publication does not merit the awarding of tenure. Sarah also thinks, however, that Patrick's teaching has been excellent, and, consequently, she thinks the final tenure decision could have gone either way. Sarah sympathizes with Patrick, although she is not angered by the denial of tenure to Patrick. Moreover, Sarah feels sorrow that Patrick was disappointed and angered by the decision to deny him tenure, and she feels regret that she and other members of the department were unable to do more to mentor Patrick so that he would be able to improve the scholarly quality of his work. Sarah also worries about Patrick's state of mind and hopes, for his sake, that he can harness his anger and redirect his efforts to ensure a better future for himself. Sarah experiences none of Patrick's emotions; she is neither disappointed nor angry, but she does feel sympathetic concern for Patrick in multiple ways: sorrow, regret, worry, hope. Sarah experiences these emotions because she cares for Patrick and desires, for his sake, to see him flourish.

Were Sarah not Patrick's friend, it is plausible that she would not experience these emotions at all. Nevertheless, even then, Sarah might still feel a form of sympathy upon hearing the news of Patrick having been denied tenure through the grapevine. Sarah sympathizes with Patrick's disappointment not because Patrick did not obtain a personal good—tenure—but because something good for all of us—the "person-neutral value" of well-being—was not advanced for Patrick (see Darwall, 1998, p. 275). Sympathy in this example moves in the direction of compassion, a species of sympathy in which the moral significance of sympathy becomes more recognizable.

Sympathy, in Stephen Darwall's view, "involves concern for another in light of apparent threats to her well-being or good" (Darwall, 1998, p. 275). This conflicts with the idea advanced previously, that sympathy is a possible response to positive situations and emotions as well as negative ones. That said, I find that Darwall's characterization of sympathy, with one important change, defines the narrower conception of sympathy that I am calling "compassion." Sympathy, in my view, should not be reduced to compassion. Compassion is a species of sympathy in its concern for the other for the other's sake. Nevertheless, it is more restricted in its scope than sympathy, and its structure differs from that of sympathy insofar as it involves some degree of emotional sharing.

Compassion, in my view, is a distressing emotion expressive of concern for another for the other's sake in response to the other's actual (not merely threatened), serious, and undeserved misfortune or suffering (Nussbaum, 2001, p. 306). Compassion, consequently, includes from the beginning the recognition that the seriousness of the harm puts at stake the other's well-being or flourishing (Darwall, 1998, p. 275; Nussbaum, 2001, p. 307), and its affective dimension is a felt distress that reflects, but is not identical to, the distress of the other. The distress of the other is a response to undeserved misfortune or suffering, whereas the compassionate distress is directed to the other as distressed in the face of the situation in which she finds herself.

Like sympathy, compassion is an instance of what Scheler calls genuine fellow-feeling (*Mitgefühl*). Since compassion, unlike sympathy, necessarily involves a degree of sameness in the affective states of the one who experiences compassion and the one for whom it is felt, compassion moves toward a shared emotion. It is important, however, to understand the sense in which and the degree to which it is shared. I shall consider this question in relation to Scheler's understanding of a shared emotion, what he calls an "experiencing an emotion in common" (*Mit-einanderfühlen*). For Scheler, emotions are experienced in common when my empathic recognition of and emotional response to the other's emotional state and the other's empathic recognition of and emotional response to my emotional state are so intertwined that the emotional responses are not experienced as distinct emotions (Scheler, 1954, pp. 12–13). Scheler's well-known example is of parents mourning their dead child. In Scheler's view, they experience the same grief. They feel it together as a *single* experience of grief. What they feel is constitutively interdependent, and this interdependence is a function of the social relation in which they stand to one another. Their relation to one another as parents of the child overcomes the separateness of their emotional responses; they share a single experience of grieving. In Scheler's view, they are a single we-subject grieving.

Thomas Szanto (2018, p. 87) has identified three ways in which one of the parents might report the experience of grief, ways that differently disclose how a shared emotion is embedded in particular social relations. First, the parent could say, "I personally grieve for our child," and here the social relation is embedded in the intentional object of the grieving—our child. Second, the parent might say, "I as a parent or family member grieve for our child," and in this case, the social relation is embedded both in the intentional object (our child) and in the intention as a parent or family member. Finally, the parent might say, "We as parents grieve for our child." Once again, the relation is embedded in both the intention (as parents) and the intentional object (our child). Szanto argues, however, that the third report, which expresses Scheler's view, is deeply problematic in a way that the others are not.

In Scheler's view, the interdependence of the consciousnesses of the parents is so complete that the we-consciousness is a single *token* of grief. As the discussion of empathy has revealed, however, the experiential stream of the other cannot be first-personally experienced. Hence, it is difficult to understand how the two experiences of grief can be so integrated as to constitute a single token of grief. The view seems contradictory on its face. We are asked to envision a single, unified, yet plural, first-personal experience in which two consciousnesses are merged into one. The third report can be meaningful only on the assumption that there is more than one individual experiencing grief, and this entails that there must be *two* tokens of grief. As Szanto puts it, "just as there can be no proper sharing without something that is common and rightly integrated, there is just as little room and no need for sharing if there is not a plurality of individuals who actually engage in sharing" (Szanto, 2018, p. 88). Moreover, "those individuals—their deep and robust integration notwithstanding—actually differ and have a clear awareness and understanding of precisely not being intermeshed, fused, let alone identical, in their affective lives. Rather . . . they exhibit intentional and experiential variations and differences vis-à-vis one another (hence self/other-differentiation)" (Szanto, 2018, p. 89). Szanto's argument makes clear that Scheler's view of shared emotions fails to maintain the self-other differentiation that empathy reveals as necessary.

This is the reason for saying that compassion falls short of a shared emotion in Scheler's sense. Compassion, in brief, does not involve a single token of distress shared by the compassionate person and the one to whom the compassion is directed. In what sense, then, is compassion a shared emotion? Given that intentionality in general is a structure involving (1) the (subjective) experience, including (2) the sensory feelings characteristic of affective experience, (3) the intended object, and (4) that intended object just as intended (= the intentional object), there are at least four different senses in which an experience can be shared. The sharing of the subjective experience, including the felt feeling-sensations, is, as we have seen, impossible, although in Scheler's example the parent's subjective experiences and their feeling-sensations have type-identity even though not token-identity. The intended object can be shared just in case the experiences of the different subjects are directed to the same object or state of affairs. And the intentional object of the experiences can be shared if and only if the experiences are directed to the object under the same aspects or conceptions.

Let us return to the example of Sarah's sympathetic concern for Patrick for whom the denial of tenure threatens a loss of livelihood. While compassion would be inappropriate when the person suffering harm to their well-being is at fault and deserves the harm, Sarah is not convinced that Patrick deserves the denial of tenure. In this context, she feels not merely sympathetic concern for Patrick but distress about Patrick's suffering this harm. Patrick likely experiences a range of emotions in response to the distressing event: anger and disappointment, as we have seen, but also anxiety about his loss of livelihood and his ability to find a new position as well as grief at the loss of his academic position that constituted a central element of his sense of his personal identity. Sarah is distressed that her friend is suffering, and she is distressed by her friend's situation that motivates that suffering. Patrick's distress targets the situation (the denial of tenure and the loss of his position and, potentially, his livelihood), whereas the target of Sarah's compassionate concern and distress encompasses both Patrick's distress and the situation targeted by Patrick's distress.

Properly speaking, the intended objects of Sarah's and Patrick's experiences differ. Patrick is directed to the situation of having been denied tenure and its consequences; Sarah is directed to Patrick's experience of distress (disappointment, anger, anxiety, grief, and so forth), which encompasses as well the intended object of Patrick's distress. Hence, there is a partial coincidence of intended objects. Similarly, there is a partial coincidence of intentional objects. Patrick's experience intends the situation as motivating his felt emotions, whereas Sarah's experience intends Patrick as understanding the situation in a certain way and as experiencing a set of affective responses. The coincidence in intentional objects, however, can come apart. Sarah might understand Patrick as primarily angry over the denial of tenure when Patrick is, in fact, primarily anxious about his prospects for finding a new position and maintaining his identity as a teacher and scholar. The intentional object of Sarah's compassion conceives Patrick as other than he is, but it nevertheless has elements that correspond to the intentional object of Patrick's experience. Patrick, after all, is angry, and the denial of tenure and its possible consequences are aspects of the intentional object of both Sarah's and Patrick's experiences. These partial coincidences in the intended and intentional objects along with the type-identity of affective experiences and feelings of distress indicate that Sarah's compassion shares a type-identical distress with Patrick that is ultimately rooted in the denial of tenure.

This relation, however, is unidirectional. Sarah's compassion incorporates the awareness of the denial of tenure and its possible consequence as a part of a larger whole. Sarah's intentional object encompasses the whole of Patrick's intentional object, even if under a somewhat different conception and, thus, encompasses the intended object of Patrick's experience as well. Patrick's experience, by contrast, is not directed to Sarah's intended object (Patrick), and, consequently, it cannot share an intentional object with Sarah. And since Patrick's experience is not directed to Sarah, it does not properly share Sarah's feeling of distress that is the response to Patrick's distress. So, although Sarah is intentionally directed to Patrick's experience and aware of the object of Patrick's experience, the converse is not true.

In this example Sarah feels compassion for her friend Patrick, but not all experiences of compassion involve those known to us. I feel compassion for those suffering in the humanitarian crisis in Yemen, for those caught in the civil war in Syria, for those that lose their homes to fires in the western United States, tornadoes in the central United States, and hurricanes in the eastern United States. In such cases, when I do not know the persons involved, what does it mean to say that my compassion expresses a concern for the sake of the other? In such cases we seem unable to think that *X* feels compassion for *Y* for *Y*'s sake as we might think regarding Sarah's compassion for Patrick for Patrick's sake. Sarah can have a fairly determinate idea of how Patrick conceives the good for himself and feel compassion for Patrick because of the negative effects the denial of tenure will have on Patrick's pursuit of that good. But, it seems, *X* can have no such determinate ideas for the refugee in the Syrian war or the orphaned child in Yemen or the now homeless person in California, Texas, or Florida.

Compassion, I have said, involves an awareness that the serious and undeserved misfortune or suffering of another harms the other's flourishing or well-being. It is a harm that touches directly and centrally on human concerns and motivates the recognition that—in the words of songwriter Phil Ochs—"There but for fortune may go you or I."[5] Flourishing or well-being is a good proper not just to some individuals but to all humans precisely as humans. And the harm to it that comes from serious and undeserved misfortune and suffering is "not just some harm or disvalue *to* another person, but . . . the *neutral disvalue* of this personal harm" (Darwall, 1998, p. 275).

I have abridged Darwall's sentence, and I will return to it in a moment. Darwall argues that sympathy—I am applying this view to compassion—is concerned not merely with harm to a particular person but the *person-neutral disvalue* of this harm. The harm is "not just terrible for him, but . . . neutrally bad in a way that gives anyone a reason to prevent it. . . . [I]t is as if there is a reason to relieve the other's suffering consisting simply in the fact that the person herself, and so her good, matters" (Darwall, 1998, p. 275). The good of others for their sake, Darwall continues, "matters categorically. . . . [C]oncern for another for her sake cannot be reduced to a desire for that person's good. Generally, it is *because* we care about someone that we desire her good, not *vice versa*" (Darwall, 1998, p. 276). We have, in Darwall's view, a concern for the person herself—the person matters to us—such that we are motivated to care for her good for her sake. Now we can see the force of the end of the sentence I abridged: "[S]ympathetic concern presents itself as of, not just some harm or disvalue *to* another person, but also the *neutral disvalue* of this personal harm *owing to the value of the person himself*" (Darwall, 1998, p. 275; last emphasis added).

I asked what it could mean to feel compassion for a person for that person's sake when we are referring to misfortune and suffering experienced by those who are at a great distance and are unknown to us. Darwall points to the answer. Empathy recognizes the other as a person like me having dignity, a value that summons and commands respect. All others (should) matter to me just insofar as they possess a dignity that commands my respect. Sympathy expresses my caring concern for the flourishing, the well-being, of other persons and of the community of persons who co-constitute a shared world just on the ground that they have value—dignity—as persons. Compassion is my sympathetic caring and shared distress for other persons experiencing undeserved misfortune or suffering that seriously harms their well-being. And I can feel compassion for those at a distance precisely because well-being is a person-neutral good. All three affective responses to the empathically recognized person—respect, sympathy, and compassion—are ways of valuing the other for the other's own sake. All three affective responses are central and fundamental moral emotions.

I have claimed (1) that recognition respect in its recognition of the dignity of other persons builds itself on empathy's disclosure of the irreducible difference of the other and (2) that sympathy (and compassion) in its concern for the well-being of other persons builds itself on empathy's disclosure of the similarity of the other and the communalization of subjects co-constituting a shared world. But sympathy too, as we have just seen, preserves the difference between A as sympathizing with *B* in *B*'s grief or joy and *B* as feeling grief or joy. In what sense, then, does sympathy bring forth the aspect of similarity to me?

Three considerations already at work in our discussion are relevant. Given that empathy reveals both similarity and irreducible difference and grounds both sympathy and recognition respect, it should not surprise that even in sympathy I preserve the sense of the other as a person who is an alternate center of rational conscious agency and, as such, has dignity. In sympathetically caring for the other for the other's sake, I do not serve only my own ends (or, if I do, my sympathy is insincere). Preserving the sense of the other as an alternate center of rational conscious agency is just a manner of respecting the other, but it also says that the other as a rational agent is like me, an agent that has cares and concerns that I can make my own ends, not for my sake, but for the other's sake.

In addition, sympathy is the most fundamental of what me might call "attractive" (Sherman, 1997, p. 175; 1998, p. 175–81) or "cooperative" or "communalizing" attitudes. Sympathy—whether commiserating with another's suffering or rejoicing in someone's joy—insofar as it recognizes the other has having cares and concerns of her own, motivates cultivating another's reason, emotions, and abilities to judge and to understand reasoned goods, all the while refraining from imposing judgments and decisions on the other. To do this is to maintain the tension between similarity and irreducible difference. To do this involves cooperative attitudes that manifest themselves in care for the other for the other's sake, a care first arising in sympathy and motivating us to help the other to realize her chosen goods and, as in Patrick's case, to sympathize with him when things do not work out well. A cultivated sympathy, in other words, inclines us to care for and to assist others in a way that recognition respect alone does not.

Finally, sympathy furthers the establishment of the community toward which empathy points. Empathy discloses that I and the other share a world; it discloses possibilities for a community of subjects who cooperate in coming to know the world, in identifying shared goals over and above their individual ends, in establishing institutions that enable the achievement of both personal and shared goals, and so forth. Sympathy is part of the fabric of this community because of its concern for the good of others for their own sake, for the sake of their flourishing and well-being along with our common flourishing and well-being.

This runs the risk of motivating paternalistic, if not oppressive, attitudes and actions. This is why, just as recognition respect must be counterbalanced by sympathy in the formation of communities, sympathy must be counterbalanced by recognition respect. We need sympathy in relation to recognition respect to move beyond the formal notion of respect for all persons as persons to care for the individual persons who not only command respect but whose well-being is a concern for us all. At the same time, however, the irreducible difference between self and other cannot be lost from view as it might be were sympathy to morph into a paternalistic attitude. Each person in the community must "decide," that is, decide in the light of the best available evidence, for herself what is true, good, and right. The other is always irreducibly other, and recognition respect of the irreducibility of the other—a conscious, free being in her own right—creates the moral space in which sympathetic concern does its work of caring for others and for the sake of others. Sympathy, in short, fills the moral space bounded by respect. Sympathy motivates other emotions, desires, and actions that preserve the "similarity and communalization in irreducible difference" characteristic of the empathy grounding it. It is an emotion that, like respect, is central to morality, most notably in the form of compassion.

In conclusion, empathy reveals the structure of all intersubjective relations, namely, similarity-in-irreducible-difference. It also underlies the two emotions of sympathy (including its subspecies compassion) and respect, emotions that manifest this structure. Sympathy is rooted in and manifests our similarity, whereas respect is rooted in and manifests our irreducible difference. Insofar as it is a single, albeit complex, structure that is intersubjectivity, sympathy and respect—in particular, recognition respect—just insofar as they are rooted in empathy are intertwined with one another. They serve as the fundamental moral emotions in respect's creating the logical space in which morality is located and sympathy's establishing cooperative and communal relations within that moral space. And that is why empathy means everything for ethics.

NOTES

1. See, for example, in Husserl's *Nachlass* Ms. A VI 26, 42a: "Mere sensation-data and, at a higher level, sensory objects, as things that are there for a subject, but there as value-free, are abstractions."

2. This view of empathy is rooted in and combines aspects of the views of several phenomenologists. See, for example, Husserl 1970, 1973a, 1973b, 1973c, 1989; Stein 1989; Scheler 1954; Szanto 2018; Szanto and Kreuger 2019; Walsh 2014; Walther 1923; and Zahavi 1999, 2008, 2014, 2015.

3. I have discussed the interplay of empathy, respect, and sympathy in Drummond 2006, 2020, 2022a, and 2022b. This essay follows, albeit with revisions, those previous discussions.

4. See Darwall (1977) for the distinction between appraisal respect and recognition respect.

5. "There but for Fortune," track 9 on Phil Ochs, *There but for Fortune*, Elektra Entertainment, 1989.

REFERENCES

Darwall, S. (1977). Two Kinds of Respect. *Ethics*, *88*(1), 36–49.

———. (1998). Empathy, Sympathy, Care. *Philosophical Studies*, *89*(2–3), 261–82.

Drummond, J. (2002). Forms of Social Unity: Partnership, Membership, and Citizenship. *Husserl Studies*, *18*(2), 141–56.

———. (2006). Respect as a Moral Emotion: A Phenomenological Approach. *Husserl Studies*, *22*(1), 1–27.

———. (2010). Self-Responsibility and Eudaimonia. In C. Ierna, H. Jacobs, & F. Mattens (Eds.), *Philosophy Phenomenology Sciences* (pp. 441–60). Springer.

———. (2013). The Intentional Structure of Emotions. *Logical Analysis and the History of Philosophy/Philosophiegeschichte und logische Analyse*, *16*, 244–63.

———. (2020). Empathy, Sympathy, Compassion. *Metodo*, *8*(2), 149–66. https://doi.org/10.19079/metodo.8.2.149

———. (2022a). Empathy, Sympathetic Respect, and the Foundations of Morality. In E. Magri & A. Bortolan (Eds.), *Empathy, Intersubjectivity, and the Social World: The Continued Relevance of Phenomenology* (pp. 345–62). De Gruyter.

———. (2022b). Sympathetic Respect, Respectful Sympathy. *Ethical Theory and Moral Practice*, *25*(1), 1–15. doi: 10.1007/s10677-021-10210–7

Husserl, E. (1959). *Erste Philosophie (1923/24): Zweiter Teil: Theorie der phänomenologischen Reduktion* (R. Boehm, Ed.). Springer.

———. (1970). *Cartesian Meditations: An Introduction to Phenomenology.* (D. Cairns, Trans.). Martinus Nijhoff.

———. (1973a). *Zur Phänomenologie der Intersubjektivität: Texte aus dem Nachlaß. Dritter Teil: 1929–1935* (I. Kern, Ed.; Vol. 3). Martinus Nijhoff.

———. (1973b). *Zur Phänomenologie der Intersubjektivität: Texte aus dem Nachlaß. Erster Teil: 1905–1920* (I. Kern, Ed.; Vol. 1). Martinus Nijhoff.

———. (1973c). *Zur Phänomenologie der Intersubjektivität: Texte aus dem Nachlaß. Zweiter Teil: 1921–1928* (I. Kern, Ed.; Vol. 2). Kluwer.

———. (1989). *Ideas Pertaining to a Pure Phenomenology and to a Phenomenological Philosophy. Second Book: Studies in the Phenomenology of Constitution* (R. Rojcewicz & A. Schuwer, Trans.). Kluwer.

———. (2004). *Einleitung in die Ethik: Vorlesungen Sommersemester 1920/1924* (H. Peucker, Ed.). Kluwer Academic Publishers.

———. (2014). *Ideas for a Pure Phenomenology and Phenomenological Philosophy. First Book: General Introduction to Pure Phenomenology* (D. O. Dahlstrom, Trans.). Hackett Publishing Company.

Kenny, A. (1963). *Action, Emotion, and Will*. Routledge.

Kriegel, U. (2017). Dignity and the Phenomenology of Recognition-Respect. In J. J. Drummond & S. Rinofner-Kreidl (Eds.), *Emotional Experiences: Ethical and Social Significance* (pp. 121–36). London: Rowman & Littlefield International.

MacIntyre, A. C. (1999). *Dependent Rational Animals: Why Human Beings Need the Virtues*. Open Court.

Mertens, K. (2000). Husserls Phänomenologie der Monade. Bemerkungen zu Husserls Auseinandersetzung mit Leibniz. *Husserl Studies*, *17*(1), 1–20.

Nussbaum, M. C. (2001). *Upheavals of Thought: The Intelligence of Emotions*. Cambridge University Press.

Scheler, M. (1954). *The Nature of Sympathy* (P. Heath, Trans.). Routledge and Kegan Paul.

———. (1973). *Formalism in Ethics and Non-Formal Ethics of Values: A New Attempt Toward the Foundation of an Ethical Personalism* (M. S. Frings & R. L. Funk, Trans.). Northwestern University Press.

Sherman, N. (1997). *Making a Necessity of Virtue: Aristotle and Kant on Virtue*. Cambridge University Press.

———. (1998). Concrete Kantian Respect. *Social Philosophy and Policy*, *15*(1), 119–48.

Smith, A. (1976). *The Theory of Moral Sentiments* (A. L. Macfie & D. D. Raphael, Eds.). Clarendon Press.

Stein, E. (1989). *On the Problem of Empathy* (W. Stein, Trans.; 3rd rev. ed). ICS Publications.

Szanto, T. (2018). The Phenomenology of Shared Emotions—Reassessing Gerda Walther. In S. Luft & R. Hagengruber (Eds.), *Women Phenomenologists on Social Ontology: We-Experiences, Communal Life, and Joint Action* (pp. 85–104). Springer International Publishing. https://doi.org/10.1007/978-3-319-97861-1_7

Szanto, T., & Krueger, J. (2019). Introduction: Empathy, Shared Emotions, and Social Identity. *Topoi*, *38*(1), 153–62. https://doi.org/10.1007/s11245-019-09641-w

Walsh, P. J. (2014). Empathy, Embodiment, and the Unity of Expression. *Topoi*, *33*(1), 215–26. https://doi-org.avoserv2.library.fordham.edu/10.1007/s11245-013-9201-z

Walther, G. (1923). Zur Ontologie der sozialen Gemeinschaften (mit einem Anhang zur Phänomenologie der sozialen Gemeinschaften. *Jahrbuch für Philosophie und phänomenologische Forschung*, *6*, 1–158.

Zahavi, D. (2015). You, Me, and We: The Sharing of Emotional Experiences. *Journal of Consciousness Studies*, *22*(1–2), 84–101.

Zahavi, Dan. (1999). *Self-Awareness and Alterity: A Phenomenological Investigation* (New edition). Northwestern University Press.

———. (2008). Simulation, Projection and Empathy. *Consciousness and Cognition*, *17*(2), 514–22.

———. (2014). *Self and Other: Exploring Subjectivity, Empathy, and Shame*. Oxford University Press.

———. (2019). Second-Person Engagement, Self-Alienation, and Group-Identification. *Topoi*, *38*(1), 251–60.

Chapter 2

Ethics, Empathy, and Vulnerability

Trust as a Way of Making Sense of Our Vulnerability and Dependability

Esteban Marín-Ávila

ABSTRACT

The chapter explores ethical problems that can be approached in the context of phenomenological analyses where the topics of empathy, violence, vulnerability, and emotivity intercross. The main question is the following: How can we attempt to live an ethical life given our awareness that we are vulnerable before others and dependent on them? In this context, it is suggested that trusting is a way of making sense of our vulnerability and dependability of others. The intentional structure of trust is examined in relation to problems that violence poses to it. It is suggested that, even though trust has a practical main direction of interest, it entails beliefs and feelings as well. On the other hand, being trusted amounts to being able to engage in social relationships with others. The final part of the chapter addresses ethical problems that appear when we assume a reflective attitude toward our capacity to trust and to correspond to the trust that others invest in us. It is argued that this reflective attitude sheds light on the beliefs, axiological assessments, and volitions that are involved in our relationships and loyalty to others. The conclusion is that acting before others in meaningful or fully rational ways involves acknowledging our vulnerability and making sense of it, that we do this by trusting, and that an ethical reflection should submit the problems raised by empathy and trust to a radical examination.

Keywords: phenomenology, violence, reflective trust, rational valuings, rational actions, social capacity

In this chapter I wish to reflect on the vulnerability that comes together with living a life structured by empathy, that is, with a life shaped by the awareness of the all-pervasive presence of others. If vulnerability is a trait of our social existence, then acting in meaningful ways in our concrete world implies being able to assume this vulnerability in rational or meaningful ways. I will argue here that trusting others can be considered precisely as a way of making sense of our vulnerability before others. This means that, when we trust, we apprehend or give meaning to our vulnerability and our surrounding world in ways in which we can be explicitly aware or not. More importantly for my argument, as such apprehension or attempt to give meaning to our vulnerability, trust can be grounded in assumptions of all kinds that can be rational or not.

By looking at how violence challenges our disposition to trust and motivates us to reflect on what is at stake in trusting, I discuss some aspects of our vulnerability that are essentially related with our capability to constitute interpersonal relationships. This should make clear that a life lived with awareness of others has a dimension of vulnerability that is not always acknowledged but that comes to the fore when we suffer from violence or face the menace of it. Thus, my conceptualization of vulnerability will be related to a conceptualization of violence.

EMPATHY, VIOLENCE AND VULNERABILITY

In Husserl's works, the problem of empathy is usually limited to the question of how it is possible for a subject to perceive other Egos, or, in other words, of how the phenomenon "other Egos" is possible. This question is intermingled with the problem of how it is possible to constitute a world that is experienced as being real in the sense of intersubjective and not reducible to what is immanent to each person's own living consciousness, that is, to what Husserl calls in the *Cartesian Meditations* the "sphere of ownness" [*Eigenheitssphäre*] (Husserl, 1973a). However, empathy is not only inseparable from our awareness of being part of the real world but also from the affective and practical meaning that it has for us. Without empathy we would not be able to grasp through feelings some of the most basic and important valuable aspects and states of affairs of this world, nor to engage in some of the most basic and important practical landscapes that it can offer to us.

Our awareness of other Egos is not only doxical or representational: It is also emotional/axiological and practical in the sense that other Egos are also referents of our emotional/axiological and practical intentions and interests, referents of our emotions and valuings, as well as of our practical assessments and resolutions. Consequently, a phenomenological inquiry into empathy should address the question of how we relate to other Egos in ways that are crucial for the appearance of social, moral, or plainly intersubjective values, as well as for the possibility of performing meaningful actions that would not be possible in isolation. Ultimately, it cannot leave aside the ethical problem of how being aware of others and engaging in different forms of relationships with them can open possibilities of living lives that are more rational or meaningful than the kind of lives that we could live in relative isolation.

Regarding this last point, the reader should keep in mind that when I write of actions that are "fully rational" or "fully meaningful," I am following Husserl's idea that for volition—be it a singular action, a set of actions, or a life—to be considered rational or meaningful, it is not enough that it be feasible. On the contrary, rational volitions are also those directed to goals that can be understood in rational beliefs and established as authentically valuable by the agent (Husserl, 1988, 2004).

Husserl claimed that the supreme topic of ethics is the renovation of individual persons and of collectivities, that this renovation consists in becoming an authentic human being by living according to reason and evidence (i.e., according to insightful reason) and that one cannot be willing to become an authentic human being without having the aspiration to belong to an authentic community and to an ethical humanity as a whole (Husserl, 1987). Let me rephrase this by saying that one cannot attempt to undertake fully meaningful actions and to live a fully meaningful life without attempting to embed these actions and this life in the more encompassing fabric of actions and lives of all the others that we grasp empathically. All the most proximate and most remote others of which we are aware inevitably co-determine the sense of the world that we inhabit, as well as the meaning of our actions.

Here I wish to make explicit some of the problems that are at stake in the Husserlian idea that the aspiration to live a fully rational life can only take place together with the aspiration that others live meaningful lives as well. Moreover, I would like to suggest that the aspiration to live a fully rational or meaningful life, the aspiration that according to Husserl is the topic of ethics (Husserl, 2004), cannot be undertaken without reflecting on the doxical, axiological and practical problems raised by empathy. Consequently, living such an ethical life implies reflecting on these matters in the concrete situations that we face in our everyday lives.

The aspiration to live ethically encounters factual challenges. The reflections that make these concrete problems explicit cannot be reduced to abstract considerations and resolved in analyses that leave out the conditions in which we live as concrete human beings. Of these factual challenges, some of the more significant and obvious ones are our own vulnerability, violence, and the kind of irrationality that the latter imposes on those who suffer it. How is it possible to live a meaningful life in the context of an intersubjective world in which we are necessarily vulnerable and in which violence cannot be ruled out? Or more concretely, how can we deal with violence and the imposition of irrationality in our attempt to live meaningful lives?

These questions point to the ways in which we can make sense of our vulnerability and, more specifically, of our situation of being exposed to violence. It is worth noting that even if our vulnerability becomes more acute and more perceptible when we face violent situations and environments, this vulnerability as such is not the result of violence. As I suggest, living in an intersubjective world implies being vulnerable. In this sense, this chapter contains a partial, initial answer to the question of how we can make sense of our vulnerability. It focuses on the more obvious traits of such vulnerability, which are the ones that can be brought to the fore when considering the practical challenges that violence imposes on us, and more emphatically, the challenges that the suffering of violence, and not its infliction, impose on us. Thus, the following remarks will be focused on the beliefs, valuings, and practical considerations that make it rational to be disposed to undertake actions without attempting to rule out vulnerability, that is, on the conditions on which it would be fully rational or meaningful to act on the basis of trust.

Let me advance at this point the two main series of ideas that compose my core argument:

1. When a person is trusted or perceived as trustworthy, this goes together with giving her the capacity to establish social relationships with the person who trusts her or perceives her in such a way.

With the term *social relationship*, I am following Husserl and alluding to something quite specific: a form of volition or practical intention in which the participants are engaged with doing something whose accomplishment implies the concurrent volitions and ultimately actions of several persons, and with it, certain forms of collaboration. Such a synthesis of volitions or collaboration presupposes, in turn, the capacity to participate in interactions that have the form of what Husserl and Reinach called "social acts": sayings, promises, orders, requests, declarations, and so on (Reinach, 1988, pp. 158–69; Husserl, 1973b, pp. 165–224).[1]

Trusting someone amounts to giving her the capacity to say, promise, ask, order or declare things to us, etc., and with this, the capacity to collaborate with us. This relates to the fact that the experiences of trusting and being trusted amplify our capacity to act in the world or, in other words, amplify the horizon of the sense that we can give to our actions, as well as the horizon of things that we can do with the concurrence of our efforts. A person that trusts others can be said to perform rational actions even when the meaning of her endeavors partially escapes her understanding because it partially depends on the intelligence of others, and she can perform these actions efficiently together with her counterparts in trust. In sum, an attitude of trust enhances our agency, but not only regarding our practical capacity or feasibility: This enhancement also concerns the understanding and valuing of ends and means and, therefore, the meaning that we are able to give to our actions. With this, trust opens the possibility of undertaking rational actions that otherwise would not be possible (Marín-Ávila, 2021).

2. To claim that trust enhances our capacity of acting rationally does not mean that it is always rational to trust or to correspond to the trust that is deposited in us. To trust someone involves making oneself vulnerable before her. If one is reflexively aware of putting oneself in a position of vulnerability before someone else and willing to do it, then this can only be rational if it is feasible, based on sound beliefs, and done for the sake of something valued. This is especially clear when considering the problems of habiting and acting in a violent society.

To trust and to accept the trust of others means to be able to engage with them in social relationships of all kinds, including those of domination. Someone who is capable of taking and fulfilling orders must be capable of promising obedience (Reinach, 1988), and to promise obedience one must be perceived, for whatever reasons, as trustworthy by the master. When these promises of obedience are not given as responses to threats of the use of force or of violence of any kind, they are given under the assumption that the person who issues the orders is worthy of our trust. An example of this is the authority of a teacher or of a moral, religious, or political leader. On top of that, the expression of trust also can give way to other more subtle and deliberately disguised forms of domination, as is the case with some forms of emotional manipulation (Steinbock, 2014).

Even though trust might be used to engage in all sorts of social relationships, to trust someone implies making oneself vulnerable before her. Another way to put this is by saying that it is not possible to trust someone without giving her the opportunity to betray this trust (Steinbock, 2014; Baier, 1992). Even when this is always the case when we trust, in violent environments the possibility of being betrayed is especially prominent and can have consequences that are especially serious. Precisely in relation with this kind of environments, populated by all sorts of menaces, trust cannot be taken for granted as something natural and spontaneous and the following questions become relevant: In who, in what matters, and under which circumstances should we trust? And since trusting implies assuming high risks in violent environments: Why is it desirable to trust? What do we "gain" when we trust someone or what do we "lose" when we do not do it? To raise these questions as practical problems: How and why should we create environments in which it is possible to trust? How can we avoid making mistakes when we take the risk of trusting? To what should we pay attention if we wish to assess whether the risk of suffering betrayal is something worth taking?

VIOLENCE

At this point, let me say a few words on vulnerability and violence to introduce a preliminary conceptualization of these phenomena and to highlight some ethical problems related with them, especially the problem of what it means and involves acting meaningfully in view of some of the challenges posed by empathy. With the term *violence* we usually identify phenomena and relationships that are so diverse that it might seem that it is not possible to obtain from them a common concept. I will not attempt to elaborate here such a unitary concept. My remarks will be limited to highlight essential aspects of phenomena that we identify with this term and play an important role in the motivations to trust and distrust and, consequently, that shed light on the problem of the rationality of trust. Since the suffering of violence and its menace makes us attentive to our vulnerability, the attempt to conceptualize essential traits of common and basic forms of violence is relevant for an inquiry into how we experience our vulnerability and how we attempt to make sense of it by trusting.

With the term *violence*, I am alluding here to the destructive character of something. To distinguish the kind of destruction that belongs to human phenomena, we can say that it is relative to human actions, forms of actions or forms of arranging actions—like habits, traditions, practices, or normative arrangements—whose realization or execution consists precisely in destroying something, even when this is done with the purpose of transforming what is partially destroyed, or of coercing (Arendt, 1970; Sánchez Vásquez 2003). In this sense, coercion is an effect of violence. However, violence can occur without the attempt to coerce but simply to damage, destroy, or annihilate the victim.

Arendt (1970) highlights a fundamental element of violence when she points out, furthermore, that it is a relationship that *has its origin* in the realm of instrumentality. We produce some things by destroying other things, and we can make people behave as we wish in the same way, through instruments and by treating them as instruments. In this sense, all infractions of the Kantian categorical imperative, in its formulation of treating oneself and others always as ends in themselves and not as means, are forms of violence (Kant, 2007).

While discussing Marshall Sahlins's exchange theory, the social anthropologist Claudio Lomnitz (2005) observes that, when violence cannot be reciprocated because the victim is powerless against the perpetrator, it can give rise to a kind of asymmetrical relationship and form of exchange that he calls "negative asymmetric reciprocity" (*reciprocidad asimétrica negativa*). In these relationships, an initial violent act—a robbery, rape, extortion, or homicide—forces the victim to get involved in a cycle of exchange with the perpetrator. The violent act is usually followed by a symbolic gift that creates a fictional debt and a cycle of exchange that is characterized by the fact that the gifts and services flow from the powerless victim to the powerful perpetrator of violence. As examples of this kind of relationship and cycle of exchange, Lomnitz mentions among others the following: After the conquest of the Aztec Empire, the Catholic Franciscan order justified the domination of American Indigenous population of the New Spain by appealing to the latter's acceptance of the gift of eternal salvation; during the raids to kidnap local workers to extract rubber, the Amazonian slave hunters distributed axes to the captive Indigenous people with the aim of creating a fictional debt; after having appropriated through violence of the northern territories of Mexico, the government of the United States "bought" them to pacify its relationship with the southern neighbor (Lomnitz, 2005). Another example mentioned by him is the persistent tradition of robbery of brides in Latin America and New Guinea during the twentieth century, as well as in eighteenth-century Britain, which resulted in forced marriage and was usually accompanied by a gift to the family of the woman who was abducted (Lomnitz, 2005, 2021). The point here is not simply that cycles of exchange can be initiated by debts but that violence can be used to claim "debts" that justify forced cycles of exchange of objects and services.

However, even when violence usually serves instrumental purposes and can be explained by an instrumental logic, it is important to notice that violence on occasions can merely aim at the destruction of the victim or the whole chain of means and ends that make up the practical structure of the world in a given society. I take this conception from Sartre's *Notebooks on Ethics* (1992). According to Sartre, absolute violence is a nihilistic way of rejecting the world understood as arrangement of means and ends. One of his examples is rape. In that case, the aggressor rejects the established ways of seduction as a means to have a sexual encounter with the desired person. However, by degrading the victim to the condition of a mere object, the aggressor does not obtain the satisfaction of the desire that originally or allegedly moves him but only the self-deceit or bad faith of a possession.[2] The aim of this kind of violent action is to destroy the world in which the rapist cannot satisfy his desire. This can be appreciated in a more caricatured way in another example set forward by Sartre: Someone tries to open the lock of a door and, when she fails, breaks the lock. Notice that this action of breaking the lock does not aim at opening the door. I want to stress here Sartre's observation that noninstrumental violence, a kind of violence that aims at the annihilation of the world, emerges when someone's strength is inadequate to achieve her aims (Sartre, 1992, p. 171). In the first example, what is desired by the rapist, the sexual encounter with another person as something distinguishable from the possession of an object cannot be obtained through force. This is why violence is a way of refusing to be born in a world that is shaped by the establishment of relationships with others (Sartre, 1992, p. 177). These thoughts revolve around certain traits of violence that have been also observed by the anthropologist Rita Segato (2010) in the context of her research on sexual violence.

Segato draws on Carole Pateman's famous work, *The Sexual Contract* (1988), to explain the sexual violence that structures contemporary societies by the tense coexistence of a persistent traditional and asymmetrical order and way of thinking, which she calls "the law of status," and another modern, egalitarian order and way of thinking that she calls "the law of contract" (Segato, 2010, pp. 28–31, 135–36). According to Segato, sexual violence against women, and particularly rape, are traditional ways of disciplining women that do not assume a subordinate position in relation to men in society. This subordination has a tributary form—of care, affect, sex, offspring, housework and other nonremunerated work, etc.—that is directly related with men's honor (Segato, 2010, pp. 38, 143–44, 230). Consequently, Segato observes that sexual violence in modern societies responds to the conflict caused by the coexistence of the premodern social orders and ways of thinking of "status," and the modern "contractual" social orders and laws. This conflict imposes on men a mandate to discipline, and more precisely, to discipline through rape, women that transgress the traditional social order that is based on their tributary subordination—or to discipline feminized subjects, if we consider the appearance of these forms of violence in male prisons (Segato, 2010, p. 23).

Segato points out that the violence of "gore rapes" [*violaciones cruentas*][3] and feminicides, which according to her are the paradigm of all other forms of gender and sexual violence, has a surplus that cannot be explained in instrumental terms. Based on testimonies of convicted rapists, she observes that this surplus of violence was for them an end that was emotionally satisfactory in itself but also a source of perplexity: They cannot explain to themselves why they committed the aggression the way they did it. While pointing out that their acts did not have a purely instrumental purpose, Segato suggests that rape is not merely the appropriation by force of a sexual service but the attempt to rob something that cannot be robbed (Segato, 2010, pp. 22, 43–44). She also suggests that the fact that many of the interviewed felt pushed to commit their crimes by imaginary others or, in some cases, described their crimes as something dictated by fate, might be explained by considering that these violent acts were related to the constitution of their very identity as male subjects before other male subjects. According to Segato, to be a man is to have a status that needs to be conquered and maintained through violence and that consists in receiving tribute from women (Segato, 2010). When this status and consequently the identity of a subject as man are menaced or even lost, they need to be restored through violence. However, in the extreme cases where violence exceeds any instrumental logic, the violent agent is often someone without identity, someone who is pushed to regain a damaged status and identity through the violent act. In this sense, the act is performed in a structure without subject (Segato, 2010, pp. 44–47).

I wish to suggest that the excess of this kind violence that cannot be reduced to an instrumental logic can also be explained by recourse to Sartre's notes on the nihilist character of absolute violence. When force is not adequate to restore the order of status, the disciplinarian man can resort to absolute violence with the aim of annihilating aspects of the world ruled by the law of contract. It can be said that the violence of the disciplinarian man is directed to the annihilation of the establishment of certain social relationships that are not compatible with the asymmetries of traditional social relationships. In its excess, sexual violence would be a symptom of the refusal of its perpetrators to be integrated into the world of what Segato calls "the contract," a world that, among other things, involves the establishment of symmetrical relationships between men and women.

If with the concept of violence we allude to acts or forms of agency that aim at destroying aspects of the world or at transforming it through destruction, then it is not obvious that all sorts of violence are reprehensible. Even Arendt (1970), who observed that violence stands in a relationship to power that is inversely proportional, acknowledged that the durability of power presupposes a certain base, even if minimal, of violence. This is explained by the fact that all sorts of power, understood as the capacity to act in concert, face internal and external violent threats to dissolve it. Coercion seems to be to some extent necessary for primary socialization and, consequently, for social reproduction. It also seems to be necessary for the establishment of laws that prohibit direct forms of violence that aim at degrading groups of human beings, sustaining forms of domination and undermining the prospects of living in an egalitarian society.

With these last remarks I wish to make clear that I do not think that all the problems and crossroads that we face when inhabiting a violent surrounding world can be solved by seeking to eliminate all forms of violence. The problem is more complex. What I wish to examine here is how violence affects our agency and how it inhibits and limits our capacity to act rationally or meaningfully or, at least reduces the practical projects in which it would make sense for us to engage. It is obvious that direct coercion makes this, but here I am interested in showing other less obvious and more fundamental ways in which this inhibition or limitation occurs. As such, they are as well forms of inhibiting or limiting our capacity to trust, that is, our capacity to apprehend or give meaning to our vulnerability and dependability from others.

The latter means that a violent surrounding world imposes a certain orography that determines the interactions or collective actions that can be meaningfully undertaken, and with it, determines the forms in which it is possible to face the menaces of violence itself and the social dynamics that sustain it. As such, violence makes our attention prominent to a more basic structure of vulnerability and dependability in which our actions and lives take root. And while violence can be theoretically eradicated and the goal of minimizing it can be embraced as a desirable ideal, the structure of vulnerability and dependability cannot be eradicated nor minimized without radically transforming who we are and renouncing to the most cherished aspects of our beings and lives.

TRUST

I wish to come back now to the topic of trust. To see how the analysis of this attitude fits in my account, it is important to point out that in our everyday lives we acknowledge our vulnerability and dependability of others and try to make sense of it in a practical way. We do it by trusting, even when we do not always reflect about it. Allow me to make explicit some elements to characterize what is meant and involved in trusting.[4]

From a phenomenological perspective based on intentional analysis, trust can be described as an attitude that involves an apprehension or understanding of the world. It involves beliefs, value assessments and practical intentions that are either correct or incorrect and that can therefore be examined from the point of view of their rationality. Consequently, I wish to introduce the problem of trusting others in a violent surrounding world in the context of the ethical question raised by Husserl and picked up by me in the opening lines of this chapter: given that each one's life is embedded in the encompassing fabric of other person's actions, forms of agency and lives that are seldom rational or meaningful, how is it possible to live a rational or meaningful life? According to Husserl, to live an ethical life (i.e., a life that is absolutely meaningful) involves the aspiration to realize an ethical humanity where actions and lives can have the greatest possible rationality or sense (Husserl, 1987). Since I will claim that the kind of attitude that I identify here as "trust" is a condition for interpersonal interactions that are as basic as communications, as well as for more complex collective actions and social relationships, my point is that one cannot commit to live an ethical life without being willing to reflect on our trust. And if the problem of empathy is not understood in the limited sense of clarifying the possibility of being aware of others but in a broader sense that includes the question of what it means to be aware of ourselves as agents situated in a world with others, then it cannot be separated from the problem of trust.

The problem of trust becomes prominent when living in a violent surrounding world. In view of the constant menace of violence, questions like the following ones cannot be simply set aside without further reflection: In whom should I trust? What matters, actions or decisions should I trust to others? When should I do it? And more concretely: Why should I trust or why does it make sense to trust in a given case?

Allow me to begin to conceptualize trust by pointing to something that might seem odd about it, at least at first glance: Trust is a preeminently practical attitude that consists in making oneself vulnerable before someone else. And here it is important to stress that making oneself vulnerable is not the same as being naïve (Steinbock, 2014). The vulnerability that characterizes trust consists in abstaining from doing some things, those that we trust to others, and in lowering the guard before the trusted people (Baier, 1992). In other words, it consists in renouncing agency and practical intelligence in some respects, as well as renouncing to be on guard for the possible evil that might come from the trusted one. When we trust that our friends, neighbors, teammates, colleagues, or institutions will protect us from violence or will support a course of action or a project initiated by us, we delegate actions and decisions to them, and we do other things that only make sense to do under the assumption that we have trust in them.

Why do we make ourselves vulnerable in these cases? We do it because we think or simply take for granted that valued things and situations depend on it: being able to walk on the streets without fear; feeling safe and nurtured at home, school, or at our workplace; introducing beneficial changes in our communities; cultivating practices like reflecting and discussing with others the topics that we find more interesting, etc. This points to another essential trait of trust: namely, a willingness to become vulnerable for the sake of creating or preserving valued things. In other words, we trust because, by making ourselves vulnerable before others, we attempt to create or take care of certain goods.

Of the goods that we create or preserve when we trust, there are some that could not exist if we were not able to adopt this attitude. Some of them are so basic, that without them our ability to live in society would be inconceivable. Without trust in the sincerity of our fellow human beings, it would not be possible to talk and the product of this activity, language, would be inconceivable. It would not be possible to engage in the most basic speech acts or social acts, like making promises and, consequently, making pacts (Baier 1986). I will come back to this point soon. However, here I wish to stress that trust is not merely an instrumental means to achieve goods: It is an essential component of some of the goods that we most appreciate, like the extremely wide variety of interpersonal relationships that are usually identified as forms of friendships and love, as well as the pleasures that are only possible in those relationships, like conversations that are plentiful of trust or other forms of intimacy and complicity that give us profound satisfactions when they take place in an ambience of mutual trust (Zirión, 2005).

Now I wish to bring attention to the fact that the capacity to speak and make promises depends on being trusted by the addressee of these acts. Furthermore, when we notice that someone trusts us, this amounts to experiencing a sort of demand (Steinbock 2014). When someone says, "I trust you in this matter," she makes this demand explicit, but it can also take place without being expressed. To acknowledge that someone trusts us implies to feel the imposition of a demand to which we are free to respond or not. We feel this demand when we notice that our significant others, neighbors, partners, or even bystanders and strangers trust us to do things and make decisions for them, to take care of them, or to support them in their initiatives and projects. Here I want to suggest that this demand is precisely a call to establish social relationships with those who trust us, relationships that begin by speaking and sharing promises. In this sense, to respond to the trust deposited in us with any sort of expression can be considered already a form of promise, that is, a form of obliging oneself to do something before the person who trusts us and thereby to give her the right to claim the fulfilment of such obligation (Reinach, 1988). In other words, what we feel as a demand in these situations is the possibility of engaging in social relationships with those who trust us. Nevertheless, and this is a point that I will elaborate on the following lines, in any given case we might very well have reasons to accept or reject this possibility opened by trust.

In sum, when we trust someone, we give her the capacity to speak and promise things to us and, through some complications of these social acts, also the capacity to accept requests and accept the authority to issue orders or to declare norms or institutional facts (Marín Ávila, 2018a). To be trusted by someone is to receive the capacity to engage with her in communications, promises, pacts, and other kinds of speech or social acts through which common will can be formed. I am alluding here to intersubjective volitions (Husserl, 1973b, 1973c) or collective intentions (Searle 2010) and, thus, to the possibility of preserving or making things that can only be preserved or created if other persons take part in this attempt. In more colloquial terms: Trust makes it possible to organize ourselves. If we think this in Arendtian language, it could be said that to trust someone is to create the conditions to act in concert with her and, thus, to share power with her; to withdraw trust amounts to extinguish power (Arendt, 1970).

VIOLENCE AND REFLECTIVE TRUST

Let us keep in mind what we examined before regarding the problem of violence, for it will allow us to grasp more clearly the motivations that lie behind the question of whether it is rational or irrational to trust in a given situation. For the sake of the argument, it is important to keep in mind that trusting is a way of apprehending or giving meaning to our vulnerability and to our surrounding world. The remarks that we picked up from Segato and Sartre are especially insightful because sexual violence often occurs in the context of relationships that involve trust.[5] When it comes to this kind of violence, it is not rare that aggressor and victim are engaged in an affective relationship as family, friends, or couple; that they are in a working, pedagogic, or academic relationship that can only be functional on the basis of trust; or that violence occurs in a context where the trust that the victim had in persons and institutions that were supposed to protect her from aggressions is betrayed. Nevertheless, it would be naïve to think that this problem could be solved by following the precept not to trust in any person or institution that could betray this trust. First, because an essential trait of trust is that it can always be betrayed. It is not possible to trust someone under the assumption that she is incapable of betraying this trust. As I have already mentioned, to trust someone involves making oneself vulnerable before the addressee of this trust, and this means tacitly or explicitly acknowledging that the trusted person is free to betray this trust. Secondly, because ceasing to trust someone implies precluding the possibility of establishing social bonds with that person, be it sincere, authentic communication, or making pacts with any hope that they will be respected. In that sense, confronting violence in the context of relationships that involve trust implies adopting a complex and critical attitude toward the trust on which these relationships depend.

To elaborate on this idea with the purpose of considering if it can be extended to other forms of structural violence or social relationships that entail violence, like those between classes, racialized subjects, people of different ethnicities or nationalities, etc., it is necessary to examine what we assume when we trust. What sort of reasons might we give to justify our trust or distrust in someone? What beliefs, valuings, and practical intentions do we assume when we trust? Of course, I do not think that trust is always the result of a decision. Nevertheless, I wish to inquire here into the meaning of trusting—to the way in which we "apprehend" or "understand" our surrounding world when we trust—by considering the doxical, axiological, and practical intentions involved in this attitude. What intentions—or habitualities—should be the focus of our attention if we wish to become aware of what it means and is involved in trusting someone or an institution at a given moment? As I have already suggested, to trust is to attempt to make sense of our vulnerability and dependability of others by acting in a certain way, according to certain valuings and to certain beliefs or doxical intentions.

Let us begin by considering trust exclusively as a practical attitude, abstracting from the beliefs and valuings that might be involved in it. We have already seen that to trust someone is to make oneself vulnerable before her and that this means renouncing agency and practical intelligence to delegate them to the trusted one. Regarding its pure practical form, trust can be inconsistent or simulated. There are situations in which someone can say, or even believe, that she trusts someone else without really being willing to become vulnerable before the allegedly trusted person. Let us say that I ask someone to do a work that is of crucial importance for me, and that, to be safe and backed from the mishaps that might follow from her bad decisions or neglections, I do the same work that I asked her to do. Can we say that I trusted her? The answer must be "no," at least if by "trust" we understand the attitude that I have been describing.

In some cases, these attitudes of false trust can have the purpose of exploring the possibility of trusting, of testing the person that we say that we trust, to see whether it is really possible to trust her or not. All the same, authentic trust implies vulnerability, and this is precisely why it is a way of making sense of our dependability of others and not a way of overcoming it. When these incongruences of trust are not done for the sake of testing, they can be practical contradictions that are based on deliberate attempts to simulate and deceive, or in self-deceit and bad faith. This amounts to attempting to escape or overcome our dependability of others without acknowledging or owning this move. In any case, it is important to pay attention to these incongruences and to make them explicit, for being mistaken or deceived on this question means to wrongly assume that there is ground for collaboration and for magnifying the capacity of undertaking meaningful actions with the aid of others. And to live in the practical intention of doing something that we are not capable of doing, that is, having the will to do what is not feasible, is a form of irrationality.[6]

Let us consider now the doxical components of trust and the beliefs that are entailed in it. To make oneself vulnerable before someone else can only be rational, or can only make sense, when one holds the belief that this person wishes to help her and not to harm her. The conviction that someone has good will toward us is a motive to trust her; consequently, to discover that she is disposed to do us bad is a motive to distrust. However, sometimes it is not enough to note the good will of someone to let that her resolves and actions determine the success or failure of our dearest practical interests, goals and projects: It is also necessary to count in that she is capable of doing what she is trusted to do (Baier 1992). To speak up against the abuses of a person with power or authority over us can have fatal consequences if this accusation is presented to someone who does not have good will toward us or that is incapable of honoring this trust by responding accordingly and taking the proper measures. Such misplaced trust gives the abuser the possibility of taking reprimands with all the advantages of the conjunction of her power and authority and the vulnerability to which we are exposed by having trusted. In sum, it does not make sense to trust someone under the false belief that the counterpart has good will toward us, as well as under the false belief that she is capable of doing what we trust her to do. Under these conditions, trusting is an irrational practical attitude.

I have left in last place the rational dimension of trust that is specifically emotional and axiological because it is often overlooked and is crucial for the conclusive part of my argument. Reflecting on the reasons or assumptions that underlie our trust is necessary to approach, from a phenomenological perspective, ethical problems raised by empathy, and particularly by our vulnerability and dependability on others. However, this reflection should include making explicit the desires and hopes that are involved when we undertake this attitude.

For trust to be rational or to make sense, practical consistency and rational beliefs are not enough. As I already suggested, the resolution to lower the guard and to renounce to practical agency and intelligence in some respect can only make sense under the assumption that such thing is something worth doing or, more precisely, that by adopting this attitude one contributes or at least allows for the realization or preservation of something that is valued. This axiological assessment is based on an explicit or tacit axiological-emotive apprehension or "interpretation" of the situation of trusting in that particular case. And just as much as beliefs and practical intentions that come together with it, this axiological assessment is susceptible of being wrong.[7] I can take for granted that making myself vulnerable before a particular person is something worth doing, perhaps because I take for granted that the relationship that this attitude makes possible is valuable. But after a more careful reflection I can discover that I do not really value that relationship anymore. To discover that by trusting we are not letting something valuable be realized or preserved is therefore a motive to stop trusting. For how could it make sense to be subject to the will of others when this does not provide any possible satisfaction, be it from the side of pleasure, power, love, and so on?

The resolve or decision to trust in a given situation depends on what one wants to do and on the desire to establish, preserve, or recreate standing or broken social relationships, as well as on the assessment of the goods that are intrinsically or extrinsically related with these relationships. In this sense, trust is based on hope. If an attitude can be described by a characteristic gaze or main direction of interest (Kessler & Staiti, 2010), then hope is an emotional attitude because it is centered on an emotional gaze that can be characterized as the desire or positive assessment of a certain future that is intended as uncertain and beyond our control. Hope also entails the practical intention to contribute to realize or preserve this future possibility or at least to endure while it comes, but this practical intention is not its main direction of interest. To have hope in something is preeminently to dwell in feelings. It would be impossible to undertake meaningful actions in our social and historical world if we were not able to be hopeful of certain things: The success of most of our projects and actions, or at least of the relevant ones, depends on whether they are supported by the toils and actions of other persons, which are to a higher or lesser degree, always beyond our control.[8]

As I have already mentioned, in contrast with hope, trust entails a main practical direction of interest. Trust is not something that we feel, even when it involves feelings but something that we do. And as such, it is a way of responding to the uncertainties that come together with coexisting with others. When we trust, we try to make sense of our vulnerability and dependability in order to navigate a world that is not under our control.[9]

TRUST AS A WAY OF MAKING SENSE OF OUR VULNERABILITY AND DEPENDABILITY OF OTHERS

What hopes do we have when we keep on trusting in the context of the general environment of distrust created by the structural violence in many of the societies of today? What goods do we hope to create, preserve, or reform by trusting? Because it motivates us to reflect about our trust, violence sets us before a fundamental ethical problem: that of the social relationships that we wish to build and the way in which we wish to own our vulnerability and dependability on others to find and give meaning to an uncertain world.

However, here it is important to be mindful of the fact that violence is not the cause of our vulnerability and dependability on others. Since we are social beings, which means that we cannot avoid trusting altogether, the violence that we inflict on others and suffer from them is always embedded in a more basic structure of vulnerability and dependability. As Butler has pointed out, violence and the suffering of loss often reveals our bonds:

> Loss and vulnerability seem to follow from our being socially constituted bodies, attached to others, at risk of losing those attachments, exposed to others, at risk of violence by virtue of that exposure. . . . When we lose certain people, or when we are dispossessed from a place, or a community, we may simply feel that we are undergoing something temporary, that mourning will be over and some restoration of the prior order will be achieved. But maybe when we

> undergo what we do, something about who we are is revealed, something that delineates the ties we have to others, that shows us that these ties constitute what we are, ties or bonds that compose us. . . . Many people think that grief is privatizing, that it returns us to a solitary situation and is, in that sense, depoliticizing. But I think it furnishes a sense of political community of a complex order, and it does this first of all by bringing to the fore the relational ties that have implications for theorizing fundamental dependency and ethical responsibility (Butler, 2006, p. 22).

Although violence might be in principle eradicated, the structure of vulnerability and dependability that comes together with the very fact of our social existence cannot be overcome without changing or undermining the human condition at its core. In any case, the light that violence sheds on our vulnerability shows what is at stake in our particular and concrete social bonds. It obliges us to raise the question as to why should we trust and why should we continue to willingly own this vulnerability before concrete others that can exploit it against our interests and that can use it to exert violence against us.

Is it possible to create the conditions for trust to emerge and, therefore, for engaging in social relationships that were unlikely before, or for reestablishing social relationships that have been broken? It is relatively common to find arguments saying that it is impossible to trust at will. Given the basic character of this attitude and its passive origin, this might be the case. However, it seems perfectly possible to create conditions to motivate others to trust us or even to trust third parties and to motivate ourselves to trust others as well.

I will leave aside for the moment the interesting and all too common case of trusting a third party, say an unknown person, as a consequence of trusting another one, for instance a friend, who trusts the third party. The fact that trust can be transmitted in this way seems to have wide ranging implications. However, in this chapter, I focus on the simpler case of generating the conditions to trust someone directly.

A person, collectivity or institution can contribute to create conditions favorable to be trusted by making evident her good will and capability to those whose trust she wants to earn, as well as by making evident that this good will and capability is grounded in hopes shared with them. This means giving those whose trust we want to earn reasons to believe that we value things that they might value as well, and that we have practical intentions (or habitualities) that are compatible with the possibility of them trusting us in a rational way. I might be inclined to trust someone to take care of my children if she has given me proofs of being willing to help me and doing me good and of being capable of responding in a responsible way if there is an emergency of any kind, but also if I know that she shares with me the hope that by taking care of them, she is contributing to the flourishment and well-being of my children. If I am convinced of her good will and capability, but think that by taking care of my children she hopes to foster a goal that I do not share—like converting them into her religion or teaching them principles or values that I do not share—this might be a good reason not to trust her with their care.

Trusting someone can make it easier for the trusted person to reciprocate the trust because the vulnerability is thus tempered: To be trusted is to receive some power over the trusting person, and it is easier to trust someone over whom we hold some kind of power. The power that we have by being trusted is a balance or check for the possible abuse of the power given to those who we trust (Baier, 1986).

Because it often takes place in intimate and trusting environments, sexual violence can be especially suitable to examine what is frequently at stake in trusting: being open to establishing, reestablishing, preserving, or renewing social relationships. It does not make sense to willingly trust someone who does not have an interest in keeping or maintaining with us a social relationship that we can consider acceptable or desirable. These and other forms of violence that are embedded in asymmetrical social relationships, like those of class, racialized subjects, people from different ethnicities or nationalities, etc., can be faced with the power or collective organization that is made possible by trust and trust networks of support. However, missing or overseeing the possibility of undertaking rational or reflexive trusting attitudes can make us fall in the mistake of considering that violence brings us to an impasse because it inhibits trust and, with this, inhibits the possibility as well of resisting or reverting violence with organized collective actions.

What I have argued is that we can leave this false impasse behind if we raise the questions as to how, who, and in what matters should we trust, and also, what kinds of relationships do we wish to establish with those who we trust by the very fact of trusting them. I hope to have given elements to show that it is possible to raise and answer these questions by considering different sorts of reasons and by adopting a reflective attitude to examine the beliefs, practical intentions, and desires that are involved in trusting someone or a group of people in a given case.

The kind of reflective attitude toward trust that I have identified as rational trust is something already present in our everyday relationships. My purpose here was to make it explicit so as to highlight a dimension of our practical rationality that is often neglected and to examine some of the implications and consequences of the fact that practical rationality involves making sense of our vulnerability and dependability on others. Moreover, I tried to show that we do this by adopting an attitude that we usually take as alien to rationality. It is seemingly obvious that violence is related to the inhibition of trust because the menace of violence makes it less likely that one will be willing to remain or become vulnerable before those who might exploit this vulnerability for their own interests. However, rather than a mere inhibition of trust, violence often causes a limitation or delimitation of it. With this I mean that violence motivates those who suffer it to draw limits about the persons (or kinds of persons) and matters (or kinds of matters) in which they can find reasons to trust or distrust. As it can often be seen in social conflicts and movements, growing distrust in some persons and matters comes together with new forms of trust and solidarities.

Trust cannot disappear altogether without undermining or transforming substantially our capability to be in the world with others (De Warren 2020). Moreover, this capability comes together with the structure of vulnerability and dependability to which I have alluded previously. It is not possible nor desirable to avoid being vulnerable and dependent on others. What does it mean to make sense of our vulnerability and dependability? To take them as ethical problems in a phenomenological vein means to inquire the following: How can we attempt to live the most rational or meaningful life that we can live considering our vulnerability and dependability on others, as well as the vulnerability and dependability of others on us? This question cannot be answered in an abstract way. It is not enough to inquire into what we should believe, desire, and do. These are already difficult questions, but the acknowledgement of our vulnerability and dependence on others makes the inquiry much more difficult because it comes with the acknowledgment that these questions should be answered in relation to what we think or know that those others believe, desire, and do. We raise and answer these questions when we reflect or converse with others about the reasons that we might have to trust them and also about the reasons that we have for wanting to earn their trust.

Before assuming that it is necessary to attempt to regain the trust that we have lost from someone, it is convenient to ask ourselves why we want this trust. It goes without saying that this applies as well for institutions that have lost or never gained the trust of the people that are supposed to serve, but it is important to keep it in mind because trust is the glue of all social relationships, be them among individuals or collectivities. Broken trust might be the consequence of rational reflections from a party that received the worst part from a social relationship. In such a case, it can only be rational or make sense to trust again if the renewed trust is based, among the other elements that I have mentioned, on signs of good will and of desires that the trusting person can share. To display signs of good will and shared desires without sincerity, with the mere purpose of earning someone's trust, amounts to perpetuating the forms of domination or violence on the basis of deceit. It is not idle to ask what we desire from engaging in relationships with others and what we desire and value when we trust and want to be trusted.

In this chapter I have attempted to elaborate on the idea that ethics should consider the fact of empathy, that is, the fact that we exist in a world whose meaning implies our awareness of others. The philosophical question of how we can make sense of our vulnerability and dependability of others is perhaps closer to our everyday experiences and concerns than what we might consider when we discuss it in philosophical texts. It is the everyday question of who and why should we trust, whose trust should we honor, and why should we reciprocate the trust that others have in us—or, in other words, why should we be loyal or in complicity with them. Should we trust persons, groups or institutions—be they relatives, friends, colleagues, bosses, government offices or officials, etc.—that are violent against us or against other people? Should we reciprocate their trust and thus be loyal to them? If we answer in the affirmative any of these questions, we should be able to say why and how we should trust them or reciprocate their trust. However, given that we often, if not always, trust before deciding to do it, these answers are already given. By trusting and reciprocating the trust of others we have always already taken a position that involves beliefs, valuings, and volitions, regardless of whether we are aware of them. If ethics involves making a radical reflection on what we ought to do in any given case, on what is most rational or what makes more sense to do (Husserl 2004), then it cannot do away with making explicit in concepts the ways in which we attempt to make sense of our vulnerability and dependability of others in our everyday lives and submitting them to a radical examination.

NOTES

1. I have elaborated elsewhere the idea that what Husserl and Reinach called "social acts" [*Soziale Akte*], a concept that resembles that of "speech acts," implies collaboration. (See Marín 2015 and 2018a).

2. For an alternative and more structural phenomenological analysis of this degradation, see Marcela Venebra (2021). Venebra argues that women's bodies are often culturally constituted as objects available for men.

3. Segato uses the concept of "rape" to allude to the use and abuse of the body of other without her participation with a comparable intention or will. She employs the term *violación cruenta* or "gore rape" to broadly allude to rapes where persuasion plays a minor role, and the act is done through the use of force or the menace of force (Segato, 2010).

4. For a more complete phenomenological analysis of trust and its relation to hope, see Marín-Ávila (2021).

5. For a phenomenological account of sexual violence as forced intimacy, see Ferrarello (2019).

6. For feasibility as a component of practical rationality and the relationship between this kind of rationality and axiological and doxical rationalities, see Husserl (1988, 2004) and Marín Ávila (2018b).

7. On the apprehension of value, see Husserl (2004, pp. 71, 74, 92 and 223; 1952, pp. 8–9)
8. I elaborate on this conception of hope with more detail in Marín Ávila (2021).
9. I take this metaphor from De Warren (2020).

REFERENCES

Arendt, H. (1970). *On Violence*. San Diego: Harcourt Brace Jovanovich.

Baier, Annette. (1986). Trust and Antitrust. *Ethics*, *96*(2), 231–60.

———. (1992). Trust. In *The Tanner Lectures on Human Values, vol. 13*, 107–174. Salt Lake City: University of Utah Press.

Butler, Judith. (2006). *Precarious Life. The Powers of Mourning and Violence*. New York: Verso.

De Warren, Nicolas. (2020). *Original Forgiveness*. Evanston, IL: Northwestern University Press.

Ferrarello, S. (2019). *The Phenomenology of Sex, Love, and Intimacy*. New York: Routledge.

Husserl, E. (1952). *Husserliana IV. Ideen zur einen reinen Phänomenologie und phänomenologischen Philosophie. Zweites Buch: Phänomenologische Untersuchungen zur Konstitution* (ed. M. Biemel). The Hague: Martinus Nijhoff.

———. (1973a). *Husserliana I. Cartesianische Meditationen und Pariser Vorträge* (Ed. S. Strasser). The Hague: Martinus Nijhoff.

———. (1973b). *Husserliana XIV. Zur Phänomenologie der Intersubjektivität. Texte aus dem Nachlass. Zweiter Teil. 1921–28* (Ed. I. Kern). The Hague: Martinus Nijhoff.

———. (1973c). *Husserliana XV. Zur Phänomenologie der Intersubjektivität. Texte aus dem Nachlass. Dritter Teil. 1929–35* (Ed. I. Kern). The Hague: Martinus Nijhoff.

———. (1987). Fünf Aufsästze über Erneuerung. In *Husserliana XXV. Aufsätze und Vorträge (1911–1921)* (Ed. T. Nenon & H. R. Sepp). The Hague: Martinus Nijhoff.

———. (1988). *Husserliana XXVIII. Vorlesungen über Ethik und Wertlehre. 1908–1914* (Ed. U. Melle). The Hague: Kluwer Academic Publishers.

———. (2004). *Husserliana XXXVII. Einleitung in die Ethik. Vorlesungen Sommersemester 1920 und 1924* (Ed. H. Peucker). Dordrecht: Kluwer Academic Publishers.

Kant, I. (2007). *Grundlegung zur Metaphysik der Sitten*. Suhrkamp.

Kessler, K., and A. Staiti (2010). Einstellung. In H. Gander (Ed.), *Husserl Lexikon* (pp. 78–80). Darmstadt: WGB.

Lomnitz, C. (2005). Sobre la reciprocidad negativa. *Revista de antropología social,* 14, 311–39.

———. (2021, March 5) *Interpretación del 'tejido social rasgado.'* El Colegio Nacional. https://www.youtube.com/watch?v=L5pzMLBQqv8

Marín Ávila, E. (2015). Social Acts as Intersubjective Willing Actions. In M. Wehrle & M Ubiali (Eds.) *Feeling and Value, Willing and Action. Essays in the Context of a Phenomenological Psychology, Phaenomenologica*, vol. 216. New York: Springer.

———. (2018a). Sobre la racionalidad del deber social. Reflexiones sobre el deber social con base en observaciones de Edmund Husserl y Adolf Reinach. In M. Crespo (Ed.) *Filosofía trascendental, Fenomenología y Derecho natural*. Hildesheim: Olms.

———. (2018b). "On axiological and practical objectivity. Do Husserl's considerations about objectivity on the axiological and practical realms demand a phenomenological account of dialogue?" In I. Quepons & R. Parker (Eds.), *The New Yearbook for Phenomenology* (pp. 212–30). New York: Routledge.

———. (2021). Hope and Trust as Conditions for Rational Actions in Society. A Phenomenological Approach. In *Husserl Studies*, 1–19. DOI: 10.1007/s10743-021-09288-9..

Pateman, C. (1988). *The Sexual Contract*. Redwood City, CA: Stanford University Press.

Reinach, A. (1988), "Die apriorischen Grundlagen des bürgerlichen Rechtes (1913)," in *Sämtliche Werke. Textkritische Ausgabe 1. Werke* (Eds. K. Schuhmann and B. Smith) (pp. 141–278). Philosophia.

Sánchez Vásquez, A. (2003). *Filosofía de la praxis*. Mexico City: Siglo XXI.

Sartre, J. P. (1992). *Notebooks for an Ethics* (Trans. Da. Pellauer). Chicago: University of Chicago Press.

Searle, J. (2010). *Making the Social World. The Structure of Human Civilization*. New York: Oxford University Press.

Segato, R. L. (2010). *Las estructuras elementales de la violencia*. Buenos Aires: Prometeo Libros.

Steinbock, Anthony. (2014). *Moral Emotions: Reclaiming the Evidence of the Heart*. Evanston, IL: Northwestern University Press.

Venebra, M. (2021). A ras de la carne: en el límite de la violencia y el sentido. In A. Bąk (Ed.) *Las fronteras del sentido. Filosofía y crítica de la violencia*. Toluca, Mexico: UAEMEX/Sb editorial.

Zirión, A. (2005). Tolerancia y confianza. In *Acta fenomenológica latinoamericana. Volumen II* (pp. 137–49). Lima, Peru: Círculo Latinoamericano de Fenomenología/Pontificia Universidad Católica del Perú.

Chapter 3

Emotion, Reality, and Ownership

Craig Derksen

ABSTRACT

The paradox of fiction has been used as a tool to study how our emotions relate to reality for a long time. I follow its form and its lesson to create the paradox of empathy and ownership. This paradox and strategies for resolving it can provide insight into how empathy works as well as possible harms due to perceptions of ownership.

Keywords: empathy, ownership, paradox of fiction, emotion

We seem to feel emotions based on the lives of others, even if they are fictional. Consider the television show *BoJack Horseman*.[1] While the show is about the life of a washed-up anthropomorphic horse who was the star of a situation comedy in the 1980s and 1990s and is voiced by Will Arnett, the show is also about sadness. The show is considered to really begin with the eighth episode "The Telescope," which sets the mood for the rest of the series.[2] Without empathy, the show does not work. Without empathy for a horse, the show does not work. Without empathy for a fictional horse, the show does not work.

There are similarities between emotions directed toward other people and emotions directed toward fiction. Emotions directed toward fiction are directed at others, fictional others. The challenges presented by our emotional responses to fiction have been used as a tool to explore the details of emotion at least since Plato. In *The Ion*, Plato claims that the only explanation for our emotional responses to fiction is that we are out of our minds. There are lessons that have been learned about emotion and our perception of reality from the paradox of fiction. Likewise, there are lessons to be learned from a similar approach to empathy and our perception of ownership.

PARADOX OF FICTION

The modern take on the paradox of fiction is usually attributed to Colin Radford but also to Kendall Walton.[3] It involves a paradox of three claims:

1. People experience emotions for fictional characters and events, without perceiving them to be real.
2. People do not believe that fictional characters and events are real.
3. To experience an emotion for a character or event, one must perceive it to be real.

This is standard paradox form, all the claims seem plausible on their own, but holding all three is a contradiction. The paradox targets the relationship between emotion and the perception of reality. Claim 1 endorses emotion for fiction, claim 2 rejects our perception of fiction as reality, and claim 3 endorses a relation between emotion and the perception of reality.

This paradox has a great history. Since its introduction, it has become a mainstay of philosophy, neuroscience, and literary theory.[4] Part of the reason it has received so much attention is that it is at an intersection of all these fields, and people love working at intersections because it allows neuroscientists to talk about literature and literary theorists to talk about brains. Another reason that it has received attention is that it is a paradox or puzzle, and people love working with puzzles. They love playing with puzzles, they love solving puzzles, they love rejecting puzzles. In fact, it is common for people to not only solve the paradox by rejecting one of the claims but also to suggest that they have rejected the existence of a paradox in the first place.[5]

There are a variety of classifications for solutions to the paradox.[6] The most common classifications revolve around which claim is being rejected.

Some reject claim 1. Some of these rejections are based on the claim that our responses to fiction are not emotions but emotion-like responses.[7] Others claim that our responses to fiction do not have objects (like moods rather than emotions) and, thus, cannot be directed at fiction.[8] Still others suggest that the responses are emotions, but they are directed at things we perceive to be real rather than the fictional objects that we know are imaginary.[9]

Others reject claim 2. This requires an explanation of how we believe that fiction is real. This approach usually relies on an irregular account of belief and reality. It inspires an investigation of alternatives, like a partial belief, a loss of reality, or a willing suspension of disbelief.[10]

The final approach is to reject claim 3. The approach to rejections of claim 3 differ based on whether they reject an intuitive approach to claim 3 or a theoretical approach to claim 3. The intuitive approach is easily rejected because most people do not have a strong intuitive commitment to the relationship between emotions and reality. The rejection of the theoretical approach (the cognitive theory of emotion) uses the paradox as a call for a theoretical revision to allow for emotional reactions to fiction.

However, the literature is far more than a decision on whether to pick claim 1, 2, or 3. The organization of the positions into rejections of different claims is a starting point for investigations. It is not a matter of rejecting claim 1 and saying that responses to fiction are not emotion; the important part is where things go from there. A solution to the paradox that posits a special emotion-like state that is not an emotion can be similar to a solution that posits a special belief-like state, if the exploration is similar. Likewise, a rejection of claim 3 is not of any value without a subsequent exploration of the rejection. The organization facilitates the exploration of the relationship between emotion and the perception of reality.

The whole point of the paradox of fiction is that there is something odd going on with our emotional responses to fiction that needs to be explored. We do not see emotional responses to fiction as odd because they are so common, just a part of life. However, the paradox is an attempt to draw attention to how odd our emotional responses would seem if they were not so common.

Our emotional responses to people and events that we perceive to be real are different from our emotional responses to people and events that we do not perceive to be real. The rejections of the claims are ways of exploring these differences. Emotion and reality do not have a simple and direct relationship, but they still do have a relationship and exploring that relationship has been the focus of the study of the paradox of fiction.[11]

A PARADOX OF EMPATHY AND OWNERSHIP

If the paradox of fiction is a tool to study the relationship between emotion and belief in reality, then a paradox of empathy could be used to study a similar relationship related to empathy.[12] The paradox of fiction is a puzzle caused by having emotions directed at things that are not real as if they were real. The paradox of empathy is a puzzle caused by having emotions for things that are not ours as if they were ours. The paradox of fiction puts an emphasis on the perception of reality, and the paradox of empathy puts an emphasis on perception of ownership. While the paradox of fiction involves a generous understanding of reality, this paradox involves a generous understanding of ownership.[13]

Why ownership? Empathy refers to the relationship between our emotions and others, their circumstances, and their actions. While it covers a wide variety of psychological phenomena, they all involve the relationship between our mental states and other people, their circumstances, and their actions. Your emotions that are directed at you, your circumstances, and your actions are just emotions, not empathy. Empathy requires emotions about others. Emotions about others require a generous understanding of ownership.

Thus, the paradox:

1. People experience emotions based on other people, their circumstances, and their actions, without perceiving the people, circumstances, or actions as belonging to them.
2. People do not believe that they own other people, their circumstances, and their actions.
3. You must believe that you are a person, are in a circumstance, or performed an action in order to experience an emotion.

The elephant in the room is number claim 3. Unlike the paradox of fiction, we do not have a cognitive theory of emotion to fall back on. What we do have is a history of discussing empathy as taking something.

Common definitions of empathy rely on certain metaphors. These metaphors include: sharing feelings, experiencing another person's experiences, placing yourself in another person's frame of reference or position, taking on another person's perspective, walking in someone else's shoes, and so on.[14] These metaphors universally rely on taking something from someone else and using it as if it were your own. They require you to claim ownership over feelings, experiences, frames of reference, perspective, and metaphorical shoes that do not conventionally belong to you.

The academic discussions of empathy rely on a similar metaphor. David Hume's discussion of how people's minds "turn into mirrors" is frequently used as a watershed moment in the discussion of empathy.[15] While mirrors might not be an obvious metaphor for ownership, they do copy an image that belongs to something else. Hume's choice to describe our mental states as "reflecting" and "reverberating" with other people's minds, further demonstrate how this metaphor is about generous ownership.[16]

Both Theodor Lipps and Edmund Husserl rely on the metaphor of "projection."[17] On the surface, projection is reaching outward, projecting yourself into someone else's mind or circumstance. However, neither is actually suggesting that we somehow send our thoughts out into the world. In both cases the metaphor is about taking in external things. We do not actually put something in someone else's shoes. We imagine that we are wearing their shoes, it is internal. For Lipps, this is clear from his emphasis on sense data and its implications for how we understand aesthetic experiences and other minds. This is also clear from Husserl's emphasis on intersubjectivity, which is accessed from a first-person point of view. Both Lipps and Husserl require an adoption rather than a projection. Since the person is adopting something that they do not own, both Lipps's and Husserl's accounts of empathy rely on a generous account of ownership.

Even the neuroscientific discovery of mirror neurons confirms the emphasis on ownership. Mirror neurons are neurons that fire both when we are the person, when the circumstances are ours, when the actions are ours, and when this is not the case.[18]

The paradox of empathy and ownership might not seem exciting because it is easy to resolve. However, how it is resolved is at issue. The easiest resolution is an appeal to empathy. The question is: What sort of appeal? Does empathy provide a rejection of claim 1? Do we only experience emotions for our own person and events, while empathy is a distinct nonemotion response? Does empathy provide a rejection of claim 2? Does empathy allow us to perceive other people and events as ours, even if they are not? Or is empathy a rejection of claim 3, a type of emotion that does not require ownership? While empathy might solve the paradox, how we use it to solve the paradox results in different accounts of empathy, with serious implications.

Just as with the paradox of fiction, the value is in the exploration rather than the strict resolution. The exploration of the paradox of fiction is an exploration of the intersection of emotion and belief. The paradox of empathy and ownership is an exploration of the intersection of emotion and perceptions of ownership. Empathy does not involve the typical perception of ownership that nonempathic emotion does, but it does involve some sort of perception of ownership. Empathy does not just require the perception of other's circumstances, but it also requires having an atypical perception of ownership toward those circumstances, making them your own to some degree.

For empathy, it is the perception of that ownership that matters, rather than actual ownership.[19] Just like our perception of reality does not always match with reality, our perception of ownership does not always match up with actual ownership. For example, we might think we own things that we do not and vice versa based on clerical errors. More than that, just like our perception of reality is complicated in different ways than reality, our perception of ownership is complicated in different ways than ownership. A house might be owned by the legal homeowner but also by the bank, an investment fund, and the government. However, the primary income earner might feel like they really own the house, as might the person who does all of the housework, as might the person who spends most of their time there, as might the person who grew up there (even if their family sold the house). Most children definitely feel like they own their rooms. Things can be ours in a variety of ways, but we can think they are ours in even more ways. These perceptions of ownership are not wrong when they conflict with ownership (the child is not wrong to feel like they own their room) nor are they correct when they align with ownership (someone who invests in the investment fund that owns your mortgage cannot demand a place to sleep). We can and do apply the perception of ownership broadly. We regularly criticize drivers who "think they own the road." We encourage people to take ownership of themselves, their circumstances, and their actions, even though this sort of ownership is not covered by conventional property rights.[20] Our perception of ownership is complicated by the complexities of ownership, as well as the complexities of perception, and the complexities at the intersection of the two.

Rather than try to capture all of these complexities, I offer the following: Empathy involves treating some element of another and their life as if it is ours. This is not conventional ownership, nor is it simple ownership. It can be applied to a broad group of entities including people, circumstances, and actions. It allows for perceived degrees of ownership. Conventional ownership is often concerned only with controlling interest, only the person who owns enough to have control matters. Perception of ownership concerns itself more broadly, all degrees of ownership matter. Perception of ownership also allows for a variety of elements, I can have some entailments of ownership without others.

THE CHALLENGE OF EMPATHY AND OWNERSHIP

Just like the benefits of a generous approach to reality (and, thus, imagination) are well-known, the benefits of a generous approach to the ownership of people, their circumstances, and their actions (and, thus, empathy) are well-known. Without empathy, it is unlikely that we as a species would continue to exist. This is probably not news to anyone, but what about the harms of empathy specifically as it relates to a generous conception of ownership?[21] Since empathy is a product of a generous sort of ownership, the harms can be identified in terms of what is being owned and how.

Empathy can be a product of a generous account ownership as directed toward a person. It can be a product of taking that person as owned in the same manner as you own yourself, taking that person as being closer than they are, or taking that person as property.

It is not uncommon to discuss our ownership over ourselves.[22] The belief that we are someone other than ourselves seems to be a failed perception of reality rather than a failed perception of ownership. However, a generous account of ownership might result in maintaining reality (I know who I am) but applying the rights, privileges, and responsibilities of self-ownership to another person. I might celebrate a child's or favorite sports team's successes as if they were my own and even talk about "our" success. While some behaviors inspired by this sort of perception of ownership might be beneficial, like empathy, others could be harmful, like using your perceived rights of self-ownership to supplant the other person's rights of self-ownership.

A weaker but related generosity of ownership would involve behaving as if that person is closer to us than they are. We apply some of the entailments of ownership to others based on our closeness to them; we have greater rights, privileges, and responsibilities toward those that are closest to us.[23] The generous account of ownership can result in the perception that others are closer to us than they actually are. We can treat strangers as if they are long-term close friends if our circumstances result in the stronger perceptions of ownership commonly associated with empathy. The best example of this is the treatment of celebrities as if they are close friends, making them more likely to be the target of our empathy.

Possibly the most dangerous version of generosity of ownership is to take another person as if they are your property. In this case the rights, privileges and responsibilities deployed would be those of property ownership rather than self-ownership. I do not think that the harms of this need to be enumerated.

This generous account of ownership can also apply to circumstances. Rather than behave as if I owned another person, I could behave as if I owned their circumstances as if they were my own. This can be extreme where I behave as if their circumstances were circumstances that I am in, or more subtle where I behave as if their circumstances were somehow closer to me than they actually are. This can be through confusion of probability (behaving as if they are more likely) or temporality (behaving as if I was or will be in the circumstances). We understand and respond to the circumstances of others differently than we understand and respond to our own. Generosity of ownership blurs this line and allows us to take on the circumstances of others as if they were our own. This sort of confusion of ownership of circumstance can also influence our beliefs about the world and thus behaviors. Owning the circumstances of a parent whose child was kidnapped can result in a person being paranoid in the protection of their own child. Just as personal experience can bear more epistemic weight, generously owned experience can bear more epistemic weight.

The generous account can also apply to actions. I can take someone's actions as if they were an action I have taken or as if they were the sort of action that I would take. This bears special interest for how we treat those actions. People tend to justify actions that they own in different ways than the actions of others. We have many psychological mechanisms developed to protect ourselves from the psychological danger of neutrally judging our own actions. Taking ownership over the actions of another will prevent neutral judgment of their actions.

Although the generosity of ownership necessary for empathy can lead to moral problems, the lack of generosity of ownership is just as dangerous. Frequently people fail to have empathy or reject their empathic feelings if they cannot take ownership of the other person, their circumstances, or their actions. People often fail to take ownership of other people if they are perceived as different.[24] People reject the circumstances of others if those circumstances are unfamiliar or interpreted in a problematic way.[25] People reject the actions of others if they do not understand them. Rejecting the ownership of these people, circumstances, and actions means the rejection of empathy. This lack of ownership often explains the failure of empathy.

THE POINT

When we study imagination, the idea of a generous approach to reality has aided the investigation for a long time. The study of empathy could likewise benefit from the idea of a generous approach to ownership. Just like with imagination, the point is not to be critical of this generous account, but to use it to inform our accounts of empathy. With it we can see the possible dark sides of empathy as well as a possible cause for a lack of empathy.

NOTES

1. https://www.netflix.com/title/70300800
2. https://www.avclub.com/at-last-we-see-who-and-what-bojack-horseman-and-bojack-1798469018
3. Radford, 1975; Walton, 1978.
4. Neill, 2005.
5. There is a common approach that involves referring to the paradox as the "so-called paradox."
6. Levinson, 1997.
7. Walton, 1978.
8. Charlton, 1984.
9. Lamarque, 1981.; Currie, 1990.
10. Taylor Coleridge, 1817, ch. 14.
11. This exploration has included the relationship among emotion and action, catharsis, and loss of reality as well as other topics.

12. I am not the first to note a relationship between the paradox of fiction and empathy, see Harrison, 2008.

13. Although not all resolutions to the paradox of fiction rely on a generous understanding of our perception of reality, they all relate to it, making it an easy way to describe a widely varied group of solutions. I will follow this practice for discussing empathy as a generous approach to ownership.

14. This is probably best demonstrated by an internet search for *empathy*.

15. Stueber, 2019.

16. Hume, 1978. For a discussion of the crimes of mirrors, see Borges, Yates, Irby, and Gibson, 2007.

17. Lipps, 1903; Husserl, 2001.

18. Goldman, 2006.

19. For a discussion of actual ownership and strong emotion, see Hick and Derksen, 2012.

20. Some tie self-ownership to personal identity; Martin, 1998.

21. I will not concern myself with the other harms of empathy here.

22. Smith, 2020.

23. Another complexity of our perception of ownership.

24. Hein, Engelmann, Vollberg, and Tobler, 2016.

25. Fricker, 2007.

REFERENCES

Borges, Jorge Luis, Donald A. Yates, James East Irby, and William Gibson. (2007). *Labyrinths: Selected Stories & Other Writings*. New York: New Directions.

Charlton, William. (1984). "Feeling for the Fictitious." *British Journal of Aesthetics*, *24*(3), 206–16.

Coleridge, Samuel Taylor. (1817). *Biographia Literaria*.

Currie, G. (1990). *The Nature of Fiction*. Cambridge, Cambridge University Press.

Fricker, Miranda. (2007). *Epistemic Injustice: Power and the Ethics of Knowing*. Oxford: Oxford University Press.

Goldman, A. (2006). *Simulating Minds: The Philosophy, Psychology, and Neuroscience of Mindreading*. Oxford: Oxford University Press.

Grit Hein, Jan B. Engelmann, Marius C. Vollberg, and Philippe N. Tobler. (2016). "How Learning Shapes the Empathic Brain." *Proceedings of the National Academy of Sciences*, *113*(1), 80–85.

Harrison, Mary-Catherine. (2008). "The Paradox of Fiction and the Ethics of Empathy: Reconceiving Dickens's Realism." *Narrative*, *16*(3), 256–78.

Hick, Darren, and Craig Derksen. (2012). "Righteous Art Anger." *The Journal of Aesthetics and Art Criticism*, *70*(4), 373–82.

Hume, David. (1978). *A Treatise of Human Nature*. Oxford: Oxford University Press.

Husserl, Edmund. (2001). *Logical Investigations Volume 1*. London: Routledge.

Lamarque, Peter. (1981). "How Can We Fear and Pity Fictions?" *British Journal of Aesthetics*, *21*(4), 291–304.

Levinson, Jerrold. (1997). "Emotion in Response to Art: A Survey of the Terrain," in Mette Hjort & Sue Laver, *Emotion and the Arts* (pp. 20–34). New York: Oxford University Press.

Lipps, T. (1903). *Aesthetik Volume 1*. Hamburg: Voss Verlag.

Martin, Raymond. (1998). *Self-Concern: An Experiential Approach to What Matters in Survival*. Cambridge: Cambridge University Press.

Neill, Alex. (2005). "Art and Emotion," in Jerrold Levinson, ed., *The Oxford Handbook of Aesthetics* (pp. 421–35). New York: Oxford University Press.

Radford, Colin. (1975). "How Can We Be Moved by the Fate of Anna Karenina?" *Proceedings of the Aristotelian Society*, *49*, 67–80.

Smith, Joel. (2020). "Self-Consciousness." *Stanford Encyclopedia of Philosophy*. Available at: https://plato.stanford.edu/entries/self-consciousness/#SensOwne

Stueber, Karsten. (2019). "Empathy." *Stanford Encyclopedia of Philosophy*. Available at: https://plato.stanford.edu/entries/empathy/

Walton, Kendall L. (1978). "Fearing Fictions," *The Journal of Philosophy*, *75*(1): 5–25.

Chapter 4

Embracing Ambiguity

Simone de Beauvoir's Responsive Ethics

Maren Wehrle

ABSTRACT

Throughout her philosophical and literary career, Simone de Beauvoir was concerned with existential problems like singularity, freedom, and responsibility. Beauvoir transforms phenomenological concepts like intentionality, situation, lived body, project, and existence from Husserl, Merleau-Ponty, Heidegger, and most of all Sartre into a genuine existential ethics based on the ambiguity of the human condition. This ambiguity of our finite existence, namely, the fact that we are both subject and object, active and passive, immanent and transcendent, is for her the precondition of real ethics. Two insights are crucial for such an approach: that existence is always embodied and situated (concretizing and complementing Husserl and Merleau-Ponty) and that freedom can never be absolute but must be realized within concrete situations and in relation with others (arguing against Sartre).

In this chapter, I will present Simone de Beauvoir's philosophy as a *responsive ethics*, in which freedom and vulnerability, mind and body, we and others, are necessarily intertwined. Her entire work, so I would like to argue, not merely her "ethics of ambiguity," can be characterized as an attempt to develop such a performative ethics—an ethics that argues for the response-ability to accept and embrace one's ambiguity to live an "authentic," that is, ethical life.

Keywords: Beauvoir, Merleau-Ponty, ambiguity, responsivity, responsibility, situation, freedom, performativity, ethics, phenomenology, existentialism

INTRODUCTION: EMBRACING AMBIGUITY

> As situated beings, all humans share this fundamental ambiguity of being at once subject and object. Beauvoir's attitude toward this condition is not to regard it or the tension it produces as undesirable, a flaw to be eliminated if possible. For Beauvoir, ideally we embrace and live our ambiguity. This belief lies at the heart of her humanism. (Card 2006, 15)

From her earliest to her latest writings, Simone de Beauvoir was concerned with existential problems like singularity and intersubjectivity, freedom and responsibility. For Beauvoir all ethical questions arise within the tension of these seemingly opposing poles, for example, the temptation of bad faith or conflicts in relation with others. Although her thought, which developed out of the intellectual environment of Paris before, during, and after the Second World War, is framed within Sartre's existentialism and highly influenced by the works of Merleau-Ponty, Heidegger, and Husserl (Gothlin 2006; Bauer 2006; Kruks 1990; Heinämaa 2003; Langer 2006; McWeeny 2017; Willkerson 2017),[1] Beauvoir concretizes, corrects, complements. and combines their concepts and approaches to produce a genuine existential ethics based on the ambiguity of the human condition.

Even before spelling out the concept of *ambiguity* explicitly and theoretically in her essay *The Ethics of Ambiguity* (1948/1947), Beauvoir pointed to the unsolvable ethical tensions that come with our concrete and finite existence: the seemingly opposing experiences of being both free subjects and an object for others, both active and passive, both separate from and dependent on others. Here, it already becomes clear, in what ways Beauvoir's notion of ambiguity departs from the ontological definitions of either Heidegger or Sartre. In using fiction as a form of expression, she emphasizes the concrete situation of individuals instead of mere ontological structures. Unlike Sartre, she develops a fine-grained analysis of concrete intersubjective relations, which cannot be reduced to a mere dualistic or dialectic approach of the "for-itself" and the "in-itself," which then either leads to an antagonistic approach or a dissolution of self and other.

In her first novel *She Came to Stay* (1984/1943), inspired by the writings of Hegel and Sartre, Beauvoir testifies to the existential antagonism of consciousness against consciousness, and freedom against freedom. About a "love triangle" among the characters Pierre, Xavière, and Françoise, the novel begins with Hegel's statement that "each consciousness seeks the death of each other" and ends with Françoise's murder of Xavière. But instead of confirming the theoretical antagonism, where each consciousness wants to objectify or even murder the other to claim its freedom, she dives into the complex realm of the concrete: the stickiness of interrelations and emotional involvements between subjects. It thus becomes clear that the murder at hand is not metaphysical but motivated by a concrete situation and aimed at a particular person. The point was not to eliminate the "other" itself, as Debra Bergoffen emphasizes, but to murder this particular other: "Existential ambiguity trumps Hegelian clarity."[2]

In her subsequent essay Pyrrhus and Cinéas (2004/1944), Beauvoir explicitly addresses the underlying ethical questions that come with existential ambiguity. She differentiates between ethically correct and incorrect realizations of singular freedoms and projects. In this regard, she starts off with an existential ontological description of the human condition as an absolute but finite freedom. She asks, how can we welcome this freedom and live it, and how is this freedom *related to or even combinable with that of others*? First, she argues that disrespect or violence against the other's freedom also affects me: I am the "face" of the other's misery; I am responsible for their situation of which I am part. Second, I need this other to realize my own freedom; I must call out, make an *appeal to the other*, that is, affect and convince them to engage with and pursue my projects even beyond my lifetime.[3] But, for this appeal to be successful, I have to respect their freedom as equal to mine.

The issues raised by these early novels—the ambiguity of our existence, the responsibilities and limits of freedom, our singularity and intertwinement with others—are explicitly stated and elaborated on in a more systematic and theoretical terms in *The Ethics of Ambiguity*, and later philosophically applied to concrete cases and situations in *The Second Sex* (2011a/1949), *Must We Burn Sade?* (2011b/1953), and *The Coming of Age* (1996/1970).

In the following, I want to show, that two insights are crucial for her unique take on ambiguity. First, existence is always embodied and situated (concretizing and complementing Husserl and Merleau-Ponty). Second, freedom can never be absolute but must be realized within concrete situations and in relation with others (arguing against Sartre). It is her focus on situatedness and relatedness that ultimately makes her existential philosophy (and fiction) into an ethical project. I thereby claim that her approach can be interpreted as a *responsive* and, ultimately, a *performative ethics*, in which freedom and vulnerability, mind and body, self and other, are necessarily intertwined and in which we constantly try to realize and perform a situated and relational freedom.

DEFINING AMBIGUITY

With the notion of *ambiguity* Beauvoir refers to the fact that we are objects and subjects alike, that we are a part of this world of which we are conscious. Although we assert ourselves as an "internality against which no external power can take hold," we simultaneously experience ourselves as a "thing crushed by the dark weight of things" (Beauvoir 1948/1947: 7). This existential condition expresses itself concretely in "the truth of life and death, of my solitude and my bond with the world, of my freedom and my servitude, of the insignificance and the sovereign importance of each man and all men" (Beauvoir 1948/1947: 9).

In this regard, humans can never be a pure thing, nor a pure subject, but find themselves somewhere in between. In other words, we are both subjective agents that freely project themselves into the world, a world that appears there for us, as well as material, visible, and vulnerable objects within that world. In this ambiguous situation, humans must realize their freedom. Freedom is made manifest by the constant possibility of failure. To fulfill one's freedom, then, one must face their ambiguity. This demands the assumption of oneself not as a fixed existence, but rather as a "lack of being" (cf. Sartre 1956), to elicit a space for being to unfold.

The use of the notion ambiguity in Beauvoir has most often been associated with the ontology of Sartre and Heidegger (cf. Gothlin 2006; Keltner 2006). Here, ambiguity refers to the temporal tension between facticity and transcendence, between what we currently are and what we are about to be. In this sense, human existence is understood as a project or becoming rather than a predefined substance or essence: In existing, one continuously projects oneself toward a future, thereby uniting past and present within one's doings. In Sartre's interpretation, this leads to the famous existential imperative that existence always comes before essence. Human being is thus characterized by a lack of being; therefore, it is forced to give itself being (i.e., it has to define its essence itself through its projects).

For Sartre, this lack of being is what is essential for subjectivity in opposition to objectivity or being. As operating subject of my experiences or actions, I transcend myself toward the world, I am consciously directed at the things in this world. As such, I am not thematic or conscious of myself or my body; therefore, strictly speaking, I am nothing. One is only something, that is, a content-determined object (part of being) of this world, that is, seen and thematized as object. However, this being and its content is primarily determined by other subjects, whose gaze objectifies us and thereby assigns us a specific objective sense and meaning.[4] This brings Sartre to the radical conclusion: Either I am subject and consciously have the world, but I myself am nothing, or I consciously have myself (as object) but lose my status as subject. In being something, I thus lose my self-evident and carefree acting in the world and recognize that I am an object among others and that there are other subjects for whom I am an object and with whom I have to share this world. Within such a dualistic framework one is either in the subject mode, where the world is "for me" (*pour soi* [for itself]), or one is in the object mode (*en-soi* [in-itself]). However, human beings are never just an in-itself, but first and foremost an object for others (*pour-autrui* [for-others]). This results in an antagonistic approach to intersubjectivity, where the relation between self and other must necessarily be conflictual. Other subjects by definition want to constrain my freedom and objectify me: One is either subject or object; either I objectify, or I am objectified.

Beauvoir follows Sartre in stating that it is precisely this lack of being that implies the possibility of transcendence (going and being beyond of what one is at the moment). But this ontological freedom and lack of determination comes at the price of needing to fill this gap with one's own projects, which in turn leads to existential anxiety. However, contrary to Sartre, Beauvoir interprets this ambiguous condition in a much more positive way: Her emphasis lies not on the desire of "wanting to be" (i.e., the often failed attempt to define one's essence by oneself). Instead, and more in the line with Heidegger, she understands this desire as "wanting to disclose being" (cf. Beauvoir 1948/1947: 12; cf. Gothlin 2006: 49). This seemingly slight change of emphasis, however, makes a big difference. It aligns ambiguity not with the attempt to overcome a paradoxical ontological condition, an attempt that is doomed to fail, but with a joyful desire to explore the world, which expresses itself as a performative praxis of disclosing and being responsive to the world.[5]

Such a disclosing must in turn not be understood as an objectification but as a pre-reflective and practical form of intentionality, a term originally coined by Husserl (*fungierende Intentionalität*) and concretely applied in Merleau-Ponty's phenomenology of the body (Merleau-Ponty 2012/1945: 441). The respective lack or indefiniteness of existence is what makes the *disclosing* of the world and *transcending of the subject* into this world possible. What Beauvoir adds to this is a specific affective dimension. The freedom and need to transcend oneself, which lies at the heart of every existence, is accompanied with what she calls a *joy of existing*. The primal state of human existence thus lies not in seeking the "death of the other consciousness," or in the wish to objectify the other but in a "free generosity" that expresses itself in vitality, curiosity, and responsiveness (Beauvoir 1948/1947: 41).

According to Beauvoir, the human condition is thus first and foremost characterized by a *passion for meaning* or a *drive toward being*, a passion that can never be completely fulfilled because we are unable to disclose the absolute meaning of the world or become its autonomous authors. Therefore, this drive "always misses its goal" (Beauvoir 1948/1947: 42).[6] The latter, the indeterminateness, can in turn cause anxiety and fear and the wish to objectify, universally define or retain a once-fixed meaning or role. On the basis of Husserl's distinction between an operating and an object-intentionality, Beauvoir here employs a two-stage model of *affective intentionality*. Joy is what accompanies the first stage of intentionality, which is defined as an operative mode of disclosure or discovery (of the meaning) of the world. The second stage comprises the explicit act of fixating or creating meaning whereby one posits oneself as an author of this meaning. The latter can be accompanied with a praxis of self-identification or an act of domination of others. Depending on which mode prevails, this "objectification" can thus either ground a movement of liberation (from a constraining or oppressive situation) or an act of exploitation (of the world and others), respectively.

In this framework, we do not have opposing forces such as consciousness on the one hand and materiality on the other. Rather, the body, as lived body and as *material* body becomes central. We experience joy because of the *affective and responsive connection* we have with the world and others. Beauvoir describes the body that feels and its sensitivity as a presence, "which is attentive to the world and to itself" (Beauvoir 1948/1947: 42). In this regard, the body is not only determined by physiological conditions but also the condition of our affective relation with the world. For Beauvoir, ambiguity is thus not merely a side effect, resulting from the ontological definition of human being as transcendence or lack of being, as it is in Heidegger and Sartre. Rather ambiguity is something concretely lived. In this latter sense, ambiguity is based on the existential fact, that as existence, we are embodied, concretely situated and, thus, affected by, dependent on and responsive to others.

Although Beauvoir merely refers to Husserl or Merleau-Ponty in her *The Ethics of Ambiguity*, I would like to argue that she develops her ethics in direct relation to Husserl's phenomenology of the body and Merleau-Ponty's concrete application of it,[7] in terms of the situated body and the body in-situation. The very fact of situatedness is thus the reason that existence is ambiguous, or to put it in transcendental terms, as Merleau-Ponty does in his preface to the *Phenomenology of Perception*, situatedness is the condition for the possibility of experience (Merleau-Ponty 2012/1947, xxvii). Because of being materially situated in the world, we are both a subject for, and an object of, this world; because of being temporally and historically situated, the past impacts our current projects, and they transcend themselves into the future; because we are socially situated, all of our meanings and doings are (implicitly or explicitly) related to others.

THREE DIMENSIONS OF AMBIGUITY

Beauvoir's idea of ambiguity comprises three essential insights, which follow from each other and which describe different dimensions of situatedness: (1) Existence is embodied: one both experiences the world through one's body, and one experiences oneself as body situated in this world. (2) Existence is historical: one is situated in time, that is, has to span an intentional arc that links an inhabited past to present actions and future goals. (3) Existence is intersubjective: in our existence we are bound up with, and dependent on, others (cf. Keltner 2006: 201).

Of Being a Subject for and an Object of Experience

The first insight can be traced back to Husserl's distinction between *Leib* and *Körper*. For Husserl, our embodiment is inherently twofold: It is lived as well as material (i.e., extended and physical), subject as well as object, of experience. This ambiguity of human embodiment is well illustrated in the famous quote, which states: "The same Body which serves me as means for all my perception obstructs me in the perception of itself and is a remarkably imperfectly construed thing" (Husserl 1989: 167). The body is what allows us to perceive, and it is in this sense the subject of perception, while at the same time the body is a perceived object. However, it can only be imperfectly perceived by oneself and, therefore, is in need of verification and signification by other subjects. Here, the crucial aspect of ambiguity that Beauvoir notes at the beginning of her *Ethics*, that we are at the same time a subject and an object for others, finds its concrete anchorage in the ambiguity of human embodiment.

Husserl highlights two related but ultimately different aspects of human embodiment. First, he emphasizes the aspect of a lived, sensing and moving body (*Leib*) in contrast to the mere extended body. Against such a dualism, he points to the necessary conjunction of the lived and physical aspects of embodiment by using the combined term *Leibkörper*. Husserl thereby intends to show how the subjective lived aspects are interrelated with the material ones. Indeed, the notion of the lived body at the same time implies that we are also physical and external, otherwise we could neither sense nor be sensed. Second, Husserl wanted to stress our ability to address ourselves thematically in terms of a physical object or *Körper*. The crucial point in Husserl's differentiation is thus not so much the difference between the nonmaterial and the material, the internal or external, but rather the difference between a nonthematic (operative) bodily being or existence and the body as thematic, explicit or intended object.

In Beauvoir, this ambiguity of embodiment not only plays a prominent role in her descriptions of the concrete situations of existing subjects but also guides her method of analysis. In her descriptions, she combines both an account of lived experiences and bodies on the one hand and represented and evaluated bodies on the other. In *The Second Sex* and *The Coming of Age*, for example, she describes the interrelation of how concrete women/aging subjects live their bodies from within and how this female or aging body is thematized, defined, and evaluated from without in philosophical, religious, or scientific discourses. How the materiality of, and discourse on, women/aging subjects defines their situation and how this in turn is lived, suffered, and taken up by the respective individuals.

From the fact that we are both a material and lived body then directly follow the other two dimensions of ambiguity (2) that we are embedded and situated in a concrete spatial, material, and temporal environment, and that we inhabit, live, and acquire this environment in a pre-reflective or practical way, and are able to reflectively relate and evaluate this situated embodiment (3) that we are affected by and responsive to others who share this environment with us, and that we are able to experience them not merely as objects but also as (transcendent) subjects.

Of Being Situated and Being In-Situation

As subject-objects we are passively located, affected, moved, or molded from the outside and subjectively feel these external affects from the inside. This is the reason why we are never indifferent to our situation and have to somehow relate to what is happening to us. In turn, we are actively disclosing the world and are able to tactually and visually explore it but simultaneously to feel when we are touched or seen. Precisely because we are never merely objects, but also living subjects—sensing, moving and experiencing—our materiality makes us open and vulnerable to the world.

While this fact of situatedness was for Husserl merely an obstacle on the way to the things themselves (early Husserl) or a starting point for an analysis of the lifeworld (later Husserl), Merleau-Ponty made this insight central to his phenomenology. In fact, what he shows, against Sartre, is that being situated is a necessary foundation for human thinking and freedom, rather than something opposed to it. In his *Phenomenology of Perception* (2012/1945), he emphasizes that human perception, and in fact, most human activities are neither reflective or intellectual, nor can they be reduced to simple stimulus response conditions. Instead, humans are through their bodily existence directed toward the world. We acquire and make sense of the world by interacting bodily with our environment. Such a receptive or practical sense-making thereby occurs before we reflect on it or establish fixed linguistic meanings. Our body thereby functions as our "anchor," as it were, to the world. This means that we are situated within, but also that we actively inhabit and relate to, this world. Being *situated* thus means being defined and shaped by the material, natural, historical, cultural, and social "habitat" into which we are born or in which we always find ourselves. Being *in situation* in turn means that we also have to actively appropriate and inhabit this situation and, by this, are able to shape or change it through our doings.

For Merleau-Ponty as well as for Beauvoir, being in the world thus has a twofold meaning; it means that we are (passively) embedded in (or thrown into) it and actively relate to it. We are both situated in an already pregiven natural as well as cultural world and in-situation, that is, related toward the world, in our actions, perceptions, and various intentions. In the wording of Merleau-Ponty's later ontology, we are both part of an already *instituted sense* and participate in the process of *instituting sense*. As concrete living and material beings we incorporate and are shaped by an already instituted meaning, a world, history, culture, or social community that was long there before we entered the picture. This past that was never present to us both impacts the way we live or exist in our bodies (implicitly) and the way we evaluate our bodies and those of others (explicitly). We have to inhabit and appropriate this world in practical and implicit ways and, in turn, relate to this world in explicit ways through affirming, questioning, rejecting, or intentionally changing the conditions we find ourselves in. In doing this, we participate (depending on the circumstances more or less) in the further institution of sense by shaping this situation (cf. Merleau-Ponty 2010/2003). Within existing passivity and activity, generativity and individuality are thus necessarily intertwined.

Merleau-Ponty points here especially to the temporal ambiguity of our embodiment and situatedness. Being situated means being part of a general history of evolution and nature, as well as an individual history of past experiences. In this regard, the lived body is comprised of two layers, an actual acting and a habitual layer (Merleau-Ponty 2012/1945:84), while the latter consists of sedimented experiences, acquired skills, and sensorial-bodily memories. Moreover, the individual body is at the same time an anonymous organic complex, to which we hardly have any conscious experiential access. As actual and habitual bodily subjects, we are thus guided and motivated by a pre-personal time that runs through our bodies and experience and a personal time that represents our current actions. In this sense, Merleau-Ponty can state that we are at the same time entirely passive and entirely active (Merleau-Ponty 2012/1945: 452). The act of explicit choice is here merely the tip of the iceberg, the final recognition and confirmation of a process or project that is already under way (cf. Wilkerson 2017: 228).

Beauvoir's famous sentence that "one is not born, but becomes woman," can be read against the background of the concept of situatedness, where habit plays a central role. Beauvoir with Merleau-Ponty does not understand habit as mere automatic or mechanical repetition but as a performativity through which one literally inhabits and incorporates one's environment via repeated doings. In such processes one's body and character are developed, and one acquires practical meanings and skills. Here, situatedness ceases to be an external condition and literally becomes embodied. This is what Beauvoir points to in *The Second Sex*, when she describes how women's characters are shaped by their situation and repetitive and "immanent" daily tasks. In this process of acquisition, one is both passive and active, shaped and shaping. This makes situatedness on the one hand a permanent, anonymous, and determining force but, on the other hand implies possibilities for change and the realization of a concrete situated freedom.

Beauvoir's focus on "becoming" is thus not a typical example of Sartrean existentialism, which sees becoming in the light of absolute freedom or the realization of a freely chosen and individual project. Rather, the focus lies on the impact of concrete situations that either constrain or enable such an "ontological freedom." Beauvoir thereby allies with Merleau-Ponty in stating that every freedom must necessarily be a situated freedom, that is, constrained but also motivated by one's historical, material, and social situation. However, Beauvoir takes this idea of situated freedom and makes it concrete in applying it to the description of existing historical subjects and their situation. In doing that, she takes the insight of situatedness more seriously than Merleau-Ponty himself when she critically questions if being embodied and being situated concretely means the same for all existing humans. What if a situation is primarily characterized by domination, oppression, or limitation, should the body not be better conceived of as a "prison" than an anchor? What if past experiences and material conditions operate not in a motivating or enabling but in a constraining or even violent way? Beauvoir thereby points to the fact that although all existing humans share a general sense of ambiguity and vulnerability, ambiguity does not mean the same for the privileged as for the oppressed (cf. Card 2006: 15). The lesson to be learned from Beauvoir is that concrete situations can limit our freedom to act, but they do so differently. The limits for some people are thus far more severe than they are for others. This is true, for example, for women in a patriarchal society, for oppressed minorities, and for people at a certain age in contrast to people in the "prime of their life" (as Beauvoir highlights in *The Coming of Age*). In these cases, freedom and one's possibilities of action and choice are not absolute but relative to one's concrete situation.

Taking her existential case study in *The Second Sex* (namely, French middle-class, white women), we can describe women's typical situation as by and large restricted to the French domestic sphere, their activities reduced to the daily repetition of household tasks. In such a division of labor, women are denied their full status as subjects, who actively contribute to their own projects or the legislative and executive dimensions of their society. Instead of being a full sovereign subject able to choose their own projects and define what they want to become, their situation defines their "essence" beforehand as the "other" with regard to men. Instead of experiencing their bodies as organs of their will and desires, they learn that their bodies are there for the desires and needs of others (men and children). Instead of actively creating and transcending themselves in the (public, social, political, or cultural) world, they are allotted the merely sustaining and caring tasks that enable others to do so. In this sense, Beauvoir argues, women are especially confronted with their existential ambiguity.

Although all human existence is both subject and object and possessed of the same ontological freedom (potential and desire to transcend themselves), due to their predetermined and limited caring tasks, women have to deal with the fact of being passive, material, vulnerable, and mortal on a daily basis. However, due to their situation they do not have the possibility of realizing their full freedom as free, creative, and sovereign subjects. Because of their economic dependence and lack of experience, skills, knowledge, or cultural capital needed to enter the public domain, women could not easily escape or transform their domestic situation. Their situation was thus especially oppressive; becoming woman in this historical, political, and economic situation thus involved a form of social determination.

With this concrete example, Beauvoir is able to show that concrete bodily practices or existential projects are not purely individual, nor always chosen voluntarily or even rationally. Certain aspects of "our own" actions are determined for us, as are the practices in which we participate for recognition and acceptance as social or legal subjects. However, one is never fully determined by one's situation; there are (dependent on the level of oppression) relative possibilities for action. Therefore, becoming refers neither to a quasi-natural development nor to a personal choice with a clear telos or aim. But neither does it entail that one is merely passively "made" a woman by society. Becoming necessarily implies a performative dimension, that is, one has to take up one's situation and enact or perform what is appropriate to it. Within this performance, however dominated or limited one is by their situation, one takes part in the becoming and, therefore can be (at least partly) be held responsible for it. Although, one cannot choose one's situation, one can (dependent on the level of oppression) choose how to live it (cf. Tidd 2006: 231).

Here, Beauvoir's existential approach becomes evident. Every existence due to a lack of being, develops or makes itself (into) being (*se faire être*) through its projects. This is why Beauvoir chooses the formulation "*se faire object*," when she describes the becoming of women in a patriarchal society (cf. McWeeny 2017: 218). Women are forced and pushed into being an object by their situation, but they also have to participate to make themselves into objects for others. The situation thus frames or determines the way in which the assigned genders have to realize their subject or object role. While women thus make themselves objects, men are encouraged to make themselves subjects (se faire subject) by "extending [their] subjectivity to the bodies of others and denying [their] vulnerability, relational, and passive aspects" (McWeeny 2017: 2019).

For Beauvoir, patriarchy is thus a societal organization, in which the existential ambiguity, which refers to all human existence, is betrayed by trying to overcome and purify it through a binary and dualist conception. Only by outsourcing the passive, material, vulnerable, mortal, and object side of existence to women, can men in turn retain the illusion of themselves as entirely active, universal, rational, powerful, and almost immortal subjects. For Beauvoir this represents an act of bad faith, where both men and women fail to concretely realize their ontological freedom and thus take responsibility for it. Women are accused of bad faith when they do not take their relative, although limited, possibilities for action but, rather, affirm a situation in which they are spared of responsibility. Men are accused of bad faith when they use "the other sex to hide from themselves their ambiguous condition" (Vintges 2006: 145). To be able to realize their ontological freedom and establish an authentic relation to each other, women should therefore reject the position of the other and take on the role of subject, while men must accept their contingent bodily existence (Vintges 2006: 145).

To deny one's existential ambiguity thus means, for Beauvoir, to deny one's freedom and responsibility. This is true, for each individual as well as for society as a whole. This Beauvoir emphasizes in her book on old age (1948/1947), where she shows, that the same categorization and discrimination applies to the elderly, who are also defined as other in modern Western capitalist societies. A societal system that tries to establish the ideal of a young, rational, strong, powerful, and high-performance male as the standard, while defining everyone else as deviant, is thus according to Beauvoir not a society that allows for the "authentic," that is, the ethical realization of the "ontological freedom" of all of human existence. For this, one must will oneself free, which means transitioning from "nature" to "morality," that is, from a potentially given freedom to an actively realized moral or ethical freedom (Beauvoir 1948/1947: 25).

Three things are thus crucial for Beauvoir's take on ethics based on ambiguity and freedom. First, to will oneself free and to act morally are one and the same. And to act this way, one must embrace one's (and the other's) ambiguity. Second, we are able to concretely realize our freedom and become ethical beings not despite our ambiguity but because of it. Although every human existence is free as well as situated (ontological conditions), one can choose how to live one's situation, that is, one can choose to take up one's freedom properly or instead reject or deny it. In *The Ethics of Ambiguity*, Beauvoir describes several psychological "types" of existence that in different ways flee from realizing their freedom. Their common characteristic is their indifference with regard to their existence; they want to withdraw from their freedom, for example, by trying to reject all values of existence (nihilist), to transfer their freedom and responsibility to a group, higher cause or ideology (serious man), or else to deny their ambiguity and thus the freedom of others (adventurer). Finally, this means, that if we want to ethically realize our freedom, we need to recognize the ontological freedom of others and practically (ethically) support it.

It is at this point that Beauvoir departs from an early Sartrean existentialism and becomes ethical. Her ethics is thereby based on the idea of ambiguity as it is found in Merleau-Ponty rather than Sartre: the entanglement of subjectivity with time, others and the world, the passive with the active, the visible with the invisible, the tacit with the explicit. However, going beyond Merleau-Ponty and Sartre, situated freedom must always be a relational freedom (cf. Andrew 1998, 2006, cf. also Kruks 1990, Fulbrook/Fulbrook 1995).

The Ambiguity of Being with Others

Intersubjectivity, in the form of an ontological dependency and difference between self and other, and in the form of concrete relations in love, reciprocity or conflict, lies at the heart of Beauvoir's ethics. Here again, beyond the common associations with Sartre and Heidegger's approaches to the topic, one can also identify an idea prominently defended by Husserl, namely that the ambiguity of our embodiment is crucial for empathy. Husserl's take on empathy thereby includes the experience of the other as both "similar" and essentially "different" from us. Both aspects are necessary for granting the other's freedom and my own.

In experiencing the other, we are aware of the other's body as material and extended object, while we are at the same time responsive to them as "bodily subjects," and we immediately grasp the other *as* "other," that is, as something that transcends us and is transcendent to us—a subject that cannot be reduced to an object of our experience but instead has its own experiences (including their experiences of us). The "double constitution" of the body as Leib and Körper thus has a mediating position not only among the thinking I, soul, and nature but also between my bodily self and the other. This is why embodiment is crucial for Husserl's account of empathy, thereby showing a different path to intersubjectivity than that taken by Sartre. Rather than cause for conflict, the ambiguity of human embodiment is seen as the precondition for every form of empathy. In our everyday life, we never see other bodily subjects as mere objects among others, although what we actually perceive is only the visible and external side of the body. However, the other is immediately accessible to us through its bodily expression (i.e., we always experience others directly as subjects like ourselves. This is possible because we ourselves have experienced this intertwinement of the exterior, material side of embodiment with an internal/subjective side (notably in the phenomenon of the double sensation; Husserl 1989: 152). Nonetheless the other is for us never originally accessible. Their feelings, emotions, or thoughts can only be anticipated. What makes the other a subject or other constantly escapes us, we can neither hold on to it nor control it. Indeed, this is what constitutes the transcendence of the other, makes them subject. If the other could be experienced originally, it would merely be one of my experiences, an immanent idea. However, the fact that we cannot in principle experience the other originally means that the other subject cannot be reduced to my experience, and it transcends my experience, existing independently and outside of it. Even more, the other has the same status and the same general abilities as I myself. Conversely, this means that I too am an object of the experience of others—so I too am dependent on others, who need to assign meaning and grant recognition to my existence. [8]

This means that our situated existence is always bound to others and comes with the ability of responsiveness to others and that this mere potential must be concretely realized as ethical freedom (i.e., a freedom that intentionally respects and supports the freedom of others). Freedom thereby concretely requires reciprocal recognition. To live in bad faith thus refers not only to individuals who deny their own freedom but also to those who deny others' freedom. That we need the other to recognize, support, or carry on our meanings and projects is the piece of the puzzle Sartre has missed: "To will that there be being is also to will that there be men by and for whom the world is endowed with human significations. One can reveal the world only on a basis revealed by other men" (Beauvoir 1948/1947: 71). To be able to grant such a recognition, legitimation, and generativity, those others must be free themselves: "Every man needs the freedom of other men and, in a sense, always wants it, even though he may be a tyrant; the only thing he fails to do is to assume honestly the consequences of such a wish. Only the freedom of others keeps each one of us from hardening in the absurdity of facticity" (71). Therefore, as Barbara S. Andrew puts it: "It is not enough to make meaning in front of slavish devotees, for their recognition is not valuable because it is not free" (2006: 36).

To disclose the world in a meaningful way, we need others. Beauvoir is the first to make this seemingly simple idea explicit. With a side kick to Hegel and Sartre, she emphasizes that the other does not merely take the world from me and limit my freedom but also gives the world (including myself as part of this world) to me. The initial feeling of hate is thus naïve, a "desire that struggles against itself," because "[i]f I were really everything there would be nothing beside me; the world would be empty. There would be nothing to possess, and I myself would be nothing" (Beauvoir 1948/1947: 71). The fact that we are situated in a historical world and that we can only disclose this world partially from our limited perspective, means in turn, that other subjects are needed to reveal the world with and for us. Moreover, the whole notion of "project" has a necessarily intersubjective dimension. "No project can be defined except by its interference with other projects" (71). So, to be able to realize and transcend ourselves toward the world in our projects, we need to appeal to others to recognize our projects as meaningful and to participate in them, support them, or take them over, beyond our finite existence.

This inter-relatedness and dependency is by no means evaluated as something negative. Quite the contrary, being authentic is not defined in individual or aesthetic terms (in opposition to an intersubjective sphere like "*das Man*" in Heidegger) but in ethical and relational terms. Living an authentic life means to realizing one's ethical and relational freedom together with others. Freedom is thus always related to the freedom of others: "To will oneself free is also to will others free" (Beauvoir 1948/1947: 73). This means not that I will the other's freedom out of self-interest. Rather Beauvoir wants to emphasize that every individual freedom is existentially tied to the freedom of all others. In willing my freedom, I must thus simultaneously will the freedom of others. If the other subjects would not be free (or full subjects), this would mean in turn that my world (that is revealed by and with others) and my projects (recognized, overlapping, dependent on others) would be empty or worthless. Here, Beauvoir's argumentation is aligned with Husserl's, in which intersubjectivity is needed to grant not only one's status as subject but also to verify the objectivity of the world. She translates this epistemological argument into a practical and ethical one: Only a being that is free can grant me my world, that is, the meaning, recognition, and freedom, I am dependent on. The world has only value and meaning for me, if it is also a world to others, in turn, "freedom has only a meaning when other people exist to recognize it" (Card 2006: 25).

However, such a realization of relational freedom does not occur without conflict. Beauvoir does not dissolve the tension between me and the other, rather she emphasizes both, that as individual existence we are ontologically separated, have different desires, projects, or situations, and that we are bound to another in a plurality of ways. Concretely, this means that I cannot will the freedom of all at the same time. I have to decide which freedom I want to support at a certain time, and this could be at the cost of—or even in opposition to—the freedom of other subjects. Here, ethical decisions become entangled with history and politics. One needs to come up with a historical reflection and political arguments, addressing the question why a certain group of subjects at this time needs the support of freedom more than others or even at the expense of others. Such a decision must thereby necessarily relate to and reflect on the concrete historical, social, economic, and political situation of subjects and cannot be made according to universal principles or a categorical imperative.

CONCLUSION: A RESPONSIVE ETHICS

In *The Ethics of Ambiguity*, Beauvoir famously states, against all accusations of existentialism as an individualistic, relativistic or antinormative approach, that "existentialism is the only philosophy in which an ethics has its place" (Beauvoir 1948/1947: 38). In her argumentation, she refers to the fact that other philosophies cannot explain the existence of evil. In a philosophy that reduces everything to prefixed physical nature, evil would be reduced to a mere epistemological error on the side of humans, while in a traditional humanism, one cannot even account for such a thing as evil as both humans and the world are supposed to be complete and perfect. Only when there is the real possibility to fail, to lose, or to win, when there are real dangers and damnations, is there room for ethical considerations. If everything is decided beforehand by nature or god, or if everything is already perfect, there is no need or room for an ethic. Therefore, an ethic presupposes a certain amount of freedom (there is something to choose or decide) but also a certain amount of situatedness that motivates specific actions (not all actions are equally relevant or good). In this sense, the situatedness and ambiguity that follow from this is not an obstacle for ethics but rather makes ethical reflection possible and needed. On this point, Beauvoir has a unique position that is the basis for her responsive ethics. Contrary to Heidegger or Merleau-Ponty, who define intersubjectivity as a neutral or harmonious state of being-with, she insists on the individuality and separateness of existence. Contrary to Sartre, for whom the self-other relation is defined in agonistic and conflictual terms, she emphasizes the relational and reciprocal aspects of intersubjectivity. Again, if we were to be equally defined and affected by a social sphere of being-with, there would be no need for an ethics. The same would hold true if every intersubjectivity were by definition antagonistic. In that case, an intrinsic ethical reflection on how we should relate to each other would be useless (instead one would only need external laws that prohibit one from killing others). However, the fact, that human existence is both subject and object, situated and free, passive and active, dependent and separate (a) is the ontological condition for responsivity and empathy for others but also the cause for anxiety, fear, and the possibility of fleeing this ambiguity by dominating others and (b) enables one to realize or reject one's concrete, that is ethical and relational freedom, and thereby makes ethical reflections necessary.

Beauvoir's ethics is thereby performative and bottom-up in that it relies both on the possibility (openness) and necessity of becoming. Taking the fact of the situatedness of human existence seriously, she has to reject a deontological ethics in the Kantian vein, which defines a priori and universal moral imperatives. Also, ethics for her is not a normative study of concepts like "good" or "bad" (cf. Heinämaa 2006: 75). Rather than understanding ethics in a top-down manner, where imperatives, concepts, values, or rules are applied to various concrete situations, she wants to understand how these values are constituted bottom-up by situated individuals in their interrelated doings. In this sense, she is closer to an Aristotelian virtue ethics, where you become virtuous only by repeatedly doing virtuous things. The insight she draws from this is that values, rules, and norms are not merely what define and determine our situation (being situated) but also develop through and depend on our activities (being in-situation). The latter entails that we have to take on a certain responsibility for them. If we affirm or passively repeat norms that are to our advantage but are harmful for others in that they constrain their freedom, objectify or dominate them, then we have a co-responsibility for them. More radically, we thereby deny parts of our ambiguity and are in consequence not free.

To concretely realize one's freedom as an ethical one is thereby neither an easy task nor something everyone is able to accomplish at all times and in all situations. In *The Second Sex* and *The Coming of Age*, Beauvoir delves deeper into the societal, economic and material conditions that stand in the way of becoming an ethical, free and relational self, while in *The Ethics of Ambiguity* or *Must We Burn Sade?*, she analyzes the psychological factors that stand in the way. Not everyone is able to face their ambiguity and, thus, realize their freedom properly. In this regard, Beauvoir describes various modes of escaping one's freedom, all of which result in an overall indifference towards one's existence and consequently to the existence of others. Such indifference is for Beauvoir the cause of all evil or unethical action. The first class of types she defines are the *subman*, the *serious man*, and the *nihilist*. All of them share a fundamental apathy or lack of vitality, which is motivated by their fear of existence. Instead of following their primary desire to disclose the world, they numb, in turn, their original sensitivity and openness to it.

The subman, whose negation of himself shows in his boredom and lack of meaningful interaction with others and the world, masks this fear and indifference by taking refuge in the ready-made values of the social world. He easily follows leaders or succumbs to ideologies (45). Because he is unable to escape his ontological freedom, he needs to find a way to engage with the world. At this point, he often turns into the serious man. The serious man focuses on an external object, social value, or ideology in which he attempts to lose himself. He subordinates his freedom under a "great" cause or esteemed value, which in turn provides him with predefined values and a stable identity (48). In giving himself over to a higher cause or acting as part of a group, however, he ceases to take any responsibility for the respective values and the probable harm they cause others. If the serious man fails to achieve his higher cause, his disappointment turns him into a nihilist, who tries to desire nothing. Although, this attitude expresses a truth about the ambiguity of the existence—that it is indeed a lack, nothingness, as well as radical finitude—the nihilist fails to live his ambiguity in refusing to become.

The second class of types are not indifferent but instead appear to be joyfully or passionately engaged with the world and others. However, they are unable to realize a truly relational freedom. The adventurer, for example, seems at first glance to affirm his freedom, and enjoys disclosing the world and transcending himself. However, he uses others for his adventures thereby negating their freedom: "His fault is believing that one can do something for oneself without others and even against them" (63). The passionate man also flees his freedom by failing to establish a reciprocal relation: Instead of being responsive and open towards the other, he rather wants to possess the other as his object (65).

A responsive ethics must condemn these "inauthentic" ways of living, not in the name of a predefined normative concept or law but because these forms neglect the relationality that lies at the heart of every existence. Although every action emanates from subjectivity, these actions at the same time transcend and thereby surpass one's subjectivity. Neither a project, a choice, a value or norm can be realized or last without the recognition, belief, and support of others: "Man can find a justification of his own existence only in the existence of other men" (72). Therefore, indifference to others or domination of others is an inauthentic and thus unethical form of existence for "a freedom will itself genuinely only by willing itself as an indefinite movement through the freedom of others" (90).

Ontologically, we are thereby bound up with others in the most fundamental way, namely, in an *affective* manner. Existence is described by Beauvoir as an "urgent interrogation," as soon as one exists one has to "answer." Existence as affectivity, transcendent movement as well as vulnerability, means that "I concern others and they concern me" (72). Therefore, intentionality as the disclosing and constituting of meaning must be affective as well as intersubjective. In disclosing the world, we connect to others affectively;

in constituting meaning or engaging in projects together. Genuine or "authentic" freedom and an ethical life is thus only possible when it is shared (cf. Wehrle 2020).

At the same time, just being affected by or being responsive to others is not enough. In the same way as we are not merely passively situated but have to take up and actively relate to this situation, we also have to engage in reflections and intentional actions to become ethical. For Beauvoir, the freedom to become (and not be totally determined by one's situatedness) comes with responsibility. One needs to learn, exercise and continuously realize one's freedom in accordance with and in support for others. In this regard one is not responsible for the biological, material, or economic situation, historical and cultural norms and values, we are born in and that shape us. But we are responsible for the way we relate to these conditions, how we live them, and whether we want to keep or change them.

Beauvoir's work is in this regard an attempt to develop such a responsive and performative ethics of freedom and responsibility. An ethic, which calls us to actively and repeatedly accept and embrace our ambiguity to live an authentic, that is, ethical, life. This is what she herself tried to accomplish in her writing and activism. Ethics for Beauvoir is thus not reduced to a certain domain of actions but is a life project, even more, it is "the existential project." Wanting to realize one's freedom, to become free or human, one needs to become ethical. Becoming ethical is thereby not merely an individual but a collective task, a shared work that is never finished and must remain open and partly ambiguous[9] because of the changing situation one has to reckon with. Embracing one's ambiguity is thereby the first step to becoming an ethical self, which implies being a sensitive and responsive self, responsive to the appeal of past, present, and possible future others.

NOTES

1. For her reading and application of Hegelian concepts as master/slave dialectics etc., cf. Hutchings 2017; Direk 2017; Gothlin 1996; Bauer 2001; Green and Roffey 2010; for influences from Marx, see Kruks 2017.

2. Cf. Bergoffen 2011.

3. Beauvoir here applies Hegel's concept of mutual recognition that can escape a master-slave dialectic, cf. Bergoffen 2011.

4. Sartre makes this clear in his famous analysis of the gaze, in which a person peers through a keyhole out of jealousy or curiosity. Initially, one is completely absorbed in the act of peering and consciously directed at the spied-on couple behind the keyhole. This suddenly changes as soon as one hears footsteps. At such a moment, one becomes aware of oneself as an object among others in the world, visible to other

subjects in a way that remains inaccessible to oneself. Here, it becomes clear that what one is, is determined by how others see us: In this case, as a person peering forbiddenly through the keyhole, or in short, as a peeping tom.

5. Gothlin argues in this regard that the notion of ambiguity in Beauvoir relies on the Heideggerian concepts of "disclosure" (*Erschlossenheit*) and "being with" (*Mit-sein*), cf. Gothlin 2006: 45.

6. Intentionality always creates new "intentions"' that again seek fulfilling, this is the motor for sensitive disclosure or perception as Husserl also emphasized in his genetic works; he termed this "passion" either "drive-intentionality" or "general perceptional interest," cf. Husserl 1973; Wehrle 2015.

7. For the influences of Merleau-Ponty and Husserl on Beauvoir, cf. Heinämaa 2006; for the similarities and differences between Beauvoir and Merleau-Ponty, cf. Wilkerson 2017; and for mutual influences of the two friends, cf. Langer 2006, McWeeny 2017.

8. As Husserl shows step by step in his description of the experience of the other (Husserl 1963), this other, who initially appears as a mere perceived body in my field of perception, must necessarily also have a sentient and moving body and, thus, a spatiality and environment. A body that is there for me but here for the other. They too have a psyche and a consciousness. They see the same things I do but from a different perspective; they stand on the same ground as I do but in their here. The very existence and experience of the other is thus the key to securing a shared objectivity. As soon as we can prove the transcendence of the other in our experience, it is true that the world and the things I experience exist not only for me but also for others (i.e., they are not only subjective but objectively valid).

9. For a critique that highlights the limits of Beauvoir's notion of ambiguity with regard to ethics, see Schott 2006: 244.

REFERENCES

Andrew, Barbara S. 1998. Care, Freedom, and Reciprocity in the Ethics of Simone de Beauvoir. *Philosophy Today* 42 (3/4): 290–300.

———. 2006. Beauvoir's Place in Philosophical Thought. In: C. Card, ed., *Cambridge Companion to Simone de Beauvoir* (pp. 24–44). Cambridge: Cambridge University Press.

Bauer, Nancy. 2001. *Simone de Beauvoir. Philosophy and Feminism*. New York: Columbia University Press.

———. 2006. Beauvoir's Heideggerian Ontology. In: Margaret A. Simons, ed., *The Philosophy of Simone De Beauvoir. Critical Essays* (pp. 65–92). Bloomington: Indiana University Press.

Bergoffen, Debra. 2011. Introduction to "Must We Burn Sade? In: M. A. Simons & M. Timmermann, eds., *Political Writings* (pp. 39–43). Urbana: University of Illinois Press.

Beauvoir, Simone de. 1948/1947. *The* Ethics of Ambiguity. Trans. by B. Frechtman. New York: Citadel Press.

———. 1984/1943. She Came to Stay. Trans. by Y. Moyse & R. Senhouse. London: Fontana.

———. 1996/1970. *The Coming of Age*. Trans. by P. O' Brian. New York: Norton & Company.

———. 2004/1944. Pyrrhus and Cinéas. In: M. A. Simons, M. Timmerman, & M. B. Mader, eds. Philosophical Writings. Urbana: University of Illinois Press.

———. 2011a/1949. *The Second Sex*. Trans. by Constance Borde & Sheila Malovany-Chevallier. New York: Vintage Press.

———. 2011b/1953. *Must We Burn Sade?* Trans. by K. A. Gleed, M. J. Rose, & V. Preston. In: M. A. Simons & M. Timmermann, eds., *Political Writings*. Urbana: University of Illinois Press.

Card, Claudia. 2006. Introduction: Beauvoir and the Ambiguity of 'Ambiguity' in Ethics. In: C. Card, ed., *Cambridge Companion to Simone de Beauvoir* (pp. 1–23). Cambridge: Cambridge University Press.

Direk, Zeynep. (2017). Simone de Beauvoir's Relation to Hegel's Absolute. In: Laura Henghold and Nancy Bauer, eds., *A Companion to Simone de Beauvoir* (pp. 198–211). Oxford: Wiley.

Fullbrook, Kate, and Edward Fullbrook. (1995). Sartre's Secret Key. In: Margaret A. Simons, ed., *Feminist Interpretations*. University Park: Pennsylvania State University Press.

Gothlin, Eva. 1996. *Sex and Existence: Simone de Beauvoir's "The Second Sex."* London: Athlone.

———. 2006. Reading de Beauvoir with Heidegger. In: C. Card, ed., *The Cambridge Companion to Simone de Beauvoir* (pp. 45–65). Cambridge: Cambridge University Press.

Green, Karen, and Nicholas Roffey. (2010). Women, Hegel and Recognition. *The Second Sex*. *Hypatia* 25(2): 376–93.

Heinämaa, Sara. 2003. *Toward a Phenomenology of Sexual Difference. Husserl, Merleau-Ponty, Beauvoir*. Lanham, MD: Rowman & Littlefield.

———. 2006. The Body as Instrument and as Expression. In: C. Card, ed., *The Cambridge Companion to Simone de Beauvoir* (pp. 66–86). Cambridge: Cambridge University Press.

Husserl, Edmund. 1963. *Cartesian Mediations. An Introduction into Phenomenology*. Trans. by D. Cairns. The Hague: Martinus Nijhoff.

———. 1973. *Experience and Judgment*. London: Routledge & Kegan Paul.

———. 1989. *Ideas Pertaining to a Pure Phenomenology and to a Phenomenological Philosophy. Second Book: Studies in the Phenomenology of Constitution*. Trans. by R. Rojcewicz, and A. Schuwer. Dordrecht: Kluwer Academic Publishers.

Hutchings, Kimberly. (2017). Beauvoir and Hegel. In: Laura Henghold and Nancy Bauer, eds., *A Companion to Simone de Beauvoir*. Oxford: Wiley, 187–98.

Keltner, Stacy. 2006. Beauvoir's Idea of Ambiguity. In: Margaret A. Simons, ed., *The Philosophy of Simone de Beauvoir. Critical Essays* (pp. 201–10). Bloomington: Indiana University Press.

Kruks, Sonja. 1990. *Situation and Human Existence: Freedom, Subjectivity and Society*. London: Unwin Hyman.

———. 2017. De Beauvoir and the Marxism Question. In: L. Henghold and N. Bauer, eds., *A Companion to Simone de Beauvoir* (pp. 236–49). Oxford: John Wiley & Sons.

Langer, Monika. 2006. Beauvoir and Merleau-Ponty on Ambiguity. In: C. Card, ed., *The Cambridge Companion to Simone De Beauvoir* (pp. 87–106). Cambridge: Cambridge University Press.

McWeeny, Jennifer. 2017. Beauvoir and Merleau-Ponty. In: L. Henghold and N. Bauer, eds., *A Companion to Simone de Beauvoir* (pp. 211–24). Oxford: John Wiley & Sons.

Merleau-Ponty, Maurice. 2010/2003. *Institution and Passivity. Course Notes from de Collège de France (1954–1955)*. Trans. by L. Lawlor and H. Massey. Evanston, IL: Northwestern University Press.

———. 2012/1945. *The Phenomenology of Perception*. Trans. by Donald A. Landes. New York: Routledge.

Sartre, Jean-Paul. 1956 [1943]. *Being and Nothingness*. Transl. by H. E. Barnes. New York, Philosophical Library.

Schott, Robin May. (2006). Beauvoir and the ambiguity of evil. In: Claudia Card (Ed.). *The Cambridge Companion to Simon de Beauvoir*. Cambridge: Cambridge University Press, 228–47.

Tidd, Ursula. 2006. The Self-Other Relation in Beauvoir's Ethics and Autobiography. In: Margaret A. Simons, ed., *The Philosophy of Simone de Beauvoir. Critical Essays* (pp. 228–40). Bloomington: Indiana University Press.

Vintges, Karin. 2006. Simone de Beauvoir: A Feminist Thinker for the Twentieth-First Century. In: Margaret A. Simons, ed., *The Philosophy of Simone de Beauvoir. Critical Essays* (pp. 214–28). Bloomington: Indiana University Press.

Wehrle, Maren. 2015. "Feelings as the Motor of Perception"? The Essential Role of Interest for Intentionality. *Husserl Studies 31*(1): 45–64.

———. 2020."Simone de Beauvoir." In: T. Szanto, and H. Landweer, eds., *The Routledge Handbook of Phenomenology of Emotions* (pp. 187–97). London: Routledge.

Wilkerson, William. 2017. Beauvoir and Merleau-Ponty on Freedom and Ambiguity. In: L. Henghold and N. Bauer, eds., *A Companion to Simone de Beauvoir* (pp. 223–36). Oxford: John Wiley & Sons.

Chapter 5

The Personalistic Attitude

Edmund Husserl and Edith Stein on Empathy as the Intuition of the Person as Value

Dermot Moran

ABSTRACT

In this chapter I discuss the close similarities among Husserl's, Scheler's, and Stein's concept of the person as an absolute value that exercises itself in position-takings. Ethics, for the classical phenomenologists, Husserl, Scheler, and Stein, concerns the whole person, including the affective and rational dimensions, intellect and the heart, as well as volition. Persons are distinctive for their free *agency*, *capacity to recognize norms*, and ability to interact responsibly with other personal agents in the context of the communal and historical life-world.

Keywords: agency, Husserl, Scheler, volition

Ethics, for Husserl, Scheler, and Stein, concerns the whole person, involving the affective and rational dimensions, intellect and the heart, as well as volition. Persons are distinctive for their free *agency*, *capacity to recognize norms*, and ability to interact responsibly with other personal agents in the context of the communal and historical life-world.[1] The whole person is ethical through and through. In his 1920–1924 *Einleitung in die Ethik* [*Lectures on Ethics*] (2004), Husserl writes:

> We name "ethical" not only willings and actions [*Wollungen und Handlungen*] with their goals, but also persisting sentiments [*Gesinnungen*] in the personality [*Persönlichkeit*] as habitual orientation of willing. . . . So, we call many joys, griefs "beautiful," noble, now evil, low, mean, and see in them ethical predicates, as well as corresponding sentiments, habitual orientations of emotion [*Gefühlsrichtungen*] like love and hate. We thus assess all properties of the heart [*Gemütseigenschaften*] and summarize the whole "character" of a person as ethical or ethically reprehensible, the inborn as well as the acquired character, and so finally and especially the person [*die Person*] itself. (Husserl 2004, 8)[2]

Persons, moreover, for Husserl, Scheler, and Stein (and Von Hildebrand; see Crosby 2002), instantiate or incorporate value, indeed an absolute value. They also apprehend and create values, stand in evaluative relations to one another, and recognize and interpret each other's intentional motivations that are interwoven with their own. As agents they have the capacity to will ends and set vocational goals for their lives (Hart 2006; Heinämaa 2019, 2020; Loidolt 2021; Luft 2006, 2012). In this chapter, I shall focus on Husserl's and Stein's conception of *persons* and *the personalistic attitude* as the basis for ethical interaction.

Persons, for the classical phenomenology of Husserl, Scheler, Von Hildebrand, and Stein, inhabit the world of spirit (*die Geisteswelt*, *die geistige Welt*), that is, the cultural world of significance and value that is disclosed only if one adopts what Husserl terms, in *Ideas* II (1952, 173), the personalistic attitude (*die personalistische Einstellung*) toward other subjects and engages in spiritual acts with them. Spiritual acts are acts that persons address to each other as persons. As Husserl writes in his *Introduction to Ethics* lectures:

> the peculiar essence of the entire spiritual sphere [*Wesen alles Geistigen*] refers *to the essence of the subjects of the whole spirituality as subjects of intentional lived experiences*; these subjects are Egos, are personal subjects" (Husserl 2004, 104, [trans. Andrew Barrette])

Edith Stein similarly writes in *On the Problem of Empathy* (first published 1917, English translation, Stein 1989)

> Our whole "cultural world," all that "the hand of man" has formed, all utilitarian objects, all works of handicraft, applied science, and art are the reality correlative to the spirit. (Stein 1989, 92; GA 5 109)[3]

Both Husserl and Stein also maintain that the person actualizes herself in *uniquely personal acts* (acts that recognize other persons such as promising, forgiving, etc.).[4] Persons, for both Husserl and Stein, operate at a unique level of their own, apprehend and experience values, take stances, and form convictions that shape their spiritual lives as a whole.[5] Persons are apprehended uniquely through a spiritual recognition from other persons. It takes a person to recognize a person (Husserl does not address the issue of whether there are nonhuman persons but Stein does allow for purely spiritual persons, for example, angels).

Persons have intrinsic value because they are unique and unrepeatable. Husserl always maintains that each consciousness is "uniquely and originally individual": "Absolute individuation enters into the *personal* Ego" (Husserl 1989b, 315; Hua IV 301).[6] For Stein (1996), similarly, each human being has "unrepeatable singularity" and uniqueness (*Eigentümlichkeit*; 182). Stein similarly maintains that every individual has a unique value-essence (*Wertwesen*) in their personhood (*Persönlichkeit*). The world would be missing this unique value-being (*Wesen*) if the person did not exist. In later writings, Stein (2002b, 363; GA 11/12 310) speaks of person-being (*Personsein*). Persons are complex but unique entities (Husserl speaks of their "double unity" of body and soul [*Doppeleinheitigen*] Hua IV 162) enfolding lived bodies, cultural belonging, personal histories, and are enmeshed in interpersonal relationships. Stein (2000b) similarly speaks of human beings doubly entangled in causality and motivation, the twofold basic lawfulness (*die doppelte Grundgesetzlichkeit*; 1). For Stein, the realm of spirit is also the realm of freedom (2002b, 372; GA 11/12 317).

Husserl, Scheler, and Stein (and Dietrich von Hildebrand) understand persons as primarily constituted through feelings and emotions that apprehend and respond to values (*Werte*) that are real and external to the person. Persons emotionally apprehend and appreciate *values* and are motivated to follow *reasons* they themselves find compelling, against a background of "ends" or goals considered defining *for them*. For the classical phenomenologists (Husserl, Scheler, Von Hildebrand, and Stein) persons are individual, unique, and of inestimable value.

THE PERSON IN SCHELER, HUSSERL, VON HILDEBRAND, AND STEIN

The first published *phenomenological* discussion of the person is to be found in Max Scheler's *Formalism in Ethics* published in two parts in 1913 and 1916 in Husserl's *Jahrbuch* (Scheler 1916; 1973). Husserl's lectures of the period (on ethics and on nature and spirit) as well as his *Ideas* II manuscript were unpublished. Husserl denied the direct influence of Scheler and maintained that he had arrived independently at his own conception of the person.[7] Husserl largely resented Scheler for copying his ideas; Scheler in turn poured scorn on Husserl's formulations in his extramural lectures delivered in front of Husserl's students at Göttingen (as Edith Stein recalls (1986, 259). Scheler claimed to have independently discovered phenomenology; Stein (259) excuses him by saying that he was a voracious reader and very likely could not recall where he had found his ideas). Nevertheless in the Preface to his *Formalism*, Scheler writes that he owes "to the significant works of Edmund Husserl the methodological consciousness of the unity and sense of the phenomenological attitude" (Scheler 1973, xix).

Scheler was seeking to lay a foundation for ethics through a concrete analysis of the relation between persons and value. A secondary aim was to critique Kant whom, nevertheless, Scheler regards as having produced the most scientific account of ethics. Scheler had an enduring influence on Stein. In many ways, she sought to harmonize Husserl's and Scheler's accounts of personal spiritual life.[8] She was particularly taken by his account of the person. It is difficult to separate the accounts of the person in Scheler, Husserl, and Stein, but I will sketch a brief account (see also Andrews 2012).

Persons, for Scheler (1973), are peculiar entities, what he calls "beings-in-act," whose nature cannot be objectified (387). The person is a performer or executor of acts [*actvollziehendes Wesen*] (384) "genuine acts in which something is 'meant'" (388). Scheler (mistakenly according to most Kant scholars; see Perrin 1974) criticized Kant for designating the person purely formally as a rational person (*Vernunftperson*), whereas, for Scheler (1973, 383), "*the person* is *the concrete and essential unity of being of acts of different essences . . . The being of the person is therefore the 'foundation' of all essentially different acts*." The person, moreover, "is not an empty 'point of departure' of acts; rather he is a concrete being" (384). For Scheler, the person is a layered unity of drives, feelings, spiritual sentiments, and desires. Most of all persons are bearers of value and apprehend value.

For Scheler, the value of a person is based on their capacity to give example as a good person and this in turn is based on their uniqueness or *haecceity* ("thisness"):

> One can therefore say that the highest *effectiveness* of the good person on the moral cosmos lies in the pure *value* of *exemplariness* that he possesses exclusively by virtue of his *being* and *haecceity,* which are accessible to intuition and love, and not in his will or in any acts that he may execute, still less in his deeds and actions. (Scheler 1973, 575)

The good person *exemplifies* goodness and this *value* motivates and inspires other persons to be good. Scheler is explicit:

> Nothing on earth allows a person to become good so originally and immediately and necessarily as the evidential and adequate intuition [*Anschauung*] of a good person *in* his goodness. (Scheler 1973, 574)

The person is the center of all acts of valuation: "That which can be originally 'good' and 'evil' . . . is the *person*, the *being* of the person itself . . . *'good' and 'evil' are values of the person*" [*Personwerte*] (28). For Scheler, there are ideal types of the good person for each social situation (and Stein follows him here). These *types* act as models because they are *values* and they are apprehended by us in *value-cognitions* (1973, 577) that are given intuitively. We love the being who is the model. Scheler writes that a model or moral exemplar is a "*structured value-complex* in the form of *unity* of the *unity* of the person, a structured thisness of *values* in the *form* of the *person*" (578). The person who *follows* the model is not under a moral law but rather a free act of consent based on love:

> Following, however, is to be understood in the sense of *free* devotion to the content of personal value that is accessible to *autonomous* insight. For we become *like* the exemplar as a person. We do not become what he is. (Scheler 1973, 580)

The person is not a thing or object; the nature of the person, for Scheler, can never be objectified. The person, furthermore, manifests him or herself in the execution of acts but is not a mere aggregate of acts. The whole person is present in and permeates their acts (Scheler 1973, 386). Scheler presents his account of the concrete person as an antidote to Kant's formalism, but he was clearly unfamiliar with Kant's much more detailed discussions of the person in his anthropology, which brings his account closer to Scheler's.

PERSONS AS UNITIES OF BODY, SOUL, AND SPIRIT

For Husserl, Scheler, and Stein, persons are unique ontological entities, distinct from material things. First and foremost, the person is a genuinely objective thing, constituted in objective time and belonging to the spatiotemporal world. On the other hand, its essence is quite distinct from that of real things (*Ding-Realitäten*; Husserl 1965, 493). Each person, for Husserl, develops a particular individual style (*Stil*) of life and acts with typicality and habituality in certain circumstances (*Ideas* II § 60).[9] As Stein (2004) emphasizes, one's individual uniqueness (*individuelle Eigenart*; 22) is expressed in one's original expression, handwriting, impact on others, as well as in one's innate.

Husserl, Scheler, and Stein claim that the person is a surplus over and above its psychophysical constitution (i.e., body and soul). We are not just embodied, material beings causally caught up in and dependent on the world (experiencing gravity, breathing air). The body is living and ensouled—an organism. Each physical thing is an instantiation of a type; its essence is universal (e.g.; water, oxygen; Hua IV 298), whereas each person as spirit has its "individual essence" in a unique sense (Hua IV 298), for Husserl:

> the spirit lives through, takes a position, is motivated [*Der Geist aber ist ein erlebender, stellungnehmender, motivierter*]. Each Spirit has its way of motivation. and, unlike a thing, it has *its motivation in itself.* It does not have individuality only by being in a determinate place in the world. The pure Ego of any given *cogitatio* already has absolute individuation, and the *cogitatio* itself is something absolutely individual in itself. The Ego, however, is not an empty pole but is the bearer of its habituality [*Träger seiner Habitualität*], and that implies that it has its individual history. (Husserl 1989b, 313; Hua IV 299–300)

Being a person is ontological; it is not just a social role. As Sophie Loidolt (2021) points out:

> it is important to note that the uniqueness of the person is not created by social interaction nor practical agency. Rather, it is actualized, formed and unfolded through them.

Persons experience themselves first and foremost as "personal egos" (Husserl 1989b, 149; Hua IV 141). In one sense, Husserl says, the personal ego is one with the psychic ego (the ego of affective life), but in another sense these egos are apperceived from different standpoints—two different "modes of apprehension" (Husserl 1989b, 150; Hua IV 142). The personal ego is related to the interpersonal world of other subjects; the psychic ego relates just to its body (*Leib*; Husserl 1989b, 149; Hua IV 142). The personal ego acts, Husserl says, as ruler of the soul (*als regens der Seele*; Husserl 1989b, 150; Hua IV 142). Stein elaborates these ideas but does not deviate substantially from Husserl.

For Stein, specifically, the individual uniqueness of a person is encapsulated in an individual essence from which the person gradually unfolds or develops (*entfaltet*) throughout life.[10] Husserl captures an essentially similar notion of the entire concrete life encapsulated in a "monad" (a term that already appears in "Philosophy as Rigorous Science" (Husserl 2002) but which achieves prominence in *Cartesian Meditations* [1950]). For Stein, the person is a center to engage the world [*ein Zentrum in die Welt hineingestellt*] (2009, 191; GA 10 128).

PERSONS IN THE NEXUS OF MOTIVATION

Persons, for Husserl and Stein, are constituted in "spiritual acts" that stand outside the causal order (Stein 1989, 109; GA 5 127). They operate by motivation (*Motivation*), which is a connectivity that works through recognizing and understanding reasons that make sense to those persons and invoke specific responses within an overall intentional nexus (*Zusammenhang*) of meanings, as Stein develops, following Husserl *Ideas* II, in her "Psychic Causality," part one of her 1922 *Beiträge* (Stein 2000b).[11] Persons respond to what has *significance* or importance (von Hildebrand's *Bedeutsamkeit*) *for them*, rather than automatically reacting to stimuli, as in the cause-effect network of the natural world. For Stein, "Motivation is the lawfulness of spiritual life" (1989, 96; GA 5 107; a similar sentence is also found in Husserl's *Ideas* II § 56: "motivation is the lawfulness of the life of the spirit," 1989b, 231; Hua IV 220). Strict causation is the law governing the natural world. Understanding the spiritual world means grasping intentional motivation and the rational laws governing the domains of feeling, valuing, willing, and acting (Stein 1989, 97; GA 5 114). For Stein (1989), this means that the human sciences require understanding through appreciating the relevant motivations, a "comprehension that relives history" (93; GA 5 109).

In her first book, *On the Problem of Empathy* (1917), Stein claims that human feelings disclose a new objective realm, namely, the world of values (*die Welt der Werte*; Stein 1989, 92; GA 5 108). Stein writes similarly in her *The Structure of the Human Person*: "We gain access to the world of values, as to the entire objective world [world of objects], through our spiritual life" (Stein 2004, 114). In *Empathy*, she writes furthermore:

> Spiritual acts do not stand beside one another without relationship, like a cone of rays with the pure "I" as the point of intersection, but one act experientially proceeds from the other. The "I" passes over from one act to the other in the form of what we earlier called "motivation." (Stein 1989, 96; GA 5 114)

Stein (1989) writes that the person as nature is subject to the laws of causality, and, as spirit, to the laws of meaning (*Sinngesetzen*; 112; GA 5 129).

STEIN ON PERSONS AND "LIFE-POWER" (*LEBENSKRAFT*)

Human beings, as embodied, belong to nature and are, in Stein's terms, bodily-bound (*leibgebunden*; 1989, 100; GA 5 118). Husserl and Stein both call human beings "psycho-physical" or "physico-psychic" entities (Hua IV

64). Indeed, Husserl and Stein in particular, acknowledge that psychophysical conditionality (*Konditionalität*; Hua IV 64), that is, health, life-energy (*Lebenskraft*), physical constitution, and capacities can influence one's psychic states (what Husserl and Stein call soul, [*die Seele*]). A person's specific drives, interests, and abilities are dictated by their given bodily, psycho-physical constitution. This is facticity. People just are drawn to, like or dislike, certain colors, tastes, sounds, or movements, Husserl says. It is one's peculiar embodiment that mediates and filters one's being-in-the-world. Both Stein and Husserl believe that we are motivated "from below" (by psychophysical conditionality) and "from above" (moved by spiritual values): "the spiritual life of the human person rises from a dark ground" (Stein 2002b, 364; GA 11/12 310). Elsewhere, she says that the soul sinks its taproot into nature. Persons are material beings as well as possessing psychic and spiritual natures.

Going beyond Husserl, Stein introduces her own novel notion of life-power (2000b, 22; GA 6 22ff), a modification of a concept that she had encountered in Theodor Lipps and Henri Bergson.[12] Life-power is parceled out in different amounts in different individuals and waxes and wanes, can be depleted or replenished, but is always finite. It determines our psychic responses to stimuli (e.g., when one is tired, a slight noise can distract one, which one might not notice in a more energetic state). Everyone only has a given amount of life-power. There is both physical and psychic life-power, for Stein. It is this life-power that can nourish the will of an exhausted person to struggle on. For Stein, it represents the deep individuality of one's union (*Verbindung*) of body and soul.

Stein is clear that my ego is experienced as not actually identical with my body. I can put myself anywhere in my body but some parts seem nearer than others (2004, 84). My hand is nearer to me than my foot, although this experienced nearness is not the same as spatial distance (Stein 1989, 42–43; GA 5 58–9). In fact, Stein says I have a personal body (*ein persönlicher Leib*; 2004, 84) in which the "I" lives and which can be personally shaped by the I. The ego is not the whole of consciousness. Following Husserl, she distinguishes the soul or psyche (*die Seele*) from both the pure ego and the person. The soul is not the same as the egoic stream of consciousness. Our soul is the center of our experiences; it includes the acuteness with which I engage in perception or the liveliness of my behavior. It accounts for the intensity of my feelings (Stein 1989, 39–40). There is a deep psychic source for consciousness that is deeper than the ego. Similarly, spirit lifts the ego beyond itself. Stein gives the example of working on a problem but feeling too dull to solve it. This feeling of dullness is different from the awareness of the ego (2002b, 365; GA 11/12 312). As she writes in *Finite and Eternal Being*: "The human ego, in short, is not only a pure ego, not only a spiritual ego, but also a bodily ego" (2002b, 367; GA 11/12 313).

HUSSERL ON THE PERSON AND THE PERSONALISTIC ATTITUDE

The I is not just a point of view or center for acts and experiences, but the I is first and foremost an embodied, spiritual person. Husserl uses the term "person," following Kant, and others, to mean the individual human subject in its full concreteness, especially in its social relations with other subjects, and in terms of agency, willing, judging, valuing, and generally exercising rational self-responsibility (*Selbstbeantwortung*; *Ideas* II § 60). Scheler similarly believes he is expanding on Kant's formal notion of the person by including the person as sensitive, valuing agent. Stein is able to bring this broadly Husserlian-Schelerian conception of the person into alignment with the traditional Neo-Thomist conception of the person.

In the late *Crisis of European Sciences*, Husserl tries to capture the uniqueness of our personal experience by speaking of the I of personal pronouns (*Ich der personalen Pronomina*; Hua VI 270). In his early *Logical Investigations* (Husserl 1984; English translation Husserl 2001a), it is noteworthy that Husserl does not mention "persons" and his focus is primarily on individual episodes in a single stream of consciousness, in a single "ego" (In the first edition, there is even little mention of the ego). Husserl's first discussion of persons in print is found in his *Logos* essay, "Philosophy as Rigorous Science" (Husserl 2002),[13] where persons are treated as unities not identical with their material bodies. The longest discussion of persons is in Husserl's posthumously published *Ideas* II (§§ 49–51), written initially in 1912, and edited by Edith Stein in the period around 1918 to 1920.[14] For Husserl, at least according to *Ideas* II, persons approach the world primarily through the personalistic attitude (*Ideas* II § 34) which considers human beings in terms of their inner, subjective, mental life and motivations.[15] The personalistic attitude is Husserl's unique phrase (to my knowledge, the term does not appear in Stein or Scheler) for the attitude human beings take towards themselves and others *as* persons (in which they treat each other as "I," "you," and "we," see *Ideas* II § 49), in specifically personal interactions, in talking to one another, shaking hands, and so on, humans adopt the personalistic attitude.[16] Husserl defines it as:

> the attitude we are always in when we live with one another, talk to one another, shake hands with another in greeting, or are related to another in love and

> aversion, in disposition and action, in discourse and discussion. (Husserl 1989b, 192; Hua IV 183)

It is an interpersonal attitude. In the *Crisis* Husserl further explicates personal life:

> Personal life means living communalized as an "I" and "we" [*als Ich und Wir*] within community horizon, and this in communities of various simple or stratified forms such as family, nation, supranational community [*Übernation*]. (Husserl 1970, 270; Hua VI 314)

For Husserl, the personalistic attitude is a basic *sui generis* attitude, perhaps the most original and fundamental human attitude to others. Husserl even thought that the personalistic attitude had genetic primacy: people were animistic in the past about events in the world. As he writes in *Ideas* II § 34:

> That which is given to us, as human subject, one with the human body, in immediate experiential apprehension, is the human person, who has his spiritual individuality, his intellectual and practical abilities and skills, his character, his sensibility. (Husserl 1989b, 147; Hua IV 139)

Note that here Husserl claims that humans have spiritual and not just bodily individuality. Stein goes further to posit a spiritual matter that individuates human beings.

In *Ideas* II, Husserl sees the natural attitude as founded on and subordinated to the personalistic attitude. Indeed, for him, one only arrives at the natural attitude through the self-forgetfulness (*Selbstvergessenheit*) of the personalistic attitude (Husserl 1989b, 193; Hua IV 183). The subject, apprehended as a person (a conscious, free, self-responsible, sense-making agent) is not visible to someone in the naturalistic attitude that sees physical entities as objects of nature (*Ideas* II § 51). In *Ideas* II § 62, Husserl speaks of the interlocking (*ineinandergreifen*) between the natural and personalistic attitudes, but he explicitly differentiates the personalistic attitude from the natural, and indeed maintains that the natural attitude is in fact 'subordinated' to the personalistic attitude (*Ideas* II § 49).[17] The natural attitude is actually reached through a self-forgetting or abstraction of the self or ego of the personalistic attitude, through an abstraction from the personal that presents the world in some kind of absolutized way, as the world of nature.

THE INTERPERSONAL WORLD OF INTERLOCKING SUBJECTIVITIES

Persons are unique individuals, yet they are also *communalized* in a world of interpersonal relationships.[18] For Husserl, we are always persons, with and for others, in permanent relations with others as friends or foes (Husserl 1989b, 192; Hua IV 183). Persons, furthermore, are embedded in surroundings (*Umgebung*) and a surrounding world or environment (*Umwelt*) that is personal and interpersonal. The person is the center of her surrounding world (*Ideas* II § 50):

> to each person belongs his surrounding world [*Umwelt*], while at the same time a plurality of persons in communication with one another, have a common surrounding world. (Husserl 1989b, 195; Hua IV 185)

There is an intermeshing between the personal world and interpersonal common world. This world is the *horizon* for my actions as I perceive and understand them. Horizons offer openness and closure. Thus, Husserl claims, the person who knows nothing of physics does not have physics informing their surrounding world (Husserl 1989b, 195; Hua IV 186).[19] This common surrounding world is "constituted in experiencing others, in mutual understanding and mutual agreement" (Husserl 1989b, 203; Hua IV 193). Persons form a communicative community (*Mitteilungsgemeinschaft*; Husserl 1973, Hua XV 461), constituted through social acts (Husserl 1989b, 204), where one addresses and recognizes others and they reciprocate through responses that recognize the address. Being a person is also an intrinsically social matter involving interpersonal relations with others. We belong to a nexus of persons (*Personenzusammenhang*; Husserl 1989b, 213; Hua IV 203). Similarly, in "Philosophy as Rigorous Science," Husserl says "the personality belongs to a cultural community and an age" (2002, 285).

Soon after it was published Edith Stein carefully read Heidegger's *Being and Time* and wrote an unpublished critical evaluation of it (2006, 445–500; English translation, Stein 2007). Stein has criticisms of Heidegger's insistence on human finitude and his highlighting of anxiety as a fundamental mood, but she agreed that human beings are beings-in-the-world (Stein 1996, 177). In *Aufbau* she maintains: "existence is existence in a world; its life is life in community" *Dasein ist Dasein in einer Welt, sein Leben ist Leben in Gemeinschaft*; Stein 2004, 134). We find ourselves as already members of social groups (e.g., family), larger societies (language-using groups), and institutions. In that sense we are thrown into community. However, our primary experience is not nothingness but the sense of fullness. We are fulfilled through others. For Stein, spiritual worlds are worlds that are subjectively experienced by the persons themselves. It is always a world for me (as we saw also with Husserl), while it also has the sense of being a world shared or shareable with others.

"Individual and Community," (Stein 2000b, 129–314), the second part of Stein's *Beiträge*, published in Husserl's *Jahrbuch* in 1922 is a deeper exploration of the nature of community (*Gemeinschaft*) and society (*Gesellschaft*). In particular, she follows Husserl in recognizing the social acts through which individuals relate to each other (Stein 2000b, 210) as well as the affective attitudes we take to one another—love, trust, gratitude (Stein 2000b, 211). Stein highlights love as a central uniting bond between humans.

THE PERSON AS TAKER OF POSITIONS

To be a person, first and foremost, for Husserl, Scheler, and Stein, is to have the capacity freely to adopt attitudes or take stances (*Stellungnehmen*). Scheler had spoken of the person coming into being by performing intentional meaning-creating acts. Husserl speaks of position-taking as an active, free decision of the ego. For Husserl, all life involves position-taking. Positions can also be altered and the ability to take different stances toward a belief is part of the nature of human consciousness. For Husserl, the concrete, free person is built up gradually through position-takings (Arango 2014), stances I take toward matters that interest me. These do not have to be intellectualistic, and, indeed, the personalistic attitude is generally speaking not a theoretical attitude ("personal life is generally non theoretic" [*kein theoretisch*]; Husserl 1970, 318; Hua VI 297). I am instinctively drawn to certain people and I make them my friends. Husserl describes this kind of practical stance-taking as *habitual*, as a pretheoretical attitude; it is primarily experienced in our emotional life that is oriented to values and in practical choosing and willing. But my stance-taking is decisive for me (Hua IV 231)

In his lectures on ethics, Husserl wants persons to become more self-aware (he even speaks of ego-splitting [*Ich-Spaltung*]; Hua I 16) and "responsible" in that they are required to recognize and give priority to *rational* motivation other and above instinctive, affective, habitual drives. A person develops as a person through specific spiritual acts. Persons are under a moral obligation to develop and perfect themselves (see Loidolt 2021). Especially in his ethics lectures (Hua XXVIII; Hua XXXVII), and in his *Grenzprobleme der Phänomenologie* (Hua XLII [Husserl 2013]), Husserl discusses persons as both instantiating value and creating values and as committing themselves through their choices to the "absolute ought" of developing their personhood to the full. Husserl says in his *Grenzprobleme* that one has to strive to achieve the unity of one's person, to set oneself goals and carry them through. For

Husserl, as his thought developed, the person is more and more viewed as an entity that is not only the "subject of acts of reason" (Hua IV, §60) but is also sensitive to feeling and oriented to value. Human beings are also attentive to what Husserl calls love values (*Liebewerte*) and have a sense of their lives answering to a call. As Husserl writes in *Grenzprobleme*:

> A distinctive feature, however, is that the I is not only a polar and centering inwardness, thereby accomplishing meaning and value and deed out of itself, but that it is also an individual I, who, in all its presenting, feeling, valuing and deciding, has a deepest center, the center of love in the distinguished personal sense; the loving I who follows a 'call,' a 'vocation,' an innermost call, which strikes the innermost center of the I itself and which is raised to new decisions, new responsibilities and justifications of the self. (Husserl 2013, 358–59; Loidolt 2021)

Ultimately, for Husserl, persons inhabit a community of love (*Liebesgemeinschaft*) where persons support each other in becoming who they are (Hua XIV, 172–75; Husserl 2013, 301–17, 512–15). In his *Grenzprobleme*, Husserl also (along with Scheler) attributes the highest worth to persons:

> The highest values are everywhere those of subjectivity as such, which is directed towards value creation and the attribution of value and which is directed, at the very highest level, towards the best that is possible. (Husserl 2013, 316).[20]

Similarly, Stein thinks the person has a responsibility to develop oneself and arrive at "fullness of being" (Stein 2004, 87). Stein is clear that attitudes are adopted habitually and not simply chosen. We built on a platform of habit.

HUSSERL ON THE APPREHENSION OF VALUES

For Husserl, besides our outer perception (äussere *Wahrnehmung*) of objects, and inner perception (*innere Wahrnehmung*) of our own states, we have an immediate, intuitive apprehension of values (*Wertnehmung*) that operates through our feelings.[21] I intuitively apprehend through feeling something *as* beautiful, *as* true, important, useful, and so on (Husserl 1988, 277). At the outset of *Ideas* II, Husserl distinguishes between the theoretical attitude (of the natural scientist) and the axiological and practical attitudes (Husserl 1989b, 9; Hua IV 7). He speaks of valuing acts and of the discipline of axiology,[22] and in his ethics lectures, he regularly discussed the nature of value or worth (*Wert*) (see Hart 1990). Admiring the blue sky as beautiful is a felt experience distinct from theoretically appreciating a blue sky. The theoretical attitude can certainly grasp values, but it does not *live through* the experience of them. One must distinguish between being moved feelingly by the tone of the violin and appreciating intellectually that the tone is beautiful without being actually moved (Hua IV 186–87).

In *Ideas* II, Husserl underscores that he had already introduced the concept of valuation or value apprehension (*Wertnehmung*; Hua IV 9, 186) before Scheler. Values are ideal objectivities, for Husserl (Hua XXVIII 277), as for Scheler, but their exact ontological status is difficult to specify.[23] Scheler maintained there was an objective hierarchy of values and that they have act-being (*Aktsein*). Values are intuitively given; value-graspings (Stein speaks of the grasping of values [*Erfassen der Werte*]), are intentional acts directed at objects, primarily in feelings and emotions. For the mature Stein, this hierarchy of values is an order of being, it belongs to ontology (Stein 2004, 25). Persons are intuitively sensitive to and oriented to *values* (beauty, truth, usefulness). Initially what is apprehended is the object and its nonevaluative features and this object produces an affective reaction that presents a value.

The experiencing of finding something beautiful seems to be a higher-order or founded act depended on a perceptual act (seeing the sun set) and then an accompanying feeling—a *being moved* to experience it as beautiful. The being moved is a *passive* experience. I simply feel myself being drawn to the beauty of the sunset. But there are many different strands to this experience. Feeling the value and responding to it are different.

In *On the Problem of Empathy*, Stein also talks explicitly about *Wertnehmen* as an original apprehension of values (GA 5 11, 33, 34, 35), and she expands on this discussion in her *Beiträge*.[24] The apprehension of a value motivates a feeling response. Moreover, an act of valuing can also motivate an act of will (Stein 1989, 108; GA 5 126). For Stein, where oriented theoretically we see "mere things" (Stein 2000b, 160; GA 6 135). Every objective thing is also a value: "every fully constituted object is simultaneously a value object" (*Wertobjekt*; Stein 1989, 160; GA 6 134). An act of valuing is primarily a felt experience, for Stein. However, a genuine act of valuing can be based on a *nonactual* experience, such as a memory or an imagining. Stein recognizes that we can be intuitively drawn to a lower value that we feel more than a higher value (Stein 1989, 105; GA 5 123). I grasp a value in a special act of feeling. This initial feeling is different, for Stein (who is following Hildebrand here), to the response or answer (*Antwort*) that the value calls for in me.

In her 1922 *Beiträge*, following Husserl, Stein carefully distinguishes between the nonaxiological (extra-egoic [*ichfremd*]) properties of the beautiful things (their color, shape, etc.) and the feeling of being moved that the specific value of beauty evokes. The evaluative properties of the thing are not sensuous or material; I could, for instance, grasp the "elegance" of a mathematical proof or the value of an inner act of pardoning (Stein 2000b, 160; GA 6 134). They are higher order properties found on the sensuous but not identical with them. I could see the thing physically without grasping its value (Stein 2000b, 162; GA 6 136). But when I grasp a value, I have a feeling that provides the matter or stuff (*Stoff*) for the value-grasping *Wertnehmen* (Stein 2000b, 160; GA 6 135). These are feelings that are felt and can never be fully articulated in words. If there is no feeling in the value-grasping, then there is no stuff on which to base a value reaction. This feeling in turn can lead to:surrender" in me and I feel "gladness" (*Freud*) at the beauty, or I can be left cold (*kalt*). This, for Stein, is analogous to an empty intuition in perception, when I grasp a thing without fulfilment of intuition (as in hearsay). To grasp a value, we need both the self-givenness of the thing in some kind of intuition but also there must be the appropriate inner condition (*innere Zuständlichkeit*; Stein 2000b, 162; GA 6 136) of the subject. For Stein, as for Hildebrand and Scheler, one can suffer from value-blindness (*Wertblindheit*; Stein 2000b, 162; GA 6 136). One can see an object and simply not be aware of its value. Or one can glimpse the value (as a kind of place holder that is not intuitively filled in but is given "emptily"; Stein 2000b, 162; GA 6 136) but not be personally affected by it (Husserl mentions this case too).

EDITH STEIN ON THE NATURE OF THE PERSON

Edith Stein elaborated her distinctive view of persons consistently over the course of her writings from 1917 to her death. Her detailed and fine-grained conception of the person draws on Husserl, Scheler, Reinach, Hildebrand, and her former teacher, the psychologist William Stern,[25] among others, but after 1922, she fused her phenomenology with a Neo-Thomist philosophical anthropology (in her writings from 1932 to 1942). She explicitly addresses Scheler already in her dissertation on empathy, but there is also the influence of Husserl's *Natur und Geist* lectures (that Stein acknowledged in her *Life in a Jewish Family*) and by *Ideas* II (on motivation) that she was helping to edit.[26] In the *Beiträge* she is also directly influenced by Dietrich von Hildebrand on value[27] and in terms of his analysis of the nature of the will.[28]

The fourth chapter of Stein's dissertation, titled "Empathy as the Understanding of Spiritual Persons" [*Einfühlung als Verstehen geistiger Personen*] (Stein 1989, 91; GA 5 108), discusses the constitution of the person in emotional experiences and the apprehension of persons in empathy. She also discusses "the being and value" of the person and the various ways persons are divided into "types." Throughout the dissertation, Stein constantly speaks of persons and of personality or personhood (*Persönlichkeit*);[29]

she speaks of experiencing a *person's* grief and acts of honesty or dishonesty of *persons*. She speaks of the understandings of foreign personhoods (*Verständnisses fremder Persönlichkeiten*) and of understanding or interpreting historical personalities (*historische Persönlichkeiten*)—for example, I can think of Caesar in his house in ancient Rome or think of him as placed in the twentieth century. But for Stein it is the one identical, individual Caesar that I am thinking of (Stein 1989, 110; GA 5 128). I grasp the unchangeable core (*Kern)* of the personhood of Caesar.

For Stein, persons are individual unities and each person is correlated to a value-world (*Wertewelt*; Stein 1989, 108; GA 5 126; cf. GA 6 174, 183, 184; "a world as pleasure and pain, as noble and common, as beauty and ugliness," Stein 2004, 81). Emotions always involve an evaluative element. Emotions are object entities but also possess subjective significance according to which these values are grasped at different depths by individuals. Feeling and emotions apprehend matters as positively or negatively significant. There is also a certain passivity (being seized [*Ergriffenwerden*]) and activity (freedom; Stein 2004, 82). Values demand a certain posture of will.

Stein writes (referencing Jaspers) that it is an old psychological tradition that the "I" is constituted in emotions (Stein 1989, 89; GA 5 109). Her 1922 *Beiträge* extends her discussion of persons, developing a layered ontology of body, soul, and spirit and discussing her concept of life-power (*Lebenskraft*) in detail. In her later works, Stein embeds her phenomenological account of conscious, embodied psychic life (developing Husserl and Scheler) into a more metaphysical (inspired by Thomas)—and at the same time concrete and existential—conception of the person. God as absolute being is an infinite person; angels and humans are persons of different orders. Persons are substances; they are self-standing. They have existence-for-themselves (*Für-sich-selbst-Dasein*; Stein 2009, 222; GA 10 148).

Stein elaborates on how persons relate to each other. I look at another person and see into his innerness (*Innerlichkeit*)—he can open up himself or shut himself (Stein 2004, 78). One's value as an individual person is, interestingly, for Stein, distinct from existence (Stein 2000b, 213). Thus, a fictional character can inspire us as much as an existing person. The hero of an epic poem inspires my imagination (Stein 2000b, 216) and may act as a model for my ethical deeds. Stein writes:

> Persons as well as their properties and actions, and indeed their stirrings of life in the widest sense, are carriers of values [*Träger von Werten*]. (Stein 2000b, 216; GA 6 180)

Values, moreover, exist independent of their bearers (this is a position also held by Scheler). One instantiates the value (e.g., honesty) but honesty as a value has independent validity.

I am drawn to persons or repelled by them. I approve or disapprove of the other person; I grasp their value or disvalue (*wert oder unwert*; Stein 2000b, 212; GA 6 177). I see someone and I say so should one be (*so sollte man sein*; Stein 2004, 91). But if I love someone—despite seeing a defect or failing—I love them for their whole stock of value, their repertoire of being (*Seinsbestand*; Stein 2000b, 212; GA 6 177). The love of a person is based on the *apprehended value* of the loved person; only the lover has access to that value (Stein 2000b, 213; GA 6 177). So the lover subjectively apprehends a value in the loved person. On the other hand, someone never exposed to love cannot experience the depth of their own souls in which love and hate are rooted (Stein 1989, 111; GA V 129). They will remain unfulfilled in their personal nature.

The soul, as bearer of a unified flow of conscious experiences as experienced in the first person (see *Ideas* II § 20) is intrinsically bound to the body (*leibgebunden*) and "interwoven" with it is a "psychophysical" unity (Stein 1989 40). At the beginning of *On the Problem of Empathy*, Stein says that souls and bodies of human subjects (including her own) need to be suspended and put to one side in the phenomenological reduction (*Ausschaltung oder Reduktion*; 1989, 3; GA 5 11). One is simply focused on felt consciousness. She begins her fourth chapter with a new declaration:

> So far we have considered the individual "I" as a part of nature, the living body as a physical body among others, the soul as founded on it, effects suffered and done and aligned in the causal order, all that is psychic as natural occurrence, consciousness as reality. . . . Consciousness appeared not only as a causally conditioned occurrence, but also as object-constituting at the same time. Thus it stepped out of the order of nature and faced it. Consciousness as a correlate of the object world is not nature, but mind. (Stein 1989, 91; GA 5 108)

Intentional consciousness operates on a new level—the level of meaning and value, where matters have significance for us. We are now in the world of persons.

In *On the Problem of Empathy*, Stein says that the soul is a "substantial unity" (1989, 40; GA 5 56) and she argues for the constitution (*Konstitution, Aufbau*) of the person in emotional experiences because feelings "announce personal attributes" (1989, 99; GA 5 117) and are connected to the I in a way that bodily sensations that are "foreign to the ego" (*ichfremd*) do not. External perceptions are not egoic as such (Stein 2009, 185). Sensations, on the other hand, are not part of the I and are foreign to the I. Stein distinguishes between sensual feelings (pleasant taste, feeling of pain) and general feelings (e.g., vigor [*Frische*] or sluggishness [*Madigkeit*]). General feelings, unlike sensations, are not localized in one bodily locale. General feelings, moreover, are rooted in the depth of the ego and also fill it out entirely. Thus, for instance, my whole being becomes suffused with joy.

From Scheler, Stein took the idea that the person is sensitive to value or evaluative (*werthaftig*; Stein 2000b, 227; GA 6 190). Humans have, Stein says, "permeability" for values in general—not just moral, aesthetic or intellectual values—but all aspects of normative life: "we see what a person *is* when we see which world of value [*Wertewelt*] she lives in" (Stein 2000b, 227; GA 6 190). A concern for truth is evaluative. Our whole sensory, affective, and cognitive lives are ordered to values. In *On the Problem of Empathy*, Stein said a person is correlated to a value world (*Wertewelt*; Stein 1989, 108; GA 5 126; or world of values [*Welt der Werte*]; Stein 1989, 92; GA 5 108). She speaks of the feeling of value (*Wertfühlen*). For Stein, a new object realm is constituted in feeling. This is the value. She writes:

> In joy the subject has something joyous facing him, in fright something frightening, in fear something threatening. Even moods have their objective correlates. For him who is cheerful, the world is baptized in a rosy glow; Even moods have their objective correlate. For him who is cheerful, the world is baptized in a rosy glow; for him who is depressed in black. (Stein 1989, 92; GA 5 108–9)

The person is an antenna for value. The person is also an inestimable value in herself, but she also creates new values. For Stein also persons express their spirit in their free spiritual acts. In *Finite and Eternal Being*, she writes: "the realm of spiritual life is the authentic realm of freedom" (Stein 2002b, 372). The I becomes creative out of the depths of its own self "in the form of free acts" (Stein 2002b, 376).[30] The whole person, however, is never exhausted in these acts (Stein 2009, 381). One can be honest without actually having done acts of honesty. One has a "predisposition," for example, to music or mathematics that may never be actualized (Stein 2000b, 199).

Stein continues to deepen her analysis of the person in her later systematic works, especially *Potency and Act* (1931) and *Finite and Eternal Being* (2002b) but also in her influential, occasional writings on women's education (Stein 1996). In *Finite and Eternal Being* she speaks of person-being (*Personsein*; Stein 2002b, 363). Persons, for Stein, are integrated into both the material and the immaterial, spiritual worlds (Stein 2009, 221; GA 10 147). The person is "conditioned both from above and from below" (Stein 2002b, 364). They have psychic wholes or totalities which must be approached as such. Soul is bound to body; spirit is conditioned by both soul and body as conditions them in turn (Stein 2002, 364). Persons are carriers of their own lives ("having oneself in hand"; Stein 2002b, 370; GA 11/12 315). The affective, emotional life is the heart of the person. For Stein, emotions have the greatest effect on the inner form of the self (2009, 381). The emotions reveal reality in its "totality and in its peculiarity"(2009, 96). Each soul has its own disposition that governs how intensely emotions are experienced, the acuteness of sensations, the amount of energy one has available for a task, and so on (Stein 1989, 40). Thus, there is a need for education as to the authenticity of sentiments. Pure emotions have to be educated with intellect to become emotions cognizant of values. Intellectual critique is needed to separate the false from the true. According to Stein, the intellect must grasp something to wake the emotions. The intellect lights the path for emotions. The emotions drive the will into action (1996, 96). But emotions need the control of the will and the light of intellect.

STEIN ON THE CORE OF THE PERSON (*KERN DER PERSON, PERSÖNLICHKEITSKERN*)

A unique and original aspect of Stein's account, in her dissertation is her claim that each has an individual personal core (*Kern der Person*; Stein1989, 109; GA 5 127; *Persönlichkeitskern*, Stein 2000b, 92; GA 6 80; Stein 2009,183; GA 10 122) that remains unchanged throughout life, despite the person's life constantly changing.[31] The core discloses itself in an unfolding (*Entfaltung*; Stein 2009, 209; GA 10 139). This core is the original personal situation (*die ursprüngliche persönliche Anlage*; GA 6 100) and is one's affective or emotional life (*Gemütsleben*; Stein 2009, 237). The core is a simple whole with no separable parts. The core unfolds or ripens (*entfaltet*) and can be heightened (*Seinssteigerung*; GA 10 146), but does not develop (*entwickelt*).[32] The personal core is never completely "disclosed or disclosable" (Stein 2009, 200). This core has a fixed stock of being (*Seinsbestand*; Stein 2000b, 92; GA 6 80) that prescribes how the person develops. The core cannot change its original "predisposition" (Stein 2000b, 233). The person's character properties are its capacities for apprehending values, and in them the core unfolds itself outward (*enfaltet sich in ihnen nach aussen*; Stein 2000b, 231). Kindliness as a character trait does not just show itself in kind actions; a person can just be kind even if he or she does not get to do kind actions (Stein 2000b, 231). This core of the person is what makes the person who he or she is and is also his or her *similitudo dei* (Stein 2009, 219; GA 10 146). According to Stein, the human being, "first of all is potential and that he himself only very gradually unfolds to actualization" (Stein 2004, 235).[33]

The person's core has actual being (*es ist wirklich*; Stein 2009, 193; GA 10 129); it is *actu ens*, *aktuell Seiendes* (GA 10 146) or being-in-act. To know a person is to be able to apprehend this core of being even if we cannot grasp it fully.[34] Only God knows each person to the core (Stein 2004, 14).

The person is constituted in layers, what Stein calls the layered structure of the human person (*Schichtenaufbau der menschlichen Person*; Stein 2004, 96). The person has a body and a soul. But being a person seems to depend on how much we live out of the soul. The soul is the true "inner" of the human, she writes in *Aufbau* (Stein 2004, 104). There is a genuineness and originality in living according to one's core (*Ursprünglichkeit und Echtheit des »kernhaften« Lebens*; Stein 2000b, 235; GA 6 197). People can live at different depth dimensions; and they can act from their soul-centers or not. External impressions have little personal involvement (Stein 2009, 185) and do not penetrate deeply into the soul. However, if, for instance, a noise disturbs me when I am concentrating on work, then it does penetrate my person and affect me inwardly. There are "depths of the I" (*Ichtiefe*; Stein 2009, 186; also discussed in *Empathy* (GA 5 120) and *Beiträge* (1922).[35] A lot of intentional relations with the object are superficial. The same sound can slip by me, but if I am concentrating, it can disturb me and make me angry (Stein 2009, 187). There are differences between people: "some live mainly at depth" (188). Humans have different degrees of vital strength—bodily power and spiritual power (Stein 2004, 110). Human beings are not just constituted from below by material corporeal powers. They also have spiritual sources of power. Each person has different degrees of depth, breadth, and power to engage with the world (Stein 2009, 192). Every free decision is performed from "the center and depth of his being" (206).

Stein thinks of the ego as rooted in a soul and this soul has a character and individuality, or peculiarity or particularity or uniqueness [*Eigenartigkeit*] of its own

> The innermost center of the soul is the 'how' of the essence itself and as such impresses its stamp on every trait of character and every attitude and action of human beings, it is the key that unlocks the mystery of the structural formation of the character of a human being. (Stein 2002b: 501–2)

CONCLUSION

The classical phenomenologists (Husserl, Scheler, Hildebrand, and Stein) all give primacy to the concrete, embodied, historically embedded, individual human person as the primary value-being (*Wertsein*), the source of moral agency, who lives primarily in a spiritual world with other persons. All these phenomenologists hold that persons relate to one another in the world of spirit understood as a value-world (*Wertewelt*). For Stein: "To be a person is to be a free and spiritual being. That the human being is a person sets it apart from all other beings in nature" (2004, 78). All three claim that persons have direct apprehension of values in their feelings and emotions. Stein, in particular, offers a detailed philosophical anthropology and psychology that explicates in detail how the affective life operates in the making of decisions and the adopting of stances towards oneself and others. Ethical life involves the person as a whole—intellect, affectivity ("the heart"), will. One's character is a unique essence that is given to one from the start and which unrolls through life.

NOTES

1. Husserl lectured on ethics throughout most of his teaching career (see Husserliana XXVIII, [Husserl 1988], and XXXVII [Husserl 2004]). His *Kaizo* articles (Hua XXVII [Husserl 1989a]), written in the 1920s, focus on ethical renewal. Husserl's starting point is Brentano and Kant. For Brentano and Husserl, the categorial imperative becomes "do the best that is attainable." As de Warren puts it, for Husserl: "Value-feelings are blind without judgments, while ethical judgments are empty without affective intuition of ethical values" (Warren 2017).

2. I am grateful to Andrew Barrette for giving me access to his unpublished translation of Husserliana XXXVII.

3. Hereafter I will refer to Edith Stein's *Gesamtausgabe* (published by Herder) as GA followed by the volume and page number.

4. Stein was deeply influenced here by her mentor Adolf Reinach's account of "social acts" (Salice 2015). Reinach in his *A Priori Foundations of Civil Law* (1983) argues that persons are the source of all legal ability (*rechtliches Können*) and thus also of all value. Furthermore, Reinach writes that persons have the right and duty to develop themselves. An absolute moral entitlement, such as the right to develop one's own personality, can have its ground in the person as such (Reinach 1983, 13).

5. As Sophie Loidolt writes: "To take a stance, to express it, to even form one's whole life and actions according to certain convictions, is at the center of Husserl's descriptions and characterizations of personhood" (Loidolt 2021).

6. Hereafter Husserl's Husserliana volumes will be abbreviated to Hua followed by the volume number in Roman numerals.

7. Stein was conscious of the tension between Husserl and Scheler and comments on it in her *Life in a Jewish Family* (1986, 259). At Göttingen, Scheler belittled Husserl's work at every opportunity and insisted on his own originality, whereas Husserl was convinced that Scheler was dependent on Husserl's work (Stein 1986, 259).

8. Stein's first book, *On the Problem of Empathy* (1917), for instance, contains references not just to Scheler's *Formalism* that had just been published in Husserl's *Jahrbuch* (1913, 1916) but also his earlier *Zur Phänomenologie und Theorie der Sympathiegefühle* (1913; later revised in Scheler 1923, trans. Scheler 1954), his *Versuche einer Philosophie des Lebens* (1915), "The Idols of Self Knowledge," *Ressentiment,*

and other works published by 1916. Stein was greatly taken by the charismatic Scheler when she attended his extramural lectures in Göttingen. She wrote in her *Life in a Jewish Family*, "One's first impression of Scheler was fascination. In no other person have I encountered the "phenomenon of genius" as clearly. (Stein 1986, 259).

9. See Goto, *Der Begriff der Person in die Phänomenologie Edmund Husserls*.

10. Stein, furthermore, insists in her *Aufbau* that the human sciences should not reduce the individual exemplar to the general type. Zoology can study animals as exemplars of a type but anthropology, psychology, must study the individual human essence (Stein 2004, 23) or singular person (*Einzelperson*; Stein 2004, 25).

11. There are of course "irrational" motivations based on feelings and associations that are not rationally motivated. Husserl in particular is concerned only with rational motivations. Husserl is critical of Kant's formalism, which does not take into account the determining factors on a person's desire and will.

12. Theodor Lipps speaks of psychic power (*psychische Kraft*), in his *Leifaden der Psychologie* (1909, 80, 124) that Stein identifies broadly with her *Lebenskraft*. Husserl does not have this concept, but it is not clear that he would have rejected it. On life-power in Stein, see Betschart 2009. Stein is also influenced by Bergson's concept of *élan vital* here (Stein's friend Roman Ingarden wrote his doctorate on Bergson with Husserl).

13. In his "Philosophy as Rigorous Science," Husserl speaks of experience as a "personal habitus" (Husserl 2002b, 284) involving the self being influenced to take positions, motivated by its experiences, accepting or rejecting the experiences of others.

14. Later persons are treated as "monads" in *Cartesian Meditations* § 32 (Husserl 1950). The person is discussed in Husserl's 1919 *Nature and Spirit* lectures (Husserl 2002a); see also his 1927 lecture series *Natur und Geist* (Husserliana 2001b), as well as his *Ethics* lectures (Husserl 1988, 2004), his *Kaizo* articles, and again plays a role in his *Intersubjectivity* volumes (Husserl 1973) and in the *Crisis* (Husserl 1954, 1970). See Goto 2004.

15. Husserl speaks of the "personalistic attitude" in *Ideas* II Sections 34 and 49. I have not found the expression in other Husserliana volumes.

16. In *Ideas* I, Husserl does not speak specifically of the personalistic attitude but includes in the "natural attitude," our normal relations to others as persons and in their social roles.

17. Here I depart from John J. Drummond (2008, 155), who claims that the personalistic attitude is a species of the natural attitude. In my view, the personalistic attitude is the whole that contains the natural attitude as a part.

18. Husserl speaks of communalization (*Vergemeinschaftung*). See Hua XV 20, 46, 57, 518. It arises initially instinctively through habit, but later there are explicit deliberate forms of community. See Caminada 2019.

19. According to *Stanford Encyclopedia of Philosophy* entry on "personalism," this would make Husserl a strict personalist—one's sense of the world emerges from an intuition about oneself.

20. *Die höchsten Werte sind überall die der Subjektivität als solcher, die auf Werterzeugung und Wertzueignung gerichtet ist und zuhöchst gerichtet ist auf Bestmögliches* (Hua XLII 316).

21. Von Hildebrand in his Habilitation thesis, "Sittlichkeit und ethische Werterkenntnis," (Hildebrand 1922, 462–602), says that *Wertnehmen* is Husserl's term of art whereas *Wertfühlen* is Scheler's preferred term (Hildebrand 1922, 468). Hildebrand speaks of value grasping *Werterfassen* and value knowing *Werterkenntnis*. Hildebrand says we see value as an objective entity of things, states of affairs, and persons, just as we see colors and hear sounds. Initially, we have an intuitive apprehension of the value. He further distinguishes between seeing a value (*Wertsehen*) and actually *feeling* it when it strikes us (*Wertfühlen*). There is, in phenomenology, a general discussion about how values are intuitively apprehended. We are immediately struck by the values of things (based on the properties of those things). Hildebrand distinguishes different kinds of familiarity with values—from knowing (*wissen*) to familiar acquaintance (*kennen*). Hildebrand thinks we need an attitude of passive reverence or acceptance to fully grasp the nature of value which speaks a "word" that demands a response in us unless we are "value blind" in which case we will be simply unmoved.

22. Axiology was also discussed by Husserl's younger contemporary Nicolai Hartmann (1882–1950). Husserl defines axiological reason as a "consciousness which constitutes value objectivities" (Husserl 1988, 266).

23. Scheler has been accused of Platonism on values posited as independent objective entities. See Blosser 2012. Husserl was deeply influenced by Brentano on value. For a discussion of Brentano's value theory, see Baumgartner and Pasquerella (2004).

24. See also Stein 1989, 31; GA 5 48; 1989, 33 GA 5 50.

25. William Stern (1871–1938) was a famous German psychologist, a student of Ebbinghaus in Berlin, who invented the intelligence quotient (IQ) measure. He wrote studies of child psychology based on observations of his own children. He was devoted to personalistic psychology and published his *Person und Sache* (Stern 1906). He taught at the University of Breslau but moved to Hamburg in 1916 until 1933, when he was forced to emigrate to the United States, where he taught at Duke University until his death in 1938.

26. The term "personalistic attitude" does not appear in Stein's 1917 work, *Problem of Empathy*, presumably because she began editing *Ideas* II only after she had completed her dissertation in 1916. She does speak of the "natural attitude" (Stein 2000b, 227; GA 6 190) and the phenomenological attitude.

27. Stein references Dietrich von Hildebrand's *Die Idee der sittlichen Handlung* (Hildebrand 1916) on values as having an extramental existence as transcendent objects, but involve an intramental or intra-egoic (*ichlich*) content; see Stein 2000b, 7; GA 6 18). Stein notes that she uses the term lived experience for both types of experience.

28. Stein references approvingly von Hildebrand's *Die Idee der sittlichen Handlung* (Hildebrand 1916) on the three-fold meaning of willing (*Wollen*) as aspiring (*das Sichbemühen*) for example, to be good; resolving (*Vorsatz*) to do something (e.g., going for a walk); and desiring (*Wollen*) to realize a state of affairs (*Realisierung*

eines Sachverhaltes), as opposed to a mere subjective wanting (Stein 2000b, 55–57; GA 6 48–49).

29. Stein speaks frequently of *Persönlichkeit* (usually translated as "personality"), but she does not mean empirical psychological personality. She means what makes a person uniquely a person. Each person is unique, irreplaceable, and invaluable. Each person has a distinct character that grows, develops, and is shaped during life. It does include one's fundamental outlook (optimism, brightness, etc.) in so far as it is essential to one. At the basis of one's personality is the core (*Kern*), which makes the person the unique individual they are.

30. Stein claims that the human being can and should form itself (*kann und soll sich selbst formen*, *Aufbau*, 2004, 93)

31. Stein speaks of the core point of the I (*Kernpunkt*) or the I-core (*Ichkern*) or core of the person (*Kern der Person*). Hering is the first to have employed the expression core (*Kern*) to designate the set of fundamental proprieties of an individual essence (Hering 1914, 168–69).

32. This concept of the unfolding or blooming (*Entfaltung*) of the person is introduced in *Empathy* (GA 5 129). Stein is influenced here by Scheler's *Formalism*, which says a person lives out of a mental center (*geistigen Zentrum*; see Stein 2000b, 200; GA 6 166) out of which he or she unfolds (*sich enfaltet*).

33. In relation to her understanding of the personal core, Stein was influenced by Teresa of Avila, and John of the Cross ("spark of the soul," the "interior castle"), as well as by Scheler and Hedwig Conrad-Martius (see Hart 2020). Many of Stein's remarks are reminiscent of Meister Eckhart's ground of the soul (*Seelengrund*), and so on. She speaks of the ground of my soul (*Grund meiner Seele*; Stein 2004, 85). This ground, she says, is where every worry lives. She sharply distinguishes it from the qualityless nature of the pure I.

34. Not everything in the person comes from the core. There are emotional and other sentient traits that are "indifferent" to the core (Stein 2000b, 228–29); they do not matter to the core. There are experiences that do not issue from the core and yet pertain to the identity of one's psyche. There are experiences that are proper to the I (*ichlich*) as opposed to external contents (e.g., sense data) that are foreign to the I (*ichfremd*; Stein 2009, 186).

35. Husserl in *Ideas* II also acknowledges depths to the ego: there is "in the obscure depths, a root soil" (Husserl 1989b, 292; Hua IV 279).

REFERENCES

Andrews, Michael F. (2012). "Edith Stein and Max Scheler: Ethics, Empathy, and the Constitution of the Acting Person." *Quaestiones Disputatae* 3: 33–47.

Arango, Alejandro. (2014). "Husserl's Concept of Position-Taking and Second Nature." *Phenomenology and Mind* 6: 168–176.

Baumgartner, Wilhelm, and Lynn Pasquerellea. (2004). "Brentano's Value Theory: Beauty, Goodness and the Concept of Correct Emotion," in Dale Jacquette (ed.), *The Cambridge Companion to Brentano*. New York: Cambridge University Press.

Beckmann-Zöller, Beate. (2008). "Edith Stein's Theory of the Person in Her Münster Years (1932–1933)." Translated by Amalie Enns. *American Catholic Philosophical Quarterly* 82: 47–70.
Betschart, Christof. (2009). "Was ist Lebenskraft? Edith Steins erkenntnistheoretische Prämissen in *Psychische Kausalität* (Teil 1)." *Edith Stein Jahrbuch* 15: 154–83.
Blosser, Phillip. (2012). "Toward a Resolution of Antinomies in Max Scheler's Value Theory: With reference to Herman Dooyeweerd." *Philosophia Reformata*77(2): 93–113.
Caminada, Emanuele. (2019). *Vom Gemeingeist zum Habitus: Husserls "Ideen II"—Sozialphilosophische Implikationen der Phänomenologie*. Dordrecht: Springer.
Conrad-Martius, Hedwig. (1921). *Metaphysische Gespräche*. Halle: Niemeyer.
Crosby, John. (2002). "Dietrich Von Hildebrand: Master of Phenomenological Value-Ethics." In *Phenomenological Approaches to Moral Philosophy*. Dordrecht: Kluwer Academic.
Drummond, John. (2008). *Historical Dictionary of Husserl's Philosophy*. Lanham, Md: Rowman & Littlefield.
Goto, Hiroshi. (2004). *Der Begriff der Person in der Phänomenologie Edmund Husserl.* Würzburg: Köningshausen und Neumann.
Hahn, Colin. (2014). "Husserl's Concept of Personhood and the Fichte Lectures." In Faustino Fabbianelli and Sebastian Luft (eds.), *Husserl und die klassische deutsche Philosophie / Husserl and Classical German Philosophy* (pp. 299–310). Dordrecht: Springer.
Hart, James G. (1990). "Axiology as the Form of Purity of Heart: A Reading *Husserliana* XXVIII." *Philosophy Today* 34, no. 3: 206–21.
———. (2006). "The Absolute Ought and the Unique Individual." *Husserl Studies* 22: 223–40.
———. (2020). "The Method of the Realontology." In: Parker R.K.B. (eds.), *Hedwig Conrad-Martius' Ontological Phenomenology*. Women in the History of Philosophy and Sciences Vol. 5. Cham: Springer.
Heinämaa, Sara. (2014). Husserl's Ethics of Renewal: A Personalistic Approach. In Miira Tuominen, Sara Heinämaa, and Virpi Mäkinen (eds.), *New Perspectives on Aristotelianism and Its Critics* (pp. 196–212). Leiden: Brill.
———. (2019). "Two Ways of Understanding Persons: A Husserlian Distinction." *Phenomenology and Mind* 15: 92–103.
———. (2020). "Values of Love: Two Forms of Infinity Characteristic of Human Persons." *Phenomenology and the Cognitive Sciences* 19: 431–50.
Héring, Jean. (1914). Lotzes Lehre vom Apriori. Eine Philosophische Studie. Typescript preserved in the Hering Archive, Fondation du Chapitre de Saint-Thomas, Strasbourg (unpublished). Cited in Daniele DeSantis, "'An Ocean of Difficult Problems' Husserl and Jean Hering's Dissertation on the A Priori in R. H. Lotze," *Husserl Studies* 37 (2021):19–38.
Hildebrand, Dietrich von. (1916). "Die Idee der sittlichen Handlung." *Jahrbuch für Philosophie und phänomenologische Forschung* 3: 126–251.
———. (1922). "Sittlichkeit und ethische Werterkenntnis." *Jahrbuch Für Philosophie und phänomenologische Forschung* 5: 462–602.

Husserl, Edmund. (1950). *Cartesianische Meditationen und Pariser Vorträge*. Ed. Stephan Strasser. Husserliana I. Den Haag: Nijhoff.

———. (1952). *Ideen zu einer reinen Phänomenologie und phänomenologischen Philosophie. Buch II: Phänomenologische Untersuchungen zur Konstitution.* Husserliana IV. Den Haag: Nijhoff.

———. (1954). *Die Krisis der europäischen Wissenschaften und die Transzendentale Phänomenologie. Eine Einleitung in die phänomenologische Philosophie.* Ed. W. Biemel. Husserliana VI. The Hague: Nijhoff.

———. (1965). *Erste Philosophie (1923/24). Zweiter Teil: Theorie Der Phänomenologischen Reduktion.* Ed. R. Boehm. Husserliana VIII. The Hague: Nijhoff.

———. (1970). *The Crisis of European Sciences and Transcendental Phenomenology*. Trans. David Carr. Evanston, IL: Northwestern University Press.

———. (1973). *Zur Phänomenologie der Intersubjektivität. Texte aus dem Nachlaß*. 3 volumes. (Husserliana XIII, XIV, XV). Den Haag: Nijhoff.

———. (1977). *Phenomenological Psychology. Lectures, Summer Semester 1925.* Trans. J. Scanlon. The Hague: Nijhoff.

———. (1984). *Logische Untersuchungen*. Erster Band: *Prolegomena zur reinen Logik*. Text der 1. und der 2. Auflage, hrsg. Elmar Holenstein, Husserliana XVIII; and *Logische Untersuchungen*. Zweiter Band: *Untersuchungen zur Phänomenologie und Theorie der Erkenntnis*, in zwei Bänden, hrsg. Ursula Panzer, Husserliana XIX 1 and 2. Dordrecht: Kluwer.

———. (1986). *Aufsätze und Vorträge 1911–1921*. Ed. Hans-Rainer Sepp and Thomas Nenon. Husserliana XXV. Dordrecht: Kluwer.

———. (1988). *Vorlesungen über Ethik and Wertlehre (1908–1914)*. Edited by Ullrich Melle. Husserliana XXVIII. Dordrecht: Kluwer.

———. (1989a). *Aufsätze und Vorträge 1922–1937*. Hrsg. Ed. Thomas Nenon and Hans-Rainer Sepp. Husserliana XXVII. Dordrecht: Kluwer, 1989.

———. (1989b). *Ideas Pertaining to a Pure Phenomenology and to a Phenomenological Philosophy. Second Book. Studies in the Phenomenology of Constitution*. Trans. R. Rojcewicz, A. Schuwer. Dordrecht: Kluwer.

———. (2001a). *Logical Investigations*, 2 Volumes. Trans. J.N. Findlay, with a new introduction by Dermot Moran London/New York: Routledge.

———. (2001b). *Natur und Geist. Vorlesungen Sommersemester 1927*. Hrsg. Michael Weiler. Husserliana XXXII. Dordrecht: Kluwer.

———. (2002a). *Natur Und Geist. Vorlesungen Sommersemester 1919* (Husserliana Materialienbande Vol 4. Dordrecht: Springer.

———. (2002b). "Philosophy as Rigorous Science." Trans. Marcus Brainard, *The New Yearbook for Phenomenology and Phenomenological Philosophy* Vol. II (2002), 249–95.

———. (2004). *Einleitung in die Ethik. Vorlesungen Sommersemester1920/1924*. Edited by Henning Peucker. Husserliana XXXVII. Dordrecht: Kluwer.

———. (2013). *Grenzprobleme der Phänomenologie: Analysen des Unbewusstseins und der Instinkte, Metaphysik, Späte Ethik, Texte aus dem Nachlass (1908–1937)*, Husserliana XLII. Eds. R. Sowa and T. Vongehr. Dordrecht: Springer.

Jacobs, Hanne, ed. (2021). *The Husserlian Mind.* The Routledge Philosophical Minds Series. New York Routledge.

Lipps, Theodor. (1909). *Leifaden der Psychologie*, 3rd ed. Leipzig: W. Engelmann.

Loidolt, Sophie. (2021). "Husserl on Personhood and Practical Agency." In Hanne Jacobs (ed.), *The Husserlian Mind.* The Routledge Philosophical Minds Series. New York Routledge.

Luft, Sebastian. (2006). "Husserl's Concept of the 'Transcendental Person': Another Look at the Husserl-Heidegger Relationship." *International Journal of Philosophical Studies* 13(2): 141–77.

———. (2012). "The Subject as Moral Person: On Husserl's Late Reflections Concerning the Concept of Personhood." In Gert-Jan van der Heiden, Karel Novotny, Inga Römer, and Laszlo Tengelyi (eds.), *Investigating Subjectivity: Classical and New Perspectives* (pp. 25–41). Leiden: Brill.

Meacham, Darian. (2013). "What Goes Without Saying: Husserl's Concept of Style." *Research in Phenomenology* 43: 3–26.

Melle, Ullrich. (2007). "Husserl's Personalistic Ethics." *Husserl Studies* 23: 1–15.

Moran, Dermot. (2016). "The Personal Self in the Phenomenological Tradition." In Rafael Winkler (ed.), *Identity and Difference Contemporary Debates on the Self* (pp. 3–35). London: Palgrave Macmillan.

Perrin, Ronald F. (1974). "A Commentary on Max Scheler's Critique of the Kantian Ethic." *Journal of the History of Philosophy* 12, no. 3: 347–59.

Reinach, Adolf. (1983). "The A Priori Foundations of Civil Law." Trans. John Crosby. *Aletheia* 3: 1–142.

Rinofner-Kreidl, S. (2010). "Husserl's Categorical Imperative and His Related Critique of Kant." In P. Vandevelde and S. Luft (eds.), *Epistemology, Archaeology, Ethics. Current Investigations of Husserl's Corpus* (pp. 188–210). New York: Continuum.

Salice, Alessandro. (2015). "Actions, Values, and States of Affairs in Hildebrand and Reinach." *Studia Phaenomenologica* 15: 259–80.

Scheler, Max. (1913). *Wesen und Formen der Sympathie*. Gesammelte Werke, Vol. 7. Bonn: Bouvier, 2005.

———. (1916). *Der Formalismus in der Ethik und die material Wertethik. Neuer Versuch der Grundlegung eines ethischen Personalismus*. Bern: Francke, 1980.

———. (1954). *The Nature of Sympathy*. Trans. P. Heath. London: Routledge & Kegan Paul.

———. (1973). *Formalism in Ethics and Non-Formal Ethics of Values: A New Attempt Toward the Foundation of an Ethical Personalism*. Trans. M. S. Frings and R. L. Funk. Evanston, IL: Northwestern University Press.

Stein, Edith (1917). *Zum Problem der Einfühlung*. Edith Stein Gesamtausgabe Bd. 5. Freiburg, Basel. Wien: Herder, 2008.

———. (1922). *Beiträge zur philosophischen Begründung der Psychologie und der Geisteswissenschaften*. Edith Stein Gesamtausgabe Bd. 6. Freiburg, Basel. Wien: Herder, 2010.

———. (1931). *Potenz und Akt: Studien zu einer Philosophie des Seins*, Edith Stein Gesamtausgabe Bd. 10, Wien, Basel. Köln: Herder 2005.

———. (1950). *Endliches und Ewiges Sein. Versuch eines Aufstiegs zum Sinn des Seins. Anhang: Martin Heideggers Existenz-philosophie & Die Seelenburg.* Reprinted Edith Stein Gesamtausgabe Bd. 11–12, 2006.

———. (1986). *Life in a Jewish Family: An Autobiography, 1891–1916.* Trans. Josephine Koeppel. CWES, Vol. 1. Washington DC: ICS Publications.

———. (1989). *On the Problem of Empathy*. Trans. by W. Stein. The Collected Works of Edith Stein, Vol. 3, Washington, DC: ICS Publication.

———. (1996). *Essays on Woman*. Translated Freda Mary Oben. Eds. Lucy Gelber and Romaeus Leuven, CWES, Vol. 2. 2nd ed., revised.

———. (2000a). *Die Frau. Fragestellungen und Reflexionen*, Edith Stein Gesamtausgabe Bd. 13.

———. (2000b). *Philosophy of Psychology and the Humanities.* Trans. by M. C. Baseheart and M. Sawicki. *The Collected Works of Edith Stein*, Vol. 7. Washington DC: ICS Publications.

———. (2002a). *Aus dem Leben einer jüdischen Familie und weitere autobiographische Beiträge*. Edith Stein Gesamtausgabe Bd. 1, 2002.

———. (2002b). *Finite and Eternal Being. An Attempt at an Ascent to the Meaning of Being*. Trans. by Kurt F. Reinhardt. CWES, Vol. 9, 2002.

———. (2004). *Der Aufbau der menschlichen Person. Vorlesungen zur philosophischen Anthropologie*. Edith Stein Gesamtausgabe Bd. 14. Berlin: Herder.

———. (2006). "Martin Heideggers Existentialphilosophie," in Edith Stein, *Endliches und Ewiges Sein. Versuch eines Aufstiegs zum Sinn des Seins*, Edith Stein Gesamtausgabe, Bd. 11/12. Freiburg: Herder, "Anhang," pp. 445–500.

———. (2007). "Martin Heidegger's Existential Philosophy." Trans. by Mette Lebech. *Maynooth Philosophical Papers* 4: 55–98.

———. (2009). *Potency and Act. Studies toward a Philosophy of Being*. Trans. by W. Redmond. *Edith Stein Collected Works*, Vol. 11. Washington DC: ICS Publications.

Stern, William. (1906). *Person und Sache*. bd. Ableitung und Grundlehre des kritischen personalismus. Berlin: J. A. Barth.

Warren, Nicolas de. (2017). Husserl on Phenomenological Ethics. In Sacha Golub and Jens Timmermann (eds.), *The Cambridge History of Moral Philosophy*. New York: Cambridge University Press.

Zahavi, Dan. (2021). "No Ego, Pure Ego, Personal Ego." In: Hanne Jacobs (ed.), *The Husserlian Mind*. New York: Routledge.

Chapter 6

The Role of Empathy in the Affective Twist of Husserl's Critique of an Axiological and Practical Reason

Carlos Lobo

ABSTRACT

To define more closely the specificity of the phenomena of ethical reciprocal recognition, with their axiological and practical dimensions, and the way in which transcendental empathy intervenes in them, it is necessary to come back to the intentional articulations at stake. On this basis, in the first and second part of this chapter, we will understand better Husserl's account of moral conscience, in terms of practical and axiological reason, and his critical discussions of Hume's and Kant's psychologic and naturalistic interpretation.

Keywords: recognition, axiology, empathy, Hume, Husserl, Kant

INTRODUCTION

The history of the concept of empathy, its origins, and metamorphoses, before, after, and around Husserl, is now if not well-known, at least well-documented. My aim is not to go back over these different metamorphoses in Edith Stein or Moritz Geiger, nor over the criticisms that the theory of empathy may have faced within the phenomenological school, be it in Heidegger or Scheler. Because of the amphibology resulting from these mutations, it is often difficult to see who is targeted by the critics, who is not always explicitly mentioned or directly referred to, as well as to discern under the claimed borrowings the misinterpretations or even betrayals. This is certainly a generic situation, but the concept of empathy, perhaps more than any other, is conducive to such equivocation.

Instead, I want to focus on a particular moment in this conceptual history and the way in which Husserl's appropriation of this concept comes to renew in depth the Kantian idea of the critique of reason, a renewal that translates into an *enlargement* of the parallelism of practical and theoretical reason, to what he calls axiological reason, and an *inversion* of the method of transcendental analytics. To begin with the latter, instead of an analytic proceeding constructively and regressively to explore the architectonics of reason and its limits, Husserl advocates constitutive intentional analysis, which in its genetic form endeavors to follow the emergence of the a priori normative functions, which define reason, from the soil, not to say the humus, of the multifaceted and multidimensional activity of consciousness. The result is a considerable *broadening* of the idea of reason, which goes far beyond a parallelism of practical and theoretical reason since the spheres of acts held to be alien or merely preliminary to rational activity also rightfully fall under a critique of axiological reason. Thus, to give a simple indication, aesthetic pleasure itself, independently of, and prior to any judgment, comes under a *sui generis* rationality (i.e., aesthetic reason), and, more broadly, any form of sentimental activity, insofar as it includes its own intentional structure, comes under a critique of specific axiological reason.

Husserl's critique of axiological and practical reason appears early in his work, as the counterpart of the critique of "logical reason," which, in its broadest sense, covers not only the sphere of judgment and reasoning, but the whole sphere of acts of representation, whether they are simple representations or founded acts of representation. The idea of a parallelism between two large classes of acts, objectifying and nonobjectifying acts, is indeed at the heart of the Fifth Logic research and its rewritings. It provides the main thread of the lessons on ethics given by Husserl from 1902 to 1918. It is taken up again in an insistent way in the introductory lectures on ethics of 1920. Commentators and phenomenologists who have debated whether any other form of act is ultimately based on representations and, therefore, subordinate to logic have either paid little attention to this massive fact or, for reasons I do not wish to discuss here, have not taken it seriously. However, it is decisive if we want to have some chance of throwing some light on the most striking schisms that have crossed the phenomenological movement, of which we should certainly not exclude the so-called "existentialist turn" in its different variants, as well as those that have occurred in its wake (theological and ethical turn).[1]

This parallelism is particularly useful if we want to understand the role that empathy comes to play in transcendental phenomenology and avoid confusing it with related concepts that have played such a great role in ethics since the eighteenth century, especially in English philosophy. The counterproof would be given by the confusions that arise again in the wake of Husserl and that he points out in Max Scheler and Edith Stein,[2] or Moritz Geiger.[3] It would also allow us to see in what way Heidegger's criticisms of the theory of empathy translate a deep misunderstanding of the nature of Husserlian transcendental idealism, to which his interpretation of Kantian Critiques barred him from access.

Husserl transforms the psychologizing and aestheticizing concept of empathy into a central element of his transcendental monadology, where intersubjectivity appears as a decisive phase of the constitution in which the norms of rationality, whether logical, axiological, or practical, are predrawn. It is thus from the eidetic of consciousness and the egological eidetic and, consequently, from the resources of self-variation, that it becomes possible to grasp the contours of the Husserlian theory of empathy developed in the Fifth Cartesian Meditation.[4] For this reason, this concept must be carefully distinguished from the derived concepts of sympathy and compassion, which make it a form of affectivity, whose role in human behavior is not to be denied but that must not be taken for all that as a criterion or, even worse, as an origin of moral behavior. The misunderstanding of these eidetic foundations leads to a misunderstanding of ethical rationality, of which two diametrically opposed historical examples are Kant and Hume.

FROM THE PSYCHOLOGICAL TO THE PHENOMENOLOGICAL THEORY OF EMPATHY

The so called "theory of empathy" is the keystone of Husserl transcendental monadology, and conversely, the Cartesian character of Husserl's monadology relies on its dependence to the specific association performed under the title of "empathy" (i.e. an analogizing pairing of myself with the other Self). This association must be understood in the frame of the transcendental analysis of intentionality (i.e., of the correlation between noesis and noema as an a priori to any ontology, any region of being, any domain of knowledge and of experience). Within this frame, empathy must be understood as a specific intentional modification, which functions as a vector of the transfer of the intentional meaning primordially constituted, within the proper sphere, into a fully objective one (i.e., an intersubjectively communicable meaning).

Consequently, and conversely, this genesis of the *objective meaning* is in return the guarantor of the possibility of the *appropriation* of any intersubjectively constituted meaning (whether it is of the order of worldly or natural realities, of idealities, or even of works and cultural institutions, such as laws, social or moral norms). Reciprocally, this possibility of appropriation is implicated in the sense of objectivity, be it posited as a categorial, natural, social, cultural, spiritual, or historical reality.

The Methodological Transformation of the Concept of Empathy

The adoption of the concept of empathy, like that of association, motivation, or first of all that of intention, is associated with a methodical transformation of a psychological and aesthetic concept into a transcendental phenomenological one (i.e., within the framework of the a priori of the correlation) and, consequently, of the relativity of any ontology (whether natural or fundamental) with respect to the consciousness.[5] To evaluate the relevance of such "borrowings" entails an examination of what this methodical transformation consists of. Perhaps in this way we will be able to do justice to certain criticisms. At least, we can then credit Husserl with the coherence of his approach. This immediately opposes him to those who, like Scheler or Heidegger,[6] reject the concept of empathy on the grounds that it would be essentially psychological, as well as to those who, in the name of a "phenomenological realism" that is most often indeterminate and diffuse, only see in it an ultimate avatar of German idealism. By distancing himself from the constitutive method, Heidegger, as early as 1927, and Scheler,[7] in his attempts of 1917, show the same "lack of discipline" and fail fatally in their pretension to substitute an ontological approach to the constitutive approach of the transcendental phenomenology and, eventually, to give an account of the spheres of the action and of historicity in their various dimensions.[8] Despite their call for authenticity and radicality, and regardless of their respective intellectual profiles,[9] this resulted in persistent misunderstandings about what could or could not be asked of the theory of empathy. This consequently concealed the usefulness of such a theory for the establishment on solid bases of a true axiology, both material and formal,[10] which neither Heidegger nor Scheler, nor Edith Stein understood and could not understand.[11] In a text, probably inspired by seminar discussions, Husserl examines this opposition by insisting, in contrast with Scheler's diffuse spiritualism, on the constraints of the constitutive method that is based at the same time on the resources of reflection, of the imaginary variation, and of the kinesthetic experience reduced abstractly to the proper. The mixture of hypothetical and aprioristic reconstructions based on external observations represents not only the antipode of the phenomenological method but testifies to an incapacity to understand that the "method of analysis of the immanent intentional structure,"[12] on the basis of an experience is the only one susceptible to supply the laws of essences of the *syntaxes of consciousness* at work in any form of consciousness, including the perception of others. Whether it is a question of "normal" or anomalous subjects, familiar or not, and, correlatively, of "real" and normal perceptions or "abnormal" experiences (illusory, hallucinatory, or paranormal such as "supposed apparitions of spirits," relationships with the dead, other animals, etc.), prior to any ontological argument, it is necessary to establish phenomenologically the laws of the "syntaxes of consciousness."[13] To ground a theory of empathy phenomenologically is indeed to clarify intentionally these forms of experience from an "*ABC of intentionality and, so to speak, from a grammar of intentionality*."[14] In this perspective, the phenomenology of normal human intersubjectivity will represent a first task and a first level of elucidation, not exclusive of more extensive forms, with the understanding that the set of configurations must be able to represent viable syntactic "compositions," justified on the basis of an eidetic of possible forms of consciousness and forms of intersubjectivity, close or distant, familiar or unfamiliar, etc., with their necessary correlates, forms of worlds and corresponding possible common natures.[15]

The Two Concepts of Empathy

The opposition between the phenomenological concept and the psychological (Lippsian) concept of empathy is thus rooted in a divergence of method.[16] But it is not enough to claim the primacy of the intersubjective constitution over any other subsequent phase of constitution. It is first necessary to account for the articulation or grammar of empathy that a psychological theory is unable to describe or even reveal, whether by direct or indirect observation. In particular, it is necessary to pay attention to the modal constituents that the psychological conceptions of imitation or association by resemblance or transference by analogy and their metaphoric do not allow[17] and to account for the vast range of the experience of others, which an approach enclosed from the outset within the bounds of experience or, supposedly, normal or average human existence conceals or fails to describe in its proper terms.[18]

Psychological empathy is an "insight" of a human psyche that has as its ultimate basis in the psycho-physical human body whose type is familiar to us in its surrounding world, all this under the noetic modal register of the presumptive, and yet almost unshakeable certainty of the given real world, characteristic of the natural consciousness. By extension and analogically, it can concern any physical reality endowed with an expressive character, that is to say with a psychic interiority similar to mine; thus, including a natural reality, like an organism, a work of art or a landscape.[19] The important word that signals a whole host of delicate problems is the term *similar*.[20] The transcendental process of empathy has its methodical starting point in the stratum of primordiality (with its intentional structure) obtained by the abstractive reduction to the proper, and the constitutive phenomenological analysis tries precisely to describe, in its proper order, the series of constitutive operations leading to the sense donation of "a foreign transcendental primordiality," in "cooperation" with which the proper ego will be able to constitute, in return, a common world, and a common nature. This implies a natural spatiotemporality, in which the transcendental ego will find him or herself constituted in return as subject situated in a common world. Consequently, it accounts for the conditions of possibility "of the world and personal existence in the world, personal acts of psychological empathy," that is, "psychological apperception, in which soul becomes conscious as soul of a corporeal body"; which "is a completely different apperception than the one by which a primordial body given in my primordiality becomes the turning point for the 'apperception' of an alien primordiality of an alien ego and ego-life, by which we constitute a common nature, a common world and ourselves in it and as we."[21]

The phenomenological theory of empathy is part of a constitutive phenomenology whose titles are: "Theory of transcendental intersubjectivity, 'transcendental aesthetics' as phenomenology of the world, taken purely as the world of experience, time and individuation, phenomenology of association as theory of the constitutive performances of passivity, phenomenology of logos, phenomenological problem of 'metaphysics' etc."[22] More specifically, it includes a genetic and an eidetic component whose articulation is anything but easy,[23] and whose intrinsic difficulties explain why, many among Husserl's disciples turned away from it to return to realism and to the psychology of the Munich school.[24] Nevertheless, from 1922 at least, Husserl affirms to have developed the essence of this "transcendental science of subjectivity" that includes these different modifications: in "social subjectivity, communalized, subjectivity connected by empathy" and therefore the "monadological" turn, where this subjectivity gives itself as an "egoic totality."[25] One understands better at the evocation of this program the ambivalence of Husserl's attitude toward the psychological approach of empathy: Despite the multiplication of critical gestures,[26] the fact that the constitutive level on which the psychological approach is placed from the start is not eliminated but becomes itself a theme and the index of a constitutive problem. Moreover, a transcendental theory of empathy will have to elucidate the constitution of a common world in all its strata: natural, cultural, and historical, which also includes its practical, axiological, and normative dimensions.[27]

Still it is necessary beforehand to isolate in its purity this sphere of primordiality, while preserving the intentional content accordingly reduced to the proper, what can be done only by the "method of primordial reduction (of the given world to its primordiality)" by which "I come correlatively to the primordial ego," and while "remaining in the abstract reduction," "build on from there" by putting "a primordial empathy into effect and gaining 'primordial others.'" This "transposition" by which the already constituted intentional content takes on a sense of possibly being-in-common, supposes constitutive resources and operations that it is necessary to glance through with some detail and to seize in their reciprocal implications. It is on this ascending path of intersubjective constitution that we encounter the first form of empathy that Husserl calls "primordial empathy." From this level, the other is given not only "perceptually," but also "as an evaluating and practical subject" and as "object of my concerns, of my activities."[28] What is called "nature" represents only one constitutive level that is co-constituted with the common world, a practical world penetrated by values, in which I and the others are objects and carriers of evaluative acts and actions. In the genetic perspective, the problem is to discern and order these levels. A theory of empathy thus requires and presupposes a transcendental phenomenology of empathy but, complementarily, a theory of empathy is necessary for phenomenology to become fully constitutive. Without it, we would not go beyond a solipsistic "phenomenism," and transcendental aesthetics would not manage to unfold into a transcendental theory of reason, and eventually into a transcendental logic. As we shall see, the old confusion between common sense and reason provides here a precious indication of the stages (and levels) that a constitutive phenomenology must and can go through.[29] It is indeed with the constitution of the alter ego that we touch the structural and intentional bases of the "principles" that give themselves to us afterwards, in the form of rational a priori principles.

We face here the problem of "normality and rationality," but before coming to this point let us recall what empathy consists of from a constitutive point of view.

EMPATHY IN THE GENETIC CONSTITUTIVE PERSPECTIVE

If we stick to the "transcendental aesthetic" level, it is initially a question of constituting a community of psycho-physical bodies and of a common world, which envelopes a common nature.[30] *Matching, transference, association, analogy* . . . so many terms that intervene in the description of empathy, and which it is advisable to hear in the constitutive perspective, by being attentive to the (noematic) meaning included in this act and these moments of acts, as well as to the implications of meaning, which the phenomenological analysis must unfold: (a) the analogizing apperception and the play of modalities, and in particular the subjunctive as index of a complex combination of possibility and impossibility; (b) the certainty on the eidetic level, the possible variants of mine, as pure variants, possibly drawn from past modifications (role of the recollection, or of the "pro-recollection") (*Wiedererinnerung, Vor-erinnerung*), but here too Husserl's insistence on the eidetic and modal character of this transfer of meaning; (c) finally the role of the kinesthetic, hyletic underpinning, and its doxic and positional vector.

The ABC of Empathy

It is thus a question of a transfer of meaning and a transfer of validity, of the belief in a being according to its own modality, a certainty of being, and the associated validity that is transferred to an alter ego. The main difficulty is summarized in these terms by Husserl: "How do we originally come to foreign bodies? Here comes the question: the body there looks similar, as my body would look from here, where I am now, if it had been moved there by me or by itself (belonging here: by others, if I had them already).—There, of course, lies the difficulty."[31]

Among the persistent difficulties on which Husserl did not cease to return and if we stick to the only representational aspect, and thus to the purely natural correlative stratum, let us mention those which touch the development of the spatiotemporal structure. Husserl mentions several of them which touch the pairing of my own body to the appearance of the own body of the other.[32] I have an experience of my own body, but it is for this reason incomplete. The multisensorial experience and the imagination certainly make up for it, but it does not remain less difficult "to understand how presentation should become possible, where the corresponding possibility of presentation is missing for me."[33]

Another difficulty: admitting that the imagination of displacements provides the link to operate the associative coupling between my body and that of the other, at the end of which I pose him as endowed with an interiority, this seems to suggest that the structure proper to a projective space, with the whole of the properties that Husserl describes under the title of "*Perspektivisierung*" is already constituted in the proper sphere, prior to the primordial empathy. Hence the hesitation: "Is it therefore not correct to talk about the external representation saying 'my body at some place in space,' since a perspectivistic representation comes about *only after* the fact that other bodies as bodies recognized as equal with my body has occurred? This idea has made difficulties for me again and again. Is there not the solution here?"[34] This central problem, at the core of the phenomenological transcendental aesthetics, leads to a clear solution in the late texts of the problem of the constitution of space. This one comprises two strata that are also two levels of enrichment of the aesthetic syntheses. It is thus necessary to distinguish between the spatiality proper to the primordial sphere and the "completely different" space constituted when the empathy comes into play. Empathy does not, therefore, rely on an effective and spatial displacement or permutation of places (my body here, that body there) because an absolute Here and Now cannot be properly displaced but only intentionally modified.[35]

The localization operated by empathy is thus the constitution of a distant place, from the "infinite distance" of a point outside space, which is an ego. What Husserl summarizes in neo-Fichtean terms. After the emergence of this insignificant thing that is the other body, as body of the other, of an alter ego, the world reduced to the own solipsist opens to the outside, acquires a true spatiality, which communicates itself transitively to my body, to the ghosts of surrounding bodies, whether they are those of simple things, organisms or similar. And more fundamentally, it is *eo ipso* the same for any ego, real or possible, arising in this common space-time: "so the general world of things is characterized in such a way, that to each body belongs an ego comprehensible by each ego as concrete world-consciousness, which thus appears objectified and realized in the common world of things, 'located' in space, in space-time, nothing really spatial, but recognizable intersubjectively as belonging to the body, expressed as comprehensible to all in the body."[36]

Finally, a third difficulty concerns the role of the imagination in the apperceptive transfer at the end of which another ego is posited there, in the spatial double, of localization in a faraway place that transforms my absolute zero (of my here) into a faraway place relative to that there. The manuscript that we follow here is particularly explicit on this point. The counterfactual (I imagine myself *as if I were there* in the body of the one that is *really there now,* and imagine standing, moving, seeing, feeling *as if I were there*) poses a question: "Do I carry out a fantasizing as if I had the second body there as my body, can I fantasize my body transformed into this other one, as if I had it as a body, this effective other body?" To which the answer is: "the apperception inherent to *all association*—the *original, positional one*, not proceeding in the as-if of pure imagination, for which then just everything valid for the original association is modified accordingly—transfer of *the sense of being*, thus real ad-perception, insofar as in the perception lies the sense of *the validity of being*."[37]And this associative pairing and transference of positionality of the absolute (here and now) to the presumptive (here and now of another) is performed and is reciprocal "without further ado, in one stroke."[38] Husserl proposes to call this specific form of "positionality" "ad-position." If we stick to passively realized empathy, and the modal composition here at play, the phenomenological analysis brings into play a composition of partly free and partly motivated possibilities, which is fundamental to a phenomenologically clarified ontology. The passive syntheses of association gather *actual* and *virtual* kinesthetic modifications, which constitute the passive ground of my "I can" (move from here and be there, where the other stands, similarly as *I would* stand, *if I would go over there*).[39] These possibilities "are pre-drawn in terms of being."[40] This validity is never definitively acquired and the possibility of a disappointment, that later experience can always reserve, affects all the constitutive levels involving empathy. And it falls to the progress of experience to confirm or infirm the presumed validity of this apperception, if it was right in shooting "beyond its 'legitimate' limits." But in the last instance: "Experience only shows what 'real analogy' may mean here in each case, i. e., the fulfillment and disappointment of the anticipation."[41] It is precisely in this hiatus that the demand for rationality is located.

Empathy, Self-Variation, and Emergence of Rationality

To understand the emergence of rationality, and the way in which it transforms in return the sense of this primordial core of empathy, it is necessary to insist on the modal substructure of this complex constitutive process that we are overviewing, trying to grasp the *ABC of empathy*, and the articulations between the transcendental aesthetic dimension and its eidetic underpinnings. This transfer of validity of being and of value opens a register of experience, which as such tends toward an accomplishment, an ultimate filling and exposes itself in doing so to a series of peripeties that are *the manifold process of modalizations (i.e., life itself)*. Each of these "possibilities" and counter-possibilities of the "being other," as far as they concern "egological ipseities" are singularizations of the ego eidos, which I must, by methodical constraint, draw from my own fund, by a self-variation that occupies the fourth Cartesian meditation and whose decisive role for the problem of empathy is so rarely or badly considered, whereas it is decisive. But we do not want to take up this whole problematic here, but simply show how it underlies the phenomenological theory of the moral will, as rational will.

I reveal myself as a transcendental fact, itself caught in a space of possibilities of being other, and this structure of mine is exemplary of what an ego is in general, as revealed by the free variation by which I obtain the eidos-ego. Every ego possesses a form of essence, by which it is a realization of its possibilities of being and contains them all in it horizontally, according to modes that we must specify. The same ego, the structure of essence of which we have just presented schematically, contains moreover *alteri* of which some have been decided from my factitious ego which includes the space of play (*Spielraum*) of the other potential possibilities (those are known or potentially known alter ego). Belong also to this space of play of realized possibilities, the other unknown ones that I presume (i.e. all anonymous others past, present, and to come). Others are undecided possibilities, of which the historical characters about whose existence I wonder for example are part. By variation of my ego thus explained, I obtain a form of eidos enriched with the structure of "*me and us*." The eidos-ego turns out to be not only the essential form of all my possible variants, but it is the same for all the egos horizontally included in my alteri space of play (Spielraum). The form of essence thus obtained is that of an ego involving in itself the alteri.

Now, as Husserl keeps repeating, *all this is intentionally and horizontally included in my transcendental factual ego*. Therefore, the transcendental ego, with its horizon, comprises in it the space of play of all the possibilities of being-other (in the two senses of the term: of becoming other than I am and of others that I am not), and is equivalent to the general form of the ego. Now, this irreducible original facticity entails the difference between the realized possible variants and the variants that remain pure possibilities, between the "other egos" (real, presumed real, probable) implying me as factitious and the other egos as pure (imaginary) variants of my ego or of that of the others, so to speak, in abeyance, that Husserl names "eidetic possibilities," follows. The former are real possible egos because they are objectified by me as known or unknown men, or as analogs of hypothetical men on other planets or star systems, in the presumed real world that *is mine*; whereas the latter are irremediably part of possible worlds and are if necessary objectified in an eidetic possible world.[42]

What the theory of empathy approaches on the level of the transcendental facticity belongs to an eidetic structure of reciprocal implication. Let us take the thing in its greatest generality, on an eidetic level. At the most general level, in contrast to a mere free possibility, "all eidetic possible transcendental I's are implied one in each other," and consequently, any possible I that I pick out: "implies immediately a universe, a totality [of other I's] coexisting with it."[43] And new consequence: Each possible variant of my ego implies its other possibilities, his or her alter egos; and the same holds in a similar way for each of his alter egos. Hence the law of essence: every ego envelops a monadic totality of co-implicated egos. Every ego taken as a possible example (whether it is real or purely possible) thus has the same essential form, belongs to the same eidos ego. Or to put it in other words: Every ego implies its universe of possible compossible egos. But incompossible possible egos are also included, as incompossible; for example, a Caesar who would not have been assassinated in the Senate, or would have been assassinated later, etc. Any position of an ego thus entails the position of a universe of compossible egos. As for the possibility of a purely possible and noncompossible ego, it implies the possibility of possible universes of other egos compossible with this ego. And in each of these universes, each ego belonging to this universe is an alter ego for all the other egos belonging to this universe; thus, he is an alter ego for these alter egos. In summary: *every egological universe implies an ego that implies the other egos and implies all the possible egos compossible of this universe*. Hence, a new eidetic proposition: the transcendental intersubjectivity eidos implies the transcendental ego. And in a trivial way: one is equivalent to the other.

But as Husserl already noticed, this equivalence posed on the eidetic level must be considered in its *sui generis* link with transcendental facticity. The "very significant thing" is that "constructing and construction (the constituted unity, the eidos) belongs to my factual holdings, my individuality." Consequently, just as the region of consciousness comprises all other regions including formal ontological spheres, here too every essentiality related to subjects is a moment of my transcendental facticity. This is the phenomenological way to understand the Cartesian truth that the cogito is a *fundamentum inconcussum* (i.e., an absolutely necessary and apodictic foundation).[44] At this very first stage, the "primal structure" "arises in its change of the primal hylè etc. with the primal kinaesthesis, primal feelings, primal instincts," and already "instinctively" is already predrawn for me "the constitution of the whole world," "whereby *the enabling functions themselves have their essence-ABC, their essence-grammar in advance*." A proper psychology not blinded by naturalism would have seen this transcendental teleology.[45]

Empathy in a Teleological Perspective

If we now turn to the teleological perspective, each transcendental subjectivity is characterized as a teleologically oriented constitutive process, which can be modally characterized as a process of elimination of contradictions (i.e., of selection of the possible ones compatible, at first, not with the best of all possible worlds, but allowing to preserve the presumed real world). But this is at least a world without contradictions. At the very least, it is a nonchaotic world, endowed with some kind of nomological order, thus with a nature.[46] This means that this subjectivity carries a will or at least an aspiration to "live," which must be understood as a process of modalization oriented toward "true being" (i.e., toward being that truly is). Any voluntary subjectivity is a carrier in its patent form of a latent "horizon of will," which develops and clears up in fact as this will develops. The form of the telos thus develops in the practical horizon of human existence by operating two fundamental changes of the will: (a) an awakening of the will to the authenticity of existence (an existence conscious of the meaning of existence) and (b) a resolution to live in accordance with the goal thus become conscious. The will is in this sense, world-creating and develops the telos in an axiological modal sense, not only to make the world continue to be possible but also to work by all its means so that this world is the best of all possible worlds. This universal absolute will, which Husserl calls divine, is the condition of possibility of the concrete existence of transcendental monadology. But conversely, this will require, not as a condition of possibility, but as a necessary condition, the existence of the structural layer that makes it possible, namely that of embodied subjectivities, thus of bodies. Another way of saying that nature is a *sine qua non* condition of the development of a practical world, but that one should not reduce the latter to the former, as naturalism wants.[47]

EMPATHY FROM AN ETHICAL POINT OF VIEW

The passage from teleology to ethics takes place as soon as one considers that the goal thus assigned to the will practically takes the form of the "supreme good" (*das Beste*) and of a life tended toward its realization: happiness. By considering practical modalizations (e.g., failures, practical impossibilities, remorse), the resolution takes the form of the "choice of the best possible life," in the world *whatever it is*, then in the world *as it is*. The practical horizon is twofold: to become a center of axiological radiance (i.e., to preserve and promote the practical goal, which formally takes the form of the formal categorical imperative "act for the best!").[48]

The thought of duty that develops then, which Husserl designates, with a Stoa name, as "*kathekon*," follows from the above considerations, which allow to develop the eidetic and transcendental substructure of ethical reflection.[49] What about the ideals of life? What is to be determined for the best life? We must distinguish between ethical reflection in relation to a hypothetical ethical goal, choosing the best paths for a *given* goal, and ethical reflection in relation to an absolute ethical goal. In the latter case, we are dealing with a categorical imperative. In essence, an ethical decision of this nature considers in a more or less articulated way the total horizon of life, and the decision corresponds to a presumed ideal of happiness. A consequent ethical reflection considers the "practical modalizations," and, thus, the reflection on the possibility and the causes of failures of the action as well as on the possibility and the means to avoid them (thus to foresee and to protect oneself, as well as it is possible, against such failures). It is here that the first form of normality appears (to oneself, to others, and to the natural conditions of action).[50]

Because of the effort and aspiration that continue to work in such a context, the demand for normality develops into a *striving toward practical rationality*, which thus becomes the essential character of a "moral nature" and a goal for the social moral world and education. Rationality understood in this way is the form of morality.[51] This practical rational regulation of life takes, in particular on the individual level, the form of a *demand for self-judgment*, preserving and cultivating the possibility of an autonomous judgment (*Selbsturteilung*), that of the *inner judge*. Because of the singular implication between fact and eidos revealed by phenomenology, we understand why this reign of ends does not tolerate any alibi but is incumbent on us here and now and is the responsibility of each one. It does not invalidate the action carried out in a blind way (guided by love or the good will), but one cannot oppose this one to the rational form that it takes because it would be unfair and pusillanimous to think that if the object of this love is worthy of it, any effort of articulation of the ABC of this affectivity would constitute a threat or even worse, an evil.

Empathy and the Foundations of a Rational Ethics

But the function of empathy in Husserl's own research in ethics is still not clearly established. Husserl insisted repeatedly, in his lessons on ethics,[52] on the fact that empathy is prior to any practical, valuative, or normative attitude. We know that one of the guiding threads of these investigations was the conflict between sentimentalist ethics and rationalist ethics, and especially the critique of Hume on the one hand, and that of Kant, on the other.

First, empathy must not be confused (as Hume and others did) with any kind of feelings, especially any kind of altruist feeling, be they moral or not. Hume was "wrong on the ethical character of feelings," precisely because he confuses "pure empathy and empathy with compassion for the other person,"[53] Feelings are not moral per se, but according to their motivation and their fulfilment as affective acts. Hume also failed to see "what class of feelings related to ego-subjects play a special role in ethics" and to which we must attribute their proper "correctness and falsity," if we don't want to renounce any ethics at all. And he did not see consequently that "*mere suggestion does not in itself justify feelings*."[54] Against Hume, Husserl argues[55] that (1) empathy is not compassion for the other person, as when someone behaves benevolently towards his neighbors. That (2) he who judges must not feel compassion, but judge in pure cognition of the action and the circumstances of the action judged: "we as judges, acknowledging his behavior, do not need to feel love for him, as judges, this is not proper in itself, it goes beyond the attitude of cognition." More generally, Hume "is wrong on the ethical character of feelings." The feelings are ethical under certain conditions (i.e., according to the fact that they are right and true or wrong and false).[56]

To evaluate *objectively*, he who judges must behave as a "mere spectator," whose judgment does not suffer from the interference of feelings, be it sympathy, compassion, or pity. "The sympathetic is a special mode of feeling and nothing other than the benevolent in the forms of sympathy and pity." Here empathy, in its strict sense comes into play: "Mere empathy with others creates for us *mere conceptions in their inwardness*," whereas sympathy goes "beyond the conceptions of their feelings"; in this case, "we sympathize, rejoice with, suffer with in our own actual feelings." Moreover, this sympathy has itself an intentional structure, it is an act, with a distinct axiological content which must not be confused, as Hume does, with anthropological and natural properties or dispositions and this is another aspect and consequence of his naturalism. When I sympathize with someone and feel compassion, I empathize with his suffering and the "object" of his or her feelings, but this has nothing to do with a quasi-mechanical transmission of emotion. The feeling has its correlate, and I feel compassion not regarding this correlate; I do not suffer from the loss of his daughter, but I understand empathically what this loss can or could mean for him, his actual feeling is the object of my compassion.[57]

But the deeper failure of Hume psychological grounding of ethics lies in the fact that he could not avoid confusion between two classes of feelings related to first-person subjects, "empathy with compassion for the other person," which both "play their *special role* for ethics" and consequently confuses thus "mere suggestion" and rational justification. The reason is that the grounds of the distinction between right and wrong judgment lies in the rightness and wrongness of feelings themselves: "if we do not ascribe to them a rightness and wrongness of their own, we can renounce any ethics at all." Conversely the one who judges must be in "the attitude of cognition" to recognize "the rightness" of the behavior, not "to feel love," or any other feel-with-the-other.[58]

Rationality of Feelings or the True Logic of the Heart

Husserl insists on the difference within the sphere of "evaluative emotional acts," which is parallel to that of judging, the difference between modes of fulfilment of the truth intended in the judgment. In the parallel sphere of feelings and of willing, we must recognize the exact corresponding difference. This applies to feelings as acts and not to "passive feelings." As acts, feelings have their own noematic correlates that are not those of the possible judgment or representation considering the "thing" or "object" of feeling or will because feelings and will are primarily orientated toward a value, and all acts of those sphere are of the genus: "taking for worth of." Now these acts obey the general laws of consciousness regarding the relations between empty intention and fulfilment. For instance: "a loving grasping of value, in which the value itself is embraced and possessed, is the originally acquiring act-consciousness as opposed to the *mere holding for value*, the ego act of loving, of rejoicing in something, etc., which just means, holds as pleasing, lovable, but just does not originally have the value in its own selfhood." And accordingly, we have the similar relations between the modes and degrees of fulfilment and the multiple forms of modalization. This holds for all evaluative acts: will and action as well as feelings, including aesthetical feelings.[59]

The field of application of rational norms and, thus, the postulate of a possible justification of practice, concerns not only the good (correlate of the will) and the will, but also the moral person as "subject of the will," "his acts, his motives, his habitual practical traits." The idea of an axiological and practical reason stems from these considerations, the idea of a "reason of the will" or "rational will" thus presupposes the possibility of a scientific justification based on the laws of essence that govern the sphere of the acts at stake, which are the analogue of the laws valid for the logical sphere of the acts. These acts of justification and the explicitly justified acts form the class of rationally motivated acts. These rational motivations are of various types: "insightful justifications, legal rejections and legal repudiations" and their correlate (i.e., the "propositions" corresponding to these positional acts which are "values"); their progressive unveiling in the eyes of consciousness corresponds to the emergence of rational norms. It carries with it a requirement of *universal* validity in their application to acts, circumstances, and acting subjects; the conquest of "*objectivity*" in the order of ethics as in that of knowledge is translated by the postulation of a "*common sense*," intersubjectively ideally communicable, by an ideal empathy. As Husserl insists: "therein lies . . . that, ideally speaking, it is at all possible for a proposition that an ego puts forward to be put forward by everyone and to be recognized as the same by everyone *through ideally possible empathy*" and "therefore, that my opinion can be understood by everyone and grasped as an opinion of the same sense" and "that, a priori, every justification or expulsion is also common property, every truth and falsity, every true value and every false value, every good decision of the will as well as every bad one with regard to these legal characters."[60]

Such are the conditions of possibility of the "everyman," which is nor the average man that Hume postulated, nor *das Man* of the existential analytics.

Empathy and Moral Justification

What is the role that empathy can and must play in ethics? If there is no such thing as a "moral of empathy" or a "politics of empathy," it is nonetheless true that empathy plays a key role in the understanding of how feelings or a will can be clarified and justified and how they can be judged right or wrong.[61] As Husserl puts it in a lapidary sentence: He "who judges must not feel compassion," but only "empathy."

If we have to overcome the naturalistic interpretation of feelings and morality and avoid believing that morality would be based on a certain kind of feelings, it remains that a morality and a knowledge of morality cannot dispense with understanding, not the mechanisms of affects and passions, but their articulation, and this one is of *intentional essence*. This is why, once the leave is given to naturalistic psychology, ethics must turn to transcendental phenomenology, if it is true that it is in the framework of a "pure and a priori phenomenology" that "all *questions of principle, not only of ethical reason, but of all reason in general, find their solution*."[62]

A theory of ethical reason requires the phenomenological investigation of reason, a system of forms of ethical life and of the forms of feeling and will and finally of life as such in its multiple forms of being.[63] Now, as we have seen, the latter is characterized as an open teleological process of modalization. The eidetic character of these investigations has its root in the phenomenon of the feeling and the will, as of the perception, namely the way in which the possible is implied in them.

The normative, then rational dimension of ethical life is based on the phenomenon of empathy taken in its transcendental sense. All the consecutive attempts to theorize morality in the course of history, as well as the first sketches that spontaneously developed from practical reflection, bear witness to this. The possibility of evaluating ethical action as well as rational ethical action supposes the resource of pure imagination, without which it is impossible to place oneself, so to speak, in the place of a "pure spectator," not disinterested in general, but neutral, possibly as a spectator of oneself, " which is empathetic with the action and attitude at stake, but not taking part in them, not involved in the affective dispositions judged." "All external feelings and practical interests must *remain out of play*," and the spectator must "only have empathy modifications of feelings and wills." The true ethical understanding of the other requires thus a pure empathy (i.e., a methodological imaginary transference).[64]

From this perspective, we understand why morality does not lie in a repression of selfish interests in favor of altruistic interests or purely in a detachment from all interests. The requirement of eliminating self-interest and selfish motives is primarily and unconditionally about the subject who makes moral judgments about an action and not the one who acts.[65] The contradictory conceptions that the historical philosophical ethics illustrate aim beyond their divergences at an operation and, more specifically, at a type of modification of the positionality, which it is advisable to identify and which explains at the same time the intervention of the imagination and the canonical forms of the staging's that it operates to give us to understand one of the central facts of the moral conscience, that is the scission (*Spaltung*) of the self in two instances. This operation is the épokhè, whose forms are however multiple.

It is indeed by it that the "the methodological meaning of pure imagination for moral judgments, and likewise the methodological meaning of placing oneself in an uninvolved spectator and in pure contemplation" is clarified. If we try to go beyond the aesthetic sense of this requirement, it means that we want to avoid judging arbitrarily, "rather, we want to gain an insightful judgment, an objectively true judgment." The "impartiality of the judgment" implies "eo ipso" that "all external feelings and practical interests" be kept "out of play" (thus an ethical épokhè of our actual feelings, will and interest). Positively, the resources of imagination are required to forge the possible variants of ourselves adjusted to the case at hand: "we have to live purely in understanding and re-evaluating and reflecting on the cognitive documents of the acting person, by which we gain the knowledge of what was in his sense, what was before him as good and as practical to strive for, and what was rightful in it and what was not." All this is accessible "only to empathy modifications of feelings and wills," and methodologically performable by transferring oneself "into a foreign uninvolved evaluator," and correlatively, "whole situation into an imagination."[66] This "transferability in the pure imagination" is the subjective and noetic resource of the claim to rationality in the order of knowledge as in the order of axiology or action. Still, it is necessary for this purpose to withdraw the imagination and the feelings from the naturalistic and psychological interpretation.[67]

Pure Imagination and Ethical *Époknai*

Whether it is by the medium of imagination or by a purely methodical act, the condition of a moral judgment, and more widely of a moral rationality resides in an inhibition of the contrary impulses, desires, and wills.[68] It is intrinsically linked to the creative character of the will, to its fiat, it is a hinge element of any will, as far as this one is exercised as a lifting of inhibition or as an inhibition. "Or an inhibition (a counter-drive of motives) is lifted or outweighed. In the contemplative question 'Is this so or not?,' 'suspension' is possibly exercised, and this suspension is lifted again."[69] But this *épokhè* can take many forms. If we push the analysis further, as Husserl requires, we arrive at a *typology of practical and axiological inhibitions*, which must be distinguished from purely *doxic inhibitions.*[70] But it gives birth to the awakened practical reason only when it takes the form of a universal ethical épokhè,[71] which opens the widest field of my possibilities of being and allows me to determine myself for the best life.

In the technical terms of *Ideas . . . I*,[72] axiological reason emerges from consciousness when the actual ego opens himself to the larger background of potentiality (of pure variants of being-other), by implementing a "*functional axiological épokhè*."[73] Épokhè is a form of inhibition, but not all inhibitions are an épokhè, and fewer are paired with a universal practical reduction.[74] Husserl is interested in this difference in the beautiful pages[75] that he devotes to the multiform phenomenon of asceticism. It is his way of revisiting in a phenomenological genealogy of morality the multiple meanings of "ascetic ideals." When épokhè exercises on and against the fulfillment of "passionate desires" or "affects," these are not suppressed, as in renunciation (when I realize that it is, for example, an impossible love or that the means to satisfy this affect are out of reach); I continue to experience them and even possibly to explore the possibilities of their fulfillment. The épokhè relating to such and such a feeling is a global and general abstention. It is a *negation* concerning the fulfillment without bearing on the act (feeling, will or opinion) on the intention. From the point of view of attention, it takes the form of a "looking away."[76]

This concerns not only the feelings in their active form but also the passive forms of affectivity, which have become passive or are primitively passive, that is to say "unconscious." "Everything concealed, every concealed validity functions with associative and apperceptive depth, *which the Freudian method makes possible and presupposes*."[77] The phenomenological analyses of the whole of these processes can thus rightly be advanced as "a *foreshadowing of Freudian psychoanalysis*, with its trapped affects, its 'repressions,' etc."[78] Seeking to relax the constraints of Brentanian psychology, from which it borrows the principles, the nascent psychoanalysis proposes a metapsychology whose metaphorical naturalism presupposes the same psychological principles as Brentano. Unable, like Brentano, to think of an intentionality specific to the affective sphere, whether active or passive, Freud comes to this central thesis of metapsychology, that the mechanisms of repression, of resistance, and more widely inhibitions, cannot be exercised directly on affects, but *only on the representations that they invest*.[79] The economic point of view follows from this.[80] Seeking to relax the constraints of Brentanian psychology, from which it borrows the principles, the nascent psychoanalysis proposes a metapsychology that falls back into a (metaphorical) naturalism. In contrast, Husserl proposes an analysis of the laws of essence governing affects, impulses, and feelings per se. Their dynamics are ruled by laws of essence of intention and fulfillment, *parallel* to those which govern the sphere of the representation and the cognitive (objectifying) activities. What is thought, in psychoanalysis, in terms of "object" (of the desire, of the impulse, of wish or will) is allowed to be decomposed according to the ABC of the passive and active affective intention, in a series of modal peripeties.

We have thus: "the drive in the mode of saturation in the positivity of the fulfillment"; and its " counterpart of full inhibition," which splits the drive into a twofold process, where an "element" receives a satisfaction and continues its underground life (in passivity, that is, sedimented under the form of hidden or "filthy" habits; while the remaining drive is absolutely inhibited, and is experienced as uncomfortably, as "driving actuality in every living present, constantly crying out for completion, so to speak."[81] These modal transformations are the real economy of the psyche:

> For here, apparently, lies the radical for the elucidation of what is really a subjective fact about these psychoanalytic things. Modes. The drive in the mode of "unconsciousness," of being unconscious to me, versus the drive in the mode of desiring attention emanating from the ego center. The life drive in its *modal transformations* uniformly in its uniform drive-temporality in a constant becoming, transforming itself—in transformation of the special drives, which therefore stand individually, in togetherness, in a constant genesis, in an "intentional" genesis, although we stand here first in a pre-intentionality, which plays its role in all explicit intentionality. [82]

Husserl's conclusion may seem excessively optimistic, but they undoubtedly fulfil one of Lacan's suggestions that a logic of desire should be akin to "modal logics."[83] The unconscious is a "mode" of desire and attention, whose deep articulation lies in the system of "modal transformations" that we have tirelessly tracked, and which constitute the fundamental core of the syntaxes of consciousness.[84]

In a manuscript on the inhibition of the drives, Husserl explicitly tackles this typology of the forms of inhibition and takes up again the problem of asceticism.[85] To the typical of the drives,[86] which has rightly interested many commentators, corresponds a theory of types of épokhai covering all the main forms of inhibition, which is required if one wants to avoid the modern forms of psychologism or naturalism that have accompanied the history of psychoanalysis. In addition to the inhibitions exerted on the drives from other drives, the partial inhibitions on the background of a fundamental aspiration that persists; the constitution of feelings based on inhibitions of drives, and so on. It is necessary to consider the higher forms that the mechanisms of projection, identification, introjection, and idealization capture only partially.

A RENEWED CRITIC OF AXIOLOGICAL AND PRACTICAL REASON

Against a general tendency to naturalization, which will be perpetuated in psychoanalysis or in the genealogies of morality that will flourish in the wake of Rousseau, even what was called previously "passive feelings" (drives, desires, inclinations, aspirations, inhibitions, etc.) comprise intentional articulations that must be described.

Naturalization of Practical and Axiological Reason in Hume

Hume's insights, suitably stripped of their naturalistic distortion, offer starting points for such investigations. In his *Treatise*, he

> gives parallel explanations of how senseless feelings and strivings in themselves are formed according to the psychological laws of nature in such a way that a seemingly objective mental world, social world, becomes and specifically that a seemingly objective mode of judgement asserts itself in all community subjects and seemingly objective categories of practice, as if (there were) domains of a genuine objective truth here on the basis of a practical reason apparently demonstrating objective correctness.

To preserve the properly rational sense of this claim to objectivity, we must pursue to its ultimate implications what Hume himself is obliged to concede: namely, that just as the truth of a judgment presupposes universal communicability, the validity of a value (the rightness of a will or a feeling) postulates the possibility of an intersubjective harmonization, a universal concordance of rational subjects. The means of this communication is, as we have seen, transcendental empathy. Because this is understood in an empirical and naturalistic way by Hume, by virtue of a principle of economy supposed to govern nature, he falls into an aestheticization of ethics. Indeed, the postulated universal intersubjectivity cannot rise beyond the *sensus communis* postulated by the aesthetic judgment according to Kant. It is thus mechanically, by virtue of a purely natural process, that the egoism of the first feelings and tendencies rises to the universality inherent in any morality worthy of the name and gives right to apparently altruistic feelings. Universality or communicability is naturalized and "purely mechanically, as the tendency of harmonization, the tendency towards the greatest possible agreement of the evaluating and judging subjects, asserts itself." There is indeed an épokhè, "in which everyone *switches off his or her self-interest* and judges as an uninvolved spectator based on pure 'sympathy.'" As a result, selfish feelings can be judged virtuous, as long as "these would be approved of in such cases by the uninvolved spectator *Everyman*."[87] Thus, even if egoism is not morally condemnable for Hume, he allows for affective behaviors, for feelings, that are not egotistical, insofar as they would be susceptible of approval by anyone who would look at these feelings with the eyes of an uninvolved observer—Everyman.

But as we have seen, this ethical consideration of others is more a phenomenon of harmonic resonance than of a true reciprocal understanding. Because of the confusion between sympathy and empathy, the figure of the moral arbiter takes on the form of a spectator who will judge according to the resonances that the feelings of others will arouse in him?

Kant's Absolutized Practical Reason

On the other hand, by excessive reaction against the empiricist psychologism in the theory of knowledge as well as in the theory of morals, Kant commits an opposite methodological error; that of a conceptualist constructivism.[88] Kant's transcendental constructivism is hardly more satisfactory because as he makes universal communicability a simple criterium of rational objectivity in the order of knowledge, so the objectivity of the rational will makes the relation to others only a criterion of the categorical imperative. What is missing is an elucidation of the aesthetic and affective conditions of possibility of such a rational will. Because of his rejection of feelings, in general, in the sphere of the pathological, except that of respect, Kant has not given himself the means to explore the subjective conditions of possibility of rational and free action. Husserl's grievance is thus about methodology.

Kant's condemnation of the intervention of feelings in ethics rests on an error diametrically opposed to that of Hume. Kant is wrong and morally rigid in banishing compassion as "pathological affection."[89] Failing to see the intentional structure of feelings, he did not see that those affective intentions, like cognitive intentions, opinions in the strict sense of the term, could be empty or filled, know degrees of filling and, in relation to that, undergo specific modalizations. Consequently, he did not see that an act of charity was not immoral, but that it could be spontaneous and, so to speak, blind, or based on an intuitive empathy "that opens the mind's eye and the heart to the inner life." Empathy in the phenomenological sense, for example, "makes compassion intimate and deep."[90]

After such a rejection of the very matter of ethical life, he could not but feel the impotence and sterility of formal rational imperatives—of which he did not have a clear idea anyway—and reject them by confusing them with hypothetical imperatives, as he admits in the introduction to the Third Critique. But above all the conception of practical reason to which he was thus led had to be enclosed in a rigid formalism, an exact analog of the transcendental principles providing the fundamental lines to the knowledge of nature. What gives content to the formal categorical imperative "Act as best you can!" is not the transcendental deduction of the categorical imperative and the postulates of practical reason, but the exploration of the resources of free voluntary action. Universality is certainly, as we have seen, an essential character of good will, but it says nothing if we do not provide "precise explanations" of the subjective performances that make it possible and effective.

One does not understand how and why practical reason gives right to some rare feelings and to the will, whose goodness it demands, and excludes all other forms of feelings. Kant misinterpreted the role of feelings in ethics,[91] by banishing even compassion from the sphere of rational ethics. We do not expect practical rationality to banish will. How could we banish feelings from the sphere of the ethical? Charity is ethical if it is right (if it is rationally motivated or *could be* rationally motivated). Yet we can demand that compassion be clear and distinct and not vague and confused.

Despite these objections, just as Husserl reveals eidetic phenomenological insights behind Hume's empiricist clothing, it is possible to discern behind Kant's logical constructions phenomenological insights of rare depth.[92]

On Moral Conscience and Épokhè

Therefore, axiological, and practical rationality presupposes an empathy performed in pure imagination, in an axiological neutrality.[93] Husserl provides thus an eidetic and transcendental clarification of the peculiar splitting (*Spaltung*) at work in the famous phenomenon of "moral consciousness" (*Gewissen*), such as it was pointed out by Heidegger in *Sein und Zeit* (§§54–60). "I have experienced a rupture of my personality, or how much a personality can split, all these splits take place as those of the identical (and through them persisting) ego pole."[94] But unlike his former assistant, the description is here developed in the frame of a critique of evaluative and practical reason, in a renewed and deepened sense. Without this kind of *functional neutrality*, which is not purely theoretical and methodological (like in Weber), the splitting would indeed be pathological and remain extra-ethical, as Kant feared.

What is the call of the conscience?[95]

Consciousness manifests itself through its imperative form, but it is not apodictic (*endgültig*). It is apodictic at the moment of decision, at the moment when the value imposes itself as absolute, or the best relative to any other. But it can undergo modalizations: it does not speak definitively at every moment; it can be "indeterminate," it can be affected by doubt, it can err, but above all it seems to be caught in relativity, which seems to compromise any claim to absolute validity. It is so if we refer to the historical intersubjectivity which is essentially indefinite. But to this we must oppose the existence of axiologically evident acts. "For example, the motherly 'I should,' the motherly love and loving motherly activity in its inner consequence" has a categorical validity. "Here we have conscience in evidence."[96] And it would be a sophism to argue that, since this evidence can undergo modalizations (e.g., conflict, doubt, error), it is not ultimate, and deprive it of axiological and practical validity. For it is exclusively in this present, in which the decision is taken, in which the *fiat* of the will is performed, that the conscience imposes itself, and not in regard to virtually future modalizations. From the point of view of practical reason, it is "the *unum necessarium*." This does not mean that we must limit our view to the present, as stated by the equivocal axiom "pick the present moment." On the contrary, a decision will have all the more chance of being sustainable and valid, if it takes into account life in its entirety, and beyond that, if it takes into account the widest intersubjectivity. A decision taken *in conscience* concerns my whole life: "I as the subject of conscience is the I of the whole life as the I of permanent values." It considers the widest intersubjectivity, and thus the widest space of possibility, which does not exclude a priori that things unfold in a different way than my actual level of knowledge or information leads me to suppose. Consciousness must deal with the principal uncertainty of life: "the possibilities of the other coming are not only fantasy possibilities."[97] Often enough "something other than what was so definitely expected came; and so, the coming otherwise also has its 'real possibility,' in which there is a belief component of an analogous kind as in the expectation." This must lead to the regulation of all hope and fear. As the sublimely banal formula says: "to all this belongs a general uncertainty of life." From this it follows that the rule of life will be all the surer that the discernment will have used the failures and surprises of life, so that each decision is inscribed in a "space of possibilities," always vaster and, yet, more determined.

CONCLUSION

In contrast to Hume, who developed, under a "sensualist clothing," some major insights into those eidetic laws that he understood wrongly as natural laws (laws of human nature, in his theoretical as in his practical behavior), Kant has not conceived and formulated the true concept of a priori. Moreover, Kant misunderstood the distinction between active and passive feelings, and thus did not understand the structure of feelings as acts. In other words, despite some interesting incursions of Mendelsohn into that field, interestingly mentioned by Husserl, Kant did not develop nor think it possible to develop a phenomenological eidetic analysis of lived experiences but limited the psychological investigations to collecting of empirical indirect observations. By taking seriously the advocated parallelism, Husserl's critique of Kant's ethics helps us to understand better his critique of Kant's epistemological positions. It is highly instructive to list and understand the major objections. The first is that Kant misunderstood the a priori eidetic laws governing the sphere of feelings, as well as those ruling the sphere of sensations. The ABC of moral consciousness and the inner court is to be found in the articulation in an insight that Hume twisted by confusing empathy as a transcendental process, involving neutrality, with sympathy.

This dissociation between the constitutive level of empathy and the experiential level of sentimental forms of sympathy or compassion (*Mitgefühl*) cannot be reconciled with the distinction between cognitive or representative functions and affective and practical functions, because the constitutive level in question is not primarily of the order of representation and knowledge. On the contrary, it is from the constitutive analyses that a certain number of fundamental ethical phenomena can be described and removed from the controversies that have fueled the field of ethical reflection from Aristotle to Nietzsche and beyond: this is the case of the phenomenon of recognition in the intersubjective and specifically ethical sense, of the postulate of an impartial judge that culminates in the figure of the inner court, the phenomenon of consciousness, etc. Armed with this distinction, transcendental phenomenology is able to recognize the respective rights of affectivity and understanding, and to arbitrate the recurrent philosophical conflicts between sentimental morals and rationalist morals, to found the parallelism of practical reason and theoretical reason, to reconcile finally the requirements of a genealogy of moral notions starting from the passive affective levels without reducing the forms of rationalities emerging thus to epiphenomena or to the damped expression of an all-mighty affectivity or will. As far as one puts into brackets the natural thesis, this emerging reason cannot be regarded as any super-ego or super-man in the naturalistic sense but as a mere human being striving for rationality, striving to bring up himself and his mates to the standard of rationality.

In empathy, a double modification of meaning takes place, corresponding to the intersubjective constitution: (a) a pairing of any imaginary variant of myself, always in principle accessible by a free variation, as a *pure possible*, which ceases to become a real proper possibility for myself because it is associated to the factual appearance of a foreign body in my environment, *there*, and by that very fact posed and projected in this environment, from my here and now, from the irreducible and original facticity (*Urfaktizität*) of my own existence; (b) from this pairing results the apprehension of this appearance of body (a phantom of physical body, at first stage) as manifestation of another real existing proper body, of a *Leib* with its interiority, which is, by essence, phenomenologically barred to me, but that he expresses in many ways. As Husserl insists, this operation is given to us as the first core of the common world with its common nature.

What is labeled here phase (a) encompasses a series of complications that Husserl did not cease to reanalyze and to deepen. The "modal formula" of empathy is a combination of a pure possibility (me if I were there and were the other) with a real impossibility (I can absolutely and actually *not* be *this* other standing there, while and since I am here), which results in a position of absolutely transcendent reality, exceeding all possible intuition but nonetheless intuitively given, inasmuch as empathy is a mode of intuition, which eventually grounds new modes of intuitions raising a pretension to a full reality. To this is added a series of reciprocal presuppositions in chiasms:

since the position of the transcendent reality of another "ego" in an alien corporeality (*Leiblichkeit*) supposes the immanent apodictic reality of my ego in its own corporeality. This is translated, into the eidetic point of view, under the form of a reciprocal presupposition of the ego eidos of which the other and me are singularizations and individuations, and the presupposition by this eidos of myself as an original facticity. Finally, from the point of view of spatiality, this modal play that is translated by the conjunction of an absolute here and now (the zero-point given by my body in its centered kinesthetic space) in the absolute present indicative and of a *there* that has a sense of localization for a body and of occupation for a body of its own, only insofar as I hypothetically project myself there, in the mode of the subjunctive. Such is the grammar, the ABC of the transcendental theory of empathy.

NOTES

1. Jannicaud (1981), Marion (1989), Ricoeur (1990, 2004) and Levinas (1992), on the footsteps of Heidegger are among major figures of this turn.
2. See Moran, 2004. Scheler, 1973.
3. Geiger, 1911a, 1911b.
4. See Lobo, 2014; de Santis, 2020.
5. Letter from Husserl to Misch, 3. VIII. 1929, Husserliana, Dokumente III, III/6, Philosophenbriefe, p. 276.
6. Heidegger, 2004, GA, 29/30, 291, 298, 302–4; and Heidegger, 1977.
7. Husserl to Grimme, 9. IV. 1917, *Briefwechsel, Die Göttinger Schule,* Husserliana, Dokumente III, Teil III/3, p. 79.
8. Husserl to Ingarden, 16. XI. 1918, *Briefwechsel, Die Göttinger Schule*, Husserliana, Dokumente III, Teil III/3, Die Göttinger Schule, p. 201–202.
9. Scheler; on Scheler, see Husserl to Grimme, 5. IV. 1918. Bernau b/St Blasien le 5 April 1918, *Briefwechsel, Die Göttinger Schule*, Husserliana, Dokumente III, Teil III/3, p. 81). Husserl à Ingarden, 9 IV. 1927 (Husserliana, Dokumente III, Teil III/3, Die Göttinger Schule, p. 232). On Heidegger, Letter from E. et M. Husserl to Ingarden, 26. XII. 1927, *Briefwechsel, Die Göttinger Schule*, Husserliana, Dokumente III, Teil III/3, p. 235–36.
10. Husserl to Koyre, 22. VI. 1931, *Briefwechsel, Die Göttinger Schule*, Husserliana, Dokumente III, Teil III/3, p. 360). Husserl an Kaufmann, 19. XII.1928. (*Briefwechsel*, Die Freiburger Schüler, Husserliana, Dokumente III, Teil III/4, p. 178).
11. Husserl à Löwith, 22. II. 1937. Freiburg i/B Lorettostr. 40 22. II. 1937, *Briefwechsel*, Die Freiburger Schüler, Husserliana, Dokumente III, Teil III/4, p. 397)
12. Hua XIV: 335–36.
13. Hua III/1, and Lobo, 2006, 2010, and 2021a.
14. Hua XIV, 335–36. Emphasis mine. In Hua XV: 385. My comment on *Ideas . . . I*, see Lobo, 2010.
15. Hua XIV: 336.

16. Hua XLIII-1: 547. This distinction is deepened in Twardowski. See Plotka, 2020.
17. Hua XIII, 342, 338–39. See Taipale, 2012: about Hua XIV: 8; Hua VIII, 495. And Heinämaa, 2014.

"Hua XIII: 338. See Husserl reply to Lipps: "I do not apperceive the other ego simply as a duplicate of myself and accordingly as having an original sphere completely like mine" (Hua I: 146; cf. Husserl XIII, 342). As J. Taipale observes: "Therefore, already from the very start, the other is expected to prove *similar* to me, as *Meinesgleichen*—or *Unseresgleichen* as Husserl and Stein also put it . . . Husserl adds that even though the other is "essentially related to me as the normally existing ego," to be sure, "*after* his being is established for me, my being is likewise related to his" (Hua XV: 34–35; quoted in Taipale 2012).

18. About these metaphors, see Taipale, 2015, and Lobo, 2012.
19. Such is the phenomenological root of the aesthetical concept of empathy in Vischer (1873), Lipps (1900, 1903, 1906), and Worringer (1911). About anesthetization of ethics, in Hume (1990), according to Husserl, see below.
20. At the root of the notion of "fellow" and "next."
21. Hua XV: 116 sq.
22. Husserl to Pfänder, 6. I. 1931. (*Briefwechsel, Die Münchener Phänomenologen*; Husserliana, Dokumente III, Teil III/2, p. 180)
23. Husserl to Bell, 13. XII. 1922, *Briefwechsel, Die Göttinger Schule,* Husserliana, Dokumente III, Teil III/3, p. 43–44).
24. *Briefwechsel, Die Göttinger Schule* Husserliana, Dokumente III, Teil III/3, p. 46.
25. Husserl to Bell, 13. XII. 1922 (*Briefwechsel, Die Göttinger Schule*, Husserliana, Dokumente III, Teil III/3, p. 46).
26. This criticism of the psychological concept of empathy doctrine starts in 1913–1915 (see, e.g., Hua XIII, p. 333–42).
27. Taken in this poor sense, of course, "empathy" is neither an existential nor an empirical phenomenon (Op. cit. p. 166). This refutes consequently Heidegger's objections, which are circular. They consider reductively psychological and cognitive forms of empathy, which *of course* presuppose the "being-in-the-world-with" the others and entails already an understanding and some form of acquaintance (*Kenntnis*) with the other. (See *Sein und Zeit*, Gesamtausgabe. Band 2, Klostermann, Frankfurt-am-Main, 1977, § 26, p. 16 & passim.).
28. Hua XV: 138.
29. Hua XV: 137.
30. Hua XV: 137, note.
31. Hua XV, Text N 37 dating from 1934, deals with the "problem of empathy."
32. Hua XV: 245, 247.
33. Hua XV: 246.
34. Hua XV: 249–50.
35. Hua XV: 655.
36. Hua XV: 657.
37. Hua XV: 251.
38. Ibid.

39. "But I am here, and remain so, if I physically 'look the same' with the foreign body, and the approach, I would be there, has only possibility as approach, I could go there now, I could have gone there, been driven etc. I control these possibilities, as well as all the manifold appearances, which would have to occur there as variations of those, which I have here" (Hua XV: 252)

40. Hua XV: 252.

41. Ibid.

42. "To every real possible other for me belongs that it *implies me as factual ego* with my real experience and world of experience. 2) But to *a purely eidetically possible other*, [it belongs] that it implies, in its possibility, the variations of the eidetic possibility of my ego. With this it is also said that the completely unknown other [is] objectified as a human being in the factual world for me, either as a human being of the earth or as a human-like being on some celestial body etc. But an eidetic possible transcendental I is objectified as a human being in an eidetic possible world." Hua XV: 382.

43. Hua XV: 382–83.

44. Hua XV: 385.

45. Ibid.

46. See Hua XV-text 22.

47. Hua XV: 385–86.

48. About this formal imperative that comes from Brentano see for instance Hua XXVIII: 142 sq. "Der formal objektive Imperativ lautet: "Tue das Beste unter dem erreichbaren Guten innerhalb deiner jeweiligen praktischen Gesamtsphäre"

49. Hua XV: 142. Supplement VII, August 1931

50. "In life one judges the others by the kathekon (at first) and is judged oneself and is motivated early to practice self-judgment - judgment of the past and possibly, the WHOLE and life past, which is in memory, or the whole professional past, the whole past from maturity, with which the 'serious' life began. *Self-reflection and self-assessment serve the regulation of life, it goes into the past for the sake of the future and goes into the future for the sake of the possibilities of life, for the sake of the possible teleological forms, among which judging assessing is and should be chosen.*" Hua XV: 145.

51. « The normal community world—the normal everyday life with other people in normal custom, in the normality of the state order, in the normality of the *common ground* of experience, the ground of the common tradition, the common mode of judgment and evaluation, the probable manner of reactions in each respective *typical situation*." HUA XV: 143.

52. Published in the volumes 28 and 37 of the Husserliana (Husserl, 1988, 2004) subsequently, and for sake of clarity, referred to as Hua XXVIII and Hua XXX-VII, respectively.

53. Hua XXXVII: 194.

54. Ibid.

55. Ibid.

56. Ibid.

57. Ibid.

58. Ibid.
59. Ibid. See also Hua XI, sections II and III.
60. Hua XXXVII:121.
61. Lobo, 2014, 2016.
62. Hua XXXVII: 196. Emphasis mine.
63. Ibid.
64. Hua XXXVII: 191
65. Hua XXXVII: 190.
66. Hua XLII: 191.
67. But this presupposes for this domain of truth that feeling and willing are not, as Hume thought in his blindness for everything specifically spiritual, merely natural facts in a naturally conceived soul, but acts that have the character of either legitimate, or illegitimate opinions and, if the former is the case, constitute truly existing values. Hua XXXVII: 192.
68. "The instincts (food instinct, sex instinct, etc.) are constantly there in the coexistence, but in different modes; but in the acting out they can inhibit each other, the one of the one can eliminate the other, in the current effect, therefore." Hua XLII: 417.
69. Hua XLIII-3: 264
70. Hua XLII.
71. See also, Lobo, 2008 and 2007.
72. Hua III/1, §§ 113–14.
73. Which in contrast with a practical and axiological skeptical épokhè (Hua XXVIII: 238, 353) which is *nonsense,* does not fall into a "performative" incompatibility. In this view, we understand to what extent, in a theoretical and practical respect, it is *unsafe* to foreclose the épokhè.
74. Hua XLII: 125–29.
75. Hua XLII: 112 Supplement XIV on "*Eingeklemmte Affekte—Askese* »"
76. "To the épokhè of allowing the possibility of the effect (in instinctive desires lies in it a periodicity of enjoyment and reawakening of the drive as desire) belongs the 'looking away' and wanting to look away," Hua XLII: 126.
77. Hua XLII: 126.
78. Ibid.
79. About the possibility for a feeling (or a pulsion) to be conscious/unconscious without the mediation of a representation, see Freud; Das Unbewusste [1905] (Freud, 1982: 135–38). And his reconsiderations afterward, that *consequently* the hypothesis that anxiety proceeds directly from the repression of libido, is not sustainable anymore, in *Hemmung, Symptom, Angst*, [1926], (Freud, 1982: 253). Freud, 1970 and 1971. See Kaiser, 1997; Pigman, 1995.
80. Hua XLII: 126.
81. Ibid.
82. Hua XLII: 126–27.
83. Lacan, *Mon enseignement*, Seuil, 2005, p. 52.
84. Et Hua XLII. Lobo, 2012.

85. On "Drive, instinct. Desire, wanting. Various notions of inhibition, of inhibiting, of holding oneself, negating, and affirming. Asceticism—'new life,' épokhè": Hua XLII: 125–29.

86. "Drives—instincts, the original drives, drive types in their general typology. Drive, need in the mode of satisfaction" (Hua XLII: 126).

87. Hua XXXVII: 193.

88. Hua XXXVII: 197–98.

89. Hua XXXVII: 228.

90. Ibid.

91. Ibid.

92. Hua XXXVII: 198.

93. Heidegger does not say much about an ethics founded on empathy transcendentally understood, and much less about its dependence on the épokhè. Yet, in his analytics of moral conscience he relates the possibility of the hearing of the call of moral conscience with a break, i.e., an interruption or suspension of the everyman hearing. See *Sein und Zeit*, § 55.

94. Hua XV: 254.

95. "The call of Conscience" and the "personal 'I have to'" (*Ruf des Gewissens. Mein persönliches "Ich soll"*). HUA XLII: 416. Where respect for the categorical imperative meets the conatus, but understood as an effort towards more permanence, and thus rationality.

96. Hua XXXVII: 419.

97. Hua XXXVII: 299–300.

REFERENCES

De Santis, D. 2020. "Self-Variation": A Problem of Method in Husserl's Phenomenology. *Husserl Studies* 36, 255–69. https://doi.org/10.1007/s10743-020-09270-x

Freud, Sigmund. 1970 [1905]. Der Witz und seine Beziehung zum Unbewussten. In *Sigmund Freud Studienausgabe*, Band IV. Frankfurt am Main: S. Fischer, 9–220.

———. 1971 [1905]. Bruchstück einer Hysterie-Analyse. In *Sigmund Freud Studienausgabe*, Band VI. Frankfurt am Main: S. Fischer, 83–186.

———. Das Unbewusste, *Metapsychologische Schriften* [1905], in *Psychologie des Unbewussten*, Studienausgabe, Band III, Fischer Taschenbuch Verlag, 1982, 119–173.

———. *Hemmung, Symptom, Angst*, [1926], in *Hysterie und Angst*, Studienasugabe, Band VI, Fischer Taschenbuch Verlag, 1982, 227–310.

Geiger, Moritz. 1911a. *Zum Problem der Stimmungseinfühlung*. In: *Zeitschrift für Ästhetik*. Band 6, 1911, S. 1–42.

———. 1911b. *Das Bewußtsein von Gefühlen*. In: *Münchener Philosophische Abhandlungen*. 1911, S. 125–62.

Heidegger, Martin. 2004. *Die Grundbegriffe der Metaphysik. Welt—Endlichkeit—Einsamkeit*. Frankfurt am Main: Vittorio Klostermann.

———. 1977. *Sein und Zeit*, Frankfurt am Main: Vittorio Klostermann
Heinämaa, Sara. 2014. Transcendental Intersubjectivity and Normality: Constitution by Mortals. In *The Phenomenology of Embodied Subjectivity*. Springer, 83–103
Hume, David. 1990. *Treatise of Human Nature*, ed. P.H. Nidditch. Oxford University Press.
Husserl, Edmund. 1984. *Briefwechsel, Die Münchener Phänomenologen*. (*Husserliana* Dokumente III, Ed. Elisabeth Schuhmann, Teil III/2).
———. *Briefwechsel, Die Göttinger Schule,* Husserliana, Dokumente III, Teil III/3.
———. *Briefwechsel*, Die Freiburger Schüler, Husserliana, Dokumente III, Teil III/4.
———. *Briefwechsel*, Philosophenbriefe, Husserliana, Dokumente III, III/6.
———. 1950. Hua I: *Cartesianische Meditationen und Pariser Vorträge*. Edited by Stephan Strasser, Haag: Martinus Nijhoff.
Hua III: *Ideen zu einer reinen Phänomenologie und phänomenologische Philosophie. Erste Buch;* Edited by Marly Biemel. Haag: Martinus Nijhoff, 1950.
Hua VIII: *Erste Philosophie. Zweiter Teil: Theorie der phänomenologischen Reduktion*. Edited by Rudolf Boehm, Haag: Martinus Nijhoff, 1959.
Hua XIII: *Zur Phänomenologie der Intersubjektivität. Texte aus dem Nachlass. Erster Teil: 1905–1920*. Edited by Iso Kern, Haag: Martinus Nijhoff, 1973.
Hua XI: *Analysen zur passiven Synthesis. Aus Vorlesungs- und Forschungsmanuskripten, 1918*–1926. Edited by Margot Fleischer, Haag: Martinus Nijhoff, 1966.
Hua XIV: *Zur Phänomenologie der Intersubjektivität. Texte aus dem Nachlass. Zweiter Teil: 1921–28*. Edited by Iso Kern, Haag: Martinus Nijhoff, 1973.
Hua XV: *Zur Phänomenologie der Intersubjektivität. Texte aus dem Nachlass. Dritter Teil: 1929–35*. Edited by Iso Kern, Haag: Martinus Nijhoff, 1973.
Hua XXVIII: *Vorlesungen über Ethik und Wertlehre*, 1908–1914, Husserliana, Vol. 28, Dordrecht: Springer, 1988.
Hua XXXVII: *Einleitung in die Ethik, Vorlesungen Sommersemester 1920/1924* Ed. Henning Peucker, Dordrecht: Springer, 2004.
Hua XLII: *Grenzprobleme der Phänomenologie. Analysen des Unbewussten und der Instinkte. Metaphysik. Späte Texte aus dem Nachlass (1908–1937)*. Edited by Rochus Sowa and Thomas Vongehr. Dordrecht: Springer.
Jannicaud, Dominique. 1981. *Le tournant théologique de la phénoménologie française*. Paris: Éditions de l'éclat.
Kaiser, Ulrich. 1997. *Das Motiv der Hemmung in Husserls Phänomenologie*. München: Fink.
Lacan, Jacques. 2005 *Mon enseignement*. Seuil
Levinas, Emmanuel. 1992. *Éthique comme philosophie première*. Paris, Rivages.
Lipps, T. 1903. *Einfühlung, innere Nachahmung, und Organempfindungen*, 1903
———. 1906. *Einfühlung und ästhetischer Genuss*. 1906
Lipps, Theodor. 1900. Ästhetische Einfühlung. *Zeitschrift für Psychologie und Physiologie der Sinnesorgane* 22, 415–50.
Lobo, Carlos. 2006. "L'*apriori* affectif (I). Prolégomènes à une phénoménologie des valeurs." *Alter* 14, 3–68.
———. 2007. Le temps de vouloir—la phénoménologie de la volonté. *Annales de Phénoménologie* 29–83.

———. 2008. Phénoménologie de la réduction et réduction éthique. In F. de Gandt & C. Majolino, eds., *Lectures de la* Krisis (pp. 123–59). Vrin.
———. 2010. Introduction à une phénoménologie des syntaxes de conscience. *Annales de phénoménologie*, 117–63.
———. 2012. La "résistance de Derrida à la psychanalyse et la phénoménologie transcendantale. *Studia Phaenomenologica* 399–425.
———. 2014. Self-variation and self-modification. In Dermot Moran and Rasmus T. Jensen, eds., *The Phenomenology of Embodied Subjectivity* (pp. 263–84. Springer.
———. 2016. "Digging out the roots of an affective fallacy." *Revista internacional, Eikasia*, Madrid, 321–47
———. 2021a. Diagrams of time and syntaxes of consciousness. A contribution to the phenomenology of visualization. In B. Luciano & C. Lobo, eds., *When Form becomes Substance: Diagrams, Power of Gesture and Phenomenology of Space*. Birkhäuser/Springer.
———. 2021b. Individual existence. A phenomenological and logical clarification. In Marco Cavallro & George Heffernan, eds., *The Existential Husserl*. Springer.
Marion, Jean-Luc. 1981. *Sur la théologie blanche de Descartes*. Analogie, création des vérités éternelles, fondement, P.U.F.
———. 1989. *Réduction et donation*. Recherches sur Husserl, Heidegger et la phénoménologie, P.U.F.
Moran, Dermot. 2004. The Problem of Empathy: Lipps, Scheler, Husserl and Stein. In Thomas Kelly & Philipp Roseman, eds., *Amor amicitiae: On the Love That Is Friendship: Essays in Medieval Thought and Beyond in Honor of the Rev. Professor James McEvoy*. Leuven: Peeters.
Pigman, George. 1995. Freud and the History of Empathy. *International Journal of Psycho-Analysis* 76, 237–256.
Płotka, W. 2020. From psychology to phenomenology (and back again): A controversy over the method in the school of Twardowski. *Phenomenology and the Cognitive Sciences* 19, 141–67. doi: 10.1007/s11097-019-09620-x
Ricœur, Paul. 1990. *Soi-même comme un autre*. Seuil
———, ed. 2004. *Parcours de la reconnaissance*. Stock.
Scheler, Max. 1973. *Wesen und Formen der Sympathie* [1912]. In M. S. Frings, ed., *Gesammelte Werke*, vol. 7. Bern: Francke. [English translation G. McAleer, 2008, *The Nature of Sympathy*. New Brunswick.
Taipale, Joona. 2012. Twofold Normality: Husserl and the Normative Relevance of Primordial Constitution. *Husserl Studies* 28: 49–60.
———. 2015. The anachronous other: Empathy and transference in early phenomenology and psychoanalysis. *Studia Phaenomenologica* XV, 331–48.
Vischer, R. 1873. *Ueber das optische Formgefuehl, Ein Beitrag zur Ästhetik*. Leipzig, Hermann Credner.
Worringer, Wilhelm. 1911. *Abstraktion und Einfühlung*. R. Piper & Co, Verlag.

Chapter 7

Phenomenology as Reverence

The Role of Reverence in the Phenomenological Method of Dietrich von Hildebrand

Alexander Montes

ABSTRACT

In this chapter, I argue Dietrich von Hildebrand's realist conception of consciousness and phenomenology leads him to propose reverence (*Ehrfurcht*) as the most fundamental moral attitude and as inherent to the very method of phenomenology. In contrast to his teacher Husserl, Hildebrand rejects any form of transcendental idealism. For Hildebrand, when we have an intuition of or "take-cognizance" of an object there is no activity in us beyond receiving what is given. Thus, when intuiting values, we receive their "call" for a proper response, including to be affectively moved by them. Reverence is the attitude of volitional, affective, and cognitive openness to receiving the world of values and responding to them properly. Reverence for value is the center of the moral life. I conclude by showing how Hildebrand, like Husserl, views phenomenology, with its attitude of reverence for what is given as true and good, as embodying an ethical way of life that grants moral freedom.

Keywords: Hildebrand, Husserl, Stein, realism, reverence, phenomenology

In his 1960 *What is Philosophy?*, Hildebrand makes a surprising claim: the fundamental moral attitude (*sittliche Grundhaltung*) of reverence (*Ehrfurcht*, literally "holy fear" or "holy awe") is essential to any phenomenological inquiry (Hildebrand, 2021, p. 174). For Hildebrand, when we have an intuition, a "taking-cognizance'" (*Kenntnisnahme*) in his terminology, of any object as having value, we intuit a "call" ("*Fordern*" in the German translation of *Ethics*, which could also be translated as "demand") to give a proper value response and/or be affected by the value (see Hildebrand, 2020, p. 40; Ger. tr., 1973, p. 43). Only with a reverent openness to accept these demands of values, in particular the value of truth, can one receive what is given.[1] This reverence for values is the "mother of all the moral life," for in it one is ready to conform both one's will and actions as well as one's heart to the demands of moral values (Hildebrand, 2017a, p. 3).

According to Hildebrand, the philosopher does not only pursue knowledge of certain, important objects (e.g. freedom, goodness). She also seeks an affective, contemplative union with the object, which Hildebrand calls a "spiritual 'wedding'" with the object (Hildebrand, 2021, p. 164). For Husserl values are apprehended in a non-objectifying, axiological, affective attitude (*Einstellung*) of "delighting abandon and surrender," but they become objects only when thematized as such in a cognitive theoretical attitude (HUA VI, §4, p. 8; En. tr., 1990, p. 10). By contrast, for Hildebrand, values are given as always already "objectified," to use Husserl's term, in the very stance of reverent openness to taking-cognizance of them, though a further reflective theoretical stance is necessary to make them objects of knowledge (Hildebrand, 1977, pp. 32–34; En. tr. 2016, pp. 20–24). Affective delight in values is not only a precondition for a proper phenomenological attitude but also part and parcel of it.

In this chapter, I will argue that Hildebrand's claim that reverence is essential to phenomenology and ethics is based on his radically realist conception of phenomenology. First, I show how Hildebrand echoes Husserl's "Principle of All Principles" in his *Ethics*, in that Hildebrand submits all theorization to intuition. Hildebrand, in part in reaction to Husserl's transcendental idealism, takes his phenomenology in a realist rather than idealist direction. Second, I explore Hildebrand's epistemology with regard to objects in general and values in particular in the second and third sections respectively. I then show how reverence functions simultaneously as what Husserl would call an "axiological" attitude and an "objectifying" attitude, though Hildebrand himself does not use these terms. Next, I show how reverence functions in and is entailed by Hildebrand's phenomenological method. Finally, in the conclusion, I will show that Hildebrand's priority of receptivity to activity in consciousness leads him to propose reverence as an ethical way of life, which phenomenology embodies. I connect this to Husserl's own conception of phenomenology as embodying an autonomous ethical life—a concern that includes much of what Hildebrand would call reverence despite Hildebrand's and Husserl's divergence on the issue of transcendental idealism.

A REALIST ECHO OF THE PRINCIPLE OF ALL PRINCIPLES

While Hildebrand and Husserl diverge on the question of realism, they agree on the primacy of intuition for any phenomenological inquiry. They agree that any theorization must strictly follow what is given in intuition. This primacy is famously articulated in Husserl's "Principle of All Principles" found in *Ideas I* §24:

> That each intuition affording [something] in an originary way is a legitimate source of knowledge, that, whatever presents itself to us in 'intuition' in an originary way (so to speak, in its actuality in person) is to be taken simply as what it affords itself as, but only within the limitations in which it affords itself there. Let us continue to recognize that each theory in turn could itself draw its truth only from originary givenness. (HUA III, §24, p. 52; En. tr., 1990, p. 43)

For both Hildebrand and Husserl "intuition" means that the object is self-given to the mind (Hildebrand, 2021, p. 200). Both understand phenomenology as a science of a priori essences, which they both refer to by the Greek term "*eidos*" (Hildebrand, 2021, p. 105; HUA III, p. 6; En. tr., 2014, p. 5). One finds in Hildebrand's "Prolegomena" to his *Ethics* a paragraph that echoes Husserl's "Principle of All Principles":

> It will be one of our chief aims to avoid any thesis that is not imposed on us by the data and, above all, to abstain from tacit presuppositions that are neither evident nor proved. We take reality seriously in the way in which it discloses itself; we greatly respect everything that is immediately given. (Hildebrand, 2020, p. 5)

However, the appearance of the word *reality* in this paragraph cannot be innocent given Hildebrand's disagreement with Husserl on the issue of realism. In *Ideas I*, Husserl holds that our normal conscious life takes place in the "natural attitude," where there is a most general positing of the world and the objects and values within it as being actual, there-on-hand (HUA III, §31, p. 63; En. tr., 2014, p. 53). Within this "general thesis of the world," objects of consciousness have the doxic modality of belief (HUA III, §103, p. 257; En. tr., 2014, p. 246). De Warren (2015) notes that, for Husserl, belief appears as being on the object, that is, as a doxic modality of the object, rather than as a subjective state of the mind. "With this genial insight, Husserl has in a single stroke de-subjectified belief from the merely subjective or psychological" (p. 246). An object at first appears to be a statue, but once it seems to move "the object itself 'appears to be questionable,' 'to be doubtful,' etc." (p. 245). The background of all doxic modalities is a general belief in and positing of the world as existing independent of the mind. Husserl proposes "bracketing" this general positing. One keeps the positing in place, but one does not go along with it. Instead of assuming the statue is real or an illusion, in this new phenomenological attitude I simply have the statue precisely as an appearance. This bracketing, Husserl claims, frees phenomenological research to be an eidetic science (HUA III, §33, p. 70; En. tr., 2014, p. 57). Majolino (2015) notes that Husserl distinguishes the individual essence of an object (sometimes called the "*So-Sein*" or "such being") from an *eidos* proper (pp. 42–43). Ruby-red is an *eidos*; this ruby-red of this cup is an individual essence. When one enters into the phenomenological attitude the focus becomes the *eidos* proper.

In *Ideas I*, Husserl claims that this bracketing involves suspending all values (*Werte*), as values are constituted as objects by the subject (HUA III, §56, p. 183; En. tr., 2014, p. 104). The way Husserl conceives of the givenness of values gives a certain value-neutrality to his conception of phenomenology, although his phenomenology both presupposes an affective givenness of values and investigates those values. In *Ideas II*, we find a distinction between the cognitive, theoretical, objectivizing attitude (*Einstellung*) that gives things as beings and an affective, axiological, non-objectivizing attitude that initially gives values (HUA IV, §4, p. 7; En. tr., 1990, p. 9). I take pleasure in the beautiful sky and admire it in "an attitude of purely delighting abandon or surrender" (HUA VI, §4, p. 8; En. tr., 1990, p. 10). I first must see the sky in a founding objectifying act of sensory intuition, and then I feel it to be beautiful in a non-objectifying feeling of value. When I come to reflectively regard the sky as a "beautiful sky" in the cognitive, theoretical attitude, I have now sedimented the value beautiful onto the object sky to constitute it as a beautiful sky, a higher-level value-object.[2] When I switch out of the axiological attitude into the theoretical attitude, I no longer live in an attitude of "delighting abandon or surrender." It should be noted that this particular passage of *Ideas II* shows the influence of Stein, Husserl's editorial assistant at the time, and it she may have written that passage. Nonetheless, it expresses Husserl's own position. Melle (2002) and Hart (1990) note that Husserl maintained this division between axiological and cognitive attitudes throughout his career. As Hart (1990) puts it, Husserl, "holds until the end of his life that although apperceptions of the heart are not reducible to apperceptions which govern the experience of objects, the evaluations are founded necessarily in the 'objectifying acts'" (p. 214). Thus, there is a certain neutrality to cognition for

Husserl. To avoid Husserl's conclusions, Hildebrand must defend a different conception of how consciousness works.

HILDEBRAND'S REALIST EPISTEMOLOGY

Hildebrand does so by means of three crucial features of his philosophy, which also undergird his ethical notion of reverence. The first is Hildebrand's acceptance of Husserl's own concept of categorial intuition found in his *Logische Untersuchungen* (*Logical Investigations*) VI §46 (HUA XIX, LI VI, §46, 673; En. tr., 2013, p. 282). Through categorial intuition, I perceive relations and states of affairs. These categorial intuitions allow what Husserl terms "material a-priori" truths to be grasped in experience. Hildebrand (2021, p. 69) uses the example of color to exemplify how these truths can be grasped. From an experience of an orange fruit, I can immediately grasp the essential truth "orange is between yellow and red." If it turns out I was hallucinating and no such fruit exists, the insight into the essence of the color orange remains valid.

Hildebrand (2021) understands these essences as "such-being" (*Sosein*) unities: the principle of unity in virtue of which various elements of a being are held together and given their sense (*Sinn*) (2021, pp. 101–116). The most important such-being unities are "highly intelligible essences" (e.g., number, justice, color, etc.), which yield synthetic a-priori truths and are the objects of philosophy (Hildebrand, 2021, p. 107).[3] The knowledge derived from these highly intelligible essences possesses three marks: intrinsic necessity, incomparable intelligibility, and absolute certainty (Hildebrand, 2021, p. 59). The necessity comes from the truth's basis in essence. The incomparable intelligibility and certainty stem from the fact that a highly intelligible essence is approached "from within" in intuition rather than observed "from without" as with observation in the empirical sciences. Following Husserl, Hildebrand (2021) understands these essences as imposing "laws" on any object that participates in that essence, e.g., a person must be a free and rational being (See HUA XVII, P, §46, A/B 170; En. Tr., 2001, p. 110).

The second feature is Hildebrand's crucial distinction between experience of existence, *Daseinserfahrung*, and experience of essence, *Soseinserfahrung* (Hildebrand, 2017b, p. 522). Though I lacked an experience of the existence of the orange fruit, I had a valid "such-being experience" of the color orange and its essence. Orange is between yellow and red is no less true even if no orange things exist (Hildebrand, 2021, p. 69). As Hildebrand puts it in his *Selbstdarstellung* (1975, translated as "Survey of My Philosophy" 2017b): "Both essence and the existence thereof are given to us through our perception" (p. 522). Like Husserl, Hildebrand allows for individual essences and *eidē* to be given in experience. Hildebrand holds that a lover can have a deep experience of the individual essence of his or her beloved (See Hildebrand, 2009). Yet Hildebrand sees no need for a reduction to make the *eidos* as *eidos* thematic.

The third, and most important, feature of Hildebrand's epistemology is his conception of knowledge as a purely receptive having (*Haben*) of the object known. By his own admission, Hildebrand here is indebted to the distinction between meaning-acts and presentations found in Reinach's essay "A Contribution to the Theory of Negative Judgement" (1981, p. xxi, see Hildebrand, 1983 for Hildebrand's acknowledgment of this influence). Reinach (1981) holds that meaning-acts are "blind" in that they do not have intuitive contact with the object. The state of affairs is not given in the assertion. For Reinach, this givenness is instead found in presentation (*Vorstellung*), which is the simple having (*Haben*) of an objective content (*Inhalt*) (1981, p. 23).[4] Salice (2019) notes that Reinach's conception of meaning marks a significant divergence from Husserl. In the *Logical Investigations* VI §37–39, truth is defined as *adaequatio rei intellectus*, which he understands as the correspondence of the meant with the given; i.e., truth occurs when a meaning-act is fulfilled in intuition (HUA XIX, LI VI, §37–39, pp. 646–656; En. tr., 2013, pp. 259–66). For Reinach and Hildebrand, by contrast, significations or meaning-acts cannot be fulfilled by intuitions. They are radically distinct forms of intentionality that cannot be assumed under a single genus. Thus, Hildebrand sees no need for "the meant" for an *adaequatio* to occur, only the simple having (*Haben*) of an object of knowledge's objective content (*Inhalt*) suffices.

As a result, for Hildebrand, knowledge is not so much the fulfillment of a signification by an intuition as it is, "a wholly incomparable contact: One being touches another and possesses the other in an immaterial manner" (2021, pp. 12). He makes two key distinctions to undergird this receptivity in his doctoral dissertation, published in 1916 as *Die Idee der sittlichen Handlung* (*The Idea of Moral Action*). First, one must distinguish two notions of "content-of-consciousness," namely (1) content as having a consciousness-of an object, for example, the beautiful landscape (*Inhalt* in *Die Idee* [objective content]), (2) content as being itself a conscious entity (*Gehalt* in *Die Idee* [experiential content]), for example, joy (Hildebrand, 1916, p. 134; 2021, pp. 12-13). Second, he distinguishes between an act of purely receptive taking-cognizance, where the subject is void (*leer*) and the objective content (*Inhalt*) of the relation is on the side of the apprehended object or state-of-affairs, and a spontaneous position-taking act (*Stellungnahme*), where there is experiential content (*Gehalt*) on the side of the subject (Hildebrand, 1916, p. 134).

For Hildebrand, all knowledge is based on taking-cognizance. In *Die Idee*, Hildebrand claims that taking cognizance is passive (*passiv*) (1916, p. 136–37), with no activity on the part of the subject whatsoever. In his *What Is Philosophy?*, Hildebrand admits there is an activity of spiritual going-with (*geistiges Mitgehen*) the object contained within taking-cognizance (Hildebrand, 2021, p. 19). This going with is an "intentional echoing of" or concerting (*konspirieren*) with the object that does not detract from the receptive character of the process of taking-cognizance (Hildebrand, 2021, p. 20; Ger. tr., 1973, p. 27). "[It] is only an active cooperation with the self-disclosure of the object" (Hildebrand, 2021, p. 20). It does not involve any positing of the object, nor is it necessarily a constitution of the object.

Hildebrand does not reject the notion of constitution for some objects. For example, the blue of distant mountains (which are green close up, and, like all colors, are dependent on light photons) or a melody (as opposed to sound waves) are aspects of intentional objects that are, by Hildebrand's admission, "constituted" for the subject (2021, p. 141). They presuppose a human mind. Nonetheless, this blue color or this melody still have "objective validity" (Hildebrand, 2021, p. 153). They are not mere semblances like a dream or the apparent bentness of an oar in water. They carry a valid "message" to humans proper to the object; mountains are *meant* to be seen as blue by most humans. The blue of mountains is no less real than the scattered photons, which exist, in part, to allow such colors to be (p. 163). They belong to reality, to the object. Moreover, Hildebrand is careful to note that highly intelligible essences are in no way constituted by the subject, in their such-being they have a full independence from the mind (Hildebrand, 2021, p. 140).

VALUES AND THEIR GIVENNESS

The radical receptivity of consciousness to the world grounds not only Hildebrand's epistemological realism but also his moral realism as well. Hildebrand terms the ability to motivate either a volitional or affective response to an object importance (*Bedeutsamkeit*, which could also be translated as "meaning" or "significance"), as opposed to mere indifference or neutrality (2020, p. 25; Gr. tr., 1973, p. 29). Things appear as having either a positive (good) or negative (evil) salience. Lacking this salience, a being is purely "neutral" and is unable to motivate an affective or volitional response. In all cases, an object's importance issues a word (*Wort*) that one can "respond" or answer to (*Antwort*) (Hildebrand, 2020, p. 40; Gr. tr., 1973, p. 43).

One of Hildebrand's most crucial innovations, which is not found in his phenomenological contemporaries such as Husserl (HUA IV) and Scheler

(1970), is his distinguishing three irreducible categories of importance: what is "merely subjectively satisfying," what is "the objective good for a person," and what "important-in-itself," which he typically terms "value" (Hildebrand, 2020, pp. 36–51). My pleasure in an undeserved, merely subjectively satisfying compliment is the *principium* of the compliment's character as important, and its importance is the *principiatum* (Hildebrand, 2020, p. 40). A healthy meal derives its importance from being in my objective true interest, it is an objective good for me. A value stands as important in itself without any relation to one's own person (*ohne jeglichen Bezug auf die eigene Person*) (Hildebrand, 1916, p. 174, translation mine). This importance is apprehended as independent of my knowledge of it or of my stance toward it. Values, when given to us, issue a call (*Fordern*) or a word (*Wort*) to the subject to give a proper value response (Hildebrand, 2020, p. 40, Gr. tr., 1973, p. 43). This response, even if not morally obligatory, "ought" or is due (*Sollen*) to be given to the value. To give an example of a value apprehension and response, when I apprehend the intrinsic importance of an act of forgiveness, the intrinsic importance of this act (i.e., its value) is given as the *principium* and my response of joy toward it is the *principiatum* (Hildebrand, 2020, p. 40).

It is crucial to note how "importance," in the sense that Hildebrand uses the term, is united to its bearer. Crosby, a student of Hildebrand, finds that all three forms of importance have objectivity in the sense of being a "distinct moment on the object" (1977, p. 247). Following Ross (2003), Crosby considers importance to be a "consequential" property of an object based on but not reducible to various "constitutive" properties of the object (1977, p. 314). Various causal and constitutive properties of coffee enable it to quench my craving, yet those properties are not the importance of the object (Crosby, 1977). Even when my desire enters into the constitution of this cup of coffee as subjectively satisfying, this "importance, once constituted, however subjective, does not exhaust itself in engendering interest" (Crosby, 1977, p. 256). I rather take interest in the coffee *in virtue of* it being subjectively satisfying for me. The importance inheres neither in the person, nor in the relation to the person, but only as standing before the person as being on the object.

Unlike the other two kinds of importance, values are fully intrinsic to the being of the object. As Crosby (1977) puts it, values "grow out of" the being, for example, human dignity out of our nature as free persons (p. 313). In an appendix to Crosby's article, Seifert (1977), another student of Hildebrand, notes that speaking of "values" is somewhat misleading, as if they were independent of their objects. It is better to speak of "the being insofar as it is precious in itself" (p. 334).

As all knowledge ultimately rests on taking-cognizance, knowledge of values must be traced back to an intuitive taking-cognizance of values (*Wertnahme*). In his habilitation *Sittlichkeit und ethische Werterkenntnis*

(1922, *Morality and the Ethical Knowledge of Values*), Hildebrand distinguishes two types of intuitive grasping of values (*intuitives Werterfassen*): the cognitive seeing of values (*Wertsehen*) and the feeling of values (*Wertfühlen*) (1922, pp. 469–71). Even in his 1965 major work on affectivity, *The Heart*, Hildebrand (2007, p. 37) insists value-apprehension is first a cognitive act rather than affective act, in contrast to nearly all of his phenomenological contemporaries. "It is a cognitive act in which we grasp the value". I can cognitively grasp the value of a virtue without being able to feel the value (Hildebrand, 1922, p. 469). By his later works, the language of *Wertfühlen* mostly drops out and is replaced by his notion of being-affected (*Affiziertwerden*) (Hildebrand, 2020, p. 219; Gr. tr., 1973, p. 243). In being-affected by a value, there is an experiential affective content (*Gehalt*) in me that is recognized as coming from the object to me (centripetal intentionality) rather than from me to the object (centrifugal intentionality) (Hildebrand, 2020, p. 219). Being-affected presupposes taking-cognizance of values (Hildebrand, 2020, p. 218).

Mulligan (2009) has suggested that, in his later works, Hildebrand abandoned his earlier position in *Sittlichkeit* that values can be given in feelings (*Wertfühlen*) for a now solely cognitivist view of value apprehension. However, I do not think that Hildebrand neglects the role of feelings in value apprehension but, rather, that he recognizes a cognitive component *included* within any act of affective value apprehension. To feel values (*Wertfühlen*) involves taking-cognizance of them. Feeling values contains an additional affective experiential content (*Gehalt*) that has a receptive and centripetal intentionality, rather than a responsive and centrifugal intentionality, which wraps around this taking-cognizance of a value. The affective *Gehalt* (experiential content) of *Wertfühlen* has a centripetal intentionality that marks it as a being-affected (*Affiziertwerden*) by values, which is why Hildebrand switches to the latter term.

If I only see a value, I can have knowledge-that (*Wissen oder Erkennen*) this object is intrinsically important, but it leaves me cold, and the value does not speak to me. I do not have a lively experience (*erleben*) of the value (Hildebrand 1922, pp. 469–76). By contrast, when I feel the value, I both experience it (*erleben*) and I can know it by acquaintance (*Kennen*). Many values call for us to be affected by them, and not just to cognitively grasp them or respond to them with either affective or volitional responses.

Finally, a third, indirect way values are given to us is through what Hildebrand calls basic attitudes (*Grundhaltungen*) and basic stances (*Grundstellungen*) (Hildebrand,1922, p. 520). Echoing Plato's *Republic* Book IV (1992, 437d–438d.), an interest in a particular good is constituted by a most general interest, for the particular good is contained in the more general *eidos*. A glutton's desire for a cake testifies to a basic concupiscent stance (*Grundstellung*) in favor of the subjectively satisfying. Hildebrand finds three basic stances: pride (*Hochmut*), concupiscence (*Begehrlichkeit*), and reverence (*Ehrfurcht*) (1922, p. 520). These stances are *Stellungnahmen*, basic position-takings that are responses directed toward the world.

With concupiscence I want to *have* subjectively satisfying goods, whereas with pride I want to *be* in and occupy an illegitimate superior, but subjectively satisfying, position (Hildebrand, 2020, p. 465). If the morally evil stances dominate the person, one is blind to values. Any attempt to awaken this person to values is met with either indifference or hostility to values (Hildebrand, 1922, pp. 514–20). This raises the questions: how can a response be prior to receiving what is responded to and how can it blind one to what it is responding to? Hildebrand's answer is that in this basic stance toward the world there is an indirect givenness of the world of values rather than an intentional relation to any particular value. Basic stances have an indirect givenness of the location (*Ort*) of values (Hildebrand, 1922, p. 522). In pride or concupiscence, the person is directed toward the world as good but only under the aspect of subjectively satisfying. The person is oriented in the direction of values but is closed to whatever may come from that direction.

THE NATURE OF REVERENCE

Hildebrand describes the basic attitude of reverence in an eponymous essay (Hildebrand, 2017a), which was first published in his *Sittliche Grundhaltungen* (1933) and then translated by his future wife Alice Jourdain as *Fundamental Moral Attitudes* (1950).[5] For Hildebrand, reverence is first and foremost a response, not to a particular value but to the world of values as such. Its active character is both affective and volitional in nature, and it is connected to cognition. I would argue that reverence is the willingness to receive values and to freely conform to their demands. It is also a readiness of one's heart to give proper affective responses or to be affected by them, rather than be hard heartedly unmoved. It involves what Husserl would call an axiological attitude of "delighting abandon and surrender" (HUA VI, §4, p. 8; En. tr., 1990, p. 10). Reverence stands as "the mother of all the moral life" (Hildebrand, 2017a, p. 3). Hildebrand distinguishes between qualitative moral values proper, such justice and honesty, and morally relevant values, such as human dignity or the beauty of art, that take on moral import in certain situations (2020, p. 137). Not every moral act is a response to a morally relevant value, for example, when I return someone a dollar he loaned me, that dollar has not become a value (Hildebrand, 1980, pp. 51–53). But even in this moral act of fulfilling a trivial promise, I respond to the general value of honesty itself. Thus, every moral act is a response to a moral value. This entails that reverent openness to values is the foundation of every moral act (Hildebrand, 1922, p. 580–83).

Hildebrand connects *Ehrfurcht* with Kant's respect (*Achtung*) by seeing it as a kind of ethically charged respect not only for the autonomy of persons, but of all beings insofar as they have value. In contrast to fantasy, a real being is "autonomous" in the sense that it is "independent of the person considering it, it is withdrawn from his arbitrary will" (Hildebrand, 2017a, pp. 5–6). Thus, all beings possess, at a minimum, the basic value of existence, which is violated in any falsehood. Second, there is the "autonomy" of the essences of values that have their own "laws" that they impose on us. Justice, in its essence, demands that I be just. The reverent person keeps a "reverent distance from the world" that allows objects to "unfold" and give themselves and the "word" of their value in taking-cognizance (Hildebrand, 2017a, p. 6). Thus, reverence involves a willingness to abandon oneself to values and to the call to give a proper value response. As Hildebrand phrases it, again implicitly referring to Kant, one is ready "to be formed by their law" (2017a, p. 3):

> Because of this autonomy, being is never a mere means for the reverent man and his accidental egoistic aims. It is never merely something he can use but he takes it seriously in itself; he leaves it the necessary space for its proper unfolding. Confronted with being, the reverent man remains silent in order to give it an opportunity to speak. (Hildebrand, 2017a, p. 6)

We can now compare Hildebrand to Husserl. Schuhmann notes that Husserl made several criticisms of Hildebrand in his notes to Hildebrand's dissertation (1992) notes. First, Husserl held that Hildebrand's claim that the subject in taking-cognizance is empty of ideas, *doxa*, and modality of executions is *nicht korrekt*. Second, Husserl notes that for him almost all intentional acts have a centrifugal intentionality, only affections have a centripetal intentionality. Third, in *Die Idee*, Hildebrand makes a distinction between *Erkennen* (recognizing) and taking-cognizance (1916, pp. 144–55). *Erkennen* can only apply to states of affairs are actually obtaining (*Bestand*); obtaining is the ontological correlate of *Erkennen* for Hildebrand. So one can take cognizance of the imagined arrival of a friend, but one cannot have an *Erkennen* this imagined state-of-affairs. While Hildebrand abandoned this distinction between *Erkennen* and taking-cognizance in *What Is Philosophy?* (2021), it anticipates his later concept of existence as being given in *Daseinserfahrung*. Husserl notes that he does not see a reason why *Erkennen* is limited to only really obtaining states of affairs. Implicitly, this indicates that Husserl would have been suspicious of Hildebrand's later notion of *Daseinserfahrung*. Fourth, in *Ideas I*, Husserl is careful to note that the positing of the general thesis is *not* a particular position-taking act (*Stellungnahme*) but is more basic and fundamental than any particular *Stellungnahme*.

Finally, Hildebrand holds that transcendental idealism, in general, considers all objects of the mind to be the creation (*Schaffen*) of the mind's constitution of them (Hildebrand, 2021, p. 21; Ger. tr., 1976, p. 28). Husserl would reject this "subjective idealist" characterization of his position (HUA III, §55, p. 134; En. Tr., 2014, p. 102). Instead, the process of constitution is often passive, where the object is constituted by the subject according to its own essence. For example, in his *Analysen zur passiven Synthesis*, Husserl claims that prior to all active and passive constitution, soon-to-be-objects entice us to notice them by means of their affective allure (*Reiz*) (HUA XI, 1966, §38, p. 148; En. tr., 2001, p. 179). Hart (1992, p. 68–72) argues that once passive synthesis is taken into account, Hildebrand's taking-cognizance is revealed to be a passive synthetic constitution. Hart notes that in *Die Idee,* Hildebrand (1916, p. 136) misses the achievement character latent in taking cognizance because he assumes that since taking-cognizance is not a *Stellungnahme* it has no activity present in it at all (Hart, 1992, p. 71). In a private email correspondence with me, Hart confirmed that he regards Husserl's constitution as "manifestation and display of being, not creation of it," *pace* Hildebrand's interpretation of Husserl (Hart, Personal Communication, February 23, 2021).

With Hildebrand's introduction of the spiritual going-with and Husserl's progressive accentuation of the receptive character of constitution, the two philosophers' positions end up far closer to each other than either man realized in his lifetime. Yet Husserl's constitution and Hildebrand's going-with are still, to my knowledge, distinct. For the spiritual going-with, need not represent an active or passive sense-giving (*Sinngebung*) activity on the part of the subject, unless the object is given as constituted (e.g., the blue of distant mountains). Further, the going-with involves not just the absence of any position-taking, but the absence of positing of any sort. Things are simply *given* in both their such-being content and their existence. Husserl sees the world as colored by belief, this statue is given to me as doubtful because it looked like it moved. For Hildebrand, it is rather that I experience a *Soseinserfahrung* of a statue, but once it moves, I doubt I had a *Daseinserfahrung* of a statue. Thus, Husserl's notion of 'positing and a general thesis is challenged by the notions of *Soseinserfahrung* and *Daseinserfahrung*. For this reason, Hildebrand holds there is no need to bracket things, for there is no positing to be put out of operation in a special transcendental attitude.

In her *Beiträge zur philosophischen Begründung der Psychologie und der Geisteswissenschaften* (1922, translated as *Philosophy of Psychology and the Humanities*, 2016), Stein herself offers a position that forms an illustrative comparison and contrast with Hildebrand's position. Implicitly referring to Hildebrand's cognitivist claim in *Die Idee* that value-apprehension rests on taking-cognizance of values (See Hildebrand, 1916, p. 137), Stein asks rhetorically, "What gives us the right to designate the grasping of the value itself as a feeling? Does not whatever have to do with feelings lie within the response-reaction?" (1922, p. 143; En. tr., 2016, p. 159). Stein notes it is possible to "catch a glimpse" of the value while being left affectively "cold," without "being inwardly filled up with it." (1922, p. 145; En. tr., 2016, p. 161). In this case:

> The missing contents (*Gehalte*) are represented by empty places, which are marked off as place holders for the specific contents (*Gehalte*), bear within themselves an intention toward those contents. . . . Analogously to the empty presentation of a thing, this value-intention isn't presented as a pure X, but rather with all of its qualities (except that those qualities aren't in your face intuitively but are presented precisely emptily). (Stein, 1922, p. 146; En. tr., 2016, p. 163)

In this case a value-apprehension of the beauty without the *Gehalt* of joy in the beauty gives only an empty presentation of the beauty (1922, p. 144, En. tr., 2016, p. 160). For Stein, the *Gehalt* is "the material on the basis of which values come to givenness for us" (1922, p. 144, En. tr., 2016, p. 160). The value itself demands a "value-grasping and affective attitude" (*Gemütstellungnahme*) in order to be intuitively grasped (Stein, 1922, p. 146; En. tr., 2016, p. 159). Thus, she states:

> Beauty . . . insists that I inwardly open myself up to it. . . . As I withhold the response beauty requires, beauty doesn't entirely divulge itself to me. The intention inhering in the mere information remains unfulfilled . . . the completely fulfilled value perception (*Wertnehmen*) is always a feel[ing] in which the value-intention and the response reaction are united. (1922, p. 143; En. tr., 2016, p. 159)

For Stein, feeling, apprehension of value, and cognition of the bearer of the value are so united that neither the bearer nor the value are given separately from each other. Yet for Stein the thematicity of the affective state (e.g., gladness) is in tension with the thematicity of the value, the beauty of the landscape. If I focus on and surrender myself to the value the gladness fades from view, but if I focus on the gladness the value fades. One's orientation toward the world determines what one will grasp in the world. Stein writes "when oriented theoretically, we see mere things. When oriented axiologically, we see values" (1922, p. 144; En. tr., 2016, p. 160).

Stein here tries to mediate a path between Husserl and the direct realism of Hildebrand and Reinach (See Lebech 2010; Vendrell Ferran 2017).[6] Whereas Husserl places cognition of things before the apprehension of values, for Stein, like Hildebrand, values are given with their bearer in a unified experience of value feeling. Similar to Hildebrand, to fully grasp the value, the proper feelings and attitude must be present, there must be an openness to what the value has to disclose. Like Hildebrand, Stein allows for a kind of value-apprehension when the proper feelings are not present. However, unlike Hildebrand, she would hesitate to call this cold value-apprehension an intuition. Stein retains Husserl's language of values as constituted, for which feelings are ultimately necessary, and the language of intention and fulfillment, all of which Hildebrand eschews. While Stein and Hildebrand are fundamentally speaking of the same experience, Hildebrand takes a more direct realist approach, the value can be directly intuited in an object-like manner.

Hildebrand makes a key distinction in his *Ästhetik (1977). I* between frontal and lateral consciousness-of (*frontales Berwußtsein-von und laterales Vollzugbewußtsein*), which allows Hildebrand to reject Husserl's division between cognitive objectifying attitudes and affective, non-objectifying attitudes (1977, pp. 32–34; En. tr. 2016, pp. 20–24). Frontal consciousness is the conscious-of some object (e.g., in intuition). However, one's own affective states (e.g., joy) are typically given in a lateral consciousness; where they are known "from within." When one falls in love, "he has a 'consciousness of' of this person, but he also learns thereby what being in love means" (Hildebrand, 1977, p. 32; En. tr., 2016, p. 21). For Hildebrand, lateral consciousness can be loosely called knowledge, but the knowledge is never thematic. When one is experiencing joy, one has not yet made joy the object of knowledge. To do this requires a reflective act where the joy becomes the object of a taking-cognizance, that is, of frontal consciousness-of. "Naturally it [the joy] ceases at that very moment to be consciously lived" (Hildebrand, 1977, p. 33; En. tr., 2016, p. 21).

Thus, whereas for Husserl the value is not given in an objectifying manner, for Hildebrand, the value is given in what Husserl would call an objectifying manner in taking-cognizance. For Hildebrand, it is not the *value* but only the *response* and *feeling/being-affected* that is not given an objectifying manner but, rather, in a lateral manner. Thus, for Hildebrand, having the very *objectivity* of the value is in no way inconsistent with an attitude "delighting abandon and surrender" (HUA VI, §4, p. 8; En. tr., 1990). Thus, in essence, Hildebrand, unifies what Husserl would have called a theoretical, cognitive, objectifying attitude with an affective, axiological attitude. As a result, Hildebrand's phenomenological cognitive attitude is in itself an axiological and an objectifying attitude in Husserl's sense. The value is given immediately in cognition of the object. Cognition directly gives values; it is not value neutral.

THE ROLE OF REVERENCE

What roles, then, does reverence play in Hildebrand's phenomenological method? For Hildebrand, phenomenology must be distinguished from the naïve, pre-philosophical attitudes that precede it. For Hildebrand, the theoretical attitude presupposes a prior "naïve" taking-cognizance (2021, p. 46). Although the subject is "void" and receptive in taking-cognizance, precisely what the subject is open to receiving is determined by the kind of attitude the subject has. For instance, suppose I take-cognizance of the window as a practical means of escape from prison. Here the object (the window) and knowledge (knowledge about the window) is only secondarily thematic, and a practical theme (escaping the room) is the main theme. This "pragmatic attitude" can lead to certain discoveries, but it always leads to a "one-sided limitation of our knowledge" (Hildebrand, 2021, p. 39). In some situations, where a great value is at stake (e.g., taking cognizance of a child about to fall into a well), the object is extremely thematic, and there is no pragmatic deformation of knowledge, but that knowledge is only thematic to the extent necessary to achieve the goal (Hildebrand, 2021, p. 41).

In theoretical taking-cognizance, knowledge is the explicit theme, though the object is often less thematic (e.g., a philologist asks if this trivial phrase in *Beowulf* is authentic) (Hildebrand, 2021, p. 40). But in specifically philosophical taking cognizance, both the object and the knowledge of the object are of great importance and thematic (Hildebrand, 2021, p. 39). For Hildebrand, the theoretical attitude is a primarily active rather than receptive stance. "One does not allow the object itself to speak. Instead one tries to acquire . . . knowledge of it by observations, reflections, inferences" (Hildebrand, 2021, p. 47). For example, from a single or multitude of experiences of free action, I posit that "freedom in general presupposes knowledge". Such theorizations can be either "organic" or "inorganic" (Hildebrand, 2021, p. 48). Organic theorization grows out of naïve contact with the objects theorized about. Such theorizations are not necessarily correct (e.g., the Little Drummer Boy's conclusion that "all people are bad" from a single traumatic experience). Yet they have an "organic link" to those experiences, which inorganic theorizations lack. For example, an undergraduate, who in his naïve living respects moral demands, may inorganically conclude that all moral values are the result of *ressentiment* from a shallow reading of philosophy. Philosophy requires organic theorization.

Reverence ensures philosophy is eminently "critical," in that these theorizations are to be continually tested by reference back to lived contact with the object in taking-cognizance. First, the object is considered "in the light of the absolute" (Hildebrand, 2021, p. 179). The such-being of the object, with its essence and its laws, determines the main theme of the inquiry according to its highly intelligible essence. The philosopher must place him or herself at a certain reverent "distance" from the object (Hildebrand 2021, p. 183). By this Hildebrand means the presuppositions and limitations of view imposed by a pragmatic interest, which might interfere with the inquiry, are suspended. This reverent distance is, therefore, an aid to lived contact with the object and its highly intelligible essence.

The main reason why reverence is essential to phenomenology has to do with a third theme over and above the object theme and the knowledge theme: the "contemplative theme" (Hildebrand, 2021, p. 165). For Hildebrand, taking-cognizance can "go" in two directions, one toward knowledge of the object, and the other toward "the direction of intimate real contact of having the object in a most immediate and full possession. Our mind touches the object and stands before it 'face to face'" (2021, p. 164). Seeing one's beloved, one can gain knowledge of the beloved, his or her traits or character. Yet one can also enjoy union with the beloved precisely through a mutual interpenetration of looks of love (*Ineinanderblick*) (See Hildebrand, 2009). Though Hildebrand does not use the language of empathy here, it is clear that this loving contemplation involves it. In analogous manner, a highly intelligible essence is intuitively before one's mind in a continual taking-cognizance of that essence (e.g., contemplating the nature of goodness). For Hildebrand, this contemplation involves not just perception but also being delighted by the contemplated object. This contemplation is the aim of the "*eros*" and wonder at the heart of all philosophy (Hildebrand, 2021, p. 219).

Yet contemplating a philosophical object, one is no longer concerned with the question "how is it?" (Hildebrand, 2021, p. 164). Here there is a parallel with Husserl's and Stein's position. Insofar as I am contemplating the object, I am not concerned with knowledge but with "delighting abandon and surrender" (HUA VI, §4, p. 8; En. tr., 1990, p. 10). Unlike Husserl, this contemplative attitude of "delighting abandon and surrender" in no way lessens the objectivity of the value, though it is not currently thematized as an object of knowledge. This delighting surrender is part and parcel of the phenomenological attitude itself. The phenomenologist "dwells in" the object, a union that Hildebrand does not shy from calling a "spiritual 'wedding'" with the object (Hildebrand, 2021, p. 164).

Had Husserl been alive to read Hildebrand's *What Is Philosophy?* in 1960, one could imagine him wondering how wedding bells have entered into phenomenology as a rigorous science. Hildebrand could respond that they have entered in virtue of the Principle of All Principles. For in intuition we grasp values as the preciousness of their objects. To experience a value includes receiving the call to give a proper value response and also to be moved by it in the proper manner. In philosophy, the value in question is primarily truth. Yet the values and beauty of the particular objects of philosophy (e.g., goodness, justice, freedom, etc.) are also to be responded to appropriately and contemplated. One finds, then, that reverence for the truth is in fact one with ethical respect for the autonomy of beings in their existence and essence. For Hildebrand, "philosophy does not pretend to assume a position superior to the being it intends to know. Rather it considers this being as a 'partner' in which it wants to participate" (Hildebrand, 2021, p. 176). Yet one also gives one's surrender (*Hingabe*) to the object's word. Thus, for the philosopher the objects of inquiry:

> Always mean something more to him than mere objects of knowledge. Hence, the unique reverence that is found in philosophical inquiry, and also the solemn character of philosophical knowledge (Hildebrand, 2021, p. 174).

CONCLUSION: REVERENCE AS A WAY OF LIFE

I wish to close by noting that despite their marked differences from each other, Husserl's and Hildebrand's philosophies ended up much closer than either realized, particularly with regard to the ethical import of phenomenology. In Husserl's *Vienna Lecture* and *The Crisis*, phenomenology is presented as the means for ethical renewal of individual human lives and the whole of human culture (See HUA VI; En., Tr. Husserl, 1970). One can find in these ethical writings of Husserl a marked attitude of what Hildebrand calls reverence. Husserl advanced the notion of an "ethical *epochē*" where one brackets one's previous life and goals and subject's them to a universal critique (See HUA XVII; HUA XXXVII, p. 198; see also Hart, 1990; Melle, 2002, 2007). One takes a distance from the values and goals posited by one's society, critically investigating they are truly founded and good. One's life and the community's life are now to be based on rational insight into ethical absolute values. The result is an autonomous and authentic ethical life. While Husserl never abandoned the distinction between the theoretical, practical, and axiological attitudes, he came to see that even the theoretical attitude itself takes place in the horizon of a practical and an axiological attitude oriented to truth and the fully rational life. For Husserl and Hildebrand, in different ways, what Husserl considers to be the axiological attitude and theoretical attitudes can be unified as two "directions" of the same phenomenological attitude.

For Hildebrand the way of life phenomenology embodies, models, and proposes is the reverent life. As I have spelled out in another work (Montes, 2019), Hildebrand in a manner parallel to but also very different from Levinas implicitly finds ethics to be first philosophy (Levinas, 1969, 1981). A reverence for what is other than the mind, which is necessarily void in taking-cognizance, is necessary for phenomenology to get off the ground. The phenomenologist must love the truth and be open to being delighted by it and responding to it in the proper manner for truth to disclose itself to her. It is precisely this submission to the truth that grants freedom from any pragmatic deformation of knowledge and from proneness to error.

This one and the same ethical attitude of reverence is also, Hildebrand notes, at the basis of love (See Hildebrand, 2009; 2017a, p. 7). One must be reverently open to the value of the beloved in his or her particular preciousness and essence. While Hildebrand does not discuss empathy (*Einfühlung*) at length as does Husserl (See HUA IV) and Stein (See Stein, 1917, En. Tr., 1989), it is clear that for him reverence is the necessary precondition for any loving, deep empathy with another person. Thus, a reverent, loving empathy along with a reverent openness to the truth about the value of the world stands at the basis of the moral life. Empathy, philosophy, and love have the same root in reverence.

Yet this life of reverence is not limited to philosophy. It is the ethical call that all values issue to us to be open to them, to be moved by them, and to respond to them. Philosophy indeed can aid those who are not philosophers by dispelling the negative influences of bad philosophy (see the case of the undergraduate above) and by confirming our deepest intuitions of the value of the world (Hildebrand, 2021, pp. 213-19). Philosophy embodies a life lived in reverent accord with the truth. Hildebrand would agree with Husserl that such an attitude of distance and seeking grounds of one's life projects, the free position-takings, to be based on evident insights grants *autonomy*. For both, there is a freedom, an autonomy, that can only be had by submitting one's life to the demands of values as grasped in insights based on their essences. Only this reverence for and submission to the truth can set us free for freedom (Galatians 5:1).[7]

NOTES

1. Like Husserl, Hildebrand considers phenomenology to simply be the method of philosophy made explicit. I will thus use the terms philosophy and phenomenology, as Hildebrand does, more or less interchangeably in this paper (Hildebrand, 2021, p. 205).

2. Dale Hobbs (2017) notes that Husserl eventually moved away from conceiving of values as given in an object-like manner and moved toward considering values to be features on the horizon of experience given in affectivity. This would only serve to further the divergence between Husserl and Hildebrand, for whom values are thoroughly objective.

3. For Hildebrand, phenomenology is concerned with a-priori truths, but only those pertaining to objects that have great importance and value (Hildebrand, 2021, p. 171). "What is two plus two?" is not an object of philosophical inquiry, but "what is number?" is (Hildebrand, 2021, p. 129).

4. I am indebted to Sergio Sanchez-Migallón's Spanish translation of *Die Idee* for the translation of *Gehalt* as "experiential content" and *Inhalt* as "objective content" (See Hildebrand, 2014).

5. The concept of *Ehrfurcht* is one that Hildebrand takes from Scheler "On the Rehabilitation of Virtue" (Scheler 1913; En. Tr. 2004).

6. Lebech (2010) places Stein closer to the direct realists; whereas Vendrell Ferran (2017) places her closer to Husserl.

7. Special thanks to Professors Dermot Moran, Jeffrey Bloechl, Elisa Magri, and John Crosby for comments on other versions of this paper. Special thanks also to Professor James Hart and my colleagues Michaela Reißlandt (née Sobrak-Seaton) and her spouse Benny Reißlandt and Andrew Barrette for discussion with me on topics covered in this chapter. Finally, thanks to Susi Ferrarello for helpful comments on a previous draft of this chapter.

REFERENCES

Crosby, J. (1977). The Idea of Value and the Reform of the Traditional Metaphysics of "Bonum." *Aletheia: An International Journal of Philosophy*, 1, 231–336.

De Warren, N. (2015). Concepts without Pedigree: The Noema and Neutrality Modification. In A. Staiti (Ed.), *Commentary on Husserl's Ideas I* (pp. 225–56). De Gruyter.

Hart, J. G. (1990). Axiology as the Form of Purity of Heart: A Reading Husserliana XXVIII. *Philosophy Today 34*(3), 206–21.

———. (1992). *The Person and the Common Life: Studies in a Husserlian Social Ethics*. Kluwer Academic Publishers.

Hildebrand, D. (1916). Die Idee der sittlichen Handlung. *Jahrbuch für Philosophie und phänomenologische Forschung*, *3*, 126–252. https://ophen.org/pub-101096. Spanish Translation Consulted: (2014). *La idea de la acción moral* (S. Sanchez-Migallon, Trans.; 1st edition). Ediciones Encuentro.

———. (1922). Sittlichkeit und ethische Werterkenntnis. *Jahrbuch für Philosophie und phänomenologische Forschung*, *5*, 462–602. Consulted Unpublished Draft English Translation by Robin Rollinger.

———. (1933). *Sittliche Grundhaltungen*. Matthias-Grünewald. English Translations Consulted: (1950) Fundamental Moral Attitudes. Longmans, Green, and Co.; (2017) *The Art of Living*. Hildebrand Press.

———. (1977). *Ästhetik I*. W. Kohlhammer. English Translation Consulted: *Aesthetics: Volume I*. (J. Crosby, Ed.; B. McNeil, Trans.) Hildebrand Press.
———. (1980). *Moralia: Nachgelassenes Werk*. Josef Habbel.
———. (1983). Reinach as a Philosophical Personality. (J. F. Crosby, Trans.). *Aletheia. An International Journal of Philosophy*, *3*, xv–xxvi.
———. (2021) What is Philosophy? (F. Wenisch, Trans.) Hildebrand Press. Other English Version Consulted: (1991). *What is Philosophy?* Routledge. German Translation Consulted: (1976). *Was ist Philosophie* (J. Seifert, Ed., K. Mertens & F. Wenisch, Trans.). W.Kohlhammer.
———. (2007). *The Heart: An Analysis of Human and Divine Affectation*. St. Augustine's Press.
———. (2009). *The Nature of Love*. St. Augustine's Press.
———. (2014). *My Battle Against Hitler: Faith, Truth, and Defiance in the Shadow of the Third Reich by Dietrich von Hildebrand* (J. F. Crosby & J. H. Crosby, Trans.). Image.
———. (2017a). Reverence. In *The Art of Living* (pp. 1–8). Hildebrand Press.
———. (2017b). Survey of my Philosophy. (J. F. Crosby, Trans.). *American Catholic Philosophical Quarterly*, *91*(4), 517–559.
———. (2020). *Ethics* (J. F. Crosby, Ed.). Hildebrand Press. German Translation Consulted: (1973). *Ethik*. W.Kohlhammer.
Hobbs, D. (2017). *Investigations of Worth: Towards a Phenomenology of Values* [Doctoral Dissertation, Marquette University]. ProQuest Dissertations Publishing.
Husserl, E. (1950). HUA III. *Ideen zu einer reinen Phänomenologie und phänomenologischen Philosophie I: Allgemeine Einführung in die reine Phänomenologie*. (K. Schuhmann, Ed.; 2nd ed.). Nijhoff. https://ophen.org/pub-137694. English Translation Consulted: (2014). *Ideas for a Pure Phenomenology and Phenomenological Philosophy: First Book: General Introduction to Pure Phenomenology* (D. O. Dahlstrom, Trans.). Hackett Publishing Company, Inc.
———. (1951). HUA VI. *Die Krisis der europäischen Wissenschaften und die transzendentale Phänomenologie*. (Biemel W., Ed.). Nijhoff.
———. (1952). HUA IV. *Ideen zu einer reinen Phänomenologie und phänomenologischen Philosophie II: Phänomenologische Untersuchungen zur Konstitution* (M. Biemel, Ed.). Kluwer. https://ophen.org/pub-108556. English Translation Consulted: (1990). *Ideas Pertaining to a Pure Phenomenology and to a Phenomenological Philosophy: Second Book Studies in the Phenomenology of Constitution* (R. Rojcewicz & A. Schuwer, Trans.). Springer.
———. (1966). HUA XI. *Analysen zur passiven Synthesis: Aus Vorlesungs- und Forschungsmanuskripten*. (M. Fletcher, Ed.) Nijhoff. https://ophen.org/pub-108669._English Translation Consulted: (2001). *Analyses Concerning Passive and Active Synthesis: Lectures on Transcendental Logic* (A. J. Steinbock, Trans.). Springer.
———. (1984). HUA XIX. *Logische Untersuchungen. Zweiter Band—II. Teil: Untersuchungen zur Phänomenologie und Theorie der Erkenntnis.* (U. Panzer, Ed.). Nijhoff. https://ophen.org/pub-108837. English Translation Consulted: (2013). *Logical Investigations: Volume 2*. (D. Moran, Ed.; 1 edition). Routledge.

———. (1988). HUA XXVII. *Vorlesungen über Ethik und Wertlehre: (1908–1914)* (U. Melle, Ed.). Kluwer. https://ophen.org/pub-109118

———. (2004). HUA XXXVII. *Einleitung in die Ethik: Vorlesungen Sommersemester 1920/1924* (H. Peucker, Ed.; Dordrecht). Kluwer. https://ophen.org/pub-109301.

Lebech, M. (2010)Edith Stein's Phenomenological Value Theory. *Yearbook of the Irish Philosophical Studies*, 139–50).

Levinas, E. (1969). *Totality and Infinity: An Essay on Exteriority* (A. Lingis, Trans.; 2nd ed.). Duquesne University Press.

———. (1981). *Otherwise than Being, or, Beyond Essence*. (A. Lingis, Trans.). Kluwer.

Majolino, C. (2015). Individuum and the Region of Being: On the Unifying Principle of Husserl's "Headless" Ontology. In A. Staiti (Ed.), *Commentary on Husserl's Ideas I* (pp. 33–50). De Gruyter.

Melle, U. (2002). Edmund Husserl: From Reason to Love. In J. J. Drummond & L. Embree (Eds.), *Phenomenological Approaches to Moral Philosophy* (pp. 229–48). Kluwer Academic Publishers.

———. (2007). Husserl's Personalist Ethics. *Husserl Studies 23*(1), 1–15.

Montes, A. (2019). Toward the Name of the Other: A Hildebrandian Approach to Levinasian Alterity. *Quaestiones Disputatae 10*(1), 82–109.

Mulligan, K. (2009). On Being Struck by Values-Exclamations, Motivations, and Vocations. In B. Merker (Ed.), *Leben mit Gefühlen: Emotionen, Werte und ihre Kritik* (pp. 141–61). Mentis.

Plato. (1992). *Republic* (C.D.C. Reeve, Ed.; G. M. A. Grube and C.D.C. Reeve, Trans.; 2nd ed.). Hackett Publishing Company, Inc.

Reinach, A. (1981). A Contribution Toward the Theory of Negative Judgement (D. Farrari, Trans.). *Aletheia. An International Journal of Philosophy 2*, 9–64.

Ross, D. (2003). *The Right and the Good* (P. Stratton-Lake, Ed.; 2nd ed.). Clarendon Press.

Salice, A. (2019). The Phenomenology of the Munich and Göttingen Circles. In E. N. Zalta (Ed.), *The Stanford Encyclopedia of Philosophy* (Winter 2019). Metaphysics Research Lab, Stanford University. https://plato.stanford.edu/archives/win2019/entries/phenomenology-mg/.

Scheler, M. (1970). *Formalism in Ethics and Non-Formal Ethics of Values: A New Attempt Toward the Foundation of an Ethical Personalism*. (M. Frings and R. Funk, Trans.). Northwestern University Press.

———. (2004). On the Rehabilitation of Virtue. (E. Kelly, Trans.). *American Catholic Philosophical Quarterly* 79(1), 21–37.

Schuhmann, K. (1992). Husserl und Hildebrand. *Aletheia. An International Journal of Philosophy 5*, 6–33.

Seifert, J. (1977). Appendix to "The Idea of Value and the Reform of the Traditional Metaphysics of 'Bonum'" (J. Barger, Trans.). *Aletheia: An International Journal of Philosophy*, *1*, 328–36.

Stein, E. (1917). *Zum Problem der Einfühlung*. Waisenhauses. English Translation Consulted. (1989) *On the Problem of Empathy* (W. Stein, Trans.) ICS Publications.

———. (1922).Beiträge zur philosophiscen Begründung der Psychologie und der Geisteswissenschaften. *Jahrbuch für Philosophie und phänomenologische*

Forschung 5: 1–283; English Translation Consulted. (2016) *Philosophy of Psychology and the Humanities* (M. Sawicki, Ed.; M. C. Baseheart, Trans.). ICS Publications.

Vendrell Ferran, I. (2017) Intentionality, Value-Disclosure, and Constitution: Stein's Model. In D. Moran and E. Magri (Eds.), *Empathy, Sociality, and Personhood: Essays on Edith Stein's Phenomenological Investigations* (pp. 65–85). Springer.

Chapter 8

"Against" Empathy

From the Isolated Self to Intersubjectivity in Martin Heidegger's Thinking and the Consequences for Health Care

Francesca Brencio

ABSTRACT

The aim of this chapter is to provide an account of Heidegger's views on intersubjectivity and to understand his critiques toward the concept of empathy. This contribution is divided into four sections. In the first section, I will reconstruct the hermeneutical shift Heidegger introduced into phenomenology and see how it contributed to the understanding of *Dasein* in terms of facticity. In the second section, I will show how Heidegger's account of subjectivity and intersubjectivity is grounded on the strong critique toward every theory of the isolated self in favor of a conception of *Dasein* ecstatically open, embedded in the world and grounded on the ontological structure of *Mitsein*. In the third section, I will explore the Heideggerian critique of empathy, and in the last section, I will show how Heidegger's account of intersubjectivity may help to enrich the dialogue between phenomenology and health care, a dialogue conceived in terms of a moral enterprise.

Keywords: empathy, intersubjectivity, *Mitsein*, hermeneutic phenomenology, health care

INTRODUCTION

Martin Heidegger's views of empathy go against the grain of the contemporary perspective, not because he did not take the issue of intersubjectivity seriously, but because his account of intersubjectivity shakes up many theories of empathy, both in the phenomenological tradition and in the field of psychology. This is due to the hermeneutical shift he introduced into phenomenology, which forged his account of *Dasein* and intersubjectivity, and his understanding of phenomenology as a method for ontology. Heidegger's relationship with phenomenology is more than a matter of philosophical education and historical circumstances; it is a landmark of his philosophical pathway. When the Klostermann publishing house started to publish Heidegger's *Gesamtausgabe* in 1975, the first volume which inaugurated the collected works was *The Basic Problems of Phenomenology* (GA24). This book compiled the lecture series that Heidegger gave at the University of Marburg in the summer of 1927 and is considered by many interpreters as a kind of precursor of *Being and Time*. Heidegger himself proposed to start the *Gesamtausgabe* with this text and to follow up this book with *Being and Time*. At the core of this decision was the will to provide a clear orientation to his works, admitting that his pathway into phenomenology was fundamental to his thinking. Before discussing how Heidegger conceives intersubjectivity and how his account has many important consequences for health care practices, I would like to briefly reconstruct his shift from transcendental to hermeneutic phenomenology between 1919 and 1925, taking into account the early Freiburg Lectures (1919–1923) and the Marburg Lectures (1923–1938).[1]

THE HERMENEUTIC SHIFT IN PHENOMENOLOGY AND ITS RELEVANCE TO THE HEIDEGGERIAN ACCOUNT OF INTERSUBJECTIVITY

The starting point of Heidegger's relationship with the phenomenological method may be found in the *Psychologismus-Streit* (the psychologism dispute), which took place in Germany between the end of the nineteenth century and the beginning the twentieth century. At the core of this dispute there were two elements: First, the relationship between logic and philosophy and, second, whether or not logic may be conceived as a part of psychology. Husserl played a cardinal role in this debate, harshly criticizing the possible transformation of philosophy into a positivistic science. It is in the *Prolegomena* of the *Logische Untersuchungen* that Husserl clarifies his position on psychologism. According to him, one of its fundamental mistakes is to ignore the difference between logic and psychology. Logic must not be regarded as an empirical science (since its objects may also be nonexistent), but at the same time it must be characterized by certainty and exactness since it deals with ideal structures and general laws. Psychology, however, is an empirical science which focuses on the nature of consciousness and may be characterized by a certain probability or vagueness. The attempt to reduce logic to psychology is a mistake related to a regular category error. One of the most evident mistakes of psychologism is that "it does not distinguish correctly between the object of knowledge and the act of knowing. Whereas the act is a psychical process that elapses in time and that has a beginning and an end, this does not hold true for the logical principles or mathematical truths that are known."[2]

In his critique of psychologism, Heidegger follows Husserl (and Carl Braig) to a certain extent on this theme, but at the same time he recognizes that the distinction between a psychic act and logical content gives anti-psychologism a dual nature that is impossible to accept. In his 1912 article titled "Recent Developments in Logic," he suggests that "the sharp delimitation of logic against psychology is perhaps not feasible (*durchführbar*). . . . It is one thing for psychology to found logic in principle and to secure its value of validity, and another for it to assume the role of becoming an initial sphere of activity, an operational basis in logic. The second is in fact the case, since we have to do with the peculiar fact that harbors problems within itself that can perhaps never be fully clarified, namely, the fact that *the logical is embedded in the psychical.*"[3] This critical consideration of the transcendental standpoint will be further elaborated: Psychology will always have a connection to philosophy,[4] and, as such, psychology must be conceived in terms of a phenomenology of meaning, providing an operational basis for logic, and remaining forever relevant to philosophy.[5] In his understanding of the relationship between philosophy (as logic) and psychology, Heidegger is planting the seeds of what in *Being and Time* becomes the existential analytic of Dasein.

As we know from a letter from Husserl to Natorp, dated October 8, 1917, Heidegger was starting his comprehensive confrontation with phenomenology at that time. The period from 1919 to 1929 has appropriately been called Heidegger's phenomenological decade,[6] reaching a point of high recognition in 1920 when Heidegger became Husserl's personal assistant. A sign of his commitment to confront the phenomenological method was the lecture course of the Winter Semester 1919–1920, titled *The Basic Problems of Phenomenology* (GA58), which deals with an extremely problematic issue: the most radical and decisive problem of phenomenology is phenomenology itself.[7] The intuitions that were elaborated in the prewar writings take the form of a radical reorientation of what we must conceive as original: the motto "experience first" is decisive only if we mean by this to have a new access to life, a theme to which he dedicated his efforts. The *Lebensphilosophie*, a dominant theme in philosophy at that time, is the theoretical occasion to combine the hermeneutical gaze with the phenomenological method. At the beginning of *The Basic Problems of Phenomenology*, we read that "phenomenology is the name for the method of scientific philosophy in general"[8] because it provides the appropriate mode of access into the issue of being.[9] In this sense, "phenomenology is our way of access to what is to be the theme of ontology, and it is our way of giving it demonstrative precision. Only as phenomenology, is ontology possible."[10] Before being considered as a reflection on the transcendental structures of experience, phenomenology is an "understanding, a hermeneutic intuition,"[11] a self-interpreting process in which factic life intuits itself. Heidegger was interested not merely in clarifying the structures of experience, but also in understanding how we can interpret, evaluate and act on what we experience.[12]

Between 1919 and 1922 Heidegger suggests that phenomenology might not necessarily be tied to the concept of the transcendental.[13] Dissatisfied with a reflective account of phenomenology, his efforts are aimed at defining a concept of factical life. This is possible by acknowledging the fundamental role of affective elements, conceived both in active and passive aspects of intentional directedness. This radicalization of the Husserlian-Brentanian notion of intentionality aims to demonstrate that the unity of intentional life must be searched for at a pre-theoretical level, namely the *pathic* dimension of existence. The hermeneutic phenomenology of factical life scrutinizes the a-theoretical domain of each lived experience, stressing the role of the pathic dimension of the givenness.[14] Far from falling into a kind of irrationalism, Heidegger insists on the foundational role of the pre-theoretical (*vorweltlich*) dimension of life, which unveils the role of moods as means of accessing the world. In *Phenomenology of Religious Life* moods are often called affections, recalling the Latin word *affectiones*. Welcoming the legacy of Aristotle's meditation on affects, Heidegger stresses how a human being is constitutively a being-in, because determined by πάθη (affection): "These πάθη, 'affects,' are not states pertaining to ensouled things, but are concerned with a *disposition* of living things in their world, in the mode of being positioned toward something, allowing a matter to matter to it. The affects play a fundamental role in the determination of being-in-the-world, of being-with-and-toward-others."[15] *Being-in* a mood indicates a situatedness and a disposition (διάθεσις) toward the world, the others, the language. These concepts, announced between the Freiburg and Marburg years, become developed in a systematic way in *Being and Time* where Heidegger introduces the fundamental structure of *Befindlichkeit* as an a priori constitutive part of Dasein's facticity and shapes his understanding of intersubjectivity and his critique of the notion of empathy.

Between 1920 and 1921 the expression "phenomenological hermeneutics" appears several times and it only changed after 1922 with "hermeneutics of facticity." Heidegger's philosophical enterprise is to theoretically and historically understand that at the core of life there is not knowledge, but rather *care*,[16] a concept that is cardinal in *Being and Time* and that unveils the structure of existence in its original intersubjective space. In Heidegger's first Marburg course, *Introduction to Phenomenological Research*, the hermeneutic change and the rejection of Husserl's transcendental ego is the result of strict historical need, rooted in the influence of Dilthey's thinking on the philosopher of Meßkirch, in the study of Aristotle and the Neo-Kantian tradition, and finally in Christian and theological education. The hermeneutic phenomenology elaborated at the beginning of the 1920s becomes a proper ontology during the elaboration of *Being and Time*: The phenomenological motto to the things themselves may be conceived as an indication of the *Seinsfrage*. In this respect, the role of hermeneutics is not confined to understanding (*Verstehen*), but rather it emerges as an independent philosophical activity that involves the human being in its constant *interrogation* of experiences, things, and relationships in the *mode* of the everyday activities. This mode is precisely what initiated Heidegger's ontological understanding of the being. This interrogation is often referred to by Heidegger as the verb "questioning," a central expression in all the many turns at work in his meditation, and summarized in the famous motto "questioning is the piety of thinking."

The *Lebensphilosophie* was one of Heidegger's main concerns. He saw in Dilthey's philosophy of life an interpretation of human existence close to that which he was striving to achieve. Particularly critical of his mentor Heinrich Rickert, Heidegger sees in life-philosophy a certain hope for phenomenological research. The ground of investigation for life-philosophy is the issue of facticity, a notion that, for Heidegger, seems to be less ambiguous than the concept of existence used by Kierkegaard and Jaspers. Facticity is the key theme of the 1923 summer semester lecture titled *Ontology. Hermeneutic of Facticity*. "'Facticity' is the designation we will use for the character of the being of 'our' 'own' Dasein. More precisely, this expression means: in each case 'this' Dasein in its being-there for a while at the particular time . . . insofar as it is, in the character of its being, 'there' in the manner of being."[17] Gadamer recalls that the word facticity was understood and formulated "in the dispute over faith in the Resurrection. This is how the word 'facticity' figures in Rothe and other theologians of the Hegelian and post-Hegelian generation. Of course, when Heidegger uses the word, it had been given the quite different stamp. . . . Facticity refers, after all, to the fact in its being a fact, i.e., precisely the thing back of which and behind which one cannot go."[18] To put it differently, facticity deals with the *naked fact of existence.* "The 'hermeneutics *of* facticity' is a possessive and not objective genitive, meaning 'facticity's hermeneutics.'"[19] Facticity means that the living being is as such because of *its being through living.* "The relationship here between hermeneutics and facticity is not a relationship between the grasping of an object and the object grasped. . . . Rather, interpreting is itself a possible and distinctive *how* of the character of being of facticity."[20] Phenomenological investigations on factical life cannot be separated from the same investigations on history, conceived as a going along with life as it is lived.

The breaking point with Husserlian phenomenology occurs with the 1925 summer semester lecture, where he charged his contemporary phenomenology with the "unphenomenological" attitude[21] of dogmatism "with respect to nothing less than the delimiting of the field of research of phenomenology itself to transcendental consciousness. The world of lived experience knows of no such duality between object and knowledge."[22] According to Heidegger when we perform phenomenological reductions, we do not deal with a natural attitude, but rather with a theoretical attitude because what we are really going to bracket is not the real experience of myself "as a living being, a zoological object, out there, present-at-hand as any other . . . , rather I experience myself as someone engaged in a particular activity, job, and the like."[23] To put it differently: our phenomenological reductions—aimed not at denying, neglecting or abandoning the world around us but rather at bracketing a certain dogmatic attitude toward reality—are dogmatic because "the question of being itself is left undiscussed."[24] The critique he raises against Husserl is that he dealt with a narrow concept of being, basically reduced to his interest in intentionality. As a result, Husserl "identified the being of consciousness with the being of objects and thereby failed to uncover the unique mode of being that characterized intentional subjectivity."[25] Heidegger aims at unveiling the hidden aspect of transcendental phenomenology in favor of a more original understanding of experience, conceived not from any psychological angle but rather as factic life-experience itself and ontology. This understanding is only roughly sketched in this lecture series but became the focus of his *magnum opus* (1927), which marks a definitive break with Edmund Husserl. The founding father of the phenomenological method recognizes how his assistant had rejected many important ideas of his own philosophy, developing completely new concepts, which, in many respects, are in contrast with fundamental principles of his phenomenology.[26] Heidegger's rejection of transcendental phenomenology is the starting point of his conception of life and history, which impacts his understanding of Dasein in terms of subjectivity and intersubjectivity.

FROM THE ISOLATED SELF TO THE *MITSEIN* OF *DASEIN*

Heidegger's account of subjectivity and intersubjectivity (*Miteinandersein*) is characterized by a strong critique of every form of dualism, as if on one hand there is a subject and, on the other hand, there is an object that requires an appropriation process. The self is never isolated nor put in front of a world in a kind of dualistic view, but rather it is always disclosed and ecstatically opened, embedded into the world which requires it to deal with certain concerns and preoccupations. The notion of *ekstasis* is used in this context as a synonym of openness, disclosedness, articulated through a double axis: a vertical one, toward transcendence, and a horizontal one, toward sociality. It is precisely this ecstatic ontological structure of the everyday Dasein that founds a concept of intersubjectivity where the Dasein is always *being-in* and *being-with*. Heidegger's meditation is aimed at overcoming the Cartesian dualism at the core of the modern philosophical tradition: The subject is never isolated from the world in which it physically lives, and it cannot process the experiential world into inner and outer spaces, but rather the subject is ontologically determined by a belonging to the intersubjective space.

In the 1923 summer semester lecture titled *Ontology. Hermeneutic of Facticity*, we find a clarification on the structure of Dasein: "the being-there of Dasein (factical life) is *being in* a world."[27] The insistence of the *being-in* is an element of Heidegger's account of Dasein; while in the *Phenomenology of Religious Life* the being-in is related to moods and affective phenomena, here it is related to the world. These indications pave the way to *Being and Time*, where we find a systematic analysis of the Dasein. In the twelfth paragraph of the second chapter of the book, Heidegger clarifies what he means with the being-in. Far from being a property typical of all entities ready at hand (*Mitvorhandensein*), the being-in of the Dasein is an existentiale: "'Being-in' is thus the formal existential expression for the Being Dasein, which has *Being-in-the-world* as its essential state."[28] There is an ontological difference between the being-in as existentiale and the category of the insideness that things have in relation to each other. The existentiale does not delimit a spatial condition, but rather this is possible only because of the existentiale being-in. "*Being-in* is not to be explained ontologically by some ontic characterization, as if one were to say, for instance, that Being-in in a world is a spiritual property, and that man's 'spatiality' is a result of his bodily nature."[29] The not being-in of Dasein is a certain property that it sometimes has or not, but rather, because Dasein is essentially characterized by the being-in, it can encounter and discover the world, because its ontological constitution is precisely the *being-in-the-world*.

Dasein is also characterized by another ontological structure: the *being-with* (*Mitsein*). Phenomenologically speaking, Dasein is always a being-with the others, and this independently from the fact that the others are perceived, visible, close to me. "Dasein as Being-with lets the Dasein of Others be encountered in its world. . . . Only so far as one's own Dasein has the essential structure of Being-with, is it Dasein-with as encounterable for Others."[30] Dasein itself is *Mitsein*, and because of this mode of being it can coexist alongside as *Mitdasein*. In its being-in and being-with, Dasein deals with the many concerns of everyday life, related to things, as ready-at-hand, and to people. In the first case, the commitment of Dasein to care for things is called *Besorgen, concern*, while in the second it is called *Fürsorge, solicitude*, an essential element for the being of the Dasein. "Dasein 'is' essentially for the sake of Others. This must be understood as an existential statement as to its essence."[31] Of course, this does not mean that Dasein always cares about the others or about the things encountered into the world. It suggests that the positive mode of Fürsorge is the original domain of the plural dimension of Dasein. We can meet two different types of solicitude, or two extreme possibilities: On one hand, there is a form of solicitude that takes away care from the other, and the other "is thus thrown out of his own position; . . . he can either take it over as something finished and at his disposal, or disburden himself of it completely. In such solicitude the Other can become one who is dominated and dependent, even if this domination is a tacit one and remains hidden from him. This kind of solicitude, which leaps in and takes away 'care,' is to a large extent determinative for Being with one another, and pertains for the most part to our concern with the ready-to-hand."[32] On the other hand, we find a possibility of solicitude, which does not deprive the other from the existential task of care "but rather to give it back to him authentically.. . . . This kind of solicitude pertains essentially to authentic care—that is, to the existence of the Other, not to a 'what' with which he is concerned; it helps the Other to become transparent to himself in his care and to become free for it."[33]

If we try to simplify the Heideggerian jargon, we can say that human beings are already born into a world and are never separated from the world. As such, they are always connected to a there, which the German word *Da* in Dasein means. Far from being a geographical determination, this there designates the *openness* of our existential constitution.[34] "By its very nature, Dasein brings its 'there' along with it. If it lacks its 'there,' it is not factically the entity which is essentially Dasein; indeed, it is not this entity at all. Dasein is its disclosedness. . . . its 'there.'"[35] A human being's being-in-the-world is not an abstraction, but rather a concrete occurrence which contributes to fulfillment through the manifold modes of human behavior.

The being *situated* into the world and being *affected* by the world is strictly related to the being's facticity, and it becomes manifest to us through our own moods and affectivity, which are the ways in which we find ourselves in the world, in relationships, in relation to things, etc. This is the role of *Befindlichkeit*,[36] one of the key structures of Dasein, together with understanding and language, explained by Heidegger in the twenty-ninth paragraph of chapter 5 (I section) of *Being and Time*. Theoretically speaking, *Befindlichkeit* is not a point of departure for Heidegger's confrontation with phenomenology; on the contrary, it is a point of arrival nourished also by his study and work on Aristotle. Disposition[37] expresses the fact that human beings are always situated in a mood and always open to the world. Moods (*Stimmungen*) are not an intentional state directed at something, but, rather, they are conditions of making such states possible. Moods are means of accessing the world and as such they have not an internal nor an external object. They are not a kind of psychological state that we experience within a given world, but rather they are a "background through which it is possible to encounter things in the ways that we do, as 'there,' 'not there,' 'mattering,' 'not mattering,' 'for this' or 'for that.'"[38] In having a mood, "existence is always disclosed. . . . 'To be disclosed' does not mean 'to be known as this sort of thing' . . . Having a mood is not related to the psychical in the first instance, and is not itself an inner condition. . . . Disposition is a basic existential species of their disclosedness, because this disclosedness itself is essentially Being-in-the-world."[39] However, it is important to stress that not all feelings are moods. Feelings might not have a disclosive value, for example as pain, which may be described as more "blinding than disclosive. Pain tends to cut the world off from us, to turn us in upon ourselves."[40]

In its average everydayness Dasein deals with concerns and solicitude. The fundamental moods (*Grundstimmungen*) of anxiety and fear disclose the very nature of Dasein: its care (*Sorge*). "Dasein's Being reveals itself as care (*Sorge*),"[41] says Heidegger. Care is used in a purely ontological and existential meaning: it does not characterize facticity in a single mode of being of Dasein or as a single subject, the "I." On the contrary, care embraces the unit of the ways in which Dasein may be characterized. "Care, as a primordial structural totality, lies 'before' ['*vor*'] every factical 'attitude' and 'situation' of Dasein, and it does so existentially a priori; this means that it always lies in them."[42] Care is ontologically earlier than every behavior, phenomena and situation in which Dasein may be involved.

Through moods *we dwell in the world:* they constitute the being-with-one-another[43] and contribute to the characterization of our social dimension. Moods "can open up questions of motivation that have been the province of moral psychology and speak to the limits of cognition in explaining or affecting moral action."[44] In their cardinal role in guaranteeing access to alterity, moods assess something important on the intersubjective nature of *Dasein*, unveiling an element of Heidegger's critique of empathy. Moods do not allow mental transposition of feelings and emotions into someone else, but rather they uncover the limits of empathy.

"AGAINST" EMPATHY

We can retrace Heidegger's interest in empathy[45] back to his lectures during his Freiburg period, when he developed a view of intersubjectivity close those of Dilthey and Scheler.[46] Generally speaking, we can say that the concept of empathy was considered in a positive way in that context. However, this perspective radically changes in *Being and Time*, where the concept of empathy is mentioned on several occasion always with a critical accent. A discussion on empathy is introduced at the end of the twenty-sixth paragraph of the 1927 book, in the paragraph titled *The Dasein-with of Others and Everyday Being-with.* There, we read: "This phenomenon, which is none too happily designated as 'empathy' ['*Einfühlung*'], is then supposed, as it were, to provide the first ontological bridge from one's own subject, which is given proximally as alone, to the other subject, which is proximally quite closed off."[47] According to him, empathy serves as a bridge from one's own feeling, thought, experience, and so on, to another subject, as if this conception of empathy allows the projection of one's own feeling, for example, "into" another subject, closed off from the original perceiver. Heidegger's critique of empathy lays precisely on the issue of projection and, we can say, is related to a cognitive approach to empathy: Dasein is always a being-in and being-with, and as such, no projective model of empathy is required to achieve an understanding of one another. This cognitivistic consideration of empathy, conceived as a form of mental transposition into other subjects, "pertains solely to a deficient mode of 'being-with-one-another,' since it involves an elaborate manoeuvre of comprehension in order to 'get' to another subject, which is only required because we usually live among one another in a mode of reciprocal indifference and concealment."[48] For Heidegger empathy is not a primordial existential phenomenon and does not represent a theme of proper philosophical investigation. Empathy risks the suppression of the genuine understanding of one another as original constitutions of the being-with-the-others.

Here it is important to make a clarification: Heidegger is not against shared feelings, nor does he affirm that they are not possible. Rather, he rejects any cognitivisitc model that assumes the self as an isolated monad in the horizon of sociality. Intersubjectivity in terms of *Miteinandersein* has an ontological originality that the phenomenon of empathy does not possess. In the *Fundamental Concepts of Metaphysics*, Heidegger asks a question very close to the function of empathy: "Can we as human beings transpose ourselves into another human being?"[49] Here, once again, the expression "transpose . . . into" underlines his conception of empathy. His answer is: It is possible that in certain contexts and situations "other human beings on average comport themselves to things exactly as we do ourselves; and furthermore, that a number of human beings not only have the same comportment toward the same things, but can also share one and the same comportment with one another, without this shared experience being fragmented in the process."[50] It is possible, says Heidegger, that people go with (*Mitgang*) others in their understanding and access to things, but it is also true that in the everyday activities this possibility appears very difficult, and "so seldom [we] find ourselves really able to go along with them."[51] Heidegger is not denying the possibility for a human being to transpose themselves into others but, rather, is stressing that this possibility already and originally belongs to man's own essence, that is in its being with the others: "The ability to transpose oneself into others and go along with them, with the Dasein in them, always already happens on the basis of man's Dasein, and happens as Dasein. For the being-there of Da-sein means being with others, precisely in the manner of Dasein, i.e., existing with others."[52] This is what Heidegger aims to clarify when he affirms that the issue of empathy is not a topic of philosophical debate. The issue of empathy "does not ask anything, because it is not a possible question. . . . It is a meaningless, indeed a nonsensical question because it is fundamentally redundant."[53]

It is important to repeat that Heidegger is taking seriously the issue of intersubjectivity, the possibility of sharing experiences and shared feelings, but his perspective is aimed at avoiding any dualism. In the general understanding of empathy, the transposition of my feelings into another's own feelings collides with a nondualistic account of subjectivity. It requires the existence of isolated selves that somehow need to communicate their own experiences, emotions, feelings, thoughts from the ground of an ontological separation, a kind of isolation in which they constitutively are. In the community of *Mitdasein* the Heideggerian dismissal of empathy finds its theoretical justification. Against any cognitivistic approach to empathy, Heidegger reaffirms the primacy of ontology—in this case, the primacy of the ontological constitution of Dasein as *Mitsein*—on every mental act conceived as a mere transportation into someone else's mind.

At this point, a question seems to be urgent: If Heidegger is "against" a cognitivistic account of empathy, does it mean that there is no room for such a concept and practice in his meditation? It seems to me that it is still possible to talk about empathy in Heidegger's thinking but we need to consider intersubjectivity from a different perspective, that is from the ontological perspective of Mitsein, and moreover, we need to say something on the issue of the self. In *Grundprobleme der Phänomenologie* (1919–1920), Heidegger asks if any experience we are committed to has an inner reference to the I, a certain mineness (*Jemeinigkeit*) related to the experiential dimension. His answer is that in every experience a certain reference to myself is present: Every experience is not an experience from nowhere, but rather it is exactly *my* experience. Here Heidegger is not talking about the ego, but rather he is referring to a self which is embedded into the factical life-experience and implicated in all the intentional behaviors, primarily encountered in and through our engagement in the world. In the 1927 lecture series, *The Basic Problems of Phenomenology*, Heidegger stresses the relationship among the self, Dasein, and the world, affirming that disclosing a world is always already a self-finding enterprise. In *The Metaphysical Foundations of Logic*, we read: "To be in the mode of a self means to be fundamentally toward oneself. Being towards oneself constitutes the being of Dasein and is not something like an additional capacity to observe oneself over and above just existing."[54] The intentional directness toward the world and the things is a co-disclosure of the self, linked to intentionality. We can say that we find ourselves primarily as a worldly situated self, and the self-acquaintance is never detached from our ontological constitution. On the contrary, it happens through non-reflective character as an expression of factical life-experience, whose foundational character is represented by the Mitsein.

This Heideggerian account of the self serves as a starting point for a different interpretation of Heidegger's view of empathy. Lawrence Hatab described empathy as an "ekstatic being-in-therewith-the-Other, [an] empathic concern as a fundamental element of Dasein's social world."[55] This ecstatic account of empathy is not a continuative condition of Dasein's everyday life, but, rather, it is a rare and occasional possibility: "there can be moments of spontaneous, direct, affective responses, wherein we are immersed in/there/with the other person: we might wince, or tears might well up, or sadness might come—all in direct response to what is seen/sensed/felt in and from the person's words, tones, gestures, facial expressions, and body language."[56] In these moments the reflective or self-conscious activity are not at work in our relationships. We are simply there for another fellow human, sharing and participating in his or her emotions, feelings, thoughts, fears, and experiences. Lou Agosta provides an extensive account of Heidegger's understanding of empathy through the lens of the hermeneutic circle. In this way, all the key existential structures of being in the world, such as human affectedness, understanding, interpretation, and speech, are considered in their mutual relationship. The careful reconstruction of Heidegger's use and refuse of empathy guides the author into a broad discussion of how a hermeneutics of empathy may enrich the interdisciplinary dialogue with psychoanalysis.[57] Some suggestions of an Heideggerian account of empathy are also provided by Kevin Aho. According to him, the experience of empathy is always mediated in advance by a temporally structured familiarity with the other; the other, to some extent, already matters and makes sense to me. Thus, for Heidegger individual experiences such as empathy are themselves made possible by Dasein.[58] Dan Zahavi devotes an extensive clarification of Heidegger's understanding of empathy, highlighting how he was the only phenomenologist to question the primacy of the empathic encounter. A Heideggerian account of intersubjectivity requires a simultaneous analysis of the relationship between subjectivity and world, in their mutual interconnection. As such, Heidegger's consideration of intersubjectivity is 'beyond empathy': "the empathic approach . . . still misconstrues the nature of intersubjectivity, since it takes it to be, first of all, a thematic encounter between individuals, wherein one is trying to grasp the emotions or experiences of the other. . . . However, the very attempt to thematically grasp the experiences of others is the exception rather than the rule."[59] In his account of intersubjectivity Heidegger emphasizes the social and cultural embeddedness of intersubjective understanding.

One of the most eye-catching elements of Heidegger's critique of empathy is that it cancels the attitude that makes people, experiences, relationships, and things meaningful to us because they can also become my possibilities of feeling as other people feel, of experiencing as other people do, of caring about relationships or things as other people care. Ludwig Binswanger has stated this point clearly: "By presenting this ontological connection, Heidegger has banished entire libraries on the problem of empathy, the problem of perceiving the foreign as such, the problem of the 'constitution of the foreign I,' and so on, to the realm of history, for what the latter want to furnish proof of and explain is always already presupposed in the proof and the explanations; the presupposition itself can neither be explained nor proven, but rather only ontologically–phenomenologically 'disclosed.'"[60] Despite the criticisms and the different perspectives, I am inclined to affirm that Heidegger's account of intersubjectivity may contribute to enriching the dialogue between phenomenology and health care, a dialogue conceived in terms of a *moral enterprise*. The therapeutic encounter, for example, may be regarded as an ongoing enterprise in which every subjectivity involved and the world are required to disclose themselves in a meaningful relationship, in an ongoing dialectic of appropriation and unconcealment of meanings.

MITSEIN AND HEALTH CARE

Heidegger's analysis of Dasein was not confined to *Being and Time*: it extended beyond the book and beyond the resonance of the name of its author. The *Daseinsanalytik* is an indication of a hermeneutics of facticity, which may reach also health care practices. Physicians, clinicians and practitioners do not merely have to observe and to describe symptoms and the clinical history of the people they meet, but they should also be trained to understand hermeneutically the facticity of each existence to provide a person-centered understanding of health in precedence to a disease-centered one. When a disease undermines our bodily or mental functions, doctors are not simply required to fix something broken but, rather, to understand *a way of existence* that can contribute toward the highest task of human existence: *being free*. This is one of many other lessons we can draw from the *Zollikon Seminars*, a series of seminars delivered between 1959 and 1969 in front of an audience of doctors, psychiatrists, and analysts in the Zollikon house of Dr. Medard Boss, a Swiss psychiatrist. These seminars were a testament to one of Heidegger's strongest hopes: that there is the possibility to inaugurate a dialogue between a certain way of conceiving philosophy, namely non-metaphysical thinking, and medicine; a dialogue able to educate physicians in thinking, not only in describing but also in *understanding*.

It is in the context of the Zollikon Seminars that Heidegger talks about intersubjectivity in terms of *Mitdaseins.* The background is the application of a new clinical approach to mental health, known as Daseinsanalysis (or *Daseinsanalyse*, in German). This approach was characterized by many elements of Heidegger's analysis of Dasein in *Being and Time*, such as the original openness of Dasein, its intersubjective structure in terms of *Mitsein*, the relationship with moods and the affective as a means of access to the world. In the *Zollikon Seminars* we read: "[I]t is therefore possible that the relationship between the one who does the Daseinanalysis and the one who is analyzed can be experienced as a relationship between one Dasein and another. This relationship can be questioned regarding how this specific being-with-one-another is characterized in a way appropriate to Dasein. . . . The decisive point is that the particular phenomena, arising in the relationship between the analysand and the analyst, and belonging to the respective, concrete patient, must be broached in their own phenomenological content and not simply be classified globally under *existentialia*."[61] The specific being-with-one-another is Heidegger's way of talking about empathy from the perspective of the more original domain, the ontological one. The seminar held on July 8, 1965, is extremely clear on this point, summarizing some cardinal ideas from *Being and Time:* "The often-quoted psychological theory of empathy rests on this obviously incorrect concept. This theory starts by imagining an Ego in a purely Cartesian sense—an Ego given by itself in the first instance who then feels his way into the other—thus discovering that the other is a human being as well in the sense of an alter Ego. Nevertheless, this is a pure fabrication."[62] Being-with-one-another (*Miteinandersein*) refers to a way of existing with the others in the manner of being-in-the-world, especially with the others and the things we encounter.

If we transfer the Heideggerian account of intersubjectivity into health care practices, we cannot deny how the ontological structure of Dasein should impact the therapeutic relationship in terms of Mitsein and solicitude. It should redirect ways of thinking, moral insight, and sensibilities, both in the theoretical descriptions and in practical ways of handling disease. Acknowledging the being-with-one-another structure of our existence and its inextricable relationship with the world, these two elements should invite professionals in the field of health care to acquire a different gaze, both toward suffering and toward treatments, exemplified by a different attitude toward thinking: "Thinking is a deed. But a deed that also surpasses all praxis. Thinking permeates action and production, not through the grandeur of its achievement and not as a consequence of its effect, but through the humbleness of its inconsequential accomplishment."[63] However, "we measure deeds by the impressive and successful achievements of praxis. But the deed of thinking is neither theoretical nor practical, nor is the conjunction of these two forms of comportment."[64] This deed is an acting, or conducting oneself toward an original ethics, toward a full accomplishment of the authenticity of one's own existence.

Heidegger's clarification of the fundamental structures of Dasein and his account of intersubjectivity may help professionals in the field of health care by offering a new approach to understanding the human being, its vulnerability, and the possibility of recovery. Hermeneutic phenomenology can also contribute to a better understanding of ourselves, of our relationship with therapists, and with illness itself. These tools may redefine the landscape of human vulnerability and maybe invite us to reconsider the epistemological constitution of medicine. Human beings are not quantifiable, causally determined objects, nor isolated selves; on the contrary, they are always situated and determined by their ongoing involvement in the world that makes self-acquaintance possible. Uncovering the profound lessons of Heidegger's account of intersubjectivity means also to redefine the task of medicine, no longer reducible to a form of praxis focused on healing and fixing, but rather as an inherently thoughtful enterprise, and a form of dialogue that illuminates the entire existence in all its modifications.

NOTES

1. In doing so, I will especially focus on the texts (a) *Towards the Definition of Philosophy* (GA56–57), which groups the *Kriegsnotsemester* 1919 course and the summer semester 1919 course; (b) the lecture course of Winter Semester 1919–1920, titled *The Basic Problems of Phenomenology* (GA58); (c) *The Phenomenology of Religious Life* (GA60), which gathers the lectures from two courses at Freiburg, *Introduction to the Phenomenology of Religion* from winter semester 1920, and *Augustine and Neoplatonism* from summer semester 1921; (d) the first Marburg course, *Introduction to Phenomenological Research* (GA17); (e) the 1923 summer semester lecture titled *Ontology. Hermeneutic of Facticity* (GA 63); (f) the 1925 summer semester lecture titled *History of the Concept of Time. Prolegomena* (GA20).
2. Zahavi, 2003, 9.
3. Heidegger, 2007, 42.
4. Ibid., 30.
5. Feher, 1994, 77.
6. Cf. T. Kisiel, 1993, 59; Cf. also T. Kisiel and J. van Buren, eds., 1994.
7. Heidegger, 2013.
8. Heidegger, 1988b, 3.
9. Heidegger, 1988b, 11.
10. Heidegger, 1962, 60.
11. Heidegger, 2002, 89 and ff.
12. Stanghellini and Rosfort, 2013, 206.
13. Heidegger, 2001a, 173, and 2013, 229.
14. Brencio, 2018.
15. Heidegger, 1989, 83.
16. Heidegger, 2001a, 89.
17. Heidegger, 1999, 5.
18. Gadamer, 1994, 24.
19. Ibid., 25.
20. Heidegger, 1999, 12.
21. Heidegger, 1985, 109–10, 128 and ff.
22. Feher, 1994, 82.
23. Ibid., 86.
24. Heidegger, 1985, 114.
25. Zahavi, 2005, 49.
26. I refer the reader to Husserl, 1968; Breeur, 1994; and Husserl, 1997. The secondary literature on this theme is immense; among the fundamental works see Beaufret, 1974; Von Hermann, 1988; Bernet, 1988, 195–215; B. Hopkins, 1993; J. Taminiaux, 1994, 269–90; Marion, 1998; Keller, 1999; Crowell, 2001; Crowell, 2005, 49–64; Boedeker, 2005, 156–72; Zaborowski, Denker, and Bernet, eds., 2012.
27. Heidegger, 1999, 62.
28. Heidegger, 1962, 80.
29. Ibid., 82.
30. Ibid., 157.

31. Ibid., 160.
32. Ibid., 158.
33. Ibid., 159.
34. Heidegger, 2001, 120.
35. Heidegger, 1962, 171.
36. I refer the reader to Brencio (2019), 344–53.
37. There many translations of *Befindlichkeit* into English, among which the most known are state of mind, findingness, and attunement. In my work on *Befindlichkeit*, I decided to translate it as disposition. This decision is grounded on the use of the German reflexive verb *sich befinden*, which literally means finding oneself. In an ordinary way of speaking, the colloquial sentence *Wie befinden Sie sich?* means How is it going? or How do you feel?. In everyday language this expression refers to the situation in which someone finds herself situated. It is starting from this situated experience that the world, things, people, and so on are disclosed to me, or in Heideggerian jargon to the *Dasein*. Disposition is thus both this *being into a situatedness*, as ontological and constitutive dimension of *Dasein*, and *being open* to the world.
38. Ratcliffe, 2010, 128.
39. Heidegger, 1962, 173–76.
40. Caputo, 1994, 337.
41. Heidegger, 1962, 227.
42. Ibid., 238.
43. Heidegger, 1995, 67.
44. Hatab, 2002, 252.
45. The notion of empathy doesn't have a long history. The German term that is translated as empathy is *Einfühlung*, and it was first used in 1873 in the domain of aesthetics by the philosopher Robert Vischer. It was later taken over by Theodor Lipps, who introduced it into the field of social cognition to designate our basic capacity for understanding others as minded creatures. Despite its distinct philosophical origin, the concept of empathy was soon adopted by psychologists.
46. On this topic, I refer the reader to C. Ferencz-Flatz, 2015, 479–96.
47. Heidegger, 1962, 162.
48. Hatab, 2002, 255.
49. Heidegger, 1995, 205.
50. Ibid.
51. Ibid.
52. Ibid.
53. Ibid.
54. Heidegger, 1984, 189.
55. Hatab, 2002, 256.
56. Ibid.
57. Agosta, 2010.
58. Aho, 2009, 66.
59. Zahavi, 2005, 165.
60. Binswanger, 1953, 66.
61. Heidegger, 2001b, 124.

62. Ibid., 111.
63. Heidegger, 1988a, 274.
64. Ibid., 275.

REFERENCES

Agosta, L. (2010) *Empathy in the Context of Philosophy*. New York: Palgrave.

Aho, K. (2009) *Heidegger's Neglect of the Body*. New York:SUNY.

Beaufret, J. (1974) *Dialogue avec Heidegger. III: Approche de Heidegger*. Paris: Les Editions de Minuit.

Bernet, R. (1988) *Transcendance et intentionalité: Heidegger et Husserl sur les prolégomènes d'une ontologie phénoménologique*. In F. Volpi et al., (eds.), *Heidegger et l'Idée de la phenomenology* (pp. 195–215). Dordrecht: Kluwer Academic Publishers.

Binswanger, L. (1953) *Grundformen und Erkenntnis menschlichen Daseins*. Zurich: Max Niehans.

Boedeker, E. C. (2005) *Phenomenology*. In Hubert L. Dreyfus and Mark A. Wrathall (eds.), *A Companion to Heidegger* (pp. 156–72). Blackwell Publishing.

Breeur, R. (1994) Randbemerkungen Husserls zu Heideggers Sein und Zeit und Kant und das Problem der Metaphysik. *Husserl Studies* 11, 3–63.

Brencio, F. (2018) Disposition: The "Pathic" Dimension of Existence and Its Relevance in Affective Disorders and Schizophrenia. *Thaumazein* 6, 138–57. DOI: http://dx.doi.org/10.13136/thau.v6i0

———. (2019) *Befindlichkeit: Disposition*. In G. Stanghellini, A. Raballo, M. Broome, A.V. Fernandez, P. Fusar-Poli, and R. Rosfort (eds.), *The Oxford Handbook of Phenomenological Psychopathology* (pp. 344–53). Oxford: Oxford University Press.

Caputo, J. D. (1994) *Sorge and Kardia: The Hermeneutics of Factical Life and the Categories of the Heart*. In T. Kisiel and J. van Buren (eds.), *Reading Heidegger from the Start: Essays in his Earliest Thought* (pp. 327–44). Albany: SUNY Press.

Crowell, S. G. (2001) *Husserl, Heidegger, and the Space of Meaning: Paths Toward Transcendental, Phenomenology*. Evanston, IL: Northwestern University Press.

———. (2005), *Heidegger and Husserl: The Matter and Method of Philosophy*. In Hubert L. Dreyfus, and Mark A. Wrathall (eds.), *A Companion to Heidegger, Blackwell Publishing* (pp. 49–64). Blackwell Publishing.

Feher, I. M. (1994) Phenomenology, Hermeneutics, Lebensphilosophie: Heidegger's Confrontation with Husserl, Dilthey, and Jaspers. In T. Kisiel and J. van Buren (eds.), *Reading Heidegger from the Start: Essays in his Earliest Thought* (pp. 73–90). Albany: SUNY Press.

Ferencz-Flatz, C. (2015) The Element of Intersubjectivity. Heidegger's Early conception of Empathy. *Continental Philosophy Review* 248, 479–96. doi: 10.1007/s11007-015-9350–4

Gadamer, H. G. (1994) Martin Heidegger's One Path. In T. Kisiel and J. van Buren (eds.), *Reading Heidegger from the Start: Essays in His Earliest Thought* (pp. 19–34). Albany: SUNY Press.

Hatab, L. J. (2002) *Heidegger and the Question of Empathy*. In F. Raffoul and D. Pettigrew (eds.), *Heidegger and Practical Philosophy*. New York: SUNY Press.

Heidegger, M. (1962) *Being and Time*. London: Blackwell Publishers.

———. (1984) *The Metaphysical Foundations of Logic* Bloomington: Indiana University Press.

———. (1985) *History of the Concept of Time. Prolegomena*. Bloomington: Indiana University Press.

———. (1988a) *Pathmarks*. Cambridge: Cambridge University Press.

———. (1988b) *The Basic Problems of Phenomenology*. Bloomington: Indiana University Press.

———. (1989) *Basic Concepts of Aristotelian Philosophy*. Bloomington: Indiana University Press.

———. (1995) *Fundamental Concepts of Metaphysics*. Bloomington: Indiana University Press.

———. (1999) *Ontology: The Hermeneutics of Facticity* Bloomington: Indiana University Press.

———. (2001a) *Phenomenological Interpretations of Aristotle. Initiation into Phenomenological Research*. Bloomington: Indiana University Press.

———. (2001b) *Zollikon Seminars*. Evanston, IL: Northwestern University Press.

———. (2002) *Towards the Definition of Philosophy*. London: Continuum.

———. (2007) *Recent Research in Logic (1912)*. In T. Kiesel & T. Sheehan (eds.), *Becoming Heidegger. On the Trail of His Early Occasional Writings 1910–1927* (pp. 33–48). Seattle: Noesis Press.

———. (2013) *The Basic Problems of Phenomenology (Winter Semester 1919/1920)*. London: Bloomsbury Academic.

Hopkins, B. (1993) *Intentionality in Husserl and Heidegger: The Problem of the Original Method and Phenomenon of Phenomenology*. Dordrecht, Kluwer Academic Publishers.

Husserl, E. (1968) *Letters to Roman Ingarden*. The Hague: Martinus Nijhoff.

———. (1997) *Psychological and Transcendental Phenomenology and the Confrontation with Heidegger (1927–1931)*. Dordrecht: Kluwer Academic Publishers.

Keller, P. (1999) *Husserl and Heidegger on Human Experience*. Cambridge: Cambridge University Press.

Kisiel, T. (1993) *The Genesis of Heidegger's Being and Time*. Berkeley: University of California Press.

Kisiel. T, and J. van Buren (eds.). *Reading Heidegger from the Start: Essays in His Earliest Thought*. Albany: SUNY Press.

Marion, J. L. (1998) *Reduction and Givenness: Investigations of Husserl, Heidegger, and Phenomenology*. Evanston, IL: Northwestern University Press.

Ratcliffe, M. (2010) The Phenomenology and Neurobiology of Moods and Emotions. In D. Schmicking and S. Gallagher (eds.), *Handbook of Phenomenology and Cognitive Sciences* (pp. 123–40). Springer.

Stanghellini, G., and Rosfort, R. (2013) *Emotions and Personhood. Exploring Fragility—Making Sense of Vulnerability*. Oxford: Oxford University Press.

Taminiaux, J. (1994) *The Husserlian Heritage in Heidegger's Notion of the Self.* in T. Kisiel and J. van Buren (eds.), *Reading Heidegger from the Start: Essays in his Earliest Thought* (pp. 269–90). Albany: SUNY Press.

Von Hermann, F.-W. (1988) *Der Begriff der Phänomenologie bei Heidegger und Husserl*. Frankfurt: Klostermann

Zaborowski, H., Denker, A., and Bernet R.(eds.) (2012) *Heidegger und Husserl*, Heidegger-Jahrbuch, vol. 6. Alber Verlag, Freiburg im Breisgau.

Zahavi, D. (2003) *Husserl's Phenomenology*. Stanford, CA: Stanford University Press.

———. (2005), *Subjectiviy and Selhood. Investigating the First-Person Perspective*. Cambridge, MA:The MIT Press.

Chapter 9

Being (N)One of Us

The Ethical and the Body

Henning Nörenberg

ABSTRACT

This chapter contributes a phenomenological analysis of our sense of dealing with another conscious being or even a person. Drawing on insights articulated by Løgstrup (1997) and Levinas (1969), I investigate the relevant sense under the name "excess phenomenon." One of this phenomenon's most conspicuous traits is the subjective sense that the other person cannot be reduced to a set of categories nor predicted in terms of their reactions. In the course of my analysis, I provide an account of the excess phenomenon's bodily dimension and outline the ethical significance of the phenomenon in question. Although the excess phenomenon is not sufficient for grounding ethical demands, it is a necessary condition for the other person's authority to hold the subject responsible because it is involved in the way in which the subject registers the other as a fellow human being. I argue that the other person's moral authority cannot be reduced to the subject's commitment to communal norms, but that such commitment may have an influence on the subject's sensitivity to the excess phenomenon in other persons.

Keywords: Levinas, Løgstrup, Strawson, ethical demand, embodiment, reactive attitudes, communities of respect, dehumanization

According to a widespread conception, the mental states of other people are hidden from us. In this view, we would have to deduce or simulate what the other person is thinking, willing, or feeling (see Leslie, 1987, p. 139; Goldman, 2005, p. 80 f.; for a critique see Gallagher & Zahavi, 2012, pp. 191–218). A promising alternative to this view has been proposed under the name of "empathy."

The discussion on empathy focuses on the question of whether and how we have experiential access to other persons' mental states. Empathy, in this sense, is a primarily bodily understanding of the other by way of expressive phenomena (see Scheler, 1973; Stein, 1922; Plessner, 1982; Zahavi, 2014; Nörenberg, 2022). To a considerable extent, it is achieved in terms of a dynamic, mutual responsiveness rather than in terms of detached observation from a third-personal perspective (Ratcliffe, 2014).

The focus of the present chapter is on a particular layer or aspect of empathy. Any attempt to explicate our access to other minds presupposes that it refers to the existence of other minds. Thus, any form of empathy as an experiential process must involve the subjective sense that one actually is in contact with another conscious being rather than with a mere object of some sort. This requirement has been spelled out in Husserl's *Cartesian Meditations* in an instructive manner (Husserl, 1950, pp. 139, 144; Zahavi, 2014, p. 125 f.): The sense of there being another person primarily refers to the bodily presence (*Leibhaftigkeit*) of that person. Further, it must retain a palpable distinction between oneself and the other according to which the experiences of the latter cannot be given to one in the same way as the one's own experiences. This distinction involves a peculiar form of appresentation in connection with the behavior of the other person's body.

What insights can we gather from analyzing the experiential quality of the subjective sense of there being another person? As some of the most distinguished Husserl scholars have argued, the *Cartesian Meditations* help establish that the other person responds to the subject in a different manner than mere physical objects do (see Smith, 2003, pp. 243, 248), and that, in contact with the other, the subject can make experiences they could not make in isolation (see Zahavi, 2014, p. 133).

In this chapter, I would like to enrich the picture by analyzing what one might call the "excess phenomenon." Phenomenologists such as Knud Ejler Løgstrup (1997 [1956]) and Emmanuel Levinas (1969 [1961]) describe the way in which the other person appears to transcend or escape the categories under which the perceiving subject attempts to subsume them. What their descriptions seek to elucidate is the peculiar sense that the other person is simply more than any categorization can grasp: "The face of the Other," Levinas writes, "at each moment destroys and overflows the plastic image it leaves me" (1969, p. 50). Løgstrup articulates a similar idea by saying that the personal presence of the other "erases" the image of themself that the subject constantly tries to form (1997, p. 13). This sense of the other as being beyond categorization is what I intend by the label "excess phenomenon."

Both Løgstrup and Levinas investigate the excess phenomenon in the context of their relevant account of phenomenologically grounding the ethical demand to take care of the other person. Thus, it seems worthwhile to revisit their proposals in the light of more recent attempts of explicating the ethical dimension in human relationships. My central claim in this regard will be that the excess phenomenon functions as some sort of warrant for what Strawson (1962) and others have called the "participatory attitude" that, in turn, constitutes an essential aspect of the web of our practices and emotions in terms of which moral norms are intelligible.

My investigation proceeds as follows. Since the notion of categorization serves as a contrastive backdrop of Løgstrup's and Levinas's explication of the excess phenomenon, I start out by sketching the general problem of categorization. Then, I explicate the excess phenomenon more thoroughly and finally discuss its meta-ethical implications.

CATEGORIZATION AS A GENERAL TRAIT OF HUMAN LIFE

To explicate the excess phenomenon more thoroughly, we first need to understand what is meant by categorization because it is this notion that serves as a contrastive backdrop in both Levinas and Løgstrup. Categorization is grounded in an important aspect of our engagement with the world: Perceiving is always already perceiving "something as something" (Heidegger, 2006, p. 149). We do not see, hear or feel entirely meaningless stuff—usually we feel a rough surface, hear a motorcycle, or see that our neighbor is angry. Sometimes we may even deal with something that is unfamiliar or does not seem to make any sense. But even these things are far from being completely devoid of meaning, insofar as they are part of an overall meaningful situation and at least pose some sort of problem for us. In this sense, perceiving is always already perceiving as . . . or, in other words, perception is not primarily about "things themselves," but about *states of affairs* that also contain the aspect in terms of which those "things" appear (see Schmitz, 2019, p. 47).

To *categorize* something is to make that "as which" something is perceived more explicit and determinate. Pragmatists and phenomenologists have emphasized that such explication and determination is only possible against the backdrop of a more diffuse and holistic meaningfulness called the *situation*.[1] In this perspective, situations are ontologically prior and semantically richer than the determinate meanings—states of affairs in various modalities (e.g., facts, problems, norms, desires, etc.)—that can be fetched from it by way of explication. However, besides engaging with situations in terms of an implicit and holistic know-how as in animalistic lifeforms, *human* forms of life depend to a great extent on the capacity to explicate situations from particular vantage points:

> Humans survive in their environment by reconstructing situations as constellations of individual factors without thus being able to exhaust the meaningfulness of situations; reconstruction remains a tentative adjustment by trial and error. (Schmitz, 2019, p. 75)

In the process of such reconstructions, particular aspects of the situation are singled out and specified in terms of stable roles such as cause, effect, character, goal, problem, solution, and so on. The stability of those reconstructions may often hide the fact that they are originally derived from and dependent on the more comprehensive situations. In this sense, situations can never be completely exhausted, for any explicit state of affairs can only make sense in the context of more implicit meanings. Thus, although our lived reality is in fact more complex, on many occasions we can and maybe even have to skip over that complexity and take a particular "as which" as the definitive thing. A forester, to quote a famous example from Uexküll (2010, p. 128), may see a particular tree as a few cords of wood, while a young girl may see the face of a demon in its bark. Generally, some particularly stable reconstructions may even sediment, turn into a perceptual practice and, thus, frame the process of perception itself (see Gallagher & Varga, 2014, p. 196). In such cases it is hard for the perceiver to become aware of the fact that that particular "as which" is not so definite after all. This is, roughly, the general *problem of categorization.*

THE EXCESS PHENOMENON IN LØGSTRUP AND LEVINAS

A particular instance of the problem of categorization occurs in the context of interpersonal relations. Even if, perhaps, *individuum est ineffabile*, we tend to form various sorts of "images" of other persons we are dealing with. We may, for instance, perceive them in terms of rather unreflected stereotypes ("working class—say no more!"), or we may, perhaps based on previous experience, get a robust impression of particular character traits ("this guy is a sycophant") (see Schmitz 2015, p. 219; Løgstrup, 1997, p. 12). In all these cases, we seem to attempt to make sense of the other person in terms of categories we are already familiar with. Levinas, more often than not resorting to hyperbolic discourse, calls this tendency "the reduction of the other to the same," or even the "suppression or possession of the other" (Levinas 1969, p. 45 f.).

The excess phenomenon, however, is supposed to trump this tendency:

> The way in which the other presents himself, exceeding the idea of the other in me, we here name face. This mode does not consist in figuring as a theme under my gaze, in spreading itself forth as a set of qualities forming an image. The face of the Other at each moment destroys and overflows the plastic image it leaves me, the idea existing to my own measure and to the measure of its ideatum—the adequate idea. (Levinas 1969, p. 50 f.)

The face of the other person, in this sense, is not their physiognomy or the spot where there are eyes, nose, and mouth, but a particular mode in which the other person appears so that they constantly escape the categories in terms of which the perceiver tries to make sense of them. To be sure, this is not supposed to mean that the perceiver would or even could stop perceiving the other person *as*. . . . Rather, the idea is that the perception of the other is accompanied by a sense that the other is *more than* or *irreducible to* the image formed of them:

> the actual presence of the other person leaves no room for a mere picture. His or her presence and my picture of him or her are irreconcilable. They exclude each other, and it is the picture that must give way. (Løgstrup 1997, p. 13)

According to Løgstrup and Levinas, this mode of appearance is supposed to be the natural ground of human interaction in a normative sense. From a descriptive point of view, however, it is often overridden by other dynamics or even unavailable under certain circumstances. I shall touch on some of those dynamics at the end of this chapter; for now, it may suffice to indicate that the excess phenomenon belongs to situations in which both persons are mutually involved with one another rather than, for instance, those situations in which one is a third-personal observer of the other. This is what Levinas (1969) suggests by saying that this mode of appearance is not connected with any "thematization" of the other person—which would be due to the detached onlooker—but with "conversation" (p. 51) which designates a "face-to-face" contact with the other (p. 39). Løgstrup, in turn, calls this the "direct association" or the personal encounter with the other person (Løgstrup 1997, p. 13).

Such direct encounters with the other person, Levinas argues, involve the sense that there is constantly something that outstrips, frustrates, or even resists the subject's anticipations of how the other will react. The face "teaches its very novelty" (Levinas 1969, p. 66) and exercises a power that feeds from the "unforeseeableness" of the other's reactions (p. 199). Løgstrup highlights the same aspect from a different angle by indicating a natural and spontaneous inclination to take the other person's expression as something new rather than as something that is a deterministic consequence of one of their earlier states (Løgstrup 1997, p. 13).

Both Levinas and Løgstrup also emphasize that the subject needs to adopt—or, because of its supposed naturalness, rather *remain in*—a particular *attitude* toward the other person in order to be sensitive to the excess phenomenon. That attitude is by tendency sympathetic to the other person, although not in any stronger sense of sympathy. Perhaps, it is best described as some kind of openness. In the direct encounter, the subject is supposed to let themself in for the other; this is "fundamental trust" in Løgstrup (1997, p. 9 ff.) and "welcoming of the Other" in Levinas (1969, p. 66). Løgstrup regards that attitude as a rather natural and fundamental one. According to him, most of us would find it difficult to leave behind that attitude unless there are indications that the other person is not to be trusted. Levinas, in contrast, who sometimes additionally links that open attitude with a particular kindness toward the other, presents it as a glorious achievement connected with a spectacular breakdown of the subject's egoism. Nevertheless, both would agree that this attitude is, at least in normative respects, more fundamental than attitudes in which the subject reduces the other person to a set of features, dispositions and reactions.

Although the open attitude is relevant to the excess phenomenon, the latter is not simply an effect of the former. Such a claim would ultimately amount to an account, according to which one could receive from the other only what one oneself has simulated and projected onto them (see Zahavi 2014, p. 112 ff.). This is certainly not compatible with Levinas's account of "exteriority," the point of which is precisely that the other is supposed to be irreducible to the subject's knowledge. Rather, the open attitude should be regarded as the right kind of sensitivity and awareness to the excess phenomenon. The attitude is the right kind of sensitivity in a similar way as a wine connoisseur is able to discern particular flavors that are *really there*, although not everyone is sensitive to them (see Zahavi 2014, p. 164). The subject's attitude is not supposed to be the cause for the "overflowing" of their categories to occur but a way for the subject to be aware of it. In this sense, the open attitude is veridical and the excess phenomenon is some sort of "warrant" for it: Experiencing the excess phenomenon makes it meaningful and sensible to adopt or to keep up that attitude, for without the relevant phenomenon the open attitude would be pointless.

MUTUAL BODILY RESPONSIVENESS AS PART OF THE EXCESS PHENOMENON

Although neither Løgstrup nor Levinas analyze it in more detail, the face-to-face interaction with one another involves a powerful dynamic that resonates in the feeling body.[2] The relevant dynamic goes under various names in phenomenological and pragmatist accounts, for instance "mutual incorporation" (Schmitz, 1980, p. 23 ff.; Fuchs & De Jaegher, 2009; Nörenberg, 2018) or "participatory sense-making" (De Jaegher & Di Paolo, 2007). The dynamic is characterized by an oscillation of dominance or activity and devouredness or receptivity between both participants, and it unfolds in terms of bodily felt instances of tension and relaxation and the concomitant shift of motor-intentional foci:

> In short intervals, the partners of mutual incorporation pass the dominance to one another like a ball. In this play, the exchange of glances, for instance in a conversation, is an important conveyer. The one who speaks in the presence of the other tends to look at him and to try to make eye contact—not primarily in order to control the effect of his words, but to catch on with his partner in a manner palpable to both of them. Until now the incorporation pertaining to the conversation is dominated by the one addressed as he is decisive with regard to the attempt to catch on. A slight signal of acceptance—not with regard to the content of the speech, but with regard to the bodily palpable way in which the speaker turns toward him—gives the dominance to the speaker, and henceforth the dominance oscillates within the incorporation in a manner hardly noticeable during the conversation. (Schmitz, 2011, p. 40 f.; my transl.)

The dynamic described here unfolds "below" what the participants are thematically aware of (they are usually focused on the topics of the conversation); it is unthematically sensed in the exchange of glances, the tone, the prosody, the gestures, the way in which one "hangs" on the other's word, and so on. The dynamic, however, does not presuppose anything like an ideal dialogue in which both participants would share equal partial amounts of the dominant and the receptive role. Harmony in this sense is not required. Rather, the point is that a palpable sense of mutual connectedness and response is constituted. However, even theorists of mutual incorporation acknowledge the relevance of an open attitude, in terms of which the subject lets themself in for the other person.[3]

In contrast, Levinas's account seems to amount to the subject's fascination for the "epiphany of the face" (Levinas 1969, p. 51)—a textbook example of "unilateral incorporation" where there is no such oscillation (see Fuchs & De Jaegher, 2009, p. 473 f.; Schmitz, 2011, p. 39 f.). Because Levinas tends to reflect the excess phenomenon against the background of that fascination, he leaves open the question whether and to what extent the "unforeseeableness" and irreducibility of the other might also be grounded in the dynamic of mutual incorporation.

On many occasions, Løgstrup touches on this dynamic in his analysis of the primordial attitude of trust in which his reflections on the excess phenomenon are embedded. To trust is, according to Løgstrup (1997), to come forward in the hope of being accepted by the other (p. 9 ff.), and he briefly indicates the complex and precarious affective dynamic that arises from mutual invitations to respond, anticipations of such responses and, of course, also from frustrations regarding those anticipations. Moreover, he offers valuable analyses of the ways in which such invitations, anticipation, claims, and demands are subtly and, by and large, even unthematically expressed and negotiated in the tones and gestures in which both persons address and respond to one another. He also clearly states that the dynamic unfolds and resonates in the feeling body, for our part in it can contribute to making the other person's world "large or small, bright or drab, rich or dull, threatening or secure" (Løgstrup, 1997, p. 18). Even Løgstrup's original description of the phenomenon of trust—the subject literally ventures forth in order to be met by the other (*at vove sig frem for at blive imødekommet*; Løgstrup 2010, p. 19)—suggests the centrality of mutual incorporation.

Thus, Løgstrup certainly pays more attention to the mutuality in the encounter between the subject and the other person than Levinas does. The latter abstracts nearly entirely from the mutual dynamic. One could say that Levinas has frozen a particular interval in that dynamic and is only paying attention to the overwhelming effect that the other has on the subject. In contrast, Løgstrup is much more aware of the mutual dynamic and even much more willing to include the notion of reciprocity in his overall ethical project. This is, by the way, why I think that his approach is ultimately superior to that of Levinas. Nevertheless, precisely when he attempts to elucidate the excess phenomenon, Løgstrup tends to focus on the unilateral effect that the other person has on the subject:

> To associate with or encounter personally another person always means to be "in the power of" his or her words and conduct. Psychology refers to this as the power of suggestion. There are many degrees of suggestion. It may be very weak, only strong enough to understand what the other person says and does, or it may be so strong that we are, as we say, grasped, or captured or devoured. (Løgstrup 1997, p. 13)

This, too, describes rather a freeze of a particular interval in the subtle oscillation between dominance and receptivity. In contrast, one could argue that the dynamic of mutual incorporation is central to the excess phenomenon. It contributes to the subject's pre-predicative awareness of being in contact with another "lived body," a conscious subject (the so-called "Thou-orientation") or even a person (see Schutz, 1967, p. 164; Husserl 1973, pp. 66, 70, 435 f.; Schmitz, 2011, p. 41; Zahavi 2014, pp. 138, 143). Husserl's famous example of momentarily mistaking a mannequin for a human person (Husserl 1973, p. 92) can illustrate this: The "halo" of kinesthetically felt possibilities for interaction afforded by the object in question "which gave the sense 'human body'" (Ibid.) in the first place vanishes as mutual incorporation cannot be established and the oscillation is lacking. Thus, the sense of having to do with a lifeless mannequin is formed. This gives us a first indication that there is more to the sense of the presence of an irreducible other than what could be explicated from the snapshot of unilateral fascination for or being in the power of them:

> It could be argued that the second-person perspective involves a relation between you and me, where the unique feature of relating to you is that you also have a second-person perspective on me, that is, you take me as your you. (Zahavi 2014, p. 246)

An example more recent than Husserl's which also reflects an encounter in which the relevant phenomenon is conspicuously absent or at least diminished can be found in the descriptions of particular interview situations.[4] Those situations are retrospectively described by the interviewers in terms of a "cool distance" between them and the relevant interviewee, as if there was something "rigid" and "dead." The very interviewees, in turn, were described as remaining "withdrawn," "uninvolved," as if they were "not really there," and proving to be a "hard nut to crack" even for experienced interviewers. These descriptions point to a certain type of communication problem that also seems to involve a bodily dimension since they refer to specific experiential qualities (e.g., rigid, dead, withdrawn, etc.) of which we are primarily aware in terms of bodily feeling (see Nörenberg 2022). In the context of our current discussion, we could conceive of the bodily dimension of the relevant communication problem in terms of absence—or at least depletion—of there being two participants continuously oscillating between activity and receptivity. This at least contributes to (if it does not fundamentally constitute) the rigid or dead character of the communication in question.

Regarding the depletion of continuous oscillation, the reported scenario seems closer to unidirectional than to genuine mutual incorporation: It is by and large the interviewer clinging on the few words of the relevant interviewee—who, on their part, do not return this favor and seem to be somehow absent from the conversation ("not really there"). To be sure, the mutuality is not completely lacking here, for otherwise this would hardly count as a conversation at all. However, the rigidity that is supposed to characterize the (non-)responsiveness of the other is quite far from the dynamic of mutual incorporation. The lack of mutual responsiveness seems to be a central factor in what the interviewers reflect as a hard nut to crack.[5] To be sure, in contrast to Husserl's example, the interviewers are in no doubt about whether they are actually facing a real person, but there is not too much that would lend itself to "overflowing" or even "destroying" the image of the other person that is formed during the interview. Like empathy, the excess phenomenon comes in many different layers. And, at least part of the phenomenon seems to involve the subject's sense of the other's responsiveness to the subject's initiatives.[6]

THE EXCESS PHENOMENON AND THE ETHICAL DEMAND

The excess phenomenon has meta-ethical significance. To put it in a rather recent terminology, the presence of the other person is supposed to exercise "deontic power" over the subject, that is, it gives the subject *reasons for action* that are *independent from what they desire* (Searle, 2010, p. 123). In the terminology of Løgstrup and Levinas, the encounter with the other person imposes a demand on the subject, a demand to take care of the other that can thwart the subject's egoism (Løgstrup, 1997, pp. 17 f., 20 ff.; Levinas, 1969, pp. 50, 197). The demand implies that the subject ought to adopt a nonviolent attitude toward the other person and act in their favor. Both Løgstrup and Levinas argue that the demand in question is the fundamental ethical phenomenon in which more specific "deontic powers," such as moral norms, conventions of courtesy, and so on are grounded (Løgstrup, 1997, p. 19 f.; Levinas, 1981, p. 185; see Nörenberg 2020, p. 201).

In Levinas's account, the demand seems straightforwardly implied in the excess phenomenon in terms of which the other is experienced:

> [H]e can oppose to me a struggle, that is, oppose to the force that strikes him not a force of resistance, but the very *unforeseeableness* of his reaction. He thus opposes to me no greater force, an energy assessable and consequently presenting itself as though it were part of a whole, but the very transcendence of his being by relation to that whole; not some superlative of power, but precisely the infinity of his transcendence. This infinity, stronger than murder, already resists us in his face, is his face, is the primordial *expression*, is the first word: "you shall not commit murder." The infinite paralyses power by its infinite resistance to murder, which, firm and insurmountable, gleams in the face of the Other, in the total nudity of his defenceless eyes, in the nudity of the absolute openness of the Transcendent. There is here a relation not with a great resistance, but with

> something absolutely *other*: the resistance of what has no resistance—the ethical resistance. (Levinas 1969, p. 199)

According to this account, the ethical demand ("you shall not kill") is supposed to emerge from the "unforeseeableness" of the other person's reaction, from the other's "transcendence" and "infinity," all of which are references to the excess phenomenon.

However, I think this account is a bit premature. One could argue that the excess phenomenon is a necessary condition for the subject to experience the relevant demand. But it is certainly not sufficient because the experience of the demand entails another aspect that is not covered by the excess phenomenon. Levinas occasionally addresses this aspect, but it is even clearer explicated by Løgstrup:

> Through the trust which a person either shows or asks of another person he or she surrenders something of his or her life to that person. Therefore, our existence demands of us that we protect the life of the person who has placed his or her trust in us. . . . Regardless of how varied the communication between persons may be, it always involves the risk of one person daring to lay him or herself open to the other in the hope of a response. This is the essence of communication and it's the fundamental phenomenon of ethical life. (Løgstrup 1997, p. 17 f.)

The demand is grounded in the exposure that is inseparable from human contact. Exposing oneself (i.e. "venturing forth") means that, to some extent, one is at the mercy of the other person, and vice versa. We have seen how this exposure is already embodied in one's attempt to catch on with the other person who then, according to the bodily dynamic, *nolens volens* finds themself in the dominant role. It is the palpable sense of assuming the dominant role on which the demand to take care for the person addressing oneself is based.

Levinas, too, is aware of this aspect. In his hyperbolical way, he refers to it whenever he presents the other person as having fallen victim to the subject who, in turn, is supposed to feel shame:

> The invisible offense . . . is produced as judgment itself when it looks at me and accuses me in the face of the Other—whose very epiphany is brought about by this offense suffered, by this status of being a stranger, widow, and orphan. (Levinas 1969, p. 244)

Thus, although Levinas often seems to suggest that the sense of the other's exposure coincides with the sense that the other "overflows" any category (see Levinas 1969, pp. 50, 87, 197, 199), he might still agree with Løgstrup that the aspect of exposure is relevant for grounding the ethical demand.

As we have seen earlier, both exposure and excess are part of the dynamic of mutual bodily resonance. Although both aspects are closely related, we should distinguish them. The roles of exposure and dominance oscillate between the participants of the encounter. It is the dominant role in the mutual relationship in terms of which the relevant participant is sensitive to the demand regarding the other person, but it is the oscillation and mutual responsiveness that underpins the excess phenomenon. And, arguably, not even any sense of being in the dominant role is sufficient for the subject's recognition of the demand. This seems to emerge from the, admittedly, extreme example of sadism. The sadist seems to have a sense of dominance and also a sense of being responded to by another conscious, sentient being (excess phenomenon), but this does not necessarily go hand in hand with a sense of there being any demand for taking care of the other. In this sense, the excess phenomenon is *no sufficient* condition for experiencing the ethical demand.

THE EXCESS PHENOMENON AND THE WARRANT OF "REACTIVE ATTITUDES"

However, the excess phenomenon at the heart of the thou-orientation seems to be a *necessary* condition for being sensitive to the ethical demand. If it is correct that the experience of the excess phenomenon makes it sensible to adopt or to keep up an open attitude towards other persons, then it is, as I will now try to show, a relevant factor in the stability and warrant of our practices of holding each other responsible, e.g., by praising or blaming.

Strawson (1962, p. 195 ff.), Helm (2017), and many others argue that our practices of holding each other responsible are grounded in particular patterns of ethically relevant emotional responses ("reactive attitudes") such as resentment, gratitude, indignation, approbation, guilt, etc. We might as well add Levinasian shame to the list (see Nörenberg 2020, p. 197 ff.). In the absence of any of such patterns, no metaphysical proof of the freedom of choice could convince us of holding ourselves, or others, responsible for what we or they have done. In turn, given the relevant patterns of emotional responses, no metaphysical proof of determinism could make us give up holding each other responsible.[7] This is, of course, not to rule out that our more theoretical considerations or changes in our culture could modify the patterns of those emotions. In a manner similar to what has been called "emotional regulation" (Gross, 1998), theories and cultural changes may be among the factors that determine under which circumstances the relevant emotions occur. For instance, these factors may shift the appropriate focus of our indignation from, say, premarital sex to racist behavior. They may even shift the appropriate target of our indignation from an outrageously ignorant teenager to the persons responsible for that teenager's development.[8] However, despite those shifts, whenever we actually experience indignation as appropriate ("righteous anger"), we hold a particular person responsible for not living up to a norm we regard as binding for us and them (see Helm, 2017, p. 14). This is what indignation is about. Likewise, the circumstances under which the other ethically relevant emotions such as gratitude or guilt occur may change over time, from culture to culture, or because of morally relevant considerations. Nevertheless, they ground our understanding of moral responsibility.

One of the central points in the argument made by Strawson and many others is that our capacity to experience such ethically relevant emotions presupposes that we adopt or keep up something like that open attitude toward those who are the appropriate target of the respective emotion. Strawson calls this the "participatory" attitude and contrasts this with the "objective" attitude:

> To adopt the objective attitude to another human being is to see him, perhaps, as an object of social policy; as a subject for what, in a wide range of sense, might be called treatment; as something certainly to be taken account, perhaps precautionary account, of; to be managed or handled or cured or trained; perhaps simply to be avoided, though this gerundive is not peculiar to cases of objectivity of attitude. (Strawson, 1962, p. 194)

According to Strawson, the objective attitude toward others allows them to become the target of emotions such as repulsion, pity, or fear. However, it excludes that those others can become the target of emotions more relevant to our practices of holding each other responsible, such as gratitude, resentment, approbation, or indignation. You may be able to talk to those others, but you cannot reason, nor even quarrel with them (Strawson, 1962, p. 195). By tendency, the objective attitude implies that kind of categorization that "reduces" the other to a set of preconceived notions one has of them or grasps them in terms of a few character dispositions (e.g., orderliness, parsimoniousness, stubbornness)[9] that predict their reactions in particular situations. In other words, it implies precisely what can only occur *in absence, ignorance or suppression of the excess phenomenon*, if Løgstrup and Levinas are on the right track.

In turn, the other person can be a proper target of ethically relevant emotions only in connection with the participatory attitude. That is, the participatory attitude is involved in, for instance, one's feelings of shame or guilt about having wronged another person. It is also involved in resenting the other person for a particular offense. What is more, this account implies that perceiving a particular state of affairs in terms of ethical evaluation (e.g., as something to take *offense* at or something that *wrongs* somebody) also requires recognizing the relevant person in terms of the participant attitude.

Whomever you perceive in the objective attitude may be able to harm you and also be harmed by you. But you cannot perceive them as offending nor as someone wronged by you in any ethically stricter sense. The participatory attitude, in contrast, implies that the relevant states of affairs are perceived as ethically relevant, because they are, among other things, perceived in the light of the "inter-personal human relationship" (Strawson, 1962, p. 194; see Helm, 2017, p. 10) between you and the other. This relationship is supposed to ground the standing of both participants as their moral status, their authority to hold each other responsible. Thus, insofar as the excess phenomenon "warrants" the participatory attitude, it underpins the moral considerableness of a person and, in connection with it, the perception of ethically relevant states of affairs. In this sense, the excess phenomenon is a necessary factor in being sensitive to ethical normativity.

SECOND-PERSONAL AUTHORITY

The excess phenomenon is not sufficient for grounding a person's moral authority. Helm plausibly argues that the rational connections between the ethically relevant responses constitute an equally relevant factor (2017, p. 11 f.). The authority of the participants to hold each other responsible involves a communal element, because it refers to particular norms both participants are committed to (Ibid., p. 13 ff.). However, there is a tension between the communal element of authority and a more second-personal source of that authority which is not sufficiently addressed by Helm.

According to Helm, one's authority to hold another person responsible has its source in one's membership in the community defined by particular rational patterns of ethically relevant responses (2017, p. 14). For instance, the demand to return your neighbors' purse you found on the pavement is intelligible only if other persons such as your neighbor have the authority to hold you responsible for not returning it. And, in simplified terms, they have the authority in question if your failure to return the purse would elicit reactive attitudes, namely resentment in your neighbor, feelings of regret in yourself, and indignation in those who witness the scene (see Ibid., p. 17 f.). That this pattern is intersubjectively projectable is supposed to mean that the same pattern would be elicited if the roles are reversed, for instance if your neighbor found your purse and would feel guilty for having failed to return it to you, while you would resent him for his failure, and so on. (see Ibid., p. 65 f.). According to Helm, it is neither the reactive attitudes themselves nor their intersubjective structure in a particular instance but, rather, the consistency of those intersubjectively projectable patterns, which warrants our authority to hold each other accountable to certain norms. Such patterns constitute a form of import to which we respond affectively (Ibid., 70). The import in question coincides with what we implicitly care for as a life worth living (Ibid., 73 f.).

However, even though Helm seems to correctly point out the relevance of that factor in his critical assessment of Darwall's position,[10] his glossing over the relevance of the second-person standpoint seems a bit premature. To be sure, the commitment to communal norms is a highly relevant factor in a person's moral authority. However, Helm's account underexposes a particular power that seems to be inherent in second-personal authority and irreducible to anybody's commitment to communal norms. Helm's account seems to imply that both the victim of a particular offense and the witness have the same authority to hold the offender responsible because in both cases their authority is warranted by their affectively constituted commitment to those norms that make the incident intelligible as an offense. Now think of the following example: A professor suggests that there is no need to prohibit particular Halloween costumes because the students on the campus seem mature enough to take responsible decisions and are capable of addressing and negotiating their concerns themselves.[11] The emotional response of a considerable group of students of color suggests that these students perceive this suggestion as an outrageously racist remark. Let us assume, for the sake of the argument, that you—in the role of a witness—found another student of color who has read that professor's suggestion carefully and sincerely negates the question of whether they have been offended by that email. You may exchange a couple of arguments on that topic with them. After a while, you get the impression that this student has carefully reflected on the matter and even understands your point, but nevertheless arrives at the conclusion that they have not been offended by that professor. Is there not something in the student's sincere negation that would incline you to stop trying to convince them of the idea that they actually have been offended (regardless of what you yourself may think of the matter)?

Løgstrup (1997, p. 21 ff.) suggests that there is. He argues that the demand that urges us to take care of the other person simultaneously "forbids that we ever attempt, even for his or her own sake, to rob him or her of his or her independence" (Ibid., p. 26), for example, by trying to convince the other of something they firmly reject. "Independence" or "individuality"—Løgstrup uses the latter term in another passage dealing with the same topic—once more refers to the sense that there is something in the other person that cannot be captured in or subsumed under the categories that the subject is so familiar with. If Løgstrup is right and the example just given is plausible, the excess phenomenon grounds a genuine second-personal authority that cannot simply be reduced to communal norms. It cannot because that very authority is involved in negotiating and, potentially, also in determining, whether and to what extent a particular communal norm applies and is violated here and now. This aspect remains underexposed in Helm's account.

DEHUMANIZATION AS INSENSITIVITY TO THE EXCESS PHENOMENON

The previous argument suggested that the excess phenomenon grounds an irreducible second-personal authority. This view, however, must be reconciled with the fact that a complex of communal norms can, and often does, moderate or diminish the subject's sensitivity to the excess phenomenon emerging in the encounter with the other. Here we are back at the problem of categorization. Just as a person sufficiently committed to the norms of forest management may tend to perceive trees in different terms than, for instance, woodland strollers, the subject's membership in particular groups and commitment to the relevant communal norms may influence their perception of other people. For instance, a great variety of empirical research provides evidence that cultural or racial in-group and out-group biases influence the subject's capacity to empathize with others (e.g., Xu et al., 2009) or their selection of partners for social interaction (e.g., Burns & Sommerville, 2014). In some cases, out-group biases can even imply more subtle or more explicit forms of dehumanization (Haslam, 2006).

To be sure, a great deal of empirical studies contributing to the field are designed in such a way that the participants do not encounter the other in the manner described in this chapter, but are more like detached onlookers responding to pre-recorded faces, scenes they witness, and so on. Nevertheless, it seems plausible to assume that particular ways of categorizing that are implicated in one's commitment to the norms valid in one's community can sediment and frame the attitude toward nonmembers of that community. In such cases, a decreased sensitivity to the excess phenomenon is a possible effect of that framing. Haslam's study on dehumanization suggests that the humanness of others that is denied in some cases involves a sense of the other's vital agency, emotionality and cognitive flexibility (2006, p. 257). Where this sense is absent, the descriptions resemble those pertaining to expected, but frustrated mutual incorporation: The other is perceived as "lacking in motionality, warmth, cognitive openness, individual agency, and . . . depth," as "rigid," as "inert and cold," as "interchangeable (fungible) and passive," as "object- or automaton-like" (Ibid., p. 258). Their behavior appears as being "caused rather than propelled by personal will" (Ibid.). What is more, there are indications that the bodily resonance with the other is indeed decreased in such cases (e.g., Likowski et al., 2008). As Gallagher and Varga put it: "We are simply less responsive to out-group members and display significantly less motor cortex activity when observing out-group members" (2014, p. 194). From an enactive point of view, this finding is best explained in terms of perceptual practices and skills rather than additional inferences: "one is not trained to make bad inferences; one is conditioned to directly perceive others as non-person" (Ibid., 196). In this sense, and pretty much in line with my previous interpretation of Løgstrup and Levinas, the open attitude is a perceptual skill (a sensitivity to the excess phenomenon) that on certain conditions is not used by or not available to the subject.

As the discussion on dehumanization suggests, in-group and out-group distinction is one of the conditions on which the subject is less sensitive to the excess phenomenon. That is, a sense of the other person as not belonging to one's own kind can interfere with or even block one's sense for the transcendence and second-personal authority of the other. From this point of view, Helm (2017, p. 17 ff.) seems to be on the right track when he insists that the other person's authority to hold the subject responsible is also linked with their mutually recognized membership in a community committed to a complex of shared norms and practices. However, as we have seen, we should conceive neither of membership nor of community in a too static or exclusive manner. The relevant normative content to which the members of a particular community are committed may indeed modify the members' sensitivity to the excess phenomenon in out-group members that, in turn, underpins the moral authority of the latter. That is, although the other's second-personal authority is not entirely dependent on our recognition of them as "one of us," it may be diminished where the other is perceived as being "none of us."

CONCLUSION

In this chapter, I have suggested a phenomenological analysis of our sense of dealing with another conscious being or a person. Drawing on insights articulated by Løgstrup (1997) and Levinas (1969), I have labeled the relevant sense as the excess phenomenon because one of its most conspicuous traits is the subjective sense that the other person transcends one's attempts to reduce them to a set of categories or to exactly anticipate their behavior. The general capacity to reduce complex situations to categories is a relevant factor in human evolution, but especially in face-to-face encounters, we may notice repeatedly that the other person exceeds our categories. This is the core of the excess phenomenon.

I have also pointed out that the excess phenomenon is related to a particular attitude of openness toward the other person and argued in which sense the attitude may be warranted by the phenomenon in question. Furthermore, I have suggested in which way the excess phenomenon might be underpinned by a bodily dynamic called mutual incorporation.

In another step, I have sketched what I take to be the ethical significance of the excess phenomenon and suggested a number of philosophical distinctions. I have argued that the relevant phenomenon is not sufficient for grounding what Løgstrup and Levinas call the ethical demand emerging in the relationship with the other person. It is not, because the excess is conceptually distinct from the aspect of exposure, and the latter is a relevant factor in the account of the ethical demand, too.

Nevertheless, it seems that the excess phenomenon is a necessary condition for the other person's authority to hold the subject responsible. I have argued that the phenomenon in question is a kind of warrant for what Strawson (1962) and many others call the participatory attitude. This attitude, in turn, is a condition of possibility for the complex web of ethically relevant emotions (reactive attitudes), in which our practices of holding each other responsible with regard to communal norms are ultimately grounded.

As a contribution to clarifying the role of the communal norms in the recognition of the other person's authority, I have argued that the excess phenomenon underpins a peculiar second-personal authority. That is, the other person's moral authority cannot be reduced to the fact that both the subject and the other person are jointly committed to a particular set of norms. It is genuinely second-personal in that it is an element irreducible to membership in any particular community of mutual respect, as it is involved in the negotiation and determination of what "our" moral norms are, how they are appropriately applied, and so on. Membership in a particular community and the commitment to that community's moral norms, however, may have an influence on the subject's sensitivity to the excess phenomenon in other persons who are perceived as nonmembers. This influence is most conspicuous in particular forms of dehumanization that seem to function as a suppression of the excess phenomenon.

NOTES

1. Dewey (1931, p. 94 ff.), for instance, argues that any existential proposition such as, for instance, "the native American was stoical" or "the stone is shaly" ultimately refers to what he calls a particular pervasive quality against the backdrop of which single objects alone and their attributes such as "native American," "stone," "stoical," or "shaly" can make sense. Such pervasive qualities holistically define the scope and context—the "situation"—by the implicit clues of which any thought, insofar as it is methodic and distinct from the lose association of ideas, is oriented or even guided ("controlled"). Schmitz (2019, p. 73) conceives of what Dewey intends by pervasive

single qualities as situations and defines them as holistic, internally diffuse syntheses of meanings consisting of "states of affairs (that something is the case), programs (that something ought to / should be the case [as a norm or as a desire]) or problems (whether something is)."

2. The feeling body is a phenomenological concept that is supposed to capture the subjective access to feelings such as pressure, tension, relaxation, swell, tightening, etc. It is to be distinguished from a third-personal perspective on one's own body such as the perspective of a physician.

3. "Whoever does not let themself be touched [by the other], whoever inflexibly sticks to their countenance, looks past the other" (Schmitz, 2011, p. 46; my transl.).

4. See Großheim, et al., 2014, p. 15; Nörenberg 2021a, p. 6 f. The relevant interviews were conducted in the context of the research project "Sense of Life and Politics in Mecklenburg-Western-Pomerania." The original focus of this project was on a connection between a region-typical "sense of life," that is, a specific way of finding oneself in the world, and regionally predominant political attitudes. In the present context, however, the focus is on the observations concerning the non-verbal interactions between the interviewees and the interviewers.

5. Caveat: Of course, by profession, the interviewers cannot afford to adopt an unambiguous attitude of sympathetic trust toward their relevant interviewees. However, a specific openness to the "novelty" and "unforeseenableness" of the other person must be part of their professional attitude if qualitative research is to have any value (see Brinkmann & Kvale, 2015, p. 193 ff.).

6. In many respects, this idea is parallel to Ratcliffe's attempt to reframe empathy as mutual empathy: "I propose that we think of 'empathy' principally as 'mutual empathy,' as a progressively sophisticated experience of mutual understanding that develops through certain forms of interaction" (Ratcliffe 2014, 277).

7. For a possible gap in the argument—and a proposal to fill it—see Schmitz, 2007, chap. 4 and 7; Nörenberg 2021b.

8. Both notions "focus" and "target" of an emotion are carefully defined in Helm (2001, p. 68 f.).

9. This is how Abraham (1923, p. 27) summarizes Freud's diagnosis of "anal retentiveness."

10. Darwall insists that the ethical demand (e.g., for not being hurt) is not only grounded in agent-neutral reasons (e.g., the duty to reduce pain as a bad state of the world) but also in the relevant persons authority to address that demand to another person (second-personal authority) (see Darwall, 2004, p. 45 ff.; 2006, 247). Helm (2017, p. 17 ff.), in turn, argues that Darwall's account must eventually concede that the relevant authority is grounded in membership in and commitment to a particular community with their respective norms.

11. See Lukianoff & Haidt, 2018, p. 55 ff.

REFERENCES

Abraham, K. (1923). Ergänzungen zur Lehre vom Analcharakter. *Internationale Zeitschrift für Psychoanalyse* 9(1), 27–47.

Brinkmann, S., & Kvale, S. (2015). *InterViews: Learning the Craft of Qualitative Research Interviewing*. Sage.

Burns, M. P., & Sommerville, J.A. (2014). "I Pick You": The Impact of Fairness and Race on Infants' Selection of Social Partners. *Frontiers in Psychology*. DOI: 10.3389/fpsyg.2014.00093

Darwall, S. L. (2004). Respect and the Second-Person Standpoint. *Proceedings and Addresses of the American Philosophical Association* 78 (2), 43–59.

———. (2006). *The Second-Person Standpoint: Morality, Respect, and Accountability*. Harvard University Press.

De Jaegher, H., & Di Paolo, E. (2007). Participatory Sense-Making: An Enactive Approach to Social Cognition. *Phenomenology and the Cognitive Sciences* 6, 485–507.

Dewey, J. (1931). *Philosophy and Civilization*. G. P. Putnam's Sons.

Fuchs, T., & De Jaegher, H. (2009). Enactive Intersubjectivity: Participatory Sense-Making and Mutual Incorporation. *Phenomenology and the Cognitive Sciences* 8, 465–86.

Gallagher, S., & Varga, S. (2014). Social Constraints on the Direct Perception of Emotions and Intentions. *Topoi* 33(1), 185–91.

Gallagher, S., & Zahavi, D. (2012). *The Phenomenological Mind*. Routledge.

Goldman, A. I. (2005). Imitation, mind reading, and simulation. In S. Hurley & N. Chater (ed.), *Perspectives on Imitation* (vol. 2, pp. 79–94). MIT Press.

Gross, J. J. (1998). The Emerging Field of Emotional Regulation: An Integrative Review. *Review of General Psychology* 2(3), 271–99.

Großheim, M., et al. (2014). Kollektive Lebensgefühle: Zur Phänomenologie von Gemeinschaften. *Rostocker Phänomenologische Manuskripte* 20, 3–77.

Haslam, N. (2006). Dehumanization: An Integrative Review. *Personality and Social Psychology Review* 10(3), 252–64.

Heidegger, M. (2006). *Sein und Zeit*. Niemeyer.

Helm, B. W. (2001). *Emotional Reason: Deliberation, Motivation, and the Nature of Value*. Cambridge University Press.

———. (2017). *Communities of Respect: Grounding Responsibility, Authority, and Dignity.* Oxford University Press.

Husserl, E. (1950) [1931]. *Cartesianische Meditationen und Pariser Vorträge*, ed. S. Strasser (Husserliana 1). Martinus Nijhoff.

———. (1973). *Experience and Judgment: Investigations in a Genealogy of Logic*. Northwestern University Press.

Leslie, A. M. (1987). Children's understanding of the mental world. In R. L. Gregory (ed.), *The Oxford Companion to the Mind* (139–42). Oxford University Press.

Levinas, E. (1969) [1961] *Totality and Infinity: An Essay on Exteriority*, trans. A. Lingis. Martinus Nijhoff.

———. (1981). *Otherwise than Being or beyond Essence*, trans. A. Lingis. Martinus Nijhoff.

Likowski, K. U., et al. (2008). Modulation of facial mimicry by attitudes. *Journal of Experimental Social Psychology* 44(4), 1065–72. https://doi.org/10.1016/j.jesp.2007.10.007

Lukianoff, G., & Haidt, J. (2018). *The Coddling of the American Mind: How Good Intentions and Bad Ideas Are Setting Up a Generation of Failure*. Penguin Books.

Løgstrup. K. E. (1997) [1956]. *The Ethical Demand*, trans. B. Rabjerg & R. Stern. Oxford University Press.

———. (2010). [1956]. *Den Etiske Fordring*. Klim.

Nörenberg, H. (2018). Mutual and Solidary Incorporation as Elementary Forms of Social Cognition. *Synthesis Philosophica* 66, 403–17.

———. (2020). Deontic Power and Bodily Felt Demands. *Phenomenology and the Cognitive Sciences* 19, 191–216.

———. (2022). Leib, Ausdruck und Rolle: Plessner, Schmitz und die Anderen. In A. Bosch et al. (ed.), *Körper—Leib—Sozialität: Philosophische Anthropologie und Leibphänomenologie: Helmuth Plessner und Hermann Schmitz im Dialog*. Springer.

———. (2021a). Deontological Feelings: The Tranquil, the Familiar, and the Body. *Frontiers in Psychology* 12, 1–14. https://doi.org/10.3389/fpsyg.2021.662675

———. (2021b). Operari Sequitur Esse: Hermann Schmitz's Attitudinal Theory of Agency, Freedom, and Responsibility. In C. Erhard & T. Keiling. *The Routledge Handbook of Phenomenology of Agency* (pp. 208–18). Routledge.

Plessner, H. (1982). *Ausdruck und menschliche Natur* (Gesammelte Schriften 7). Suhrkamp.

Ratcliffe, M. (2014). The Phenomenology of Depression and the Nature of Empathy. *Medicine Health Care and Philosophy* 17, 269–80.

Scheler, M. (1973). *Wesen und Formen der Sympathie* (Gesammelte Werke 7). Francke.

Schmitz, H. (1980). *Die Aufhebung der Gegenwart* (System der Philosophie V). Bouvier.

———. (2007). *Freiheit*. Alber.

———. (2011). *Der Leib*. De Gruyter.

———. (2015). *Selbst sein: Über Identität, Subjektivität und Personalität*. Alber.

———. (2019). *New Phenomenology: A Brief Introduction*, trans. R. O. Müllan & M. Bastert. Mimesis International.

Schutz, A. (1967) [1932]. *The Phenomenology of the Social World*, trans. G. Walsh & F. Lehnert. Northwestern University Press.

Searle, J. (2010). *Making the Social World: The Structure of Human Civilization*. Oxford University Press.

Smith, A. D. (2003). *Routledge Philosophy Guidebook to Husserl and the Cartesian Meditations*. Routledge.

Stein, Edith. (1922). Beiträge zur philosophischen Begründung der Psychologie und der Geisteswissenschaften. *Jahrbuch für Philosophie und phänomenologische Forschung* 5, 1–283.

Strawson, P. F. (1962). Freedom and Resentment. *Proceedings of the British Academy*, 48, 187–211.
Uexküll, J. V. (2010). *A Foray into the Worlds of Animals and Humans: With a Theory of Meaning*. University of Minnesota Press.
Xu, X., et al. (2009). Do You Feel My Pain? Racial Group Membership Modulates Empathic Neural Responses. *Journal of Neuroscience* 29 (26), 8525–29.
Zahavi, D. (2014). *Self and Other: Exploring Subjectivity, Empathy, and Shame*. Oxford University Press.

Chapter 10

Tomasello, Husserl, and the Cognitive Foundations of Morality

Stefano Vincini and Andrea Staiti

ABSTRACT

One of the strongest theses in Michael Tomasello's *A Natural History of Human Morality* (2016) is that morality presupposes the constitution of a "we" (i.e., a plural agent). Yet, the precise nature of this plural subject, what exactly the we is, is something that Tomasello wisely leaves open for further philosophical debate. The goal of this chapter is to elucidate Edmund Husserl's contribution to this debate and clarify, from the Husserlian perspective, in what way the plural subject can constitute the basis for morality. A thoroughgoing comparison with Tomasello helps evaluate what can still be considered to be valid in Husserl's view. Accordingly, the present chapter has both an exegetical and a systematic component. For both Husserl and Tomasello, although morality is based on shared intentionality, shared intentionality is founded on affective empathy in its turn. Broadly consistent with Tomasello, Husserl suggests that, in some fundamental cases, the we is the carrier of a communal intention or other kinds of communal mental states. The plural subject coincides with the individuals insofar as they communicate with each other and form a phenomenological unity. The specificity of Husserl's contribution lies in the clarification of how a communal mental state is individuated. This clarification relies on Husserl's own theory of how experiences in general are individuated through a synthesis of distinct components. Husserl's position is thus radically anti-Cartesian because it challenges the assumption that a mental state can have only one individual subject. The chapter also points out that this anti-Cartesian position was common to other early phenomenologists such as Max Scheler and Edith Stein.

Keywords: shared intentionality, anti-Cartesianism, the first-person-plural, collective intentions, early phenomenologists

INTRODUCTION

Michael Tomasello's *A Natural History of Human Morality* (2016) draws on an impressive range of contemporary empirical evidence and traditional philosophical reflection. Tomasello's book provides references to historical figures such as Rousseau, Hume, and Kant, as well as contemporary moral thinkers such as Darwall and Korsgaard. Moreover, because Tomasello assigns a primary role to the cognitive foundations of morality (i.e., what he characterizes as the capacities for shared intentionality), he engages the major figures of the so-called analytic debate on "collective intentionality," that is, Searle, Bratman, Gilbert, and Tuomela. Tomasello liberally draws on their arguments, accommodating them to empirical data and his own psychological intuitions. Tomasello (2016, p. 147, 153, 162–63), however, in no way falls prey to the illusion of having finally solved the problem of the origins of morality; he rather shows awareness of its depth and complexity. On the whole, Tomasello provides a characterization of the natural-historical evolution of our species to which philosophers can easily relate, possibly to offer back insightful ideas from which the cognitive-psychological explanation of morality could then benefit.

One of the strongest theses in Tomasello's book is that morality presupposes the constitution of a "we" (i.e., a joint or plural agent). Roughly, the idea is that a subject can come to have a moral obligation toward another only if she experiences herself as a member of a community with shared values and goals. Yet, what it means to be part of a community that has goals, what it is to be part of a we is something that is systematically investigated in the phenomenological tradition, both by its early and its contemporary exponents. For example, Scheler (1916, 1973) distinguishes different experiences contributing to the constitution of a we and investigates different forms of community corresponding to such experiences. In her meticulous inquiry into the forms of shared intentionality, Stein (1917, 2000) repeatedly discusses the plural subject, and in Husserl (Hua XIV, XV) one can find an equivalent to Tomasello's assertion of the dependency of morality on the we. In our present, Schmid (2009) and Zahavi (2019) locate the first-person-plural at the core of their debate on the phenomenology of sharing. Therefore, it makes sense to look for a philosophical clarification of Tomasello's conception of morality as dependent on the we precisely in this tradition, although Tomasello only shows scant awareness of the value of phenomenology for his line of research. In the present chapter we want to focus on Husserl and assess how Husserl's phenomenology and Tomasello's phylogenetic-ontogenetic psychology may enhance each other with respect to the connection between shared intentionality and morality.

A difficulty that we have to face is that Husserl, like other early phenomenologists, had rather radical views on shared intentionality. The phenomenological approach to shared intentionality challenges usual ways of thinking. It is thus imperative to engage in a close analysis of Husserl's texts to avoid a facile interpretation that would assimilate them to preconceived views. Despite valuable work in this direction (e.g., Caminada 2019; Schimd 2009; Zahavi 2019), we are still far from having sufficiently understood and examined the resources that Husserl and other classical phenomenologists produced in the field of shared intentionality. The goal of this chapter is to elucidate Husserl's view on the plural subject and clarify, from the Husserlian perspective, in what way the plural subject can be said to constitute the basis for morality. Accordingly, the present chapter has both a textual and a systematic component.

The chapter is divided into four sections. The first section summarizes Tomasello's discussion of the relationship between morality and the we. Since several elements of Tomasello's view are present in Husserl's too, this section prepares us to appreciate what can still be considered to be valid in Husserl. It also offers a first clarification of the relationships between morality and empathy, which represents a key topic for a phenomenological (meta) ethics. The next section briefly presents considerations from Scheler and Stein as a first phenomenological option to clarify the notion of the we. This section invites the question as to whether Husserl, too, pursued Stein's and Scheler's path. The third section elucidates Husserl's conception of the we. It examines a relatively underdiscussed manuscript written between 1918 and 1921, which unequivocally expresses the radicality of Husserl's view. It also refers to later texts that confirm the ideas discussed in that manuscript. Finally, the fourth section revisits the relationship between morality and the we, but this time to discuss Husserl's own thoughts on the matter.

TOMASELLO ON MORALITY AND THE WE

The starting point of Tomasello's analysis is the morality* of the last common ancestor between humans and chimpanzees (six million years ago). Such morality* is assumed to be essentially of the same kind as that of contemporary chimpanzees. The asterisk indicates that it is not a morality in the human sense of the term. The human sense implies reason (i.e., it implies recognizing a moral obligation), an "ought," as valid for any peer that would find herself in the given situation. Chimpanzees (and our common ancestor with them) may feel well when another individual feels well, feel bad when the other feels bad, help the other and act prosocially at the cost of sacrificing other impulses, but, in the last analysis, this is nothing more than acting in accord with a psychophysical impulse, in this case a prosocial one. This prosocial impulse is usually called *empathy* in ordinary English, but Tomasello uses the old Humean term: *sympathy*. A morality* of mere empathy has certainly its own dignity, but it ultimately boils down to just following an inclination of one's own, as opposed to following a rule that is recognized to be valid for any partner in the use of reason (Tomasello 2016, pp. 32–34, 39).

Empathy is nonetheless the basis of morality in the specifically human sense. Tomasello argues not only that human morality would be impossible without the empathetic foundations that are found in other primates but also that the capacity for empathy must have increased significantly for humans to end up having the morality they currently have. Following Tomasello, the first process that contributed to such human surplus of empathy—and that we mention here for a reason that will become apparent in the fourth section—is mating via pair bonding (2016, p. 42). Among other things, pair bonding made a male capable of recognizing the ones who, like him, "hung around" the female he was bonded to, and this greater recognition of one's own relatives (in particular, one's offspring) led to being "less indiscriminately aggressive." As this example suggests, humans had to become more empathetic than their ancestors before they could develop a true morality of "intellectual powers" (p. 50). Overall, Tomasello's account does not seem to underestimate the function of empathy.

The "intellectual powers" that brought about morality did so by making "joint action" possible, a kind of action that is carried out by a "we" (Tomasello 2016, p. 40, 50–51, 64–65). As Korsgaard, quoted by Tomasello (2016, p. 40), writes:

> The primal scene of morality is not one in which I do something to you or you do something to me [this is reciprocal helping; chimpanzees can do it too] but one in which *we* do something together. (Our emphasis)

The prototypical example of the kind of action that Tomasello analyzes is stag or antelope hunting. This was a primary means of survival for *homo heidelbergensis* already about 400.000 years ago. This kind of action requires (a) more than one individual participant and (b) defined roles that can be fulfilled by different individuals and are known to all participants, for example, "chasing the antelope" and "waiting ahead to spear it" (Tomasello 2016, p.

54). In an action of this kind, each individual knows not only that achieving the communal goal is beneficial to his or her own existence, but also that each participant, including the self, *ought* to do his or her part (in order for the action to be successful). Hence the moral ought derives, at least in part, from having identified one's own goals with a communal goal:

> The only possible source for a personal sense of "ought" of this genuine kind is my identification with and deference to a larger (even idealized) social body of which I myself am a part. I freely grant authority—legitimate authority—over "me" to the supraindividual entity that is "we," and indeed, I will defer to that "we" to the point that if you rebuke me for nonideal behavior [for not fulfilling my role], I will join you in this rebuke (either overtly or in a personal feeling of guilt), judging that it is indeed deserved. (Tomasello 2016, p. 64)

Furthermore, full-fledged morality requires recognizing the parity among participants: I acknowledge that your protest is legitimate if I do not fulfill my role just like my protest is legitimate if you don't fulfill yours. The attitude by which one expects the other to acknowledge one's legitimate requests is what Stephen Darwall calls the second-person standpoint. This standpoint requires conceiving of the "we," since a subject can meaningfully advance a claim on someone else only if she considers both self and others as part of the community of people who can equally advance their protests when the situation legitimatizes it ("I expect you to address my demand because *we all* accept that this kind of demand is legitimate").

> The standing to make claims and demands on one another as free and rational persons is something to which *we* are *jointly* committed whenever *we* take up the second-person stance. (Darwall, quoted by Tomasello 2016, p. 39; our emphasis).

The cooperation of early humans was a dyadic, small-scale cooperation. Thus, the moral ought appeared, for example, as applicable only to me and my hunting partners. In other words, the "universality" of the morality of reason—which was never just following a prosocial impulse—was initially restricted to the small number of collaborating peers. This universality underwent an extension when humans developed large cultural groups (starting about 150.000 years ago) perceived as large collaborative enterprises (Tomasello 2016, p. 85). At that point, the moral ought became "objective," that is, recognized to be valid for "all members of one's culture," who—in the minds of humans until, unfortunately, not too long ago—coincided with "all human beings" or "all rational beings" (pp. 92–97).[1]

Morality, then, would require a we, be it the we of a small-scale cooperation or the we of "all rational beings." However, Tomasello's statements on the we are somewhat unsatisfactory. For example, what does it mean that, in a joint action, an individual is "both the 'we' . . . and at the same time an individual"? Indeed, as mentioned, Tomasello does not claim to have fully clarified the nature of the we. He explicitly states that the "jointness" of a joint action, or "we-ness," is still an open question "on which reasonable people may disagree" (Tomasello 2014, p. 152) and Rakoczy (2017, p. 409), a prominent developmentalist influenced by Tomasello, characterizes it as "notoriously difficult to spell out." In the last analysis, it would be unfair if we demanded of Tomasello the clarity that philosophers are still unable to provide. Yet, further philosophical scrutiny with the aid of phenomenology may shed further light on this admittedly puzzling matter.

A RADICAL OPTION: THE "WE" IN SCHELER AND STEIN

If we look for more clarity in the phenomenological tradition, it is not possible to neglect the early systematic works on shared intentionality and the we by Max Scheler (1916, 1973) and Edith Stein (1917, 2000). These works were largely written earlier than the Husserlian manuscripts discussed in the third and fourth sections, they were rather comprehensive and well-structured, and were published between 1913 and 1922, which is long before the publication of Husserl's research manuscripts on the same topics. For these reasons, before focusing on Husserl's texts, we shall briefly examine the main features of Scheler's and Stein's notion of the we. In the third section, we shall then test whether a notion of this kind is present in Husserl's too.

To start with, we notice that both Scheler and Stein assigned a key role to emotion sharing, though Scheler (1973, pp. 23–24) called it feeling-together (*Miteinanderfühlen*) and Stein (1917, pp. 16–18) called it feeling-(as-)one (*Einsfühlen*). This centrality of emotion happens to fit our purposes very well because both Tomasello (2019, pp. 54–55) and Husserl (XIV, p. 198, lines 4–8) posit emotion sharing as a basic form of shared intentionality. Stein observed that Scheler stressed two fundamental features of emotion sharing and she endorsed both of them:

1. In emotion sharing, different people have "strictly the selfsame feeling" [*streng dasselbe Gefühl*] (Stein 1917, p. 18). Scheler (1973, p. 249, see especially p. 252) and Stein (1917, pp. 17–18; 2000, pp. 135–136) employ the distinction in Standard German between *derselbe/dieselbe/dasselbe*, which indicates selfsameness, or numerical oneness, and *gleich*, which denotes the mere type-identity between a plurality of things, to emphasize the numerical oneness of the shared emotion.

2. In emotion sharing, the distinct subjects are preserved [*erhalten bleiben*] (Stein 1917, p. 18). This is because each participant has his or own way of experiencing, or individual perspective on, one and the same overarching emotion (Scheler 1973, p. 249; Stein 2000, pp. 135–36). In vain, one will oppose the numerical oneness of the shared emotion to the differentiation of its subjects and the corresponding individual perspectives: Scheler (1973, pp. 23–24) and Stein (1917, pp. 17–18) suggest not just that the two are compatible, but that it is precisely the combination of distinct individual contributions that allows for the constitution of a unitary emotion as shared, as co-owned (Scheler 1973, p. 48, pp. 251–53; Stein 2000, pp. 136–37; Vincini 2021).[2]

Scheler emphasized these two features for distinct but complementary reasons. He stressed the differentiation of individuals and perspectives to counter metaphysical theories that undermined the ultimate ontological autonomy of the individual, reducing it to a mere component of a supra-individual entity (Scheler 1973, p. 75). He emphasized the numerical oneness of the shared emotion to challenge the Cartesian assumption that a mental state can only have one subject (1916, p. 544–45; Schloßberger 2020, p. 79). This assumption postulates that, because the bodies of individuals are separate, so must be the mental states of these individuals, and there cannot be a unitary mental state that spans across separate individuals (Scheler 1973, p. 239). This assumption is certainly still widespread in contemporary philosophy and psychology and, therefore, it is challenging this assumption that makes Scheler and Stein's thought particularly radical.

Stein (2000) went further by applying the general principles identified by Husserl in his theory of inner time consciousness to the clarification of the synthesis of communal experiences (cf. Caminada 2019, p. 349). As most contemporary interpreters of Husserl's theory agree (De Warren 2009; Brough 2011; Zahavi 2011; etc.), the pre-reflective stream of consciousness entails a pre-delineation of temporally extended individuated experiences. This pre-delineation implies that each component of the synthesis represents a distinct perspective on the unitary experience: it is not possible to experience an experience as beginning or ending if the current phase does not contain a reference to the whole of the experience (Brough 2011, p. 34). Some circumstances in which phases or segments of experience are pre-reflectively unified are the following: (i) when they have identical sensory content; (ii) when they have the same intentional object, but the way in which it is presented differs (e.g., the different sides of a perceived thing); (ii) when they manifest the same whole, but shift from the whole to a (non-self-standing) part of the whole; and (iv) when they manifest a complex of (self-standing) objects (e.g., when inspecting a room or an apartment) (Hua XXXVIII, pp. 63–67). These examples point to the idea that phases or segments of an experience—even if not all strictly temporally continuous—are pre-reflectively assigned a certain unity on the basis of a certain overlap (*Deckung*), or similarity, between their structures (intentional object, sensory content, affective quality, etc.) (cf. Hua IX, p. 286; Hua XVII, p. 168).

Stein's original move was to suggest that the same kind of synthesis occurs in the pre-reflective pre-delineation of a unitary shared emotion, where the different components or perspectives are experienced to belong to different individuals. It is a passive associative synthesis occurring in virtue of the similarity between the emotional responses of the different individuals. This synthesis of similar but distinct components is nothing new (*nichts Neues*) because it already occurs for individual experiences (Stein 2000, p. 136). To explain how a unitary shared emotion results from the synthesis of components experienced to belong to different individuals, Stein (2000, p. 137) resorts to the synthesis pre-delineating a unitary individual perceptual experience:

> The relationship of the different partial contents [belonging to different participants] is illuminated by the parallel coalescence of one individual experience. . . . If I come close to an object in the dark and, while steadily keeping it in view, I at first take it to be a crouching man, then an animal, but at last I recognize that it's a milestone, then this altogether continuous experiential series merges into the unity of one perception.

Through this example, Stein emphasizes the considerable differences between the phases pertaining to an individual experience (they correspond to different object categorizations) because she wants to clarify how various responses of different individuals can be synthesized as components of a unitary emotional whole. However, this emphasis is utterly compatible with the acknowledgement (and the investigation) of the constraints of such a synthesis—the crouching man, the animal, and the milestone are relatively similar compared to a totally different object (e.g., a skyscraper) that would be experienced as giving rise to a new experience. Analogously, the examples of emotion sharing discussed by Scheler, Stein, Krebs, and others show that some similarity between the individual responses is needed in order for these to be taken to be part of a whole. When an individual is not sufficiently attuned, has a reaction of opposite valence, emotes in regard to a different target, etc., the individual is often *not* taken to participate in the emotion of the group. Hence Stein (2000, p. 169) suggests that communal experiences are assembled through the same process of association via similarity that functions in individual experiences.

This is not the place for an examination of the phenomenological evidence provided by Scheler and Stein, nor of other arguments that can be elaborated in support of their view (see, however, Vincini 2021). It suffices to say that the force of Scheler and Stein's view of emotion sharing resides in bringing to the fore a question that is often neglected (the question of the pre-delineation of individuated experiences) and in clarifying the nature of shared emotions not by means of some ad hoc principle, but in light of a general process of synthesis concerning all experiences.

For our purposes, what is most important is that Scheler and Stein's view implies a fundamental conception of the we in line with the phenomenological method. This method requires refraining from positing anything that does not belong to the phenomena, or experiences, under reflective examination. Thus, the method excludes positing the (questionable) existence of a subject independent from its experiences. Rather, one talks about a subject only because the shared emotion is given as lived by someone, as belonging to the plurality of individuals that take part in it. The we as the plurality of co-subjects of a unitary emotion is nothing other than the result of the synthesis constituting the emotion, which combines responses undergone by different subjects:

> In place of the individual ego we've got a subject in our case that encompasses a plurality of individual egos. Certainly I the individual ego am filled up with grief. But I feel myself to be not alone with it. Rather, I feel it as *our* grief. . . . *We* are affected by the loss, and *we* grieve over it. (Stein 2000, p. 134)

It is clear that this conception of *the we as the co-subjects of a unitary mental state* contradicts the Cartesian assumption that every mental state can only have one subject.[3] Now, Scheler's challenge did give rise to a certain debate in the German speaking world in the late 1910s and 1920s (Schmid 2009, p. 78), Husserl certainly read Stein's dissertation (Caminada 2019, p. 167), had her treatises on the foundations of the human sciences in hand in May 1920 and eventually accepted to publish them in his *Jahrbuch* in 1922 (Stein 1993, p. 43). Therefore, it is unlikely that Husserl was totally unaware of the radical conception of shared intentionality that was elaborated by these younger phenomenologists he inspired, especially if one considers that Stein engaged in the very Husserlian method of clarification through elucidation of experiential syntheses (Hua IX, p. 286).

Nevertheless, we shall not assume any direct influence of Scheler and Stein on Husserl, but rather consider their radical view on shared intentionality just as a phenomenological option that Husserl may have possibly chosen to pursue in his own thinking. Specifically, then, the next section will address the following question: does Husserl in his manuscripts actually endorse the radical, anti-Cartesian conception of the we as co-subjects of one and the same mental state? We can anticipate one reason to expect the answer to be in the affirmative. Husserl criticized the very same Cartesian assumption that Scheler challenged, the idea that, because the bodies of individuals are separate, their mental states must be separate too and there cannot be a unitary mental state spanning across different individuals (Hua IX, p. 356–57, lines 35–21). Husserl designated this way of thinking as "*Individualpsychologie*" and deemed it incapable to account for genuine shared intentionality (Hua IX, p. 627). Thus, we can expect that Husserl's positive view also converges with Scheler's on this radical point.

HUSSERL'S RADICAL CONCEPTION OF THE "WE"

Husserl did not write a systematic work in the domain of shared intentionality. We thus have to reconstruct his view from his posthumously published research manuscripts. Because we do not have reasons to believe that the "mature" Husserl (say, from 1913 onward) substantially changed his mind with regard to the issue of the anti-Cartesian conception, we can follow for most of our discussion a thematic line of reasoning, referring to earlier or later manuscripts as it best fits the logic of our analysis. Nonetheless, the reference to late texts (written after 1930) remains important because it bears witness to a relative stability in Husserl's position.

Communication and the We

Before addressing the question of the anti-Cartesian conception of the we, in this subsection we should examine Husserl's view of the relationship between the we and communication. In this manner, when we will tackle the question of the anti-Cartesian conception in the next subsection, we will already be familiar with crucial elements of Husserl's view of shared intentionality.

In a late manuscript, Husserl makes the notable claim that reciprocal awareness of the other and her mental states is not sufficient for the second-person perspective; rather, this perspective also requires an act of communication (Zahavi 2019, p. 254). Recall that we observed that the second-person perspective operative in the moral phenomenon goes together with a sense of the we (Darwall/Tomasello). Analogously, Husserl treats the "I-You-Connection" (the second-person perspective) as a "*social unification*" (a we) presupposed in genuine personal-level communities (Hua XV, p. 472; Staiti 2010, pp. 205–11). Thus, in suggesting that the I-You-Connection requires communication, Husserl is proposing that, even at a fundamental level, the we requires an act of communication. Indeed, for Husserl, the etymology signals that the act of communication has precisely the function of engendering a community (Hua XV, p. 473; cf. Hua XIV, p. 199: "communication creates unity").

But what is an act of communication and how does it establish a community? An act of communication is an act aimed at motivating a co-executing (*Mitvollzug*) of a certain intentional act (e.g., thinking that "today is a beautiful day"). The addresser's act targets a completing act in the addressee, the act of taking up (*Aufnehmen*) what is meant in the message. Therefore, a successful, completed act of communication implies an overlap (*Deckung*) between addresser and addressee, of which both are reciprocally aware; for example, each is aware that they both think that it is a beautiful day (Hua XV, p. 476). Communication creates a community in virtue of this overlap; it engenders the we of the people who intentionally refer to the same content or object.

However, it seems that, for Husserl, the relationship between the we and communication is one of co-implication. In other words, Husserl seems not only to say that the we requires communication but also that communication requires the we. The reason could be that communication is experienced as an action that *we* do, a veritable joint action with roles, the addresser and the addressee (cf. Schmid 2014, p. 11):

> In addressing and in taking up the address, the other "I" and "I" come to a first unification. . . . Speaking, listening, and responding, we already form a "we," which is unified and communalized in a particular manner. (Hua XV, p. 476)

> In communication, "we" all come in touch with one another, we build a personal unity of a higher level. (Hua XIV, p. 194)

It should not surprise that Husserl may suggest that communication both creates and presupposes the we. For the we that results from communication is not the same that realizes it, or, better, the former is a modification of the latter: we communicate and, by doing this, we come to be a group of people with a new content or intentional object in common.

In any case, Husserl explains that communication presupposes a common world, that is, a world that is "ours," to which we both intentionally refer and to which each bodily subject with his or her communicative gestures belongs (Hua XIV, pp. 196–97). In this way, Husserl points to another dimension of experienced overlap between subjects: Each is taken to be, in principle, an object of intentional reference for others and the self (i.e., for all).

Let us consider an anecdotal example. When a child belonging to the family of one of the authors was learning to speak, he first used the second personal pronoun (*tu*, the Italian for "you") to refer to himself. He thus first referred to himself with the personal pronoun which he heard others using to refer to him. Presumably, there was communication and overlap already at this level.

The child experienced communication when the other responded; he could not be the subject of the communicative action by himself (although he could play his own part by himself, for example, as the addresser). Furthermore, the child himself and the other family members understood each other to refer to the child with the same pronoun. When the child learned the correct use of personal pronouns, they understood this commonality at another level, the level of using indexical personal pronouns in the same way.[4]

The anecdote also points to another aspect of the interconnection between communication and community discussed by Husserl. Since, for Husserl, a person is a subject that can take herself as an object of consideration (reflection) and can take a practical stance toward herself, her impulses, her actions, etc. (freedom), Husserl (e.g., Hua XIV, p. 175; Staiti 2010, pp. 193–205) insists that a subject becomes a person through communication with others (the child was first the "you" of others). Moreover, considering the foregoing, the idea of a communicative intertwinement (*Verflechtung*) originating one's being as a person does not seem to be an exaggeration (XV, p. 603). Communication engenders the overlap or coincidence (*Deckung*) between subjects, that is, the experienced intentional reference of both self and others through communicative signs to the very same objects or contents, including the self.

A Focus on a Particularly Important Text

We can now start examining texts in which Husserl asserts that a certain kind of we, the plural agent in a strict sense consists in the plurality of co-subjects of a unitary communal mental state. Since the temptation to fit Husserl's view into the mainstream Cartesian conception is strong for the contemporary reader, in this subsection we closely examine a text where Husserl defines his position and identifies the textual elements that forestall a Cartesian misinterpretation. The text is Number 10 of Hua XIV, also known as *Gemeingeist II* (but not to be confused with the homonymous text discussed by Caminada 2019, pp. 217–53). In the next subsection, we will consider other texts that confirm its assertions.

Text Number 10 starts with recalling the context and the ultimate goal of the inquiry (i.e., the phenomenological-ontological foundations of the human sciences). This phenomenological ontology clarifies "the parallel constitution of community-subjects and of community-accomplishments" [*Gemeinschaftsleistungen*] (XIV, p. 192). Since community-subjects are nothing independently of their concrete functioning (cf. XIV, p. 204, lines 4–6; Caminada 2016), Husserl begins precisely with a list of "community-acts." Note that the emphasis is on the plurality of the *kinds* of community-acts:

> Community-acts. Community-evaluations, but, before that, community-presentations and community-convictions, communal practical "to dos" or rather communal decisions, etc. (XIV, p. 192)

Then, to start explaining the idea of a community-conviction, Husserl begins with a paragraph analyzing the conviction of the individual as a group-member (XIV, pp. 192–93). This is analogous to Stein's approach (2000, p. 134; cf. Krebs 2015, p. 144): She first considers the emotion of the individual "as a member of" or "in the name of" the group, where the latter expression does not denote a representative-institutional function, "but merely the relation to the community that is contained in the experience itself." Indeed, for Stein (2000, p. 141, 164), the individual's emotion can be considered as an emotion in itself or as a component of a communal emotion, depending on what one aims at in her or his acts of reflection. Hence, when Husserl analyzes the individuals' convictions, he finds a structure of overlap (*Deckung*) and reciprocity between different individual convictions. However, he concludes the paragraph by suggesting that this does not at all mean that there is no unitary conviction of the community:

> In any case, there is a community-conviction, a community-evaluation, a community-decision, a community-action. (Hua XIV, p. 193)

Note that the reiteration of the singular indefinite article emphasizes the numerical oneness of the communal mental state in contrast to the plurality of the individual states. Indeed, this quote is different from the previous one, where the list had no singular indefinite article and thus emphasizes the plurality of the *kinds* of communal states. This passage is the first indication of Husserl's anti-Cartesian conception. It should prepare us for the more forceful ones that follow.

Husserl continues by examining the phenomenology of a communal action. When the individual wills are also reciprocally directed at one another—each wants that the other wants X—the individual actions are individualized as "one complex action" (Hua XIV, p. 193; cf. Stein 2000, p. 193). The total action (*die gesamte Handlung*) is both "mine" and "his" (i.e., *ours*) although each of us has a "part" that is "exclusively his own." Here it is difficult not to recognize the very same structure of individual roles that constitutes a joint action for Tomasello (see first section of this chapter).

Then, Husserl hints at the idea that role-structured joint actions are characterized by a communal will (Hua XIV, p. 193, lines 28–29). The hint is given through the contrast with community accomplishments without a communal will, such as the production of a language, a legal system, and also, to some extent, a science. This distinction is discussed more extensively at various points in the text, and we shall now pay attention to it because it hinges on the numerical oneness of what is today called "a collective intention." Moreover, this distinction is crucially important because it would be a serious misunderstanding of Husserl's view to ascribe to him the idea that all communities are plural agents.

The distinction is formulated at pages 194–195 as follows: there are (1) personal-level connections characterized by "the unity of a will of the community" and (2) personal-level connections without such unity. Whereas in the first case the individual intentions are taken to be part of a unitary will, in the second the performance of an individual is imitated and spreads across the group independently of the individual's will. Examples of the two kinds are the community of people writing the constitution of a parliamentary state and the community in which a language is (constantly) molded, respectively (Hua XIV, p. 201). If Tomasello's "plural agent" seems to be an apt contemporary expression to designate the first kind of community—that is, the subject of a joint/collective action and of the communal will bringing it about—the second kind of community can by no means be regarded as a plural agent.

In certain respects, a science can be a group accomplishment of the second kind because the accomplishments of a single scientist can cause repercussions in a way that is independent of the intentions of the original scientist or of anyone else. Yet, Husserl also points to the "one-sided communication" between scientists of past generations and present scientists who continue their work and share their ultimate goals (Hua XIV, p. 198). This can perhaps already be considered as a collaborative action and a communal will enduring through the generations (Hua XIV, p. 194, lines 29–31; p. 200, lines 15–18). More clearly, however, the case of "reciprocal communication" between scientists of the same generation (Hua XIV, pp. 198–99) who collaborate to serve the same goals counts as prototypical example of a community accomplishment of the first kind, that is, a joint/collective action executed through a communal will (see Hua XXVII, pp. 52–53).

Husserl calls a plural agent "a higher order personal unity" (Hua XIV, p. 194). In the context of clarifying the constitution of such a communal subject through the unifying effect of communication, Husserl provides a statement that underscores the (anti-Cartesian) numerical oneness of the communal mental state through the use of quotation marks:

> It is a personal-level connection—founded on the awareness of the other—in which (in every genuinely social respect that constitutes a specific layer of sociality) "a conviction" lives, "an evaluation," "a will," with all their preconditions of unity of a similar kind. And as correlate we have the unity of "an" accomplishment, "a" [communal] work. (Hua XIV, p. 194)

That the quotation marks including a singular indefinite article and a noun underscore the numerical oneness of the communal mental state—in contrast with the plurality of the individual states that constitute it—is made even clearer by the analogous use of quotation marks in the following passage:

> Everywhere we have a plurality of people with many personal capacities, streams of consciousness, acts of consciousness that enter and insert themselves in those streams—and yet "a mind" [*und doch "ein Geist"*], a personality of "higher order" . . . with a consciousness that encompasses—in some selection—all individual consciousnesses. (Hua XIV, p. 199)

The idea of a communal mental state encompassing functional components from all individual consciousnesses is clarified through the phenomenon of *Deckung*, overlap or coincidence, established through communication:

> Separate [material] things remain external, they can stand one next to the other and be in contact with each other, they can never have *something identical* in common. Consciousness, however, truly coincides with consciousness [*Bewusstsein aber deckt sich wirklich mit Bewusstsein*], a consciousness that understands another consciousness constitutes within itself the selfsame that the other consciousness constitutes. Both are one in the selfsame.

In other words, because the acts of consciousness of different *communicating* individuals *overlap*, that is, because they have a content or intentional object in common, these acts are experienced as components of a unitary, intrinsically interconnected, mental state—and, in line with the epistemological assumptions of the phenomenological tradition, the communal mental state must be considered as a unitary social event manifested through a phenomenological synthesis. Clearly, Husserl is talking about a synthesis of components from different individual consciousnesses as the following passage shows. The German "*so*"—translated here as "in this way"—refers to the overlap with a "foreign consciousness," which nonetheless "mirrors" one's own (lines 18–28):

> In this way, consciousness unifies itself with consciousness, overflowing all the time, encompassing time in the form of simultaneity as in the form of succession. Personal consciousness becomes one with the other, with a consciousness that is necessarily separate from itself, and thus becomes a unity of supra-personal consciousness. (Hua XIV, p. 199)

Husserl is not employing an ad hoc principle of unification for communal experiences. On the contrary, it is "the intentional essence of acts" (Hua XIV, p. 199) that allows for the encroaching of an act on another, both in the case of past, present, and future acts of the same individual, as in the case of acts of different individuals. In both cases, different acts of consciousness are synthesized in "encroaching acts" [*übergreifenden Akte*] (Hua XIV, p. 200):

> As active functioning act, my thinking encroaches other thinking, my own just like the thinking of others. My willing encroaches the willing of others. (Hua XIV, p. 200)

Thus, Husserl can state that each communal state—or, more precisely, each communal "act" (a communal presentation, evaluation, or will)—is a unitary phenomenon distributed among a plurality of individuals:

> Within the multiplicity of wills distributed among the individuals, it [the connected multiplicity of persons] has a will identically constituted for all of them. This will has no other location, no other substrate than the plurality of communicating people; and the same is true for other "unitarily," socially constituted acts. (Hua XIV, pp. 200–201)

Husserl had emphasized the difference among convictions, evaluations, and volitions as enduring properties of the subject and the single acts in which these enduring properties actualize themselves (Hua XIV, p. 195, lines 22–24). For example, a person knows how large her apartment is (enduring property): she does not think about it all the time, but, if you ask her, she can think about it (actualizing act) and let you know; an academic has committed to teaching a course (enduring property), every time she goes to campus to do it she is merely actualizing her enduring intention. These enduring properties are necessary for a subject to be a rational subject and not just prey of its impulses (Hua XIV, p. 196, lines 12–22).

Husserl explicitly states that, just like the individual subject, the plural one has both enduring properties (*bleibende Akte*) and particular acts that actualize those properties ("*Akte*" *als Akteinzelheiten*) (Hua XIV, p. 201, lines 4–9). Consider a few examples from our own times. The European Medicines Agency (EMA) has the enduring intention to approve all COVID-19 vaccines that meet certain scientific and public health requirements. For any vaccine-candidate that is subjected to its evaluation, EMA takes a particular decision (either approval or rejection) that actualizes its enduring intention. In spring 2021, the German government was made up of a coalition of parties and had the enduring intention to do what was reasonably doable to dampen the health and economic damages of the pandemic (it had already ordered two comprehensive "lockdowns"). When Easter 2021 was approaching, the government announced a targeted lockdown concerning the days surrounding Easter, the so-called "Easter Rest" (*Osterruhe*). After a few days, given the protests and confusion that the first announcement gave rise to, the government officially backed off from the Easter Rest. Though one reversed the other, both decisions were actualizing a (more or less well-specified) enduring intention.

There are collective actions that occur at a particular time and place (e.g., approving a vaccine-candidate, announcing a targeted lockdown, carrying out a counterattack at a particular point of a European football match, etc.). The collective intention that realizes these actions actualizes enduring intentions of the group and it is an open question whether it can be considered to be actualized by other intentions in its turn. Husserl states that individual intentions have a relation of foundation, or of functional components, with regard to the communal intention—this is true for both enduring and actualizing intentions (Hua XIV, p. 201, lines 9–11). But it seems that an *individual* enduring intention can be actualized only by an *individual* actualizing intention and a *communal* enduring intention can be actualized only by a *communal* actualizing intention. My enduring intention to teach a semester-long course is not founded on my actualizing intention to go to campus this morning; analogously, our enduring intention to perform counterattacks in the right circumstances (to score and win the game) is not founded on our actualizing intention to realize a counterattack at this point of the game. For these reasons, it would be wrong to say that there is no communal actualizing intention but only individual actualizing intentions. If there is no communal actualizing intention (as *founded on* individual *components*), the group simply does not carry out the particular action (the particular counterattack).[5]

What is perhaps most striking in *Gemeingeist* is the parallel between the individual and the community at the level of the phenomenology of synthesis. Husserl does not refrain from recalling the unity of individual acts of perception (Hua XIV, p. 201, lines 27–32), or how they undergo "immanent 'associative' interweavings . . . before any reflection" (Hua XIV, p. 202) to shed light on how components from different individuals may be configured into unitary communal mental phenomena. Furthermore, the parallel also consists in the idea that all subjectivities, including the individual subject who performs an act of perception, can appear only through a synthesis of experience (Hua XIV, p. 201, lines 31–32; p. 203, lines 25–28): They all are unities of phenomenological constitution (*konstitutive Einheiten*). On this basis, one can begin to see how, once a joint action is individuated, the subject of the action can be individuated as well: The awareness concerning the individuals is synthesized as manifesting a plural agent (e.g., the group of people who are participating in a philosophy seminar or the group of friends who are having dinner together). Indeed, who realizes a collaborative action is not just the individuals, who by themselves may have no connection with each other, but the individuals insofar as they communicate and interact with each other, i.e., insofar as they form a *unity* (Hua XIV, p. 201, lines 3–8).[6]

To sum up, there is overwhelming evidence that *Gemeingeist II* espouses an anti-Cartesian conception where the we can be the plural subject of a unitary communal mental state: the individuation of a joint or collective action precisely as one in opposition to the plurality of roles; the fundamental distinction between community accomplishments characterized by a communal will and those that are not; the unequivocal assertions that components from different individual consciousnesses are synthesized into a unitary phenomenon of consciousness through the process of *Deckung*; the emphasis that this process of unification applies to individual experiences just like communal experiences; the assertion that a unitary communal state is distributed among a plurality of subjects as its substrate; the parallel between the individual and the communal with respect to both enduring properties and actualizing acts, as well as the general idea of a subject as a unity of phenomenological constitution (all of this strengthened by reiterations with or without quotation marks).

It is—at least to a large extent—the same anti-Cartesian conception that one encounters in Scheler and Stein. Indeed, as for Scheler and Stein, the participants in a unitary communal state remain "individual people" (Hua XIV, p. 202, lines 33–37), they have their own individual ways of appearance (*Erscheinungsweisen*) of the same social whole. Even when characterizing "the unity of total life and striving that is communalizing itself" as a fusion of people (*Verschmelzung der Personen*), Husserl maintains that each of these people has its own individual life and point of view (*deren jede doch von ihrer Stelle aus ihr Leben hat*; Hua XV, p. 599).

Other Texts

Husserl espouses the anti-Cartesian idea of unitary communal mental states in other texts, too. For example, he states that plural agents can have mental functions just like individuals (Hua XIV, p. 205, lines 10–16) and that the acts of an individual are unified with those of others to form a unity of communal consciousness, thinking, or action (Hua XIV, p. 206, lines 17–21). He also insists on the analogy between individual and group insofar as they both have consciousness and "acts" (Hua XIV, p. 217, lines 13–15; p. 218, lines 33–34).

As a further exemplification, however, we shall turn to the fourth of the more famous *Kaizo* articles. In this text, after noting that a community can have a unity of life that is not "a mere collection" of the lives of the individuals, though it is founded on them (Hua XXVII, p. 48), Husserl writes:

> A community has a consciousness, as community it can also have a self-consciousness in a pregnant sense, it can have a self-evaluation and a will targeting itself, a will to shape itself . . . a will-direction, which is a will-direction

> belonging to the community itself and is not a mere sum of the founding individual wills.[7] (Hua XXVII, p. 49; cf. Hua XXVII, p. 50, lines 19–20)

A few pages later, Husserl insists that he is not talking about a collection of individuals with type-identical will in accord with type-identical ideals (*Individuen mit gleichem Willen gemäß gleichen Idealen*), but rather precisely about "a will of the community" (Hua XXVII, pp. 52–53). At this point, Husserl uses the example of the community of scientists interacting with each other to achieve the common goal (though, as mentioned, science is also in certain respects an example of a community-accomplishment without communal will). Husserl characterizes the unity of will of such a scientific community as being, at least in the ideal case, "a communistic unity of the will." This expression effectively suggests that there is no individual ownership of the communal will—as if it were private property—but only a co-ownership.

Overall, we have no reason to think that this anti-Cartesian conception of a unitary communal mental state may be contradicted in some other text written by Husserl. Nonetheless, even if there were a few passages contradicting it, this conception must be regarded as fully Husserlian, because, as observed previously in this chapter, it derives from a consistent elaboration on Husserl's general phenomenology of synthesis, which capitalizes on Husserl's most original insights concerning inner time-consciousness and synthesis via overlap (*Deckungssynthesis*).

HUSSERL ON MORALITY AND THE WE

We have noted the similarity between Husserl's and Tomasello's characterizations of a joint action. Altogether, the previous section presented Husserl's anti-Cartesian conception as a candidate for clarifying Tomasello's notion of the plural agent, the we—keeping in mind Husserl's distinction from groups that are not plural agents. This section examines Husserl's view on the relationships between shared intentionality and morality. Here the similarities with Tomasello's theory are possibly even more noticeable.

The first similarity regards the affective basis of morality. Although Husserl often talks about "love" and love should arguably be distinguished from empathy, we can treat love and empathy as analogous in that they both entail positive feeling for others. It is not only that, for Husserl (Hua XXXVII), just as for Tomasello, morality requires a combination of prosocial inclinations and the cognition of norms valid for all (where this "all" can extend as humanity evolves). Just like in Tomasello's phylogenetic story, prosocial affection is considered by Husserl (Hua XIV, pp. 165–84) as a precondition for shared intentionality (cf. also Scheler 1973, p. 24). Love does not imply the existence of a community, but can unify people into a community (XIV, p. 175, lines 5–12; Hua XV, pp. 588–99).

As pointed out, the first step, mentioned by Tomasello, toward the evolution of a specifically human morality concerns mating and kinship relations. Husserl, too, seems to assign a fundamental significance to family, and he analyzes the sexual relationship. In the ideal case, each sexual partner is not only taking pleasure in the other's embodied subjectivity but also wants the other to take pleasure in oneself too and values the interaction as a joint activity in which he or she wants to participate (XIV, p. 177, lines 2–13). Through this overlap of the individual wills, the partners experience that "a unity of will embraces both of them and brings about a unity of reciprocal action" (lines 13–14). Analogously, the communal meal and its shared joy is one of the activities founding the unity of the family (p. 178, lines 30–35; p. 179, lines 13–14). In these activities, "a unity, a whole, is constituted, composed of I-subjects who penetrate each other by connecting with each other, insofar as the life of one I co-lives in the life of the other, it is involved in it" (p. 179).

In the context of a family community instituted through such affectively charged experiences (e.g., sex, communal meals, play, etc.), a family member can become aware of having a *function* within it, for example, the function of caring for the partner or the children (Hua XIV, p. 180, lines 14–20). Indeed, Husserl describes the family as a community with its communal goal and where each member has his or her function or role (Hua XIV, p. 181, lines 4–9); thus, in this respect, family life is described as a collaborative action (lines 9–12).

On the basis of the givenness of one's own function in the family, the ought "*arises*," it comes to be given, too: One ought to fulfil one's own function for the sake of the family (Hua XIV, p. 180, line 24). This is the "the naturally grown duty" (line 38). Just like the duty to do one's own part in a small-scale collaborative action of *homo heidelbergensis* (Tomasello 2016, pp. 39–84), it can in principle arise before and independently from the existence of an organized cultural group. Nonetheless, already in the context of the family, one's own duty is delineated in a general way and thus it constitutes an enduring property of the person (Hua XIV, p. 180, lines 35–37; cf. Tomasello, pp. 55–57). Since each member has a function within the family, each member can demand from the other the fulfillment of his or her role, knowing that the other could demand the same from oneself in an appropriate circumstance: This "personal demand" (Hua XIV, p. 180, line 23) is essentially the second-person standpoint presented in the first section.

The move to the ethics of "larger associations," where a member does not personally know all other members, can also be understood in terms of functions within the community (Hua XIV, p. 182, lines 24–32; cf. Tomasello's idea of cultural groups as "collaborative enterprise"). For example, there are "state functions" (e.g., tax-paying, voting, complying with traffic laws, etc.) that a citizen of a state *ought* to fulfill (lines 7–11). This metaethical discourse applies to the "communities of will," or plural agents, such as a state, a family (lines 9–10, 22–32) and, to a significant extent, a scientific community (Hua XIV, p. 183, lines 25–31), but not to groups that are not plural agents, the communities of the second kind discussed previously. For example, a linguistic community does not constitute a "personal whole" (p. 182, lines 21–22, 35–39), although it does constitute a social reality where a message can spread widely (p. 183, 19–21).

To conclude this section on Husserl's view on the relationship between morality and the we, it should be noted that, in this kind of metaethical discourse, ethical demands become the more inclusive, the more one recognizes oneself as part of a larger whole. Hence in Husserl (Hua XIV, p. 204; XXVII, pp. 54–59; XXXVII, pp. 237–43), the idea of "humanity" as the community of rational beings to whom one recognizes oneself to be bound plays an ineliminable regulatory role, but the idea of ethics as based on function is also present in contemporary environmental-ethical discourse, where one is called to recognize oneself as part of the community of all living beings or even as part of the cosmos.

Furthermore, in Husserl, the individual has the ethical demand of trying to make one's own community as ethical as possible (Hua XXVII, p. 46, lines 17–21). Thus, the ethical progress of a community depends on the ethical attitude of individuals (Hua XXVII, p. 49, lines 14–17). The ethical reflections of individuals—usually after a first communalization in a group with common goals—propagate in a social movement (*in einer sozialen Bewegung*)—for a contemporary example, think about the Fridays for Future "movement." Certainly, this propagation also occurs through mimetic processes characterizing groups that are not plural agents. Nonetheless, in the ideal case, the final result consists in the individuation of a will-direction that belongs to the community and that aims at the renewal of the community itself (lines 17–26). The individuation of the communal will occurs through the overlap of the individual wills in a process of communication (Hua XIV, p. 182, 30–34).

CONCLUSION

In the first section, we ascertained that for Tomasello morality implies the we (i.e., it implies a form of thinking characterized by the phenomenological constitution of collaborative actions, roles, and plural agents). The full clarification of these cognitive foundations of morality is wisely left open for further philosophical investigations.

In the attempt to retrieve the conceptual resources provided by the phenomenological tradition, we came across a somewhat paradoxical result that unifies Scheler, Stein, and Husserl with Tomasello: if morality has its cognitive foundations in shared intentionality, shared intentionality has in turn its own *affective* foundations. Tomasello and Husserl posit the basis of social participation in empathy and love, respectively; Tomasello, Husserl, Scheler, and Stein treat emotion sharing as the fundamental form of shared intentionality. Scheler and Stein's analysis of emotion sharing offered an option for clarifying the notion of we: *We* are the co-subjects of a unitary affective phenomenon, conceived as a synthesis of components experienced to belong to different individuals. Hence, we came to formulate the central question of the chapter: whether Husserl too endorsed this radical challenge to the Cartesian assumption that a mental state can only have one subject—not just as a critique, but by formulating a positive conception contradicting that assumption.

To address this question, the first step was to consider the role Husserl assigns to communication. Communication creates *Deckung*, that is, overlap or coincidence, between individual minds who come to have an intentional content or object in common. Then, through the close examination of a text from Hua XIV and other texts, we ascertained that, for Husserl, this *Deckung* makes the individuation of a joint action and of a communal mental state possible. The texts propose the anti-Cartesian conception according to which individual consciousnesses are (passively) taken to constitute a unitary communal consciousness. This is in any case a fully Husserlian conception because it derives from a consistent application of Husserl's theory of mental phenomena as syntheses.

Accordingly, Husserl's contribution to clarify the we as the cognitive foundations of morality can be formulated as follows: In some cases—to be distinguished from other kinds of social reality—the we is the "who," the plural subject, the substrate that carries out a collaborative action and possesses a communal will or any other kind of communal mental state. The we does not simply coincide with the individuals, who, by themselves, may not be connected with each other but coincides with the individuals insofar as they communicate and interact with each other (i.e., insofar as they form a phenomenological unity).

With a striking resemblance to Tomasello's theory, Husserl posits the emergence of the "first" ought in the family as a collaborative context: It is because I share the value of the family with the other members that I know what I and them ought to do. The family is constituted through communal experiences (e.g., sex and communal meals) which realize anti-Cartesian "unities of life."

New moral imperatives emerge as one takes oneself to be part of larger and larger wholes. Although in certain cases the unity of the will can only be disclosed through philosophical reflection because the overlapping individual wills are too variously distributed, in other cases the communal will—to which the individual, for Husserl, ought to contribute—can become the object of public discourse and sociological explanation (Tollefsen 2015). For example, if a state or a corporation sets its short- and long-terms goals to counteract the environmental crisis and consistently realizes them in the short and long run, then this may be because a unitary state of will has become attributable to the community, via the converging of individual wills through a process of communication.

AUTHOR CONTRIBUTIONS

Stefano Vincini is lead author. He wrote the Introduction and from the first section to subsection "A Focus on a Particularly Important Text" (pp. 207–224). Andrea Staiti wrote the remaining sections (pp. 224–229). Both authors reviewed and accepted all sections of the chapter.

ACKNOWLEDGMENTS

SV's work on this chapter was made possible through the generous support of the Alexander von Humboldt Foundation.

NOTES

1. In Tomasello's story one can see only the first steps toward a truly universal and inclusive morality. We will come back to this topic in the fourth section.

2. We follow Krebs's (2015, pp. 109–50) meticulous discussion in considering Stein's work as an original development of Scheler's. Obviously, there are also differences between Scheler and Stein, and they may be taken to be significant, but, for the most part, they do not concern "emotion sharing"; rather, their differences revolve around the topic that is designated today as "Direct Social Perception" (Dahlstrom 2021). In footnote 6, we will point out a relatively minor difference between Scheler and Stein concerning emotion sharing.

3. In an interdisciplinary spirit—which implies the effort to accommodate different terminologies and domains of investigation—we follow the currently widespread use of the expression "mental state." It goes without saying that phenomenologists would preferably talk about "*Erlebnisse*" (lived experiences) and that *Erlebnisse* are always a process, never a static phenomenon (but is this not true also for a mental state as understood, for example, by a neuroscientist?). Deliberately, employing the

expression *mental state* leaves open the question of whether this phenomenological theory of individual and communal lived experiences may also be fruitfully applied to mental states that are not considered to be "conscious."

4. In general, learning a language may be said to entail joining the "we" of those who share a common linguistic practice to refer to the world and to achieve intended effects through each other (Hua XIV, p. 194). However, see Section four for distinguishing the linguistic community from the plural agent in the strict sense.

5. Caminada (2019) is right that there is nothing "spooky" in Husserl's conception of communal consciousness or communal mental states. Indeed, Scheler (1916, pp. 544–45, see especially footnote 1) too distinguishes between a legitimate conception of communal consciousness and a "mysterious" one, and Stein (2000) opts for reserving the term *consciousness* for the individual mind, who alone is "originally constituting." Caminada (2019, pp. 287, 347) shows that Husserl's conception is fully intelligible and bereft of any spookiness just as much as Scheler's and Stein's. However, Caminada seems to worry that if one took Husserl's assertion on communal actualizing acts seriously (Hua XIV, p. 201, lines 4–9), one would have to admit some spookiness in Husserl's conception. This worry seems ultimately unwarranted. Once one acknowledges that all experiences (both individual and communal) are a synthesis of components, a communal actualizing intention appears as nothing else than the synthesis of the overlapping and reciprocally complementing individual actualizing intentions. Clarifying the relationships between foundation and actualization in this context is an interesting and complex task for future research. However, in the last analysis, it seems that it is the general phenomenology of synthesis, not the distinction between enduring properties and actualizing acts, that gets rid of the spookiness.

6. Stein (1917, p. 18) sides with Husserl on this and complains that Scheler did not realize that it is only insofar as the subjects form a (interacting)unity that they can be co-subjects of a communal action or mental state.

7. The term will-direction (*Willensrichtung*) is used for individuals as well (e.g., Hua XIV, pp. 213, 422).

REFERENCES

Brough, J. B. (2011). The Most Difficult of All Phenomenological Problems. *Husserl Studies 27*: 27–40.

Caminada, E. (2016). Husserl on Groupings: Social Ontology and Phenomenology of We-Intentionality. *Phenomenology of Sociality: Discovering the 'We.* (Vol. 3; pp. 281–95). Routledge; London/New York.

———. (2019). *Vom Gemeingeist zum Habitus: Husserls Ideen II. Sozialphilosophische Implikationen der Phänomenologie*. Springer: Heidelberg.

Dahlstrom, Daniel. (2021). Experiencing Others: Stein's Critique of Scheler. *American Catholic Philosophical Quarterly* 95(3): 433–53.

De Warren, N. (2009). *Husserl and the Promise of Time: Subjectivity in Transcendental Phenomenology*. Cambridge: Cambridge University Press.

Hua IX. Husserl, E. (1962). *Phänomenologische Psychologie.* The Hague: Nijhoff.

Hua XIV. Husserl, E. (1973). *Zur Phänomenologie der Intersubjektivität II.* The Hague: Nijhoff.

Hua XV. Husserl, E. (1973). *Zur Phänomenologie der Intersubjektivität III.* The Hague: Nijhoff.

Hua XVII. Husserl, E. (1974). *Formale und transzendentale Logik.* The Hague: Nijhoff.

Hua XXVII. Husserl, E. (1989). *Aufsätze und Vorträge (1922–1937).* Dordrecht: Kluwer Academic.

Hua XXXVII. Husserl, E. (2004). *Einleitung in die Ethik. Vorlesungen Sommersemester 1920 und 1924.* Dordrecht: Kluwer Academic.

Hua XXXVIII. Husserl, E. (2004). *Wahrnehmung und Aufmerksamkeit. Texte aus dem Nachlass (1893–1912).* Dordrecht: Springer.

Krebs, A. (2015). *Zwischen Ich und Du. Eine dialogische Philosophie der Liebe.* Berlin: Suhrkamp.

Rakoczy, H. (2017). Development of collective intentionality. In K. Ludwig & M. Jankovic (Eds.), *The Routledge handbook of collective intentionality* (pp. 407–19). London: Routledge.

Scheler, M. (1916). *Der Formalismus in der Ethik und die materiale Wertethik. Neuer Versuch der Grundlegung eines ethischen Personalismus.* Halle: Niemeyer Verlag.

Scheler, M. (1973). *Wesen und Formen der Sympathie*, in: Max Scheler, Gesammelte Werke. Vol. VII.

Schloßberger, M. (2020*). Max Scheler. The Routledge Handbook of Phenomenology of Emotion* Edited by Thomas Szanto. Hilge Landweer.

Schmid, H. B. (2009). *Plural action. Essays in philosophy and social science.* Dordrecht: Springer.

Schmid, H. B. (2014). Plural self-awareness. *Phenom. Cogn. Sci.* 13(7):7–24.

Staiti, A. (2010). *Geistigkeit, Leben und geschichtliche Welt in der Transzendentalphänomenologie Husserls.* Würzburg: Ergon Verlag.

Stein, E. (1917). *Zum Problem der Einfühlung.* Halle: Buchdruckerei des Waisenhauses.

———. (1993). *Self-Portrait in Letters 1916–1942*, tr. Josephine Koeppel. Washington: ICS Publications.

Stein, E. (2000). *Philosophy of Psychology and the Humanities* (M. Sawicki, Ed., M. C. Baseheart & M. Sawicki, Trans.). Washington, DC: ICS Publication.

Tollefsen, D. (2015). *Groups as Agents.* Cambridge, UK: Polity Press.

Tomasello, M. (2014). *A Natural History of Human Thinking.* Cambridge, MA: Harvard University Press.

———. (2016). *A Natural History of Human Morality.* Cambridge, MA: Harvard University Press.

———. (2019). *Becoming human: A theory of ontogeny.* Cambridge, MA: Harvard University Press.

Vincini, S. (2021). Pairing and sharing: The birth of the sense of us. *Phenomenology and the Cognitive Sciences.* https://doi.org/10.1007/s11097-021-09793-4.

Zahavi, D. (2011). Objects and Levels: Reflections on the Relation Between Time-Consciousness and Self-Consciousness. *Husserl Studies* 27:13–25.

Zahavi, D. (2019). Second-person engagement, self-alienation, and group-identification. *Topoi 38*(1): 251–60.

Chapter 11

Fiat cura, et pereat mundus

Husserl's Phenomenology of Care and Commitment

Nicolas de Warren

Novelty must be inspired
for Jonathan Imber

ABSTRACT

In this chapter, I propose to explore "the importance of what we care about" from a phenomenological angle in the spirit but not necessarily in the footsteps of Harry Frankfurt's seminal essay. My overarching claim is that Frankfurt's threefold distinction—knowing, ethical conduct, caring—is equally central to Husserl's phenomenology of reason and, more directly, underlies Husserl's phenomenological ethics of values and vocation in his Freiburg manuscripts of the 1920s and 1930s. As I argue, Husserl seeks to ground acting with respect to right and wrong and hence, norms and obligations, on the lived experience of valuing, of what it is to find something important worth caring about, as well as the uptake of such values for a person along a distinctive course or in a particular manner, which presupposes agency, responsibility, and self-consciousness. As I examine, care is indexed phenomenologically to the affectivity of values; we would not care for something, let alone uphold the importance of what (or who) we care about, were it not valuable to care, were not the things and persons I care for experienced as valuable. It is arguably this dimension of value that remains largely ignored in much of the literature in "care ethics" but which proves essential for, indeed, distinctly defines a phenomenology of care and commitment.

Keywords: Husserl, Harry Frankfurt, care, ethics, values, responsibility

In an essay providing a catalyst for my present effort to motivate as well as delineate a phenomenological ethics of care and commitment, Harry Frankfurt identifies what he terms a "third branch of inquiry" concerning a "fundamental preoccupation of human existence," namely, "*what to care about*." This branch of inquiry stands in contrast to inquiries regarding how to act according to what is right and wrong or what to believe regarding what is true or false about the world.[1] Whereas the latter falls under the remit of epistemology and questions of right and wrong are the domain of ethics, concerns falling under the heading of "the importance of what we care about" cannot be subsumed to either of these traditional domains of thinking. While ethics deals primarily with acting in relation to other human beings (as well as other sentient life-forms) in terms of what I *ought* to do, the arena of care, of what and who one cares for, involves "deciding what to do with *ourselves*." Not everything that a person cares about necessarily possesses or implies ethical relevance or conduct. In fact, much of what we care about is not distinctively ethical in significance; indeed, we are often conflicted when faced with the imperatives of ethical obligations, on the one hand, and the demands of our cares, on the other. The relation between ethics and cares is both complex and variable, at times direct, at times indirect, and would seem to be asymmetrical in this regard: Whereas not everything that importantly matters to me possesses ethical import, striving to act according to duties and norms—*wanting* to lead an ethical life—would have to represent something I care for, to wit, caring about acting with moral rectitude. This overlapping notwithstanding, Frankfurt suggestively argues that "the question concerning what is most important is distinguishable from the question of concerning what is morally right." What these three domains of inquiry nonetheless share is that "providing fully articulated analysis" of their respective "defining notions" proves no easier in one case than with the others. With the third domain, what proves challenging is understanding the operative meanings of *caring* and *importance* without falling into circularity (i.e., we care for what is important because what is important defines what we care about) or begging the question of what it *is* to care for something, what caring about entails and involves, as well as how we become compelled into caring about somethings, or persons, rather than others (or not), of how, in other words, what we care about makes a claim on us. These and other questions reveal the existential depth of care, or, as Frankfurt remarks, that care "guides the person in what she does with her life and in her conduct." What we care about shapes how we dispose of our lives, its conduct and pursuit, defining who we are in our distinct way of being. In broaching the fundamental significance of our cares and concerns, we recognize ourselves as "caring beings," beings for whom things and other persons matter in a host of ways, and with such purchase in our lives that puts into play and, indeed, places at stake, the kind of person we aspire to be.

In what follows, I propose to explore the importance of what we care about from a phenomenological angle in the spirit but not necessarily in the footsteps of Frankfurt's seminal essay. As with Frankfurt's own reflections, I shall reflect on "in a somewhat tentative and fragmentary way a few of its central concepts and issues" within a Husserlian frame of analysis. My overarching claim is that Frankfurt's threefold distinction—knowing, ethical conduct, caring—is equally central to Husserl's phenomenology of reason and, more directly, underlies Husserl's phenomenological ethics of values and vocation in his Freiburg manuscripts of the 1920s and 1930s. A phenomenological ethics of care and commitment can be mapped from Husserl's ethics of value and vocation. Husserl's materialist value ethics, along with his conception of the person and associated notions, articulates in a phenomenological key the fundamental dimension of caring. Husserl seeks to ground acting with respect to right and wrong, and hence, norms and obligations, on the lived experience of valuing, of what it is to find something important *worth* caring about, as well as the uptake of such values for a person along a distinctive course or in a particular manner, which, as Husserl stresses, presupposes agency, responsibility, and self-consciousness. The argument at hand is that what we care about stands under the operator of valuing. Care is indexed phenomenologically to the affectivity of values; we would not care for something, let alone uphold the importance of what (or who) we care about, were it not *valuable* to care, were not the things and persons I care for *experienced as* valuable—value-laden—in some way; yet, it is this dimension of value that, arguably, remains largely ignored in much of the literature in care ethics, but which proves essential for, indeed, distinctly defines phenomenological ethical thought. We might in this regard speak of the forgottenness of the problem of value in what is commonly called care ethics. By contrast, Husserl grounds his phenomenology of care—the term *Sorge* crops up in his manuscripts—in a theory of values, without which relations of dependency and attitudes toward vulnerability would lack axiological basis. An ethics of care should provide a robust account of values, their ordering, mode of experiential givenness, and forms of uptake in our lives. What we care about, or who we care for, stands under an operator of value, and values, in Husserl's parlance, are operative ("functional intentionality") in our everyday lives and can become a theme of reflection, assessment, and critique, open to rational and deliberative adjudication.

Even in its outline form in his manuscripts, Husserl offers the means for a suggestive account of valuing as a nexus of experiencing involving the affectivity of values, care for others, and self-valuing—valuing oneself as the kind of person for whom values are important, for whom caring about something, or someone, gives substance and significance to one's own life. Within this framework, a bond obtains between caring for someone under the operator of value and disposing of one's own life, *having a life rather than merely being a life*. Given Husserl's argument for values of love as the highest values, caring for others ranks above all other forms of caring; and hence, relations with others are integral to the domain of caring and self-valuing. Valuing is thus constitutive of interpersonal relations *as well as* establishing a relation with oneself. One cares not only for others, but for oneself, indeed, for the values as such in terms of which relations with others are constituted as axiologically salient, that is, valuable. To care about someone (or something) is, moreover, inherently prospective and directed toward the future. In Frankfurt's expression, what we care about defines what "a person's life is in whole or in part *devoted* [to]," or, in Husserl's vocabulary, what (or who) we care about is tethered to a *vocation*. Guided under the directionality of vocation, the pursuit of personhood becomes temporalized in a distinctive manner: "The moments in the life of a person who cares about something, however, are not merely linked inherently by formal relations of sequence. The person necessarily binds them together, and in the nature of the case also construes them as being bound together, in richer ways."[2]

For Frankfurt, caring "presupposes some degree of persistence," as instilled by the commitment of devotion that undergirds the sustained importance of what, or who, we care about. In Husserl's thinking, this crucial dimension of "persistence" is addressed with a conception of ethical striving as self-persistence (*Selbsterhaltung*) and the corresponding challenge of corroborating or enduringly confirming (*Bewährung*) the values that orient and shape our lives. In his ethical reflections, Husserl accentuates this temporal dimension of caring as an issue of sustaining the values instantiated in caring headlong into a future fundamentally marked uncertainty and contingency. This exposure of the importance of what (or who) we care about to the basic uncertainty of the future provides a counterpoint to the paradox, touched upon by Frankfurt, that "it certainly cannot be assumed that what a person cares about is generally under his immediate voluntary control" and, moreover, that "the fact that someone cares about a certain thing is constituted by a complex set of cognitive, affective, and volitionary dispositions and states."[3] For Husserl, we must be "affected" or "impacted" in some manner, in a way that is not merely equated with an emotion (not all emotions are keyed to values) and yet which is experienced in a form of felt affectivity, which, in turn, is not equivalent with feelings such as pain or pleasure. A defining phenomenological challenge consists in characterizing and mapping the various ways in which values are disclosed in affective experiences. Given this disclosive function of affectivity, the uptake of caring hangs on the curious situation that what we hold near and dear, whether other persons, objects, values, ideas, and so on is generally not initiated by our voluntary choosing or deliberation. On the contrary, we are first, in some affective way or another, touched or impacted by what, or who, we care for. Our cares are at first "not under our immediate control," as Frankfurt observes; values, in Husserl's parlance, "call" on us and announce themselves in our lives in a form of solicitation. In speaking of the "affectivity" of values, we must equally speak of the attachment of values *to us*, its hold on us, so that much as we are bound to this attachment, we rarely experience this bonding of value, as with the bonds of love, as an infringement or constraint on our freedom, but, on the contrary, as its condition and enrichment. As with love, we are "struck" by the person and yet this is not experienced as coercion or constraint on freedom, and indeed, requires exercise of self-reflection, deliberation, and choice into order for uptake in our lives. In a twofold sense: not under our immediate control in terms of origin and future not under control in terms of destiny; and so, framed with a horizon of future beyond ourselves. This constitutive paradox of care, as both outside and inside our freedom, as both *given* and *claimed*, is captured in Husserl's expression *Vernunftglaube* with which, among other reaches, Husserl characters the peculiarity of "absolute values" in relation to his recasting of Kant's "fact of practical reason."

Studies of Husserl's ethical thought, still piecemeal and relatively nascent compared to the wealth of literature on other signature facets of Husserl's phenomenology, have yet to situate Husserl's ethical thought within the broader cultural landscape of the late nineteenth and early twentieth centuries. Three considerations, flagged here in passing, are especially significant for a proper contextualization of Husserl's phenomenological ethics: the ideals of *Bildungsbürgertum*, the rich debate concerning "vocation" among Husserl's contemporaries (one thinks especially of Weber's celebrated lectures), and values as a defined domain of philosophical inquiry.[4] Husserl shares with other contemporary thinkers such as Scheler the ambition of establishing a phenomenological alternative to Kantian deontological ethics, consequentialism as well as utilitarianism and eudaimonism. In Husserl's prewar lectures on ethics, he positions his efforts, largely in the vein of Brentano's ethical thinking, between Kantian "formalism," with its argument for moral conduct as determined by formal lawfulness of the will, and British moral sentimentalism, with its insight into the basis of moral distinctions, or values, in feelings. Husserl accepts the grounding function of moral feelings for the shaping and directing of moral action; with Kant, Husserl remains bound to understanding moral obligation and normative demands as irreducible to subjective caprice or mere feelings. What characterizes a wide range of phenomenological ethics (Scheler, Hildebrand, Stein), including Husserl's own, is an indispensable significance accorded to the experience and uptake of values for the formation of ethical life. Values, however, are not arbitrary or relative to mere subjective experience, but, on Husserl's axiological argument, are structured into essential and a priori configurations. The domain of "care," understood as standing under the operator of values, anchors the disposition and capacity for moral conduct according to obligations and norms. To care about something, or someone, is to care under the operator of something or someone *being* valuable.

Husserl's breakthrough work of the *Logical Investigations* is routinely lauded as launching the project of phenomenological philosophy with its subsequent evolutions, iterations, and course corrections. Less recognized, however, is Husserl's own understanding of the significance and direction of his phenomenological *Durchbruch*. As Husserl writes in 1906: "In the first place, let me state the general task that I must realize for myself, if I am ever to call myself a philosopher. I mean a critique of reason. A critique of logical and practical reason, *above all* a critique of valuing reason (*der wertenden Vernunft*)." Rationality manifests itself in three irreducible forms: Human beings can know the world, act in the world, and value the world. Cognition, action, and valuing are three basic orientations of human existence as shaped by reason, here understood as domains of human experience where, in each respective case, the question of truth can meaningfully be raised and—in principle—answered with reference to evidence, that is, of how the world shows up, or discloses, itself. Husserl's projected threefold critique of reason does not refer to a system of faculties, however. Instead, the *Leitfaden* for a phenomenology of reason is intentionality, more specifically, an analysis of consciousness as a manifold of forms of intentionality. Accordingly, Husserl preserves while setting on a new methodological basis Kant's original questioning: What can I know, what should I do, what can I hope for? These orientations of rationality in the world are irreducible to each other, and yet belong to a concordant system of phenomenological reason. Kant's fourth question ("What is a human being?"), said to encompass philosophy as such, becomes in turn with Husserl restated into an encompassing conception of humanity, indeed, in the aftermath of the First World War, into the renewal of an aspiration for the attainment of a genuine human culture. Above all, the trajectory of Husserl's thinking moves toward—never accomplished in his life-time—a host of ethical-religious themes adumbrated in his research manuscripts during the 1930s. As Husserl announces in the "concluding word" to the *Cartesian Meditations*, "phenomenology indeed *excludes every naïve metaphysics* that operates with absurd things in themselves, but *does not exclude metaphysics as such*." The possibility of genuine (*echten*) human life, "demanded as 'meaningful' (*sinnvoll*) in a particular sense . . . and all the further and still higher problems," namely, "ethical-religious problems," represents the guiding telos of phenomenological striving.[5] In this manner, phenomenological *Selbstbesinnung* gives "new significance" to the Delphic motto "know thyself!" as the imperative for reflection on the importance of what matters most in an age of crisis marked by the forgottenness, first and foremost, of the value of philosophical reflection itself.

Husserl inherits from Fichte and, more broadly, the nineteenth-century discourse on *Bildung*, a conception of human life as animated by striving. The significance of Fichte's ethical writings on the formation of Husserl's thinking cannot be underestimated, especially *Die Anweisung zum seligen Leben* and *Die Bestimmung des Menschen*. In answer to the question of what, or who, is a human, Fichte speaks of the "destiny," "vocation," and "drive." A person is not a given but a task (*Aufgabe*). As Husserl himself echoes, "all life occurs in the broadest sense in striving" (*im Streben*), in terms of instincts, drives, and the "authentic volitional life of ego-acts."[6] To be a subject is to become a person, not merely to exist, or "be a subject," but to pursue and attain a life in the sense of constituting oneself as a knowing, acting, and valuing person in a community of other (like-minded striving) persons. Here is not the occasion, for reasons of space and scope, to consider the complexities of Husserl's conception of personhood. Throughout his writings, Husserl speaks of the transcendental person, person as substrate of habituality, the ego, the community of persons, communities as persons of "higher order," personal attitude, and position-taking. What is clear, however, is that the person needs to be spoken of phenomenologically in many ways, with each declination gravitating around a basic contention that what it is to be a person, or better: *who* is a person, involves becoming we who are to be. Enmeshed within a phenomenological configuration of personhood are different forms of striving: *Trieb*, *Streben*, *Tendenz*—Husserl occasionally speaks as well of *Triebsintentionalität*. In these different manifestations, striving remains tethered to teleology; strivings, in turn, reflect different accentuations of teleology. Striving and telos run hand in hand: we strive to become who we are "to be" under the regulative guidance of an idea that becomes discovered—awakened to—sui generis in the adventure of becoming oneself. As Husserl writes: "Each of us has . . . his own Idea which, in a practical respect, constitutes his higher life-task, his higher determination and vocation."[7]

Cast in terms of vocation, the relation between striving "to become a person" and the telos of "being a person" inscribes life into a back-and-forth motion between the push of striving and the pull of an Idea. We are separated from ourselves, from who we *ought to be* as a function of who we genuinely become. The notion of vocation tailors the Idea as individualized to each person under schematic configurations of normative ideals. Striving to be this or that *kind* of person becomes motivated in terms of a vocation's calling—its pull on life, which in turn becomes clarified in view of striving toward its achievement—its push on life. We are stretched and shaped along the course of life, calibrating, and navigating, what to do with oneself in the world, in a perpetual tension between striving to become and called on to be. Throughout this constant push and pull, Husserl contends that the ideal of personhood entails striving to achieve concordance (*Einstimmigkeit*) with oneself, thus implicitly recognizing a plurality to personhood in its pursuit of unity with itself. This emphasis on unity and concordance attests to the pervading sense in which a person seeks to be at home with itself, but, equally, at home in the world as well as at home with others. Concordance is here a matter of integrity and self-coherence, managing the various value commitments and cares into a unified project of life. The ideal of life as an *achievement*, integral to pursuing oneself in self-becoming, informs Husserl's philosophical orientation, including, the conception of himself as a philosopher. In Husserl's terminology, the unity of life represents a monad, not, however, bereft of windows, but shot through and through with structures of intentionality. In this appropriation of Leibniz's term, Husserl in his own way conceives of the unity of life in terms of uniqueness and wholeness. The unity of life, under the operator of vocation, is not pre-given or pre-determined; it stands before oneself as a task (*Aufgabe*) and hence challenge. Of special note is the temporalization of life's self-constitution as a unique whole. An accomplished life is formed through the temporalization of experiences and episodes into a whole, not merely in chronological sequence, but, more saliently, into a living stream, or coursing, of life with diversified temporalities, rhythms, and vectors. In his analysis of inner time consciousness, for example, Husserl speaks of the sedimentation of one's pasts (in the plural), as different traces and trajectories of one's becoming that form a textured depth. Is my past simply behind me, or also still ahead of me, indeed, remaining within me, as the unfinished genesis of my presence in the world? Setting aside further consideration of Husserl's sophisticated conception of inner time consciousness—the integral temporalization of consciousness as living—the idea of a "genuine life" consists in striving to attain attuned unanimity (*Einstimmigkeit*) with oneself and, hence, in this sense, "genuine satisfaction" with oneself. This *ideal* of attuned unanimity with oneself accentuates the plural senses, or lack of unanimity, and hence, different vectors of self at play, in the unfolding of a life. Different senses and vectors of self are keyed to respective, and often, conflicting vocations, which, on Husserl's thinking, correlate to a hierarchy of values, at the top of which stand intellectual and spiritual (*geistige*) values and vocations.

In striving to find unanimity with oneself, the course of life is necessarily split from itself. As Husserl notes, "in vocational life (*Berufsleben*) there is a split, so to speak, within the person of the vocation-person (*Berufsperson*)."[8] This split within oneself, striving under the operator of a vocation, can be understood in two related senses: as the split between who one is and who one is to become, between, in other words, *striving to become* and *called to be*; as the split between a determinate vocational sense of self (as father, teacher, etc.,) and oneself as a determinate whole in attuned unanimity. Throughout a life, a person toggles back and forth between different vocational personas: professor at the university, father at home, and so on. Each of these vocational dispositions and orientations are keyed and set into different spaces of normative demands and obligations, but likewise, different landscapes of value. Husserl's evocation of "splitting" in this context echoes his conception of *Ich-Spaltung* in his phenomenological analyses of phantasy (*Phantasie*); unlike imagining that I am Superman, when consciousness doubles itself into both the subject who imagines and the object imagined, experiencing itself at a distance from itself, as other than itself, when called upon and striving "to be a father," I am distant from myself in a constitutively different sense, for I open a space (and time) within myself that I am able to traverse and, hopefully, if successful, arrive at myself, as the future father I want to be. A vocation sets life on a trajectory of determinate becoming. In striving to be the kind of person I am presently not yet, I aim for myself, to be myself, on the horizon of my vocational aspiration. We might speak here of virtues of accuracy, adroitness, and aptness in evaluating the felicity conditions for achieving oneself: accuracy in the sense of attaining the idea of oneself, adroitness in cultivating the requisite capacities of one's character, and aptness of fit between accuracy and adroitness. The father who fails to appreciate the *values* entailed in the vocation of fatherhood, even as his conduct might formally satisfy the norms and duties of fatherhood, might be deemed to be "stupid," for example, in spending his discretionary income on Warhammer figures rather than providing for his child; in this case, a father would have confused the order of values (pleasure of wargaming versus caring for child's well-being), and can thus be said to have acted stupidly. A father, on the other hand, who would be indifferent to the values entailed on the vocation of fatherhood as such would be judged "foolish" in his failure, neither hitting the mark (accuracy) nor exercising any degree of competence (adroitness).[9] In the perpetual taking stock of oneself in terms of who I want to become, phantasy must necessarily exercise a critical role for self-formation, or *Selbstbildung* (much as one finds in Fichte's thinking) because a vocation opens a space of possibility *for me* that I must, through a employment of eidetic variation and self-reflection (*Besinnung*)—indeed: ethical reduction—explore and map in imagining *who* I must become in striving to be a good and caring father.

On this basis, Husserl's ethical ideal reaches toward *Seligkeit*, as more than satisfaction or happiness, and this entails that one strives to realize the best possible person that one can be, given the range of possibilities (of oneself) that one can become under given historical and cultural conditions, but, more significantly, under the value operators of one's chosen vocation. A person must cultivate the "I can" (*Ich kann*) of competencies and abilities, within an available range of possibilities, in view of the target space of norms and duties of their called upon vocations. The attainment of Seligkeit would thus represent a state of *joy* in having lived an accomplished and valuable life in meaningful relations to others. In the felicity of caring, there is joy without numbers and ode to the importance of what, or who, we care about.

Insofar as vocations are keyed into values, they are geared into relations with others (as parent, teacher, etc.), and hence, constitutive of intersubjectivity in its axiological and practical dimensions. Given that Husserl considers values of love *to be* the highest values as indispensable for attaining Seligkeit, Husserl's personalism stands firmly embedded within an ethics of love, where "fulfilled love" entails not only that I value myself (as self-valuing) to be the best possible person I can be, but, as guided by vocational calling, to be the best possible person in relation to those whom I care about. Measured by the idea-vocation of who I should be, and hence striving to become who I am to "to be," I can (more or less) fail at achieving myself yet by the same token I can (more or less) be successful as accomplishing myself. Genuine life requires cultivating one's own "style" of existence as a distinctive sense of meaningfulness of life as a whole within which experiences and episodes, even if failed, thwarted, or disappointed, nonetheless find place within oneself as "satisfied" regarding life as whole. Regrets and disappointments are "erased" or "crossed-through," not thereby ejected from one's life but, on the contrary, given place and perspective, as the scars of one's past, within the concordance of life *with* itself; one lives *with* one's failures and failings, not against them. As Husserl writes: "My life as a whole must conform to this style that I have freely formed for myself such that all particular disappointments can be fitted into this style (*einfügen lassen*), which I have, be it in terms of crossing-through (*Durchstreichungen*), distributed into the sense of style (*Stilsinn*) and function for the form of the whole."[10] In appealing to the notion "style," Husserl avoids any accusation of formalism or intellectualism; genuine life does not merely consist in formally living according to lawfulness. It involves cultivating one's own distinctive manner and course ("streaming") of becoming a person, of finding and achieving oneself, and hence, of the possibility of missing and failing oneself. Much as Husserl's ethics insists on "material values" (i.e., values as content of volition, decision, and conduct), this notion of style insists on a "materialism" of personhood, that is, the values and vocations that uniquely shape *my* life as a whole. In these various aspects, we find Husserl's phenomenological inscription of the idea of *Bildung* with its emphasis that *becoming* a person must be "freely shaped from me."[11]

Husserl's implicit *Bildungsphänomenologie* is framed within a distinction between "ethics" and "axiology," or, in Frankfurt's terms, between the domain of ethical inquiry and the "third domain" of inquiry into the importance of what we care about. This distinction, central to Husserl's thinking, represents a version of widely operating distinction between "morality" and "values" found in other (Husserl's) contemporary thinkers. In his 1913 essay "Moral Fruitfulness," Robert Musil, for example, takes issue with the "grumpily dignified scheme" of Kant's categorical imperative. As he writes: "Act in such a way that your acting can be a recipe for everyone—this Kantian morality is the German morality, is conscientiousness personified."[12] Against Kant's Pharisaism, Musil proposes: "Do not act so that your acting is a recipe for everyone, but so that it is valuable." What is valuable, in contrast to what is moral (in terms of formal lawfulness) refers to the pursuit of Seligkeit, which, as Musil portrayed in the relationship between Ulrich and Agathe in *The Man Without Qualities*, is founded on experiences of the erotic-mystical—"the other condition." To be sure, Husserl's conception of Seligkeit stands removed from Musil's "other condition," yet this point of contact between both on Seligkeit as the apex of *valuable existence* proves instructive for situating Husserl's thinking within his Central European-German cultural context. Husserl, for this part, distinguishes between "ethical attitude" and "axiological attitude" by contrasting the question "am I an ethical person?" from "am I a valuable person?" The ethical attitude is predicated on acting and volition along with reflective self-assessment and decision-making. As Husserl writes, "what belongs first and foremost to ethical willing and acting (*Tun*) is that it is not a naïve acting, but also not a naïve willing, but that the same rational object is willed consciously in its normativity and motivated through normativity."[13] As significantly, the ethical attitude refers to other persons, since, on Husserl's thinking, to adopt an ethical attitude toward the world and, hence, with regard to oneself (self-regard and self-valuing), involves not only one's "genuine ethical volition"—wanting to be ethical and deciding accordingly, that is, for the sake of norms—but includes as well "lived empathy for such [another's] will"—and hence, for any and all other ethical persons—"in which we put ourselves in the place of the one who wills ethically, and will with him, as it were." The disposition to deliberate and decide according to ethical norms reaches beyond the horizon of one's own life, for, as a "monad"—a unique and whole life in becoming—I am inextricably *implicated* (in Husserl's technical terminology: "intentional implication") in the lives of others, and hence, interwoven into a nexus of other monads. This intersubjective interweaving (*Verwebung*) places my own striving to attain concordance with myself on the stage of contributing toward the concordance of humanity with itself, that is, the community of *all other* striving persons (or "monads").

For Husserl, "the intrinsically first being, the being that precedes and bears every worldly objectivity, is transcendental intersubjectivity: the universe of monads, which effects its communion in various forms."[14] Anchored in a description of the natural attitude from the orientations of valuing and action (axiological and practical), a person finds themselves in relation to other persons as their neighbor (*seine 'Nächsten'*). The other person stands opposed (*gegenüber*) to me not in the same manner as perceptual objects. Indeed, other persons are not objects (*Gegenstände*) but neighbors in the sense of standing next to me as another member (*Mitglied*) of a community (the family, the team, etc.) to which I belong myself. Insofar as another person is a member of "a near community"—the near horizon of the community of my family, my teammates, my tribe, and so on,—that person *also* belongs to the community as its zero-link or zero-element (*Nullpunkt*) of orientation. Each member-person understands themselves as the center of the community, or, in other words, as the first-person perspective, yet insofar each member-person equally understands other member-persons as a zero-element, each in turn understands themselves as "Mit-Glied." I understand myself as "being-with" other members of the community to the degree that I understand the members as themselves a zero-element along with me. In this manner, a person stands opposite (*hat sich gegenüber*) *not only* his neighbor but at the same time his near community as such. Within the family, for example, I stand opposite and apposite (not opposed) my neighbor (brother, etc.) *and* the community of the family as such (or what Sartre would call "the third").[15] The community is not so much an object of my consciousness, as it is a cardinal point of bearing in my orientation in the world: I think, act, and value with regard to the family insofar I understand myself as a member of *this* family along with my brothers, parents, and so on How the family is construed remains a variable and cultural question; *that* a person stands in relation to their family (or tribe, team, etc.) as well as its members represents a formal structure of what it is to exist in the world as an intersubjective being. Each member is both a center of orientation (zero-point) and part (or member) (*Mit-Glied*). A near community can in turn stand as a central-link (*Zentralglied*) within an encompassing community, which, in turn, can stand as a central link in a more encompassing community: My family can stand as a central-link in the community of New Yorkers; being a New Yorker can in turn stand within the community of being an American; being an American can stand within the community of humanity.

These observations on the natural attitude, characterized from the angle of acting and valuing, are meant to establish Husserl's basic consideration of what we would recognize as social being, or social existence, in terms of orientation, membership, and standpoint. The natural attitude is structured according to a social topology: orientation toward the world as determined by community membership; terms of encounter with others as determined by demarcations of inclusion and exclusion (my family and your family, us and them, etc.), and standpoints onto the world of social existence as rooted in social orderings. Most remarkably of all is Husserl's insight that each individual person, as both a zero-link and a member (i.e., recognizes themselves as belonging to the community and is recognized by others as a member and, hence, recognizes themselves as a member along with other members), is invested as a speaking member, who can speak for themselves as well as for the community as such. To be social being is *eo ipso* to be a speaking being, and it is in the capacity of being able to speak *for* the community, *to* other members of the community, and *of* oneself as community member, that the individual is both "subject" and "object," and, moreover, the community gains "objectivity" through speech-acts that constitute social objects. Much as the lived-body is both a zero-point of orientation *and* an object in the world in relation to other bodies and, hence, in this sense, a "link" or "part" of the world in its spatial (and causal) nexus, the social being of the person is both a zero-point of orientation *and* an object (i.e., a member in the figurative and literal sense) of orientation. As Husserl writes: "Thus, the human world as individual and communal is objective in subjective orientation for the individual as well as for himself."[16]

The distinction between axiological and ethical attitudes—between values of our caring and actions of our deciding—frames Husserl's conception of a rank ordering of values spanning from (lower) sensual values and (higher) spiritual values. Not all values are of equal standing relative to each other. In adopting a traditional partitioning of values from "lower to higher," Husserl understands higher values as "absorbing" lower values, i.e., when values come into conflict with each other. In this manner, Husserl leverages a hierarchy of values against hedonism and utilitarianism, given their respective adherence to lower values. Husserl argues, however, that a theory of values is not sufficient for a theory of ethics, since the latter refers to questions of duties and obligations, the general form of which is the question: What should I do? (*Was soll ich tun?*)[17] The ethical operates under the imperative of ought (*Sollen*). Husserl's basic contention is that formal lawfulness of the ethical will—self-determined autonomy for the sake of ought—is based on an affective apprehension of a value. The disposition to act according to a norm or duty presupposes, on this argument, the affectivity of a corresponding value; only when affected by the value of Black lives, given (and against) their historical subjection to oppression and racism, do I become disposed to act on the injunction "Black Lives Matter!" For Husserl, the question what should I do? implicates the question "what is the most valuable (*das Wertvollste*) among those things that I can do?," and hence, "which of these decisions would be the decision of a valuable and most valuable human being?" In this sense, the question of conscience "am I a moral human?" is distinct from the question "am I a valuable, that is, meaningful human being?" Not all questions of meaning, of what gives value to my life is of an ethical significance. On the other hand, striving to become an ethical person would entail that placing my life under an operator of value, enhancing my life as valuable and, indeed, striving to attain Seligkeit, the most valuable and hence meaningful—authentic—form of human existence in the manner of my own unique style.

Noteworthy is Husserl's emphasis on striving to become "the best possible person" that I can in relation to myself, that is, myself considered from the standpoint of an Idea. This requires not only the exercise and habituality of self-reflection, but, moreover that I take stock of my life as whole in terms of what Husserl calls *Überschau*.[18] Self-reflection needs to be exercised along with taking stock of life under the horizon of one's idea, or vocation, thus involving the mapping of one's possibilities, namely, possible versions of the kind of person one can and should become. To lead a life is thus to strive to become the best among possible different life narratives, shaped through different choices, adversities, and consequences. Husserl recognizes that a life pursues different vocations simultaneously, each with different demands, values, and norms (father, scientist, husband, friend, etc.), such that living a life is not reduced to proper conduct, but becoming a certain kind of person, becoming the best person I can be within the space and time afforded to me, circumscribed by the idea of how I can become, as if with every decision, I am choosing not just "to be this person" but also "not to be this person," not another person, but me. Different possible scripts and versions of myself, which I must author, inform and infirm the chosen course of life, along with, notably, the discarded ghosts of myself, of who I could have been, or could not, given the fortunes of the world, not have chosen to be.

In striving to become a whole person, Husserl suggests that this expansive becoming would require the transforming of one's "special vocation"—to be a scientist, for example—into a complete universal vocation (*vollen Universalberuf*), where Husserl understand this universal vocation as comprising "to be human, the most complete, authentic, and true human."[19] However a vocation is willed, it must be willed "for eternity," as it were, that is, sustained in its importance and purchase such that this decision to this kind of person is not impulsive or one-off. The decision for a vocation must become one's *devotion*; a person must become invested in and committed to the values one cares about and hence the kind of person who embodies and lives through and in these values. To be sure, the decision "now and forever," based on the vocational call of values, can in the future become abandoned, neglected, and betrayed. In binding to who I should be, I bind myself in advance to an idea of myself in the future, and must thus anticipate myself as well as, in striving, reach out to myself. Ultimately, Husserl's temporality of vocation and commitment (or devotion) dovetails with his phenomenology of volition, where willing entails deciding to act, enactment, and follow-through of action.

Personhood is self-constituted in terms of *Selbst-Erhaltung*—self-conservation or self-persistence—which entails repeatedly (and sustainingly) choosing to become myself under the operator of values and vocation, namely, choosing to be a certain kind of person (father, teacher, etc.), through whose thoughts and deeds, a corresponding set of values gains traction and presence in the world (in relation to others). Underlying the sustained importance of what (or who) I care about must be an existential choice regarding what to do with myself, of who I want, and ought, to become, thus implying self-valuation and caring for oneself. Husserl, in this regard, speaks of responsibility for oneself, in view of one's vocation, and loyalty toward oneself, in view of one's cares and commitments. When I fail to heed the call of values and vocation, I have betrayed myself. I stand irresponsible toward *both* myself as well as implicated others.[20] Self-valuation (*Selbstwertung*) and self-responsibility are integral to the self-directed attitude of "caring for life," namely, my own, or what Husserl calls *die Einstellung der Lebenssorge*.[21] To shoulder responsibility for oneself is to care for oneself and place importance on oneself as caring and valuing; it is to burden oneself with oneself in the cause of one's own self-becoming, that is, *freedom*.

One of the more substantial transformations in Husserl's phenomenological ethics occurs with the introduction of "absolute values" in the aftermath of the First World War.[22] A crucial difference between objective values and absolute values consists in that the latter are tethered to vocations; an absolute value "calls" on a person "to be," and, in this sense, we might speak of an implicit "ideal ought" expressed in the interpolation of absolute values: the affectivity of love for one's child calls the self as "father" into being. The uptake of absolute values thus takes the form of responding to the call of an associated vocation, namely, to become the *kind* of person who has invested themselves in shaping their lives, in thinking and action, according to an absolute value. Conversely, failing to heed the call of vocation represents a failure of oneself and abdication of both responsiveness to an absolute value and responsibility toward who one *ought to be*. Husserl's paradigmatic example of absolute values is of a mother's love for her child. A mother's love for her child engages intertwined conditions. Although grounded in the affectivity of love, it necessarily involves cognitive and ethical dimensions, or conditions. The absolute value of "caring for the child" issues neither solely from a rational decision nor is it reducible to mere instinct, and this because Husserl considers that instincts, as with hunger, lack within themselves guidance or direction toward a *determinate* object: When I feel pangs of hunger and need to eat, the instinct for food is geared toward any determinate kind of nutrition.[23] However, if I desire steak tartare, there is a determinate desire, not just an indeterminate instinct for food; although responding to a basic instinct, it is nonetheless constituted as a desire given its directionality toward a particular kind of object or range of objects. This can be illustrated with the experience of disappointment: If my desire to enjoy lamb is disappointed, an alternative might nonetheless satisfy my hunger and hence instinct, but therefore not my desire *for lamb*. My instinctual need for food is satisfied yet I am nonetheless unhappy and unsatisfied in terms of what I desire, if even I am satiated foodwise. For Husserl, motherly love is both an instinct and a desire. I am struck as it were despite myself by the affectivity of love for my child, they are irreducible not only, however, to my own subjectivity but, in a different sense, are also irreducible to objective values (i.e., cannot be placed in rank ordering and rational comparison): A mother's love for her child cannot be weighed against another mother's love, even though both mother's love their respective children "absolutely." The absolute, as singular, cannot be declinated in terms of either "universality" or "particularity," or a type-token relation.

A peculiarity of what Husserl terms absolute values consists in the elusive manner to which such affective values cannot be placed on either side of a conventional distinction between subjective feeling and objective state of affairs. Nor are absolute values to be confused with perceptual attributions of color, size, and so on to objects. Strictly speaking, we do not perceive values in the way we perceive colors, and yet, Husserl argues that the intake of values is intuitive and affective, or better: affectively intuitive, for which he adopts the term of *Wertnehmung*. As with other kinds of intentionality, experiential "value-intaking" transpires according to the structuration of "empty" and "fulfilled" intentionality. Caring for a child as yet unborn, in expectation of their birth (or arrival, as with adoption), represents in Husserlian terms an "empty intention." We might only have of the child their name, as a signifying intention, or a set of expectations and emotions, that refer to the as yet unborn child; a mother might feel in herself the kicks and shuffling of the baby; we can see an image of the child; we can hear their heartbeat. These represent different "empty intentions" that becomes "fulfilled" with the birth of the child; and yet, even once born to the world, the child remains in a phenomenologically crucial sense "to be encountered," since, on Husserl's account, the ego of the other is never given to us "in flesh and blood," and hence, we are, as it were, always intending in a manner that remains "to be fulfilled." Absolute values are thus irreducible to the self for they place a demand on the self "to be." Setting aside the manifold complexities and problems gather around this conception (and which admittedly Husserl himself did not adequately explore), the affectivity of an absolute value can be fruitfully characterized as an original impression that opens a trajectory of self-temporalization. As with an original impression, the initial arrival, as it were, of a disclosed value in affectivity is unmotivated but also neither passively received or actively self-posited. The affective announcement of an absolute value is, further, more akin to an original institution (*Urstiftung*) that opens not only a space of reasons and action, but a determinate course of becoming within which there exists a leeway of the possibilities. As Frankfurt observes: "If we consider that a person's will is that by which he moves himself, then what he cares about is far more germane to the character of his will than the decisions or choices he makes. The latter may pertain to what he *intends* to be his will, but not necessarily to what his will truly *is*."[24] The apparent paradox is that what we (should) care about the most is not at its inception mostly something we decided ahead of time, or chose in the manner in which subsequent choices, opened and situated within a space of willing and doing by the original institution of absolute value, comes about. And yet, on the other hand, we are not, as Husserl writes, merely moral machines who register and follow the impacts of values; there needs to be genuine uptake of value into our lives in terms of investment on our behalf. An absolute value must be *claimed* all the while that an absolute value *calls* upon us. In this sense, an absolute value can be said to *choose us* in announcing itself, to borrow a term from Scheler, as a kind of anointment. There is thus a baptismal quality to the affectivity of an absolute value. We can fail to heed the call, fail in persisting to care, or misrecognize what is asked of us, but, in a critical sense, the "call of the absolute value" is there from the beginning, and thus, unlike a desire with genesis in a nexus of motivations, it is "immemorial" in one sense, and yet, anchored in an "original impression," thus implying a coefficient of surprise and contingency. An absolute value becomes "given" as a futural task (*Aufgabe*) for me to become, shepherding, as it were, its reality into the world, including, my own.

A dawning of awareness accompanies the affective awakening of an absolute value. Under the spell, as it were, of a value's solicitation, the self becomes aware of itself in terms of its directing vocation or calling. Within this awareness, or realization, "I am a father," for example, the self becomes attentive to an object, or person, in the light of its value. Affected by love for his child, a father becomes attentive the child in its dependency and vulnerability. Different forms of attention became set within an encompassing awareness, and, indeed, sustained and cultivated, through habituality and reflection, over time, that is, the course of the caring relationship to the child.

In the vocational awareness of "being a father," the self *attends* to the child in certain ways, rather than not: the cup on the edge of the table is a possible spillage, a street-crossing becomes seen as a potential hazard, the preferences and pleasures of the child become salient, and so on. Proverbially speaking, we have eyes for the child *through* our caring and hence valuing, and thus become disposed to see things, attend to things, and respond to things for which we otherwise would not have perspicuous concern. In Husserl's thinking, the value of attention is inseparable from attending and tending to the values that have affected us, yet in attending to the things, or persons, we care about, we value not only the well-being (in this example) of the child, by just as much, the intrinsic value of valuing itself in relation to valuing ourselves as the kind of person for whom it is important to value and care for things, or persons. Attending, in this sense, is a threefold relationship: attending to the well-being of the child; attending to the value of caring for the child; attending to oneself as self-valuing. To a significant degree, the self becomes responsible not only for the child "to be cared for," but for the value of "caring for the child" itself as well as for oneself as a valuing and caring person. Indeed, values only gain traction and weight in the world—"reality"—in terms of our attending and tending to them, much as those whom we care for only have traction and weight in the world—real presence—as a function of their value.

What is remarkable is that those persons and things for which we care most about are those persons and things that we never deliberatively decided *to care about*. This is the sense in which it is to be understood that an absolute value is itself "unmotivated," that is, without genesis and in this sense immemorial (not always there from the beginning, but once there, there already from the beginning), and yet, it functions like an *Urstiftung* that opens a space for motivations, and to which motivations retrospectively refer. An absolute value can thus to be understood as both an "original impression" and "original institution," for I have been myself "instituted," that is, invested, "to care." In this temporalization, an absolute value is neither passively received from the outside nor actively posited from the inside. An absolute value opens a timeline for living; once affected by the impact of love for the child, a course and version of who I am to become becomes disclosed to me, and hence, a form of self-temporalization in conjunction with the temporalization of the child. Frankfurt observes that "there are occasions when a person realizes that what he cares about matters to him not merely so much, but in such a way, that it is impossible for him to forbear from a certain course of action." Revealingly, Frankfurt references in this regard Luther's declaration "Here I stand; I can do no other" and thus we can say: Husserl adopts the Protestant idiom of "calling" to speak of the affectivity of value as "calling upon" the mother. Struck by my love for the child, I am called to be father, and hence, a course for my life and version of who I am becomes imparted to me. As Frankfurt for this part notes, "an encounter with necessity of this sort characteristically *affects*" (my emphasis) a person not by "impelling him into a certain course of action than by somehow making it apparent to him that every apparent alternative to that course is unthinkable."[25] An absolute value propels a person into a course of action and version of themselves without thereby *prescribing or dictating* a particular course of action and particular instantiation of oneself. Rather, the person becomes impelled "to be a father" within a space of possibilities, impelled to realize "the best possible," yet within a circumscribed horizon where an alternative ("not being a father") is *unthinkable*.

Unthinkable, yet not betrayable by our own hand. Each of us harbor secrets about ourselves haunting us from within, returning as ghosts of our past with the acute sense of self-betrayal, when, under whatever circumstances, we have in the past forsaken our own vocation. At time unthinkable that there could be an alternate to the importance of what, or who, we care about, the realization that we have betrayed ourselves, of having instigated or caused the ruin of our vocation, poignantly reveals how what was once unthinkable becomes nonetheless possible. In betraying what had been most important, we blame ourselves and feel ourselves to have failed ourselves in an intimate manner. The depth of this sense of having wronged oneself (as well as the persons wronged: lovers, friends, etc.), cannot be measured in purely ethical terms of right and wrong, though it includes this as well (cheating on a spouse, etc.). The affliction of having wronged oneself and violated not just moral norms, but our cares and commitments, and this is just another way to arrive at the distinction between moral right and wrong (norms and duties) and the valuing of what is important to us—the importance of what we care about—our cares and commitments. It is this distinction between moral right and wrong and care and importance that we find in Husserl's distinction between moral duties and obligations (and the associated objective values) toward others and what he calls absolute values that do not directly pertain to our relations with others, but, to adopt here Frankfurt's felicitous expression, what to do with ourselves, the kind of life we want to lead, the kind of person we want to be. Here, then, the idea is that "wronging" oneself in this fundamental sense of self-betrayal, when we betray what we ourselves hold to be important and care for, when we first and foremost betray ourselves, cannot be understood merely in terms of *moral wrongdoing*, but a wrongdoing against the importance of what we care about, a wrongdoing against we might say our own singular essence. This wounding is not easily repairable; and it would seem that it exceeds the bounds or reach of justice, and we can wonder what kind of atonement would here dispel the ghosts of our self-betrayal, as if we are haunted by the person *who we could have, and wanted to continue to be*, a person committed to fundamental cares—cares that defined us in an essential and singular manner; we are haunted not just by possibilities that never materialized—the could have been—but we are haunted by being the kind of person we wanted to be, a person we have forsaken and betrayed. I wonder about these ghosts that cannot be expiated from our lives, and who return, often with a vengeance, the broken pieces (and fragments of memories) of who we could have been, but have not become, on account of our own doing.

The gravity and grievousness of self-betrayal reveals the intimate sense in which a vocation opens a space and time for becoming a certain kind of person according to one's own unique style of being. The mother becomes "called" into being "a mother" through an interpolation of value in relation to the specific child standing before he. The self as "mother" does not preexist the interpolation of value and, hence, caring. In responding to the solicitation of valuing her child, inseparable from the singular being of her beloved, a temporal trajectory of possible versions and narratives of oneself becomes open as well as a space of norms and duties. This calling into being of the self, or interpolation of subjectivity, is not, however, experienced as a constraint or coercion to one's freedom. Frankfurt is thus right to notice that "the suggestion that a person may be in some sense liberated through acceding to a power which is not subject to his immediate voluntary control is among the most ancient and persistent themes of our moral and religious traditions."[26] This suggestion is reflected directly in Husserl's lexicon of affectivity, calling, and vocation: We must accede and submit, become subjected to, a vocation in terms of which I become a subject; subjectification in this dual sense of acceding and attaining, for in acceding to the call of the value I must attain myself through its investment in my life. My life is bound to an investiture of caring. As Frankfurt observes: "The formation of a person's will is most fundamentally a matter of his coming to care about certain things, and of his coming to care about some of them more than about others."[27]

When fully developed in terms of Husserl's axiological and ethical conception of the self, a person is not merely reducible to an ego pole in terms of an empty, or formal, "dead substrate for attributes." In addition to understanding the self, as an ego or "I," in terms of a center of action (*Ich kann*) and volitional, as well as in terms of "character," "disposition," "temperament" (*Gemüt*), the self possesses, in caring and valuing absolutely, *intimacy* (*Innerlichkeit*). The intimacy of the self—in the typical Christian image of "heart"—is understood as a center of love and, in this regard, is considered by Husserl to be "personal" in an exceptional sense. The self who responds to the call of their vocation (under the operator of an absolute value) accedes the profound interiority of self-responsibility. A vocation (*Berufung*) speaks and indeed discloses this intimacy of personhood, but as Husserl stipulates, it is the value that calls us: *Das Rufende sind schon geahnte oder erschaute Werte*.

One hears a call to the ego (*ein Ruf an das Ego*), a call to final, absolute binding decision.[28] As with Frankfurt who notes that a person who cares about following a certain course of action must also care about caring about it, this is what Husserl means by "self-valuation" and "personal ought" (*Sollen*) that forms the authentic center of gravity of individuality. As Husserl remarks: *Das Ich, als welches ein solches innerstes Ich hat, an das Berufungen ergehen, die seine, dieses Ich, Berufungen since, hat Individualität.*[29] I must value myself as the kind of person who values taking care of my child. And this is the sense in which this "volitional necessity" (Frankfurt's term) or vocation calling is not experienced as alien or coercive since the person identifies themselves with it in an absolute self-responsibility. I see *myself* as the father who I should become and not as another. Here I stand, I can *be* no other.

Husserl in his own manner, arguably more richly textured than Frankfurt, establishes that what characterizes the *importance* of what, or who, we care about, under the operator absolute values and correlating vocations, consists in the self-persistence (*Selbst-Erhaltung*). A person committed to valuing cares, in its threefold configuration (care for values, care for others, care for oneself) must exercise, habitually and reflectively, consistency and constancy in their commitment ("devotion" for Frankfurt). What, or who, we care about must garner more uptake and traction that a mere fleeting impulse, occasional decision, or momentary enthusiasm. What, or who, we care about must continually animate, that is, affect our soul (Gemüt). Yet, aside from Husserl's account of the drive for *Selbst-Erhaltung*, Husserl recognizes that ethical striving, shaped within the axiological mold of absolute values and vocations, remains haunted by the general uncertainty and contingency of future becoming of the world.[30] Husserl's experience of the war, the death of his youngest son as well as students in combat, profoundly affected his thinking in this respect: *Kann ich leben in einer 'sinnlosen' Welt*? he repeatedly asks himself through-out Freiburg manuscripts As he wonders: "How [can I have hope] if I must judge the world to be without reason [*vernunftlose*], if the beauty of nature breaks apart due to natural evolution and my appreciation of humanity [goes out the window [*mir abhanden kommt*], perhaps as the result of such a war?"[31]

In response to this repeatedly posed question, Husserl argues that a mother "knows for certain" that, even if tomorrow would herald the end of the world (*Weltuntergang*), that a flood shall devastate the earth, it would be foolish and futile to insist that the mother should forsake her child; would we tell such a mother to curtail attending to the needs of her child, caring for her child—in a word: actively loving her child? Would a mother nonetheless uphold in an intimate manner, despite the onsetting end of days, with absolute conviction and commitment the importance of caring for her child? As Husserl dramatically declares: "Let the world be hell, I shall still resist this hell and do my duty!"[32] It would fall dramatically short of Husserl's contention were one to say: the duty to care for her child trumps over empirical determinations; this, of course, is part and parcel of absolute values, namely, that they anchor and disclose, indeed: insert the subject, into a space of reason and obligations. But this would represent what Husserl calls a "performance machine" (*Leistungsmachine*) who follows duties based on the formal lawfulness of volition.[33] The mother resists against hell because she has been affected, and this affectivity, as it were, has elected or chosen her; she we rise to sustain the caring person she has (been) chosen to be. We have seen that caring for something and placing an importance, living this importance, of what and who we care about, demands a certain disposition of the self to persist in this caring and thus, orients the person toward the future. Caring becomes a project in the adventure of the self. But now we come to Husserl's nexus of concerns: how can we be assured that the future will align with the sustaining of our cares and significance? What if the future thwarts our projects of caring: we care for our child, yet our child might die. Husserl contends that nonetheless, we resist this hell of the world and "do our duty," that is, we insist on the importance of what and who we care about, come what may. Caring becomes in this manner a transcendental principle and condition for the meaningfulness of life itself, regardless of empirical contingencies. What, however, becomes of Husserl's reformulated categorical imperative: "Always act in such a way that your action contributes as well as possible to the best (the most valuable) you recognize yourself to be able to achieve in your life, given your individual abilities and environment"?[34] Especially given Husserl's insistence on the "open future horizon" toward which this imperative is primarily oriented. What would this imperative to act for the sake of "the most valuable" once we find ourselves situated at the end of the world? If, as it were, the space of possible practical action becomes suspended and destroyed, what remains of caring and valuing, their importance?

As evinced with Husserl's paradigmatic reference to the mother's love for her child and his stirring declaration *Mag die Welt eine Hölle sein*, regardless of whether *I can* act on, and thus sustain, an absolute value and vocation, it nonetheless remains important not only for me, but as such. Even if I knew "for certain" that the world would end tomorrow, or my child perish tomorrow, the *value* of caring would not become diminished; indeed, on the contrary, we might even say that the value of caring becomes *enhanced*. The measure of the importance of what we care about as persistence despite the empirical course of the world, so if, on the one hand, Husserl underlines the aspect of self-persistence over time into the future, given that the future is inherently contingent and uncertain, this temporal dimension extends as it were "to infinity."[35]

In Husserl's phenomenology of care and commitment, the declaration *fiat iustitia, et pereat mundus* becomes transformed into *fiat cura, et pereat mundus*.

Where, then, do we arrive, in delineating the contours of a phenomenology of care and commitment? These exploratory reflections, it is to be understood, are presented in the spirit of paving a way into Husserl's ethical thought, leaving much to be further elaborated, explained, and examined. In lieu of a definitive statement of conclusion or position of arrival, we can look back over the course and ground covered in these reflections and highlight, or note, what characteristic features of the *problematic* condition of human life, once anchored in the "third domain of inquiry" into the importance of what (and who) we care about. Husserl's reflections on the sustaining and cultivating the *importance* of what we care about, or, in his terminology, the enduring *Bewährung* (corroboration) of the uptake of absolute values and our associated vocations in our lives, points to the tragedy of destiny: how can we instill trust in ourselves, our cares and commitments, given world's ineradicable contingency? How can we *hope* that our values will continue to be upheld and corroborated given the uncertainty and indeterminacy of the world, that, in other words, the world may not go our way, and, indeed, strike against all that we cherish and hold dear? In addition to this tragedy of destiny, that is, a challenge to concordance of our values and sense of life as accomplished, as a whole, there is what Husserl explicitly identifies as the "tragedy of the person." While, on the one hand, Husserl insists on concordance with oneself as the ideal of a blessed life (Seligkeit), he equally recognizes, on the other hand, and stemming directly from his notion of (plurality) of absolute values, the irreconcilability of absolute values, and, hence, tacitly, *the impossibility* of complete self-concordance with respect to what (and who) one values most. Two dimensions of impossibility haunt the pursuit of felicity (Seligkeit): the impossibility of concordance between the importance of what *I* care about and the world; the impossibility of concordance within myself between the manifold things and persons who are important, in terms of care and commitment, *for me*.

It is here that the existential significance of the twin problems of trust and hope take hold. Trust matters to us as a function of sustaining the importance of what we care about; hope becomes an imperative for us as a function of the tragedy of destiny. In his sketchy reflections on God, Husserl entertains the thought of hope as a practical postulate of reason, referring to the idea of God, as providing for the concordance of absolute values that we human beings are unable to reconcile for and within ourselves. But this leaves in our hands, that is, as a function of our persisting and enduring strivings, the problem of trust. For as Husserl writes: "I can be happy in the sense that on the basis of a correctly (*recht*) gained self-trust at the same time can trust in the world, [and] this consciousness I can gain [win], that I belong to human world in the framework of objective world, which allows for [renders possible] unending possibilities of ethical striving and a rational configuration of the world, a configuration in which humanity can achieve through one's own work continuing [progressing] and best possible happiness."[36] This cornerstone of phenomenological ethics is itself exemplified in the ethics of phenomenology itself, of the importance of caring for truth and Seligkeit for the meaningfulness of human life itself.

NOTES

1. Harry Frankfurt, "The Importance of What We Care About," in *The Importance of What We Care About* (Cambridge: Cambridge University Press, 1998).
2. Ibid., 83.
3. Ibid., 85.
4. For a suggestive meditation on "vocation" in a broader context, Jonathan Imber, "The Vocation of Reason: Wallace Stevens and Edmund Husserl," *Human Studies*, 9 (1986): 3–19.
5. *Cartesian Meditations*, trans. D. Cairns (Dordrecht: Kluwer, 1991), 156.
6. Hua XXXVII, 248.
7. Hua XXV, 289.
8. Hua XLII, 416.
9. For this distinction between stupidity and foolishness, as well as the three-fold distinction of accuracy, adroitness, and aptness (borrowed from Ernest Sosa's virtue epistemology), see Pascal Engel, "The Epistemology of Stupidity."
10. Hua XLII, 491.
11. Hua XLII, 491.
12. Robert Musil, *Precision and Soul*, 39.
13. Hua XXXVII, 247.
14. *Cartesian Meditations*, 156. For Husserl's intersubjectivity as the veritable transcendental subject, see Dan Zahavi, *Husserl and Transcendental Intersubjectivity* (Ohio University Press, 2001). See also Nicolas de Warren, "The Only Refuge: Refutations of Idealism in Kant and Husserl," in *Acts of the XI International Kant Congress* (Berlin: Walter de Gruyter, 2013).
15. See Nicolas de Warren, "We Are, Therefore I Am—I Am, Therefore We Are: The 'Third' in Sartre's Social Ontology," in: *Embodiment, Enaction, and Culture*, ed. Thomas Fuchs and Christoph Durt (Cambridge: MIT Press, 2016).
16. Hua XLII, 298. The homologous structure of belonging to a community and the subject-object configuration of the lived-body, that is, the former is not derived from the latter.
17. Hua XXXVII, 245.
18. See Andrea Staiti, "A Grasp From Afar: Überschau and the givenness of life in Husserlian phenomenology."

19. Hua XXXVII, 252.
20. Hua XLII, 488.
21. Hua XLII, 472.
22. See Ulrich Melle, "Edmund Husserl: From Reason to Love," in *Phenomenological Approaches to Moral Philosophy*, eds. J. Drummond and L. Embree (Dordrecht: Springer, 2002): 229–48, and Nicolas de Warren, "Husserl and Phenomenological Ethics," in *The Cambridge History of Moral Philosophy*, eds. S. Golob and J. Timmerman, (Cambridge: Cambridge University Press, 2017): 562–76. For the impact of the war on Husserl's thinking, Nicolas de Warren, *German Philosophy and the First World War*, (Cambridge: Cambridge University Press, 2022).
23. Hua XLII, 86.
24. Frankfurt, 84.
25. Ibid., 86.
26. Ibid., 89.
27. Ibid., 91.
28. Hua XLII, 359.
29. Ibid.
30. For a more detailed analysis, see Nicolas de Warren, "*Mag die Welt eine Hölle sein.* Husserl's Existential Ethics," in *The Existential Husserl* (Dordrecht: Springer Verlag, forthcoming).
31. Hua XLII, 307.
32. Ibid., 310.
33. Ibid., 309.
34. Hua XXXVII, 251.
35. This means then, not the primacy of practical attitude, but the primacy of axiological—theoretical attitude, and in this sense; as Cassirer writes: "The term 'prudence'. . . . means the ability to foresee future events and to prepare for future needs. But the theoretical idea of the future—the idea which is a prerequisite of all man's higher cultural activities—is of quite a different sort. It is more than a mere expectation; it becomes an imperative for life." (*Essay on Man*, 54–55). Cassirer calls this the prophetic future (not empirical) but in Husserlian terms we might call this the vocational future; the future to which I am devoted despite the devastation of the world and this then will connect to hope; the importance of hoping for what and who we care about.
36. Hua XLII, 331.

REFERENCES

Cassirer, E. (2021). *An Essay on Man*. Yale University Press.

de Warren, N. The Only Refuge: Refutations of Idealism in Kant and Husserl. In *Acts of the XI International Kant Congress*. Walter de Gruyter.

———. (2016). We Are, Therefore I Am—I Am, Therefore We Are: The "Third" in Sartre's Social Ontology. In: Thomas Fuchs and Christop Durt, eds., *Embodiment, Enaction, and Culture*. MIT Press.

———. (2017). Husserl and Phenomenological Ethics. In: S. Golob and J. Timmerman, eds., *The Cambridge History of Moral Philosophy*. Cambridge University Press.

———. (2023) *German Philosophy and the First World War*. Cambridge University Press.

———. *Mag die Welt eine Hölle sein.* Husserl's Existential Ethics. In *The Existential Husserl*. Springer Verlag.

Engel, P. (2016). "The Epistemology of Stupidity." In: Miguel Vargas, ed., *Performance Epistemology: Foundations and Applications*. Oxford University Press.

Frankfurt, H. (1998) *The Importance of What We Care About*. Cambridge University Press.

Husserl, E. (1988). *Vorlesungen über Ethik und Wertlehre 1908–1914*, Husserliana XXVIII. Ed. U. Melle. Kluwer Academic Publishers.

———. (1989). *Aufsätze und Vorträge* 1922–1937, Husserliana XXVII. Eds. H. R. Sepp and T. Nenon. Kluwer Academic Publishers.

———. (2004). *Wahrnehmung und Aufmerksamkeit, Texte aus dem Nachlass* (1893–1912), Husserliana XXXVIII. Eds. T. Vongehr and. R. Giuliani. Springer.

———. (2013). *Grenzprobleme der Phänomenologie: Analysen des Unbewusstseins und der Instinkte, Metaphysik, Späte Ethik, Texte aus dem Nachlass* (1908–1937), Husserliana XLII. Eds. R. Sowa and T. Vongehr. Springer.

———. (2014). *Cartesian Meditations* (trans. D. Cairns). Kluwer Academic Publishing.

Imber, J. (1986). The Vocation of Reason: Wallace Stevens and Edmund Husserl. *Human Studies*, 9.

Melle, U. (2002) Edmund Husserl: From Reason to Love. In: J. Drummond and L. Embree, eds., *Phenomenological Approaches to Moral Philosophy*. Springer Verlag.

Musil, R. (1995). *Precision and Soul* (Trans. B. Pike and D. Luft). University of Chicago Press.

Staiti, A. (2013). A Grasp From Afar: Überschau and the Givenness of Life in Husserlian phenomenology/ *Continental Philosophy Review*, 46.

Zahavi, D. (2001) *Husserl and Transcendental Intersubjectivity*. Ohio University Press.

Chapter 12

On the Problem of the Idealization of Empathy and Ethics

Magnus Englander and Susi Ferrarello

ABSTRACT

In this chapter, we seek to disclose how empathy and ethics have been constructed to idealized forms through the process of naturalization and relativization in science and professional practice. The chapter begins with a historical investigation of how the natural attitude continues into Galileo's technologization of nature. Following the basic structure of the natural attitude, we can also see how it shapes our interpretation of empathy. The authors disclose a paradox that seems to be unacceptable by the sciences related to modern psychology. This has resulted in the scientific community explaining empathy by sophisticated models (e.g., simulation, mirror neurons, etc.), in which the trace of the natural attitude continues, such as can be seen in the naturalization of empathy in the contemporary cognitive neurosciences. This idealization of empathy is then carried over from the sciences to professional practice resulting in a technological approach toward empathy. As a contrast, we argue for a return to our fundamental relation to others as interpersonal understanding and a reflection of empathy that would open for the development of professional ethics as a reflective human activity, instead of a set of guidelines and principles that are, more often than not, sophisticated, bureaucratic processes thought to prevent unethical action and issues of liability. Only reflection of our being with others will lead us to self-responsibility.

Keywords: empathy, self-responsibility, idealization, intentionality

> In the natural attitude, in which for ourselves and for others we are called and are humans, to everything worldly there belongs the being-acceptedness: existent in the world, in the world that is always existent beforehand as constant acceptedness of a basis. So also man's being is being in the world that is existent beforehand. In phenomenology, this being-beforehand is itself a problem.
>
> —Edmund Husserl (*Sixth Cartesian Meditation*, Section 59, 136)

As Sebastian Luft (2011, 59) has highlighted, "The natural attitude consists in viewing the world as 'nature,' as existing independent of an experiencing agent." The natural attitude indicates a naive way in which we experience life without reflecting on it. In doing so, our understanding of the world becomes a construction or at best an idealization[1] of it. The world becomes an object, a construct, an artifact in some way separated from us that we discover, observe, and keep at a distance from us. This way of experiencing the world is often at the basis of more sophisticated attitudes in both science and in our professional life. For example, the natural attitude provides the ground for the independent observer in the natural sciences, an ideal role that has since extended to our modern sense of professionalism and with an ought of being personally detached from the recipient of one's work. The worldviews generated from the natural attitude have a tendency to serve as models of idealizations in which we often fail to recognize our role in these models. Edmund Husserl (1989, p. 69) himself noted, "Reality and irreality belong together essentially in the form of reality and subjectivity, which on the one hand mutually exclude one another and on the other hand . . . essentially require one another." In other words, the way in which we experience the reality of the world—including nature, animals, and other humans—is deeply connected to our subjectivity even if it is ontologically independent from us. This generates a paradox. For example, we might believe that we are isolated islands and only our subjective experience counts as true or that we are independent observers of nature and that there is such a thing as knowledge in itself. As a consequence, the ideas that we form from our subjective experience becomes an idealization, that is a model that can explain the world. As a theme of the natural attitude, our sense of *the self* becomes naturalized into an ideal self, a model, *independent of our experience of being*. Ideal models of the self is apparent in contemporary roles such as the scientist and the professional. When faced with a complex ethical issue at work, we are encouraged to follow guidelines instead of taking a closer look at ourselves in relation to our role. We are encouraged to be professional, which is an ideal self. For example, we might be judged as a liability for not having followed prescriptive guidelines, policies, laws, and tradition; rather than as a person failing to reflect on our *self-responsibility* toward ourselves and others.

In encountering others through the natural attitude, *we also naturalize others and take for granted that they exist independently of us*. They become an ideal, a model, a construction whose existence and well-being stands out as independent of us. Edith Stein (1964, 11) captures the genesis of this as she writes, "The subject of the empathized experience, however, is not the subject empathizing, but another. . . . These two subjects are separate and not joined together, as . . . , by a consciousness of sameness or a continuity of experience. And while I am living in the other's joy, I do not feel primordial joy." In other words, at the moment that we are able to empathically perceive the emotion as it comes through in the expression of the other, we do not have a first-person experience of the other's emotion, yet we instantly recognize the meaning of the expression. Once again, the natural attitude sets us up with a paradox, resulting in the problem of empathy. Contemporary explanations of empathy extend the problem of empathy to the approach of the natural sciences and refer to empathy as implicit simulation activated by mirror neurons (Gallese, 2003) or explicit simulation through cognitive processes (Goldman, 2006).[2] Even though one could interpret the popular term simulation as (only) using a metaphor, the meaning of the term originates from the context of computer science and implies that interpersonal understanding is analogous to a technological achievement. The natural attitude and its extension to the sophisticated models of the sciences separate us from seeing our fundamental being-in-the-world and being-with-others. Nevertheless, we also have to realize, as Luft (2011, 51) reminds us, that "the natural attitude is the correlate to the lifeworld." This means that the natural attitude is fundamental in generating our ideal models of the world and also what presents us with our paradox of existence. In other words, phenomenological reflection provides us with the possibility of catching a glimpse of what seems to be an inescapable human paradox.

In this chapter, we will seek an understanding how empathy and ethics relate to the natural attitude. We will at times relate our inquiry to modern professions. However, we do not intend to cover the literature concerning professional studies.[3] Instead, we only refer to modern professions here in its general sense, so as to provide an applied context to our theoretical exploration.

THE ORIGINS OF NATURALISM

In the *Crisis of the European Sciences*, Husserl's (1970) study of Galileo's work warned us about naturalism becoming the taken-for-granted model of reality, replacing the a priori condition of the concrete lifeworld—which means that we first need our life in the world for reality to be experienced as its correlate. Instead of being a true liberator from our Idols, Galileo's naturalism was founded on a mathematization of Nature (Husserl, 1970, section 9) according to which the world exists as a geometric or mathematical entity independent of us. This mathematization of nature has led us to a new type of idealization of the world[4] expressed in the abstract construct of Nature (Husserl, 1970, 26, 34, 38, 87, 140, 221). Naturalism resulted in us ignoring the way in which intentionality—that is, the subject-object referential relation to the world—shapes the content of our knowledge. However, nature cannot be an abstract construct because we interact with it and at each interaction we make sense of its being. As a matter of fact, the continuation of the natural attitude and the objectivity constituting this idealization hides the personal components[5] that makes the ideal type possible in the first place and allows us to forget the human being behind the "construction" (Husserl, 1970, p. 49). The idealization, a word that Husserl often pairs with construction, is identified with numbers, geometrical shapes, or any seemingly neutral token that makes us forget about the human being and the natural attitude that hides behind it. Hence, Galileo's geometrization and mathematization of Nature meant that any science would have to surrender to a naturalistic methodology for which the lifeworld becomes *life independent* of our interaction with it. We had to pretend that as scientists we are not involved in the numbers we produce.

According to Husserl, the Galilean world is populated by spatiotemporal forms whose contents are established by measurements of their extensions (Husserl, 1970, section 8, p. 56). Galileo's world (*Natura*) is out there, independent of consciousness, waiting to be transformed into a mathematical and geometrical language; whereas Husserl's world (*Lebenswelt*) is the world of our lived experience which includes the possibility of Galileo's world (once transformed into numbers and geometrical forms). However, Husserl's world is a space of meanings as they result from the intentional lived experience that living beings have of this world. Galileo had to sacrifice the lifeworld to construct the starting point for modern physics. Different from the time in which Husserl was living, during Galileo's Zeitgeist, religious knowledge was believed to have a focus on the matter of spirit, while scientific knowledge was to have a focus on nature—a way to emancipate science from the Bible. Therefore, in search of objective principles to account for nature, science became τέχνη (*techne*), a technology, and no longer the realization of human spirit (Saggiatore, section, 33, p. 150). In Husserl's lifeworld (*Lebenswelt*), to measure means *inventio* (from Latin, finding), that is, to discover the meaning in the given moment of the interconnection of that living being. In the system of nature (Husserl, 1970, section, 8, p. 57) of Galilean science,[6] to measure is an objectivating tool that transforms natural beings into objective forms separated from human spiritual matter. For Husserl, "the world is not just totality but it is a whole (*Allenheit*)" (Husserl, 1970, p. 74,) whose interconnected contents and forms cannot be discarded without risking a significant loss of both meaning and values.[7]

A few years later, Galileo's intuition was systematized by Descartes. According to Husserl (1970):

> After Galileo had carried out, slightly earlier, the primal establishment of the new natural science, it was Descartes who conceived and at the same time set in systematic motion the new idea of universal philosophy: in the sense of mathematical or, better expressed, physicalist, rationalism—philosophy as universal mathematics. (p. 74)

In other words, Descartes systematized Galileo's empirical understanding of nature by officially separating nature from spirit, *res extensa* (body) from *res cogitans* (mind) and by assigning an organizing function to the latter. The mind became the main processor through which the natural findings are ordered and stored in knowledge—a scientific knowledge that once again goes beyond the limits of the human mind. According to Husserl (1970, section 17, 103), Descartes was on the verge of finding a truly meaningful ground for knowledge, a form of objectivism capable of integrating meanings with measures, values with data. Nevertheless, he seemed to be in a rush of providing a solid ground for Galileian objectivism that was also respectful of religious beliefs, consequently forgetting to question the contents of the mind and its thoughts. He used evidence (*clara et distincta perceptio*) of the *ego cogitans,* the thinking mind, to prove that there were two distinct categories of the objects of knowledge—the spiritual and the material.

Centuries later, according to Husserl, it was Dilthey (1833–1911) who organized Cartesian substance dualism into a system of science. More specifically, Dilthey sorted out scientific knowledge into two groups that still impact the way we pursue education today—that is, as science of nature (*Naturwissenschaft*) and as science of the spirit (*Geisteswissenschaft*). Husserl wrote, "Dilthey, one of the greatest humanists, devoted the energies of his whole life to a clarification of the relation between nature and spirit" (1970, Appendix 1, 1). Husserl believed that Dilthey organized science into two separate groups, reflecting the Cartesian distinction of *res extensa* and *res cogitans*: natural science as the study of the *res extensa* and human sciences as the study of *res cogitans*. While the natural sciences had the task of discovering law-based causal explanations, the human sciences would seek to understand and to describe the organizational structures of human and historical life. Once again, one science is devoid of spirit, the other one is devoid of its matter. During the late nineteenth century, the social sciences and modern psychology began to surrender to empiricism and mathematization, a systematic process that was completed following World War II. The order of the sciences was lost, psychology and the social sciences became second to the natural sciences. Modern psychology, in particular, seemed to embrace a naturalistic attitude[8]. As Giorgi (1970) convincingly pointed out, modern psychology took the natural scientific approach for granted. According to Gurwitsch (1974), the fundamental mistake of the social sciences, as seeking to adopt the theory of science of the natural sciences, is rooted in that the social sciences are prior to the natural sciences, meaning that it is possible to carry out a study on, for example, the sociology of natural science, whereas the reverse effort would result in absurdity.

ETHICS

Husserl's ethics establish itself in continuity with this systematization of the sciences. Although it is difficult to state whether we can talk about one ethics and its coherence as a system,[9] Husserl's ethics is both a science and a practice; it is a phenomenological theory grounded in a specific *region of being* that he referred to as the volitional body (Hua-Mat IV, 186)—the corporeal layer from which our body awakes in decisional acts. In continuity with his criticism of the Galilean system, Husserl's ethics eludes the strict mind/body, spirit/nature distinction. His ethics is an ethics of biological bodies (*Natur*) and an ethics of these bodies as reflective units (*Geist*). Although he also saw ethics as a theoretical and reflective science, for Husserl, ethics is a practice that should align with our intentions and to the meanings that we assign to the intentions in our life. Ethics was an embodied, practical answer to a situation, and was simultaneously a reflective—and hence theoretical (from the Greek θεωρέω, to look at)—analysis of our decision in response to a situation. On the one hand, there is the ethics of our bodies that is continuous *in fieri*. One of us has previously referred to this ethics as *Practical Intentionality* (Ferrarello, 2015). Also pointing to this are the ethics of the mind and of reflection, a meta-ethics called: *Ethical Science* (Ibid.). Separating the mind from the body, reflection from intention, and theory from practice would make our decisions empty and dull. In fact, we need to be aware of what moves the will of our body and assign a meaning to it and also come to understand how such a complex process is consistent with its intention. To investigate ethics, the scientist needs to hold a rigorous attitude toward this region of the volitional body and use the phenomenological method to clarify willings, decisions, feelings, emotions—in a word, the *Gemüt* (heart), which defines the region of ethical phenomena. Reflection here is not the same as merely theoretical reflection. Thinking of the two as synonymous would be a great error. Indeed, Husserl's ethics invites us to consider that an essential part of ethics is free from the formalization of cognition. Husserl's novelty as an ethical thinker is to have articulated an ethics that is not to be considered a logic of ethics. Husserl described ethical objects with the same rigorousness with which he described the intentional essence of objects like trees or a mat in the *Logical Investigations*. Volitions are like the redness of a mat, they can be conceived in virtue of a body that bears them and a mind that expresses them, but at the same time their essentiality exists independently of the body and the mind through which they can be expressed. Husserl seeks to describe the reflective stratum of ethics as distinctly as possible from the theoretical voice that conveys it. As such, it protected his ethics from the form of idealization and mathematization we saw developing in the sciences because our ethical intentions cannot be considered forms independent of their bodies.

In fact, during the twentieth century, the mathematization of nature and the dualistic organization of science manifested itself into a new phase: the scientifically informed professionalization of social life. However, it is not clear what place ethics holds in this dualistic organization. Following this separation, professional philosophers became the scientists of the spirit somewhat disinterested in what nature meant for the spirit; natural scientists instead focused on the behaviors of nature without questioning its mind. Knowledge about human beings was seen as distinct from knowledge about their existential context as human beings in a world, a mark of separation still prevalent today, especially for what informs the course of our basic education, as rooted in a natural scientific approach to inquiry. The result is an unquestioned belief in the disconnection between mind and nature, a consequence that still influences the way we refer to professionalism. Consequently, ethical principles became a fact for professionals, as practical guidelines that existed independent of the subjects with which their profession was interacting. This means that the ethical principles guiding professional ethical choices are, unfortunately, at best, idealizations or abstractions similar to the mathematical principle guiding the calculation of a mathematical problem and, at worse, steps to consider in maintaining a bureaucratic process. Ethics in such sense became devoid of human depth and its intention. Therefore, the professional was at a loss of a deeper reflection. The professionalization of social life in the twentieth century followed the organization of human knowledge in the sciences, which also had an effect on the continuous formation of ethics. Professionalization as an extension of a naturalistic attitude transformed ethics into an itemized list of principles that the professional was meant to follow in order to avoid problems with the liability of one's own profession. As a consequence, the conceptualization of human relationships had changed, making it instrumental to maintain a beneficial, but somewhat sterile, professional exchange.

Today, we attribute the term *professional* to individuals who are called to exercise their professions according to science, but we also use this term in relation to items and tools that could be freely manipulated for a specific purpose, such as, the market, surveys, and statistics. Inevitably, this robs the professional of personhood and responsibility, thus laying the ground for a social crisis and an object-like oriented economy. The word *professional* stems from Latin *professio* which is derived from *pro* (before) and *fatēri* (to acknowledge). The professional is one who is skilled in a certain area and devoted to it. Professor is *qui pro tetur* that is, the person who takes the responsibility to profess what they believe to be true (Czeżowski, 1989, p. 232). Therefore, the critical question becomes: In what way can we distinguish a professional from a craftsperson, a profession from a mechanical activity, an ethical person from a technician?

During the time when Galileo was doing his writing, human activity was organized into the liberal arts (*artes liberales*) and the vulgar arts (*artes vulgares*), the latter were also referred to as the mechanical arts (*artes mechanicae*). As for science, this organization, too, depended on Biblical precepts. The distinction was mostly based on the kind of labor that was connected to the given goal to be accomplished (Tatarkiewicz, 2009, I:221, 345–46). This meant that *liberal arts* were regarded as incomparably more valuable than vulgar arts—the latter were referred to as sordid arts (*sordidae*) by Cicero—since the former allowed for the development of the typically human traits that made the human being closer to God. Hence, the medieval curriculum organized liberal arts in a *Trivium* (Grammar, Logic, and Rhetoric), followed by the more advanced *Quadrivium* (Arithmetic, Geometry, Astronomy, and Music). The original distinction between the humanities and the hard sciences refers to this religious goal, to achieve a full understanding of *Theology*[10] (the Queen of the Sciences). Being experts in one of these arts was exceptionally rare and was a sign of the person's proximity to God (Jervell, Crouzel, Maier, Peters, 1980, 491–515). In the twelfth century, the emergence of the first universities allowed people vowing devotion to one of these liberal arts to become professionals.

> There were all in all four professions: a scholar, a lawyer, a physician and a priest. . . . The supreme culture based on studying the works of classical literature and philosophy. What mattered in all those professionals was not only the "expertise/technical knowledge," which—being closely related to earlier philosophy—was distant from empirical and scientific approach, but most of all what matters were some ethical attitudes and the world-view. (Sobota, 2017, 10).

The professional then was different from a normal craftsperson because, at their core, this person was an ethical leader who vowed their own actions to

God's will. It is at this point that the history of science described above originally intersected with the history of professionalism and education. Animated by the goal of separating the Church from the State,[11] God from the matter, spirit from the body, it seemed reasonable to organize knowledge around the principle of technological reproduction (Benjamin, 1935; Heidegger, 1954). Larson (1977) has shown that the rise of professionalism was connected to the rapid growth of natural science, the industrial revolutions, and the need to provide for an equal distribution of resources. Under the blanket of technology, both artes liberales and artes sordidae became an opportunity to increase individual wealth and provide for individual needs. As Weber (1964) writes, this shift marks the birth of the *homo oeconomicus* who perceives the meaning of life as a permanent professional at work, whose goal is ceaseless accumulation of wealth.

The deep-rooted humanistic values and ethical worldview that professionalism represented were later lost as a result of the process of secularization that separated God from political and scientific life.[12] If it is still true what Emile Durkheim wrote (1957), that professionalism in modern society provides the basis, not only for the division of labor, social roles and classes but also for the moral order. One can say then that moral values became corporate values for professionals, idealized constructions presented under the label ethical guidelines that would teach professionals how to be detached from the human world. Ethics became a technology, that is, a repeatable technique to avoid losing its own allowance to exercise the profession in society. Professional ethics replaced the values and meanings of traditional ethics, and ethics as guidelines could be taught by senior professionals ignoring any notion of moral philosophy. Ethics became an apparatus parallel to that of laws, as an accessory to avoid lawsuits and to enable peaceful coexistence among individuals. In this sociological milieu, empathy became another tool to achieve wealth and professional stability.That is not to say that we should not have any ethical principles, but to point out that we cannot treat such principles as similar to a corporate policy.

Like Galileo's geometrical model of nature, social scientists created models for every purpose; models that could be evaluated, often referred to as evidenced-based models. These were organizational and theoretical models that became the reality in which society, organizations, and professionals functioned and were evaluated. Professionals needed to adopt and act from a professional role based on such models to implement what later could be evaluated. For example, instruments were being developed, such as checklists, psychological tests, diagnostic manuals, ethical guidelines, and (in some organizations) even standardized expressions. This strongly impacted the way in which human behavior was socially organized. For example, as the historian of psychology Kurt Danziger pointed out in his book *Constructing the Subject* (1990), the development and general acceptance of psychological testing, such as intelligence tests and scholastic aptitude tests, made us change the format of our educational system, that is, so that education would fit the tests, instead of the other way around (perhaps even laying the ground for a new model of thought at an early age). Like everything else that followed such an idealization of reality, lifeworld phenomena were now methodologically packaged into a third-person type of model that could be measured and evaluated, as if the professional had become the practical extension of the scientist. The professional was therefore forced to perform the impossible, that is, to maintain a theoretical attitude toward the client or the patient as if the latter was a separated physical body and soul in a separated ideal external world. The professional who now adopted the scientific attitude also started to act like a natural scientist, that is, as an *independent observer* facing a *reified* patient or client.

As stated, Galileo not only founded physics in its modern form but also the possibility of technology (see also Moran, 2012, 67). His geometry was not only an area of study in mathematics but became a model for actual reality that humanity took for granted and started to imitate. Living in the natural attitude became an idealization with the potential to set up the mathematization of "real" and professional life. The adoption of the naturalistic attitude also made it possible to approach the human being as a piece of machinery, her relationship with others as understood by causality, and her actions and interactions as technological achievements. Therefore, by following the trajectory of naturalism, it should not come as a surprise that phenomena, such as empathy, has become a technical encounter captured by computer metaphors such as simulation or mirror neurons (e.g., Gallese, 2003). A technological type of thinking has also set up situations in which ethics has sometimes had to weigh towards the benefit of science, clearly showing us the danger of the separation between ethics and science. This has forced institutions to stake out ethics as formal policies, that is, as guidelines to precede instrumentally within the context of professional situations. However, guidelines do not help professionals to reflect on ethical dilemmas but only to match the guidelines to a set of circumstances, similar to how an operating system runs its programs in relation to the data as input.

In other words, the whole underlying methodology of naturalism seems to have been taken for granted, at least in the Western world, meaning a cultural world not bound by geography but by a way of technological life. Of course, phenomenology is not against technology as such, but, as Dreyfus (1972) once pointed out, we want to remember "what computers can't do" and should not do. Technology is not the same as a reflective life. To simulate, imitate or to match is not the same as to reflect and to disclose, because the former implies a naiveté that takes distance for granted as its ground. Science might lead to technology, but it cannot turn into technology, because then the reflective purpose of science is lost to the pragmatic and reproductive purpose of technology. As one of us has previously pointed out, "Different from science, technology does not involve any investigation of nature because technology's goal is to reproduce the object of its activity in an unquestioned manner" (Ferrarello, 2020, p. 15).

However, *techne* (τέχνη) as a model of thought has been reinforced over and over again in our educational system. In other words, we have been told that to rediscover basic life phenomena such as empathy and its relation to ethics, we have to follow the workings of a cognitive model instead of learning how to reflect on our lifeworld. If we could realize that any model of thought is just that, a model which provides us with a measured and ideal mirror of nature (as in geometry) or the human being (as in a role), we might be free from the chains of the dogma of one historical era, even though we will always risk turning it into the dogma of the next. Philosophical reflection and the phenomenological way to elucidate the natural attitude, as it relates to empathy and ethics, can help us to see that a model is an addition to the lifeworld and not the reality behind it. Without this realization there would be no ground upon which to stand, to be self-critical, and to resume a sense of *self-responsibility* toward one another.

EMPATHY

The whole history of empathy cannot be accounted for here, so let us instead seek its brief historical meaning and how it relates to the natural attitude. The English term *empathy* was an attempt by Edward B. Titchener (1867–1927) to translate Theodor Lipps' (1851–1914) use of the German term *Einfühlung* (originally used by Robert Vischer, 1847–1933), a concept that points to the process of imitation and projection.[13] As indicating a process of imitation and projection, *Einfühlung* or *empathy* was already interpreted from within the natural attitude. Understood as such, empathy, as a concept and term, became part of the new sophisticated model of the empirical sciences, grounded in the natural attitude as *the taken for grantedness that others exist independently of our experience of them.* This meant that we would only understand the other through an act of imitation. This particular meaning of the term empathy spread quickly to the new empirical science of psychology and to the emerging profession of psychotherapy. As Coplan and Goldie (2011, xviii) have pointed out, Freud was influenced by Lipps' interpretation of empathy, which seems reasonable considering that imitation-projection seem to fit right into psychoanalytic theory. Even though there have been countless psychotherapeutic systems since Freud, there is little doubt that the imitation theory of empathy, in one form or another, seemed to prevail within the professional context of psychology. According to Zahavi (2010, 2014), by the time Titchener's new term had reached the English-speaking world, the debate about empathy had just about started in Germany, meaning that Titchener's sense of empathy was premature, unfortunately missing the accounts of Husserl, Scheler, and Stein.

When applied to modern psychology, empathy as imitation easily found its place within the new type of modern individualism of the twentieth century Western world, a natural scientific approach towards psychology, and the growing profession of psychotherapy. Empathy was frequently discussed in the works of Heinz Kohut (1913–1981), a psychoanalyst and founder of self-psychology and, perhaps more famously, as a central theme in the development of a person-centered therapy (initially labeled, client-centered therapy) by humanistic psychologist Carl Rogers (1902–1987). The development of Rogers's thought should be noted here, especially since he changed his way of describing empathy later in his career in, which he provided an account of empathy similar to that of the phenomenologists (see Rogers 1989a). Even though Rogers had a clear humanistic purpose towards psychotherapy and was a constant critic of reductionism, initially he professionally contextualized empathy as a skill within counseling psychology and psychotherapy, even though he meant it as a way of being. Empathy was to be trained as a technique and would be used by the psychotherapist and aid in the work toward what Rogers's (1989b, 226) described as an "as if" experience of the client's mental states. Therefore, Rogers's unfortunate way of describing empathy was welcomed into a natural scientific psychology as a way to solve the problem of the distance between the therapist and the client, using a technical solution, as in the act of imitation. In such sense, the idea of empathy in psychotherapy also harmonized well with Descartes original systematization of Galileo's project, as "the human soul (*res cogitans*) . . . became a natural object among many, detached from its body (*res extensa*) and isolated from other souls" (Ferrarello, 2020, p.18). In other words, and as we argued in the previous section, modern physics, modern philosophy, and modern society are all driven by a technological attitude toward life in which real life is understood as independent of our experience of it, and thus separate from us, including our original relation to others. As such, the natural attitude makes its presence felt in modern science and extends to a technological attitude of modern professions, such as psychotherapy. In the late twentieth century, empathy turned into a necessary piece of the machinery, especially for successful professionals. The modern psychologists started to operationalize and measure empathy using paper and pencil tests, as in, for example, Rogers's (1957, 1989c) Q-sort technique. The geometrization of empathy was now initiated, meaning that our basic relation to other minded beings had become part of Galileo's overall model. In his humanistic attempt at freeing psychology for its chains from reductionism, Rogers contributed to the naturalization of empathy. In reading Rogers's (1989b) life work, there is little doubt that his overall work as a psychotherapist and educator in no way was meant in a sense of *techne*. Unfortunately, Rogers's work was incorporated into the context of mainstream psychological science and education (except at certain existential-humanistic oriented universities), meaning that, in the end, empathy turned into a technique for the modern psychologist to master. Nevertheless, at the end of the twentieth century, empathy had become a technical instrumentation inside the empirical realm of the human being, becoming finalized by the cognitive neuroscientists in the late twentieth century with their discovery of the mirror neurons as implicit neuronal simulation as the naturalization of empathy (e.g., Gallese, 2003). It becomes difficult to disagree with Heidegger (1985, p. 240) when he wrote that "the problem of empathy is just as absurd as the question of the reality of the external world."

As a result of the discovery of the mirror neurons and the reign of cognitive neuroscience, simulation theory also began to influence the professional psychotherapist. For example, contemporary attachment theorists and psychoanalysts (e.g., Fonagy & Target, 1997) followed a similar trajectory and began conceptualizing empathy as mentalization, in which they specifically referred to studies based on simulation theory to support their own theory. As part of the cognitive science movement, some scientists used a more academic metaphor in which they proposed empathy as someone having a theory of mind, as in understanding others demanded that we were using theories. However, theory, simulation, or mentalization all fall victims of the same problem, which is to ground its account of empathy on naturalism. In other words, these attempts become examples of a representational theory of mind, that is, neither of these theories are able to explain how theories, simulation, or mentalizations are being formed in the first place. As part of this debate in the beginning of the twenty-first century, contemporary phenomenologists, such as Gallagher and Zahavi (2012), among many others, returned to classical phenomenological accounts of empathy, providing insight into the original debate in Germany that extended beyond Titchener's visit. Gallagher and Zahavi (2012) showed us what psychology and cognitive science had taken for granted for a whole century. For example, just being able to state something like, 'That I can never understand,' actually indicates that some type of understanding had already taken place. Or, as Scheler (2008) pointed out in his argument against Lipps's account of empathy as imitation: If anyone would be able to imitate another person, they must first have been present to an expression for an act of imitation to be possible at all. This means that caring, agreeing, imitating, or anything else for that matter, follows empathy.

In other words, and as Stein (1964, 11) wrote, "empathy is a[n] . . . act of perceiving . . . [and] . . . is the experience of foreign consciousness"

Empathy as perception can thus be seen as part of the lifeworld and thus prior to explanations such as imitation, matching, mentalization, simulation, or theorizing. However, and as Gallagher and Zahavi (2012) have pointed out, there is no need to rule out the possibility of imitation as a more sophisticated act in understanding others, but that we have to return to empathy as perception, which is the foundation in how we know others. Empathizing perception (as Husserl, 2006, called it) can be seen as the embodied experience of another embodied, minded creature. This means that the basic understanding of others constitute a different type of perception than a non-living object. As Stein (1964, 6) states,

> This individual is not given as a physical body, but as a sensitive, living body belonging to an "I," an "I" that senses, thinks, feels, and wills. The living body of this "I" not only fits into my phenomenal world but is itself the center of orientation of such a phenomenal world. It faces this world and communicates with me.

Let us consider an everyday example.

At least once in our life, most of us have probably had the experience of approaching another person on, for example, a sidewalk and finding ourselves caught in an awkward situation where we both start to rock from side to side, unable to tell if we should both go right or left. First, let us consider this type of situation from the perspective of naturalism and simulation theory in mainstream psychology and the cognitive neurosciences. Following such a stance, we are already by default separated from the other, as two minded substances, and our ability to understand the other can only be accounted for by simulating the other; that is, the two substances are in need of a cognitive technology to understand each other. The other is external in relation to me, independent of my experience of her. As this analysis progresses down the path of empiricism, I will need a technological achievement based on an image of the other in order to understand her. Similar to Varela's (1996) famous response to Chalmers's (1995) "hard problem of consciousness," the natural scientific psychologist and cognitive scientist pose the question about empathy from the perspective naturalism, meaning that it becomes a problem in which a solution only can be found by turning to the project of naturalization.

Let us take a look at the phenomenology of the situation on the sidewalk. First of all, and as Stein (1964) pointed out, the other is not given to me as a physical body. If that would be the case, approaching either a lamp post or a minded creature on the sidewalk would not make any difference. The truth is that we are hardly imitating each other when we are standing there rocking from side to side. What we are actually doing is *being present to each other as embodied-minded creatures and following each other's meaning-expression.* And we are following meanings as these present themselves through the expression, not as if these were located inside the other person because meanings transcends the individual act in which they appear. How else would we be able to see that somebody is sad or happy without being sad or happy ourselves? In other words, following and imitation are different acts. Therefore, it does not matter how implicit an act of imitation (or simulation or mirroring) is, because empathic perception, as in following the other's meaning-expression, always precede such an act. How else would the neurons know what to imitate? Even if *following the other's meaning-expression* might seem obvious, such a finding is impossible to report if one is bound to naturalism. The other is already in my phenomenal world and it is via reflecting on my lived-experience that I discover her. As Schutz (1967) would later point out, empathy is reciprocal, meaning that interpersonal understanding of the other is already there within the we-relationship.

In what way does empathy as imitation, simulation, matching, mentalization, and theorizing relate to modern professionalism. As a professional seeking to understand my client, do I have to take for granted that we humans operate on the basis that there is a distance between minded substances? When understanding then presents itself, do I explain this as me running a copy of the other person's internal working model? As such, all types of imitation theories become explanations based on the assumption that our subjectivity operates analogously to physical distance (as in modern physics). Understanding then becomes reduced to the matching of the other's mental content. But as Davidson (2018) has recently pointed out, even in severe cases of schizophrenia we are able to understand the other, which is based on the phenomenological fact that we are able to see that the other is different from us. In other words, being able to see that somebody is different from us already indicates some form of understanding has taken place, meaning that that understanding can be described through an act of reflection. Therefore, interpersonal understanding is already taking place in all human encounters, especially in relation to any help professionals who are in daily contact with other minded, human beings. Empathy is not something that needs to be constructed. Empathy is already there when faced with a meaning-expression of a minded being. In such a sense, there is no problem of empathy, but there is a problem of the lack of reflecting on one's empathy—and as we have seen—the problem of the idealization of empathy by those who aim at naturalizing it.

Following this line of reasoning, one could argue for the possibility to reflect on one's empathic act as opposed to the technologization towards interpersonal understanding. As one of us has proposed, using such a phenomenological insight makes it possible to design a professional training in which participants (e.g., professionals and university students) are educated on how to reflect on their empathy (Englander, 2014, 2019). This would mean that we would be able to reflect on how we follow somebody's meaning expression in professional practice (Englander, 2014, 2018, 2019). Such a phenomenological approach to empathy training stands in stark contrast to trying to adopt the abstract role of the professional—that is, following the techniques and guidelines aligned with that role—and the constant attempts to overcome the distance between two substances. Instead, the professional can now begin with the experience of the other, followed by a reflection of that experience. Engaging in a reflection on our presence to meanings, we would be able to elucidate interpersonal understanding in the context of the professional situation (Englander, 2020). As Zahavi writes, (2001, 154), empathy is "taken to disclose rather than establish intersubjectivity." Consequently, interpersonal understanding could serve as the ground (as in figure-ground) for the professional role. As such, our professional judgment and communication would be grounded in what Alfred Schutz (1967) once referred to as the *we-relation* or *we-relationship*. According to Schutz,

> The basic We-relationship is already given to me by the mere fact that I am born into the world of directly experienced social reality. From this basic relationship is derived the original validity of all my direct experiences of particular fellow men and also my knowledge that there is a larger world of my contemporaries whom I am not now experiencing directly. (1967, p. 165)

The we-relationship is not just about disclosing two humans in an interpersonal context, but also intersubjectivity as such, and its many layers of the social world. What could be disclosed in a professional situation from such an inter-*action* is an original alliance or a participatory partnership as the ground for the professional work that is ahead. As the phenomenological psychiatrist Erwin Straus once stated,

> The orientation to partnership is an original one: being oriented to something together—that is, with-each-other or against-each-other. I am not aware of the "alter ego" as an object, nor can I be by making it the object of my study; I learn to know it in my action. I experience the alter ego as a partner of my intentions; we meet on the same path in meaningful cooperation or in meaningful opposition. We find our self in one world with the other, our fellow man, sharing the orientation toward some third entity. (1958, p. 156)

As we can see, Straus emphasizes the concrete interpersonal world as the context that allows us to work on something together. In contrast, acting on the basis of the natural sciences would involve the abstract formalization of the role of the ideal professional. In the naturalist's way of interpreting empathy, the other (or even the problem of the other) will have to be reified and taken as part of an abstract system explaining her as opposed to understanding her; it will measure and solve the other's problem, as opposed to helping her to solve the problem. In other words, the concreteness of interpersonal understanding is lost in the abstract play between the professional and client, as they are being engaged in the written and unwritten rules of their roles. The professional role acts on the assumptions of the profession, meaning that we become servants of a machinery and seek to follow the ideal image of the professional. Empathy, as it is part of the natural attitude of the other, will not automatically disclose our intersubjective interconnectedness with the other, such as our feelings for the other or our moral obligation to the other. But can a reflection of empathy do so?

REFLECTION AS SELF-RESPONSIBILITY

Let us now turn to our last theme in relation to the natural attitude, and how it pertains to empathy and ethics. We saw that our idealized view of the knowledge of nature also extends to sophisticated theories on how we know others and how such theories are transferred to modern professional roles. The cognitive movement has generated an internalized working model of *the self*, as if the system of the self was acting independently of the person. Once again, we recognize the natural attitude at work as in *taking for granted that the self is independent of our experience*. This naïveté extends to the idealization of human roles in the society, such as a professional role; but also to roles of ideal being, as in being a healthy person, an empathic person, an intelligent person, a leader, and so forth. In other words, our sophisticated models of the self are the extension of our natural attitude into the abstract realm, and, just like Galileo's system, it provides us with a technological attitude. The taken-for-grantedness has a price, that is, it alienates us from our lived and volitional bodies, our ground for being able to ethically reflect on our self-responsibility.

For this reason, we encourage a reflection on one's empathy that would help professionals recover their connection with the other as two minded creatures, but also as a means to return to their own volitional body, thus overcoming the dichotomy between body and mind (nature and spirit, science and humanities). Applying this form of reflection on one's empathy would enable us to return to what it means to be a human being in a lifeworld interconnected to others and would consequently help us to reflect on the values that are at the core of the human choices guiding their decisions. In one of Husserl's manuscripts (Ms. F I 24), the philosopher points to this form of reflective empathy when writing about love-values. He claims that our personal values of love (*Liebeswerte*) oblige us to promote and enhance the *love-valuings* of *all others* who have similar egoic obliging values, such as the people closest to us or our kindred spirits, and be empathic toward them:

> Of course, the fulfilment of my personal absolute ought is an originary lived experience only for me and as such preferential. But the law of love reigns here. As soon as I have the other given as the subject of her personal ought in empathy. . . . I 'have to' sympathize with her, love her; and to encourage or promote her is my absolute ought. (Ms. F I 24, 38a, b, cited in Loidolt 2012, 25, cf. 13–14; cf. Hua 42, 337)

In an analogy with his genetic theory of meaning (Husserl 2004), the values of love are seen in his later ethics (Hua, 42), as organized and as organizing principles that function as an ongoing source of meaning for our intersubjective lifeworld. In other words, the roots of these values must be branched out deep down in our psyche for them to offer true ethical guidance to us. The shallower these egoic roots are, the less is the care that a human being feels for others and one's own self. Love-values have as Melle (2007, 13) points out, "an absolute priority over the objective values." In fact, different from objective values (*ein gegenständlicher Wert, ein objektiver Wert*), the values of love are deeply connected with the intentional sources of our being (Hua 27, 11, 68). The relationality that the values of love address do not derive from external objects but from deeper feelings that connect us to a certain way of being. Hence these values are neither static nor individual, rather they are highly relational and dynamic, because they grow and change as the life of the person changes (cf. Williams and Smart 1973, 100ff.; Frankfurt 2004). A child needs the love of her caregiver to live a good life and to become a good member of society. These love-values are not mathematical functions toward which we are indifferent as a non-participating, independent observer, instead, we are their living source (Hua, 42, 351; cf. Hahn, 2009; Drummond, 2018, 142). Thus, love-values are not abstract elements, but constitute the changes in our life, meaning that these cannot be quantified, compared, or traded (Hua 42, 356–537, 390). Trying to make a list of pros and cons involving love-values would be a hopeless task.

Husserl (2004) argues that the empathic apprehension of the other as a *subject of her own genuine love-values* is enough to oblige me to care for her as such, that is, as a loving subject with her own objects, goals, and projects which are not mine and may radically differ from my own. In so far as I love something from my own egoic depths, then I can empathically understand that others love in a similar manner. This care is, itself, an obligation to love them all, independently of possible differences in the contents of the emotions involved. Here Husserl is not suggesting that we imitate the other as a way to recognize that others love in a similar manner. The minimal understanding of the other as a living, minded creature, that is, as provided by empathizing perception, also discloses the deepest sense of intersubjectivity in us (Zahavi, 2001, 154). Hence, we recognize the other as someone like us, who love like us. If one is capable to connect with one's own deeply rooted love-values, such a professional helper can recognize the humanity in others and take responsibility for the other's well-being. However, if we, as professionals, live in such a way that our own being is separated from ourselves, in which we further add sophisticated models of the self, some even artificial, what will remain of the original meaning of self-responsibility?

When we truly understand our own values through self-reflection and deep connection to our self-values, then intersubjectivity will necessarily disclose what goes beyond a mere understanding of the other. The obligation of loving the other and the root for their well-being becomes an absolute ought. Husserl explicitly says that the care for loved ones follows from a certain kind of empathy, an empathic apperception and intuitive appresentation of the other as a subject of genuine emotion; from here, the absolute ought emerges as her love, that is, as if I were her and her deepest values and obligations were mine (Hua 42, 337, 470). Such acts cannot be confused with imitation and to simulate the other, as acts of technology. In the natural attitude, if the other is taken as independent of me, even if my self is independent of my life, no ethical behavior would be possible because there would be literally no one to encounter in my lifeworld. A self-responsible act would be empty, and it would be, at best, responsible according to external idealizations (ethical guidelines, corporate codes, or both of these, that are made into an algorithm) but not as self-responsible for one's own choices and decisions. There would be no ethical use for my empathy, just dogmas to follow whose validity is as long lasting as a *Zeitgeist* can be. Let us return to the awkward situation on the sidewalk. What if one person reflected on one's empathic perception as reciprocal and communicated this to the other, saying: "Look, we are following each other." Chances are that you are now closer to the meaning of what is taken place and for a few seconds you are standing face-to-face in a present moment (*Augenblick*) in the life of a stranger, but also intersubjectively, in the life of all others.

In their ethics, Aristotle and Kant tell us that ethics would not be an ethic if no choice would be involved. The core of an ethical mind-set is the freedom with which one takes responsibility in following a specific course of action. This would hardly occur in an empathy conceived as sheer imitation. Husserl's ethics, especially the one expressed in his Kaizo articles (1922–1923), is strongly focused on the notion of responsibility (*Verantwortlichkeit*), that is, the ability to provide an *answer* to what you are doing. Such an answer does not involve just myself, but is placed in an I-thou relationship, whose roots can be traced back to the lifeworld, and it takes place in the flow of time. This means that Husserl's categorical imperative, "Do the best among what is attainable," (Hua 28, 153)[14] is the result of a responsible choice that one makes after reflecting on the meaning that connects me and the other person in that given moment of reversibility.[15] The moment in which the professional realizes that she is in an I-thou relationship is hardly a moment of imitation or simulation, as in a machine-like behavior that makes the empathic connection between the client and the professional possible. Rather it is the professional's own ability to reflect on the I-thou relationship (that takes place in that present moment). It is also her decision to communicate the meaning of that reflection, that is, genuine, ethical empathy. In other words, the moment in which the empathizer is present to true ethical content is when the reflection of one's empathy elucidates the deeper layers of intersubjectivity. The professional who remains in the natural attitude and goes through a check-list or questionnaire or providing the client or patient with a self-rating scale that has been devised to prompt an empathic behavior is only acting on an idealization of empathy and ethics. Even though such action is a type of reaction that is ethically acceptable, as in the context of preestablished ethical guidelines, it is to assume a third-person position that robs the professional of any ethical position. This is because no personal responsibility is related to the questions being posed. In other words, self-responsibility is lost. Instead, a return to the reflection of empathy is a way to return to the ethical matters themselves and to connect to the meanings we produce in and through the lifeworld.

CONCLUSION

In this chapter we described how the natural attitude influences our way of conceiving empathy and negatively impacts our ethical worldview. In fact, instead of focusing on a worldview embedded in the life-world that would foster an ethics capable of reflecting on our whole being in the world as interconnected human beings, we tend to produce ideal models that detach humans from themselves and encourages dichotomic views that separate mind from bodies, spirits from nature, humanities from science and technology. Hence, ethics reduces itself to an ideal code of conduct and empathy to a technology serving the code. Different from this, we believe that professionals dealing with problems relating to a social and psychological context should integrate the natural attitude with a phenomenological reflective one, to reflect on their empathy, this to provide for an ethical understanding that is truly beneficial for the community that they serve.

NOTES

1. Husserl (1970, §9, 23–59) uses the terms *construction* and *idealization* interchangeable.

2. As Zahavi's (2010, 2014) extensive research on the phenomenology of empathy has shown, the sophisticated notion of *simulation* can be traced to previous psychological theories of empathy as *imitation*, and already critiqued in the works of Husserl, Stein, and Scheler.

3. We can refer here to this initial literature: Abbott (1983), Breed (1955), Cullen (1983), Dimmick (1977), Gross (1978), Greenwood (1957), Khowy (1970), Klegon (1978), Levy (1974), Liebermann (1970), Moore (1961), Nilson (1979), Orzack (1959), Vickers (1974), and Watson (1976).

4. By idealization we mean here with Husserl: "The conceptual method of idealization is the fundament of the whole method of natural science (i.e., of the pure science of bodies), the latter being the method of inventing 'exact' theories and formulae and also of reapplying them within the praxis which takes place in the world of actual experience." (Husserl, 1970, 221) "The geometry of idealities was preceded by the practical art of surveying, which knew nothing of idealities. Yet such a pre-geometrical achievement was a meaning fundament for geometry, a fundament for the great invention of idealization; the latter encompassed the invention of the ideal world of geometry, or rather the methodology of the objectifying determination of idealities through the constructions which create 'mathematical existence.' It was a fateful omission that Galileo did not inquire back into the original meaning-giving achievement which, as idealization practiced on the original ground of all theoretical and practical life—the immediately intuited world (and here especially the empirically intuited world of bodies)—resulted in the geometrical ideal constructions." (Husserl, 1970, 49)

5. See Staiti (2014, 83–108) for an excellent account of how attitudes must be already present within the lifeworld for more sophisticated attitudes within the sciences to evolve.

6. According to Husserl, Galileian science was mostly organized around mathematics, geometry, and physics. Mathematics was assigned the task to recognize the pure forms of nature, to geometry the duty to measure them, and to physics to acknowledge the causality through numerical forms. None of these sciences took into consideration the role of scientist in science nor the sensuous interconnected content of these forms. (Husserl, 1970, 67).

7. "The difficulty here lies in the fact that the material plena—the 'specific*' sense-qualities—which concretely fill out the spatiotemporal shape-aspects of the world of bodies cannot, in their own gradations, be directly treated as are the shapes themselves. Nevertheless, these qualities, and everything that makes up the concreteness of the sensibly intuited world, must count as manifestations of an 'objective'

world. Or rather, they must continue to count as such; because (such is the way of thinking which motivates the idea of the new physics) the certainty, binding us all, of one and the same world, the actuality which exists in itself runs uninterrupted through all changes of subjective interpretation" Husserl, 1970, 33.

8. On the difference between natural and naturalistic attitude we can say that although the natural attitude considers the world as already present to us without questioning the way in which appears to us, the naturalistic attitude "'reifies' and it 'absolutizes' the world such that it is treated as taken-for-granted and 'obvious'" (Moran, 2008, 401).

9. Ferrarello is one of those who believe in the coherence of Husserl's ethics. To have an idea of Husserl's ethics, as science and practice, one must begin to read from volume XXVIII of the Husserliana, edited in 1988 by Melle, and then move on to the other volumes of Husserliana. Before 1988 only Roth—and Paci, with his Italian translation of *Krisis*—stirred a debate regarding Husserl's ethics. Besides them, few authors worked on ethics. An ideal path to approach Husserl's ethics is, after reading volume XXVIII, to turn to volume XXXVII in which ethics is framed within a historical and theoretical context. In volume XXXVII, the reader can also grasp Husserl's project of grounding ethics on a scientific basis, its historical and theoretical framework. After this, the reader ought to consider the ethical excerpts collected in volumes XXXV, XXXIX, XLII, and XLIII, in which it is possible to come in contact with interesting but generally brief texts that Husserl wrote on specific issues related to ethics, axiology, willing, life-world. From Ferrarello's perspective these texts are useful to strengthen the understanding of the project described in more depth in volumes XXVIII and XXXVII.

10. Marrou, 1969, 18–19.

11. On this point the history of contractualism and liberalism would be extremely needed to understand how the notion of individualization versus the communitarian sense of life developed, but there is no space for this here.

12. Here we refer to this problem: When Locke writes that the human being (implying not the Monarch whose power comes from God) is the owner of its own work, he is planting the seeds for the kind of capitalism, socialism, and individualism that Marx will, in great clarity, describe in his *Grundrisse* (1857). The human being (and not God) owns its own *caput* (from Latin, head) and its job is to accumulate the necessary wealth to keep its *caput* and the *capita* of its own family alive. Hence, the professional became anyone with the technical ability and the university certificate that allowed them to achieve wealth.

13. For a standard historical account see for example, Coplan and Goldie (2011, ix–xlvii). For a comprehensive phenomenological account, see Zahavi (2014).

14. And its variant in his later ethics "Do your best among what is attainable" (See Hua XXXVII, 342)

15. *Reversibility* in a term borrowed from Merleau-Ponty's (1968) ontology, which is also captured by terms such as chiasm and the intertwining. According to Dillon (1997, 155), "The figure called forth by these terms is that of the crossing and turning back on itself of the single thread that emanates from the spider's body when she spins her web. This web-matrix, the whole cloth, the flesh, of the world is an interweaving,

an elementary knotting, which is always prior to its unravelling in language and thought. The world is primordially phenomenon, primordially woven and weaving: and autochthonous organization, a Gestalt-contexture."

REFERENCES

Abbott, A. (1983). Professional ethics. *American Journal of Sociology*, 88: 855–85.

Benjamin, W. (1935). The work of art in the age of mechanical reproduction." In Hannah Arendt, ed., and Trans. Harry Zohn, trans., *Illuminations: Essays and Reflections*. Schocken Books, 1968.

Breed, W. (1955). Social control in the newsroom: A functional analysis. *Social Forces*, 33: 326–35.

Chalmers, D. (1995) Facing up to the problem of consciousness. *Journal of Consciousness Studies*, 2, 200–19.

Coplan, A., & Goldie, P., eds. (2011). *Empathy*. Oxford University Press.

Czeżowski, T. (1989). *Pisma z etyki i teorii wartości, Zakład Narodowy im. Ossolińskich*, PAN.

Cullen, J. B. (1983). An occupational taxonomy by professional characteristics: Implications for research. *Journal of Vocational Behavior*, 22: 257–67.

Danziger, K. (1990). *Cambridge Studies in the History of Psychology. Constructing the Subject: Historical Origins of Psychological Research.* Cambridge University Press.

Davidson, L. (2018). Transcendental intersubjectivity as the foundation for a phenomenological social psychiatry. In M. Englander (Ed.) *Phenomenology and the Social Context of Psychiatry: Social Relations, Psychopathology, and Husserl's Philosophy*, pp. 7–26. London: Bloomsbury Academic.

Dillon, M. C. (1997). *Merleau-Ponty's Ontology*. Northwestern University Press.

Dimmick, J. (1977). Canons and codes as occupational ideologies. *Journal of Communication*, 27: 181–87.

Drummond, J. (2018). Husserl's middle period and the development of his ethics." In D. Zahavi, ed., *The Oxford Handbook of the History of Phenomenology* (pp. 135–54). Oxford University Press.

Durkheim, E. (1957) *Professional Ethics and Civic Morals*. Routledge.

Dreyfus, H. (1972). *What Computers Still Can't Do.* MIT Press.

Englander, M. (2014). Empathy training from a phenomenological perspective. *Journal of Phenomenological Psychology*, 45: 5–26.

———. (2018). Empathy in a social psychiatry. In M. Englander, ed., *Phenomenology and the Social Context of Psychiatry: Social Relations, Psychopathology, and Husserl's Philosophy* (pp. 49–64). Bloomsbury Academic.

———. (2019). The practice of phenomenological empathy training. *Journal of Phenomenological Psychology*, 50, 42–59.

———. (2020). Phenomenological psychological interviewing. *The Humanistic Psychologist*, 48(1): 54–73.

Ferrarello, S. (2015). *Husserl's Ethics and Practical Intentionality*. Bloomsbury.

———. (2020). *Human Emotions and the Origins of Bioethics.* Routledge.

Ferrando, F. (2019). *Philosophical Posthumanism*. Bloomsbury Academic.
Fonagy, P., & Target, M. (1997). Attachment and reflective function: Their role in self-organization. *Development and Psychopathology*, 9(4): 679–700.
Frankfurt, H. G. (2004). *The Reasons of Love*. Princeton University Press.
Gallagher, S., and D. Zahavi. (2012). *The Phenomenological Mind.* London: Routledge.
Gallese, V. (2003). The roots of empathy: The shared manifold hypothesis and the neural basis of intersubjectivity. *Psychopathology*, 36: 171–80.
Giorgi, A. (1970). *Psychology as a Human Science.* New York: Harper and Row.
Goldman, A. I. (2006). *Simulating Minds: The Philosophy, Psychology, and Neuroscience of Mindreading*. Oxford University Press.
Greenwood, E. (1957). Attributes of a profession. *Social Work*, 2: 45–55.
Gross, S. J. (1978). The myth of professional licensing. *American Psychologist*, 33: 1009–16.
Gurwitsch, A. (1974). *Phenomenology and the Theory of Science.* Northwestern University Press.
Hahn, C. J. (2009). The concept of personhood in the phenomenology of Edmund Husserl. PhD diss., Marquette University.
Heidegger, M. (1954). The question concerning technology. In W. Lovitt, trans., *The Question Concerning Technology: And Other Essays* (3–35). Garland Publishing.
———. (1985). *History of the Concept of Time.* Indiana University Press.
Husserl, E. (1970). *The Crisis of European Sciences and Transcendental Philosophy: An Introduction to Phenomenological Philosophy* (Trans. D. Carr). Northwestern University Press.
———. (1982). *Ideas Pertaining to a Pure Phenomenology and to a Phenomenological Philosophy*, First Book. G. Trans. Fred Kersten. Kluwer.
———. (1989). *Ideas Pertaining to a Pure Phenomenology and a Phenomenological Philosophy.* Second Book. Trans. R Rojcewicz and A. Schuwer. Kluwer
———. (2006). *The Basic Problems of Phenomenology: From the Lectures, Winter Semester, 1910–1911* (Trans. Farin & Hart). Springer.
Husserl, E. Hua XXVII. (1988). *Vorlesungen über Ethik und Wertlehre 1908–1914*, Husserliana XXVIII. Ed. U. Melle. Kluwer Academic Publishers.
Husserl, E. Hua XXVII. (1989). *Aufsätze und Vorträge* 1922–1937, Husserliana XXVII. Eds. H. R. Sepp and T. Nenon. Kluwer Academic Publishers.
Husserl, E. Hua XXXVIII. (2004). *Wahrnehmung und Aufmerksamkeit, Texte aus dem Nachlass* (1893–1912), Husserliana XXXVIII. Eds. T. Vongehr and. R. Giuliani. Springer.
Husserl, E. Hua XLII. (2013). *Grenzprobleme der Phänomenologie: Analysen des Unbewusstseins und der Instinkte, Metaphysik, Späte Ethik, Texte aus dem Nachlass* (1908–1937), Husserliana XLII. Eds. R. Sowa and T. Vongehr. Springer.
Jervell, J., Crouzel, H., Maier, J., an Peters, A. (1980). "Bild Gottes I-IV." In: *Theologische Realenzyklopädie* (Bd. 6, pp. 491–515). de Gruyter Verlag.
Khowy, R. (1970). Demythologizing the professions. *International Review of History and Political Science*, 17: 57–70.
Klegon, D. (1978). The sociology of professions: An emerging perspective. *Sociology of Work and Occupations*, 5: 259–83.

Larson, M. S. (1977), *The Rise of Professionalism: A Sociological Analysis*. University of California Press.

Levy, C. (1974). On the development of a code of ethics. *Social Work*, 3: 207–16.

Liebermann, J. (1970). *Tyranny of the Experts: How Professionals Are Closing the Open Society.* Walker and Co.

Loidolt, S. (2012). A phenomenological ethics of the absolute ought. Investigating Husserl's unpublished ethical writings. In M. Sanders & J.J. Wisnewski, eds., *Ethics and Phenomenology* (pp. 9–38). Lexington/Rowman and Littlefield.

Luft, S. (2011). *Subjectivity and Lifeworld in Transcendental Phenomenology*. Northwestern University Press.

Marrou, Henri-Irénée. (1969). Les arts libéraux dans l'Antiquité Classique. In *Arts libéraux et philosophie au Moyen Âge*, pp. 6–27. Paris: Vrin; Montréal: Institut d'études médiévales.

Melle, U. (2007). Husserl's personalistic ethics. *Husserl Studies*, 23: 1–15.

Merleau-Ponty, M. (1968). *The Visible and the Invisible* (edited by C. Lefort and trans. A. Lingus). Northwestern University Press.

Moore, J. (1961). Occupational anomie and irresponsibility. *Social Problems*, 8: 293–99.

Moran. D. (2008). Husserl's transcendental philosophy and the critique of naturalism. *Continental Philosophical Review*, 41(4): 401–25

———. (2012). *Husserl's Crisis of the European Sciences and Transcendental Phenomenology: An Introduction.* Cambridge University Press.

Nilson, L. B. (1979). An application of the occupational "uncertainty principle"; to the professions. *Social Problems*, 26: 570–81.

Orzack, L. (1959). Work as a "central life interest"; of professionals. *Social Problems*, 7: 125–32.

Rogers, C. R. (1957). The necessary and sufficient conditions of therapeutic personality change. *Journal of Consulting Psychology*, 21(2), 95–103.

———. (1989a). *A Way of Being*. Houghton Mifflin Company.

———. (1989b). *The Carl Rogers Reader* (Ed. H. Kirschenbaum & V. L. Henderson). Houghton Mifflin Company.

———. (1989c). *On Becoming a Person: A Therapist's View of Psychotherapy*. Houghton Mifflin Company.

Scheler, M. (2008). *The Nature of Sympathy*. Transaction Publishers.

Schütz, A. (1967). T*he Phenomenology of the Social World*. Northwestern University Press.

Sobota, Daniel. (2017). Antinomies of professionalism: The philosophical and historical considerations. *Journal of Corporate Responsibility and Leadership*, 3: 79.

Staiti, A. (2014). *Husserl's Transcendental Phenomenology: Nature, Spirit, and Life*. Cambridge University Press.

Stein, E. (1964). *On the Problem of Empathy* (trans. W. Stein). Springer Science+Business Media.

Straus, E. W. (1958). Aesthesiology and hallucinations. In R. May, E. Angel, & H. F. Ellenberger (Eds.), *Existence: A New Dimension in Psychiatry and Psychology* (pp. 139–69). Basic Books.

Tatarkiewicz, W. (2009). Classification of arts in antiquity. *Journal of the History of Ideas*, 24(2), 231–24

Valadas Ponte, D., & Schäfer, L. (2013). Carl gustav jung, quantum physics and the spiritual mind: a mystical vision of the twenty-first century. *Behavioral Sciences (Basel, Switzerland)*, 3(4), 601–18.

Varela F. J. (1996) Neurophenomenology: A methodological remedy for the hard problem. *Journal of Consciousness Studies*, 3: 330–35.

Vickers, G. (1974). The changing nature of the professions. *American Behavioral Scientist*, 18: 164–89.

Watson, T. J. (1976). The professionalization process: A critical note. *The Sociological Review*, 24: 599–608.

Weber, M. (1964). *The Theory of Social and Economic Organization*. The Free Press.

Williams, B., & Smart, J. J. C. (1973). *Utilitarianism: For and Against*. Cambridge University Press.

Zahavi, D. (2001). Beyond empathy. *Journal of Consciousness Studies*, 8: 151–67.

———. (2010). Empathy, embodiment and interpersonal understanding: From Lipps to Schutz. *Inquiry*, 53, 285–306.

———. (2014). *Self and Other*. Oxford University Press.

Chapter 13

Sharing and Other Illusions

Asymmetry in "Moments of Meeting"

Joona Taipale

ABSTRACT

This chapter tackles the question of interpersonal understanding from the point of view of so-called "moments of meeting." Coined by Daniel Stern and his colleagues, this term refers to specific and particularly intense experiential situations, where two (or more) persons attune to each other's affective experiences, thus "cocreating" an experiential area that exists to these two individuals exclusively—a "shared private world," as Stern puts it (Stern, 2004). While moments of meeting have attracted a lot of interest in research on psychotherapeutic change, clinical effectivity, and outcome, the usefulness of the concept in nonclinical discussions has been overlooked. The chapter fills in this lacuna by underlining the applicability of the concept of descriptions of everyday experiences of emotional sharing. The core argument is that moments of meeting have an *asymmetric* structure that complicates the structure of self-other relationships. By opening new perspectives to interpersonal understanding—its successes and shortcomings—this chapter contributes both to nonclinical and clinical discussions.

Keywords: interpersonal understanding, affect attunement, emotional sharing, reparation, mutuality, illusion, Daniel Stern, illusion, truth of solipsism

INTRODUCTION: THE SUBJECTIVE BIAS

One of the necessary (though not sufficient) conditions of an ethical relationship lies in the effort of recognizing others *in their own right*, in contrast to viewing them emphatically *in the light of our subjective experiential situation*. Considering the full scope of our daily interactions, however, unbiased experiences of others count as *exceptions* rather than comprising the *rule*. Our social experiences are usually more or less colored by our dynamically vacillating and largely unconscious needs, desires, interests, associations, inhibitions, and other psychic factors. In the light of this idiosyncratic "psychic reality," other people are, by rule, introduced to us in a *subjectively biased* manner.

The subjective bias significantly complicates our experience of others. On the one hand, it affects our grasp of others in their *outer* appearance. To illustrate, whether we consider someone's behavior as bold or arrogant, active or pompous, hilarious or politically incorrect, and also whether and how such features stand out in our experience—in all this, a constitutive role is played by our factical bodily condition, state of alertness, idiosyncratic preferences, habitual prejudices, and indeed our whole developmental history. On the other hand, and more to the point, the subjective bias plays a part in our interpretations, expectations, presuppositions and suspicions concerning *others' self-experience, their experience of the world, and their experience of us* (including our external appearance and our respective experiential relations). To be sure, in many kinds of social encounter, our grasp of others' experiential life may remain rather vague and general: in an urban setting, we may fleetingly perceive tens or even hundreds of people every day, and in these perceptions we mostly build on social typifications—considering others as passers-by, cashiers, businessmen, drunkards, and so on—without pondering on how these particular individuals feel about themselves, the world, and us (see Taipale 2016). By contrast, in personally significant forms of interaction, we also reach into the other's experience and busy ourselves with how our companion thinks and feels about herself and her body, how she thinks, how she perceives and values her surroundings, and how she represents us and our intentions directed at her.

In these latter forms of interaction, to which I will be focusing in the following, the subjective bias plays a particularly central role. Namely, given that we cannot simply step into the other's mind to see how she experiences everything, in our respective sense-making efforts we can only rely on our subjective grasp that is already colored by the aforementioned idiosyncrasies. To be sure, we can consciously *aim* at recognizing the share of our idiosyncratic associations, reach beyond the subjective bias, and, thus, strive for a more neutral and "objective" assessment of others. While in the present context, we need not take a stand on whether we ever *completely* succeed in such abstraction, two observations regarding this issue can nonetheless be made. First, given that affects and emotions play a central role in the subjective "coloring" of experience, and given that the share of affects and emotions is greater in cases with personal involvement, it seems safe to note that *the subjective bias tends to be underlined in our significant social experiences.* Differently put, maintaining an unbiased attitude is particularly challenging in relation to our significant others. Second, even if we can *momentarily* recognize, more or less exhaustively, our subjective biases, and hence consider others more objectively, this abstraction is not constantly at our disposal. Indeed, considering the nuanced and vivid flow of social experiences, unbiased attitudes toward others count as exceptions: Notwithstanding the importance of the *capacity* for neutral observation, this potentiality is *not predominantly actualized* in our social life.

The subjective bias complicates the structure of interpersonal understanding and mutuality. For one, it modifies each individual's grasp of their *own* feelings and thoughts. And so, whereas *our grasp of the other's experience* is colored by our idiosyncratic psychic reality, *the other's grasp of her own experiences* is determined in the light of the other's idiosyncratic psychic reality.[1] A comprehensive and exhaustive "match" between the two seems highly unlikely. As much as we know of the other and of her history, as much as we are familiar with the other's habitualities, inclinations, and styles of reacting, and as much as we can empathically feel our way into their experiential situation, we are forever "outsiders" when it comes to *the other's idiosyncratic experience as lived through by the other.* The same naturally holds for ourselves: Others are equally "outsiders" when it comes to the inviolable core of our self (cf. Winnicott 1965, 187). Differently put, given the subjective bias, each individual lives in his or her idiosyncratic version of reality—an issue that Merleau-Ponty touches upon when speaking of "the truth of solipsism" (2012, 374). We meet, we perceive each other, and we communicate—and yet we can only relate to the other, and to what we take to be shared with them, *from our biased subjective viewpoint.*

Reciprocity complicates matters even further, given that the mentioned bias simultaneously figures *on both sides.* The other's grasp of how I think and feel likewise unfolds from the other's idiosyncratic viewpoint, and my subjective feelings and thoughts are most likely not identical with the other's representation of them. And so, while an exhaustive grasp of someone else's thoughts and feelings in all their nuances and associations, and conversely someone else's accurate grasp of my idiosyncratic feelings and thoughts as they unfold in my life, seems highly unlikely, a *reciprocal match* seems even less probable. On both sides, experiences of being with the other are at once subjective and, hence, idiosyncratically outlined experiences, and each individual has their own peculiar representation of what is shared with the other. Formally put, what Individual A considers as shared with Individual B is not identical with what Individual B considers to be shared with Individual A. In this sense, intersubjectivity has an *asymmetric structure.*[2]

While this asymmetry renders the *shortcomings* of interpersonal experience rather understandable, even expected, it appears perplexing in the light of *successful* ones. After all, in personally significant social encounters, we occasionally feel we have a good sense of *what the other is going through*, we may find ourselves *joining in the other's feeling*, and we may conversely *find our own affects met, recognized, and understood*, thus *feeling intimately connected with the other.* What should we make of such experiences in the light of subjective bias? More precisely: *What happens to the structural asymmetry in such experiences?*

The theoretical consequences of the *subjective bias* and of the ensuing *asymmetry* have not been sufficiently recognized in the philosophical and multidisciplinary literature on intersubjectivity.[3] To analyze how asymmetry underlines and complicates emotional understanding, I will focus on those intimate cases of nonverbal and emotional sharing that Daniel Stern has called "moments of meeting" (e.g., Stern 2004, 166ff.). The concept emerges from Stern's work in developmental psychology and psychoanalysis, and it has attracted a considerable amount of interest in research on psychotherapeutic change and outcome. However, the usefulness of the concept in non-clinical discussions on interpersonal understanding has been overlooked. In Stern, moments of meeting refer to particularly intense experiential situations, where two[4] persons reciprocally attune to each other's affective experiences, thus "co-creating" a shared experiential space that exists to these two individuals exclusively—a "shared private world," as Stern also puts it (Stern 2004, 173). Focusing on these particularly intensive cases enables highlighting a general structure in interpersonal experience: If moments of meeting involve an asymmetric structure, this can be expected to hold also for the less intensive, fleeting, and casual social encounters, where self/other demarcation tends to be more pronounced—this, however, will be left for further studies.

The chapter is structured as follows. In the following section, I will explain what Stern means by moments of meeting, extending his analysis beyond the psychotherapy setting. In the third section, I will engage in a critical analysis of the notion from the viewpoint of the aforementioned subjective bias. In the fourth section, I will illustrate the volatile nature of moments of meeting, and argue that they repeatedly require "acts of repair." Arguably, what continually threatens to interrupt the sense of connection is precisely the underlying asymmetry, which can make itself felt to a greater or lesser degree. Being constantly on the verge of shattering, moments of meeting presuppose a *reciprocal ignorance* concerning the asymmetric setting. I expect this account to prove useful in analyzing the successes and shortcomings of interpersonal understanding.

INTO THE UNKNOWN: STERN ON MOMENTS OF MEETING

Stern introduces the moments of meeting as occasionally arising out of *specific responses* to what he calls "now moments": spontaneously and hence unexpectedly emerging moments where the routined course of interaction is suddenly put into question (e.g., Stern 2004, 245). Such moments restore the sense of presence of the engaged individuals, by challenging the implicit "rules" or the "grammar" of being together. Stern illustrates this with an anecdote of an analysand who in one morning suddenly says that she wants to sit up and see her analyst's face:

> And with no further ado she sits up and turns around. The therapist and patient find themselves staring at each other in startled silence. That is a *now moment.* The patient didn't know she was going to do it right before . . . that moment. It was a spontaneous eruption. Nor did the therapist anticipate it, just then, in that way. Yet they now find themselves in a novel intersubjective situation. *Kairos* hangs heavy (Stern 2004, 166).

The unexpected gesture "disequilibrates" the familiar intersubjective context and calls for *action*: "something must be done" (Stern, Bruschweiler-Stern, et al., 1998, 305). It is as if an ethical claim was imposed: 'I am here—your move.' On the face of the pressing "now moment," doing nothing would equally be an act (Stern 2004, 166).

Whether a moment of meeting grows out of such now moments is contingent on the nature of the reaction of the *recipient* of the disequilibrating gesture (Stern 2004, 169). In this sense, the spontaneous eruption can be compared to an *invitation.* The unexpected gesture shakes the routined course of interaction, "pushes the intersubjective state into a zone of transition that is unstable" (Stern, Bruschweiler-Stern, et al., 1998, 305), and challenges the manner of being-with. Hence, the other member of the interactive situation is put into a position where she has to either *accept* or *turn down* the invitation, as it were. Stern's anecdote continues:

> The therapist, without knowing exactly what she was going to do, softened her face slowly and let the suggestion of a smile form around her mouth. She then

> leaned her head towards slightly and said "hello." The patient continued to look at her. They remained locked in a mutual gaze for several seconds. After a moment, the patient laid down again and continued her work on the couch, but more profoundly and in a new key, which opened up new material. The change was dramatic in their therapeutic work together (Stern 2004, 169).

The patient's spontaneous gesture combined with the therapist's personal adjustment to the unexpectedly emerging situation together established a moment of meeting. With her "authentic response finely matched to the momentary local situation" (Stern 2004, 168), the therapist *entered* the new intersubjective situation opened by the patient's spontaneity, and encountered the patient *where she currently is* (170). In other words, if the patient's initial communication to the therapist was, "I am here," the therapist's responsive communication to the patient was, "I am here with you." With her adjustive gesture, the therapist thus turned what initially emerged as a *disruptive gesture* into a *relational move* to be built upon. In short, the patient issued an invitation, and the therapist accepted it and played along.

To continue with this metaphor, we could think of various ways in which the recipient might *turn down* the invitation. As Stern exemplifies, the outcome of the now moment would have been different if the therapist had rigidly maintained or underlined her professional role, retained an observational distance and reacted to the patient with a "neutral, technical response" (Stern 2004, 168)—for example, "what are you thinking now?" In this case, the therapist would have indirectly, yet very clearly, expressed both *her reluctance to enter the new situation* created by the patient's spontaneous eruption and *her wish that the patient would return* to the routined course of interaction—or, the space that the therapist never left, as it were. By thus turning down the invitation, the therapist would have rendered the patient's spontaneous eruption as a *disruption to be overcome*, as something that does not fit the grammar of the situation at hand. In this case, the spontaneously emerging opportunity for an intersubjective meeting would have been lost. Instead, the therapist accepted the uncontrollability of the event, momentarily stepped out of her role as a therapist, and encountered the patient not so much *as a patient* but *as another human being* (see Stern, Sander, et al., 1998, 912). As Stern put it, with her spontaneous and authentic response, she resolved the sudden crisis created by the now moment (Stern 2004, 169).

Stern underlines that the intersubjective space opened by such moments is co-created (Stern 2004, 158). With this, he aims to highlight two things. For one, "each move and moment creates the context for the one that follows," and this "mutual context-creating goes on and on, one relational move after one another, such that the *direction* of where the moves go together is very largely dyadically determined" (Stern 2004, 158). That is to say, both parties *constantly* find themselves building on *something unexpected* while heading toward an *uncharted territory*. Neither of the interacting partners is *pre-acquainted* with the area they are traversing; neither of them knows what kind of intersubjective space will be co-created—if any. Each *move,* hence, presumably requires a great deal of courage and trust: After all, the other's adjusting response is needed for the spontaneous eruption to be established as a "relational move" in the first place, and the fate of one's spontaneity cannot be known in advance. Second, "each relational move and present moment is designed to express an intention relative to the inferred intentions of the other. The two end up seeking, chasing, missing, finding, and shaping each other's intentionality" (Stern 2004, 158). That is to say, while Individual A does not have direct access to the mind of Individual B, nor the other way around, what they adjust themselves to is the other's thoughts and feelings *as they subjectively conceive of them* (see Stern 2004, xvi). In the previous example, the therapist does not *know for sure* what the patient is heading with the gesture of suddenly sitting up and turning around; in her responding, she can only rely on her *own* sense of the situation and her vague grasp of the other's intention—and "misreadings" are therefore constantly possible.

Co-creation is accordingly a *recursive* process, where the engaged individuals—in a "hit-miss-repair-elaborate fashion" (Stern 2004, 156)—strive to achieve intersubjective "fittedness" (168):

> Because the process of chaining together (sometimes very loosely) relational moves in present moments is largely spontaneous and unpredictable from move to move, there are many mismatches, derailments, misunderstandings, and indeterminacy. These 'mistakes' require a process of repair (Stern 2004, 157).

In a related context, Stern talks about "missteps in the dance" (1977, 109ff). The metaphor is illustrative: when stepping on your partner's toe while dancing, for instance, there is an interruption, a kind of now moment ensuing from your clumsiness. To continue dancing, mutual adaptation is needed: your partner has to adjust her movements to your misstep, while this in turn forces you to refit your movements to her unexpectedly altered movements. Along with such *reciprocal acts of repair*, the flow of dyadic movement is retained, whereby you mutually continue each other's movements, or complement each other's motor intentionalities (see Sander 2014, 199). Likewise with interpersonal communication. To react to a patient's spontaneous gesture of sitting up by leaning forward and saying "hello" is not something one can read from a psychologist's manual; insisting upon a "specific fit to a specific situation" (Stern 2004, 168–69), moments of meeting can only be "created on the spot to fit the singularity of the unexpected situation" (Stern, Bruschweiler-Stern, et al., 1998, 305). Such "intentional fuzziness" and the ensuing need for recurring reparation render human interaction a "sloppy" process (Stern 2004, 156–57).[5]

In his account, Stern mainly maneuvers in the psychotherapeutic context, but the same applies to everyday interaction. Insofar as there are unexpected spontaneous eruptions on behalf of Individual A, there must also be room for spontaneous deviations from the preestablished setting on behalf of Individual B. Nonclinical interaction is equally a sloppy process. And while certain inviolable parameters—in psychotherapy as well as in everyday life—are necessarily needed for communication (Stern 2004, 164), the spontaneous and personal nature of the required reaction renders moments of meeting impossible to plan. The conversing individuals can only balance "at the boundary between sloppiness and coherence" (182) and, hence, repeatedly repair their missteps and adjust to those of others. As said, if the therapist was not open to the sloppy nature of the process but kept strictly with her occupational role, the patient would have felt neglected or dismissed, finding herself met *as a patient*, yet less *as a human being*. Likewise in nonclinical interaction, moments of meeting require that the other is met "where she is." While the significance of moments of meeting is particularly underlined in the psychotherapeutic setting, and while it has been mainly examined in this context, moments of meeting can be equally found outside the consultation room. We could perhaps even say that, notwithstanding their immense clinical significance, in their capacity to temporarily do away with hierarchical settings, *moments of meeting essentially are nonclinical encounters.*

In contrast to casual cases of joint action that do not deeply alter our relationship with the other, Stern underlines moments of meeting as transitional moments or experiences of a sudden shift *in implicit relational knowing* (Stern, Sander, et al., 1998, 905; Stern 2004, 242), that significantly alter or "rearrange" our way of being with the other (Stern, Sander, et al., 1998, 905, 917; Stern 2004, 176). If the now moment is like an invitation to reorganize the ground rules of being together, acceptance of the invitation amounts to an expansion of the *scope or range* of being with the other: it transforms both members' implicit sense of togetherness (Stern, Bruschweiler-Stern, et al., 1998, 305) and moves the relationship "to a deeper level of intersubjectivity" (Stern 2010, 140).

Though mainly giving clinical examples, Stern illustrates this "transitional" nature of the moments of meeting with a beautiful narrative of two persons, not knowing each other, going out for their first date. It is winter and, on the spur of the moment, the two persons decide to go ice skating; stumbling onto the ice, they engage in a sort of a clumsy dance:

> She almost falls backwards. He reaches out and steadies her. He loses his balance and tilts to the right. She throws out a hand and grabs it. . . . And each of

> them knows, at the moment, that the other knows what it feels like to be him or her. . . . There is much laughing and gasping and falling. There is no space in which to really talk. . . . At the end of a half hour, tired, they stop and have a hot drink at the side of the rink. But now their relationship is in a different place. They have each directly experienced something of the other's experience. They have vicariously been inside the other's body and mind through a series of shared feeling voyages. They have created an implicit intersubjective field that endures as part of their short history together. . . . They will talk across the table and share meanings. And while they talk, the explicit domain of their relationship will start to expand. Whatever is said will be against the background of the implicit relationship that was expanded before, through the shared feeling voyages they had on the ice (Stern 2004, 174–75).

Like in the clinical examples, here too the intimate sense of doing something together "expands" the intersubjective field (Stern 2004, 189). The expanding proceeds both horizontally and vertically, as it were: On the one hand, new dimensions of interaction open up, thus widening the horizon of possible interaction, whereas, on the other hand, the already established dimensions of interaction increase in depth. And so, once an implicit relational space has been pioneered through the joint experience, explicit interaction is altered as well (Stern, Bruschweiler-Stern, et al., 1998, 305).

Stern's emphasis concerning the *implicit* nature of moments of meeting also has a normative dimension: Moments of meeting not only *often are* implicit, but they also *need to remain* such. For one, Stern underlines that what is at stake is not a reflective experience, explicit recognition, or conscious awareness of fittedness (Stern 2004, 172; see also Lyons-Ruth 2000, 92). It is only in retrospect that moments of meeting can be grasped as such (see Sander 2014, 231). Moreover, Stern underlines that conscious attention also tends to *compromise* the experience in question: "an attempt to make this moment of meeting explicit, especially immediately after it occurred, could undo some of its effect" (Stern 2004, 191). Just consider the ice-skating couple enjoying the intimate moment, laughing and gasping carelessly, feeling enchanted by the intimate emotional connection with the other—and then consider one of them exclaiming cheerfully: "It seems that we are falling in love with one another, isn't that marvelous?" The experience is at once "disenchanted," and this is because, by *reflectively explicating* the experience, one at once introduces an observational distance to it.

To sum up, moments of meeting are implicit, nonverbal, transitional episodes in the ongoing process of implicit relational knowing, "shared feeling voyages" that significantly expand the intersubjective space among the ones involved. Metaphorically speaking, moments of meeting are not about *moving forward as one unit* but about *heading to the same direction together with someone*—even if in a sloppy manner, by way of a clumsy dance, and without knowing where one will end up. What is at stake is a rather volatile or fragile phenomenon. Like immersive experiences of playing, moments of meeting insist on remaining unreflective and unknown as such. Just as playing is interrupted as soon as one becomes explicitly aware that one is playing, moments of meeting similarly build on an *illusion*.

THE INFINITELY COMPLICATED MATCH

The topic of illusion brings us back to the question we set out with: What happens to asymmetry in moments of meeting? Some of Stern's characterizations seem to imply that in successful moments of meeting the structural asymmetry is displaced by a symmetrical sense of mutuality. Stern not only argues that moments of meeting involve an intense sense of sharing (Stern 2004, 168) and a sense of specific "fittedness" (151, 171) that build on "reciprocal mindreading" (xvi) and the sense of sufficiently "similar mental landscapes" (151). He also claims that moments of meeting build on "other-centered-participation" (Stern 2000, xxii; cf. Bråten 1998; Trevarthen 1979), whereby the interacting partners entertain a "dyadic form of consciousness" (Stern, Bruschweiler-Stern, et al., 1998, 305) and are momentarily "aware of what each other is experiencing" (Stern 2004, 151). Accordingly, moments of meeting are "cocreated by both partners and lived through originally by both" (173); they are "shared feeling voyages" (172–74), in the course of which the participants "vicariously inhabit" each other's mind and body (174) and directly "experience what the other is experiencing" (174, 241). These "cocreated islands of intentional fittedness" (164) or "shared private worlds" (173) allegedly emerge out of dyadic interaction with a "roughly equal contribution of two minds" (159). In this manner, moments of meeting allegedly relocate the interacting partners "in a no-man's land" (174), in *a neutral area equally given to both*.

Such characterizations make it seem as if Stern was thinking of a *symmetrical* setting. The preceding discussion on the subjective bias puts some pressure on many of these claims. If the experiences of the individual are inseparably veiled in idiosyncrasies—that is, if each of the engaged individuals experiences themselves, the other, and the shared area differently—it seems unavoidable that *what one individual considers to be shared with another does not perfectly coincide or match with what this other individual considers to be shared with the first one*.

The subjective bias significantly complicates interpersonal experiences by modifying the individuals' grasp of self and others. For one, instead of a homogeneous "other," the interactive situation involves both *the other in the light of my idiosyncratic psychic reality*, and *the other in the light of her idiosyncratic psychic reality*—two idiosyncratic representations that might not coincide with each other. Likewise, instead of a homogenous self, there is *idiosyncratic self-awareness and self-representation*, on the one hand, and *my self as I am portrayed in the other's idiosyncratic representation of me*, on the other. These two representations might not harmoniously coincide with each other either. Thus, instead of *two* poles, we already have *four*. Moreover, the issue is exponentially reiterated given that "my experiential relation to the other" is conceptually divided into *this relation as lived-through by me* and *this relation* as *represented by the other.* And, in turn, "the other's experiential relation to me" divides into *this relation as grasped by the other* and *this relation as I experience it.*

In this fashion, the subjective bias complicates the self-other relation. The latter unfolds as a complex structure involving internal relations, dynamics, and tensions between *numerous* poles of reference (see figure 13.1).

To verbalize this table, the overall experience of Individual A covers her *subjective self-experience* (A1), her *subjective experience of the environment* (A2), and her *subjective experience of the other* (A3). Each of these is permeated and burdened by an idiosyncratic coloring. Moreover, Individual A's experience of Individual B (A3) can be conceptually divided into A's grasp *of B's subjective self-experience* (A3-1), A's grasp *of B's subjective experience of her surroundings* (A3-2), and A's grasp *of B's subjective experience of A* (A3-3). Given that all these elements respectively figure in Individual B's overall experience (B1, B2, B3-1, B3-2, and B3-3), which is equally subjectively biased, the picture gets highly intricate.

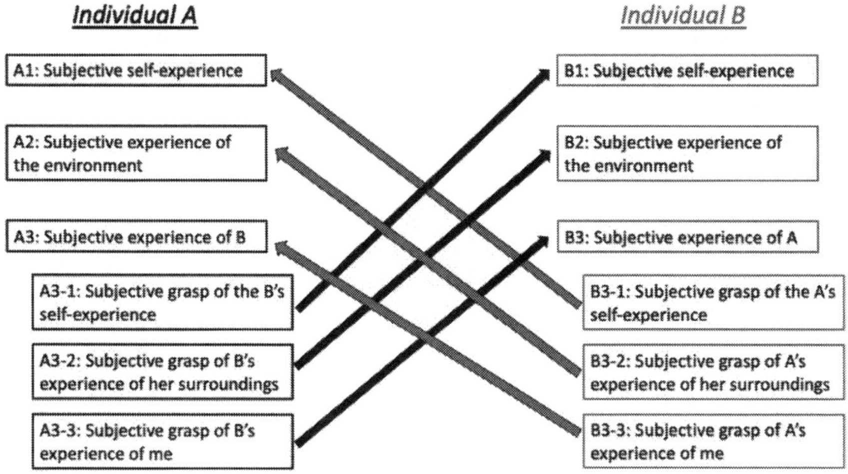

Figure 13.1.

Moreover, personally significant social experiences harbor *implicit and unconscious assumptions* concerning a match between various poles (these assumptions are indicated by arrows in figure 13.1). For instance, whenever one feels that she is "experiencing what the other is experiencing"—a trait that allegedly characterizes moments of meeting—a match is implied between *how I take the other to be feeling* (A3-1) and *how the other is feeling* (B1). In other words, while intensely feeling that we experience what the other is experiencing, we tend to assume that we are grasping the experiences of the other *as they appear in the life of the other*. The reciprocal setting complicates the issue further, increasing the number of the assumed matches. Namely, in my subjective experience of the other, I am intentionally reaching not only into the other's *subjective experience of me* (A3-3 → B3), but also the other's *subjective experience of my experience of her* (A3-3 → B3 → [B3-3 →] A3), and so on. The infinite recursive loop (see Stern 2004, 243) opening here would allow for drawing a much more complicated picture, but this level of detail is sufficient for our purposes.

Instead of busying ourselves with the further complexities of this field, we only need to note that, in the light of the subjective bias, the term *dyad* seems like a gross simplification. To be sure, from a third-person standpoint, there are *two* poles of interaction (Individual A and Individual B), whereas from first- and second-person standpoints, the number of poles is much higher. And, accordingly, *numerous* assumptions of a match may be involved, including ones between A3-1 and B1, between B3-1 and A1, between A3-3 and B3, and between B3-3 and A3. These insights motivate a critical analysis of the moments of meeting.

By suggesting that moments of meeting are built on a direct glimpse into the other's mind, or on directly grasping the other's experience (e.g., Stern 2004, 174), Stern comes to raise the bar for successful intersubjective experiences rather high. To be sure, he accordingly notes that moments of meeting are "fairly rare occurrences" (178), and he underlines that reparation is constantly needed—within the process of going along, moments of meeting are literally *moments,* even if personally significant and often unforgettable (see Sander 2014, 230). However, conceptualized in this manner, the subjective bias and the complexity ensuing from it seem to render moments of meeting not only rare but practically impossible. Namely, if already the possibility deems highly unlikely that my idiosyncratic grasp of how the other feels (A3-1) could ever *exhaustively match* with the other's subjective self-experience (B1), in reciprocal cases the complexity of the situation is exponentially increased. In the form of an argument: if an exhaustive match between the poles was required for moments of meeting, there would *not be* moments of meeting; and while moments of meeting do exist, the requirement for a comprehensive and mutual grasp of each other's intentionalities therefore must be dispensed with.

ON THE VERGE OF CONNECTION: HIT, MISS, REPAIR

In the light of what has been argued thus far, the term *dyad* strikes as a simplification. Rather than as a setting with *two* poles, interpersonal experience has been introduced here as a dynamic web of references between *numerous* poles. This complexity is owing to what I have termed *the subjective bias*. Each person experiences themselves, the world, and others in the light of their idiosyncratic experiential circumstances, and a comprehensive match across all of the respective poles seems highly likely.

While this complexity renders *mis*understandings rather understandable, what to make of *successful* interpersonal experiences? Given the subjective bias, how should we interpret *experiences of grasping what the other is going through*, *feelings of taking part in the other's feeling*, or *the sense of being understood by others*? To narrow down the scope: *what happens to the unavoidable structural asymmetry in moments of meeting?*

To examine this question, note that depending on the circumstances, the aforementioned tacit assumptions may *remain unnoticed* or *stand out*. In the latter case, suspicion tends to arise whether one's grasp of the other, or the other's grasp of oneself, is misguided one way or the other. In moments of meeting such suspicions are altogether absent. Importantly, as long as no mismatch *stands out*, the interacting partners can act *as if* there was none. To be sure, for an assumption to remain unchallenged is by no means a guarantee of its veracity. It is one thing to say that a match between subjective experiences *is ensured* and another thing to say that a match between subjective experiences *is not compromised*. My suggestion is that moments of meeting—and interpersonal understanding in general—presupposes the latter but not the former. That is to say: As long as the respective tacit assumptions are not compromised, the engaged individuals can *build on* them—regardless of their veracity. As I will suggest, this introduces an ingredient of *illusion* into the heart of intersubjective relations.

To clarify this issue, for starters, consider *verbal interaction*, which is sometimes taken to have the power to *rid* the mismatch between idiosyncratic representations of two individuals, providing interaction with a firm, symmetrical setting. For instance, in telling Individual B about a dog that I (Individual A) saw earlier, it might turn up at some point that B has a different kind of dog in mind. This prominent misunderstanding (i.e., an overt mismatch between B3-2 and A2) disturbs and interrupts the sense of sharing, and calls for "acts of repair." The prominent sense of mismatch can be rid by verbally specifying further that it was a poodle that I saw. The increased sense of precision ensuing from this act of repair might well satisfy the purposes of the interactive situation: further details, and hence, any additional mismatch between our idiosyncratic representations, *might not matter*. This often is the case in casual everyday encounters: Mutual understanding on a rather general level suffices, while idiosyncratic differences remain unimportant. However, should the nature of the conversation so demand, any recurring sense of mismatch could again be "repaired" by way of additional verbal specifications. Nonetheless, the generality of words can never exhaust the full richness of the idiosyncratic experience. No matter how detailed our specifications (i.e., verbal acts of "repair"), there will always be more to be specified.

While the mismatch between A2 (i.e., my perception of the dog) and B3-2 (i.e. the other's representation of the dog I perceived) thus *no longer makes itself felt*, the joint contentment hardly guarantees an exhaustive coincidence between the two—after all, A and B might well (and most likely do) have a *different kind* of poodle in mind. Instead of undoing the mismatch, therefore, verbal communication only pushes the mismatch one step farther: It rids the *sense of mismatch* but not the mismatch itself. The disproportion of the idiosyncratic experiences may in fact be constantly flickering beneath the surface, as it were, but without standing out to interrupt the interaction. The *level of required specificity* is what matters; interaction is disturbed only when the mismatch breaches these situational parameters and thus breaks the surface. As long as it does not stand out, the interacting partners enjoy and build upon a *sense of sharing*, without being prompted to decide on its objective veracity. In the sense that the factual mismatch is *overlooked*, the sense of sharing rests on an *illusion*.

This idea can be applied to cases of nonverbal experiential sharing, such as occurring in moments of meeting. Nonverbal interaction, too, strives for a sense of mutuality and togetherness; here, too, acts of reparation are needed; and here too the required level of specificity is determined by the nature of the interactive situation. However, without verbal communication, *how can we tell* whether our subjective intentions align with one another to a sufficient degree? Stern's response is "affect attunement" (Stern, 1985). Whereas in verbal interaction *explicit specifications, clarifications, and corrections* function as kinds of beacons that enable fitting together the idiosyncratic experiences of the conversing individuals, in nonverbal interaction the needed beacon resides in the *feeling of attunement.*

Originating in Stern's work in developmental psychology, affect attunement is a phenomenon familiar to most parents (and infants). As Stern exemplifies:

> a nine-month-old boy is sitting facing his mother. He has a rattle in his hand and is shaking up and down with a display of interest and mild amusement. As mother watches, she begins to nod her head up and down, keeping a tight beat with her son's arm motions (Stern 1985, 141).
>
> A ten-month-old girl is seated on the floor facing her mother. She is trying to get a piece of puzzle into its right place. After many failures she finally gets it in. She then looks up into her mother's face with delight and an explosion of enthusiasm. She "opens up her face" [her mouth opens, her eyes widen, her eyebrows rise] and then closes back down. The time contour of these changes can be described as a smooth arch [a crescendo, high point, decrescendo]. At the same time her arms rise and fall at her sides. Mother responds by intoning, "Yeah" with a pitch line that rises and falls as the volume crescendos and decrescendos: "yeeAAaahh." The mother's prosodic contour matches the child's facial-kinetic contour (Stern 2010, 41; cf. Stern 1985, 140).

Though not identical, the two gestures "fit together" like pieces of a diachronic puzzle: one gesture *continues* the other and, thus,establishes it as a relational move. The situation is basically similar in the case of the therapist/patient example: the therapist's gesture of leaning forward and saying "hello" is a "specific fitted match" (Stern 2004, 169) that *complements and continues* the patient's gesture of sitting up and turning around. This phenomenon also underlies the nonverbal coordination of the movements of the dancing partners, as well as the intense nonverbal exchange of the ice-skating couple. The common denominator is that the other *plays along* and establishes the gesture as a *relational move* to be built upon, so that the engaged individuals find themselves in a shared area cocreated in the course of this ongoing interaction.

Stern characterizes affect attunement as a cross-modal match between *vitality forms* (Stern 1985; 2004, 84). In both examples, instead of simply *imitating* the child's gesture, the mother gives an alternative expression to it. And, by so doing, she communicates to the child that she grasps not only how the child's behavior *externally looks like*, but also *how the child is feeling* (Stern 2010, 43). Such communication can be conveyed in various ways, making use of different sensory modalities: "extremely diverse events may thus be yoked, so long as they share the quality of feeling" (1985, 58). That is to say, it does not matter whether the mother rhythmically nods her head, produces a sound pattern, or does something else—as long as the mother's response *matches the vital quality of her son's feeling*, and thus gives an alternative expression to it (see Stern 1985, 56; 2010, 42; cf. 43, 113; Stern 2004, 84):

> What is being matched is not the other person's behaviour per se, but rather some aspect of behaviour that reflects the person's feelings state. The ultimate

> reference for the match appears to be the feeling state (inferred or directly apprehended), not the external behavioural event. Thus the match appears to occur between the expressions of inner state. These expressions can differ in mode or form, but they are to some extent interchangeable as manifestations of a single recognizable internal state (Stern 1985, 142; cf. Stern 2004, 241).

Feeling of attunement is achieved when the responding individual—be it the caregiver, the therapist, one's dancing partner, or one's friend—selectively reproduces "the dynamics of the form but not the modality" (Stern 2010, 41):

> In affect attunement, the mother matches the dynamic features of how the baby acted. This ensures the baby that she grasps what he did. However, she does not match the content and modality of the infant's action. Instead, she makes her own choice of modality and content. This assures the baby that she understood, within herself, what it felt like to do what he did. It is not an imitation, because she put it 'into her own words'—it carries her signature. It is something she felt, too. She wants a matching of inner states (Stern 2010, 114).

As long as the vital form remains the same, the alternative ways of attuning with the child will *feel the same* in the child.

Whereas these examples are somewhat one sided, in the sense that there is the child whose feelings are being mirrored by the caregiver, in moments of meeting, such *attunement occurs reciprocally*. Experiential sharing, accordingly, is not primarily a matter of knowledge but a matter of feeling. It is from the other's attuned expressions that we can tell when the other has grasped how we feel and when our subjective intentions align with one another to a sufficient degree. In short, we *feel different* when we are attuned and when we are not attuned with the other (Stern 2004, 180; cf. Sander 2014, 198–99). As Stern puts it, in the spontaneously cocreated, uncharted interpersonal space, the sought-for attunement "acts as a sort of non-conscious compass to guide" the course of interaction (Stern 2010, 138). Just consider the still-face experiment (Tronick et al., 1978) and the immense trouble that the baby experiences when the mother is still physically present but no longer attunes with her; and consider, in turn, how the baby's feeling alters when the mother re-attunes with her and thus repairs the interrupted sense of connection. No words are needed for this, and if words are involved, *how* something is said tends to matter more than *what* is said (see Stern 2004, 191).[6]

Attunement is a subtle issue, and it requires balancing between *intimacy* and *distance*. Stern illustrates this in terms of *over-attunement* and *under-attunement* (1985, 148–49). For instance, if you are telling someone about a personal loss, you would feel awkward if the other would respond with an overblown gesture as if the loss was her own; conversely, you would feel dismissed if the other would maintain an unchanged face and respond with an official tone of voice, "I see that you are sad" (see Stern 1985, 136). In both cases, you would experience *mis*attunement, but in two different senses—in the case of under-attunement, you would not feel supported by the other, whereas in the case of over-attunement you might end up supporting the other. While such obvious missteps are easy to pinpoint, mis-attunements are not always that extensive and emphatic. *Attunement is a matter of more/less, not a matter of either/or* (see Stern 2004, 189). Sometimes the sense of interpersonal connection may be only slightly disturbed by a minor detail that marginally makes itself felt without altogether interrupting the interaction. As Stern puts it: "There are many 'missteps' every minute in the best of interactions, and the majority of them are quickly repaired by one or both partners" (157).

Also, the engaged individuals might have partly different parameters for a "sufficient attunement." To illustrate, if one of the dancers is much more skilled than the other, she might be much more sensitive to missteps that her partner does not even notice: whereas the less skilled dancer may be elevated by a sense of attunement, the more skilled dancer may be vexed by what she grasps as missteps. Likewise, in verbal interaction a disproportion of representations might be disturbingly felt by one individual, while remaining altogether unnoticed by the other: whereas the current level of specificity might well be sufficient for one, the other might be troubled by the lack of further details (e.g., "what kind of poodle was it?"). In moments of meeting, there is mutual sense of fittedness and, hence, a series of relational moves that *consecutively and reciprocally build on each other.*

Whether in a literal or in a metaphorical sense, the experience of "moving along" is a *shared experience*—yet one *appearing differently* to both parties. Even if sufficient attunement was felt on both sides, and no mismatch would *stand out*, the interactive situation will nonetheless appear differently to both. As Merleau-Ponty puts it, solitude and communication are two sides of the same phenomenon (2012, 376). Given the unique experiential background of each individual, feelings of togetherness, too, awaken differing associations, memory traces, and idiosyncratic ideas. In this sense, interpersonal relationships are always *uneven* or *asymmetrical*: Each individual creates the common space in his or her own way, and hence experiences it differently. That is to say, insofar as the two do not have an exactly identical experiential set up and same idiosyncratic associations, the mismatch is constantly there, flickering beneath the surface. Even in moments of meeting, each individual first and foremost relates to his or her own idiosyncratic version of the cocreated area or shared private world. On the one hand, moments of meeting build on a sense of a match; on the other hand, this sense is partly owing to ignorance concerning the mismatch. In this sense, moments of meeting build on an *illusion* (see also Taipale 2021).

CONCLUSION

To wrap up, consider two musicians engaging in spontaneous improvisation. On the one hand, the two are *sharing an experience*: Both give and both gain. There is a felt coordination between what they hear and what they play. They are repeatedly confirming each other's "relational moves" by building on each other's spontaneous output, and hence both participate in the cocreation of *one and the same* "dynamic flow" (see Stern 2010, 140). On the other hand, each individual views the cocreated piece of music from their own idiosyncratic standpoint: Each has their own idiosyncratic representation or version of what is being co-created with the other. As long as the spontaneous musical "eruptions" of the two are sufficiently attuned with one another, the noncoincidence between the idiosyncratic "versions" may flicker beneath the surface without standing out. To be sure, generally speaking, we can say that each musician "contributes equally" to the co-creation of the piece of music: After all, both are successively issuing invitations and adjusting to those of the other. Yet, *in each moment*, the setting is asymmetrical and both relate to the co-created space differently. No matter how intense and comprehensive the feeling of attunement, the two musicians have partly differing musical background and personal taste, the music awakens partly different associations in them, and hence the two will experience the one and the same cocreated piece of music differently. Moreover, even if in the long run both individuals would take turns in inviting and adjusting, nonetheless *in each moment* one individual either *presents an invitation* or *adjusts to that of the other*—and (like in dancing) the feeling is different depending on whether one is presently leading or following. From this perspective, the claim of "equal contribution" strikes as an idealization.

Even when the established sense of attunement is felt by both, leaving lesser mistakes and rhythmic flounderings within agreeable parameters, *the sense of mismatch is only pushed aside*. Like in verbal interaction after a certain point there is no longer *need* to increase the level of specificity, in nonverbal interaction, too, the sense of attunement can reach a point where the *need for acts of repair* no longer makes itself felt. The mismatch and asymmetry is still there, but it only dimly flickers below the surface, and interaction is not disturbed by it. Like with verbal interaction, what is rid is not the mismatch but the *sense of mismatch*. Like the two musicians sufficiently attuned for an experience of co-creation to unfold, in moments of meeting, more generally, the interacting individuals are close enough to ignore the mismatch, as it were. Within the situationally outlined implicit parameters, the "emotional landscapes" of the interacting partners are similar enough for a *sense of match* to occur. Whether we are thinking of dancing, musical improvisation, infant/

caregiver dialogue, therapist/patient communication, or some other type of intense interpersonal interaction, given the subjective bias a factual match between "inner states" is highly unlikely, as was argued previously.

In this light, it seems that even in moments of meeting, the individuals may dwell *on the verge of mutually matching connection.* In short, the asymmetry is there, but it does not stand out, and hence the interacting partners may act *as if* there was none. This tension introduces an ingredient of *illusion* into moments of meeting. After all, while we *know* that a match between inner states is practically impossible, yet we occasionally *feel* a match. Notwithstanding their partly *illusory* quality, such feelings of connectedness entail an affective sense of "completion" (Stern 2004, 178) or "vitalization" (Sander 2014, 198–199), and hence comprise "the high spots of life" (Winnicott 1987, 43):

The ideas presented here have consequences for our interpretation of *ethical encounters*. If what has been said here is on the right track, it follows that we can never *exhaustively grasp* how others experience themselves, how they relate to the world and to us, and how they grasp our experience of them. In our efforts to understand others, we can only rely on our subjective experiences that are colored by idiosyncratic associations and representations, even if these might not do justice to the other "in her own right." The truth of solipsism, that Merleau-Ponty is speaking about, refers to this essential inability to transcend the boundaries of our own experience. What we can do, however, is to increasingly challenge our own presuppositions concerning others. To be sure, it might be that we never manage to *free* ourselves of our idiosyncrasies, and grasp the other without subjective biases; it may be that the other in her own right is like a *limes* in the mathematical sense, something that orients our experience without being able to be reached. Be that as it may, it seems that our occasional *feelings* of understanding others and of being understood by them—as illustrated in moments of meeting in particular—can teach us something important about *our need* for interpersonal connection. I will end with quotes from Winnicott and Merleau-Ponty, that capture some of what I have tried to analyze here:

> Although healthy persons communicate and enjoy communicating, the other fact is equally true, that *each individual is an isolated, permanently non-communicating, permanently unknown, in fact unfound. . . .* The question is: *how to be isolated without having to be insulated?* (Winnicott 1965, 187).

> Like polytheistic gods, I must reckon with other gods . . . . Consciousnesses present the absurdity of a solipsism-shared-by-many, and such is the situation that must be understood" (Merleau-Ponty 2012, 376).

NOTES

1. This idea relates to the clinical concepts of transference and countertransference (see, e.g., Ogden 1982; see also Taipale 2015a and Taipale 2019).

2. I have elsewhere discussed the asymmetry of interpersonal experience from two related angles (see Taipale 2015b and Taipale 2021).

3. When it comes to this widespread and multifaceted discussion, giving a comprehensive list of references is not possible. For just a few examples, consider, for example, Tuomela 2007; Zlatev 2008; Schmid, Shulte-Ostermann & Psarros 2008; and Rizzolatti and Sinigaglia 2018.

4. I will limit my analysis on cases with *two* individuals, thus leaving the question open whether Stern's notion can be applied to larger groups.

5. Stern makes this point vis-a-vis psychotherapeutic interaction, but hurries to note that he is not conveying a theory-hostile opinion: "sloppiness is potentially creative only when it occurs within a well-established framework. . . . I am not advocating 'wild analysis' at all. Rather, I am pointing out that even within the normal boundaries of any approach there is plenty of room for sloppiness" (Stern 2004, 164). Stern thinks that whereas "theory alone only provides the bones, sloppiness [in two-person psychology] and irruptions of unconscious material [in one-person psychology] are two different ways of providing the flesh" (Stern 2004, 159).

6. I have elsewhere analyzed this issue with respect to music listening (see Taipale forthcoming).

REFERENCES

Bråten, S. (1998). "Infant learning by altercentric participation: The reverse of egocentric observation in autism." In S. Bråten (ed.), *Intersubjective Communication and Emotion in Early Ontogeny* (pp. 105–24). Cambridge: Cambridge University Press.

Lyons-Ruth, K. (2000). "'I Sense that You Sense that I Sense . . . ': Sander's Recognition Process and the Speficity of Relational Moves in the Psychotherapeutic Setting." *Infant Mental Health Journal*, 21(1–2), 85–98.

Merleau-Ponty, M. (2012). *Phenomenology of Perception.* Translated by Donald Landes. London: Routledge Academic Publishers.

Ogden, T. (1982). "The Concept of Projective identification." In T. Ogden, *Projective Identification and Psychotherapeutic Technique* (pp. 11–37). London: Karnac.

Rizzolatti, G., & Sinigaglia, C. (2018). *Mirrors in the Brain.* Translated by Frances Anderson. Oxford: Oxford University Press.

Sander, L. (2014). *Living Systems, Evolving Consciousness, and the Emerging Person. A Selection of Papers from the Life Work of Louis Sander.* Edited by G. Amadei and I. Bianchi. London: Routledge Academic Publishers.

Schmid, H. B., Shulte-Ostermann, K., & Psarros, N. (2008). *Concepts of Sharedness: Essays on Collective Intentionality.* Frankfurt: De Gruyter.

Stern, D. (1977). *The First Relationship. Infant and Mother.* Cambridge: Harvard University Press.

———. (2000). "Introduction to the paperback edition." In D. Stern, *The Interpersonal World of the Infant* (pp. xi–xxxix). New York: Basic Books.

Stern, D. N. (1985). *The Interpersonal World of the Infant: A View from Psychoanalysis and Developmental Psychology*. New York: Basic Books.

———. (2004). *The Present Moment. In Psychotherapy and Everyday Life*. New York: W. W. Norton & Company.

———. (2010). *Forms of Vitality. Exploring Dynamic Experience in Psychology, the Arts, Psychotherapy, and Development*. Oxford: Oxford University Press.

Stern, D. N., Bruschweiler-Stern, N., Harrison, A. M., Lyons-Ruth, K., Morgan, A. C., Nahum, J. P., Sander, L. W., and Tronick, E. Z (1998). "The Process of Therapeutic Change Involving Implicit Knowledge. Some Implications of Developmental Observations for Adult Psychotherapy." *Infant Mental Health Journal*, 19(3), 300–308.

Stern, D. N., Sander, L. W., Nahum, J. P., Harrison, A. M., Lyons-Ruth, K., Morgan, A. C., Bruschweiler-Stern, N., and Tronick, E. Z. (1998). "Non-Interpretive Mechanisms in Psychoanalytic Therapy: The 'Something More' Than Interpretation." *The International Journal of Psycho-Analysis*, 79, 903–21.

Taipale, J. (2015a). "The anachronous other: Empathy and transference in early phenomenology and psychoanalysis." *Studia Phaenomenologica*, vol. XV, 331–48.

———. (2015b). "Similarity and asymmetry. Husserl and the transcendental foundations of empathy." *Phänomenologische Forschungen 2014*, 141–54.

———. (2016). "From types to tokens: Empathy and typification." In: T. Szanto and D. Moran (eds.), *Phenomenology of Sociality. Discovering the 'We'* (pp. 143–58). London: Routledge.

———. (2019). "Anonymity of the 'Anyone.' The Associative Depths of Open Intersubjectivity." In Frode Kjosavik and Christian Beyer (eds.), *Husserl's Phenomenology of Intersubjectivity: Historical Interpretations and Contemporary Applications* (pp. 193–209). London: Routledge.

———. (2021). "The illusion of contact. Insights from Winnicott's 1952 letter to Klein." *The International Journal of Psychoanalysis*, 102(1), 31–50.

———. (forthcoming). "The modifying mirror: Binding one's experiences through music." In Wiskus and De Souza (eds.): *The Oxford Handbook of Phenomenology of Music*. Oxford: Oxford University Press.

Tuomela, R. (2007). *The Philosophy of Sociality. The Shared Point of View*. Oxford: Oxford University Press.

Trevarthen, C. (1979). "Communication and cooperation in early infancy: A description of primary intersubjectivity." *Before Speech: The Beginning of Interpersonal Communication*, 1, 530–71.

Tronick, E. Z., Als, H., Adamson, L., Wise, S., & Brazelton, T.B. (1978). "The infant's response to entrapment between contradictory messages in face-to-face interaction." *Journal of the American Academy of Child Psychiatry*, 17, 1–13.

Winnicott, D. (1987). *The Spontaneous Gesture. Selected Letters by D. W. Winnicott*. Edited by Robert Rodman. Cambridge: Harvard University Press.

Winnicott D. W. (1965). "Communicating and not communicating leading to a study of certain opposites," In: *The Maturational Processes and the Facilitating Environment* (pp. 179–92). New York: International Universities Press.

Zlatev, J. (2008). *The shared mind: Perspectives on intersubjectivity*. Amsterdam: John Benjamins Publishing Company.

Chapter 14

Thinking with the Heart

From the Responsiveness of the Flesh to the Ethics of Responsibility

Elodie Boublil

ABSTRACT

By analyzing more specifically the notion of the heart and how it may offer a dynamic and open conception of interiority, this chapter aims to offer a phenomenological description of empathy based on responsivity and ethical sensitivity that may design a response ethics of vulnerability. The chapter starts with examining the notion of *Gemüt* (heart) in Kant's anthropology and Husserl's phenomenology of affective life to underline the specific kind of intentionality associated with the heart and its ethical implications. Then, I turn to Stein's anthropology and analyze her conception of *Gemüt*. This notion helps her recast the metaphysical conception of interiority within the phenomenological framework of empathy and intersubjective experience. Stein's later writings point to an ethical sensitivity to the world and others important in our political, social, and personal relations. Such ethical sensitivity paves the way for a renewed understanding of the relation between love and suffering. The heart becomes the synecdoche that symbolizes the whole person and its commitment to the world and others—anchored to compassion and responsibility. Finally, contemporary phenomenological accounts of embodied cognition (Fuchs 2018) and affective intentionality (Steinbock 2021) back up this analysis by stressing the relationship between the affective disposition involved in extended empathy and the dynamics of resonance and resilience that allow for responsibility and mutual recognition. The last section explains how dialogical phenomenology sketches out a response ethics of vulnerability grounded in a conception of empathy based on the heart's disposition rather than on the sole cognitive or affective level of experience.

Keywords: empathy, vulnerability, heart, Stein, resilience, resonance, response ethics, embodied cognition

INTRODUCTION

Can we generate empathy? In a contemporary world shaken by violence, crisis, and all kinds of uncertainty and inequality, this question emerges as a potential solution to foster mutual understanding, reciprocity, and an ethical sense of recognition that would allow all of us to live in peace. However, the definition of empathy and the relation between empathy and ethics have been at the center of philosophical controversies, especially in the continental tradition. In this chapter, I will draw on some phenomenological approaches to empathy to investigate their relation to response ethics and the ethics of responsibility. In *The Course of Recognition*, Paul Ricoeur (2005) analyzes the opposite ways Husserl and Levinas have addressed the question of intersubjectivity. According to Ricoeur, Husserl provided an account of empathy built on perception, especially in *The Cartesian Meditations* (1960). In contrast, Levinas rejected any epistemological or ontological investigation of the other to focus on the sole ethical value of the subject's vulnerability and expression (Levinas 1998). Ricoeur sums up the opposition as follows:

> Phenomenology gives two opposed versions of the original *dissymmetry*, depending on whether it takes the ego or the other as a pole of reference; one that of Husserl in *The Cartesian Meditations*, remains a phenomenology of perception; its approach is in this sense theoretical; the other that of Levinas in *Totality and Infinity* and in *Otherwise than Being: Beyond Essence*, is frankly ethical and, by implication, deliberately anti-ontological. The two approaches have each their legitimacy, and our discourse in no way requires us to decide in favor of one or the other; what matters to us is the seriousness with which of the two partners endeavors to overcome the dissymmetry which, in a certain way, persists in the background of the experiences of reciprocity and does not fail to show the reciprocity as a *going beyond* the asymmetry forever unfinished. (Ricoeur 2005: 246)

In other words, when reflecting on the conditions of possibility of empathy, Ricoeur considers that we could either start from the ego (Husserlian perspective) to reach the alter ego and recognize her precisely as an *alter* ego, or we could start from the other (Levinas's perspective) as precisely the one who resists my will to understand and empathize with her if empathizing would mean "representing" or "reducing" the lived-through reality of her experiences—more specifically her painful or traumatic experiences. Consequently, going beyond the paradox of "dissymmetry and reciprocity"—which is the title of Ricoeur's essay—beyond the tension between empathy and vulnerability amounts to elaborating a philosophical and phenomenological framework that would allow reciprocity, dialogue, and mutual understanding without requiring a kind of identification or equalization between the subjects involved. In this chapter, I will argue that the paradox of dissymmetry and reciprocity could be understood as a paradox of polarity and porosity: the polarity (or polarization) of self and other—(conditions of their responsibility and mutual recognition)—and the porosity of affective life and the lifeworld through the dynamics of response and resonance that sustain intersubjective constitution. Concern for others would not call for identification but rather demand reconnecting with the asymmetrical space necessary to its expression. The most recent example of the coronavirus disease 2019 (COVID-19) pandemic and the way it has disrupted our relation to the world and others have shown the pressing need to preserve the intersubjective and embodied dynamics through which the lifeworld could indeed become an inclusive *yet differentiated* "home-world." By analyzing more specifically the notion of the heart and the way it may offer a dynamic and open conception of interiority, this chapter aims to offer a phenomenological description of empathy based on responsiveness and ethical sensitivity that may design a response ethics of vulnerability. This chapter will notably focus on the works of Edith Stein and her understanding of interiority.

Contemporary phenomenology has shown a growing interest in Edith Stein's analysis of empathy (Magri & Moran 2018; Szanto 2015) and has more recently underlined her phenomenological and epistemological analysis of values and emotions (Vendrell Ferran 2018) and their roles in intersubjective dynamics and community formation. As developed in her lessons on the human person (2004) and her last treatise, *Finite and Eternal Being* (2002), Stein's later anthropology presents us with an innovative way to understand our inner experience. The way she rethinks interiority in contrast with Husserl's concept of the ego has been investigated (Moran 2018; Sepp 2018), yet the references to the heart (*Gemüt* / *Herz*) in her philosophical writings have been underexplored. Stein's conception of interiority can contribute to elaborating a phenomenology of the heart (Gemüt), able to overcome a persistent divide between the cognitive and the affective dimensions of experience while describing our intentional relation to the world.[1] Indeed, the notion of the "heart," which is simultaneously symbolic, anthropological, and metaphysical, fleshes out an ethical sense of personal individuation that correlates the uniqueness of the person and her relational and ethical vocation.

The chapter starts with examining the notion of Gemüt in Kant's anthropology and Husserl's phenomenology of affective life to underline the specific kind of intentionality associated with the heart and its ethical implications. Then, I turn to Stein's anthropology and analyze her conception of Gemüt. This notion helps her recast the metaphysical conception of interiority within the phenomenological framework of empathy and intersubjective experience. The notion of Gemüt is situated at the crossroads of the anthropological (natural world), ethical (intersubjective world and world of values), and metaphysical (spiritual world and notion of soul) fields. Stein's later writings point to an ethical *sensitivity* to the world and others important in our political, social, and personal relations. Such ethical *sensitivity* paves the way for a renewed understanding of the relation between love and suffering. The heart becomes the synecdoche that symbolizes the whole person and its commitment to the world and others, anchored in compassion and responsibility. As Stein puts it: "the more the life of a man is lived from the deepest interiority of its soul, the more the light that radiates from him and attracts other people in his path will be powerful" (Stein 2002: 437–38). Contemporary phenomenological accounts of embodied cognition (Fuchs 2018) and affective intentionality (Steinbock 2021) back up this analysis by stressing the relationship between the affective disposition involved in extended empathy and the dynamics of resonance and resilience that allow for responsibility and mutual recognition. The last section explains how dialogical phenomenology sketches out a response ethics of vulnerability grounded in a conception of empathy based on the heart's disposition rather than on the cognitive or affective level of experience.

ANTHROPOLOGY AND PHENOMENOLOGY OF THE HEART (GEMÜT)

Rendered by spirit, soul, or sometimes by the heart, depending on the context, the German concept of Gemüt is one of the most difficult to translate. Nevertheless, the reflections on the Gemüt have a common denominator. According to most authors, the Gemüt refers to a faculty whose state allows or prevents the unification of the subject and its existential achievement as a person. It correlates the affective and the cognitive levels of experiences in emotions or aesthetic experience.[2]

In Kant's *Critique of Pure Reason*, for instance, Gemüt is translated by "consciousness," "spirit," or "soul," referring to "the sentient aspect of the psyche," as opposed to the spiritual principle (*Geist*) or the soul (*Seele*).

Although it directly refers to the affective life of subjectivity, this concept nevertheless implies a mediation between the "cognitive" and the "affective" levels of human experience. The Gemüt articulates three primary faculties of the human being: namely, the faculty of knowledge (*Critique of Pure Reason* 2007), the faculty of desire (*Critique of Practical Reason* 2015), and the capacity for feeling pleasure or displeasure, which Kant describes in The *Critique of Judgment* (1983).

Indeed, Kant's *Critique of Judgment* and his *Anthropology* (2006) analyze the role of the Gemüt in our aesthetic experience explicitly. The "state" and "movements" of the Gemüt impact the subject's situation and her interactions with others. The Gemüt is explicitly related to the faculty of imagination. In this sense, it shapes our experience of the world and lays the ground for its understanding and interpersonal communication. For instance, in paragraph 47 of the *Critique of Judgment*, Kant indicates that the Gemüt needs to be "healthy . . . to gather its strength." In paragraph 48, Kant analyzes the case when the Gemüt is not balanced and suffers from some deficiency (*Gemütschwächen*). Kant explicitly correlates the bodily dimensions and expressiveness of the Gemüt with its ability to be "impressed" by the world and others. In a pre-phenomenological style, Kant goes on:

> For if we assume that all our thoughts are, besides, in a harmonious connection with some agitation in the body's organs, then we can pretty well grasp how, as the mind suddenly shifts alternately from one position to another in order to contemplate its object, there might be a corresponding alternating tension and relaxation of the elastic parts or our intestines that is communicated to the diaphragm (such as ticklish people feel). (Kant 1983: 205)

Moreover, the forces of the Gemüt are not only restricted to the immanence of their sensitive expression. They are also involved in the artistic genius's productions, as they can sustain the free interplay of the faculties. Therefore, Kant insists that the ability to communicate one's feelings and share aesthetic experiences is ultimately a matter of pondering and balancing one's Gemüt, one's heart, so that feelings can be communicated sensitively—overcoming thereby the primary and immanent level of physiological experience. Such characterization anticipates the twofold interpretation of empathy (*Einfühlung*) from Theodor Lipps to Edmund Husserl as an aesthetic process and an intersubjective one allowing the subject to communicate with the other. Nevertheless, when it comes to morality, in *The Critique of Practical Reason* and *The Metaphysics of Morals* (2009), Kant considers the forces of the Gemüt as pathological because they may counterbalance negatively the decisions made by practical reason. Nevertheless, Kant's anthropology stresses an essential parameter of our experience that will be taken up by

German idealism, vitalism, and early phenomenology: the fact that the life of the spirit is anchored in the Gemüt and its reactions is the very condition of its communicability to others. Indeed, in the appendix of the *Critique of Judgment*, Kant notes that:

> It seems that for all fine art, insofar as we aim at its highest degree of perfection, the propaedeutic does not consist in following precepts but in cultivating our mental powers by exposing ourselves beforehand to what we call *humanoria*; they are called that presumably because humanity means both the universal *feeling of sympathy* and the ability to engage universally in very intimate *communication*. When these two qualities are combined, they constitute the sociability that befits our humanity and distinguishes it from the limitation of animals. (Kant 1983: 31).

The Gemüt is conceived as the intermediate space where aesthetic and moral experiences intersect, where intimacy and universality can be correlated, as it is the faculty of "sympathy," or the medium of empathic experience in phenomenological terms. It points to a kind of intentionality that is neither purely objectifying nor solely constituted through intersubjective experience, namely, affective intentionality (*Gemütsintentionalität*). In Kant's philosophy, affectivity does not have an epistemological value—quite the opposite. The descriptions of aesthetic experiences are meant to illustrate the possible transition from an anthropological feature of human existence to its adequate moral response.

Husserl did not consider that affective intentionality had an epistemological value, yet he contends that affective intentionality contributes to the unification of experience at a pre-reflective level. For Husserl, affective intentionality (Gemütsintentionalität) implies the correlation between an impression's affective reception and its spontaneous evaluation. In a series of texts from 1911, Husserl describes the various forms of such an experience, depending on the affective disposition of the subject (Husserl 2021). The expressiveness of a person, for instance, can delight me once and displease me the following five times. Husserl introduces a fundamental distinction between the structure of this experience, anchored in a fundamental and primordial form of affectivity, and the variability of its content, often relative to the specific contingency of the movements and dispositions of the subject. He introduces the idea of a unity of affective disposition through time that occurs at the pre-reflective level, based on the responsiveness of one's Gemüt. In other words, our ability to empathize with others depends on the complexity of our inner experience insofar as it correlates emotions, values, and affective intentionality. This correlation is a precondition for understanding the lifeworld and what guarantees the consistency of my own experience as an individuated human being.

Edith Stein takes a step further. For her, such correlation is a condition of possibility of empathy and freedom. Indeed, the three forms of affective intentionality that Husserl describes as axiological, practical, and spiritual (three levels of Gemütsintentionalität) are rephrased and re-elaborated by Stein (Vendrell Ferran 2018). If Stein remains value-neutral in her doctoral dissertation, *On The Problem of Empathy* (Stein 1989), while providing a phenomenological analysis of empathy, her later reflections on the person's structure connect more explicitly the structure of our inner experience and the way we interact with others. Within the context of her analysis of freedom and the structure of personhood. In this sense, I contend that she lays the ground for a revaluation of the ethical status of the heart (Gemüt) within the phenomenological debate on empathy, engaging thereby a discussion with Scheler (Vendrell Ferran 2015).

INTERIORITY, EMPATHY, AND THE HEART

One of the main innovations of Stein's contribution to the debate on interiority in early phenomenology lies perhaps in the way her conception of interiority helps her rephrase the intentional correlation in an ethical sense which would link together singularity's constitution as a person (subjective pole) and the formation of the lifeworld as a community of persons (objective pole).

One can understand the relation between interiority and empathy from a cognitive and reflective perspective by understanding interiority as introspection. This experience relates to the perception of "other minds," as it has recently been done in contemporary phenomenology. Nevertheless, in this section, I would like to focus on Stein's anthropological picture of subjectivity to show the ethical capacity at stake in empathy entailed by her understanding of affective life and intentionality. Moreover, such a picture would reveal the irreducibility of the self—constituted through the life of the Gemüt—to the ego and potentially contribute to contemporary debates on self-constitution, affective life, and responsibility (Sepp 2018).

Throughout her entire works, Edith Stein has consistently affirmed that the central question of her philosophy was that of the human person. From her reflections on the ontological structure of the person to those on her ethical vocation, the human person is characterized by her relational and spiritual nature and inalienable freedom.[3] The human person is responsible for her individuation; she has to conquer her freedom to fully develop her vocation. As Stein writes:

> My existence is a continuous movement, a fleeting and, in the strictest sense, a *transitory* kind of being and thus the extreme opposite of *eternal* and *immutable* being. The being of the ego is alive only from moment to moment. It cannot be quiescent because it is restlessly in flight. It thus never attains true self-possession. And we are therefore forced to conclude that the being of the ego, as a constantly changing living present, is not autonomous but *received* being. It has been *placed into existence* and is sustained in existence from moment to moment. This, however, implies the possibility that this being may have a beginning and an end and that it may suffer a break. (Stein 2002: 54–55)

This processual understanding of individuation implies that a generative force shapes the various layers of the self—that Stein calls the lifeforce (*Lebenskraft*)—related to the individual core of the person.

Throughout her life, the person must build herself and constantly renew herself in a permanent process of transformation, without ever reaching a final state (Sepp 2018). According to Stein, several levels compose the human being: the physical level and the psychic level are subject to the regime of causality and external and physical-biological determinations, the mental-intellectual level and the personal-spiritual level structure the human being and are ultimately free of any determinations. Such structuration of the person echoes her phenomenological analysis of feelings and emotions. However, it also makes sense of her analysis of action and interpersonal relations. "Motivations" are established and defined in this last sphere (personal-spiritual) and are correlated to the values endorsed by the subject. When freedom is actualized and when the subject "consents" to her motivations, the latter become decisions for which she is responsible (Calcagno 2014). Edith Stein does not deny—quite the contrary—the weight of situational constraints (oppression, precariousness, etc.) or psychophysical ones (fragility, physical weakness) since the vital force (Lebenskraft) of the individual allows for the actualization of her freedom.

Nevertheless, the consent given to the meaning (*logos*) attributed to a given situation is deemed inalienable. The subject is always in a position, reflecting *from within*, to consent or refuse to adhere to the values presented to her. So, making room for interiority in her anthropology allows Stein to develop a phenomenological ethics that is both practically and spiritually bound. This lived space becomes a place of anchorage and dwelling, the locus from which unfolds personal individuation, at the intersection of affective life and ethical evaluation.

In this context, education plays a central role in her thinking. It allows the individual to become a free person and society to become a community, which means to share common values that guarantee everyone the free expression of their humanity and the unfolding of what Stein calls their "personal note."

This irreducible singularity stems from the "core of the person" (*Kern*) expressed through the life of the Gemüt. As Sepp recalls:

> For Stein "self" / "soul" seems to be the unifying element of a person, a "center" as we can read already in her study on *Individual and Community* (*Individuum und Gemeinschaft*, 1919); the soul "grows out of a root that characterizes the entire being of the ensouled individual entity in all its dimensions" though its "central position" does not "shape and determine the totality of the I" (Stein 2004: 191). This root or center, which Stein here also calls "core," is the "shaping" "by which the being of the individual forms itself. (Sepp 2018:52)

As mentioned, Stein's doctoral dissertation on the problem of empathy analyzed the intentional structure of empathy to highlight its invariants. She did not study this phenomenon from an existential and ethical point of view. Nevertheless, in her *Lessons on the Human Person*, she wrote: "the anthropology that we are proposing as a ground for pedagogy must be a philosophical anthropology that remains in vivid contact with the general philosophical approach, yet it will investigate the structure of the human being and its insertion in existential formation and in the existential domain to which it belongs" (Stein 2004: 25). She then uses the phenomenological method to elaborate a philosophy of freedom, which addresses the dynamics of affective intentionality and gives them existential meaning ("existential formations," "existential domains").

Here lies a twofold innovation in Stein's approach to interiority and educational *praxis*: (1) affectivity is not reduced to the flesh, corporeality or the sensible, or its disqualification from the point of view of speculative reason or practical reason, and (2) freedom is precisely freedom when it assumes the "integral" humanity of the person and the relational dimension intrinsic to affectivity that characterizes its existence and its being in the world with others. In other words, the irreducibility of the self that manifests itself through the enactment of its individuation as a person neither prevents her from being shaped by interpersonal and inter-affective relations nor makes her fail to achieve her universal vocation as a human subject.

Interiority becomes the other name of a free capacity to dwell in the affective depth that imprints on the flesh and the intersubjective world its way of being. As Stein explains:

> This inner world must not be separated from the sphere that feels, thinks, and wants, making the body a living human body and formed in a personal way. The German language says, "*Gemüt*" to designate this dimension. If it also calls it "*Seele*" (soul), then it is "the soul of the soul," where it is with itself, where it is itself and where it is as it is and according to the state in which it is at such or such moment; this is also the sphere where it collects internally what

> it grasps by the senses and the understanding, where it understands it in all its meaning, confronting it, where it keeps it, drawing force from it or by which it undergoes aggression. If we had quarreled over whether to consider the *Gemüt* and the will as two faculties of the soul or as one, it is proof that there is a strong link between the two. . . . It is the same soul which knows, which, by the will, goes out of itself, and which, in the "*Gemüt*," is with itself and confronts itself inwardly with what it collects in itself. (Stein 2004:129)

In this text, the Gemüt appears as the intermediate faculty that allows for the overcoming of the antinomy between passivity and activity—receptivity and spontaneity—to the benefit of a dynamic expressiveness of the self. It links together a capacity to bestow meaning on the world around me and a kind of transcendental affectivity that guarantees its communicability. Consequently, one of Stein's main innovations thus consists of rephrasing the intentional correlation in a properly ethical sense that links together the ethical becoming of the individual as a "person," on the one hand, and the meaningful co-constitution of the lifeworld.

The Gemüt designates the space where values, emotions, and will are interrelated, and they disclose themselves. Values shape affectivity and affectivity fleshes out the set of motivations that the will contributes to "freely and voluntarily" express. The freedom at stake does not rely on a solipsistic understanding of the subject conquered in introspection, nor does it reduce affectivity to the sphere of ego-consciousness.

To Stein, personal individuation is profoundly relational and responsive. It does not oppose the formation of the political community but, on the contrary, becomes the ethical condition of political and cultural coexistence, linking together responsiveness and responsibility.

ETHICAL SENSITIVITY: THINKING WITH THE HEART

The concept of Gemüt allows Stein to overcome the antinomy between passivity and activity, receptivity and spontaneity, immanence, and transcendence to show the dynamic and relational individuation process through which a person becomes who she is meant to be. One of the main innovations of Stein's contribution thus consists of rephrasing the intentional correlation in a properly ethical sense that links together the ethical becoming of the individual as a "person," on the one hand, and the intersubjective constitution of the lifeworld.

The heart and the will are linked together because values and affectivity are interrelated. But if our relation to the world and others penetrates interiority, the latter is irreducible to the elements it processes. Consequently,

Stein defines the person as a "free and spiritual being" (Stein 2004:78). The movements of the heart, the affective life, make freedom concrete because the person must dwell on the unfolding of her individuation process and her ethical vocation in the world. The life of the heart shows the embodied dimension of the person and underlines the relational dynamics of inter-affectivity schematized by imagination. This vividness requires a sense of distance, as the critique of *Einfühlung* (emotional contagion) in the *Problem of Empathy* already showed. The subject is *exposed* to the needs and especially to the suffering of the other, who then becomes an irreducible "you." In other words, the receptivity of the heart calls for the responsiveness of the person.

In *Finite and Eternal Being*, Stein describes this correlation between receptivity and responsiveness:

> Two human beings may listen jointly to the same news and that both have an intellectually clear grasp of its contents, such as, for example, the news of the Serbian regicide in the summer of 1914. However, the one who 'thinks no more about it' goes calmly on his way and, a few minutes later, is again busy with his plans for a summer vacation. The other is shaken in his innermost being. He envisages the impending general European war with his mind's eye, and he sees himself uprooted in his professional life and involved in the great world-historic events. His thoughts cannot detach themselves from what has happened, and he lives in feverish anticipation of the things that are to come. In his case, the news has struck deeply at his inner life, and he understands the external events from the point of view of his interiority. And because his full intellectual power is alive in his understanding, his mind penetrates into the context and into the 'consequences' of the external event. In this latter kind of thinking, "the entire human being" is engaged, and this engagement expresses itself even in the external appearance. It affects the bodily organs, the heartbeat, and the rhythm of breathing, the individual's sleep, and digestion. He "thinks with the heart," and his *heart* is the actual *living center* of his being. And even though the heart signifies the bodily organ to whose activity bodily life is tied, we have no difficulty in picturing the heart as the inner being of the soul because it is evidently the heart that has the greatest share in the inner processes of the soul, and because it is in the heart that the interconnection between body and soul is most strikingly felt and experienced. (Stein 2002: 437–38)

Stein underlines the responsive dimension involved in our interactions. Thinking with and from the heart necessarily implies an existential-ethical standpoint that initiates and impacts our decision-making processes. In other words, affectivity is not opposed to rationality. Instead, it is what makes it ethical and sensible as it is shaped by alterity and the awareness of our interdependence. It mediates and reveals the meaning that makes the community the locus of personal freedom and the place of solidarity, the place of a relation characterized by responsiveness and reciprocity.

Living from within does not separate us from the world but instead contributes to making its transformation possible. Contrary to Kant, Stein does not consider individuality as a potential threat to the harmonious growth of humankind. Contrary to Husserl, Stein does not consider that the ego is the last resort of any possible transformation through the meanings it bestows upon the world. Instead, she opens an original philosophical path.

Stein's phenomenological anthropology of the heart leads us to an ethical sense of personal individuation that might lead us to recover the Kantian universality within the concrete experience of lived-through solidarity and to find beyond the various types of "humanism" or *Weltanschauung* the true meaning and vibrant force of our humanity. Her analysis of interiority unveils an ethical *sensitivity* to the world and others that is key to our political, social, and personal relations. Such ethical sensitivity paves the way for a renewed phenomenological and ethical understanding of empathy. The heart becomes the *synecdoche* that symbolizes the whole person and its commitment to the world and others, anchored in compassion and responsibility. To illustrate this articulation between the affective and ethical aspects of interiority, the final sections of this chapter will develop further two dimensions explored by contemporary philosophy: (1) Stein's intuitions about the heart and ethical sensitivity seem to be confirmed by anthropological and phenomenological accounts analyzing the relations between intercorporeal resonance and ethical response, and (2) consequently, reevaluating the schema of the heart (Boublil, 2018; Steinbock, 2021) could help overcome what may be called the rationalist-humanist paradigm and elaborate anew a "response ethics" that may reframe the kind of *sharing* involved in empathy.

RESONANCE AND RESPONSE: THE ECOLOGICAL GROUND OF EMPATHY

An ecological approach to embodiment, cognition, and intersubjectivity (Fuchs 2018) may provide us with the resources needed to elaborate a conception of "extended empathy" (Fuchs 2017) that nonetheless includes an ethical approach to individual differences. Moreover, taking into consideration the embodied and responsive background of resilience may, for instance, lead us to move from a cognitive/rational framework of responsibility based on autonomy and recognition to a responsive/relational framework of responsibility based on interdependency, resonance, and care.

Following Thomas Fuchs (2018), we could call this relational framework the "ecological" dimension of subjectivity, according to which the dynamics of resonance and response describe the living and existential functioning of subjectivity and intersubjective relations. In this view, resilience could characterize the individuation process of subjectivity. Resilience describes homeostatic mechanisms through which the embodied subject constantly transforms and recreates itself to adjust to her social and natural environment. From an anthropological and phenomenological perspective, Fuchs insists on the relational and responsive structure of subjectivity as well as on the intertwining of the biological level and the ethical/existential level in the way we respond to ourselves, through reflection, but also to our environment and to others through what may be called a pre-reflective sensitivity:

> On this basis, emotions may be regarded as *circular interactions* or *feedback cycles* between affection, perception, and movement. Being affected by the value features or affective qualities of a situation triggers a specific bodily resonance ("affection") which in turn influences the emotional perception of the situation *and* implies a corresponding action readiness ("e-motion"). Embodied affectivity consists in the whole interactive cycle, which is crucially mediated by the resonance of the feeling body. In this way, bodily resonance, as James already emphasized, serves as the *medium of our affective engagement in a situation.* As we can see, the different components of the affection–resonance–emotion cycle mutually influence each other. Only through their ongoing circular interaction do they create the fully-fledged phenomenon of emotional experience, which therefore cannot be located "in the brain." (Fuchs 2018: 124)

The responsive structure of embodied subjectivity appears then as a pre-reflective layer that resists the risk of objectification by preserving the asymmetry between self and other yet makes room for interpersonal relation, participation, and reciprocity. According to this framework, there is no frontal opposition between the *ego* perspective (Husserl), and the *alter* perspective (Levinas) but a dynamic co-regulation that sets the ground for an ethical sense of personal and collective individuation processes. Consequently, extended empathy relies on an ethical sense of interdependency that fosters mutual recognition and collective responsibility. Stein's description of the heart, presented in the previous sections, seems to fit with such an anthropological and phenomenological description of resilience and resonance mechanisms. The heart would thus become the actual site—through affective life—and the symbolic site—through extended empathy—where responsiveness (to others), attunement (to the world), and responsibility (for one's action) could be correlated. As Bernhard Waldenfels explains, responsiveness is the name of that very openness irreducible to objectifying intentionality and meaning-making constitution. It refers to passivity.[4] It expresses our ability to be affected by an event and our capacity for responding to it: "Responsivity goes beyond every intentionality because responding to that which happens to us cannot be exhausted in the meaning, understanding, or truth of our response. All this is not restricted to the affective background of our cognitive and practical modes of comportment; it concerns these modes in their essence" (Waldenfels 2011: 28).

In other words, acknowledging the "responsive structure" of human interactions aims to guarantee that the interpersonal relationship displayed in extended empathy remains a "subject-to-subject" relationship. The paradigm of the heart allows for such openness as it is animated by a "transcendent depth" (Stein 2006: 68) that makes responsiveness, as a form of vulnerability, the "transcendental condition" of our being in the world "pointing to an openness and plasticity that makes possible transformation" (Gilson 2014: 10). In a recent book, Anthony Steinbock argues that the heart has its schema that allows us to *know* the world and others in a specific way. Beyond the divide between cognitive and affective empathy, the heart entails a particular discernment grounded in feeling: "the feeling as responsive originates from the 'creative' center of the person, for instance, through incitement, and in an interpersonal nexus." (Steinbock 2021: 23). The archetype of genuine interpersonal interaction is love insofar as "mutual recognition is founded in loving as participating the other" (45). In this framework, vulnerability consequently appears as a precondition for the "cognition of the heart" in the same way that "naïveté" and the "natural attitude" were the preconditions for the epistemic cognition carried out by the phenomenological *epochè* (95). As Steinbock explains: "I can be vulnerable and not love, but I cannot love and not be vulnerable: vulnerability is a structure of loving. In loving, I directly, immediately, devotionally participate others. I so accompany others, I so participate them, that I am already immediately bound up with their becoming-being" (96). A relation that is, so to speak, "heart-grounded" is characterized by several criteria identified by Steinbock: attention, resonance, interdependency, self-transformation, and humility (102). In other words, the phenomenological anthropological paradigm described by Fuchs and Steinbock centered on embodied cognition, ethical sensitivity, and the heart replacing affective intentionality at the core of interpersonal relations and, more specifically, at the core of care relationships and the clinical encounter. They foster a new understanding of empathy that overcomes the potential dichotomy between the cognitive and affective levels of experiences to draw an ecological ethics of vulnerability that opposes the rationalist framework of classical humanism (Steinbock 2021: 161). The last section of this chapter will offer some reflections on the ethical consequences of such ecological anthropology. More specifically, the responsive structure of our embodied interactions may impact our understanding of dialogue and responsibility in care strategies.

RESPONSE ETHICS, VULNERABILITY, AND RESPONSIBILITY

A phenomenology of dialogue may help us progress in our understanding of the relationship between empathy and ethics. Dialogue conceived as a higher form of empathy could be understood as a way to *restore the other's capability to respond for herself and to others*. In several essays, Ricoeur refers to Dutch phenomenologist Stefan Strasser. Strasser elaborated what he called a "dialogical phenomenology." The intersubjective encounter is not a subject-to-object kind of relationship—which means that it is not a relationship based on perception—but rather a subject-to-subject kind of relationship implying an ethical approach to communication and feeling. According to Strasser, the intentionality involved in genuine intersubjectivity must be understood as an "open" co-constitution of meanings, called "reciprocity," which is anchored in the expressiveness of inter-affective resonance. Strasser writes:

> The "encounter" is for us the communication between people in a significant situation for them. . . . It is not sure that the situation that gives rise to the meeting must have the same meaning for the people who meet. Friedrich Otto Bollnow rightly points out that an encounter involves reciprocity since it is based on a subject-to-subject relationship. But the intentions of the people meeting don't need to be identical. *In other words, reciprocity does not imply symmetry.* Let's take, for example, a completely banal case: A goes to a specific restaurant to have his meal. B knows this. He goes to the same restaurant to talk to A. The encounter is not accidental; it was provoked by one of the two partners. The situation is meaningful to both, but it has for B a different meaning than for A. (Strasser 1967:157)

This distinction between reciprocity and symmetry is fundamental. The interpersonal encounter is, therefore, the first condition of possibility of dialogue, put forward by Strasser, since it involves a reciprocity between two subjects, which is reciprocity of availability, a quality of presence and attention to the situation or to the relationship that is offered to both, in other words, a specific manner of attending a common situation. The fact that reciprocity is not equivalent to symmetry refers to the idea of a disposition, a structure of openness and availability that characterizes a well-understood sense of sharing. Others are not given to me; they give me the world. Moreover, the dialogical structure implies the possibility of difference and conflict. As Strasser explains:

> The concept of dialogue must be broadened. It includes not only communication employing symbolic sounds but any form of reciprocal communication

> between subjects. In accordance with what we have said before, we will speak of being dialogical when my presence to a "you" is sensitive to the presence of a "you" towards me. A dynamic definition corresponds to this ontological-static description: dialogue as an active-receptive interaction arises when my way of "dealing" with a "you" agrees with the way the "you" "deals" with me. This relationship may be of a pre-rational nature; it can be done without a world; it may be based on a bodily subject's understanding of another bodily subject. 1. "Reciprocity is not symmetry, and agreeing does not mean conforming to" 2. "The partner of dialogue is the you" 3. "Listening is not the same as being in harmony with what is heard. On the contrary, without tensions, differences of opinion, divergences of practical and theoretical approaches, the dialogue would soon stop. A "you" who cannot contradict the other cannot really talk to her. In addition, opposition, enmity, and conflict are among the fundamental ways in which I can manage a "you"; they are an integral part of the dialogue. (Strasser 1967: 65)

The critical notion analyzed by Strasser is that of "disposition." It articulates the level of resonance and response through keen attention with the level of responsibility and resilience through our capacity for self-transformation, attunement, and decision-making.

Inter-affectivity is not an obstacle to cognitive empathy or empathic understanding but rather the very constitutive feature that leads us to achieve mutual understanding. In this context, *meaning* does not proceed from a reflective and intentional act of objectification. Instead, it "emerges" as a *personal response* from the encounter and dialogue between embodied subjects taking responsibility for their engagement in the situation. As such, it lays the ground for a "creative kind of empathy," which correlates emotional responses with their context of occurrence, to acknowledge the affective yet ethical interdependency of the persons involved. As Kelly Oliver wrote: "therefore, the primary obligation of response ethics is the responsibility to engender response or facilitate, rather than close down, the ability to respond in oneself, other living beings, and the environment. Response ethics is based on taking responsibility for the other's ability to respond, which is to say, not only listening to the other but also taking responsibility for that listening and the consequences of it" (2018: 101).Interiority does not refer to a private sphere that would be cut off from the world and others. Instead, it points to the *space* of lived experience, creating conditions for both radical alterity and intimacy. This claim bears ethical consequences as acting, thinking, and loving *from within* might help us avoid any form of *grasping* that would unveil and violate the other's freedom and responsibility. The heart (Gemüt) ultimately appears as a deep and encompassing interiority that is not opposed to empathy but rather frames it. It is not a new dimension within the person's structure. However, it brings to light the lived dynamics of resonance and response through which the unification of the person reveals itself and makes itself sensible to others and the world through its capacity to love.

ACKNOWLEDGMENTS

The author would like to thank the Alexander von Humboldt Foundation and the University of Cologne for funding and hosting her research work on Edith Stein's works (2018–2020).

NOTES

1.Cf. Anthony Steinbock: "By emotions, I understand those experiences that pertain to the domain of feelings (or what some would call the order of the 'heart'), but which take place or are enacted on the level of spirit. Emotional enactments uniquely open up the sphere of the persons, that is, that specific sphere of givenness through which the human being is revealed not merely as subject, but a person, having its distinctive sphere of evidence" (Steinbock 2014: 12).

2. For previous versions of this analysis, see Boublil (2018 and 2021).

3."Right at the beginning, one finds a concise definition: 'To be a person means to be a free and spiritual being.' A person is a '*free spiritual person*.' 'Being free' refers to the simple yet originary capacity of the ego, the 'I can,' whereby there is an 'ought' that follows from this 'can.' Human beings '*can and should shape themselves*,' in other words, humans can and should be 'responsible for themselves' (Stein 2004: 78 f.).One finds the same notion in Husserl's *Ideas II* where he says in §60 that a person grasps himself or herself as that subject that is '*self-responsible*' because he or she is 'free' in the sense of 'I can.' (Husserl 1989: 269) The 'I can' that gives rise to freedom in an original sense characterizes Husserl's '*specifically spiritual*' dimension of subjectivity." (Sepp 2018: 50–51).

4. "In sum, everything that appears [to us] as something has to be described not simply as something which receives a sense, but as something which provokes sense without being meaningful itself yet still as something *by which* we are touched, affected, stimulated, surprised and to some extent violated. I call this happening *pathos*, *Widerfahrnis* or affect, marked by a hyphen to suggest that something is done *to us*." (Waldenfels 2007: 74).

REFERENCES

Boublil, E. 2018. Mystique du Coeur et Vocation de la Personne. *Le Philosophoire* 49, 151–186.

———. 2021. Stein's perspectives on the heart at the crossroads of phenomenology, anthropology and Carmelite mysticism. In H. Klueting & E. Klueting (eds.),

Edith Stein's Itinerary. Phenomenology, Christian Philosophy, and Carmelite Spirituality, Aschendorff Verlag.
Calcagno, A. 2014. *Lived Experience from the Inside out: Social and Political Philosophy in Edith Stein*. Duquesne University Press.
Fuchs, T. 2017. Levels of empathy—Primary, extended, and reiterated empathy. In V. Lux & S. Weigel (Eds.), *Empathy: Epistemic Problems and Cultural-Historical Perspectives of a Cross-Disciplinary Concept* (pp. 27–47). Palgrave Macmillan/ Springer Nature.
———. 2018. *The Ecology of the Brain. The Phenomenology and Biology of the Embodied Mind*. Oxford University Press.
Gilson, E. 2014. *The Ethics of Vulnerability: A Feminist Analysis of Social Life and Practice*. Routledge.
Husserl, E. 1960. *The Cartesian Meditations. An Introduction to Phenomenology*. Translated by Dorion Cairns. Springer.
———. 1989. *Ideas Pertaining to a Pure Phenomenology and to a Phenomenological Philosophy*. Second Book: *Studies in the Phenomenology of Constitution*. Translated by R. Rojcewicz and A. Schuwer. Kluwer.
———. 2021. *Studien Zur Struktur des Bewusstseins*. Edited by U. Melle & T. Vongehr. Springer.
Kant, I. 1983. *Critique of Judgment*. Translated by. W. S. Pluhar. Hackett Publishing.
———. 2006. *Anthropology* from a pragmatic point of view. Edited by R. Louden. Cambridge University Press.
———. 2007. *Critique of Pure Reason*. Penguin Classics.
———. 2012. *Groundwork of the Metaphysics of Morals*. Translated and Edited by Mary Gregor and Jens Timmerman. Cambridge University Press.
———. 2015. *Critique of Practical Reason*. Translated by M. Gregor. Cambridge University Press.
Levinas, E. 1998. *Otherwise than Being: Or Beyond Essence*. Translated by A. Lingis. Duquesne University Press.
Magri, E., & Moran, D. 2018. *Empathy, Sociality and Personhood: Essays on Edith Stein's Phenomenological Investigations*. Springer.
Moran, D. 2018. Edith Stein's Encounter with Edmund Husserl and Her Phenomenology of the Person. In E. Magri & D. Moran (eds.), *Empathy, Sociality and Personhood: Essays on Edith Stein's Phenomenological Investigations*, 31–48. Springer.
Oliver, K. 2018. *Response Ethics*. Edited by Alison Suen. Rowman & Littlefield.
Ricoeur, P. 2005. *The Course of Recognition*. Translated by David Pellauer. Harvard University Press.
Sepp, H.-R. 2018. Edith Stein's conception of the person within the context of the phenomenological movement. In E. Magri & D. Moran (eds.), *Empathy, Sociality and Personhood: Essays on Edith Stein's Phenomenological Investigations*, 49–64. Springer.
Stein, E. 1989. *On the Problem of Empathy*. Springer.
———. 2002. *Finite and Eternal Being: An Attempt at an Ascent to the Meaning of Being*. Translated by Kurt F. Reinhardt. ICS Publications.

———. 2004. *Der Aufbau der menschlichen Person. Vorlesung zur philosophischen Anthropologie* (ESGA 14). Freiburg.

———. 2006. *Endliches und ewiges Sein. Versuch eines Aufstiegs zum Sinn des Seins* (ESGA 11/12). Freiburg.

Steinbock 2014. *Moral Emotions. Reclaiming the Evidence of the Heart*. Northwestern University Press.

———. 2021. *Knowing by Heart. Loving as Participation and Critique*. Northwestern University Press.

Strasser, S. 1967. *Phenomenology and Human sciences, Towards a New Scientific Spirit*. Translated by A. L. Kelkel. Publications universitaires de Louvain.

Szanto, T. 2015. Introduction: Empathy and Collective Intentionality—The Social Philosophy of Edith Stein. *Human Studies* 38, 445–61.

Vendrell Ferran, I. 2015. Empathy, Emotional sharing and Feelings in Stein's early work. *Human Studies* 38, 481–502.

———. 2018. Intentionality, value disclosure, and constitution: Stein's model. In E. Magri, & D. Moran (eds.), *Empathy, Sociality and Personhood: Essays on Edith Stein's Phenomenological Investigations*, 65–86. Springer.

Waldenfels, B. 2007. *The Question of the Other. The Tang-Chun I Lecture for 2004*. Chinese University Press.

———. 2011. *Phenomenology of the Alien. Basic Concepts*. Translated by T. Stahler. Northwestern University Press.

Chapter 15

What Is Moral about Empathy?

Some Considerations about the Link between Empathy and Moral Judgment

Manuel Camassa

ABSTRACT

Over the last thirty years, there has been a growing enthusiasm about the moral potentialities of empathy in many different fields such as moral philosophy, psychology, psychopathology and ethology. Several scholars have highlighted the supposed necessary role that empathy plays in moral development, moral conduct, and moral judgment.

However, this phenomenon has recently been called into question, if not openly criticized, by both philosophers and psychologists such as Jesse Prinz (2011a, 2011b) or Paul Bloom (2013a, 2013b, 2014, 2016), who are among the harshest and most influential critics of empathy. They maintain a position in which empathy is unnecessary to the three aforementioned dimensions of morality, and furthermore that, due to its many biases, it is deleterious. This chapter will try to show why empathy should not be regarded as useless or even detrimental for morality and to propose a special role for it. The idea is to defend a "third path" (i.e., a view on empathy that provides an alternative reading and responds to both the naïve optimism of what I call the pro-empathists and to the unwarranted pessimism of the anti-empathists).

To do so, I will briefly sketch my conception of the term *empathy*. In this sense, a brief phenomenological analysis of this psychological mechanisms will be conducted. I will then examine the case of moral judgment and contend contra Prinz that although empathy is not always and directly necessary for moral judgment, it can play an irreplaceable role for moral perception, which is in turn closely related to moral judgment. Finally, I will conclude by claiming that empathy should be considered as part of the fundamental features, which define a morally virtuous person.

Keywords: empathy, pro-empathists, anti-empathists, Edith Stein, Jesse Prinz, moral judgment, moral perception, virtue, mental states, emotions

EMPATHY: THE WAY TO A DEFINITION

Saint Augustine famously said once: "What then is time? If no one asks me, I know what it is. If I wish to explain it to him who asks, I do not know."[1] It seems that approximately the same would happen to any scholar of empathy who was asked to define what empathy de facto is. Empathy is a hot topic, and it has managed to enter the field of inquiry of disciplines ranging from philosophy to the neurosciences, from psychology to zoology, from anthropology to economics. Of course, given the incredible amount of work made during the years by scholars with so different backgrounds and opinions on the matter, it cannot be a surprise to observe how blurred the definition of empathy is, both among laypeople and academics.[2]

Nevertheless, I think that a good definition of empathy can be found. In particular, I want my definition to maintain important insights stemming from traditional researchers on it (those of David Hume, Adam Smith, Edith Stein, Max Scheler, especially) and at the same time to be in line with the latest characterizations of empathy and with the normal use people make of this concept. This will also help to highlight a coherent evolution of the discussion around this phenomenon that, although it becomes more and more problematized and problematic, it revolves nonetheless around the same features. In particular, I think that a famous representative of the phenomenological tradition, namely Edith Stein, perfectly paves the way to what will be our working definition. In her masterpiece *On the Problem of Empathy*, Stein writes:

> [W]e are dealing with an act which is primordial as present experience though non-primordial in content. And this content is an experience which, again, can be had in different ways such as in memory, expectation, or in fantasy. When it arises before me all at once, it faces me as an object (such as the sadness I "read in another's face"). But when I inquire into its implied tendencies (try to bring another's mood to clear givenness to myself), the content, having pulled me into it, is no longer really an object. I am now no longer turned to the content but to the object of it, am at the subject of the content in the original subject's place.

> And only after successfully executed clarification, does the content again face me as an object.
>
> Thus in all the cases of the representation of experiences considered, there are three levels or modalities of accomplishment even if in a concrete case people do not always go through all levels but are often satisfied with one of the lower ones. These are (1) the emergence of the experience, (2) the fulfilling explication, and (3) the comprehensive objectification of the explained experience.[3]

Let us try to break down this quote. In the first phase (the emergence of the experience), we perceive the experience of the other person thanks to the so called *Ausdrucksbewegungen*, which are (for Stein as well as for Scheler, Merleau-Ponty and for modern phenomenologists like Zahavi or Overgaard) the direct behavioral expression (and integral part) of her experience. In the second phase, it is the turn of perspective-taking. Notice that for Stein the perspective-taking is different from a projection (although in the modern literature "projective empathy" and "perspective taking" are often conflated). In fact, she uses the term *hineingezogen*, which means something like dragged or drawn. The empathizer is therefore dragged, as it were, into the other's experience. While this occurs, and because this occurs, the empathizer tries to "presentify" (using a phenomenological neologism) what the target experiences. This is an intentional and conscious process, in which also imagination plays a crucial role. To understand the third and last phase of the empathic process according to Stein, we have to briefly sketch a difference essential in her reflections on empathy: that between *originär* and *nicht-originär.*

For Stein, originär and nicht-originär are the qualities of all our experiences, that is, all our acts can be either primordial or not. In particular, primordial are all acts that are carried out in a precise moment and in that same moment are experienced by the agent who is doing them; and primordial are the contents of cognitive acts in the actual moment in which they are carried out. Quoting her on this issue: "The memory of joy is primordial as a representational act now being carried out, though its content of joy is non-primordial. This act has the total character of joy which I could study, but the joy is not primordially and bodily there, rather as having once being alive. . . ." What is implied by Stein here? A practical example might help to shed some light on the problem. Imagine the following situation: Suppose that I find myself in Lucerne (where I actually am, writing these lines), waiting for the bus. It is winter, and I have the impression that the cold and damp air that pervades the Swiss city is actually penetrating my own bones. Suddenly, I start to think of my summer holidays in Tuscany, where I come from. I remember the sweet hills full of cypresses, olive trees, and vineyards in the Florentine countryside, kissed by the strong Mediterranean sun. I remember that day on the beach near Livorno and the smell of brackish water. Now, the sensation of coldness I feel is primordial; primordial is also the perception I have of the bus finally approaching, and primordial is the remembering of my holidays in Tuscany. What is nonprimordial, instead, is the content of my remembrance: the hot weather, the hills, the sea, and that joyful mood in which I was and I no longer am, while waiting for that slow bus. Thus, we can state that for Stein, empathy, memory, and fantasy are all primordial acts in which facts are nonprimordially represented.

Subsequent to this account, we should be able to understand the third phase of the empathic process. In the second phase, Stein says explicitly that the empathizer is not directed toward the target anymore: they are, as it were, in the target, in her position and they are directed toward the same object the subject is directed to. This also means that the empathizer's experience of the experience of the target here is original. However, and this is crucial, in phase three the target becomes once again an object, the object the empathizer is directed toward (*tritt es mir wieder als Objekt gegenüber*). This means to say that the primordial experience the empathizer has at phase two is only a stage in the process: that, at the end of the process, in what we might want to call the attribution phase, this experience becomes nonprimordial, for the good reason that the empathizer knows that this is in fact the experience of another and consciously understands that what they feel is not primordial. This is the reason why Stein describes empathy as an original act with nonprimordial content.

While for some authors, like Adam Smith and Edith Stein, imagination is of central importance for carrying out the empathic process, it is not so for Lipps, who instead argues in his texts for an immediate, direct, and conceptually poor process.[4] This creates a tension that remains unsolved even in the works of authors all belonging to a tradition that is far from being unitary like the phenomenological one. In fact, a modern and influential phenomenologist like Dan Zahavi tends to adhere to a philosophical interpretation of empathy that departs from that of Stein and has much more in common with the reflections of Merleau-Ponty.[5] Following this reading, the mind of others does not have to be considered as something alien to this world and that must be for this reason inferred. The mind, in fact, expresses itself in behavior, gestures, vocalizations, facial expressions. Empathy does not have, in this sense, to bridge a gap—thanks to imagination—from the visible to the invisible, from what can be observed to what cannot be observed because everything can be observed. Mental states are not cut off the world; they exist in it and can be examined by means of the common context of experience.[6]

As you can see, there is a rift between the scholars who tend to see empathy as a conceptually rich and imaginative process and those that conceive it as an immediate and conceptually poor mechanism. Of course, I could choose to give my preference to one of these positions and reject the other, however, my intention is to do something different. My aim is to offer a definition of empathy that can accommodate both positions in its formulation. This definition is able to correctly describe both the conceptually poor and unmediated kind of empathy theorized by some phenomenologists—what I will call *low-level empathy*—and the conceptually rich and imaginative variation typical of approaches valuing the phenomenon of the perspective-taking, namely *high-level empathy*.

Empathy, according to my definition, *is an intentional psychological process that allows us to tune into others and thereby understand and feel with a variable degree of approximation mental states and emotions that we deem consonant with those experienced by them, while maintaining a sense of self-other differentiation*.

With the term *intentional* I want to imply that when we empathize we always empathize with another (a human being or an animal); therefore, our focus is directed to the other and not turned to ourselves. Empathy is an other-centered mechanism and not an egocentric mechanism. It should also be added that intentional must not be read as necessarily implying an intention, a will on the part of the empathizer to really empathize with the other. In point of fact, sometimes the process of empathizing occurs so immediately that we cannot presuppose a deliberation on the part of the empathizer; rather, it configures itself as a kind of reaction. It is therefore the phenomenological meaning of intentionality that I have in mind here.

I also specified that empathy occurs with "a variable degree of approximation." Why? Schematically, this amounts to say that:

1. Empathy, like emotions, comes in different degrees (it can be more or less strong and more or less accurate in its understanding and feeling of the others' mental states);
2. Different people have different empathy levels (they are not, in other words, all equally skilled).

Specifying all that is of crucial importance because it helps us to clearly delineate what is a case of empathy and what is not, and to answer some questions regarding the extent of empathy. So, for example, imagine the following situation. Suppose Ryan tries to empathize with his friend Josh, who is disappointed and sad. And suppose that Ryan believes Josh is angry, so he goes to him and says: "I know how angry you feel at this moment. I can understand if you want some kind of retaliation and I totally share this sentiment!" As you can imagine, Josh would look at Ryan with an expression of surprise and confusion on his face and tell him that he does not feel angry at all but, rather, sad and disappointed. Now, would you be ready to affirm that Ryan has really empathized with Josh?

To answer this question, we should first ask ourselves what, inherently, empathy is. Is empathy constituted and defined by its outcome (that is the actual reaching of a feeling consonant with that of the target) or rather by its process (i.e., by the fact that we voluntarily engage in an empathic process by projecting ourselves in the target's position, trying to feel what they might be feeling?) Arguably, the majority of people (both scholars and laypeople) would agree on judging empathy by its outcome: It seems rather odd to affirm that Ryan has really empathized with Josh and that, for instance, someone who constantly draws the wrong conclusions about the mental states of others (but who nevertheless always tries) is a good empathizer. However, it seems also unfair to say that someone who has made all the correct moves to empathize with a subject but who fails to reach the right conclusion has not empathized at all. This is a complex dilemma, and many academics have decided either to follow one of the two horns of the dilemma by highlighting, respectively, the outcome dimension or the process dimension,[7] or else by widening their definition of empathy, thereby simply avoiding the dilemma altogether.[8] In light of these considerations, I think that the model I propose can be a valid way, not of bypassing the problem, nor of capitulating to one of the two options, but of providing a solution to the impasse entirely.

Following my model, empathy cannot depend just on its outcome, or we would be forced to label as acts of empathy all those cases in which there is only a mere isomorphism regarding the emotions of both the empathizer and the target (e.g., the cases of emotional contagion, in which, inter alia, there is sometimes no self-other distinction and, above all, no intentionality, and thus cannot count as empathy). But empathy cannot depend solely on the undertaken process either, or we ought to accept that a person who genuinely thinks and feels that another is happy when they are actually sad has really empathized because he or she did all the "good steps" (e.g., imaginative enactment, clear self-other distinction, etc.). So, how do we solve this dilemma? My claim is that if we think of empathy as a performative act we are in a good position to solve the problem. Take a performative act like playing football (or soccer for the U.S. reader). One can play football masterfully, as Lionel Messi or Cristiano Ronaldo do, or rather mediocrely, as I do, for instance. Are Messi, Ronaldo, and I doing the same thing when we play football? It seems that in some sense we are, and in some sense we are not, but generally, we tend to agree that we are all playing football. Only, we are inclined to make an important difference that we stress using two thin concepts: We say that Messi and Ronaldo play football *well* (even very well) and that I play football *badly* (even very badly). This means that although we are carrying out the same performative act (pro forma), I do it at a certain level and with a certain outcome, and they do it at a whole other level with entirely different outcomes. However, imagine that I start to use my hands to take the ball (outside of the box and without being a goalkeeper) and shoot a goal, or imagine that I am simply too incompetent to even control the ball with my feet and defend it with my body or to make a run. Would it still be possible to agree that I am really playing football? Arguably not.

Why so? The point is that for all performative acts the rule applies that there is a certain boundary within which a performance can still be considered valid (i.e., it can still be considered as a valid instance of a given performative act, although it is not a good or a perfect one); on the contrary, all actions falling outside of this range cannot be judged fitting with regard to the undertaken performance. My argument is that the same goes for empathy. To a certain degree, instances of empathy in which the empathizer does not perfectly match the target's mental states can still be considered cases of empathy. Yet, above a certain threshold, they cannot.[9] So, for example, the person who says to feel the happiness of the other when the other one is actually sad does not meet the minimal requirements of the consonance condition (the incongruence is too great), whereas the empathizer who feels the other is sad when the target of their empathy is depressed has (although not perfectly) met those minimal requirements. Of course, this also entails that there will be "borderline cases" in which judging if a certain act counts as empathy or not will be harder than in others (e.g., academics might debate as to whether Ryan has really empathized with Josh), but because matters of emotions are rarely simple and clear-cut, this inherent difficulty cannot be taken as sufficient to reject this view. On the contrary, I think that this view can help to solve complex cases, such as that of Ryan and Josh, without resorting to dogmatisms (like that of isomorphism). A possible solution for the Ryan and Josh case could be the following: Is there in the mixture of sadness and disappointment experienced by Josh an element of (maybe not entirely conscious) anger? If there is, then we could agree on the fact that Ryan has, to some extent, empathized. Otherwise, we can deem his act as a mere attempt at empathy (like a failed performance).

I think that the choice to be more flexible regarding the isomorphism condition, making it an issue of consonance and not of perfect equality not only makes our concept of empathy more similar to that of David Hume and Adam Smith, but it can make the discussion about empathy more productive because requiring perfect equality would be a nonstarter, like it is for Peter Goldie's concept of empathy.[10] In one of his latest articles before his death, in fact, Goldie defended an intransigent position for which empathy ("empathetic perspective-shifting" to be exact) was unable to operate with the appropriately "full-blooded notion of first-personal agency" that is involved in deliberation.[11] His argument is complex and well-described, and it is not easy to summarize it in a few words. But, to put it as succinctly as possible, because it is impossible for the empathetic person A to take on the full-blooded notion that is typical of the first-personal agency and deliberation of B in conditions of confusion and conflict (when, that is, decisions are not easy to be made), then either A is forced to usurp B's agency or they have to conceive of it in an unrepresentative "double-minded" way. It is not my aim to deepen this issue here because this will take us far away from our primary focus, but it suffices to say that the concept of empathy held by Goldie is uselessly restrictive. No one requires from empathy to be that accurate and to give us the complete full-blooded access to the first-personal agency of the other. To believe it is to ask too much from a notion that is widely used to describe a more modest understanding and sharing of the other's mental states. Thus, Goldie's criticisms can clearly be tackled by refusing to expect from empathy outcomes and effects that it simply cannot deliver.

THE MORAL FACE OF EMPATHY: EMPATHY AND MORAL PERCEPTION

Until now we have depicted our definition of empathy and specified its essence, as it were, at an epistemological level. By doing this we have saved both the views which want it, alternatively, unmediated and conceptually poor, and conceptually rich and grounded on imagination and perspective-taking by introducing the difference between low-level empathy and high-level empathy. We also showed how being more ecumenical with our definition of empathy allows us to recover the old view on empathy by Edith Stein and should thereby be welcomed even by modern phenomenologists. Finally, our position on empathy can dodge the criticisms advanced by Goldie. It would prima facie seem that we are finally out of the woods. But we are not, because during the last decade, empathy was harshly criticized even at the ethical level for the supposed moral role it can play. In particular, Jesse Prinz[12] and Paul Bloom[13] are surely the most hostile and internationally well-known critics of empathy. Because it would be impossible to respond appropriately to all their criticisms in one single chapter, I decided here to focus on one criticism only, the one moved by Prinz about the supposed role played by empathy for moral judgment. Let's reconstruct the argument briefly.

If empathy were necessary for moral judgment—so Prinz—then we could not be able to express a moral verdict without making use of empathy. However, it seems that we are capable of judging something as moral or immoral without resorting to empathy. For instance, we can judge that we have been wronged, or, to put it another way, that someone treated us immorally, without the need to empathize with ourselves. Furthermore, there are cases, such as bootlegging CDs or DVDs or evading taxes, that are commonly seen as morally wrong, even though there is no salient victim to empathize with. There is also a series of transgressions that are generally judged as immoral without thereby having grounded this judgment in empathy or compassion. Prinz offers the following list: "necrophilia, consensual sibling incest, destruction of (unpopulated) places in the environment, or desecration of a grave of someone who has no surviving relative."[14] In all these cases, empathy can hardly be the cause of our moral disapprobation because we have no one to empathize with.

If we consider all these critical points, empathy turns out to be contingent on moral judgment because we can express moral judgments without having to rely on empathy. However, one might object, empathy turns out not to be necessary in these cases, only because they are all cases in which others are not really involved. Specifically, if we take empathy to be fundamental only for the regulation of moral behavior between two or more individuals, then we may discover a necessary moral role for it. In other words, empathy might be necessary for a special class of moral judgments: those made in a social situation between real people, as opposed to juridical people, like the government, or material goods, like the environment, are examples of these. However, even in this context there are some issues. Prinz has an interesting way of illustrating this. He imagines the following state of affairs: Suppose that I come to eat the last delicious cookie from a packet I have been sharing with a friend of mine. After doing it, I feel a pang of guilt. Is this feeling of guilt coming from empathy for my friend? It does not seem to be the case. To feel guilty, I just have to construe my actions as greedy. Quoting Prinz on this issue:

> Morally significant actions can be recognized without empathy, even if those actions are ones that involve harm. We need not reflect on the harm to see that the action is bad. Perhaps you are delighted that I ate the last cookie. I recognize that, empathetically, and I still feel guilty; I still think that I should have offered the cookie to you.[15]

In other words, Prinz is persuaded that on any given occasion, our judgment that something is morally good or bad derives from a sentiment that leads to feeling the appropriate emotional response. Sentiments are in fact for Prinz "dispositions to have emotions." Hence, if I have a sentiment of disapprobation toward greed, I will feel anger or scorn when I see someone acting greedily, and guilt or shame when I myself have performed a greedy action.

Now, I believe Prinz is partially right: There are various moral judgments that we daily make without employing empathy; this is an undeniable truth. Nevertheless, I also believe that his position can be tackled on at least three fronts: The first way is by highlighting how empathy and its influences on moral judgment can sometimes be hidden, but, despite that, very much active.

The second is by showing a noteworthy role that empathy can play in moral judgment which, far from making empathy the foundation of moral judgment, makes it nonetheless a crucial faculty when it comes to judging the behavior of a moral agent, thanks to its connection with a notion that is normally related to morality and moral behavior: that of intention. The third, finally, consists in underlying the role empathy can play for *moral perception*, which is in turn strictly connected to moral judgment. I talked about the first two arguments elsewhere,[16] in this chapter I am going to discuss the third.

Empathy, so my claim, works as an information-gatherer,[17] enriches our apprehension of a certain situation. Indeed, rarely are the situations that we face and in which we can act comparable to the kind of elementary feedback we find in basic physics, where to a precise action inevitably follows a fixed reaction. Human psychology is a complex matter, and empathy is the best GPS we have that can drive us across the others' inner world. No matter what conception of empathy we defend, it is certainly the best way to understand what the actors in a certain context of experience might be feeling and thinking. In what follows, I am going to show how empathy can play a central role for what is normally known in the literature as moral perception and how this can assist our moral judgment. To reach this goal, I am going to analyze three emblematic examples and in conclusion I will try to substantiate the results by engaging in dialogue with suggestions stemming from Edith Stein (1989), Iris Murdoch (1992), Lawrence Blum (1994), and Rainer Forst (2011). However, before moving any further, we have to ask a crucial question: What is moral perception and how does it differ from moral judgment?

Rivers of ink could be written about what precisely is intended by moral judgment, but, to not uselessly complicate matters, we could describe moral judgment as that process by means of which we can judge the morality of an action or a subject. Put in another way, moral judgment is the process that should bridge the gap among moral rules, principles, or values on the one hand, and particular circumstances on the other, between the general and the particular, the axiological and the factual, the theory and the praxis.[18]

In this sense, moral perception can be deemed to be similar to moral judgment because it also deals with moral values and qualities. Indeed, moral perception could be described as the faculty to intuitively discern (to perceive, as it were) the morally salient qualities in particular situations. However, whereas moral judgment analyses the morality of, let us say, a certain action, moral perception is what makes this action appear intuitively moral. Moral perception comes on stage before moral judgment[19] and can sometimes even bypass moral judgment entirely by leading to moral action without bringing the particular circumstance in front of the courthouse of moral judgment. Notice that, for the sake of simplicity, I have defined moral perception as a faculty. Nevertheless, as we will see, moral perception should not be conceived as a unitary capacity but, rather, as a cluster of multifarious moral and psychological processes of which empathy is an integral part.

The most typical (and most powerful) potentiality of empathy is its capacity to make us step into the shoes of another, to make us understand another not *from the outside*, in a cold and detached manner, like a scientist describing the behavior of a particular animal, but, as it were, *from the inside*, in a hot and attached way. Thanks to empathy we wear the skin of the other—maybe only for a few moments, and in any case without losing the fundamental awareness of who we are—and take on a double-perspective: my own one, and that of the target of my empathy. This is what I call the *lingering in the world of others*, which is a fundamental component of empathy (at least in its high-level form): trying to recreate the perspective of the other, dwelling in the other's persona, almost in an ecstatic manner, and then come back with an enriched awareness. We are now going to see that empathy can in fact correct our biases and help us to act morally, in particular, empathy can adjust our biases regarding other people and those regarding the (moral) appreciation of certain situations.

In his 1994 book, Blum has developed an illuminating way of showing how the characteristics of moral perception are distinct from those of moral judgment and how the task of moral perception does not overlap with that of moral judgment. Blum imagines the following:

> John and Joan are riding on a subway train, seated. There are no empty seats and some people are standing; yet the subway car is not packed so tightly as to be uncomfortable for everyone. One of the passengers standing is a woman in her thirties holding two relatively full shopping bags. John is not particularly paying attention to the woman, but he is cognizant of her. Joan, by contrast, is distinctly aware that the woman is uncomfortable. (1994, 31–32)

Now, the first feature that should stand out with a certain degree of clarity from this example is—in Blum's opinion—that John and Joan clearly perceive the situation differently. In other words, different aspects of the situation are salient for John and Joan.[20] Using Blum's words: "what is fully and explicitly present to John's consciousness about the woman is that she is standing holding some bags; what is in that same sense salient for Joan is the woman's discomfort."[21] Now Blum is convinced that this difference is due to a difference in salience, which means that John and Joan perceive the same situation differently because they have different perceptions of what is salient in the situation. It should not be so difficult to notice the circularity of his argument: John and Joan perceive the situation differently because they have different perceptions of what is salient in the situation, and they have different perceptions of what is salient in the situation because they perceive the situation differently. The question to ask is therefore: Why is that? Why is Joan aware of some elements that John seems to ignore?

Now, although I agree with Blum about the difference in salience between Joan's and John's perception, I think that the only way we have to break the circularity of the argument for which we perceive a situation differently because we have different saliences, and we have different saliences because we perceive the situation differently, is to ground this diversity of salience in one of our most fundamental psychological mechanisms: empathy. Empathy is, in fact, intrinsically connected to what was rightly defined as the *salience effect*.[22] This means, using the words of Oxley, that: "empathy makes salient another's particular emotions, concerns, reasons, interests, and considerations in such a way that they are relevant and important to the empathizer, so that she is motivated to respond to these concerns."[23] This special characteristic of empathy allows us to explain how empathy can influence our moral perception: Different empathic levels in different people produce different saliences, which, in turn, provoke dissimilar (moral) perceptions of the same situations. To be more concrete, let us return to Blum's example.

Blum correctly observed that where Joan sees a woman in discomfort, John only sees a standing woman holding two shopping bags. There is, thus, a sense in which both of them see the same situation, constituted by the same elements (the standing woman in the subway train with her bags) and another in which they see two radically different things. The factor that shifts Joan's perception, as it were, to another level, is empathy. Joan feels the discomfort of the woman; she is aware of it in a way in which John is not. Having this awareness, although it is admittedly possible for Joan to refuse to give up her seat, it is nonetheless harder, surely than for the unaware John. However, it would be a mistake to stress the link that empathy can have with action uniquely, as if the only element to have moral value were a practical act. On the contrary, there is already (moral) merit in the perception of the morally significant aspects of a situation, and in the same way, we have to distinguish the moral shortcoming of a *failure to see* from the moral shortcoming of a *failure to act*. I have stressed more than once that morality is, inter alia, a matter of degrees. Now, Blum's example allows us to observe it very clearly. Contrast, in fact, the behavior of Joan with that of John and that of another man: Ted.

Joan empathizes with the woman and perceives her discomfort. She is not merely *aware* of her discomfort (i.e., in a cognizant but not emoting way), she is instead *moved* by the representation of her discomfort and consequently chooses to give up her seat. Ted, in turn, has no problem in unambiguously and correctly perceiving the woman's discomfort, but, contrary to Joan, he is not moved by it. He is, that is, cognitively aware of her discomfort, but he does not feel affective empathy for her. Probably, his own comfort has a stronger salience for him. John, in this sense, does not display the same egoism and insensitivity showed by Ted. He is simply unable to see the woman as in a discomforting position. However, if this discomfort would be brought to his attention, he would promptly empathize with the woman, feel her distress and act similarly to Joan. Hence, as it should now be clear, John finds himself in the middle between a truly morally virtuous person like Joan, who is able both to see all the moral aspects of a situation and to act accordingly, and a morally bereft person like Ted, who, though he notices the same moral aspects, refuses nonetheless to act. To make the scenario even more interesting, we could think of a character even worse than Ted, for example someone who is unable to perceive the moral elements of a situation and that even if these were brought to his attention, he would nevertheless refrain from helping: Bob.[24]

In this state of affairs, we might choose to describe the differences between the four characters as differences in moral perception (this is for example what Blum seems to do), but I claim that, in so doing, we would be at loss. In fact, we would be forced to acknowledge that the two pairs, built up by Joan and Ted on the one side and John and Bob on the other, have the same moral perception, which is incidentally true, but it does not help us to draw any fine-grained moral differentiations between them. Nor would it be an astute move to consider the act of helping the woman as the only criterion to identify the differences in moral weight I hope to have highlighted previously. Here, in fact, we would be compelled to attribute moral merit only to Joan and to put John in the same pot as Ted and Bob.

My claim is that the best criterion we have to unequivocally distinguish the nuances in the moral merit and the moral disposition of these four characters is empathy. Taking empathy as a yardstick permits us to affirm that Joan is the more empathic person of the group: She feels affective empathy for the woman, which makes the woman's discomfort transparent to her (she feels it the moment she observes her) and this in turn motivates her action. The second in the scale of moral virtue is John, who, possessing a lesser degree of empathy (compared with Joan) is unable to perceive the woman's distress, but who would be ready to help if this distress would be pointed out to him. Then it is the turn of Ted: He is able to acknowledge the woman's discomfort, but this recognition never crosses the cognitive boundary; it remains at a purely cognitive level ("I know that she is uncomfortable") and never reaches the emotional one ("I feel her discomfort"). The exclusion of affective empathy for the woman leaves Ted apathetic, unmoved and unmotivated, without triggering any reactive behavior. Finally, at the lower stage, we find Bob, who not only displays the same deficit of affective empathy shown by Ted, but also exhibits an absence of cognitive empathy because he is even unable to recognize the woman's general state of discomfort.

If we take the example of Joan as a paradigm of "perfect"[25] moral virtue, then we may assert that the three other subjects are at different distances from the perfect virtue: John has to work on his cognitive empathy, so that it can help him, inter alia, to detect the moral aspects in which the emotions of another living being are at stake; Ted has to work on his affective empathy, so that the recognition of the suffering of others can trigger a similar emotion in him and motivates him to help; Bob, finally, has to work on both forms of empathy if he wants to have a chance improving his seriously callous and unemotional character.

But before continuing our discussion about character and touching on the theme of virtue, it is useful to make a step back and consider once again the words of Stein. In *On the Problem of Empathy*, she writes, analyzing the phenomenon of the experience of a psycho-physical individual:

> This individual is not given as a physical body, but as a sensitive, living body belonging to an "I," an "I" that senses, thinks, feels, and will. The living body of this "I" not only fits into my phenomenal world, but is itself the center of orientation of such a phenomenal world. It faces this world and communicates with me.[26]

What does it mean to experience another human being as the center of orientation (in the original: *Orientierungszentrum*) of their own world? It means to experience the other as a being, a *Wesen* that has their own perspective on things and that perceives the world primarily in relation to themselves; a being that has needs, an emotional life, and vulnerabilities as we do. This kind of experience is the opposite of the egocentric kind of experience; it is the opening to a horizon consisting of mutual relationships. The others are not perceived as mere shadows of myself, as individuals that I can objectify to pursue my ends but as autonomous subjects. It is thanks solely to this kind of perception (or experience) that I can not only simply *acknowledge*, inter alia, the desires and interests of others, but that I can even *respect* them. Notice another important passage in this citation. Stein affirms that the other is also always in communication with me, which means that they cannot be conceived merely as the Orientierungszentrum of their own world but as a being that can observe me, relate to me, and even make requests of me from their singular world. This means that I am seen by the other, judged by the other, appealed to by the other in a way that I would never be able to experience without leaving my egocentrism behind and opening toward the others and the world through the use of empathy. Namely, what I think that can be argued on the basis of the reflections of Stein is that empathy works as a *precondition* to moral judgment and moral behavior. Empathy, in fact, helps us with correct understanding of the moral scenarios we have to face. It helps us to interpret the situation at hand morally. If I know that I am constantly dealing with finite and vulnerable beings that have desires, emotions, interests, and needs as I have, then this awareness constitutes the first and most fundamental (being the most original) call to a moral responsibility on my part and to the instantiation of moral behavior. In the words of Rainer Forst:

> [The insight into finitude] is an insight into the various risks of human vulnerability and human suffering, bodily and psychological. Without the consciousness of this vulnerability and the corresponding sensibility . . . , moral insight that is an insight into human responsibility remains blind.[27]

This feature of empathy is a crucial one for morality. Thanks to empathy we do not simply come to understand and feel the mental states of other people, as if they were some type of object that we can manipulate to our will; by means of empathy, as has been said repeatedly, we assume the perspective on the world of another person, we see what matters for this subject. Moreover, for the time in which we empathize, we see these things as mattering for us as well, because we have abandoned our perspective to gain access, as it were, "by the inside" to that of the other. As Stein states, we become, by way of empathy, the same other's Orientierungszentrum. I want to quote the words of John Deigh on this issue, as I find them quite appropriate:

> In taking another's perspective, the agent sees the purposes that give extension and structure to the other's life and sees those purposes as worthwhile, as purposes that matter. In this way it comes to recognize others as autonomous agents and to participate imaginatively in their separate lives.[28]

As you can see, Deigh is clear on the matter: To empathize with another person means not only to simulate her feelings and her mental states in general, but also "understanding his purposes as generating reasons for action." In other words, empathy offers us an insight into the agency of the other person, into the ways in which they act, based on certain reasons. We could add, also into the ways in which, for example, they believe, love, fear something based on certain reasons.

CONCLUSION: EMPATHY AS A NECESSARY FEATURE OF THE VIRTUOUS PERSON

Following what I have said so far, it should be easy to notice that empathy plays indeed a fundamental role for moral perception, and *a fortiori* for moral judgment. Our judgment of the behaviors of others will not be a truly moral one without insights coming from empathy, and our actions toward others will benefit from these insights, in addition. Consider, in fact, the image we normally have of the morally virtuous person. We think (and rightly so) that such a person is, for instance, someone who gets angry from time to time but—to say it as Aristotle would do—with the right people, at the right moment, for the right reasons, and to the right extent—and the same applies to any other emotion. My claim is that without empathy it will be difficult for the morally virtuous person to be truly morally virtuous: how would they know that—to use the same example—*X* deserves their anger (and how much, at which moment and for what reasons) because of something they did, if they do not know what passed through *X*'s mind and what it is like for *X* to be in the situation he or she is in? Our judgments about others would be unrefined and approximate. What is more, without empathy our morality would be short-sighted; we could have, that is, moral intentions, but we would find difficulty in converting these good intentions into actual good moral deeds for the same reasons I outlined previously: We would be lacking important information that would help us to know exactly what to do. Continuing the analogy with Aristotle, empathy covers, following my proposal, part of the field (and of the tasks) that are characteristic of the *phronesis*. Phronesis was for Aristotle a type of practical wisdom or intelligence, akin to, if not even analogous to, the concept of prudence, which carried out the role of the guide of the virtuous person, the inner advisor who told them how and when to act, thereby orienting all of their virtues. Phronesis is distinct from *sophia*, as this one is a pure theoretical knowledge directed toward universal truths typical of the sciences; for example, it is by having and developing our sophia that we learn the principles of mathematics and geometry. On the contrary, the phronesis is concerned with particulars and with praxis, in the sense that it is concerned with how to act in particular situations. One can, of course, learn the principles of action in the same way in which one learns the principles of arithmetic, that is, in a theoretical way, but applying them to the real world, in situations one could not have foreseen, requires more than theoretical knowledge; it requires a practical wisdom. My claim is that this practical kind of wisdom or intelligence would be incomplete (and thus imperfect) without the indispensable contribution of empathy, which is, after all, a kind of *emotional intelligence*. Without empathy a true phronesis cannot exist, which means that the morally virtuous person must also develop their capacity for empathy. Take the case of sincerity, for instance. It is a common assumption that morally virtuous persons are by definition and ipso facto honest and sincere. However, what does it mean to be sincere? Sincerity certainly does not require saying openly everything one has in one's heart, to any person, at any moment, and without any kind of filter. In fact, such a behavior would easily result, inter alia, in the assertion of indelicate and inopportune comments that would hurt others' feelings. Far from considering a person acting in this way as being morally virtuous, we would think that they are indeed inappropriate, ill-mannered, and asocial. Hence, the morally virtuous person, anything but insincere, would nevertheless be a person able to tell the truth "in the right way," meaning that they would be capable of doing it without hurting others (or at least by reducing this eventuality to the minimum). To carry out such a task they are going to need more than wisdom; they need empathy to perceive the emotionality of others and give voice to more appropriate, honest comments. The same applies to all the other virtues: Empathy comes to be an integral part of the phronesis and, driven by it, a necessary component of the ethos of the morally virtuous person.

To say that empathy is a necessary constituent of the ethos of the morally virtuous person implies that a *defective* empathy would mutilate the moral excellence of this person, and it would compromise their capacity to act morally. Furthermore, as we have seen in the previous discussion, a *complete lack* of empathy would prevent us from exiting from our egocentric perspective and developing a moral stance about others and the world—a world in which others are taken into account in our actions.

The fact that empathy can be of such a crucial importance for the ethos and for the moral development of a person should not strike anyone as surprising. In fact, principles are not the sole constituent of morality, or, more specifically, morality does not merely consist of the development, justification, and application of moral rules and principles. There are times in which our principles are wrong and need correction, but, above all, we need to develop a moral perception to know which kind of rule of conduct (and when) ought to be applied to the actual situation at hand. Does this mean that we should use our empathy *instrumentally*, that is, with the aim of correcting our perspective or refining our moral perception? Yes and no. Yes, because this is indeed useful and it can be definitely helpful to try to overcome our perspectives in some situations. No, because this would not happen in every situation where it is needed. To overcome one's own perspective, one needs, in fact, the willpower to do so, and the capacity to do so. These are elements that can be developed only by means of training, in other words, by the development of a good character (ethos). The aim of a good moral education should hence be the enhancement of empathy *tout court*, so that it can always be present together with our moral principles. We should strive to make a *habitus* out of empathy because it is only when empathy becomes a habitus that it can substantially (and not contingently) change our way of seeing. Iris Murdoch once said:

> The selfish, self-interestedly, causal or callous man sees a different world from that which the careful, scrupulous, benevolent, just man sees; and the largely

> explicable ambiguity of the word 'see' here conveys the essence of the concept of the moral.[29]

In these few sentences, a philosopher who was not a phenomenologist at all gives voice to an exquisitely phenomenological thought: The world is not the same for everyone because the world is *seen*, and every one of us *sees* it differently. In particular, the world is axiologically and sometimes even ontologically different for the virtuous and the unvirtuous/vicious person. And it goes without saying that a different world requires different courses of actions. Following this line of thought, if we want to correct the vicious acts of the vicious person we need to modify the way in which this person sees the world in which she lives in. And to do it, we need to expand her perspective, making her see the world through the eyes of others, making her (cognitively and emotionally) aware of the others' inner worlds: with their needs, desires, fears, intentions. This is a hard and ever perfectible task that only empathy can accomplish. And this is why empathy is so important for morality.

NOTES

1. Augustine (1960), book XI, chapter XIV.
2. See for instance Coplan (2011), pp. 4–5, and Batson (2011), pp. 11–19.
3. Stein (1989), p. 10.
4. See Lipps (1903, 1905, 1907).
5. See Merleau-Ponty (1962).
6. See Zahavi (2011, 2014) and Zahavi & Overgaard (2011).
7. For the first case see for instance de Vignemont and Singer (2006), who defined empathy as the capacity to vicariously share another person's emotion, in particular, see their condition of "isomorphism" (p. 435), according to which the empathized emotion must be isomorphic to the emotion experienced by the target. For the second one, see, for example, Coplan (2011), p. 5, who described empathy as "a complex imaginative process in which an observer simulates another person's situated psychological states while maintaining clear self-other differentiation," where the emphasis is set on the process of simulation.
8. It is the case, i.a., of Martin Hoffman (2000), who famously referred to empathy as "an affective response more appropriate to another's situation than one's own," (p. 4).
9. Of course, the view I am defending—as already mentioned *supra*—is not the only one to be found in the literature. Controversy still exists concerning the degree to which the empathic response needs to be isomorphic to the original affective state. Does a coarse-grained congruency (e.g., only the same emotional valence) suffice, or is there need for a more fine-grained equivalence (e.g., same valence, intensity, and components)? My suggestion is that isomorphism must allow for a certain flexibility, otherwise, if taken *stricto sensu*, it is just a utopic condition. In other words,

there has to be *Spielraum*, a margin for nuances. This is why I refrain to talk about "isomorphism" (which seems to imply an equivalence, a perfect and implausible match of feelings between the empathizer and her target) and I prefer to use the word *consonance*, which depicts the case where the feeling obtained through empathy must be in accordance with the feeling of the target.

10. See Goldie (2011).

11. Ibid., p. 303.

12. See Prinz (2011a, 2011b).

13. See Bloom (2013a, 2013b, 2014, 2016).

14. Prinz (2011a), p. 214.

15. Prinz (2011a), p. 215.

16. See Camassa (2019a, 2019b).

17. This is exactly what I call (partially following Slote 2016) the *epistemic role* of empathy, that is, its capacity to provide us with data about others (how do they feel?, what do they think?, sometimes even the reasons behind certain feelings and thoughts).

18. See, for example, Blum (1994), pp. 30–31.

19. It is, in phenomenological terms, more "original" more "primordial" than moral judgment.

20. But it could also be stated that the same aspects of the situation have a different salience for John and Joan. The point is that the focus of their attention is set on distinct elements that make them perceive the situation differently.

21. Blum (1994), p. 32.

22. See Oxley (2011), p. 78.

23. Ibid.

24. Notice that Bob is a character I made up and that is not present in Blum (1994).

25. I use the quotation marks because moral perfection can never be reached and it constitutes just an objective for which every virtuous person should strive.

26. Stein (1989), p. 5.

27. Forst (2011), p. 39.

28. Deigh (1996), p. 175.

29. Murdoch (1992), p. 177.

REFERENCES

Augustine, St. (1960). *The Confessions of Saint Augustine* (trans. J. K. Ryan). Image.

Batson, C. D. (2011). *Altruism in Humans*. Oxford University Press.

Bloom, P. (2013a, May 13). The baby in the well. *The New Yorker*. http://www.newyorker.com/magazine/2013/05/20/the-baby-in-the-well

———. (2013b, May 16). Feeling sorry for Tsarnaev. *The New Yorker*. http://www.newyorker.com/news/news-desk/feeling-sorry-for-tsarnaev

———. (2014, September 10). Against empathy. *Boston Review*. https://bostonreview.net/forum/paul-bloom-against-empathy

———. (2016). *Against Empathy: The Case for Rational Compassion*. The Bodley Head.

Blum, L. A. (1994). *Moral Perception and Particularity*. Cambridge University Press.

Camassa, M. (2019a). The importance of being empathist: Why empathy matters for morality. *Quaderni della ginestra 22*(1), 1–20. http://www.la-ginestra.com/wp-content/uploads/2019/09/Mediatazione_filosofica_Empathist_Ginestra.pdf

———. (2019b). "I don't want your compassion!" The importance of empathy for morality. *HUMANA.MENTE Journal of Philosophical Studies 12*(35), 42–70. https://www.humanamente.eu/index.php/HM/article/view/221

Coplan, A. (2011). Understanding empathy. Its features and effects. In: A. Coplan and P. Goldie (eds), *Empathy. Philosophical and Psychological Perspectives* (pp. 3–18. Oxford University Press.

Deigh, J. (1996). *The Sources of Moral Agency. Essays in Moral Psychology and Freudian Theory*. Cambridge University Press.

De Vignemont, F., & Singer, T. (2006). The empathic brain: How, when and why? *Trends in Cognitive Sciences 10*(10), 435–41.

Forst, R. (2011). *The Right to Justification: Elements of a Constructivist Theory of Justice*. Columbia University Press.

Goldie, P. (2011). Anti-empathy. In: A. Coplan and P. Goldie (eds), *Empathy: Philosophical and Psychological Perspectives* (pp. 302–17). Oxford University Press.

Hoffman, M. L. (2000). *Empathy and Moral Development: Implications for Caring and Justice*. Cambridge University Press.

Lipps, T. (1903). *Aesthetik*, vol. 1. Voss Verlag.

———. (1905). *Aesthetik*, vol. 2. Voss Verlag.

———. (1907). Das Wissen von fremden Ichen. *Psychologische Untersuchungen 1*, 694–722.

Merleau-Ponty (1962). *Phenomenology of Perception*. Routledge and Kegan Paul.

Murdoch, I. (1992). *Metaphysics as a Guide to Morals*. Penguin.

Oxley, J. C. (2011). *The Moral Dimensions of Empathy: Limits and Applications in Ethical Theory and Practice*. London: Palgrave Macmillan.

Prinz, J. J. (2011a). Is empathy necessary for morality? In: A. Coplan and P. Goldie (eds), *Empathy: Philosophical and Psychological Perspectives* (pp. 519–38). Oxford University Press.

———. (2011b). Against empathy. *The Southern Journal of Philosophy 49*(s1), 214–33.

Slote, M. A. (2016). The Many Faces of Empathy. *Philosophia* 45(3): 843–55.

Stein, E. (1989). *On the Problem of Empathy*. ICS Publications.

Zahavi, D. (2011). Empathy and Direct Social Perception: A Phenomenological Proposal. *Review of Philosophy and Psychology* 2(3): 541–58.

———. (2014). *Self and Other: Exploring Subjectivity, Empathy, and Shame*. Oxford University Press.

Zahavi, D., & Overgaard, S. (2011). Empathy without Isomorphism: A Phenomenological Account. In: J. Decety, ed., *Empathy: From Bench to Bedside* (pp. 3–20). MIT Press.

Chapter 16

Embodiment, Empathy, and the Call to Compassion

Engendering Care and Respect for "the Other" in a More-Than-Human World

Scott D. Churchill

ABSTRACT

This chapter addresses the question of how our embodiment—with its aptitude for empathy, mutuality, and communality—enables us to transcend solipsism toward moral and ethical engagement. Even before we engage in an ethics there is the ethos of the social world itself, which serves as backdrop for all my actions. Within this ethos, we encounter what Levinas (1969) called "the face of the Other." The other's face is an appeal, a call to action. This would be in principle true across all dimensions of otherness: gender, race, species. Within this "call to compassion," there is an important shift from first person to second- and third-person awareness, especially when we embark on the task of an ethics. One might say that the second-person experience emerges when we first engage the other as a "thou," which typically occurs at the moment we first address or are addressed by other sentient beings, whether as speaking or nonspeaking "subjects" (Churchill, 2006, 2007). Illustrations drawn from real life, including interactions among animals and between humans and animals will be used to illustrate the theme of empathy as a call to action.

Keywords: empathy, ethics, the Other, compassion

> It is man's sympathy with all creatures that first makes him truly a man.
>
> —Albert Schweitzer

> In the relations of man with the animals, with the flowers, with all the objects of creation, there is a whole ethic scarcely seen as yet, but which will eventually break through into the light and be the corollary and the complement to human ethics.
>
> —Victor Hugo

In this chapter, I reflect on how our *living experience* of other sentient beings becomes a "call to action." More specifically, I am addressing how it is that we move from perception to *action* and *advocacy*. I am interested here in better understanding how perceiving and knowing can move us into a position of *caring*, and of *caring-for*.

Among the challenges for phenomenological psychology in the modern era is the crucial one regarding how we break from our first-person-singular experience to encounter and engage with others in a communal world. At the heart of this is the question of how our embodiment—with its aptitude for empathy, mutuality, and communality—enables us to transcend solipsism (and simple self-absorption) toward moral, ethical, and practical engagement. Even before we engage in an ethics, there is the *ethos* of the social world itself, which serves as a backdrop for all my actions as well as for all my reflections. Within this ethos, we encounter what Levinas (1969) called "the face of the Other." The other's face, for Levinas, is an appeal, a call to action. This would be in principle true across all dimensions of otherness: gender, race, species, and possibly even phylum and kingdom.[1]

FROM ENCOUNTER TO ENGAGEMENT

Alphonso Lingis (1994) speaks directly to the current theme in his brief but compelling book *The Community of Those Who Have Nothing in Common*, as does David Abram (1996) in *The Spell of the Sensuous: Perception and Language in a More-Than-Human World*. More recently, Maxine Sheets-Johnstone (2011) in *The Primacy of Movement* and Maria Puig de la Bellacasa (2017) in *Matters of Care: Speculative Ethics in More Than Human Worlds* have found their way from philosophy to praxis. All of these thinkers, and many others, have advanced our understanding of the body as a *mode of access* to the meaning of experience, whether our own or somebody else's. Each of them has prepared compelling descriptions of lifeworld experiences to communicate to their readers in a palpable way how it is that we are not only connected to other sentient beings but also able to understand these other beings through a kind of communion with them.

Kenneth Shapiro (1985) in his book *Bodily Reflective Modes: A Phenomenological Method for Psychology* was one of the first U.S. psychologists to begin to develop a methodological foundation for an embodied understanding of other persons—and eventually other species—through careful reflection on Husserl's and Merleau-Ponty's phenomenologies of the body. In fact, each of these authors has drawn from the work of Husserl, Merleau-Ponty, and other phenomenologists to develop richly embodied approaches to their perception of self and others. But beyond their reflections on "methodological access," all of these thinkers have eventually taken their phenomenology out into the world, in varying degrees of engagement. In the case of Shapiro, he took his concern for animals, grounded in his profound empathy for the lives of others, and made animal welfare his lifelong commitment as attested to by the journals, book series, summer training institutes, and ethical practices that he has established over the past four decades (see Animals and Society Institute at www.animalsandsociety.org). In his own research, he has applied a phenomenological perspective to the study of human-animal relationships (1990), vegetarianism (2015), the experience of animal advocacy (1994), and atheism (2018). Sheets-Johnstone (2011) took her extensive forays into the phenomenology of movement into the applied realms of movement workshops and dance therapy, while Abram (2010) would develop his reflections on the phenomenology of expressive life into his compelling and expansive *Becoming Animal: An Earthly Cosmology*, which further invites us to leave our anthropocentrism behind in our encounters with our more-than-human world.

Lingis (2018) has taken his lived understanding of Husserl's coupling (*das Paarung*) and intertwining (*die Verflechtung*) into his encounters with others throughout his journeys around the world. In his travels to India, he spent time inside the hospices where elders had been left to spend their final days in solitary waiting—in many cases forlorn and abandoned. He sat with the dying, sometimes tending to them. When he returned home to the United States, he was asked by others, "Why would you do such a thing? Why would you spend your time attending to those with whom you have nothing in common?" The irony of the question is captured in the title of his (1994) book, *The Community of Those Who Have Nothing in Common.*

As in the case of Lingis, Puig de la Bellacasa's (2017) sense of the ethical imperative derives from the concrete "situatedness" of oneself in the world, one that is at once experiential and open to possibilities of ethical engagement. She reimagines our current ecological ethics in a world under crisis by calling on us to take responsibility and to take action, "broadening the frame beyond the human, to the scale and temporality of the ecological" (Ticktin & Wijsman, 2017). Puig de la Bellacasa characterizes her own ethical position:

> it makes of ethics a hands-on, ongoing process of recreation of 'as well as possible' relations and therefore one that requires a speculative opening about what a possible involves. And thus the thinking in this book is moved by a generic appeal of care that makes it unthinkable as something abstracted from its situatedness. (p. 6)

This almost sounds Heideggerian, in the way that our situatedness or thrownness serves as context for our caring relationality within a totality of involvements. In his early (1921–1922) lecture course on Aristotle, Heidegger presented "care" as the meaning of human life, and a few years later in *Being and Time* (1962), he presented us with his "care structure" in which our modes of involvement, our projection into our own most possibilities, are never without their situated context. Our potentiality-for-being is grounded in our dwelling alongside (*Sein-bei*) entities encountered within the world. Even Heidegger's (1971) description of a pair of peasant shoes in "The Origin of the Work of Art" is laden with the very earth that Puig de la Bellacasa (2017) in her final chapter "Soil Times: The Pace of Ecological Care" sees as essential to our experiences of 'being touched by' and 'getting in touch with' our biosphere.

However, before going deeper into Heidegger's approach to the nonhuman world, I want to pause to make a point with respect to *how philosophy matters in framing the 'conditions of possibility' for our actions.*

DO OUR ONTOLOGICAL COMMITMENTS SOMEHOW PRECONDITION OUR CAPACITY FOR COMMUNALITY?

The relationship between embodiment and ethics is not just a theoretical question for philosophers to contend with: in his critique of humanistic psychology in the *American Psychologist* (the flagship journal of the American Psychological Association), positive psychologist Alan Waterman (2013) suggested that because of their grounding in an existentialist ontology, humanistic psychologists were hopelessly "individualist," and he expressed the concern that epistemologically and practically speaking, humanistic psychologists cannot really know (or even communicate effectively with) other people because of their fundamental "appreciation of individual isolation and aloneness" (p. 127). In light of his mistaken idea that there is a kind of solipsism at the heart of humanism, Waterman wrote:

> Experience is viewed as something inherently individual and thus intersubjectivity is a problem that can only be partially resolved. Communication is, by necessity, unreliable. . . . For humanistic psychologists, establishing connections between people is seen as problematic, whether in normal social interaction or . . . psychotherapy (Waterman, 2013, p. 127).

Similarly, Seligman and Csikszentmihalyi (2000) in their proposal for a "positive psychology," a term that they had appropriated from the field of humanistic psychology (Maslow, 1970) stated (almost derisively):

> Unfortunately, humanistic psychology did not attract much of a cumulative empirical base, and it spawned myriad therapeutic self-help movements. In some of its incarnations, it emphasized the self and encouraged a self-centeredness that played down concerns for collective well-being. (p. 7)

I have critiqued these positions elsewhere (Churchill, 2014; Churchill & Mruk, 2014), so I am only using them here as a point of reference. With Waterman, we have a positivist suggesting that humanistic psychologists are really not so humanistic after all, given their predilection for self-preoccupation (as implied by a presumed underlying philosophy of individual isolation) *that consequentially precludes contact and communication.* Let's think about what this critic is saying: If "experience is viewed as something inherently individual," then "establishing connections between people" becomes problematic, "whether in normal social interaction . . . or psychotherapy." Those are powerful words. If as a result of our philosophical foundations we are unable to really establish connections with each other in "normal social interaction," then one can only imagine how inept we would be connecting and relating to people from other cultures. And then, what about our relationships with animals? Or with the natural world itself as an ecosystem? Although the critique of humanistic psychology by these positive psychologists is based on their erroneous assumptions about our philosophical commitments, it is the rationale for their critique to which I am drawing attention because it points to *a presumed role that philosophical foundations have with respect to both personal and professional practice.*

So, let us first set the record straight: The hallmark of humanistic psychology's foundation in phenomenology is its fundamental emphasis on relationality, beginning with Heidegger's early lectures on Aristotle, in which he argued vehemently against the Cartesian starting point in favor of a "relational" philosophy that would direct us toward those aspects of human existence that are always already grounded in "caring" and "encounter" (Heidegger, 2001, pp. 61–97). Around the same time, Husserl wrote thousands of pages on intersubjectivity, portions of which were published in the three volumes known as his "Intersubjectivity Papers" (Husserl, 1973). The works of Husserl and Heidegger on the fundamentally *intersubjective* and *relational* dimensions, respectively, of human experience have informed the later phenomenological ethics of Levinas, who (like Sartre before him) emphasized *human responsibility* and *accountability to others*. Especially the more "existentialist" among those sitting at the table of phenomenology were driven quite passionately by their sense of solidarity with the oppressed, perhaps most notably Sartre and Beauvoir (see Bakewell, 2016). Finally, to further secure the foundations for a phenomenological psychology within the humanist tradition, Merleau-Ponty's later ontological reflections on "expression," "institution," and "history" would preclude any slippage into isolationism, and his concept of "the body as speech" further recognizes that communication between persons happens quite spontaneously and is certainly not hampered by any presumption of existential self-absorption. So, indeed, philosophy matters in offering to humanistic psychology its foundation in an ontology that naturally leads to a call to communality and compassion. It is to a deeper appreciation of that ontology that we shall now turn.

Phenomenology of Relationality

> With a look of her eyes, a gesture of her hand, and with a word of greeting, the other faces me and appeals to me—appeals to my welcome, to my resources, and to my response and responsibility. With the vulnerability of his eyes, with empty hands, with words exposing him to judgment and humiliations, the other exposes himself to me as a surface of suffering that afflicts me and appeals to me imperatively. (Lingis, 1994, p. 33)

In one of his early lecture courses, Husserl provided for a special reduction to bring us to the experience of others—or, more specifically, to our capacity for viewing (*erschauen*) and resonating with meaning in the lives of others. It is not an egological reduction (or reduction to the first person) but an intersubjective one (Farin & Hart, 2006, xxvi; Husserl, 2006). In this case, our point of reference is not our "own" experience, nor is it our imagination of the other's experience—it is rather what Husserl called a phenomenon of "coupling" where, to paraphrase Merleau-Ponty, "the other's gestures furnish my own intentions with a visible realization." In his first lecture course on *Nature*, Merleau-Ponty cited Husserl's (1952) definition of Nature presented in *Ideen II* in which Husserl refers to "a domain of common primal presence for all communicating subjects" as the first and original sense of 'nature' and thereby of intersubjectivity (Merleau-Ponty, 2003, p. 78). Zahavi (2003) observes:

> Husserl continues his analyses (in his *Intersubjectivity* Papers) by describing a special kind of experience of the Other, namely, those situations where I experience the Other as experiencing myself. This kind of 'original reciprocal co-existence' where I take over the Other's objectifying apprehension of myself, that is, where my self-apprehension is mediated by the Other, and where I experience myself as alien, is of decisive importance for the constitution of an objective world. . . . The absolute difference between self and Other disappears. The Other conceives of me as an Other, just as I conceive of him as a self. (p. 237)

Husserl's (1973) approach to the inter-experience of multiple subjects is that we "originally" experience both our bodies and the bodies of others—including humans as well as animals—as *expressive*. In *Ideas II* Husserl (1989, p. 252) wrote: "Each movement of the Body is full of soul, the coming and going, the standing and sitting, the walking and dancing, etc." It is interesting that it is in movement—and in our living experience of observing movement (Lloyd & Smith, 2015; Smith, 2017, 2018)—that the phenomenologists direct our attention to bring us closer to the threshold of our encounters both with the Otherness of others and our *Ineinander* with others. What we are talking about here is our *mode of access* to a living encounter with the "alien" existence. In his *Phenomenology of Perception*, Merleau-Ponty (1962) wrote: "Here again I have only the trace of a consciousness which evades me in its actuality and, when my gaze meets another gaze, I re-enact the alien existence in a sort of reflection" (p. 353). Merleau-Ponty was making implicit reference to Husserl's *eine Art der Reflexion* (a kind of reflection), an elusive concept that refers less to an act of consciousness than to what he later called the "reversibilities of the flesh."

PHENOMENOLOGICAL REFLECTIONS ON OUR ACCESS TO ANIMALITY

> Suddenly there breaks forth the evidence that yonder . . . life is being lived . . . another private world shows through, through the fabric of my own, and for a moment I live in it. . . . [And finally,] my private world has ceased to be mine only; it is now the instrument which another plays. (Merleau-Ponty, 1968, p. 11)

In his 1929–1930 lecture course later published as *Fundamental Concepts of Metaphysics: World, Finitude, Solitude*, Heidegger (1995) delved into the question of our human *access* to animal life. He stated: "For the substantive problem with which we are concerned is precisely that of accessibility itself, the question concerning the potential access that man and animal characteristically have to other beings." He continues: "In seeking access to the experience of an animal, we must first ask the substantive question concerning what kind of being the animal has, such that they permit, resist, or possibly forbid any such self-transposition into them in each case?" (p. 201). I am reminded here not only of my own efforts to "connect" with bonobos at the zoo (Churchill, 2003, 2006, 2007) but also of the experiences of countless others who have engaged with animal others, as documented in endless YouTube videos. Most recently, Craig Foster in the Oscar-winning documentary *My Octopus Teacher* has presented viewers with his startling encounters with a young octopus that put its own life on the line to grant him access to its world.

Heidegger was correct in asserting that an animal might even forbid such a threshold to be established. When I first met David Abram at a Merleau-Ponty Circle meeting in 2005, he asked me if I would approach a bear in the woods in the same way that I might a bonobo in captivity (or even face-to-face in the wilds)? He was asking on the basis of his own experience with bears, but he raised implicitly the issue of perhaps needing more than empathy—something like a carefully measured respect for what is *wild* in any wild animals we might encounter—to know what the limits of safety are in approaching other species in their own habitats. Often we come uninvited and yet we are hopeful that we will be well received, such as when nature lovers free dive in the open sea to swim alongside Whale Sharks and Humpback Whales. Steve Irwin learned the hard way (in his lethal encounter with the stingray), as did Werner Herzog's *Grizzly Man*, the limits that some other species will demand of us.

If granted access to the animal other, we still must ponder the nature of the encounter itself. Heidegger observes that the "self-transposition" of self into the animal "does not mean actually putting oneself in the place of the other being and displacing it in the process" (1995, p. 202). Rather, it means "to follow the movement of showing" (Heidegger, 1972, p. 2). Heidegger (1995) elaborates: "transposing oneself into this being means: *going along with what it is* and with *how it is*. . . . Such going-along-with means directly learning how it is with this being, discovering what it is like to be this being *with* which we are going along *in this way*" (p. 202). When Heidegger spoke to his lecture audience like this, he was putting emphasis on *our being together in the moment with the animal other*. And in this being-with-one-another (*Miteinandersein*) a shared disposition (*Mitbefindlichkeit*) becomes manifest in our experience, such that in this living moment we share in the *way* of its being, in the *how* of its existence.

Heidegger's reflections on our capability *to go along with* the animal other in its expressive behavior are given deep grounding in Sheets-Johnstone's (2011) notion of *primal animation* (p. 218), which she defines as "the foundational liveliness coincident with being movement-born" (p. 218). She continues:

> Incipient intentionalities play out along the lines of this body precisely through movement that is already there, through primal animation. . . . It is through these incipient intentionalities of primal animation that creatures who must learn to move themselves, learn to move themselves. By the very nature of their task, they make sense of their own bodies first and foremost. . . . *sheer movement* is the ground on which intentionalities initially develop. . . . From the very beginning, we sense ourselves moving, we feel ourselves kinetically.

Perhaps this is why when we stand before an animal at the zoo, like an elephant swaying its head and trunk, or a gorilla beating its chest, or a young chimpanzee doing pirouettes, or even a dog wagging its tail, we feel almost moved to engage in similar behaviors. The dog vigorously wagging its tail in anticipation of receiving a treat inspires us to lean over, almost imperceptibly wagging our own rear quarters, reflecting the dog's enthusiasm back to it gesturally. And, at that moment, the dog "knows" that we grasp its intention, through the mirroring of gestures. Sheets-Johnstone continues:

> From the very beginning, we sense ourselves moving, we feel ourselves kinetically. . . . We are a moving-in-the-world being, a *Da-bewegung*. On the basis of movement, we develop an inchoate sense of ourselves [and others] as *animate forms*. . . . Through our kinesthetic consciousness we constitute ourselves as epistemological subjects. . . . Our tactile-kinesthetic bodies are an epistemological gateway, our opening way of making sense of ourselves and of the world through movement. (pp. 218–19)

Sheets-Johnstone cites the work of psychiatrist René Spitz (1983) who was interested in how the infant learns to distinguish the living from the inanimate, revealing two visual stimuli that are reliably associated with the infant's attention to and response to the living:

> The first such stimulus, he says, is "the percept of the human face and eyes"; the second such stimulus, he says, is "the perception of movement of any kind" (149). [Then] he goes on to speak of *dialogue*—"action and response" dialogue, not verbal dialogue (152)—as the pivotal factor in an infant's distinguishing the animate from the inanimate. (Sheets-Johnstone, 2011, p. 222)

It is no wonder, then, that Heidegger (as quoted previously) directs us to engage in such nonverbal dialogue, "directly learning how it is with this being, discovering what it is like to be this being *with* which we are going along *in this way* . . . while remaining other to it." Heidegger warns against what one hears other philosophers say about the possibility of truly 'knowing' an animal other. They reduce it to being something we 'do in our head' as a way of 'standing in' for the animal, in the animal's place:

> It is said of course there is no question of *any actual* transporting oneself into another being, as if we could somehow vacate our own position and directly fill out and occupy the place of that being. The transposition is not an actual process but rather one that merely transpires *in thought*. And this in turn is easily understood to mean . . . an 'as if,' one in which we *merely act as if* we were the other being. (1995, p. 202)

Heidegger wants to move beyond a mere "thought experiment" (p. 203) here: our connecting with other animals is not at all something that we can simply do in our heads. We have to bring our bodies with us (for illustrations, see Churchill 2003, 2006, 2007). Heidegger stated:

> The question as to whether we can transpose ourselves into the animal assumes without question that in relation to the animal something like a *going along with, a going along with it in its access to and in its dealings with its world* is possible *in the first place* and does not represent an intrinsically nonsensical undertaking. We do not question that the animal as such carries around with it, as it were, a sphere offering the possibility of transposition. The only question concerns our factical success in transposing ourselves into this particular sphere. The only question concerns the steps we have factically to take in order to accomplish the self-transposition and the factical limits to such an undertaking. (1995, p. 204)

Our self-transposition into the animal's being "consists precisely in we ourselves being precisely ourselves, and only in this way first bringing about the possibility of ourselves being able to go along with the other being while remaining other with respect to it" (pp. 202–3). In remaining "other" with respect to the animal, we can nonetheless allow ourselves to address or to be addressed by the animal. The steps that we have to take do not, however, require any further philosophical reflection.

The first of these steps might be nothing more than a simple curiosity about the nature of the animal other standing before us, as beautifully illustrated in Bernd Jager's (2010) anecdote presenting us with the case of a toddler contemplating a young goat:

> *Recently I happened to walk past a little improvised children's zoo in the corner of a metropolitan shopping center. Enclosed within a circular space marked off by bales of straw I noticed a dozen chickens, a few rabbits, a sleeping pig undisturbed by her litter of suckling piglets, a young calf and a most beautiful, fairy-tale white young goat. The zoo had no doubt been arranged to amuse the city children, many of whom had never before seen a rooster stride across a*

> *barnyard or heard a piglet squeal. The zoo appeared a popular attraction and it was a delight to see the great interest with which young children observed the various animals enclosed within the circle.*
>
> *As I entertained myself by watching the children a young girl of perhaps four years old drew my particular attention. The child looked with uncommon concentration at a white goat that, as if in response to the girl's curiosity, slowly walked over to where she stood and then stuck her head across the bales of straw in her direction. The animal appeared as curious about the children as the children were about her. It is hard to say what it was that so transfixed the girl's attention on this particular animal.*
>
> *Perhaps it was the extraordinary shiny whiteness of its coat, or the rosy white snout or perhaps the tiny beard. The girl kept a little distance from the straw encirclement but now, with the animal so close to her she ventured a further step in her direction. She then hesitated for a few more moments before stretching out her arm and gingerly touching the neck of the animal. As she began to stroke the goat stretched her neck, closed her eyes and then stood completely still to receive the child's caress. It was at that moment that I saw the child's face break out in a very broad and triumphant smile.*
>
> *If we ask what made the child smile we question at the same time what made her reach out to the animal and what made her want to caress it. She was obviously too young to be gathering scientific data about a particular kind of mammal, but she already understood how to enter into a dialogue with others and to form a bond with an attractive stranger. She did not approach the young goat as a material object contained within a natural universe but as a fellow creature inhabiting a common, cosmic world. The broad smile announced that the goat had consented to be her neighbor and that from that moment on they would no longer fear each other or treat one another as complete strangers. She smiled because the animal had entered her world and because two separate and mutually indifferent domains had come together to form an inhabitable whole. This cosmos came into being at the very moment when the child reached out, touched the animal and found it receptive to her touch. A threshold was established at the very spot where the child's hand touched the goat's neck and at the very moment when the goat acknowledged the girl's presence and permitted her to enter her domain.* (pp. 85–86)

Indeed, the key to understanding the reversibilities of the flesh is realizing that *it works in both directions at the same time.* It becomes a "condition of possibility" for *reciprocity*, in which we experience the true miracle of intersubjectivity.

Before returning to our discussion of animal others, we shall pause to consider some of the vicissitudes of our more general perceptual access to the lives of others.

Resonating Identification with the Other

Merleau-Ponty (1968) observed in *The Visible and the Invisible* that without the other, "I am always on the same side of my body; it presents itself to me in one invariable perspective" (p. 148). With the appearance of the other, I discover a "miraculous prolongation of my own intentions" (1962, p. 354) wherein the other's gestures furnish my own intentions with a visible realization—even if I might fail to recognize what I contribute to the qualities that I perceive in my partner (see Churchill, 1997). Sartre (1948) observed: "To love delicate hands is, we might say, a certain way of loving these hands delicately" (p. 99). The "delicate" quality perceived "over there," in the beloved's hands, is thus co-constituted by a corresponding "delicate quality" characteristic of the lover's regard for his beloved. In like fashion, the delicacy of the little goat's existence was made manifest in the delicate way that the little girl reached out to the goat.

Phenomenologists understand that perception is not a matter of passively sensing what is "over there," nor of "projecting" autistic fantasies onto another being; rather, in "experiencing the other within the we," there can be a kind of resonating identification with the other (see Churchill, 2006, 2007). It is in perception that the other is given to me, and for Merleau-Ponty, each sense is (borrowing from Husserl) *eine Art der Reflexion* (1968, p. 256), a distinctively empathic reflexivity that opens itself to the other and invests or reenacts itself in the other: "I gradually become aware of my body, of what radically distinguishes it from the other's body, at the same time that I begin to live my intentions in the facial expressions of the other and likewise begin to live the other's volitions in my own gestures" (Merleau-Ponty, 1964a, p. 119). Thus, when my gaze meets another gaze there results a de-centering of the locus of my experience, wherein we crisscross and "function as one unique body" (Merleau-Ponty, 1968, p. 215). When the other appears, our meeting is a "chiasm" in which we exist as "two opennesses, two stages where something will take place" (Ibid., p. 213). What does take place is a "strange encroachment by reason of which my visible, although it is not superposable on that of the Other, nonetheless opens upon it." (Ibid., p. 216). The chiasm is a doubling-up of two reversibilities—a conjoining of my flesh and the other's flesh, an opening into intercorporeal being.

The point here, in the current context, is that I spontaneously bring my own animality to my encounter with the animal other, just as I simultaneously bring my own humanity to the encounter. The challenge for the human perceiver is to become at least partially aware of their own animality so that it does not appear to exist solely in "the other"—in which case, the perceiver would be alienated from the nature of the animal, perceived "over there." Just as the beloved's delicate hands can appear only to the lover who looks delicately on them, so also it is the animality that exists within my own being that is the condition of possibility for my recognizing the animality that exists around me.

THE SECOND-PERSON PERSPECTIVE

Is there something that we can call a second-person awareness that exists *between ourselves* (Thompson, 2001) by means of which we are able to bear witness to a more penetrating truth about the other than by neutral observation alone? Within the call to compassion referred to in my title, there is an important shift from first-person to second-person awareness (Churchill, 2003, 2004a, 2004b, 2010, 2012, 2016, 2018), especially when we embark on the task of an *ethics*. Within the we-relationship (the first-person plural), one can adopt a second-person perspective with regard to the other, when we are addressing or being addressed by the other. Whether in word or in gesture, this exchange taking place between two people constitutes a special relationship—a portal or threshold through which meanings and intentions can become shared—as conceptualized by Dilthey (1977) with concepts like *Nacherleben* and *Sichversetzen*. It is a medium that allows for everything from empathy to microaggression to occur. For example, when I "feel my way into" the eyes of the other who is looking at me—which is the original meaning of empathy [*ein-fühlen*]—I may feel the other's warmth (and thus perceive them to be "empathic"), or I may feel the other's cool disdain (and thus believe they have "microaggressed" upon me). My own 'feeling into' the other's expression—regardless of whether I perceive warmth or aggression in the other's expression—represents what Husserl called an "empathizing perception," insofar as empathy enables me to co-experience [*nach-erleben*] the other's expression, though from my other-sided point of view.

One might say that the second-person experience emerges when we first engage the other as a "thou," which typically occurs at the moment we first address—or are addressed by—other sentient beings, whether as speaking or nonspeaking "subjects" (Applebaum, 2022; Churchill, 2006, 2007; Jager, 2010). Empathy can be possible, however, within both second- and third-person perspectives. Third-person empathy occurs when the other is not addressing me directly, but, for example, when I am observing them from a distance or reading their journals (or when they read mine) and one of us feels the other's joys and sorrows. When we are reading a handwritten letter that is addressed to us from a friend or loved one, do we not experience the other's *living presence* in their written words?

Why is it that I can be moved to delight (or even tears) when I pick up one of my mother's old handwritten letters to me? Is it not because in being addressed by her, even from afar, I feel myself present to her living intentionality? Is it not her loving me, her first-person experience while she was writing me the letter—that I am "viewing" when I read her words (to use Husserl's preferred term *erschauen* in reference to when we take note of someone else's experience)? Is not the meaning of her words precisely the love that she was so clearly experiencing and manifesting in her act of writing? And finally, is not this *loving intentionality*, which alone was capable of animating her words, the very "object" of my empathizing perception? (Churchill, 2022, p. 7)

If handwritten letters can provide a window into the soul of others, what about photographs? We all are familiar with the experience of "reading" a person's expression in a photograph, in which the other is engaged in some situation. The person who is looking at the photograph is not personally involved in the situation, and yet can empathize with the meaning perceived in the face of the other. We are indeed capable of such empathy toward others, even at a distance. Susan Sontag (2003) wrote about this in her captivating little book *Regarding the Pain of Others* where she discusses the impact and function of war photographs in communicating suffering. We are often spared exposure to images of war horrors for just this reason: that they bring us too disturbingly into the psychological horror of human cruelty and destructiveness. I will never forget the horror I witnessed during my first year in Dallas, forty years ago, at the SMU Meadows Museum where Goya's etchings depicting scenes of indescribable horror from the Spanish War made me aware simultaneously of not only the brutality endured by the victims but also of the unfathomable cruelty and sadism of the victims' tormentors. Indeed, the recent video image of George Floyd slowly being asphyxiated by a police officer kneeling on his neck was enough to mobilize millions in a resurgence of the Black Lives Matter movement.

My point is that even in these examples of third-person empathy where the suffering other is not addressing me directly, it is possible to *see through* the image to the suffering itself. There is also, in addition, a second-person empathy at work in our being directly addressed by the artist here, through his etchings. One resonates with not only *the pain of the victims depicted* but also *the horror of the artist* who reaches out to the viewer with an appeal to us to never allow this to happen again.[2]

Let's look a little closer at this primordial experience of the other. Inspired by his reading of Husserl, Merleau-Ponty (2003) observed: "*Einfühlung* is a corporeal operation. . . . to perceive the other is to perceive not only that I shake hands, but that he shakes my hand" (2003 N 76). This would mark the move from *first-person* to *second-person* perception, insofar as it involves a recognition of the subjectivity—and not merely the objectivity—of the other. This is what allowed Merleau-Ponty (1964d) to write:

> We must reject that prejudice which makes "inner realities" out of love, hate, or anger, leaving them accessible to one single witness: the person who feels them. Anger, shame, hate, and love are not psychic facts hidden at the bottom of another's consciousness: they . . . exist on this face or in those gestures, not hidden behind them. (pp. 52–53)[3]

He tells us here that it is not a matter of trying to coincide with the other, to see the world through their eyes, but rather a matter of seeing the other's experience *from the outside*, for what it is. It is by maintaining the perspective of a "witness," which we typically think of as a third-person point of view, that we enter into an awareness of the other's experience. Merleau-Ponty had laid the foundation for a new understanding of bearing witness in the *Phenomenology of Perception* where he spoke of the other's experience as it becomes known to me in my experience:

> There *is* no privileged self-knowledge, and other people are no more closed systems than I am myself. What is given is not myself as *opposed* to others . . . it is the doctor *with* the patient, myself *with* others. . . . I misunderstood another person because I see him from my own point of view, but then I hear him expostulate [or witness his behavior], and finally come round to the idea of the other person as a center of perspectives. . . . In this bipolar phenomenon, I learn to know both myself and other. (1962, p. 338).

From the standpoint of my ego, I can empathize with you, with whom I am speaking—so, within the first-person plural (you and me together), I can adopt a second-person perspective, whereby I let my own first person experience fade to the background—I forget about my anxieties or current agenda, for example, to allow something else to come into view: your happiness, or your sadness, which I can "see" in your facial expressions. You are looking at me, inviting me to laugh with you, or inviting me to feel your sadness, and your appeal to me as your "second person"—the one with whom you are speaking—puts me into a privileged perspective where I can see deeply in your eyes either the joy or the sadness that the other person over there cannot see from a third-person distance.

Thus, we conclude that within the first-person plural, empathy is possible from both second-person and third-person perspectives. Merleau-Ponty (1964d) in his essay on "The Film and the New Psychology" talks about the perspective of a witness of behavior—and how we can see, for example, in the gestures and lack of balance of the person stumbling around over there that he is dizzy. And that such an image in a movie is enough for the viewer to have a sense of the inner experience of the character. This is what made me realize that he is not describing the second person experience where we are addressed by the other or appealed to by the other. Rather, he is describing a particular kind of third person perspective where we are looking at someone whom we do not know and with whom we are not personally involved—whether we are looking across the street at something that is taking place, or watching it on video—we are capable of empathy from the third-person perspective, looking at what is going on "over there". And we are capable of and even more intimate empathy from the second-person perspective, when we look into the other's eyes and experience the call of the other. Either way, what is indeed special about these two modes of empathy is that they become a condition of possibility for a deep and immediate apprehension of the others soul.

Thus, I refer to second-person and third-person empathy to differentiate these two possibilities for experiencing the other's experience. It is important to be able to acknowledge that this difference exists; otherwise, we might think we cannot empathize unless the other looks me in the eye, or speaks to me on the phone, writes a letter to me, constituting me as a "second person" other (i.e., the one being addressed). Englander (2018) captures it quite well when he describes empathy as "following the meaning-expression of the other" (p. 54). Although his example was situated within the face-to-face therapy encounter, his characterization of empathy here is eidetic enough to embrace both second- and third-person experiences of empathy.

In the essay on film, Merleau-Ponty is talking about something other than the situation of two people entering into a face to face encounter; rather, he is talking about when we are watching a film from a third-person point of view. To use Erving Goffman's (1959) dramaturgical analysis as a point of reference, there are the actors on the stage (or in the film) and then there is the audience observing the performance, and while the actors address each other as "second persons" (I-you), the audience remains in a third person perspective as outsiders to the drama, that is, as "witnesses of behavior." And yet, even from that outside perspective, empathy is still possible—as, for example, when we watch the disturbing video of George Floyd with the officer's knee on his neck. We are not in personal relation with Floyd; he is not looking into our eyes appealing for help (which would represent our entering into a second-person relationship with him). Rather, he is over there being filmed on the street, unaware of me and my existence—I am completely third person (anonymous observer) to him. The point here is that the other does not need to be looking into my eyes in order for me to empathize. I can "feel my way into" (*ein-fühlen*) his bodily experience, even "feeling at one" with the other. Compassion comes from this feeling-in or feeling-at-one (*eins-fühlen*) with the other (Scheler, 1954, 1973), which we are quite capable of feeling from a third-person distance. This just might be what Husserl meant about empathy being a "bridge" to the other, especially in these third-person circumstances. Empathy can almost makes it *seem* as though the third person over there has entered into the I-thou with me, even when we have no such relation. We all know the experience of this kind of empathic connection with images of others' suffering, as Sontag points out in her aforementioned work, where she uses Goya's prints as examples, as well as reference to Holocaust photos as important for others to experience empathy in relation to the suffering of others.

COMPASSION AND ALTRUISM

Empathy as an epistemological posture is not just a perceptual experience but one which leads to a *primordial conviction* about something—a pathway to truth, if you will. At some point we realize that the knowledge we gain of the other through empathy is not simply information or data in a neutral sense; but rather, once it becomes conviction—something we feel in our bones—we are convinced that we must act honorably, and decisively, on the basis of that conviction. When I feel it in my bones that this person standing next to me in line at the train station is truly another "me"—a center of intentions, sensations, feelings, desires—then how can I *not* act toward them in a way that acknowledges their humanity?

We observe on YouTube videos animals of different species that are astonishingly altruistic toward each other, such as:

- The captive bear at the zoo that sees the drowning crow struggling to get itself out of a moat of water littered with debris and lumbers over to scoop it out, placing the bird gently on the pavement.
- The elephant in the wild that sees a calf stuck hopelessly in mud at a watering hole and does everything in its power to stave off the circling wild dogs and hyenas waiting to devour it.
- The water buffalo that sees one of its herd attacked by lions, and appears to "know" immediately what to do, leading a collective charge to attack the lions.
- Or, when the rhesus monkey jumps in front of an oncoming train to push on the chest of another monkey that's been electrocuted by the track, in an effort to resuscitate it, eventually pulling his comrade to safety just in the nick of time.
- The same goes for the dog on the highway in India desperately barking at oncoming traffic to stay clear of the dog hit by a car. Risking its own life to try to drag his ailing comrade to safety on the side of the road. *Whence comes this impulse to save the dog that has been run over on the busy street?*

- And, why does the dog filmed at the pier in a Mediterranean fishing village desperately try to use its own snout to shovel water onto the bodies of the fish left behind on the pavement by the fishermen, the dog clearly disturbed and mobilized by the sight of a fellow sentient being struggling to breathe—while the fishermen sit and laugh?

None of these animals had to take a course on virtue ethics to know how to act in these situations. They were simply called to do what they do. They acted on impulse, risking everything. We must ask ourselves why?[4]

In his blog on the subjective world of moles, Craig Holdrege (2003) observed:

> Any human being who has not been totally blinded by dogma knows that cats, squirrels, mice, and deer are all creatures that experience the world. This knowing is not intellectual; it is a kind of felt-knowing based on the direct interactions we have with animals. The cat looks at us when we walk by and purrs when we stroke it; it raises its tail, arches it back, hisses and focuses intently on the little puppy trying to come near. The gaze, the utterances, and the movements of the body are all gestures. They are expressive of the animal itself. . . . Each animal has a perspective, a point of view through which it lives in the world. When we observe an animal, we observe how it is living out this perspective, how it is living its unique way-of-being. (p. 16)

Stacey O'Brien (2008), in her best seller *Wesley the Owl: The Remarkable Love Story of an Owl and His Girl*, once bonded to the baby barn owl that she had found with a broken wing and rescued, would remain its caregiver and companion all its life; and reciprocally, the owl on one occasion would risk its life to comfort her by lying next to her when she was deeply sad, wrapping its vulnerable wing around her while resting together on her bed. The owl knew what to do. The impulse to protect, to comfort its perceived "mate," was given to the bird through a kind of empathy intrinsic to animals ranging from mammals to birds and even down to invertebrates like certain cephalopods: When in *My Octopus Teacher* the nature photographer Craig Foster has a close encounter with an octopus, the octopus in turn reaches out to him, risks its life to explore his body with its sentient tentacles, feeling, tasting, communicating all at once. The exchange between man and creature here is as intimate as two hands clasping each other—what we referred to earlier as the *reversibilities of the flesh*: the touching/touched. Likewise, it was in the gentle touch of a little girl's hand on the neck of a young goat that a bond was established, a threshold traversed. Richard Kearney (2021) in his latest book remind us of the importance of this most basic sense and its role in establishing our communion with our fellow beings.

From Empathy to Action

At what moment precisely does what Husserl (2006) called an "empathizing perception" (p. 164) become a call to action? Wherein lies the source of the impulse that led the small and vulnerable octopus to attach its own body to the bare skin of the adventuresome wildlife photographer swimming twenty feet underwater in a kelp forest off the coast of South Africa? It most likely had never seen a human being before, in the thick underwater forest that the octopus called its home. And yet, this vulnerable cephalopod, weighing no more than a few ounces, swam toward and literally reached out to touch and attach itself to the relatively enormous body of the mysterious sentient being who suddenly appeared within its habitat. Does the call to action only come when we witness life up close and personal? Is being a witness perhaps the first step? And might the next step be advocacy—where we "speak to" or "call ourselves toward" (*ad-vocare*) the other being who requires some assistance? Once again, on YouTube we observe the parrot on the kitchen counter that is feeding pieces of its own food to the hungry dog below. The bird does not just cry out on behalf of the hungry dog; *it acts*. What does it take to call on people to act?

Intercorporeal Compassion

> All zoology assumes from our side a methodical Einfühlung into animal behavior, with the participation of the animal in our perceptive life and the participation of our perceptive life in animality." (Merleau-Ponty, Themes from the Lectures, 97–98)

Ralph Acampora's (2006) *Corporal Compassion: Animal Ethics and Philosophy of Body* draws on our everyday experiences to call us to care about "those individuals, species, or systems . . . with which we . . . carry on an association of soma-esthetic conviviality" (p. 91). The *felt-knowing* alluded to here resonates with Polanyi's (1966) "tacit knowledge" and Gendlin's (1978) "bodily felt sense" as well as with Abram's (1996) "spell of the sensuous." Like Abram, Acampora's work draws heavily from both Heidegger and Merleau-Ponty—and a multitude of other deep influences. In a tour de force of intellectual effort, Acampora presents to the reader a most intriguing and challenging exploration of the ontology of animal life and of our relations to animals—as well as a discussion of the ethical imperatives that issue forth from this experience. He built his thesis on an inventory of every imaginable way of conceptualizing animal life and human-animal relations, reviewing all the subtleties and shadings of the existing ontological and ethical discussions. Acampora's thinking does not stop at the level of ontology but utilizes his insights into animal being to chart the course for an articulation of ethical principles that would guide our comportment toward animals.

Instead of seeking a cognitive or rational commonality with animals (which would be doomed from the start), he posits a commonality at the level of the lived body. And it is this resonance *with* the world that we learn to trust as informing our reflections on *what it is* that surrounds us, and on *how it is* that we are challenged to comport ourselves vis a vis our surroundings. This phenomenology of experience is our starting point for our encounter with others (and hence the deep and abiding value of phenomenology for those who work professionally with others, as in health care settings); it is also our starting point for our encounters with works of art (in Merleau-Ponty's writings), for our encounters with other cultures (in the work of Alphonso Lingis)—indeed, for our encounters with all universes of experience. In the case of Acampora, he is using phenomenology to orient us toward our living encounters with animal life, and for that matter, with any sentient beings that might one day be encountered. To quote from Bernd Jager's cited anecdote, "We are fellow creatures inhabiting a common, cosmic world."

Feeling connected ethically to other sentient beings indeed transcends interhuman relations as we enter into interspecies communication. At a North American zoo, a man observed JoJo, an adult male chimpanzee, slide down an embankment into the moat separating the chimpanzees from the human observers. And seeing that the chimpanzee could not swim and was slipping under the water, he did something quite remarkable: Incredibly, he climbed over the barrier, entered the water, and pushed the chimpanzee back to safety all amid the cries and screams from the onlookers who observed several adult males with hair on end approaching from the side of the enclosure. Once more fearing the worst, the human onlookers could only seem to expect that the other chimpanzees, and possibly even JoJo himself, would only intend to hurt the man, unable to recognize his heroic act as anything but a threat. JoJo, exhausted from the ordeal, slipped once more into the water; the man turned around, again amid the screams coming from the growing crowd, and once more pushed JoJo to safety and waited until he was certain that JoJo was not going to slide back into the moat, before high-tailing it back to safety. Later, the director of the Jane Goodall institute, Hans Cole, called the man on the phone and said, "That was a very brave thing you did. You must have known it was dangerous, everybody was telling you. What made you do it?" And the man replied, "Well, you see, I happened to look into his eyes and it was like looking into the eyes of another a man. And the message was, 'won't anybody help me?'" (Jane Goodall, personal communication, May 18, 2005).

CLOSING REMARKS

In his article on "The Poetics of Intersubjective Life," Peter Rosan (2012) presented accounts of empathy and stated:

> These vignettes represent variations on the theme of the subject as an engaged participant, indeed as an instrument, attuned and thereby illuminating an interiority, the other's as well as his/her own, not otherwise accessible had the subject remained a dispassionate or neutral observer of the other. (p. 116)

This is really quite brilliant: "attuned and thereby illuminating"—as if to say that our ontologically disclosive powers (our powers to illuminate, to "logos") are themselves derived *from our embodied attunement* to others. In addition, Rosan's observation—that the interiorities illuminated belong both to myself as perceiver and the other as perceived—points in the direction of a common foundation with all of Husserl's claims regarding the intersubjective realm: this would be the matrix of the aforementioned "double reduction" whereby we become present, in the reduction, to not one but two intentionalities: mine and that of the other whose experience I am "viewing."

In "The Child's Relations With Others," Merleau-Ponty observed:

> Thus, in today's psychology we have one system with two terms (my behavior and the other's behavior) which function as a whole. . . . And since at the same time the other who is to be perceived is himself not a "psyche" closed in on himself but rather a conduct, a system of behavior that aims at the world, he offers himself to my motor intentions and to that "intentional transgression" (Husserl) by which I animate and pervade him. Husserl said that the perception of others is like a "phenomenon of coupling" [*accouplement*]. The term is anything but a metaphor. In perceiving the other, my body and his are coupled, resulting in a sort of action which pairs them [*action a deux*]. This conduct which I am able only to see, I live somehow from a distance. I make it mine; I recover [*reprendre*] it or comprehend it. Reciprocally I know that the gestures I make myself can be the objects of another's intention. It is this transfer of my intentions to the other's body and of his intentions to my own, my alienation of the other and his alienation of me, that makes possible the perception of others. (1964b, p. 118)

What we learn from the more contemporary thinkers cited throughout this chapter is that our phenomenological connection to others through perception is only the starting point for the development of an ethics. These broadly speaking "perceptual" acts are gestalt experiences that are interwoven with feeling (Scheler'*s Einsfühlung*), intuition (Husserl's *Anschauung*), and even meditative contemplation (Heidegger's *andenkende Denken, Besinnung*). Together, these phenomenological concepts refer us to our own relational experiences and move us closer to what Sheets-Johnstone called "primal animation" and what Acampora called "corporal compassion." It is ultimately this primal dimension of our embodied experience of others in our more-than-human world that calls us to compassion and invites us to reach out to other sentient beings to establish a threshold or portal through which we can begin to engage in advocacy and stewardship on behalf of those with whom we share our communal world.

NOTES

1. In the Oscar winning documentary, *My Octopus Teacher* (2020), wildlife photographer Craig Foster takes us into his shared world with a cephalopod belonging to the Mollusca phylum, while Peter Wohlleben's (2015) *The Hidden Life of Trees: What They Feel, How They Communicate* and his (2021) *The Heartbeat of Trees: Embracing Our Ancient Bond with Forests and Nature* take us into his encounter with "feeling beings" from another kingdom altogether. And the recent documentary *Fantastic Fungi* (2019) takes us into the world of yet another kingdom, Fungi, to show us the multitude of ways that animal and plant life are all in ongoing communicative exchange with the Earth's fungi.

2. There is a poignant scene in the film *The Diving Bell and the Butterfly* where a stroke victim suffering from "locked-in syndrome" is approached by his speech therapist, who is teaching him how to communicate by blinking his eye, to signal which letter of the alphabet that she is reading aloud to him is the next letter of the word he wishes to "say." The scene, which consists of one continuous shot (that begins at 00:32:40 and ends at 00:34:30) in which the stroke victim is looking through his one good eye into the face of his speech therapist, is a perfect example of second-person perspectivity in its double reversibility. We see the therapist leaning in toward "our" eye (because "subjective camera" gives to us the physical point of view of the character) and we are able to "read" *her* emotions as she begins to realize what it is that he is communicating to her. At the same time, she is looking *from her perspective* into his one open eye, which still serves as "the window of his soul." When he begins to spell out "I want death," she turns away quite dramatically—not from his physical eye but from the despairing soul that she is *looking into* through his eye. As tears form in her own eyes, her expression turns from welcome receptivity to a troubled and even angry rejection of his words, which she calls an "obscenity." Mediated by the camera's point of view, we see into *her* grieving soul as she looks into his. The eyes are the medium of this exchange, and neither we nor the speech therapist are at this moment conscious of our own first-person experience, so much as we are present to the (second person) experience *of the other who is looking into our eyes* (Churchill, 2016). In the same way, the etchings by Goya present to us not only the brutality of war but also the artist's horror. There is a "double reduction" at work here, leading us back not only to the suffering of the person perceived by the artist (or therapist, in the film) but also leading us phenomenologically into the experience of the observer.

3. Likewise, for Scheler we are always confronted with a unified whole, not an expressive body that is the surface of a hidden psyche. He called it an "expressive unity" (*Ausdruckseinheit*).

4. I had an opportunity three years ago to discuss this with Jane Goodall when she was visiting Texas. I was invited to her birthday dinner, and we got to talking about these acts of altruism among different species, and she asked me why I thought these animals engaged in such acts, and the only word that came to my mind was "compassion." (She suggested that this might be a good theme for a book!)

REFERENCES

Abram, D. (1996) in *The spell of the sensuous: Perception and language in a more-than-human world.* Vintage Books.

———. (2010) *Becoming animal: An earthly cosmology.* Vintage Books.

Acampora, R. R. (2006). *Corporal compassion: Animal ethics and philosophy of body.* University of Pittsburgh Press.

Applebaum, M. (2022). Saying before the said: Phenomenological reflections on Gertrud Schwing's "A Way to the Souls of the Mentally Ill". *The Humanistic Psychologist.* Advance online publication. https://doi.org/10.1037/hum0000268

Bakewell, S. (2016). *At the existentialist café: Freedom, being, and apricot cocktails.* Other Books.

Bellacasa, M. P. (2017) *Matters of care: Speculative ethics in more than human worlds.* University of Minnesota Press.

Churchill, S. D. (1997). The alchemy of male desire: Femininity as totem and taboo. In S. Marlan (Ed.), *Fire in the stone: The alchemy of desire* (pp. 179–206). Chiron.

———. (2003). Gestural communication with a bonobo: Empathy, alterity, and carnal intersubjectivity. *Constructivism and the Human Sciences* 8(1), 19–36.

———. (2004a, July). Exploring the "in between": Second person perspectives on interpersonal life. In F. C. Richardson (Chair), *Relationality in theory, practice, and research—Exploring the space between.* Invited Symposium presented at the 112th Annual Convention of the American Psychological Association, Honolulu, July 30, 2004.

———. (2004b, October). Through a looking-glass—The bonobo and I: A "second-person" perspective on interspecies communication. Paper presented at the 29th International Meeting of the Merleau-Ponty Circle, Muhlenberg College, October 1, 2004.

———. (2006). Encountering the animal other: Reflections on moments of empathic seeing. *The Indo-Pacific Journal of Phenomenology: Special Issue on Methodology* 6, 1–13. Retrieved from http://www.ipjp.org/index.php?option=com_jdownloads&Itemid=25&task=view.download&cid=60

———. (2007). Experiencing the other within the we: Phenomenology with a bonobo. In L. Embree and T. Nenon (Eds.), *Phenomenology 2005,* vol. IV, *Selected Essays from North America* (pp. 147–70). Zeta E-Books.

———. (2010). "Second person" perspectivity in observing and understanding emotional expression. In L. Embree, M. Barber, & T. Nenon (Eds.), *Phenomenology 2010,* vol. 5: *Selected Essays from North America. Part 2: Phenomenology beyond Philosophy* (pp. 81–106). Zeta Books/Arghos-Diffusion.

———. (2012, September). Teaching phenomenology by way of "second-person perspectivity." *Indo-Pacific Journal of Phenomenology* 12, Special Edition.

———. (2013). Heideggerian pathways through trauma and recovery: A "hermeneutics of facticity." *The Humanistic Psychologist* 41(3), 219–30.

———. (2014) At the crossroads of humanistic psychology and positive psychology. *The Humanistic Psychologist* 42(1), 1–5. DOI: 0.1080/08873267.2014.891902

———. (2016). Resonating with meaning in the lives of others: Invitation to empathic understanding. In C.T. Fischer, R. Brooke, & L. Laubscher (Eds.), *The Qualitative Vision for Psychology: An Invitation to a Human Science Approach* (pp. 91–116). Duquesne University Press.

———. (2018). On the empathic mode of intuition: A phenomenological foundation for social psychiatry. In M. Englander (Ed.), *Phenomenology and the social context of psychiatry* (pp. 65–93). Bloomsbury.

———. (2022). *Essentials of existential phenomenological research.* American Psychological Association.

Churchill, S. D., & Mruk, C. J. (2014). Practicing what we preach in humanistic and positive psychology. *American Psychologist* 69, 90–92.

Dilthey, W. (1977). The understanding of other persons and their expressions of life (K. L. Heiges, Trans.). In W. Dilthey, *Descriptive psychology and historical understanding* (pp. 121–14). Martinus Nijhoff. (Original work published 1927).

Englander, M. (2018). Empathy in a social psychiatry. In M. Englander (Ed.), *Phenomenology and the social context of psychiatry: Social relations, psychopathology, and Husserl's philosophy* (pp. 49–64). Bloomsbury Academic.

Farin, I., & Hart, J.G. (2006). Translators' preface. In E. Husserl, *The basic problems of phenomenology: From the lectures, winter semester, 1910–1911* (trans. I. Farin & J. G. Hart, pp. xiii–xxxvi). Springer.

Gendlin, E. T. (1978). *Focusing*. Bantam Books.

Goffman, E. (1959). *The presentation of self in everyday life.* Anchor Books.

Heidegger, M. (1962). *Being and time* (J. MacQuarrie & E. Robinson, Trans.). Harper & Row. (Original work published 1927)

———. (1971). The origin of the work of art (A. Hofstadter, Trans.). In M. Heidegger, *Poetry, language, thought (A. Hofstadter, Trans.)* (17–87), Harper & Row. (Original lecture delivered 1935 and revision published 1960)

———. (1972). *On time and being* (J. Stambaugh, Trans.). Harper & Row. (Original work published 1969)

———. (1995). *The fundamental concepts of metaphysics: World, finitude, solitude* (W. McNeill & N. Walker, Trans.). Indiana University Press. (Original lecture course given 1929–1930 and published 1983)

———. (2001). *Phenomenological interpretations of Aristotle: Initiation into phenomenological research* (R. Rojcewicz, Trans.). Indiana University Press. (Original lecture course given 1921–1922 and published 1985)

Holdrege, C. (2003, Spring). How does a mole view the world? *In Context #9* (The Nature Institute), 16–18.

Husserl, E. (1952). *Ideen zu einer reinen Phenomenologie und phenomenologischen Philosophie II: Phenomenologische Untersuchungen zur Konstitution* [Ideas pertaining to a pure phenomenology and to a phenomenological philosophy. Second Book: Phenomenological investigations of constitution]. In *Husserliana*_(Vol. 4). Martinus Nijhoff.

———. (1973). *Zur Phänomenologie der Intersubjektivität* [Towards a phenomenology of intersubjectivity]. In E. Husserl, *Husserliana* 13, 14, 15. Martinus Nijhoff. (Original works written 1905–1935)

———. (1989). *Ideas pertaining to a pure phenomenology and to a phenomenological philosophy, Second Book: Studies in the phenomenology of constitution* (R. Rojcewicz & A. Schuwer, Trans.). Kluwer. (Original work written 1928 and published posthumously in 1952)

———. (2006). *The basic problems of phenomenology: From the lectures, winter semester, 1910–1911* (trans. I. Farin & J.G. Hart). Springer.

Jager, B. (2010). About "doing science" and "contemplating the human condition": Address to the International Human Science Research Conference at Molde, Norway, June 2009 *The Humanistic Psychologist* 38, 67–94.

Kearney, R. (2021) *Touch: Recovering our most vital sense.* Columbia University Press.

Levinas, E. (1969). *Totality and infinity* (A. Lingis, Trans.). Duquesne University Press. (Original work published 1961)

Lingis, A. (1994). *The community of those who have nothing in common.* Indiana University Press.

———. (2018). *The Alphonso Lingis reader* (T. Sparrow, Ed.). University of Minnesota Press.

Lloyd, R. J., & Smith, S. J. (2015). Motion-sensing phenomenology. In K. Tobin and S. R. Steinberg (Eds.), *Doing educational research: A handbook* (2nd ed., pp. 255–78), Sense Publishers.

Maslow, A. H. (1970). *Motivation and personality* (2nd ed.). Harper & Row.

Merleau-Ponty, M. (1962). *Phenomenology of perception* (C. Smith, Trans.). Routledge & Kegan Paul. (Original work published 1945)

———. (1964a). *Signs* (R. C. McCleary, Trans.). Northwestern University Press. (Original work published 1960)

———. (1964b). The child's relations with others (W. Cobb, Trans.). In M. Merleau-Ponty, *The primacy of perception* (J. Edie, Ed.). Northwestern University Press. (Original work published, 1961).

———. (1964d). The film and the new psychology (H. L. Dreyfus & P. A. Dreyfus, Trans.). In M. Merleau-Ponty, *Sense and non-sense* (pp. 48–59), Northwestern University Press. (Original lecture delivered March 13, 1945)

———. (1968). *The visible and the invisible* (A. Lingis, Trans.). Northwestern University Press. (Original work published, 1964).

———. (1970). *Themes from the Lectures at the College de France 1952–1960* (J. O'Neill, trans.). Northwestern University Press.

———. (2003). *Nature: Course notes from the College de France* (R. Vallier, Trans.). Northwestern University Press. (Original work published 1995)

O'Brien, S. (2008). *Wesley the owl: The remarkable love story of an owl and his girl.* Simon & Schuster.

Polanyi, Michael. (1966). *The tacit dimension*. Doubleday.

Rosan, P. J. (2012): The poetics of intersubjective life: Empathy and the other. *The Humanistic Psychologist* 40(2), 115–35 DOI: http://dx.doi.org/10.1080/08873267.2012.643685

Sartre, J.-P. (1948). *The psychology of imagination* (B. Frechtman, Trans.). Philosophical Library. (Original work published 1940)

Scheler, M. (1954). *Wesen und Formen der Sympathie* [Essence and forms of sympathy] (P. Heath, Trans.). Yale. (Original work published 1923).

———. (1973). *Wesen und formen der Sympathie*. Francke Verlag.

Seligman, M. E., & M. Csikszentmihaly. (2000). Positive Psychology: An Introduction.*American Psychologist* 55(1): 5–14. doi: 10.1037//0003-066x.55.1.5.

Shapiro, K. J. (1985). *Bodily reflective modes: A phenomenological method for psychology*. Duke University Press.

Shapiro, Kenneth J. (1990). Understanding dogs through kinesthetic empathy, social construction, and history. *Anthrozoos* 3(3), 184–95. Reprinted in C. Flynn, Ed., *Social creatures: A human and animal studies reader* (pp. 31–49). Lantern, 2008.

———. (1994). The caring sleuth: Portrait of an animal rights activist. *Society and Animals 2*, 145–67.

———. (2015). "I am a vegetarian": Reflections on a way of being. *Society and Animals* 23, 128–47.

———. (2018). A faith built on awe: Reframing atheism. *Worldviews: Global religion, culture, and ecology* 22, 199–215.

Sheets-Johnstone, M. (2011) *The primacy of movement* (expanded second edition). John Benjamin Publishing Co.

Smith, S. J. (2017) The vitality of humanimality: From the perspective of life phenomenology. *Phenomenology & Practice* 11(1), 72–88.

———. (2018). Bringing up life with horses. *Indo-Pacific Journal of Phenomenology* 18(2), 1–11.

Sontag, S. (2003). *Regarding the pain of others.* Picador.

Spitz, R. (1983). *Dialogues from infancy* (R. N. Emde, Ed.). International Universities Press.

Thompson, E., ed. (2001). *Between ourselves: Second-person issues in the study of consciousness*. Imprint Academic.

Ticktin, M., & Wijsman, K. (2017). Maria Puig de la Bellacasa. *Matters of care: Speculative ethics in more than human worlds*. University of Minnesota Press. *Hypatia Reviews Online,* Cambridge University Press: October 1, 2021.

Waterman, A. S. (2013). The humanistic-positive psychology divide: Contrasts in philosophical foundations. *American Psychologist*, 68, 124–33.

Wohlleben, P. (2015) *The hidden life of trees: What they feel, how they communicate—Discoveries from a secret world* (J. Billinghurst, Trans.). Greystone Books.

———. (2021) *The heartbeat of trees: Embracing our ancient bond with forests and nature* (J. Billinghurst, Trans.). Greystone Books.

Zahavi, D. (2003). Husserl's intersubjective transformation of transcendental philosophy. In D. Welton (Ed.), *The new Husserl: A critical reader* (pp. 233–51). Indiana University Press.

Chapter 17

Fictional Empathy, Imagination, and Knowledge of Value

Íngrid Vendrell Ferran

ABSTRACT

This chapter maintains that empathy with fictional characters, or fictional empathy, is morally valuable insofar as it can provide the empathizer with knowledge of values. More precisely, it argues that fictional empathy enables the empathizer to become imaginatively acquainted with the other's values, even if these values are different from one's own. After motivating the topic in the introduction, the chapter presents some thoughts about the epistemology of value and empathy, establishing a distinction between direct and imaginative acquaintance with values. Next, it argues that empathy can lead the empathizer to co-experience the other's values and, in so doing, make her directly or imaginatively acquainted with them. The chapter then discuss a possible challenge concerning the epistemic function of the imagination and explores different ways in which we can become imaginatively acquainted with values. It then examines features of fiction that explain why fictional empathy might be better suited than empathy for real others in pursuing this task. The chapter closes by providing some reasons why we should regard the imaginative acquaintance with value attained through fictional empathy as morally valuable.

Keywords: empathy, fiction, fictional empathy, value, knowledge of value, acquaintance, empathic acquaintance, imaginative acquaintance, imaginative scaffolding, testimony

INTRODUCTION

Empathy with fictional characters, or fictional empathy, has mostly been regarded as a crucial aspect of our aesthetic experience and its role in appreciation has been widely discussed.[1] Yet, fictional empathy is not just an aesthetically relevant aspect of our engagement with fictions; it can also have moral significance. In the literature on the moral value of fiction, it has been argued that fictional empathy enables the empathizer to explore minds which are different from one's own, leads the empathizer to understand central aspects of the human condition, and helps the empathizer to train abilities, which are necessary for empathizing with real others (see, e.g., Feagin 1996; Gabriel 2014; Nussbaum 1990). Without denying that fictional empathy can be morally significant in all these different respects, this chapter explores an aspect that has received far less attention. In my view, one of the reasons why fictional empathy is morally valuable is that it can provide the empathizer with *knowledge of values*, (i.e., of evaluative properties such as the unfair, the brave, the threatening, etc.).[2] More precisely, as I shall argue, fictional empathy enables the empathizer to become *imaginatively acquainted with the other's values* even if these are different from one's own values.[3] To give an example: Suppose that your life has been a bed of roses and you have never experienced the unfair, empathizing with Silas Marner's indignation in George Eliot's novel of the same name, you might become acquainted with it.

The idea that empathy with real others and fictional characters enables us to "co-experience" the other's experiences and, in so doing, give us access to the other's world of values was already formulated by Stein (1989) and further developed for the specific case of the cognition of literary works by Ingarden (1973). Though I adopt this idea here, I will elaborate my account not by means of an historical investigation of these authors (for an accurate analysis of both, see Mitscherling 2020), but by employing recent developments in the philosophy of empathy, emotion, and imagination. Moreover, I will not only argue that fictional empathy, like empathy for real others, can make us acquainted with values but also that on certain occasions the former seems to be better suited than the latter to pursue this task.

The chapter starts with some thoughts about the epistemology of value and empathy, establishing a distinction between direct and imaginative acquaintance with values. Next, it argues that empathy can lead the empathizer to co-experience the other's values and, in so doing, make her directly or imaginatively acquainted with them. It discusses a possible challenge concerning the epistemic function of the imagination and explores different ways in which we can become imaginatively acquainted with values. The chapter then examines features of fiction that explain why fictional empathy can be better suited to this task than empathy for real others. It ends by providing some reasons why we should regard the imaginative acquaintance attained through fictional empathy as morally valuable.

THE EPISTEMOLOGY OF VALUE AND EMPATHY: DIRECT AND IMAGINATIVE ACQUAINTANCE

Knowledge of value might come in different forms: acquaintance and truth (for a similar distinction, see Hildebrand 1982: 28). We can attain knowledge of values by *becoming acquainted with them*. This happens for instance when we have an immediate consciousness of values without the intermediation of inferences. This is the case when we see the unfairness of a situation, perceive the braveness of an action, or experience the wrongness of an emotional response (see Drummond 2009; Engelsen 2018; Mulligan 2010). Yet, we can also obtain knowledge of value by learning *propositional truths about them*. For instance, we can learn that certain types of situations are usually unfair, certain actions brave, and certain emotional reactions wrong, and so on, and apply these learned truths to particular contexts.

I take here acquaintance and truth to be distinct cognitive achievements. It can happen that we know many propositional truths about a value, and yet we have never experienced it. For instance, we can know a lot of things about unfairness while never having been a victim of it. Moreover, even when we know many propositional truths about a value, the experience of a value adds something new to our propositional knowledge about it. The first time we experience an instance of unfairness, this experience adds something new to the knowledge of truths we had about it. We can also have the experience of something being unfair and though this experience might lead us to propositional truths about unfairness, the experience itself is not reducible to these truths.

Acquaintance and truth might influence one another. By being acquainted with a value, we can derive truths about it. Having experienced the unfair, we might obtain propositional truths about unfairness. Moreover, knowing truths about a value, this might shape our acquaintance of it. For instance, having learned many truths about unfairness can help us to recognize it when we first experience it.

From both kinds of knowledge, this chapter will be concerned only with *acquaintance with values*. I am interested in cases in which a value is presented to our mind without inferences. More specifically, it will investigate how *empathy* can make the empathizer acquainted with values and the role that *imagining* plays in it. This use of the term *acquaintance* in the context of empathy, in particular fictional empathy, and of imagination prompts the question of what exactly is meant by this term.

The cases of acquaintance with value described previously (e.g., seeing the unfairness of a situation) are cases in which there is a *first-personal* experience of value. The term *acquaintance* here is employed in a similar sense to that set out by Russell (2013). According to Russell, we can become acquainted with sense-data, with the contents of our minds by memory and introspection and with universals (i.e., general ideas such as whiteness, diversity, and brotherhood) (46). Acquaintance with an object can be precise and accurate without being reducible to a sum of statements about it. We are acquainted with a color (e.g., blue) when we see it, not when we have learned many truths about the color (the latter would be "knowledge by description"). Though Russell does not speak about acquaintance with values, my thought here is that just as we can get acquainted with a color by seeing it, so too we could think about becoming *directly* acquainted with a value by experiencing it (e.g., experiencing unfairness). This acquaintance is a form of cognitive achievement that is not reducible to the acquisition of truths about values. Moreover, it comes in different degrees of precision and accuracy.

However, insofar as I defend the claim that empathy can make us acquainted with values, the use of the concept of acquaintance here differs from Russell's understanding of the term. While for Russell we cannot be acquainted with another's mind (for him, we can have knowledge of another's mind only by description), I regard empathy as a way of becoming acquainted with another's mental states (and, in so doing, with the other's values). The kind of acquaintance provided by empathy is not the first-person acquaintance that Russell has in mind in his examples. Indeed, the object we become acquainted with through empathy is not given first personally to the empathizer because it belongs to the other's experience. In this respect, Zahavi has insightfully described empathy as providing "a special kind of knowledge by *acquaintance*. It is not the standard first-person acquaintance, but rather a distinct other-acquaintance" (2017: 39). In brief, for Zahavi there is what I want to call here an *empathic acquaintance*, which differs from the first-person acquaintance provided by our own experience.

Are all kinds of empathic acquaintance of the same kind? For Zahavi, in face-to-face encounters, the empathized experience is given to us directly (i.e., we *perceive* it in the other's expression). In his view, what first-person acquaintance and empathic acquaintance have in common is that in both cases we are directly acquainted with things. Therefore, there is what can be called a *direct empathic acquaintance*. In perceiving the other's mental states in empathy, I become acquainted directly and immediately with what the other is going through.[4]

In my view, empathic acquaintance is also possible when there is no direct perception of the other and we have to imagine what the other is going through. The empathic acquaintance in these cases is not direct but mediated by the imagination, and therefore, it has nothing to do with Russell's concept of acquaintance. These cases involve *imaginative acquaintance*,[5] which I take here to be a special kind of acquaintance in which we do not directly experience a thing but rather experientially imagine it. This form of acquaintance plays an important role in our psychology. For instance, we might try to imagine what maternal love feels like even if we do not have a child, or how it is to experience unfairness even if we ourselves have never been victims of it. We use all that we know about these things (this involves knowledge of propositional truths about these things as well as acquaintance with similar things) and try to generate imaginings about them to get imaginatively acquainted with the mentioned experiences. Though we can question how far or how good we can get acquainted with a thing via imagining, my thought is that when our imaginings are correctly guided and we have enough imaginative powers, we can get imaginatively acquainted with a thing and, in so doing, get close to direct acquaintance with a thing.[6] Some might regard the use of the term *acquaintance* in the cases in which imaginings are involved as derivative or even inappropriate, but I want to stick to the term for two reasons. First, because it indicates that we are aware of something presented to our mind without the use of inferences. Moreover, in my view, the imagination, when correctly applied, can provide us with a kind of surrogate experience of something and, in so doing, make us imaginatively acquainted with it. When imaginative acquaintance takes place in the context of empathy, we can speak of an *imaginative empathic acquaintance*.

In my view, imaginative empathic acquaintance can occur in two different contexts. The acquaintance is imaginative when we empathize with real others who are spatiotemporally beyond the reach of our perception and when the other is a fictional character. In both cases, empathy requires that we imagine what the other is going through, but in the former our imaginings are guided by the *testimony* of others, while in the latter they are guided by the *fictional work* (in this respect, the distinction between direct and imaginative acquaintance does not overlap with the distinction between real and fictional empathy).

In what follows, I will concentrate on the following three cases of empathic acquaintance with values:

1. *Direct* empathic acquaintance with value via *perception* (e.g., in seeing the other's indignation, I become immediately and directly acquainted with the unfairness she is suffering);

2. *Imaginative* empathic acquaintance with value via *testimony* (e.g., in reading about what a person who lived in the fifteenth century went through, I become imaginatively acquainted with the unfairness she suffered);
3. *Imaginative* empathic acquaintance with value via *fiction* (e.g., in reading about what a fictional character is going through, I become imaginatively acquainted with the unfairness she is suffering).

Table 17.1

Direct Acquaintance	First-Person Acquaintance	
	Empathic Acquaintance	Perception (1)
Imaginative Acquaintance	First-Person Acquaintance	
	Empathic Acquaintance	Testimony (2)
		Fiction (3)

In the next section, I will examine how cases 1, 2 and 3 are possible. I will then analyze how, via imaginings, we can get acquainted with something new in cases 2 and 3. Then, I will argue that case 3 can more probably, easily, and accurately provide us with acquaintance with values than cases 1 and 2.

EMPATHY, CO-EXPERIENCE, AND ACQUAINTANCE WITH VALUES

I argue that on certain occasions (fictional and nonfictional) empathy might enable the empathizer to co-experience the other's values.[7] As I shall demonstrate, it is by virtue of this co-experience that the empathizer can become (depending on the case, directly or imaginatively) acquainted with the other's values. To this end, I will examine key features of empathy and elaborate a model that explains how (direct and imaginative) *empathic acquaintance* with the other's values is possible.

In Empathy, We *Apprehend* the Other's Experience

In empathy, the empathizer grasps what the other is going through. In this respect, empathy has been described as a "success term" (Feagin 1996: 3; Gibson 2016: 238; John 2017: 307). The question about the mechanism at work in this apprehension has been highly controversial. Proponents of the "theory-theory" endorse the view that the empathizer has a folk-psychological theory of mind about the other (Carruthers and Smith 1996);

"simulationists" claim that the empathizer recreates and reenacts the other's experience (Goldman 2006; Stueber 2006); and proponents of "perceptual accounts" argue that we are able to directly perceive the other's experience in her expression (Zahavi 2011)—for an overview, see Schmetkamp and Vendrell Ferran (2020).

I adopt a pluralist view according to which the other's experience can be provided by perceptions or imaginings. The version of pluralism that I have in mind defends a direct perception account of the other's mental states in face-to-face interactions, while simultaneously acknowledging that on other occasions the apprehension of the other's experience requires the use of imaginings. Indeed, though the perceptual account works well for those cases in which we immediately and directly see the other's shame in her blushing, or the sadness in her bodily expression, without necessarily having to adopt the other's perspective, the perceptual account cannot be applied to the case of empathy with others who are outside our perceptual horizon. In the latter cases, empathy requires that we adopt the other's perspective and experientially imagine what they are going through. Indeed, we cannot perceive the mental states of someone living on the other side of the world, or someone who lived in the fifteenth century, or a fictional character; in these cases, empathy necessitates our ability to imagine.

This Apprehension Is Oriented toward *the Other*

The empathizer not only apprehends the other's experience but is also aware that the apprehended mental states belong to the other's experiential horizon (no matter whether the other is a real human being or a fictional character). Empathy is not a question of putting ourselves in another's shoes and experiencing what it would be like "for us" to be in the other's situation (self-orientation). Rather, for empathy it is necessary that we apprehend how it is "for the other" to be in her situation (other-orientation). Note that though this distinction between self- and other-orientation frequently appears in contributions that regard empathy as involving perspective-taking (see, for instance, Coplan 2011), the pluralist view adopted above acknowledges the possibility that in cases in which we directly perceive the other's mental states, empathy occurs without perspective-taking. However, perspective-taking is always involved in cases of empathy with others who are spatio-temporally distant from us or fictional characters. That said, it is crucial for my argument here that, by virtue of this other-orientation, the empathizer can come into contact with aspects of other's psychology even if these are very different from one's own.

The Empathizer Targets *the Other's Affective States*

To become acquainted with the other's values, the empathizer has to target the other's affective states. This includes not only emotions (e.g., fear) but also the wide array of states belonging to the affective family such as moods (e.g., anxiety), sentiments (e.g., hate), vital feelings (e.g., vitality), and so on. I do not claim here that all instances of empathy target the other's affective states, i.e., that it involves an "affectivity requirement"; rather my claim here is that for the possibility to become acquainted with the other's values, empathy has to focus on the other's affective states. Thus, a detractor of the "affectivity requirement" can nonetheless accept my model as a particular case of empathy.[8]

The Empathizer Can Apprehend the *Values* Linked to the Other's Affective States.

A general point on which cognitive theories of emotion of phenomenological and analytical provenience agree is that affective states are linked to values. More precisely, affective states present us their objects not as being neutral, but as having an evaluative character that invites us to take a pro or contra attitude (for representatives of this view, see Scheler 1973; Goldie 2000). In this view, it is intrinsic to the intentional structure of affective states that they are linked to values. In this vein, values have been regarded as the "formal objects" of the affective states (e.g., de Sousa 1987). The key idea is that each affective state is linked to a value or to a series of values. For instance, the objects targeted by fear are always threatening; the objects targeted by disgust appear always to be disgusting, and so on. The formal objects have been distinguished from the "material objects" of affective states (i.e., the things, animals, persons, situations, etc.) targeted during an affective state (the locus classicus of this distinction can be found in Kenny 1963). For instance, my fear can be directed toward a lion, a neighbor, a storm, and so on. Unlike the formal objects, the material objects are not restricted, and they are also subjected to cultural, social, individual variations.

I take this intimate link between affectivity and value to be crucial to understand why in empathizing with the other's affective states, the empathizer can become acquainted with values. My thought is that if you empathize with the other's fear (affective state), you will also be able to apprehend that the other experiences something as threatening (value). Indeed, given that fear is intrinsically linked to the threatening (i.e., the threatening is the formal object of fear), when you apprehend the other's fear, you apprehend that she is experiencing something as threatening.

Fear is an example of emotion. In my view, the same thought can be extended to affective states other than the emotions. However, it should be noted that not all affective states are linked to values in the same way. In fact, the relation between affective states and values varies in light of the type of affective state we are dealing with. These variations have not been sufficiently investigated in current research because the latter has mainly studied the emotions and has not attempted to develop a map of the affective mind. Yet, the rough picture that I have in mind here is the following: (a) emotions *respond to evaluative properties* of the objects they target (my fear responds to a threat); (b) moods make us *more sensitive to clusters of evaluative properties* (my anxiety makes me more sensitive to the menacing, threatening, disappointing, etc.); (c) sentiments are responsible for *presenting* their objects *under a certain evaluative light* (hate makes me apprehend the hated object as repugnant, odious, evil, etc.); (d) general feelings are ways in which we experience the *evaluative possibilities* of our environment (vitality makes the world appear full of positive possibilities). These differences are important when it comes to concrete cases of empathy. When I empathize with the other's fear, I am aware that this fear is a response to a threat; when I empathize with the other's anxiety, I am aware that she is more prone to experience the menacing, the threatening, and so on; when I empathize with her hate, I apprehend also that the hated object appears to her as embodying a series of disvalues; in empathizing with the other's vitality, I apprehend that for her the world is full of positive opportunities; and so on. But for my argument in this section, these differences are irrelevant since what counts is that by virtue of an intrinsic link between affectivity and value, when we apprehend the other's affective states we can also apprehend the evaluative character of the other's experience. Thus, even if one does not agree with the map of the affective mind provided above, one can accept the general idea of my argument.

Does this apprehension of values involve an apprehension of the objects in which these values are given? The answer is no. Empathizing with the other's fear, I comprehend that something is threatening for her. However, I do not necessarily know what this something is. It could be that the other's fear is directed toward receiving bad news about a medical diagnosis, being haunted by a ghost or being bitten by a rabid dog. Empathizing with the other's fear does not involve necessarily knowing what the material object of her fear is.

The reason why the empathizer can get a grasp of the formal object (i.e., the values linked to the other's experience) but not of the material objects is that the material objects of affective states are contingent, individual, and culturally learned, while the formal objects of affective states are delimited. There are many things which can be the material object of fear, but the formal object of fear is always threatening. Therefore, in empathizing with the other's fear, it is clear to the empathizer that the other has apprehended something as threatening. The central thought of my argument is that the empathizer can get a grasp of the evaluative properties linked to the other's experience.

Can we apprehend values that we have never experienced before? Insofar as we can apprehend via direct perceptions or via imagining the other's affective states even if we have never experienced them, we can apprehend the values linked to these affective states in virtue of the intrinsic link between affective states and values. Thus, insofar as I can apprehend that the other is experiencing fear, anxiety, hate, or vitality even if I have never been in these states, I can get a grasp of how the world appears to her as not being neutral but as evaluatively tinctured in a certain way.

Can the value(s) linked to the other's affective states be apprehended in detail? The apprehension is in my view a question of degree. The formal object, that is, the value(s) linked to the other's affective state, might be complex and fine-grained. I do not claim here that in empathy we can always apprehend it with precision and in its full richness. On certain occasions, the empathizer can apprehend the value linked to the other's experience only coarsely, for instance, identifying that it is something positive or negative (i.e., as a value or disvalue). On other occasions, by contrast, the empathizer can get a more precise grasp of it. In short, empathy admits degrees of accuracy.

The Empathizer Experiences Something *Similar* to the Other's Experience

Empathy requires that the empathizer "resonates" with the other by experiencing something similar (see Stueber 2017). This has been called the "interpersonal similarity requirement." In my view it would be odd to claim that we are empathizing with the other's suffering without somehow experiencing what the other is undergoing. This does not necessarily imply that we suffer. Rather it means that we come to co-experience what the other is going through. I would describe cases in which we apprehend the other's suffering but remain unaffected about it as instances of mindreading rather than empathy.

This requirement must be distinguished from two similar but fundamentally different phenomena. On the one hand, empathy should be distinguished from emotional contagion. While in emotional contagion we are not aware that we have been infected by the other, empathy requires the preservation of the self-other differentiation. For empathy, the other's mental states are experienced as belonging to the other. On the other hand, empathy, unlike sympathy, does not require that we care for the other. The empathic torturer is aware of the target's pain, she co-experiences the other's suffering though not herself being in pain, but does not care about her.

By Virtue of This Similarity, The Empathizer Can *Co-Experience the Other's Values*

To explain how a co-experience is possible, we have to elucidate which aspects of both experiences are similar. Most accounts argue that the similarity concerns the "qualitative character" of the empathizer's and the other's affective states. This view has been defended in different versions by Coplan (2011: 6), Feagin (1996: 100), and Stueber (2016: 372). While the former two authors argue that the qualitative character must be the same, Stueber defends a more reasonable view according to which it suffices that both experiences are qualitatively similar. Yet, though intuitively plausible, this account does not provide us with clear-cut criteria to determine the qualitative similarity between the empathizer and the other's mental states.

One possible way to deal with this problem would be to focus on the different dimensions responsible for determining the quality of an affective experience such as intensity, depth, or hedonic valence (to name but a few), and elaborate criteria on their basis. Yet, none of these qualitative dimensions can provide us with clear criteria to determine whether two affective states are similar. For instance, both envy and sadness can be intense, deep, and unpleasant. However, we would not say that an empathizer who feels envy in empathizing with the other's sadness is undergoing a similar experience.

Alternatively, we could focus on a further qualitative dimension of affective experiences: the phenomenal nature or the "what it feels like." Each affective experience feels a certain way: how sadness feels differs from how envy feels. Could a focus on the "what it feels like" explain the qualitative similarity between the empathizer's and the other's affective states? This alternative is attractive because at the intuitive level we can easily state that the phenomenal character or the "what it feels like" of sadness is similar to worry, disappointment, and concern but is dissimilar to envy whose phenomenal quality is similar to jealousy. Yet, to pin down the specific criteria on the basis of which we consider two states similar regarding their respective "what it feels likes" is more difficult because an analysis of the constitutive elements of the phenomenal character of emotional experiences is missing.

A further alternative consists in focusing on the "intentional structure" of the empathizer's and the other's affective states. This alternative has some advantages. One point in its favor is that the intentional structure of affective states has been widely studied in current research, and we possess the necessary conceptual resources to analyze it in more detail than its phenomenal character. Moreover, since the phenomenology of an experience is intimately linked to its intentionality (Horgan and Tienson 2002), this alternative would explain why both experiences are also qualitatively similar. Such an approach has been developed by Gallagher (2012: 360). In his view, in the empathizer knowing that the other feels sad about an injustice, she is also sad about it. The intentional structure of the empathizer's sadness is similar to the other's affective state, but their experiences are not the same since both are in different situations. This idea is insightful, yet it needs refining because the complex structure of intentional states can be analyzed in more detail.

In my view, this similarity concerns two aspects of the intentional structure of the empathizer's and other's states. First, as seen previously, in empathizing with the other we can apprehend with different degrees of accuracy the evaluative character of her experience. Thus, one aspect which is similar between both is this evaluative content (i.e., the value linked to her affective experience). In empathizing with the other's sadness, I not only apprehend that the other is responding to a disvalue, but my experience must also have as evaluative content this disvalue too. Second, the attitude adopted by the empathizer toward this evaluative property must be of the same evaluative kind as the other's attitude. Thus, if the target's sadness involves an attitude of disapproval, disliking, rejection toward the disvalue, the empathizer must adopt an attitude which is of the same negative evaluative kind toward it. Therefore, all negative attitudes (which might be one of rejection, disapproval, dislike, etc.) toward the disvalue fulfill the similarity requirement.

By virtue of this similarity of content and attitude, the empathizer can co-experience the other's values even if these are different from her own. Indeed, the empathizer comes to co-experience with different degrees of accuracy the evaluative content of the other's experience and the other's attitude toward it. Since intentionality has a phenomenology too, the empathizer's experience is similar to that of the other in terms of their respective experience of "what it is like". In so doing, the empathizer experiences something similar to what the other is going through without being herself in the same state as the other.

This Co-Experience Gives the Empathizer an *Acquaintance with the Other's Values*

Insofar as empathy involves a co-experience of what the other is going through, it can make the empathizer acquainted with the other's values. Though the other's experience belongs to her experiential horizon and not to mine, I can co-experience, either in direct apprehension or mediated by imaginings, the values linked to the other's experience.

As stated, acquaintance is a question of degree. Thus, while the other's acquaintance with value can be precise, the acquaintance that empathy can provide admits degrees of accuracy. While the other can fear something threatening and this threat can be given to her with many nuances and shades (e.g., the threatening-disgusting), our empathy with her fear can provide us with a less detailed view of the quality experienced by her. However, it can also be the case that our empathy is accurate and we grasp the shades in which the threat is presented to her.

EMPATHY, IMAGINATION, AND IMAGINATIVE ACQUAINTANCE WITH VALUE

In the previous section, I argued that empathy can make us acquainted with values. This involves cases in which we directly co-experience the other's values in face-to-face encounters as well as cases in which we imaginatively co-experience them via testimony or fiction. This poses the following question: Can the empathizer through imagination become acquainted with new values in the same way as an empathizer through face-to-face encounters can? In direct empathic acquaintance, that is, when we see the other's fear, anxiety, hate, vitality in her bodily expression, we can become acquainted with aspects of values we were not previously acquainted with. This includes new value bearers, value nuances, value constellations, value hierarchies, and even new values.[9] Take for instance the case in which you see the other's fear in her face when she hears about her medical diagnosis: Here you can become acquainted with a situation in which a medical diagnosis presents a threat, the nuance of the deadly threat, the hierarchy in which health is the most precious value, the constellation in which the threat appears to be linked to the sadness, and so on. Or take the case in which you have never experienced unfairness, but in seeing the other's indignation about an injustice you come to directly co-experience the unfairness. Can our imagination also make us acquainted with all this? For many philosophers such as Sartre (2004), we cannot learn something new from the imagination because imagining presupposes that we already know what it is to imagine.

To overrule this objection let me specify first some ways in which imagining can put us in contact with something new. Kind, one of the most prominent authors in this field, has argued that we can learn something new from the imagination via the process of "imaginative scaffolding." This process consists of imagining combinations of additions, subtractions, and modifications of experiences we have already undergone (Kind 2020). I take Kind's idea of an imaginative scaffolding as a point of departure, but instead of speaking of a unique process, I regard imaginative scaffolding as comprising a set of distinct processes which deserve to be analyzed separately.

The first process is the "application" of a known feature to a novel situation. What changes here is the situation but not the feature which is already familiar to us. This process consists of an imaginative transposition of already known features to a different context.

The second process comprises a "variation" in the imagination of an aspect already familiar to us. Here the feature is known to us, but we try to modify it slightly via imagination so that we can become acquainted with a new aspect or shade of it.

The third process is a "combination" of features that are already known to us but that are compounded in a novel manner. The imagination here mingles in a novel way with features which are already familiar to us. As a result, one can become aware of features which can vary from those one already knows to different degrees.

These three processes can be applied to the case of an imaginative acquaintance with values of others who are distant from us and who are fictional characters. In my view, what we know about the other's experience through testimony or through fiction can guide the empathizer in these imaginative processes suggesting how to construe new scenarios in which values are involved. The empathizer uses what she already knows about values and applies this knowledge to new contexts, varying it in different respects, and combining it in new forms according to the indications of testimony or fictional work. In so doing, she can become acquainted with aspects of values which are new to her.

So that these imaginative processes make the empathizer acquainted with the other's values, the testimony of the other and the fictional work must be good guides to our imaginings. Not only must they provide us with the key elements of what we have to imagine, but the experiential imaginings that they generate must also be close to the direct experiences of the values in question. Moreover, we must be good imagineers too.

There are some factors which might propel and support the imaginative processes that lead to acquaintance with values. On the one hand, the process will be easier if the empathizer, despite not having experienced the values or similar values before, possesses propositional knowledge about them. This knowledge of propositional truths about the values would enable the empathizer to more precisely construct the other's experience and the values linked to it. On the other hand, acquaintance with value will be favored by the fact that the empathizer is already acquainted with similar values or similar situations in which the value is given.

By virtue of these imaginative processes, the aspects of values that the empathizer might become imaginatively acquainted with are in principle the same as the empathizer might become directly acquainted with in face-to-face encounters.

New Value Bearers

Using the first route of applying an already known feature to a new context, testimony, and fiction might enable the empathizer to become acquainted with new bearers of value. Consider the case that an empathizer is familiar with experiencing something as threatening but has never experienced a medical diagnosis as representing a threat. Yet, the testimony of others or fiction might lead her to apply this known evaluative property to a different context and in so doing come to know that a medical diagnosis can be fearful. In this case, she will discover a new value bearer for a value that she was already familiar with.

New Value Nuances

Following the second route which comprises a variation of an already known feature, the empathizer might become acquainted with a new value nuance. For instance, we might know of threats but not be familiar with the nuance of a deadly threat. Via imagination, we might come to experientially imagine this new nuance by modifying an already familiar value.

New Value Hierarchy

Also employing the second route, the empathizer might become acquainted with hierarchies of value which are new for her. Imagine an empathizer for whom beauty occupies a higher rank in her system of values empathizing with another for whom health is the most important value. In this case, the empathizer can become imaginatively acquainted with the other's values by modifying the order of values already known to her.

New Value Constellations

By the third route, which involves combining already known features in a novel manner, the empathizer might become acquainted with value constellations in which values already known to her are mingled in a novel way. Thus, she can imagine a situation in which something threatening appears to be linked to something sad.

New Values

Finally, also by the third route, we can become acquainted with new values. This presupposes a strong involvement of the imagination which, guided by testimony or fictional work, can bring the empathizer into contact with an evaluative property never experienced before. Empathy in these cases might lead us to apprehend certain features of a situation as salient which were previously not salient for us (for a similar point, see Novitz 1987: 139). For instance, it might be that an empathizer has never experienced unfairness but is familiar with situations of injustice in which some person is disfavored or at a disadvantage regarding another, and with situations in which one can become indignant or angry. This empathizer would then be able to become acquainted with unfairness by combining these different features.

In short, empathic acquaintance with values can be provided not only by direct co-experiencing of the other's values in face-to-face encounters but, as shown in this section, also by imaginatively co-experiencing the other's values, no matter whether these others are real people or fictional characters.

IMAGINATIVE ACQUAINTANCE WITH VALUE THROUGH FICTIONAL EMPATHY: ADVANTAGES

Let me now tackle the question whether knowledge about the ontological status of the other, that is, the fact that the other is a human being or a fictional character, has some influence on becoming acquainted with the other's values. In the current debate, some authors think that knowledge that the other is fictional will make empathy less likely because we have aesthetic obligations toward fictional characters that we do not have toward real persons (Petraschka 2021: 229).[10] By contrast, others such as Berninger (2021: 246) argue that fiction enables empathy, making it "more probable" and "easier." In this section, I will align myself with Berninger. More precisely, I will argue that fictional empathy makes acquaintance with values not only more probable and easier but also more accurate than empathy for real others. In short, the imaginative acquaintance with values provided by fictional empathy can be more probable, easier, and more accurate than the direct acquaintance provided by face-to-face encounters and the imaginative acquaintance provided by testimony.

I will argue for this claim by examining a series of *ontological*, *aesthetic*, *modal*, and *epistemic* features of fiction.

Ontological

The awareness that a fictional character is ontologically different from a real person might lead to a series of advantages when it comes to empathizing. We know that fictional entities are artifacts created with a specific purpose, that they do not really have mental states, that they lack a lived body, that they do not suffer as a human being does, and so on. In my view, this knowledge influences how the empathizer engages with the character's destiny and affective life.[11] Indeed, when we are confronted with a real other's suffering, we feel the ethical obligation to alleviate her pain. We also feel compelled to sympathize with her, to pity her, and to be compassionate toward her. By contrast, when we are aware that the target of our empathy is a fictional character, we can leave aside these ethical obligations; we know that the character does not suffer like a real human being. This enables the empathizer to focus on what the other is experiencing rather than on her responses toward it. While this focus can lead the empathizer to explore the evaluative dimension of the other's experience, to adopt such a stance toward another person in pain would be morally impermissible. For instance, reading Tolstoy's *The Death of Ivan Ilyich* we can take our time to explore the world of a dying person, scrutinize how Ivan Ilyich experiences his life coming to an end, and the realization that he has not yet started to live. We can perform this analysis without being concerned about alleviating his pain or showing compassion for him.

In addition, the empathizer can empathize with morally problematic characters because she knows that they have not perpetrated any real crimes. Cases of imaginative resistance aside, we seem to be more open to empathize with morally reproachable others when we know that they are fictional (a similar point can be found in Feagin 2004: 192).[12] For instance, we usually feel repulsed by imagining an infanticide. However, while reading or watching Victor Català's (Caterina Albert) play *La infanticida* (*The Infanticide*) we can empathize with the young protagonist Nela who is so afraid of her father discovering that she is pregnant and has thereby "lost her honor" that she throws the newborn under the wheels of a flour mill after giving birth. Each evening she hears the noises of the baby's bones being crushed. Empathy enables us in this case to experience a new value nuance of the morally disgusting and to enter into contact with a value system in which honor occupies a higher rank in the hierarchy of values than it would do in our everyday lives.

Aesthetic

Two further features are of an aesthetic nature. First, many fictions strive to evoke specific responses in us. To this end, they use a wide array of devices to make some aspects more salient than others. By contrast, our encounters with other human beings might lack salient elements or, in contrast, they can be so strongly imbued with salient elements as to make empathy challenging and difficult. Second, fiction presents the other's experiences as clearly articulated so that empathy is easier when compared to the fragmentary and chaotic structure often exhibited by the mental lives of real human beings (Walsh 1969: 90, 105).

Turning again to Tolstoy's Ivan Ilyich: The novel presents us with a human being who negatively evaluates specific moments, decisions, and encounters in his life such that certain key elements are made salient. This means that in empathizing with him, we can understand how, at the end of his life, Ilyich realizes that he has to die without having started to live. However, if instead of empathizing with the dying Ivan Ilyich masterfully depicted by Tolstoy, we try to empathize with a dying person who on her death bed evaluates her life in the light of its imminent end, it can be the case that her mental life is so strongly imbued by fear and despair that it becomes chaotic and inaccessible to us.

Modal

Fiction enables us to explore human possibilities that we would not usually encounter in our ordinary lives (Nussbaum 1990: 47). In this vein, we can co-experience values which are beyond the reach of our daily possibilities, i.e., values which are temporally, spatially, socially, intellectually, and emotionally distant from us. For instance, in watching the movie *Planet of the Apes*, we imagine what happens to a group of astronauts who have landed on a planet dominated by apes and who are held captive in cages. In so doing, we can empathize with their fear and how this fear has led them to perceive the planet as threatening. This is, of course, an almost unthinkable scenario outside of a fictional context. Yet, empathizing with the human protagonists of the film, we can understand the suffering of apes held captive in cages by humans on our own planet. In this way, we can become acquainted with an order of values that differs from our usual way of regarding nonhuman animals, one in which we treat other animals as being just as worthy of respect as humans.

Epistemic

In addition, while the mind of real others can be quite impenetrable, fiction can provide us with detailed inside perspectives of the character's inner life (Berninger 2021: 246; Nussbaum 1990: 46). This access to the character's inner perspective enables the empathizer not just to align herself with the other's perspective but also to imagine what the other as such is living through. As shown by Wollheim, this kind of imagining might lead to a recreation of the other's mental states and make us end up experiencing something similar (1984: 79).[13] This enables the empathizer to experience the world from the point of view of the character. Applied to our case regarding the acquaintance with values, this means that the empathizer can experience the world from the point of view of the other's value system, even if this is different from our own. Thus, in empathizing with Eliot's Silas Marner we can combine and modify what we know about situations of injustice and inequality and relate this to cases in which we become angry and indignant to get an inside grasp of Marner's mind and imagine what he is going through. In this way, we come to experience unfairness even if we have never suffered from unfairness in our own life.

By virtue of these features, when we empathize with a fictional character, we can *focus on the value* rather than on our responses toward the other's experience; we can *focus* on values *very different from our own*; values are made *salient*; and they are presented in an *articulated manner*; we can enter into contact with values which are *probable* but unusual in our life; and we can apprehend the other's values from an *inside perspective*. Beside the ontological difference between real and fictional others, some of the features mentioned involve questions of degree (they are generally, though not always, more accentuated in fiction than in real life) or frequency (they appear more often in fiction). Yet, the fact that they appear more prominently and more often in fiction suggests that empathy based on fiction makes us more probably, more easily, and more accurately acquainted with values than empathy for real others. Indeed, as mentioned, the acquaintance with values admits degrees of accuracy; sometimes the acquaintance is coarse; at other times it is more precise. Yet, by virtue of the "focus" on values, their "salience" and "articulation" provided by fiction, empathy based on fiction can make us acquainted with values in a more precise way than empathy for real others.

IMAGINATIVE ACQUAINTANCE WITH VALUES THROUGH FICTIONAL EMPATHY: MORAL SIGNIFICANCE

I have argued that empathy can make us acquainted with the other's values and that fictional empathy seems particularly well-suited to this task (insofar as the fictional work correctly engages the empathizer's imagination. In this final section, by way of conclusion, I want to offer two reasons why I think that becoming imaginatively acquainted with values through fictional empathy is morally valuable. These reasons are not exhaustive but they are significant enough to consider fictional empathy not only aesthetically but also morally relevant.

To begin, imaginative acquaintance can enable the empathizer to understand not only what the fictional character is going through and how the character evaluatively apprehends the different elements of the fictional universe but also what a real human being in a similar situation would experience. What I mean by this is that the values the empathizer becomes imaginatively acquainted with are not restricted to the fictional world. The empathizer might incorporate these values, which were previously hidden to her, into her own value system. This might lead to an "enlargement" and broadening of her own value horizon.

Second, this imaginative acquaintance can enable the empathizer to co-experience ways of apprehending the world which can strongly differ from her own. In this way, she might become aware of the existence of a plurality of value views. This might lead her not only to abandon egocentric value views, but also to "revise" her own value system. Indeed, in becoming aware of other value views, she might reflect upon the particular way in which she apprehends the world (i.e., the values that become salient for her, the hierarchies of values that reflect her preferences, etc.). In this way, the empathizer might discover that her value system is flawed or biased or full of prejudices, and she is moved to change it.

In both cases, a self-critical and self-reflective empathizer is required. Indeed, an empathizer who uncritically and unreflectively adopts the other's value views could end up becoming a racist, misogynist, or whatever other flaws are exhibited by the fictional characters. In any case, when accompanied by self-criticism and self-reflection, the acquaintance with the other's values provided by fictional empathy, though imaginative, can have real moral significance for the empathizer herself.

ACKNOWLEDGMENTS

Early drafts of this paper were presented in Vienna (September 2019) and Zürich (July 2021). I am indebted to the audiences at these conferences and in particular to Jochen Briesen and Eva Schürmann for insightful remarks. I am also grateful to Simon Mussell for copyediting this paper.

NOTES

1. While for intellectualized views of appreciations, empathy distracts us from the aesthetic values of a work, affective-oriented accounts consider that empathy has a positive function for appreciation (for a discussion of both positions and a defense of the latter view, see Feagin 2013: 368).

2. In this chapter, I work with an objectivist view of values which was originally put forward by some early phenomenologists such as Scheler (1973) but which retains some prevalence in current research (e.g., Mulligan 2010).

3. In Vendrell Ferran (2021), I have argued that fictional empathy enables the empathizer to appreciate the aesthetic values of a work by virtue of making us

acquainted with the character's values. In this paper, I expand on this argument by exploring how this acquaintance is possible and why it is morally relevant.

4. For Zahavi, when we claim to empathize with fictional characters, we make a derivative use of the concept of empathy (2017: 40).

5. In the debate on the cognitive value of fiction, we can find the expression "imaginative acquaintance," which I apply here to the case of values (see, for instance, Gaut 2007: 159).

6. This aspect has been underscored by Gabriel (2014) and Walsh (1969: 101).

7. Note that I am not claiming that all instances of empathy can make us acquainted with value. Rather I focus here on a possibility regarding a complex case of empathy focused on the other's affective states.

8. Interestingly, Stein, who put forward the view that we can empathize with the other's world of values, considers that empathy is not reducible to the other's affective states. However, as recent debate on her work has shown, there is in Stein a strong focus on affective experiences (see Magri 2015: 131).

9. For an analysis of how fiction can make us more sensitive to the apprehension of values, see Vendrell Ferran, 2018: 299–302.

10. Petraschka develops his argument by taking intellectualized views of appreciation as point of departure. According to these views, we need to avoid empathy if we appreciate the aesthetic value of fiction.

11. The ontological difference between fictional characters and real human beings persists even in cases in which real others are beyond the reach of our perceptual horizon, and as happens in the case of fictional characters, we have to imagine their experiences.

12. This does not mean that we have no moral constraints in the case of fiction. In fact, empathizing with morally dubious figures can lead to an undermining of our self-trust (Berninger 2021) or impact our self-understanding (Szanto 2020).

13. The inside perspectives provided by fiction are not always complete. Indeed, the fictional empathizer must fill the information gaps using her imaginative powers. In this process she is guided by the fictional work that indicates to her what is proper to imagine and what does not fit into the fictional world.

REFERENCES

Berninger, A. 2021. How Empathy with Fictional Characters Undermines Moral Self-trust. *Journal of Aesthetics and Art Criticism* 79, 245–50.

Carruthers, P., and Smith, P. K. 1996. *Theories of Theories of Mind.* Cambridge: Cambridge University Press.

Coplan, A. 2011. Understanding Empathy: Its Features and Effects. In A. Coplan and P. Goldie (eds.), *Empathy. Philosophical and Psychological Perspectives*, 3–18. Oxford: Oxford University Press.

de Sousa, R. 1987. *The Rationality of Emotion.* Cambridge, MA: MIT Press.

Drummond, J. 2009. Feelings, Emotions, and Truly Perceiving the Valuable. *The Modern Schoolman* 86(3–4), 363–79.

Engelsen, S. 2018. Feeling Value: A Systematic Phenomenological Account of the Original Mode of Presentation of Value. *The New Yearbook for Phenomenology and Phenomenological Philosophy* 16, 231–47.

Feagin, S. L. 1996. *Reading with Feeling*. Ithaca, NY: Cornell University Press.

———. 2004. The Pleasures of Tragedy. In E. John and D. McIver Lopes (eds.), *Philosophy of Literature. Contemporary and Classic Readings*, 185–93. Oxford: Wiley Blackwell.

———2013. Affects in Appreciation. In P. Goldie (ed.), *The Oxford Handbook of Philosophy of Emotion*, 635–50. Oxford: Oxford University Press.

Gabriel, G. 2014. Fiktion, Wahrheit und Erkenntnis in der Literatur. In C. Demmerling and Í. Vendrell Ferran (eds.), *Wahrheit, Wissen und Erkenntnis in der Literatur. Philosophische Beiträge*, 163–80. Berlin: De Gruyter.

Gallagher, S. 2012. Empathy, Simulation, and Narrative. *Science in Context* 25(3), 355–81.

Gaut, B. 2007. *Art, Emotion, and Ethics*. Oxford: Oxford University Press.

Gibson, J. 2016. Empathy. In N. Carroll and J. Gibson (eds.), *The Routledge Companion to Philosophy of Literature*, 234–46. London: Routledge.

Goldie, P. 2000. *The Emotions. A Philosophical Exploration.* Oxford: Oxford University Press, Oxford.

Goldman, A. 2006. *Simulating Minds: The Philosophy, Psychology, and Neuroscience of Mindreading.* Oxford: Oxford University Press.

Hildebrand. D. von. 1982. *Sittlichkeit und ethische Werterkenntnis. Eine Untersuchung über ethische Strukturprobleme.* Vallendar-Schönstatt: Patris.

Horgan, T., and Tienson, J. 2002. The Intentionality of Phenomenology and the Phenomenology of Intentionality. In D. Chalmers (ed.), *Philosophy of Mind: Classical and Contemporary Readings*, 520–33. Oxford: Oxford University Press

Ingarden, R. 1973. *The Cognition of the Literary Work of Art*. Evanston, IL: Northwestern University Press.

John, E. 2017. Empathy in Literature. In H. Maibom (ed.), *The Routledge Handbook of Philosophy of Empathy*, 306–16. London: Routledge.

Kenny, A. 1963. *Action, Emotion, and Will*. London: Routledge and Kegan Paul.

Kind, A. 2020. What Imagination Teaches. In J. Schwenkler and E. Lambert (eds.), *Becoming Someone New: Essays on Transformative Expereince, Choice, and Change* 133–46. Oxford: Oxford University Press.

Magri, E. 2015. Subjectivity and Empathy. A Stenian Approach. *Discipline filosofiche: Figures, Functions and Critique of Subjectivity beginning from Husserlian Phenomenology* 25(2), 129–48.

Mitscherling, J. 2020. Empathy and Emotional Coexperiencing in the Aesthetic Experience. *Horizon* 9(2), 495–512.

Mulligan, K. 2010. Emotions and Values. In P. Goldie (ed.), *The Oxford Handbook of Philosophy of Emotion*, 475–500. Oxford: Oxford University Press.

Novitz, D. 1987. *Knowledge, Fiction, and Imagination*. Philadelphia: Temple University Press.

Nussbaum, M. 1990. *Love's Knowledge. Essays on Philosophy and Literature*, Oxford: Oxford University Press.

Petraschka, T. 2021. How Empathy with Fictional Characters Differs from Empathy with Real Persons. *The Journal of Aesthetics and Art Criticism* 79(2), 227–32.
Rorty, R. 2001. Redemption from Egotism: James and Proust as Spiritual Exercises. *Telos* 3(3), 243–63.
Russell, B. 2013. *The Problems of Philosophy.* Mansfield Centre, CT: Martino Publishing.
Sartre, J.-P. 2004. *The Imaginary*. London: Routledge.
Scheler, M. 1973. *Formalism in Ethics and Non-formal Ethics of Values*. Evanston, IL: Northwestern University Press.
Schmetkamp, S., and Vendrell Ferran, Í. 2020. Introduction: Empathy, Fiction, and Imagination. *Topoi* 39, 743–49.
Stein, E. 1989. *On the Problem of Empathy*. Dordrecht: Springer.
Stueber, K. 2006. *Rediscovering Empathy: Agency, Folk Psychology, and the Human Sciences*. Cambridge, MA: MIT Press.
———. 2016. Empathy and the Imagination. In A. Kind (ed.), *The Routledge Handbook of Philosophy of Imagination*, 368–79. London: Routledge.
———. 2017. Empathy and Understanding Reasons. In H. Maibom (ed.), *The Routledge Handbook of Philosophy of Empathy*, 137–47. London: Routledge.
Szanto, T. 2020. Imaginative Resistance and Empathic Resistance. *Topoi* 39, 791–802.
Vendrell Ferran, I. 2018. *Die Vielfalt der Erkenntnis.* Paderborn: Mentis.
———. 2021. Empathy in Appreciation: An Axiological Account. *Journal of Aesthetics and Art Criticism* 79(2), 233–38.
Walsh, D. 1969. *Literature and Knowledge*. Middletown, CT: Wesleyan University Press.
Wollheim, R. 1984. *The Thread of Life*. Cambridge, MA: Harvard University Press.
Zahavi, D. 2011. Empathy and Direct Social Perception. *Review of Philosophy and Psychology* 2(3), 541–58.
———. 2017. Phenomenology, Empathy, and Mindreading. In H. Maibom (ed.), *The Routledge Handbook of Philosophy of Empathy*, 33–43. Oxford: Routledge.

Chapter 18

Affective Depth and Value

On Theodor Lipps's Theory of Aesthetic Empathy

Jannik M. Hansen and Tone Roald

ABSTRACT

The ethical implications of empathy have been debated for more than a century. In this chapter, we restore this debate in the context of aesthetics, where it first originated. Focusing on the aesthetic developed by the psychologist and philosopher Theodor Lipps, we investigate how empathy allows for works of art to be experienced as revelatory of personal and ethical value. We start by presenting Lipps's description of feeling of depth and then consider how this feeling is constituted through aesthetic empathy. The feeling of depth is characterized by the saturation of mood and a sense of "living out." Furthermore, the feeling of depth is a relational feeling enacted and felt by the spectator and seen in the work of art. The basis for this are moments of evaluation and resonance, which unfold through a dynamic fluctuation between alteration and self-identity. We end by considering the particular significance of aesthetic value. It is argued that aesthetic empathy involves an epistemic modification allowing the work of art to reveal value with a clarity specific to aesthetic experience and that the empathic constitution of value qualifies as an affective becoming of the person as ethical.

Keywords: aesthetics, empathetic constitution, self-identity, Lipps

AESTHETICS, ETHICS, AND EMPATHY

Normally when considering the relation between empathy and ethics, the central question is to what extent the empathetic response facilitates altruistic or otherwise positive behavior. The basis for this coupling was first provided by David Hume in 1739 (2203) and Adam Smith in 1759 (2002). In their works, we find descriptions of psychological mechanisms similar to current conceptions of empathy, which were considered to be formative of moral responses and sentiments.

As noted by Moritz Geiger (1911), this idea was generally adopted and developed further by scholars working on empathy around the turn of the nineteenth century. However, not everyone agreed that empathy always functions in the service of the good. According to Geiger, Henri Bergson, for instance, argued that empathy should be understood as an ability that could also be used for negative purposes.

The debate on the moral implications of empathy was granted a new lease on life in the 1980s, when Batson et al. (2015; see also Batson 1987, 2011) introduced the so-called empathy-altruism hypothesis, which says that "empathetic concern produces altruistic motivation." Today, this debate is still lively, and proponents of both positions can be found. Within care ethics, for instance, Michael Slote (2007, 2010) has argued that caring motivation involves empathy and that "empathic caring is critical for morality across a wide range of individual and political issues" (Slote, 2007, p. 8; cited in Coplan and Goldie, 2011, p. xxviii). Coplan and Goldie (2011), however, claim that many accounts of empathy do not include prosocial motivations.

In this chapter, we wish to restore the discussion of empathy and its potential ethical implications in the context from which it first originated, namely the context of aesthetics.

By now, it is well-known that empathy first appeared as an aesthetic term. It is, however, less well known that the empathic experience of art was considered revelatory of personal and ethical values. Consider, for instance, the following statement to be found in the work of one central figure of aesthetic as well as early empathy research, the psychologist and philosopher Theodor Lipps:

> The deepest aesthetic value is also the highest ethical value. . . . I feel in the beautiful what makes me human; it bestows on me value as human, constitutes humanity in me (1903, p. 524).

Today the relation between aesthetics and ethics is still debated. The philosopher, Dorthe Jørgensen (2003), in her extensive treatise on the history of aesthetic ideas, concludes that aesthetic experience leads to an experience of understanding that something has value in itself: There is something outside you that is valuable, and therefore, you live your life more ethically.

Within a phenomenological context, different positions on the relation between aesthetic experience and the ethical are also to be found. Geiger, for instance, argues throughout his work that value (and thereby the ethical) is central to aesthetics (1976). Though empathy after almost a century of benign neglect has once again become a topic of aesthetics (Koss, 2006), its role as a founding instance of the positive relation between aesthetics and ethics remains in the background.

Late in the nineteenth century, a range of scholars argued that empathy played a central role in the aesthetic experience of value. Lipps, for instance, argued that aesthetic empathy incorporates a moment of evaluation, which under the right circumstances affects a particular kind of feeling, so-called feeling of depth, which is said to reveal value in pure form. Though the use of depth to describe the aesthetic experience is to be found throughout the history of aesthetics, Lipps was the first to provide an actual description of it as a lived affective experience revealing personal value. Based on this description, we will investigate the relationship between empathy, depth, and value, that is, how experiences of affective depth can be said to reveal value through aesthetic empathy.

We will start by situating Lipps's notion of empathy in the context of the beautiful, value, and activity. We will then give an exposition of his description of the feeling of depth as a special kind of pleasure characterized by a personal engagement with the aesthetic object. In the third section, we investigate how these experiential aspects are constituted and intertwined through empathy. We will end the chapter by discussing the particular significance of aesthetic value as it is conceived by Lipps.

BEAUTY AND VALUE AS POSITIVE LIFE ACTIVITY

In the introduction to his *Ästhetik*, Lipps defines beauty as "the name for the ability of an object to produce a certain effect in me" (1903, p. 1). This effect manifests itself experientially as a particular kind of pleasurable feeling, which Lipps calls the feeling of beauty (*Schönheitsgefühl*). The feeling of beauty comes in great varieties, but it generally features affective feelings of force, greatness, freedom, and depth-aspects that together articulate a basic sense of the self as active, alive, and harmonious. Lipps (1907), therefore, also conceives beauty as the free confirmation of life felt within the perceiver as well as the work of art. Stated differently, we could also say that beauty arises from the particular way in which the work of art activates the person's feelings.

In Lipps's conception of beauty, feeling and value coincide.

> In the context of aesthetics, "beautiful" means aesthetically valuable. For me, at least, the fact is this. Therefore, it is the same whether I say that aesthetics is the doctrine of the beautiful or that it is the doctrine of the aesthetically valuable (Lipps, 1903, p. 6).

The basis for this correspondence is Lipps's general determination of value as something pertaining to life activity: "The value of my life activity (*Lebensbestätigung*) is . . . the basic value of all values or is the value in the truest sense of the word" (1909, p. 341). Life activity here refers to the inner striving movement toward the termination of a given act, for instance, of perceiving, apprehending, or imagining. Activity becomes manifest to the person as a momentary felt sense of being, what Lipps also refers to as activity feelings (*Thätigkeitsgefühle*). As such, activity feelings are also said to articulate the person's experience of vitality: "Everyone experiences it [life] in himself as the vitality of the ego, as its eternal restlessness, as the ever-continuing flow of consciousness, in short, as the ongoing activity" (1909, p. 38). Activity feelings are, therefore, also conceived as the basic feeling (*Grundgefühle*) through which the person becomes aware of herself as living. The felt sense of being pertaining to activity does not, however, in itself qualify as value. It must, as Lipps writes, be in accordance with that which is afforded by the person's nature.[1] To qualify as value, the activity must therefore actualize the life potentials[2] that are in accordance with being as human. As such, Lipps's conception of value is in line with ethical naturalism, according to which something is considered to be good if it is in harmony with its nature (Johansen, 1998, p. 458). In the present context, Lipps's conception of value as the actualization of positive life potentials is particularly interesting. It is namely said to be constituted in empathy and as terminating in sympathy, or what he calls "sympathetic empathy" (1900, 1906a, 1906b). By doing so Lipps's notion of empathy takes on a broad sense. As we shall she, it incorporates both the experience of another person's subjective being and an experience of enacting and participating in this subjective being. Lipps refers to the first moment as basic empathy and the latter moments as sympathetic empathy. Taken in its full sense, empathy is, therefore, also said to denote an experience of oneself as living in and with the empathized object—be it a person or a work of art. This experience is made possible through a particular kind of self-activity that involves evaluation and resonance. When we draw attention to aesthetic experience, it is not just because it reveals how empathy as a particular kind of self-activity constitutes value. Aesthetic experience and, in particular, aesthetic empathy prove an interesting case also because value is said to be revealed with distinct clarity in so-called feelings of depth which affects the perceiver in his being in several ways. Lipps's account, therefore, not only provides an account of the relationship between empathy and value, but it also reveals how aesthetic experience can aid the becoming of an affectively coherent and ethical person.

FEELING OF DEPTH

In Lipps's work, we find a first attempt at an actual description of depth as something experienced. Lipps (1903) describes depth as a specific felt aspect pertaining to the feelings of beauty manifesting itself directly or immediately in aesthetic experience. As an experiential aspect, depth obtains a significant status. We can experience all kinds of feelings and desires in front of a work of art, writes Lipps. The desire we experience when enjoying feelings of beauty stands out, however, by its depth (Lipps, 1900, p. 434). Without the qualitative aspect of depth, an object is not experienced as aesthetic. For this reason, Lipps conceives depth as the most important felt aspect in the realm of aesthetic feelings (1903, p. 523). Stated differently, depth, in its Lippsian sense, qualifies as the experiential or phenomenological characteristic, marking the transition or passing over from "just seeing" to enjoying aesthetic pleasure.

Depth in the Narrow Sense: Experience of "Living Out" and Freedom

Depth in the narrow sense refers to the extent to which the empathetically experienced content of the work of art also belongs to the "ground" of the spectator's personality. This ground Lipps determines as that which constitutes the spectator as human, which reveals the person as what he or she is, qua human: his or her active striving toward actualizing life.

The revelation of the ground of the person, his or her active striving toward the actualization of life, therefore, reveals itself through an affective dynamic, as something felt:

> In the beautiful, I feel a strength or a longing—respectively the movement and work of it—which, above all else, denotes what makes me a human being, above all else gives me human value, constitutes humanity in me. Or I feel in the beautiful the uninhibited *living out* of such strength and longing, an experience and enjoyment of what such strength and longing, the *liberation of a need*, the fulfillment of which is made possible by the other, allows me to be happy as a whole person. (Lipps, 1903, p. 525)

In the feeling of depth in the narrow sense, the spectator obtains the feeling of living out, that is, she has a feeling of being liberated in her activity and of actualizing her human nature. Lipps also describes this as an experience of being in agreement with oneself, as a state of self-identity which makes itself felt as inner freedom (1903, p. 531; 1900). This living out and liberation articulate a form of catharsis in which "I experience within myself," as Lipps writes, "a cleansing, a καθαρσις των παθηματων"[3] (Lipps, 1900, p. 431). In light of the description of self-identity, the sense of cleansing obtains a positive sense. It is not a matter of removing something, of freeing the perceiver *from* x, rather catharsis in the Lippsian must be understood as a becoming, as a being freed *to* x.[4]

Lipps thus determines value as something experienced in harmonious self-activity, that is, a self-activity, which is in accordance with a person's nature. Depth in the narrow sense can, therefore, also be said to qualify as the first aspect of value-experience.

Depth as Mental Saturation: From Feeling to Mood

Lipps calls the second dimension of depth "mental saturation." It is described as the experience of feelings irradiating into other domains of the self, thereby developing into a mood (*Stimmung*), saturating the entire consciousness of the person. As such, this second dimension of depth can also be said to denote a way of experiencing in which the self becomes wholly occupied with a particular activity manifesting itself as a novel and specific kind of feeling.

The basis for the saturation of mood is resonance. It was described previously how the objects we perceive, according to Lipps, enforce on us an activity, and this activity becomes manifest as a particular kind of felt sense of being. The flow of the activity is characterized by a rhythm that is said to carry a tendency to irradiate into other mental domains where it effects a similar rhythm.[5] In feelings of depth, the activity from which it originates is said to resonate with and rhythmify the entire activity of the self. All the person's activity is aligned, now moving in the same direction, thus allowing the experienced feeling to saturate the self as an all-embracing mood. As Lipps also writes:

> The more extensive and richer the mood is, the more all possible strings resonate in me, thus bringing the manifold contents of my present and past personality to life by the individual experience, the more the content of the beautiful becomes characterized by psychological saturation. (1903, p. 526)

In accordance with the description of rhythm and resonance, Lipps (1903) determines mood as a state of attunement and argues that it constitutes a feeling of its own kind, the so-called feeling of mood (*Stimmungsgefühle*). As such, feelings of mood must be distinguished from externally experienced feelings (*gegenständliche Gefühle*) as, for instance, the joy I see in my friend's smile, or the anger seen in the gestures of Michelangelo's Moses as he stares ahead while convulsively holding on to the table of the ten laws (Gammelgaard, 2000, p. 25). According to Lipps, feelings of mood do not fasten, lie, or exist in the expression of the object in the same immediate way. Or, stated differently, they do not take a concrete object as their only point of reference. Whereas the statue of Moses is experienced as the object expressing the feeling of anger and, consequently, as the gestalted owner of the anger, feelings of mood do not articulate the same sense of unequivocal ownership. The reason for this is that the structure of the directedness is changed so that it no longer has only a single object—the expression. According to Lipps, the main focus of the person's attention is now affixed to the total flow or mode of progression of mental occurrences and the way in which the rhythm of the flow manifests itself affectively. Lipps, therefore, also determines mood as the felt state or symptom arising from the total state of mental affection. We shall see that this is the effect of positive evaluation. Given this origin, feelings of mood do not manifest themselves in the same objectively given way as feelings often do:

> This general way of progressing of the mental life is not something that I can have in mind or face as an image, like a mountain or house that I perceive or imagine, or like an act of my will, or the affects linked to a certain experience of anger. (Lipps, 1903, p. 221)

Following Lipps, moods evade reification and do so because the object of attention is not a perceptual object but a current progression of activities, including the feelings they give rise to. Lacking such immediate anchoring in the object also means that they appear as fluid, hovering, ineffable, in short, as a diffuse "something." Therefore, it is also possible to say that mood is meaningful in its own specific way and distinct from how perceptual objects such as a mountain or house are experienced as meaningful. As Lipps notes, it is possible to find general names for different kinds of moods. We speak, for instance, of melancholia, joyfulness, cheerfulness, seriousness, or gloominess. Despite such attempts, the particular instance of a given mood remains something that we cannot fully capture through imagination or mental representation.

When experiencing mood in relation to works of art, we are so to speak aware of it as object-dependent, that is, as something which presupposes the existence of a perceptual object, yet it is experienced, as Lipps (1903, p. 222) writes, as "a feeling that appears in *me,* it is *my* mood." Experientially, this means that we are aware of this origin: Despite being experienced as an ineffable something, the feeling of mood is immediately related to the object qua its actualizing activity. When we cannot provide feelings of mood with the same clear objectivity, it is exactly because mood is an attunement, and as such, something occurring in interaction with the surroundings, which involves or engages the self in a particular way by activating the general flow of mental progression. In a certain sense, it is, therefore, possible to speak of objects as carrying or eliciting moods. Mood is, however, not something actually existing in the work of art but an affective potential of the work of art in the form of "a general enlivening effect" that can be actualized when entering into the spectator's general life activity. Importantly this means that the feeling of mood is not only determined by the experienced content as such—the expressive configuration. It is determined by its relation and, in particular, likeness or similarity of the enlivening effect of the work art and the general activity of the person—if the effects, so to speak, are in or out of tune with the activity of the person. Stated differently, feelings of mood are characterized by a different directedness: a bifurcated directedness in which an awareness of the object is maintained, but the focus is on the mode of experience, that is, the general way in which the object activates the self-activity of the person. We might, therefore, also say that in the experience of the feelings of mood, the *what* is subordinate to the how or the modus of experience, its flux.

Whereas depth in the narrow sense refers to an experience of self-identity and harmony—of being in accordance with one's nature in activity, depth in the wide sense refers to the experience of this harmony as something attuning the entire activity of the person and developing into a saturating mood. As such, depth in the narrow sense can also be said to be the moment in which the value is established, whereas depth in the wide sense as mental saturation articulates the force or weight, and eventually, the significance with this value makes itself felt.

Depth and Aesthetic Sympathy

Though depth, both in the narrow and wide sense, articulates a focus on the person's subjectivity, depth is not something that pertains to the person alone:

> Depth is the felt personality content. It is the depth within my own being into which I descend in aesthetic contemplation. As such, it is my depth or the depth of my being. But it is at the same time precisely the depth of the object, or depth of the object into which I, in aesthetic contemplation, go down. (Lipps, 1903, p. 523)

This is important because it emphasizes the inherent sympathetic character of the experience. Without recognizing the relational aspect, depth and eventually also the kind of value it reveals would be idiopathic or egocentric. If this were the case, it would be legitimate to say that depth is nothing but "something which we project into the object" (Spiegelberg, 1960, p. 215), and consequently that what we experience in the work of art "is merely an echo of our own [voice]" (Gilbert and Kuhn, 1953, p. 538). This is not the case, however. Being true to its pleasurable nature, the feeling of depth is neither something that can be explained on behalf of the subjectivity of the spectator, nor the objectivity of the aesthetic object, alone. We should thus be careful not to confuse what must be considered a basic and necessary constitutive asymmetry with the experiential givenness of the object.

According to Lipps, the work of art becomes manifest as an analogon to a personality (Lipps, 1898). As such, it is possible to argue that depth is not just something co-constituted and eventually shared by the person and the work of art; when experienced aesthetically, it also incorporates an awareness of a foreign subject. When descending into the depth of the work, we not only experience a feeling as something existing in and of its own, but we also come to experience, Lipps writes with reference to Goethe´s Faust, "the ground from which the affect arises, the roots from which it springs, that is, we experience the grief or despair as an inner emotion of this personality" (Lipps, 1906b, p. 49). Importantly, we not only come to experience this or that affect of Faust. We come to experience the particularity of his inner being as a person, the way in which he, in his despair, strenuously strives with force and greatness (Lipps, 1906b, p. 49). Thus what we, according to Lipps, find, or maybe more precisely encounter, in the depth of the object is the experience of another human being; however, not as such. In accordance with Aristotle's description of the tragedy, we could say that the work of art "is not the depiction of humans, but of actions and life" (Aristoteles, 2016, p. 21). Eventually, the value revealed by the depth is not a value that adheres to the sensuous but to another human gestalted in the sensuous expressive articulation of life or activity (Lipps, 1903, p. 157). Trying to capture the duality with which depth manifests itself in experience, Lipps writes:

> This experience is an experience of myself: I feel myself as human in the gestalt that appears before me, feel the harmony between myself and the human being that penetrates into me. In some way, I feel the fulfillment of the longing to be active and feel myself throughout as human. I feel the harmony between myself and the human that penetrates into me. (1906b, p. 49)

This harmony between the spectator and the artistically gestalted other, Lipps refers to as aesthetic sympathy (p. 50). Consequently, the feeling of depth is not constituted by the person alone. The person is not the original source of the feeling of depth: It involves the other, though in a modified way, as a constitutive and experiential cofounder.

Deep Dialogues and Affective Echoes: The Empathetic Constitution of Depth as Value Experience

We have now presented Lipps's description of depth as a particular kind of felt quality pertaining to feelings of beauty. We have seen that depth experientially is characterized by a saturation of mood and actualization of basic life-potentials and that these two aspects taken together provide the person with a sense of self-identity. Furthermore, it was described how feelings of depth, according to Lipps, arise relationally through a particular kind of interaction with the interior of the aesthetic object, understood as life activity pertaining to an artistically gestalted person. In what follows, we will unfold the nature of this relation. By doing so, the constitutive role of empathy, as Lipps conceived it, will become evident. In particular, we shall see that aesthetic value arises in the intersection between what Lipps refers to as basic empathy and sympathetic empathy and does so through the evaluative acts of negative and positive empathy.

Indirect Apprehension and Affective Positioning

Mood was said to involve a bifurcation of attention: that the attention of the perceiver, when having feelings of mood take the flow of progression of mental occurrences as the primary object while maintaining an awareness of the object. Lipps also describes this bifurcation as indirect apprehension (*mittelbar Auffassung*). Whereas the person in direct apprehension (*unmittelbar Auffassung*) is devoted to the apprehension of the object and, as Lipps writes, finds her gaze going outward, toward the object, without returning back, in indirect apprehension, the perceiver directs her gaze toward the object while simultaneously directing a sidelong gaze back at herself (Lipps, 1907). Importantly, the dual gaze or attention of indirect apprehension should not be understood as if the perceiver has two different experiences simultaneously. Rather, what occurs is an inner self-thematization or self-objectification, which articulates a way of relating to oneself as devoted to actualizing the demand yielded by the object. The person is thus simultaneously the actively apprehending ego and the ego that perceives and relates to itself as an ego actualizing the activity. As Lipps also notes, the numerical identity of the ego remains intact, yet a splitting occurs so that person now stands vis-à-vis herself. Consequently, the ego is bifurcated into partial egos, that is, a primary and perceived ego and a secondary and perceiving ego. This taking of itself as an object modifies the experience so that a novel kind of self-awareness emerges. As Lipps writes, "I perceive myself with a peculiar closeness and intimacy. . . . I become a fellow human being to myself" (Lipps, 1907, p. 230). This articulates the somewhat paradoxical fact that self-objectification both incorporates a self-distancing from the immediately perceiving and active ego while, on the other hand, resulting in a sort of self-presence to this ego. It is important here to emphasize that the novel kind of self-awareness is not to be taken as the instantiation, origin, or constitution of self-awareness as such. In accordance with later phenomenological conceptions of minimal self-awareness or ipseity (e.g., Zahavi, 1999), Lipps argues in *Leitfaden der Psychologie* that the ego is always present to itself or self-manifesting in experience:

> The sentence, that I experience myself in every conscious experience, is simply a tautology. "Consciousness experiences," that means experiences of an ego, belonging to a consciousness is belonging to, or appearing to an ego; the real sense of the word—consciousness—is ego. (Lipps, 1909, p. 6)

This kind of basic self-awareness is obviously different from the kind effecting from the experiences in which the ego makes itself the object of attention, that is, the kind of self-awareness arising from the self-objectification just described.

This kind of self-awareness is important in the present context for at least two reasons. First, because it (qua splitting) allows for self-evaluation: "I can, if we now return the use of the term evaluation, experience myself and my way of actualizing in the activity, positively and negatively" (Lipps, 1907, p. 229). Secondly, because this evaluation is said to constitute a central moment in aesthetic empathy by allowing for its completion as aesthetic sympathy, that is the experience and feeling of myself in the other, in a pure and free way facilitated by the aesthetic object (1900, p. 433 ff.). Stated differently, self-evaluation is what allows for basic empathy to develop into sympathetic empathy.

Evaluation as Positive or Negative Empathy

The positive or negative way of experiencing oneself in indirect self-apprehension Lipps also describes as positive and negative empathy:

> "Positive empathy" is that absorption of what penetrates into me, or the fusion of the grasping ego, as it is in itself, with that which penetrates into it. Negative empathy, on the other hand, is that the grasping ego disputes what is intruding,

> repeals, or contradicts it, that it demonstrates itself as incompatible with itself. (Lipps, 1907, p. 236)

The fusion and contradiction are exactly what we above described as harmony or dissonance between the two partial egos. As we have already described, activities of the ego carry a tendency to irradiate into other domains of the mental, enforcing an attunement of these other domains. In this present context, it means that the activity of the primary actualizing ego is enforced on the secondary perceiving ego, thus attempting to attune it and make it identical in its activity. This raises the question of how the secondary perceiving ego relates to this demand, that is, whether it is able and willing to oblige such demand without protest; if the demand, so to speak, is in harmony or conflict with the ego´s basic nature, its "tendencies, dispositions, desires" (Lipps, 1906a, p. 104). As also mentioned previously, the higher-order ego's way of relating to the demand colors the experience affectively: Conflict elicits displeasure and harmony elicits pleasure. More important in regard to the understanding of the constitution of value is that the affective coloring arising from this empathic self-relation articulates "an affective inner positioning toward the present or past own activity (Lipps, 1907, p. 233). As Lipps notes, such positioning is, without doubt, a kind of valuation (Ibid). According to Lipps, the affective positioning revealed by the pleasure of harmony or conflict can, therefore, also be understood as feelings of approval or disapproval of the activity that the ego is actualizing within. Such approval or disapproval qualifies as basic value judgments, which can be transformed into utterances such as "it is right that I position myself in this way, I ought to position myself like this" (Lipps, 1907, p. 233). That the feelings of pleasure or displeasure can be transformed into utterances demonstrates that the ego achieves a rather clear or strong sense of self.

According to Lipps, the affective approval or disapproval articulates only one aspect of the empathic evaluation. In addition to manifesting an affective positioning of the person toward its own actualizing activity, pleasure and displeasure also articulate a sense of willingness or unwillingness to co-experience (*miterleben*). To co-experience in this context means to *participate* in the actualizing activity of the objectified ego so that what was first objectified now also becomes enacted (Lipps, 1900, p. 421). If we return to the statue of Moses, the perceiver no longer just sees the anger. The anger now takes possession of the perceiver so that she experiences it with Moses. Basic empathy has thereby developed into sympathetic empathy: "So we understand by [sympathetic] empathy . . . the penetration of an activity or mode of activity of the I, which is opposite to me or is my object, into the experience of the grasping I" (Lipps, 1907, p. 236).

Based on this clarification of affective positioning, as containing an evaluative and reflexive moment of aesthetic empathy, we can call empathic evaluation reflective self-evaluation.

The Role of the Other in Affective-Aesthetic Positioning

Though the affective positioning is a self-evaluation in which the person grasps itself as actualizing an activity, this self-grasping is, to borrow a phrase from Husserl, "the ego's original (self-grasping) being in the presence of the object itself" (Husserl, 1989, p. 11). Stated differently, to grasp oneself in the presence of the object itself, is to grasp oneself affectively as actualizing the activity demanded by the object. Though the given description does legitimize the talk of *self*-evaluation, we must be cautious not to neglect the fact that in the present context, at least, what is evaluated though being an activity of the ego, is an activity which does not have its source in the motivational ground of the ego. Indeed, it is the ego's activity, but it is, as Lipps writes, an activity that has its own particular origin by not emerging from the measure of the person's own being (1906a, p. 113). Instead, it is something "communicated, something penetrating into the person from the work of art" (Ibid.). If we are to speak of self-evaluation, we must thus understand that it is a kind of self-evaluation that is founded in a more basic relation between the I and the object. Importantly, in the context of aesthetics, we saw that the object appears as an analogon to a person, that is, as an object manifesting through its expressive exterior and interior, eventually qualifying as a perceptual equivalent to a person. Thus, the actualized activity of the person, to which she relates in self-evaluation in truth, springs from a foreign person to whom it carries a reference. This is important. When Lipps writes that to empathize is to live in the other, it means, constitutively speaking, to let the other penetrate into and determine the activity of one's actively apprehending ego. From a phenomenological point of view, we can speak of this determination of activity as a form of basic "alienation." In the apprehending activity, the person is, so to speak, othered; that is, by actualizing the activity, the person is actualizing the other within and becomes "an other" to herself. We can say that she becomes an other in activity. Once again drawing on phenomenological analysis, we could say that such active othering constitutes an "alter-ation" (*Veranderung*; Theunissen, 1986, p. 89). In Lipps's conception, such alteration occurs in the actualizing activity of the apprehending ego, where it manifests itself affectively as a basic felt sense of the activity. When Lipps occasionally speaks of a fusion of the self with the other or that the self and the other are one, it is this actualization of a demanded activity originating in a foreign subject he refers to. Indeed activity in this sense constitutes coming together in inter-action.

Based on this interpretation, the spontaneous active ego (the primary ego) of the person is characterized by a permeability, basic receptiveness, or openness to the world, which manifests itself affectively in the flux of different activity feelings. This ego is in a certain sense out in the world—in the object or the other, and less within the person to whom it tacitly refers or belongs.[6] Importantly this does not mean that its basic sense of self as an ego dissolves in experience, only that it is less articulate. The clear articulation occurs, as we saw above first when—through self-objectification—the person explicitly relates to itself in acts of evaluation.

Based on this, the ground for the following two claims is provided. First, what first appeared as a reflective self-enclosed process of empathic evaluation ensues as a dynamic fluctuation between alteration and (positive or negative) self-identification, thus incorporating a sort of I-though relation, which in its positive form qualifies as a sort of communal activity that exceeds the domain of the "mere" self-relational. Second, self-identification understood as articulating personal values in aesthetic experience is fundamentally conditioned by otherness seen in the aesthetic object. One way to capture the sense of the constitutive grounds of depth experience and value elicited therein is to describe it as altero-aesthetic participation or, indeed, as aesthetic sympathy.

BEING IN DEPTH AND THE ILLUMINATION OF THE POSITIVE GROUNDS OF HUMAN EXISTENCE: TOWARD A CHARACTERIZATION AESTHETIC VALUE AND ITS EXISTENTIAL SIGNIFICANCE

Taking its proper sense aesthetic value and ethical value, according to Lipps (1909), mean the same thing. They are both personal values, understood as the activity of life actualized in accordance with human nature (Ibid.). This now raises the question of whether the aesthetic is in service of the ethical.

In this last section, we wish to consider the particular significance of aesthetic value as an ethical value as opposed to ethical value experienced outside the domain of aesthetics, that is, in practical life. Based on these considerations, the distinct significance of aesthetic empathic experience will be demonstrated.

Aesthetic Modification and Pure Value

We have shown how aesthetic value in the experience of depth also qualifies as personal value and that ethical value and aesthetic value coincide in aesthetic empathic experience of self-identity and feelings of freedom saturating the person as mood. It was also shown that this experience could be described as attunement effecting from an engaged relation with the aesthetic object as gestalting an aesthetic other, and that value, therefore, also could be understood as something constituted through attunement in which the other plays a significant role.

Importantly, the commonality between ethical and aesthetic value should not be mistaken for identity—that aesthetic value and ethical value are the same things. Though Lipps considers aesthetic value (taken in itself) to qualify as ethical value, he also argues that an "absolute contrast" exists between the two (1909, p. 343). A clarification of this absolute contrast is important if we wish to obtain an understanding of the distinct significance of aesthetic value.

The basis for this clarification is an epistemic modification brought about by the aesthetic symbol. According to Lipps, this modification has a dual consequence:

> On the one hand, the connection between the reality outside of me is eliminated for me. And, on the other hand, in that this is the case, I myself withdraw, as the one who lives and interweaves in this world of reality. (1900, p. 432)

The modification effecting the symbolic status of the aesthetic object is a suspension of reality belief. As a consequence of this suspension, the perceiver is said to enter into a novel reality, what Lipps (1900) refers to as the aesthetic reality (*ästhetische Realität*). The aesthetic reality is a reality characterized by its distinct epistemic modality. It is an "as-if" reality, and thus, in a certain sense, illusory. Yet, it is not a semblance-reality or a fantasized reality. The perceiver cannot see the object as it suits him or her in the same subjectively determined way. The symbolized content (some or other activity) is there with the same necessity as the joy in a smile. Stated more generally: The perceptual and affective degrees of freedom are the same in aesthetic perception as normal perception. For this reason, Lipps also writes that the aesthetic illusion shares an affinity with the consciousness of or belief in reality (they are both conditioned strictly by the materially or physically given).

This "suspension of reality" has a significant effect on the actualization of value, which is now allowed to appear in itself. Our awareness of ethical values outside the aesthetic reality is experienced as embedded in the context of concrete life events and also other values. This means, according to Lipps, that experiences of value also articulate a demand upon us to act in accordance with it. In the aesthetic reality, this demand of realization through action is suspended. The person still experiences activity and the feeling it gives rise to, but the feelings no longer carry the same motivational power. The reality suspension thus effects a detachment from the normative demands of practical living. Importantly, this detachment is not only to be determined as a sort of negative freedom—a freedom from the demand of realization in concrete action. The detachment also articulates a positive freedom to follow, live out, and actualize the demand yielded by the aesthetic object in a way that is not possible under the demands of practical life. Thus, the detachment can also be said to provide the condition for completion of aesthetic empathy as a form of sympathy, that is, as Lipps writes, a kind of empathy characterized by a purity, completeness, and clarity that empathic experiences immersed in the reality of mundane life cannot have and which, therefore, is specific to aesthetic empathy (1900). Because of the particular epistemic modification pertaining to the object experienced within the aesthetic reality, the person obtains the possibility to devote his or her entire mental activity to participate in and actualize the concrete feeling effecting from the aesthetic object, thereby coming to experience a given life activity in a clear affective way. The person is, Lipps writes, lifted beyond her empirical I; she has become an over- or outer-empirical ego, an ideal ego detached from mundane life and is in turn allowed to experience the activity and the value it manifests with a purity and completeness, which cannot be achieved from within any other epistemic modus. When it comes to the constitution of value, aesthetic empathy thus, as Lipps (1898, p. 17) writes, presents a "favorable moment" that reveals the fact of pure value, thus allowing us to recognize its true nature.

Importantly, this value does not remain personal. As we saw, the experienced depth pertains not only to the perceiver, but it is also seen in the object; it involves a reference to a foreign object and is sympathetic. Accordingly, depth not only provides the possibility to obtain a personal value-awareness. The perceiver not only gains the possibility to experience himself or herself in harmonious self-activity, and thus a positive personal value. The perceiver also becomes aware of this positive value as pertaining to other persons, as a general value, as Lipps writes: "It [depth] shows me in all possible human emotions the positive human being or the positive ground for his being, the gold of humanity lying beneath the surface" (1906a, p. 114).

Following Lipps, the person achieves insight into basic grounds of the human as such, that which every human is conditioned by, a striving toward the actualization of life.

Now, Lipps is not explicit about how we get from personal value to general human value, that is values that exceed the domain of that which is relative the person. Based on the preceding interpretation, it is possible to argue that this generality arises from a sympathetic state of harmony between the self and the gestalted other. Based on such interpretation, we could also say that the self- and life-affirmation that the perceiver obtains is obtained through the interaction with the other, in particular through the evaluation of actualizing activity as one having foreign subjective origin. Eventually this gives the value a shared or communal character. Thus, by entering into a relation with the gestalted other, the spectator comes to experience depth as illuminative of not only the basic condition of her personal being but the basic conditions of being as such, that is, the conditions that are shared with other persons qua human, that is the positive human, the positive ground of its nature.

Following Lipps' analysis, aesthetic value not only generates clear awareness of personal value; the particular kinds of affective constitution also reveal personal value as something achieved in communion with other persons.

Affective Becoming

We saw that the revelation of aesthetic value involves a dual activity: the actualizing activity of the functioning ego and an evaluative thematization or participation of the reflective ego in the felt sense arising from actualizing activity. We also saw that positive evaluation resulted in sympathy, irradiation of the feeling into other domains of the psyche, and eventually a sense of self-identity, whereas negative evaluation resulted in antipathy, maintenance of the bifurcated self, and eventual rejection of the activity. In aesthetic empathy, all of this, we have just said, occurs within a distinct epistemic modality, the aesthetic reality, where the ego in experience is lifted above or beyond the normative demands of mundane life. This division of the empirical ego and the ideal or aesthetic ego could suggest that the feelings arising are also ideal. We saw that aesthetic feelings, according to Lipps, do not carry the same motivational force as that of other feelings. The lack of such motivational force does not make them ideal; however, as Lipps writes:

> Ideal feelings are imagined feelings. . . . The imagined color does not shine; the imagined tone does not sound; the imagined pain does not heart. Thus, the imagined joy is not joy, and in the imagined anger, we are not angry. Imagined feelings lack the warmth and the coolness, the sweetness and the bitterness, the uplifting and depressing character of the real feelings. They are no longer feelings, but shadowy afterimages of such, bloodless, colorless, and soundless. (1900, p. 430)

Recognizing that feelings can be experienced in different modes without losing their determination as feeling, we should moderate this statement by saying that feelings experienced aesthetically exceed the level of imaginative presence qua depicted to a level felt presence. This, however, means that aesthetic feelings have a peculiar duality to them; they are felt and as such qualify as lived feelings, yet they do not motivate action, at least not immediately. This is important because, according to Lipps, it means that the aesthetic reality also becomes a psychological reality; the person experiencing aesthetically is, as Lipps writes, not only made larger in the aesthetical reality, but she is also made larger in the empirical reality. The reason for being so is that the actualizing and participating processes are actual or real mental processes. Under the circumstances that the person carries within the disposition to feel deep feelings, the symbol is said to provide the possibility to actualize or realize that which before existed only as a potential to feel, thus providing it with existence as a lived feeling. As such, the demand of the symbol on the person to actualize a given activity is a formative demand, that is, a demand that provides the feeling with form. We could also say the perceiver's affective life becomes the substratum for the form giving potential of the symbol. To use form in this way is to use it differently from how it is normally used in theories of art, that is, as something pertaining to the particular way of depicting. Following the determination of activity as a rhythmic flow, form here refers to the particular instance of such rhythm. As such, form is not an objective feature but the name for the progression of a mental dynamic that makes itself felt in the actualizing activity as it occurs in the interaction between the person and the aesthetic object. Paraphrasing Aristotle (De Anima, 1968, p. 429, cited in Johansen, 1998, p. 364), we might also say that the place of form is consciousness and, in particular, the rhythmic activity of consciousness and that this formation qua lived qualifies as a sort affective becoming of the person. As such, the illumination of the personal qua human also obtains an ontological status as something that comes into existence. This, in turn, means that the person not only obtains a particular kind of personal and general value-awareness; it also means that the person is actualized affectively in accordance with his or her ethos. Following the principle of identity, which states that the good is a sense of being in accordance with one's nature, the person not only becomes aware of this identity but, through its actualization, comes to live it in the aesthetic moment.

Based on these considerations, the specificity of the aesthetic value is to be accounted for by the following three aspects. First, aesthetic value is specific because it is given in the occurrence of a constitution in the person's affective life that cannot occur outside the aesthetic sphere, which second, is in accordance with his or her nature. Therefore, it can be considered as an actualization of the person's ethos or character and as providing the person with a strengthened sense of self. Lastly, this actualization generates an awareness that exceeds the personal sphere providing insight into the general positive ground of human existence as such, the striving toward the actualization of life.

CONCLUSION

Based on Lipps's aesthetic theory, aesthetic experience transpires as an important ethical experience. It provides us the possibility to actualize and become that which we, according to our nature as humans, are supposed to be, and as such, to have the self- and life-affirming experience of being in harmony with this nature. Conceived as such, aesthetic experience also becomes an experience in which we are allowed to explore our human ethos, that is, the deep aspects of existence revealed in the striving toward the actualization of life. Lipps has shown how depth as an essential affective aspect of beauty discloses this opportunity. In feelings of depth, the person experiences the saturation of freedom and harmony and importantly does so through the other. The person thus experiences being in harmony with himself and the other through the shared nature as humans, and this is exactly the experience of the good.

ACKNOWLEDGMENTS

Research for this paper was supported by the Independent Research Fund, Denmark under grant number DFF-6107-00273.

NOTES

1. Lipps does not specify what he means by the person´s nature, but resorts to psychological concepts such as dispositions, desires, tendencies and interests (see for instance Lipps (1900; 1906a; 1907)). Following our interpretation below of Lipps theory of value as aligning with ethical naturalism, this vague determination of the person´s habitus should not cause misgivings. Following Aristotle and to our understanding also Lipps, it is possible to argue that a more specific determination of the persons nature as well an experience of something as valuable reveals itself only in the conduct of life, that is, in the unfolding practice of lived life activity and the affective experiences they give way to.

2. The point made about life-activity also holds for life-potentials.

3. καθαρσις των παθηματων, Greek, translates into cleansing of diseases. Lipps probably obtains this from Aristotle´s poetics.

4. We will address this aspect of becoming in the last section of the paper.

5. The basis for such saturation has also been unfolded in chapter 19 of this book, by Hansen, Høffding and Krueger, titled Music and Empathic Spaces in Therapy and Improvisation. Here the notion of saturation is described as kind of "resonance" or "rhyhtmification" of the entire soul occurring in accordance with, what Lipps refers

to as the "law or irradiation" (Lipps, 1900, p. 442). We will not expand this further here, but refer to this chapter.

6. Though Lipps, following an introspective tradition also divided reality up into an outer and inner, his description of the active ego, seem to imply that this distinction should not be taken too seriously. Stated more precisely it might be legit to speak of an experiential inner and an experiential outer.

REFERENCES

Aristoteles. (2016). *Poetik*. Hans Reitzels Forlag.

Batson, C. D. (1987). Prosocial Motivation: Is It Ever Truly Altruistic? In L. Berkowitz (Ed.), *Advances in Experimental Social Psychology*. Vol. 20, 65–122.

———. (2011). *Altruism in Humans*. New York: Oxford University Press.

Batson, C. D., Lishner, D. A., & Stocks, E. L. (2015). The empathy—Altruism hypothesis. In D. A. Schroeder & W. G. Graziano (Eds.), *The Oxford handbook of prosocial behavior* (pp. 259–81). Oxford University Press.

Coplan, A., & Goldie, P. (Eds.). (2011). *Empathy: philosophical and psychological perspectives*. Oxford University Press.

Dufrenne, M. (1973). *The Phenomenology of Aesthetic Experience*. Northwestern University Press.

Gammelgaard, J. (2000). *Mellem mennesker: træk af indfølingens psykologi*. Gad.

Geiger, M. (1911) Über das Wesen und die Bedeutung der Einfühlung. In: Schumann F. (Ed.) *IV. Kongress für experimentelle Psychologie*, 29–73. Verlag J.A.

Geiger, Moritz (1976). *Die Bedeutung der Kunst. Zugänge zu einer Materialen Wertästhetik.* Wilhelm Fink Verlag.

Gilbert, K. E., & Kuhn, H. (1953) *A History of Esthetics.* Thames and Hudson.

Hume, D. (2003). *Treatise of Human Nature*. Project Gutenberg.

Husserl, E. (1989). *Ideas pertaining to a pure phenomenology and to Phenomenological Philosophy. Second book. Second Book Studies in the Phenomenology of Constitution.* Kluwer Academic Publishers.

Johansen, K. A. (1998). *Den europæiske filosofis historie - Bind 1, Antikken.* Nyt nordisk forlag Arnold Busck.

Jørgensen, D. (2003). *Skønhedens metamorfose—De æstetiske ideers historie.* Syddansk Universitetsforlag.

Koss, J. (2006). On the limits of empathy. *The art bulletin*, *88*(1), 139–157.

Lipps, T. (1898). *Die ethischen Grundfragen: Zehn Vorträge*. Verlag von Leopold Voss.

———. (1900). Aesthetische Einfühlung. *Zeitschrift für Psychologie und Physiologie der Sinnesorgane*, *22*. 415–450.

———. (1903). *Ästhetik. Psychologie des Schönen und der Kunst. 1. Band: Grundlegung der Ästhetik.* Verlag von Leopold Voss.

———. (1906a). Einfühlung und Ästhetischer Genuss. *Die Zukunft*, *54*, 100–114.

———. (1906b). *Ästhetik. Psychologie des Schönen und der Kunst. 2. Band: Die Ästhetischen Betrachtung und die Bildende Kunst.* Verlag von Leopold Voss.

———. (1907). *Vom Fühlen, Wollen und denken. Versuch einer Theorie des Willens. Dritte mit der Zweiten Übereinstimmende Auflage.* Verlag von Johan Ambrosius Barth.

———. (1909). *Leitfaden der Psychologie*. Verlag von Wilhelm Engelmann.

Slote, M. (2007). *The Ethics of Care and Empathy*. Routledge.

———. (2010). *Moral Sentimentalism*. Oxford University Press.

Smith, A. (2002). *The theory of Moral Sentiments.* K. Haakonssen (ed.). Cambridge.

Spiegelberg, H. (1960). *The Phenomenological Movement: A Historical Introduction. Volume one.* Springer Science & Business Media.

Theunissen, M. (1986). *The Other. Studies in the Social Ontology of Husserl, Heidegger, Sartre and Buber.* The MIT Press.

Zahavi, D. (1999). *Self-Awareness and Alterity. A Phenomenological Investigation.* Northwestern University press.

Chapter 19

Music and Empathic Spaces in Therapy and Improvisation

Jannik M. Hansen, Simon Høffding and Joel Krueger

ABSTRACT

The term empathy (*Einfühlung*) is rooted in philosophical aesthetics. It was used by German philosophers toward the end of the nineteenth century to describe our ability to imaginatively "feel into" works of art, which speak to us in a certain humanlike way insofar as they contain traces of what Mikel Dufrenne calls a "quasi-subjectivity" (1973, 393). In this chapter, rather than looking to art as an *object* of empathy, we instead consider art—and more specifically, music—as a resource that can *facilitate* empathy. More precisely, we turn to two cases in which music seems to establish spaces that enable and sustain empathic connectedness, as well as the ability to explore and experiment with different forms of social understanding and affective sharing.

The first case comes from the music tradition of free improvisation. Based on ethnographic fieldwork with the saxophone player, Torben Snekkestad, we become acquainted with an approach to performance that does not concern music primarily as an aesthetic product, but as a shared process of communicating and connecting nonverbally with others—a process that is essentially about exploring and experimenting with different forms of intersubjectivity and empathy. The second case comes from music therapy and autism, which can involve listening, singing, or joint music-making. We discuss studies indicating that musical interventions positively address core impairments in capacities required for empathy: for example, joint attention, social reciprocity, and verbal and nonverbal communication, as well as comorbidities of atypical perception, motor performance, and behavioral problems.

Although these two cases are different, they share the trait of using music to establish spaces of nonverbal communication and empathic understanding. Drawing on these two cases, this chapter analyses how musical-empathic spaces emerge and how these spaces solicit the integration of both low-level affective and bodily resonance mechanisms as well as high-level acts of meta-reflection, imagination, and planning that contribute to different forms of empathic understanding.

Keywords: music, empathic spaces, Lipps, rhythm, resonance, free improvisation, autism, music therapy

INTRODUCTION

Playing and listening to music performances is uplifting, inspiring, and perhaps even empowering. A live rock concert for instance can establish bonds of imaginative empathy associated with having had a significant shared aesthetic experience. Looking beyond such immediate aesthetic pleasure and zooming in on the process of playing music, however, another decisively empathic dimension emerges. Beyond and before the production of an aesthetic product, playing—or more specifically improvising—music together can ground and enhance communicative and empathic forms of mentality, expanding our interactive repertoire, whether among professional musicians or in a music therapist working with autistic individuals. At least, that is what we purport to demonstrate in this chapter. At the same time—moving from the level of live musical experience to that of fundamental theorizing on aesthetics and empathy—at the outset about 150 years ago, the term, *empathy* (*Einfühlung*) was coined as a term concerning aesthetic objects and processes. It is in itself a source of fascination that empathy, which in our everyday understanding has come to indicate an ability to comprehend and live well with others, originally concerned processes of aesthetic judgment. What we have then, is theoretical work and as well empirical cases making aesthetic or musical practices essentially bear on and develop aesthetic capabilities.

Our chapter first introduces the point of origin of aesthetic empathy with Lipps's work. Asking how Lipps might describe the metal process involved in a live musical event, we isolate three core concepts from his rich work, namely rhythm, resonance, and activity, and we trace their operation in our musical cases. At this point, it becomes evident that Lipps is a thinker of interaction and should perhaps be reassessed as a proto-enactivist rather than a *prügelknabe* reduced to simulationist and projectivist theories of empathy, as is often the case.

Our two cases are of rather different origin. The first builds on Høffding's earlier work with the improvising saxophone player Torben Snekkestad in the form of ethnographic observations and "phenomenological interviews." The second relates to Krueger's theoretical work on empathy, enactive musicking, and autism studies. Though based on different kinds of empirical backgrounds, both cases show how music improvisation can enable and enhance both basic and sophisticated empathic processes—what we call "empathic spaces"—that most likely would be otherwise inaccessible. Further, the aim of opening these spaces, we believe, constitutes a kind of ethical practice. These considerations in turn allow us to reconnect with Lipps showing how some empathic and aesthetic processes, notably resonance and rhythm, are inherently intertwined and mutually supportive.

EMPATHY AND AESTHETIC EXPERIENCE: A BRIEF HISTORICAL SKETCH

The term *empathy* dates to German aesthetics. It originates from the German noun *einfühlung*, which literally translates into "feeling-into." In 1911, the psychologist Edward Titchener developed the neologism empathy to introduce the term to English-speaking audiences. The use of empathy to account for aesthetic experience can be traced back to the Enlightenment and Romanticism, where prefiguration is to be found in poetic as well as philosophical texts as a form of animation of nonhuman objects occurring through projection.[1] In his habilitation *On the Optical Sense of Form* (1994), the philosopher Robert Vischer introduced empathy as a technical term. Drawing on findings generated by the then-novel sciences of physiology and psychology, Vischer described empathy as a kind of objectification of the body into spatial forms resulting from kinesthetic reproduction of external stimuli (1994). According to Vischer, this reproduction generated sensations of movement, which by entering into relation with the emotional and imaginative life of the person effected a "spiritual sublimation of the senses" in which "the entire body subject is moved" (p. 99, translation modified).[2] Vischer's account is important for several reasons. Not only did it provide an account closely aligned with a tendency within nineteenth-century German aesthetics toward thematization of the psycho-physical conditions for the experience of a beauty. It also provided an account in which empathy was not reduced to other mental functions, such as association, as had been attempted by thinkers like Gustav T. Fechner (1876) and Paul Stern (1898). Situating empathy within a psychological and physiological context, and insisting on its specificity,[3] Vischer would eventually furnish the psychological ground for the field research that would later become known as *empathy aesthetics* (Friedrich & Gleiter, 2007).

Sharing the basic assumption with Vischer that investigations of empathy could elucidate the psychological grounds from which experiences of aesthetic pleasure arise, a range of scholars set out to investigate the relation between empathy and aesthetic experience. The point of departure for their investigations was the general question: *How is it possible that a nonhuman object can appear with human sense*? (Geiger, 1911, see also Lipps, 1900, p. 416). For a period of approximately fifty years, with a peak around the end of nineteenth century and the beginning of the twentieth century, a diverse range of theories of aesthetic empathy emerged, most of which are not known to contemporary debates on empathy and aesthetics.[4]

Before presenting the concepts of *activity*, *rhythm,* and *resonance*, we will have to make a short detour around Lipps's conception of beauty. That is because a brief exposition of the relational nature of beauty shall help us make a convincing case that low level aspects of aesthetic empathy solicits basic affective and communicative processes, and importantly does so within an intersubjective awareness of the spectator.

THEODOR LIPPS ON THE RELATIONAL NATURE BEAUTY

Lipps (1903) defines beauty as the ability of an object to evoke a particular kind of feeling, a so-called *feeling of beauty* (*Schönheitsgefühl*). Beauty is thus conceived as an emotional effect (*Wirkung*) experienced by the person. As the science of beauty, the aim of aesthetics was, for Lipps, to describe, analyze, and explain the lawful nature of this effect: on the one hand, the objective features that an object must possess to evoke feelings of beauty; and on the other, the subjective conditions that allows for such emotional evocation within the subject. Accordingly, beauty for Lipps is neither an intrinsic quality of the object nor a quality that can be accounted for by the subjectivity of the person alone. Rather, it is a co-constituted, relational, and in-between phenomenon; it is emotionally enacted in "reciprocity," "interaction," or "dialogue" with the object, as Lipps puts it (Lipps, 1903, p. 191, cf. Lipps, 1909).

Engaging with the work of art, the spectator experiences being receptive to expressed feelings and is motivated to reproduce and re-experience the feelings of another human. This reproduction is described by Lipps as an affirmation of the other which becomes joyful by simultaneously confirming the vitality of the spectators own being as a human. When enacting the feeling of beauty, the spectator comes to experience a positive ground of being, shared by every human being. The experience of beauty is therefore at its core an experience unfolding as an intersubjective relation. The spectator not only experiences feelings, but the feelings of another human; it is as Lipps (1906, p. 112) puts it, an experience in which an echo of the other reverberates in me.

According to Lipps, the *body* holds the key to the understanding of beauty (1903, p. 102). Through its perceptual appearance—its form, color, actions, behavior, utterances, and so on—the body becomes manifest as the bearer of human life. Importantly all of these bodily expressive appearances can be symbolized aesthetically in music, poetry, painting, sculpture, and so on. Sensitivity to this expressiveness of vitality is, according to Lipps, an ability initially developed through a reciprocal relation of self- and other-experiences, the nexus of which are impulses of imitation (1903). As Karsten Stueber (2006, p. 7) writes, this means that "our aesthetic appreciation of objects in the end is grounded in seeing their form in analogy to the expressive quality of human vitality." The crucial point here is that aesthetic empathy occurs analogously to the type of empathy that allows us to experience, develop, and understand the life of other persons. For Lipps, then, the way from the latter form of empathy (i.e., in relation to others) to the former (i.e., aesthetic empathy) is therefore not far. Although the objects are different in the two cases, they both nevertheless follow the same dynamic patterns of activity.[5] It is this similarity that makes Lipps's analysis interesting to the question of how music as an art form facilitates empathy. The experience of beauty thus proves to be a relational experience in the dual sense, as founded in intersubjective awareness and progressing through interactive and interaffective processes. We will demonstrate how the low-level aspects of aesthetic empathy that Lipps calls activity, rhythm, and resonance, which together constitute the relational character of our aesthetic experiences, can help clarify how music can establish we-spaces that facilitate empathetic connectedness, social understanding, and affective sharing.

ACTIVITY AND FEELING IN BASIC EMPATHY

Lipps (1900) divides aesthetic empathy into two levels: a primary and general level he calls "basic empathy" and secondary and specific level he calls "sympathetic empathy." Though feelings of beauty first arise at the latter level, it is at the first level that the relational and rhythmic-dynamic basis for the experience of resonance is laid bare. In opposition to sympathetic empathy, which in Lipps's use refers to co-experiencing, sharing and importantly also a joy of such sharing that primarily occurs in relation to works of art or other persons, he considers basic empathy a function of consciousness occurring in relation to natural objects, sounds, and even simple spatial objects as lines. According to Lipps, an aesthetic object experienced through empathy is the product of two factors: the sensuous demand (*Forderung*) of the object on the one hand, and the activity of the person on the other.

Lipps also describes the experienced object as the result of a co-constitutive process (1909) as well as a product of interaction or a dialogue between the person and the object (1903, 1905).

Through this interaction the person and the object are mutually affected. To understand this affective transformation, we will have to delve into the basic feelings arising in the dialogue between the object and the person, between demand and activity, which is the feelings that Lipps calls feelings of activity (*Tätigkeitsgefühle*; e.g., Lipps, 1906, 1909).

In its most fundamental sense, activity can be determined as any inner mental work (Lipps, 1906). Lipps describes it dynamically, as an inner striving movement toward the termination of a conscious act. By virtue of its inner nature, this movement is not a spatial movement, rather, it is a movement between different qualitative episodes unfolding in consciousness (Lipps, 1907, p. 19). To speak of activity without its phenomenological manifestation as the feeling of being active is as Lipps writes an abstract idea (1905). He therefore also emphasizes that the meaning of the term *activity* is best understood by reference to the way it is experienced rather than to bodily or kinesthetic sensations. To capture the felt aspect and eventually the full sense of activity, Lipps employs the term feeling of activity. Here is a felt sense of inner striving, the work toward the termination of any act, as such, be it a bodily action, or reflexive acts of perceiving, imaging, reflecting or even willing (Lipps, 1907, 1905, 1909).[6] Feelings of activity can also be described as the felt sense of the I's movement toward the termination of an intended act and, hence, articulate the basic sense of vitality of the I (Lipps, 1909, p. 38). From there, Lipps goes on to describe feelings of activity as feelings of life (*Lebensgefühle*,) as well as feelings of self (*selbstgefühle*).

Importantly, the movement between a qualitative episode, which makes up the activity and provides it with its felt sense, is not determined exclusively by the person. As noted, the aesthetic object is an achievement of a co-constitutive process involving the sensuous demand of the object and the activity of the person. That the object enforces a sensuous demand on the person simply means that its appearance is not completely independent on the constituting achievement of the person, but that the object asserts and preserves its "right" to be experienced as that what it is (1909). This means that I cannot experience the object as just anything but that the I is required or requested to experience the object exactly as *this object* (Lipps, 1906, p.16). It is in recognition of this basic reciprocity that Lipps also describes the object and the feelings it gives rise to as products of "interaction," "dialogue,"

(Lipps, 1903, 191) or "co-operation" (Lipps, 1905, p. 191). Though feelings of activity, always are felt states of the person, their origin in this basic dialogue means that they are simultaneously characterized by a basic relatedness (Lipps, 1909). In emphasizing this basic relatedness, Lipps also describes activity as way of experiencing oneself as attuned (*gestimmt*; Lipps, 1907, p. 18). Lipps's account of this basic constitution of attunement circles us back to the idea that both person and object are transformed affectively. Whereas the person comes to feel herself as attuned in the feelings of activity, the objects, as the cofounder of the activity, simultaneously appears as the bearer of the activity. As Lipps writes: "it is my movement and my activity. It arises not spontaneously, but is given through the object, tied to it. As such, it appears as something belonging to the object, and belonging to it with necessity" (Lipps, 1908, p. 358). Eventually the person and the object are affectively intertwined in activity: on the one hand that object is "permeated by the person′s activity," and on the other hand, the person comes to find herself attuned in her feeling of activity and eventually her basic sense of self.

RHYTHM AND FEELING: THE MEDIUMS OF JOINT NEGOTIATION

The way in which the person comes to experience a feeling of activity and eventually also her engagement with the aesthetic object is determined by the progression of the inner movement of the activity, that is, its particular rhythm (1909, p. 38). Lipps provides us with two determinations of rhythm, both of which must be considered if we wish to understand the specific sense of resonance he tries to carve out and how it relates to the basic affective aspects of feelings of activity as they appear in aesthetic empathetic experiences of music. The first determination is narrow, rather simple, and specific to music: the successions of beats and tones (Lipps, 1903). The second is wide, complex, and expresses a core psychological concept: the progression of a given psychic event, what Lipps also characterizes as "the varying movements of psyche" (Lipps, 1900, p. 442). We saw that activity was described as a movement. According to Lipps, this movement is made up of a flow of elements, successively following on each other (p. 444). The temporality following from such succession gives the activity a linear character (Lipps, 1909). The linear character does not mean that the movement follows a straight line, however. Rather, the flow of elements constitutes a stimulation (*erregungsweise*) particular to the event. For instance, when listening to a piece of music, the highlighted tones capture our apprehension more strongly and permanently than do the moderated tones. According to Lipps, the interaction between these different modes of appearance of the tones generate a variation of dynamic qualities of "forwards striving and calmness, or between tension and relaxation, conflict and overcoming, opposition and balance" (Lipps, 1900, p. 442). These dynamic qualities are, psychologically considered, the matter of fact of rhythm as inner or mental movement. So, when listening to music we experience a duality of rhythms: the rhythm of the succession of beat and tones, along with the simultaneous awareness of the rhythms of our mental movement *in response* to these beats and tones. To speak of two rhythms is to draw an analytical distinction. Experientially the rhythm of the music and the analogue actualized mental rhythm are fused into an experiential unity. Thus each mental event is not only characterized by its particular rhythm, it is also characterized by a particular affective correlate or emotional response, which Lipps also describes as "reflex of consciousness" (*Bewusstseinsreflex*; Lipps, 1909, p. 316).

RESONANCE

As such, the mental rhythm and its dynamic qualities can have an effect beyond the apprehending activity itself. This effect Lipps describes as the "law of psychic resonance of the like" (1900, p. 442. see also Lipps 1903, p 419ff). To follow up on the example with music, the apprehension of regularity of a beat may motivate analogue bodily movements, as when we tap our foot along the rhythm of the beat of some song. Lipps claims that such tapping cannot be explained by saying that each single tap is a motor impulse motivated by the single beat. Rather, the mental rhythm of apprehension, as he writes, "awakens the rhythm of movement . . . I am not responding to the single beats, but I am repeating a basic rhythm, retained within succession of beats." (1903, p. 420). As Lipps also notes, it is curious that such awakening can take place because motor impulses and auditory impressions of beats pertain to two different sense modalities the content of which cannot be reduced to one nor the other. When the rhythm of the beat shares an intuitive similarity with bodily movement, this is according to Lipps so, because the former as actualized mental rhythm constitutes a rhythmic pattern which shares a similarity with the actualized rhythmic patterns of movement, and this to such an extent that they can have an effect on each other.[7] In Lipps's account, resonance is exactly the establishment of this similarity across these domains as well as the following mediation of sense from one domain to the other, wherefore he also refers to the law resonance as the law of radiation (1900, p. 442).

If we return to aesthetic empathy, resonance is important because it, in Lipps's use, describes how the rhythm resulting from the interaction between the demand of the object and the person's activity can extend to and activate other domains of psyche. Resonance thus allows for the attunement occurring in activity, to develop into more pervasive state, what Lipps also describes as saturating mood characterized by depth and harmony.[8]

ENACTIVE ASPIRATIONS OF AESTHETIC EMPATHY

Given the preceding exposition, it is curious that Lipps has been framed as a simulationist in modern cognitive neuroscience. Because of this simulationist or projectivist reading has been set up as *prügelknabe* throughout the history of phenomenology from Husserl and Stein to Zahavi and Gallagher (cf. Zahavi 2010). Based on the exposition of activity, rhythm, feeling, and resonance it should be clear that Lipps's notion of empathy does not articulate a subjective projectivism, nor is reducible to a matter of imitation or simulation. Indeed, it seems more fitting to interpret Lipps's account as being in line with enactive perception that, as Gallagher (2011, p. 104) writes "is perception for interaction and—rather than simulation." Importantly, this interaction was shown to be a dynamic process unfolding through *rhyhtmification* of consciousness the experiential correlates of which is a kind of feeling—so called *activity feelings*. As such, the interactive process occurring in aesthetic empathy is simultaneously an interaffective process, which mediates feelings between the object and the spectating subject. This mediation can also be described as an aesthetic affect attunement. This allows for feelings to be experienced simultaneously as both mediated/communicated and felt (i.e., as a shared and *resonant* state enhancing both self and other-awareness). The summary of Lipps's position vis-à-vis his framing as simulationist and criticisms hereof does not constitute a proper argument and presentation of the relevant debates. The purpose of presenting this reading of Lipps is to prepare the ground for thinking about our cases, and a full exposition of his potential as a proto-enactivist must be left for another occasion. Now, we will apply Lipps's account of the relational or co-constituted basis of aesthetic empathy to two musical practices. Here we will see how various kinds of turn-taking constitutive of intersubjective patterns of communication can be used in scaffolding musical we-spaces.

CREATING EMPATHETIC SPACES IN THE MUSICAL LANDSCAPE: THE CASE OF FREE MUSICAL IMPROVISATION

Even if trends in musicology and the philosophy of music have started to look at music as a process rather than as an aesthetic object (for instance with Small's [1998] influential notion, "Musicking"), it is fair to assume that most musicking has aesthetic aims. In some sense, and as this section of our chapter demonstrates, this is not straightforwardly so for the musicians in free improvisation. Though they certainly do explore aesthetic dimensions with their improvisations, the main exploration seems to concern an intersubjective, communicative process.[9]

To accomplish this demonstration, we have to first give a brief overview of free improvisation as a genre and then, also briefly, present the method and case study that produced the empirical material supporting the claim.

The reader might initially associate free improvisation with some kinds of jazz improvisation. But that hinders rather than clarifies the nature of the former. Jazz improvisation, even in avant garde forms, will usually be based in a chord progression, a key, a melody or even just a certain rhythm to improvise from. Relative to such structures, free improvisation starts from scratch. Musicians who might meet for the first time on stage, simply begin to play without any explicit agreements. This makes for an unusual kind of music, so unusual that "listening guides" (Corbett 2016) have been written to help the audience in their search for form (i.e. in their effort to make sense out of the tones coming at them).[10] Snekkestad's style is associated with what the Modern American music icon George Lewis calls the "European free improvisers" (Lewis 1996, p. 112) performing alongside artists such as Joelle Léandre, Barry Guy, Agusti Fernandez, Nate Wooley, and Evan Parker. Snekkestad is an accomplished saxophonist, mastering all "Western" styles from classical to jazz standards. He, however, has a special affinity for free improvisation, because of its communicative potential, and excels in solo improvisation, exploiting a number of "extended techniques" (Høffding & Snekkestad 2021).

The following presentation and analysis are based on empirical, qualitative data in the form of "phenomenological interviews" (Høffding & Martiny 2016) contextualized by ethnographic field observations. Snekkestad and Høffding started discussing issues of musical absorption and improvisation in 2017. In 2018, they did an exploratory, thorough interview of about ninety minutes. To get a contextually informed understanding of Snekkestad's practice, Høffding attended a number of concerts and eventually followed him on tour in the Ruhr district in Germany for seven days. Here he observed concerts every evening, experienced the daily life and culture around the free improvisation community, and conducted another five hours of interviews. This chapter relies explicitly on the 2018 interview.

There are many approaches and methods describing how to combine qualitative data and phenomenological analyses.[11] This one is based on a combination of ethnographic criteria of validity and phenomenological analyses as described by for instance Ravn (Legrand & Ravn 2009; Ravn 2021) and

Høffding and Martiny (2016). This form is particularly useful for understanding expert practices (Ravn & Høffding 2016; Ravn 2021). The interviews seek to elicit as many rich and detailed descriptions from the interviewee as possible. The focus on descriptions seeks to move the interviewee's focus away from opinions, theories and explanations. For it is exactly the job of the researcher to use the interview data to arrive at such explanations and theories. And here phenomenology, as the philosophical tradition initiated by Husserl, comes into play. The analysis of the interview aims at getting beyond the mere content of various past experiences to the *structure* of those experiences (Gallagher & Zahavi 2008, p. 28). When it comes to musical absorption (and also artistic absorption in general), the interplay between habitual, bodily, pre-reflective acts, one the one hand, and reflective acts, on the other hand, as well as changes in one's sense of agency, are particularly enlightening. For this chapter, however, we want to investigate the data from the phenomenological perspective of empathy with the idea that a central purpose of free improvisation is to establish *empathic spaces* or communicative processes. Here, we show how two different groups engage in this space and process. The first group is the musicians themselves, while the second group consists of both musicians and audience. For both groups, we see Lipps's core concepts operate, insofar as musicians as well as audience are perceived as making demands and offering artistic possibilities inaccessible for instance when practicing on one's own. This activity structure of the performative situation obviously relies on both of Lipps's notions of rhythm and as such enact a space of resonant mental-musical activity.

Most of the interviews with Snekkestad concern how he communicates in these groups and what tools he has to influence and be influenced by his co-players and audience members. Remember, when no musical agreements are made in advance, performing on stage is not merely a matter of deciding on the spot what to play given what the others are playing. Simultaneously, Snekkestad must find out how to establish patterns of communication in order to agree on where to go in the music. Snekkestad call this a "negotiation":

> A free improvisation concert is more about that everyone is in an open process and can monitor closely how the spontaneous communication between musicians change the trajectory of the music, how they are sort of negotiating the material along the way. And here we are into this, which is about human communication and relation, it is about all sorts of emotions and aesthetics you are negotiating when you are in that space. Not that it has to be about something in particular. It is a way of being together.

Improvising freely is an art of learning to surprise oneself, or rather learning to let one's fellow musicians open a space of surprise and playfulness that one can enter into. "Negotiating" in just the right way, can allow for a "pulling of the rug":

> For instance with a really good drummer, who can align himself very closely with your playing and ideas, and then suddenly create a friction. Suddenly he can perhaps stop playing at the moment where it is most predictable that we're building to a climax and in that way *pull the rug from underneath your feet,* in order to create those openings in the music where something can happen. Create new paths in the music, create new forms. Create that moment where you lose control, were you have to reorient yourself in the musical landscape.

Snekkestad's preferred metaphor for the music he performs is a "landscape" with different "zones." When the ensemble manages to pull the rug in just the right way—which is far from always the case—new landscapes and zones are opened almost as epiphanies. In this way, and much in the style of 4E cognition,[12] interactions with other musicians enable or scaffold individual transformative experiences together with new musical abilities and visions. Considering free improvisation in this way, gives it an idealistic ring: Together the musicians enable one another to expand their consciousness, by supporting and challenging each other. This, however, requires a finely attuned sensitivity and an empathic intentionality. To work, it also presupposes technical mastery over one's instrument.

The audience members of course do not play on stage, but they nevertheless play a central role in the shaping of the music, because Snekkestad is intent on communicating with them as well. His empathetic stance toward the audience is clearly seen in the following:

> A concert is more about [the fact that] that everyone [musicians and audience] is in on that process—can follow, can see the communication the musicians are going through—how you are sort of negotiating the material, whether you are in on this journey. And here we are into this, which is about human communication, relation—it is about all sorts of emotions you are negotiating when you are in that space. Not that it is about something in particular. It is about a way of being together.

This democratic ideal of sharing and co-developing the musical space is also found in the following:

> When playing improv music, I have a strong feeling that we all are in the same place. It is not like "I possess this dramaturgy and can manipulate you," it is not that kind of situation. You observe a process we are searching for, we are looking for something together, we are together, we are in the same space when this happens.

What we consistently learn from Snekkestad is that even though he has refined aesthetic preferences and savor exploring new musical zones, the music ultimately is a means to engage in a certain kind of communication. It is a way to express and receive, a tool of attunement and Lippsian resonance.[13]

It is an empirical question how often and to what degree the audience members perceive this communicative intention. It is, however, beyond doubt that these ideals of attunement or responsivity are widely shared in the free improvisation community. The famous guitarist Derek Bailey, mentions that, "to improvise and not to be responsive to one's surroundings is a contradiction if not an impossibility" (1993, p. 44). And music theorist, David Borgo, so nicely sum up the essence of free improvisation:

> Free improvisation, it appears, is best envisioned as a forum in which to explore various cooperative and conflicting interactive strategies rather than as a traditional "artistic form" to be passively admired and consumed. Improvisation emphasizes process over product creativity, an engendered sense of freedom and discovery, the dialogical nature of real-time interaction, the sensual aspects of performance over abstract intellectual concerns, and a participatory aesthetic over passive reception (2002, 184)

This brief exposition of free improvisation shows its functioning as an empathic space, providing a finely attuned room for experimentation, playfulness, and care. The communicative and interactive intension built into the free improvisation mentality, effectively transforms the music from an aesthetic product to an empathic space full of jointly perceived rhythmification and resonant possibilities. We will leave the last word to Snekkestad, who fundamentally perceives of his musical practice as an ethical commitment: "Improvisation is not solely an intuitive art form, but a socially engaged ethical practice that directly influences [my] ability to make creative decisions, engage in critical dialogue, and take risks that allow for the discovery of new insights and changed social relationships." (Høffding & Snekkestad 2021, 165)

CREATING EMPATHETIC SPACES IN THE MUSICAL LANDSCAPE: THE CASE OF AUTISTIC SPECTRUM DISORDER MUSIC THERAPY

We now apply this Lippsian perspective to a second case study: an analysis of how musical empathy develops in the context of musical therapy and autistic spectrum disorder (ASD). As with the case of free improvisation analyzed previously, we show that within these therapeutic spaces, shared episodes of musicking create opportunities for interactive experimentation, playfulness, and care. In short, they similarly involve an ongoing *negotiation* of shared aesthetic space. This is because within a therapeutic context, these spaces are not simply spaces where music is performed and experienced. More than this, they become rich spaces of empathy—spaces of shared experience and social connection that are, as Snekkestad helpfully puts it, "about human connection and relation, about all sorts of emotions and aesthetics you are negotiating when you are in that space."

While this focus on ASD and music therapy continues themes considered in the previous section, it also brings something new to the table. It highlights some *ethical* dimensions of musical-empathic spaces. It does so for two reasons: first, insofar is it concerns forms of sensitivity and responsivity to others, it foregrounds music's role in shaping the *quality and richness* of interpersonal relations within that space; second, it emphasizes the need to develop more *inclusive* spaces in everyday life, spaces more finely attuned and responsive to the needs—including the sonic needs—of neurodivergent ways of being in the world. Following the Lippsian perspective we've been developing, we argue that musical spaces in ASD music therapy potentially scaffold the development of rhythm, resonance, and responsivity among participants. Consequently, these spaces enable autistic persons to connect with others to a degree and with a felt richness that they may struggle to achieve outside of these musical spaces.

First, some brief background. ASD spans a range of impairments that are wide-ranging and vary by individual. These impairments tend to cluster around social, communicative, and imaginative difficulties (Frith 2003). Autistic people[14] often prefer order, predictability, and routine and can become preoccupied with specific subjects, activities, and habits. They may also have various communication difficulties, struggle attuning to others' emotions and intentions, and find it challenging to flexibly respond to shifting social environments (Bader 2020; Krueger and Maiese 2018).

It is still widely assumed that social difficulties in autism result from neurocognitive differences found in all autistic individuals (Chapman 2019). These differences are said to cluster around a specific trait: a diminished capacity for empathy, or *mentalizing*, when compared to neurotypicals (Baron-Cohen 1995). The core idea is that social difficulties in autism arise because autistic people struggle to cognize the existence of other minds. This empathy deficit leads to difficulties interpreting and predicting others' behavior and smoothly integrating with the shared practices and environments that make up everyday life.

What is important for our purposes is that many therapeutic strategies reflect this cognitivist assumption. With names like "mind-reading training," "picture-in-the-head teaching," and "thought-bubble training," they are designed specifically to help individuals develop and refine their mentalizing capacities so that they can more effectively represent the mental lives of others. However, recent work challenges this cognitivist approach (e.g., De Jaegher 2013; Gallagher & Varga 2015). Two shortcomings are highlighted: First, this approach overlooks the key role *embodied and interactive* factors play in shaping social impairments in ASD and offers few resources for addressing these features. Second, it presupposes that social impairments in ASD consist in a failure to conform to normative expectations of neurotypicals, without acknowledging or offering resources to address the *two-way nature* of some of these impairments.

This is where music therapy, which can involve listening, singing, or joint music-making, may help. Music-based interventions are attractive for individuals with ASD for at least three reasons (Srinivasan & Bhat 2013). First, they can address core impairments in joint attention, social reciprocity, and verbal and nonverbal communication, along with comorbidities of atypical perception, motor performance, and behavioral problems. Second, children with ASD often have enhanced pitch processing abilities and musical memory compared to typically developing children and, therefore, may find these interventions particularly pleasurable (Heaton 2003). Third, music-based activities can provide non-intimidating contexts to interact with musical instruments and other people by engaging in predictable, musically guided interactions with social partners (Darrow & Armstrong 1999).

Evidence suggests that these kinds of musical interventions positively impact various forms of development, including communicative, social-emotional, and motoric development. For example, music therapies can facilitate verbal and gestural skills in children with ASD; enhance social skills such as eye contact, joint attention, mimicry, and turn-taking; and support the improvement of fine and gross motor skills (Srinivasan & Bhat 2013). These effects can help subjects with ASD to strengthen their ability to gauge fine-grained social cues and their capacity for "body-reading." In a musical setting, subjects do rely on bodily expression to communicate—but eye contact, bodily expressions, and mimicry tend to be more exaggerated than in standard neurotypical settings. And because they are punctuated by changes in musical tone and rhythm, these expressions are easier for subjects with ASD to detect.

In this way, musical activities like listening, singing, and joint music-making can enhance patterns of rhythm, resonance, and responsivity among participants. Musical activities furnish regulative contexts in which children with ASD can work with neurotypicals to co-construct alternative musically guided forms of social connection. Musically generated auditory and rhythmic signals can regulate attention and movement in several ways: by influencing the timing of motor neuron discharge; decreasing felt muscle fatigue; facilitating automatic movements by providing predictable temporal cues; improving reaction time and response quality through facilitated responsive anticipation; and providing auditory feedback for proprioceptive control mechanisms (Thaut 1988, 130). In this way, music can serve as scaffolding for the development of selective attention and strengthen subjects' ability to detect social cues (van der Schyff & Krueger 2019). As participants lock into these shared rhythms and play an active role in shaping their development and character, they feel a deepened sense of resonance with one another, as well as a heightened responsivity to what the other is doing on a moment-to-moment basis as the music guides their interaction.

Musical spaces in a therapeutic context can have empathy-enhancing effects in other ways, too. The opportunity to interact in a musical setting may help counteract the tendency of some subjects with ASD to withdraw from social interaction. Because subjects with ASD are sometimes overreactive and feel overwhelmed by visual or auditory stimuli, they may avert their gaze, put their hands over their ears, or avoid interaction with others (Shanker 2004). Similarly, McGeer (2001) suggests that to manage sensory experiences, subjects with ASD might feel the need to shut out other people; however, that makes it difficult for them to develop social and communicative skills. The more a child with ASD avoids interaction with others, the more he or she is deprived of the sorts of experiences needed for social development.

Musical spaces provide a flexible and inclusive place where individuals with ASD can come together with other people and begin to develop an intuitive understanding of what others are thinking and feeling. Coordinated musical improvisation, for example, may help give participants a felt sense of being part of meaningful shared activity. There are often moments in music therapy where there is a palpable energy or "buzz" between the two players, for example when they spontaneously come together at a cadence point or somehow know when to end or where to go next (Maratos et al. 2011, 92). This kind of collective, communicative musicking allows participants to experience forms of social connection and emotional sharing that are different than talking, and yet offers them an avenue to overcome social isolation. In addition, it allows those who feel alienated from or out-of-sync with the social world to get back into the bodily groove of interacting with others.

Finally, the relational efficacy of music therapy—and the comfort and confidence people with ASD often exhibit within these shared musical-empathic spaces—has ethical significance. It reminds neurotypicals of the role they play in shaping the character and intensity of social impairments of ASD (Krueger 2021). A lesson of these relational therapies, we suggest, is that to better connect with autistic people, neurotypicals should move beyond attempts to "fix" the heads of single individuals (e.g., such as we find in cognitivist approaches) and instead consider ways of adjusting and recalibrating material and normative features of the social world. These strategies can include constructing more inclusive ASD-friendly spaces that consider how things like colors, lights, textures, sounds, and smells may negatively impact ASD styles of embodiment and sensory processing, and potentially impede their ability to find their way. It may involve social skills training not just for autistic persons but also neurotypicals—for example, sensitizing the latter to characteristic ASD patterns of interaction (e.g., delayed conversational response) to become more flexible and responsive to such differences. Finally, it may also involve exploring alternative (i.e., noncognitivist) forms of therapeutic interventions such as music therapy.

CONCLUSION

Among artists, and perhaps more widely held in the population, one can trace a folk-psychological idea that engaging with art, or more specifically music, makes one a better person and enhances one's empathic capacities. Few studies have been able to justify just an inch of that romantic notion.[15] We are certainly not advancing such a general claim. Rather, we believe that our analyses justify a narrower claim, namely that certain specialized forms of musicking, not least some of those associated with improvisation, highlight interaction and open empathic spaces that are otherwise hard to enter.

For Snekkestad, he can move from a low-level gut feeling of forcing the musicians to change musical direction to enable different artistic or aesthetic spaces to emerge. Or he can do so by accessing a rich repertoire of reflective processes to adjust the level of unpredictability of the music, feeding off impulses and perceived expectations from audience or musicians. The therapist improvising together with an ASD client can likewise play with the level of rhythmic and melodic predictability nudging interaction and exploration and thus helping and explicating otherwise normal interactive processes of turn-taking or rhythmical gesticulation. In both cases, musicking is used as a means of communication, speaking the same language as empathic processes.

If we revisit Lipps, we understand that this refurbishing of aesthetic means for empathic ends is possible because the two domains from the outset share significant characteristics or engage the same mental structures characterized by activity, rhythm, and resonance. Opening oneself to the demand structures of the other, be it artwork or human, while preserving one's sense of identity, enables rhythmic processes of turn-taking and resonance. When these are impaired as is the case in ASD, they can be explicated and partially restored by making aesthetic improvisatory practices a kind of placeholder. And when operating normally, they can be stretched, challenged, and further attuned in even more sophisticated performative practices, essentially making free improvisation musicians experts of interaction. We certainly expect similar parallels to exist in other artistic or improvisatory practices, but the language of rhythm and resonance is particularly applicable in our musical cases.

NOTES

1. See, for instance, Herder, 2011, part four, especially pp. 78 and 81, as well as Novalis, 1837, p. 99, Cited in Stern, 1898, p. 3).

2. The original texts says *der ganze leibmensch wird ergriffen*. (Vischer, 1873, p. 11)

3. This is a thought that would later appear more explicitly in the work of Lipps, Husserl, and Stein; cf. Stein (1989, p. 11) where she characterizes empathy as a *sui generis* form of intentionality.

4. See for instance, Currie, 2011, for descriptions of this neglect. For two reviews of the different positions within the empathy aesthetics see Meumann, 1908, and Geiger, 1911.

5. In Husserl's *Phenomenological Psychology* (1977, p. 84). we find descriptions of cultural objects, which suggests something similar. Consider for instance the following passage: "The sense (the mental significant sense expressed by cultural objects) is not found next to the matter which expresses it; rather, both are experienced concretely together. Thus, a two-sided material-mental object again stands before our eyes. Therefore, there is an analogy between the way these objects are experienced and the way in which in experiencing fellow-man, we experience a unity of body and psyche."

6. Lipps points out that bodily activity is of a special significance since the feeling of being active in bodily movement is central to the constitution of the I and the body as unity, or what he refers to as the Body-I (*Körper-ich*; Lipps, 1901, 1909). By body-I is an immediate organ of volitional activity, through which the I can engage actively with the things of the world. As Lipps notes, the active body plays a significant role in establishing the awareness of competence of activity or ability (*Tätigkeitskönnen*), that is, the awareness of being the master of the body and as such of having the power to make change through the body (Lipps, 1909, p. 41, see also Lipps 1901). The phenomenological importance of this account was recognized by Husserl in *Ideas II* (1989, p. 270) where he in his description of the "I-can" refers to Lipps as the one who first presented this fundamental discussion.

7. Consequently, we might say that Lipps's account of mental rhythm provides a theory of *sensus communis*.

8. Lipps's concepts of depth and mood are central to the experience of aesthetic and ethical value. In chapter 18 of this book, titled "Affective Depth and Value: On Theodor Lipps's Theory of Aesthetic Empathy," Hansen and Roald have described these aspects of Lipps's theory in more detail.

9. Høffding has written a number of pieces, describing and analyzing free improvisation. For a detailed presentation of the exact techniques employed in the art form, see Høffding & Snekkestad, 2021. For more theoretical analyses focused on

exploration and 4E cognition approaches to free improvisation, see Høffding & Schiavio 2021, Høffding & Satne 2019; Ravn & Høffding 2021.

10. To get a sense of such music, here is a link to a concert with Torben Snekkestad, https://www.youtube.com/watch?v=W6DCnMLSYns

11. The most well-known will be Giorgi's "phenomenological psychology," van Manen's "hermeneutic phenomenological interview" or "Interpretive Phenomenological Analysis." See Heimann, Høffding, and Martiny (in press) for an overview.

12. For lovely 4E takes on music, see Wheeler 2018; Linson & Clarke 2017; Torrence and Schumann 2019; and Krueger 2009, 2014.

13. As argued elsewhere, this is the case even in solo-improvisation (Høffding & Satne 2019).

14. We here follow the terminological preferences of neurodiversity proponents who endorse identity-first language ("autistic persons") instead of person-first language ("persons with autism") to stress the connection between cognitive styles and selfhood (Pellicano and Strears 2011).

15. See, however, Zelechowska et al. (2020).

REFERENCES

Bader, O. (2020). Alterations of Social Attention in Mental Disorders: Phenomenology, Scope, and Future Directions for Research. *Consciousness and Cognition*, 79, 102884.

Bailey, D. (1993). *Improvisation: Its Nature and Practice in Music.* Da Capo Press.

Baron-Cohen, S. (1995). *Mindblindness: An Essay on Autism and Theory of Mind.* MIT Press.

Borgo, D. (2002). Negotiating Freedom: Values and Practices in Contemporary Improvised Music. *Black Music Research Journal*, 22(2), 165–88.

Chapman, R. (2019). Autism as a Form of Life: Wittgenstein and the Psychological Coherence of Autism. *Metaphilosophy*, 50(4), 421–40.

Corbett, J. (2016). *A Listener's Guide to Free Improvisation.* University of Chicago Press.

Currie, G. (2011). Empathy for Objects. In A. Coplan & P. Goldie (Eds.), *Empathy: Philosophical and Psychological Perspectives*. Oxford University Press.

Darrow, A.-A., & Armstrong, T. (1999). Research on Music and Autism Implications for Music Educators. *Update: Applications of Research in Music Education*, 18(1), 15–20.

De Jaegher, H. (2013). Embodiment and Sense-Making in Autism. *Frontiers in Integrative Neuroscience*, 7(15), 1–19.

Dufrenne, M. (1973). *The Phenomenology of Aesthetic Experience*. Northwestern University Press.

Fechner, G. T. (1876). *Vorschule Der Aesthetik.* Druck und Verlag Breitkopf und Härtel.

Friedrich, T., & Gleiter, J. H. (2007). *Einfühlung und phänomenologische Reduktion: Grundlagentexte zu Architektur, Design und Kunst*. LIT Verlag Münster.

Frith, U. (2003). *Autism: Explaining the Enigma*. Wiley-Blackwell.
Gallagher, S. (2011). Aesthetics and Kinaesthetics. In H. Bredekamp & J. M. Krois (Eds.), *Sehen und Handeln* (pp. 99–113). Akademie Verlag.
Gallagher, S., & Varga, S. (2015). Conceptual issues in autism spectrum disorders. *Current Opinion in Psychiatry*, 28(2), 127–32.
Gallagher, S., & Zahavi, D. (2008). *The Phenomenological Mind: An Introduction to Philosophy of Mind and Cognitive Science* (2nd ed.). Routledge.
Geiger, M. (1911). Über das Wesen und die Bedeutung der einfühlung. *Bericht über den IV. Kongress für experimentelle Psychologie*, 29–73.
Heaton, P. (2003). Pitch Memory, Labelling and Disembedding in Autism. *Journal of Child Psychology and Psychiatry, and Allied Disciplines*, 44(4), 543–51.
Heimann, K., Høffding, S., & Martiny, K. (in press). "Working with Others' Experiences: Theory, Practise and Application." Special Issue of *Phenomenology and the Cognitive Sciences*.
Herder, J. G. (2011). *Sculpture: Some Observations on Shape and Form from Pygmalion's Creative Dream*. University of Chicago Press.
Husserl, E. (1977) *Phenomenological psychology*. Lectures, summer semester, 1925, (Scanlon, J. Trans.) Martinus Nijhoff.
———. (1989) *Ideas Pertaining to a Pure Phenomenology and to Phenomenological Philosophy. Second Book*. (R. Rojcewics and A. Schuwer, Trans.) Kluwer Academic Publishers.
Høffding, S. (2019). *A Phenomenology of Musical Absorption*. Palgrave Macmillan.
Høffding, S., & Martiny, K. (2016). Framing a Phenomenological Interview: What, Why and How. *Phenomenology and the Cognitive Sciences*, 15, 539–64.
Høffding, S., & Schiavio, A. (2021). Exploratory Expertise and the Dual Intentionality of Music-Making. *Phenomenology and the Cognitive Sciences*, 20, 811–29.
Høffding, S., & Snekkestad, T. (2021). Inner & Outer Ears—Enacting Agential Systems in Music Improvisation. Dance Improvisation and the Metaphysics of Force. In. S. Ravn, J. McGuirk, & S. Høffding (Eds.) *Philosophy of Improvisation: Interdisciplinary Perspectives on Theory and Practice*. Routledge.
Krueger, J. (2009). Enacting Musical Experience. *Journal of Consciousness Studies*, 16(2–3), 98–123.
———. (2014). Affordances and the Musically Extended Mind. *Frontiers in Psychology*, 4, article no. 1003: 1–13. doi: https://doi.org/10.3389/fpsyg.2013.01003
Krueger, J., & Maiese, M. (2018). Mental Institutions, Habits of Mind, and an Extended Approach to Autism. *Thaumàzein*, 6, 10–41.
Krueger, J. (2021). Finding (and Losing) One's Way: Autism, Social Impairments, and the Politics of Space. *Phenomenology and Mind*, 21, 20–33.
Legrand, D., & Ravn, S. (2009). Perceiving Subjectivity in bodily Movement: The Case of Dancers. *Phenomenology and the Cognitive Sciences*, 8(3), 389–408. https://doi.org/10.1007/s11097-009-9135-5
Lewis, G. E. (1996). Improvised Music after 1950: Afrological and Eurological Perspectives. *Black Music Research Journal*, 16(1): 91–122.

Linson, A., & Clarke, E. (2017). Distributed Cognition, Ecological Theory and Group Improvisation. In E. Clarke & M. Doffman (Eds.), *Distributed Creativity: Collaboration and Improvisation in Contemporary Music* (pp. 52–69). Oxford University Press.

Lipps, T. (1900). Aesthetische Einfühlung. *In Zeitschrift für psychologie und Physiologie der Sinnesorganen*, 22, 415–50.

———. (1901). *Das Selbstbewusstsein; Empfindung und Gefüh.* Weisbaden: Verlag von J. F. Bergmann.

———. (1903). *Ästhetik: Psychologie des Schönen und der Kunst. Erster Teil: Grundlegung der Ästhetik.* Verlag von Leopold Voss.

———. (1905). Bewußtsein und Gegenstande. In Lipps, T (Ed.) *Psychologische Untersuchungen.* Vol 1, 1–203

———. (1906).. Einfühlung und ästhetischer Genuss. *Die Zukunft*, *54*, 100–114.

———. (1907). Vom Fühlen, Wollen und Denken. Versuch einer Theorie des Willens. Zweite Völlig umgearbeitete auflage. Verlag von Johan Ambrosius Bart.

———. (1908). Ästhetik. In P. Hinneberg (Ed.), *Die Kultur der Gegenwart. Ihre Ent wicklung und ihre Ziele. I. Teil, Abt. 6: Systematische Philosophie*, 351–88. Druck und Verlag von B.G. Teubner.

———. (1909). *Leitfaden der Psychologie* (Dritte teilweise umgearbeitet Auflage). Verlag von Wilhelm Engelmann.

Maratos, A., Crawford, M. J., & Procter, S. (2011). Music Therapy for Depression: It Seems to Work, But How? *British Journal of Psychiatry*, 199(2), 92–93.

McGeer, V. (2001). Psycho-Practice, Psycho-Theory and the Contrastive Case of Autism. How Practices of Mind Become Second-Nature. *Journal of Consciousness Studies*, 8(5–6), 109–32.

Meumann, E. (1908). *Einführung in die Ästhetik der Gegenwart.* Verlag von Quelle und Meyer.

Pellicano, E., & Stears, M. (2011). Bridging Autism, Science and Society: Moving toward an Ethically Informed Approach to Autism Research. *Autism Research: Official Journal of the International Society for Autism Research*, 4(4), 271–82.

Ravn, S. (2021). Integrating Qualitative Research Methodologies and Phenomenology—using Dancers' and Athletes' Experiences for Phenomenological Analysis. *Phenomenology and the Cognitive Sciences.* https://doi.org/10.1007/s11097-021-09735-0

Ravn, S., & Høffding, S. (2016). The Promise of 'Sporting Bodies' in Phenomenological Thinking—How Exceptional Cases of Practice Can Contribute to Develop Foundational Phenomenological Concepts. *Qualitative Research in Sport, Exercise and Health*, 9(1), 56–68.

———. (2021). Improvisation and Thinking in Movement: An Enactivist Analysis of Agency in Artistic Practices. *Phenomenology and the Cognitive Sciences.* https://doi.org/10.1007/s11097-021-09756-9

Shanker, S. (2004). The Roots of Mindblindness. *Theory & Psychology*, 14(5), 685–703.

Small, C. (1998). *Musicking—The Meanings of Performing and Listening* (Music/Culture Wesleyan).

Srinivasan, S., & Bhat, A. (2013). A Review of "Music and Movement" Therapies for Children with Autism: Embodied Interventions for Multisystem Development. *Frontiers in Integrative Neuroscience*, 7(22), 22.

Stern, P. (1898). *Einfühlung und Association in der Neuren Ästhetik—Ein Beitrag zur Psychologischen Analyse der Ästhetischen Anschauung*. Verlag von Leopold Voss.

Stueber, K. R. (2006). *Rediscovering Empathy: Agency, Folk Psychology, and the Human Sciences*. MIT Press.

Thaut, M. H. (1988). Rhythmic Intervention Techniques in Music Therapy with Gross Motor Dysfunctions. *The Arts in Psychotherapy*, 15(2), 127–37.

Torrance, S., & Schumann, F. (2019). The Spur of the Moment: What Jazz Improvisation Tells Cognitive Science. *AI & SOCIETY*, 34, 251–68.

van der Schyff, D., & Krueger, J. (2019). Musical Empathy, from Simulation to 4E Interaction. In A. F. Corrêa, ed., *Music, Speech, and Mind*, 73–108. Associação Brasileira de Cognição e Artes Musicais.

Vischer, R. (1873). *Ueber das optische Formgefühl. Ein Beitrag zur Aesthetik.* Hermann Credner.

———. (1994). On the Optical Sense of Form: A Contribution to Aesthetics. In H. F. Mallgrave & Ikonomou, E. (Eds.), *Empathy, Form, and Space: Problems in German Aesthetics, 1873–1893*. University of Chicago Press.

Wheeler, M. (2018). Talking about more than Heads: The Embodied, Embedded and Extended Creative Mind. In B. Gaut &M. Kieran (Eds.), *Creativity and Philosophy*, 230–50. Routledge.

Zahavi, D. (2010) Empathy, Embodiment and Interpersonal Understanding: From Lipps to Schutz. *Inquiry*, 53(3), 285–306.

Zelechowska, A., Gonzalez Sanchez, V., Laeng, B., Vuoskoski, J., & Jensenius, A. (2020). Who Moves to Music? Empathic Concern Predicts Spontaneous Movement Responses to Rhythm and Music. *Music & Science*, 3, 1–16. doi: 10.1177/2059204320974216

Chapter 20

To Step into the Life of Others

Professional Action, Empathy and an Ethics of Engagement

Eva Schwarz

ABSTRACT

What does it mean to "understand each other" in the framework of a concrete plurality of subjects? What are the limits of our moral concern? In current philosophical discussions on the ethical relevance of empathy, the concept of empathy is largely discussed in an individualist framework with some standard examples of face-to-face-meetings. The encounter with another is often thinly described, with a focus on the feelings or experiences of persons, rather than on the wider situation and complex interaction in which they are involved. Instead, I will start from real-life situations, using examples from professional practice where subjects do not only relate to each other, but where they also step into each other's lives. In taking my starting point in practices, I hope to develop a more realistic understanding of empathy that is not only directed at an understanding of another subject but also of complex situations. This exploration will be rooted in two examples, one from policing and the other from nursing. The cases will be discussed in the light of Simone de Beauvoir's idea of engagement and Hannah Arendt's concept of plurality. Ultimately, a notion of empathy will emerge from out of an ethics of engagement.

Keywords: empathy, ethics, professional action, Beauvoir, Arendt, engagement

Without a sense of the world, you also have no sense of people.

—Meløe, 1983, 48

INTRODUCTION

What does it mean to relate to each other in the framework of a concrete plurality of subjects? There is today an ongoing debate surrounding the role of empathy in the idea of a "morally good action" and ethics in general. On the one hand, we have what I want to call *ethical approaches* that argue for the importance of empathy for our understanding of ethics. To understand what it means to act morally good in relation to another person, empathy is taken to play a crucial role. To have the ability to empathize with someone else is said to be of utmost importance for understanding ethics and moral action (e.g., Hamington 2017; Slote 2007). Empathy is defined as a capacity of relating to another subject in a way that includes a caring for the other, often in the sense of an impulse to relieve her suffering (Svenaeus 2014, 294), or in a reflective judgment of thinking one ought to help (Slote 2007). Within many professional educations, it has become common to educate students in empathy, to teach them "basic skills" of ethical encounters (Englander 2019). On the other hand, we have what I want to call *epistemological approaches*, which argue that empathy has either no or little ethical significance but is a concept that depicts the way we perceive other subjects. Dan Zahavi (2001) has argued that empathy, "in its basic form," is a concept that allows us to describe the way intersubjectivity is constituted. It is about being directly experientially acquainted with an experience that is not my own. Empathy itself says little about the way we relate to each other in morally significant ways, or about enhancing "prosocial behavior" (Zahavi 2022 [chapter 22 of this volume]). All the same, empathy, according to Zahavi, remains constitutive for our understanding of other morally significant phenomena, such as compassion or sympathy (Ibid.). From a phenomenological point of view, he argues, there is yet an important difference between empathy and other phenomena such as an impulse to help, imaginative perspective taking or affective sharing (Darwall 1998; Decety & Lamm 2006). It is not about creating similarity or fusion or an overcoming of suffering and distance, but about an experience of difference (Zahavi 2022).

The debates surrounding empathy circle around an adequate description of the phenomena, as well as around the relation between epistemological and ethical perspectives, and also between experience or perception and action (Krueger & Overgaard 2022).[1] What is common to the different approaches is that empathy is largely discussed within an individualist framework (Morgan 2017), including some standard examples of face-to-face-meetings, often with a perceiver or helper, positioned on the one side, and the person being perceived or helped on the other. The encounter is often thinly described, with a focus on the feelings or experiences of the other (often suffering!) subject. I want to approach the relation between empathy and ethics from a slightly different angle. I will start from real-life situations, using examples from professional practices (i.e., policing and nursing), where subjects not only relate to each other but are involved in a more or less complex situation requiring action. In my approach, is not only an experience, perception or understanding of the other that is at stake but an understanding of the situation and, in the long run, an understanding of a common world. Thus, I proceed from the idea that our relations to and with others are not primarily epistemic or moral in nature, but practical. This differs from ethical approaches, insofar that I take my starting point from within complicated situations requiring *mutual* interactions and (self-)understandings. When one thinks of oneself as acting together with others, the suffering (or whatever they are going through) of others is obviously one part of the ethically salient situation or world. However, it is not the only part, and, indeed, whether it is the most relevant part will depend on the situation. In taking one's starting point in a practical attitude (Husserl 1982/1913), we can also see, as I hope, how epistemological and ethical perspectives on empathy are related to one another. From a practical perspective, both understanding others as well as acting well toward them are *aspects* of an ongoing interaction in a shared world that concerns us, and whose objectivity is negotiated via interactions. This ongoing interaction and negotiation requires active engagement in both marking limits (limits of my concern, limits of my responsibility) and transcending limits (e.g., in the shape of routines). This means that "practice" is not primarily defined as institutionalized goal-directed actions (e.g., Berger & Luckmann 1966) but in the Aristotelian sense of praxis, i.e., as the sphere of interaction that is intrinsically meaningful to the agents, independent of the results or external goal (as in poiesis; Aristotle 2011). This idea of practice points to a certain ambiguity. The ambiguity consists in our relation to a world that is open to my choices, actions, and epistemic judgments and the meanings I ascribe to certain objects, persons, or routines. Yet, the practical world is also already formed and challenged by meanings, actions, and judgments of others. An understanding of empathy situated in concrete practices and defined as an "experience of difference," includes thus not only concrete others but also others who leave traces in the form of routines, styles and habits of acting, seeing, and judging that transcend my own sphere of life.

How, then, to approach empathy from within practice? I take it that the challenge of empathy consists in situations where one more or less willingly "steps into the world of another" (Meløe 1974).[2] This is not meant in terms of either a perspective-taking or imagination but in the form of a confrontation with a world of another that is strange to me. When I end up in a situation where I do not know what is going on, what others are doing or thinking, it is often not helpful to look at the person but to follow the gaze of the person toward the world with which she or he is engaged and see what might cause her concern. Following this intuition, I will begin my inquiry by investigating examples where empathy is said to be an utmost important dimension for skillful and morally good action and where subjects are confronted with each other in challenging situations.[3] The examples raise questions, such as: How to relate to one's engagement in the life of others? Who are we to one another and what are we doing once we have stepped into another's life? How to construe an understanding of a common world in relation to a plurality of perspectives that are strange to me? In a second step, I will turn to two philosophical concepts, engagement and plurality, as formulated by Simone de Beauvoir in her text "Pyrrus and Cineas" and Hannah Arendt in her major work *The Human Condition.* Both concepts shall help me to develop on the questions that arise from the examples. In the last part of this inquiry, I will develop an idea of the ethical sphere as not merely the sphere of "good action" but as the space for engagement into each other's lives. The ethical sphere thus becomes the place where our actions and interactions are at stake, where we negotiate who we show ourselves to be in our interactions in each other's lives. The interesting question is thus not *how much* empathy matters for ethics but *how* it matters.

TO STEP INTO THE LIFE OF OTHERS: EXAMPLES FROM PROFESSIONAL LIFE

The first example is taken from an essay written by a police student at Södertörn University in Sweden, Therese Botvidsson. In her essay, which also serves as the final examination paper for her studies, the police student recounts an event during her six-month internship period that was especially significant to her.[4] One night, together with her experienced instructor and a student colleague, she is called to an apartment with a psychotic and potentially violent person with a knife. While two others take care of the psychotic man, Botvidsson searches through the man's apartment where she is confronted with an unexpected situation:

> Already with my first step into the apartment, the heat hits me, I wonder if it's burning in the apartment. When I pass the hallway, I come to a long passage, the whole floor has broken light bulbs and, with every step taken, it crackles

> from my boots. I see that there are drops of blood on the shards of glass and I have my pepper spray directed in front of me as I continue into the apartment. Suddenly I see something moving and a face appears from the left side. It's a little boy who looks at me with big eyes and says "hello." I find myself pointing the pepper spray at the boy. I lower it while I greet and tell him who I am. The boy answers "sorry for the shards of glass, but Dad has to have them there to be able to hear when the demons come. (2021, p. 109, my translation)

Botvidsson describes the situation as extremely difficult. She knows not how to relate to the boy. She starts a conversation about his dog and his father and the chaos in the apartment. The boy talks to her without expressing fear. He seems to be used to the situation, the chaos, and the psychic hallucinations. Should the boy really be left in this misery, with his seemingly equally helpless grandmother? When Botvidsson leaves the apartment, she meets with her instructor who "shrugs his shoulders, waves with his arms" and says "Report of concern" (Ibid., p. 112). For the instructor, the right way to handle the situation is a matter of routine. Botvidsson wants to tell the instructor to take the boy away from the place. But she remains silent; she does not dare to question her instructor.

In this example, the inexperienced police student steps into the life of a family that appears radically different from what she is used to or could have imagined beforehand: blood and broken glass, unbearable heat, signs of psychotic actions. Still, it is part of her professional work as (becoming) a police officer to enter into the innermost private sphere of others, to be involved in ongoing relationship dramas, crime, violence, misery, and abuse. And even though the group of police officers are informed beforehand, they never quite know what they can expect. Besides, situations can change fast. (One thing police students learn from the beginning is to mentally prepare for "the best, the worst and the most likely situation" at once [Lappalainen 2021]). In the example, the police student expresses an insecurity in how to relate to the boy's expression of "normality" and the instructor's unwillingness of doing something for the boy. The police student is a beginner; she has not been in a similar situation with nothing to compare to. For her, as she writes, to enter the apartment is to enter a strange and unknown world. She is surprised by the boy's seeming indifference toward the father's behavior and does not know how to interpret it. In her world, she writes, the boy should be afraid and shaken by the situation (Botvidsson 2021, p. 115). The instructor does not see the boy's life as a police concern but, rather, of social services, but the student has not established an independent and well-grounded understanding of how to react to the situation.

With respect to the notion of empathy, we can describe this as a challenging situation for the police student. Both as a direct encounter with another subject's expressions, as formulated in epistemic accounts and as a challenge in terms of morally correct action. To her, the boy is in need of help. Yet, it is the combination of both dimensions, the direct experience of the boy's expression of feeling seemingly alright and her impulse to do something about the situation as a whole, that are puzzling. Her experience of the boy's expressions stands in contrast to the rest of the situation, including her relations to the judgment of the instructor, the grandmother, and the child and the possibility of getting help from social services. Maybe a direct expression of fear or suffering would have made it easier for the police student to judge the situation?

Before we examine this further, let us look at another example: An essay written by a nurse, Christina Olofsson, who at the time of her writing works in a home for elderly people, many of whom suffer from dementia. Right from the beginning, the nurse develops a quite close relationship with one of the women living there, Svea. For most of her life, Svea has been engaged in physically demanding labor, causing chronic back pain. She is helped every morning with her hygiene while someone follows her to the toilet. Yet, maybe, as Olofsson speculates, it is because of her increasing state of dependency that Svea is sometimes in a bad mood, berating the nurse with offensive names, and telling her that she is useless. Olofsson describes one of those days when she helps her to the toilet and is subject to verbal abuse:

> One day when I was a "wood-louse" again, it broke for me and I got angry. I left her on the toilet and thought she could sit there. The anger subsided quickly and I went back and opened the toilet door. When I went in I said: "Hello, so this is where the old crow is hiding?"
>
> This was a conscious case of disrespect and certainly a breach of integrity. But Svea's eyes lit up. She learned to recognize me, but she never said my name. Maybe this was a way for her to distance herself from the help I gave. She also became increasingly demented. (Olofsson 2011, p. 21, my translation)

In this example, just as in the previous one, the situation involves a professional taking part in the life of another person. Working with elderly people with dementia as a nurse, Botvidsson takes part in the old woman's intimate sphere of life such as washing and toilet visits. A sphere with which often not even close relatives are involved (Ibid., p. 22). Olofsson reflects on her relation to the old woman and how hard it is to take care of someone who does not want to be cared for. The nurse describes the woman as a person of integrity who wants to handle things on her own, as she was used to. She even asks herself whether it is possible to care in a good and skillful way for someone you do not like. It is obvious that she herself is affected by the way the old woman treats her and keeps her at distance (Ibid., p. 25). In the situation described she takes leave of the "professional" relation of a helper, who "empathetically feels with" the helpless woman and reacts angrily.

Both examples are characterized by a certain "gap" between the professional's practice, on the one hand, and the situations the professionals encounter on the other. In the case of the nurse, we have a practice based on routines and structures of helping and care, of assisting people with their most private routines such as going to the toilet or showering. On the other side, it is the everyday life of a woman who is used to handling things on her own, who reacts angrily to the caring attitude of the nurse, addressing her derogatorily. The nurse in turn is affected by the woman's anger; she leaves the room. But as the irritation subsides she soon returns, choosing to use an unusual phrase: "Hello, so this is where the old crow is hiding?" When the nurse steps outside her routines and handles the situation with humor and adopting unexpected phrases, the old lady reacts positively; Svea seems to appreciate the reaction and, as Olofsson writes, "she lit up." It seems as if once the nurse leaves the professional role of caring and places under suspension any "empathetic" understanding (e.g., She could have said: "I understand that it must be hard to be taken care of.")[5] things open up between the two women. Eventually, the situation can even be described as a game-changer, fundamentally altering the relationship between the two women. Regarding the situation with the boy, the gap consists not only in the difference between the boy's world and the inexperienced police student's but also between her and the instructor. The police student does not tell the instructor what she has seen and dares not to tell him to remove the boy from the apartment. Both the nurse and the police student are insecure about the situation retrospectively. The boy and the woman disappear from the sphere of interaction, the boy abruptly, the woman gradually with the onset of dementia.

These two examples pose different questions, which for various reasons are interesting for the debate on the ethical role of empathy. They can be taken as examples of performing empathy both from an ethical and epistemological perspective. They are about subjects who are being directly experientially acquainted with an experience that is not their own (Zahavi 2022). They are also examples that are, at least from the beginning, characterized by an asymmetry between a helper and someone who is in need of help. Yet, both examples also show the limits of the epistemological and ethical perspectives. The police student and the nurse are confronted with more than the presence of another subject in need of help. They are challenged by a complex situation that constitutes the life of this person, involving other subjects, objects that are meaningful to her, a prehistory, social and interpersonal relations, and so on. They are thrown into a whole world, which disjoins expression from context, and which serves to question their role within the situation in which they are engaged. In the case of the police, this difference shows itself between the boy's expression of indifference and the total chaos of the apartment and, in the case of the nurse, between her own expression of anger and a situation of care. One question with which the professionals are confronted and which is of relevance for an understanding of the ethical significance of empathy is how to relate to the world of others one happens to be thrown into and become engaged with. The examples show that the question of empathy is not only about an understating of an "other" but involves even challenges of *self*-understanding *and self*-interpretation. The professionals *and* the ones in need of help are affected by the situation, though in different ways. Both parties find themselves in a more or less confusing situation with mutual problems of understanding, such as: Who am I in the situation? How to relate to each other? A second form of question raised by the examples concerns the idea of a joint world and objectivity. Professional action seems—by definition—to proceed from a certain asymmetrical relation between the one who acts and the one who is the recipient of the act or is in need of professional action. Yet, there is also an asymmetry not only constituted by the different roles but also by the very positions of all agents involved in the situation at stake. In the police example there is an asymmetry of knowledge and experience between the student, who has actually talked to the boy and experienced the chaos in the apartment, and the supervisor who has not been involved in the same way because he took care of the father outside. For the police student, it is difficult to understand what is really going on. Is she right about her interpretation of the situation, namely that they should take the boy with them, or was the experienced supervisor right? The "special question of empathy," namely how to relate to the otherness of another subject, seems to be intertwined with the question of the constitution of subject-world-relations as such in a way that makes it difficult to distinguish the one from the other: How to construe an understanding of a common world in relation to a plurality of perspectives that are opaque and strange?

In the following I will address these questions, that is, the questions of engagement in the world of others, self-understanding and the possibility of a shared world/objectivity, with the help of two thinkers, Beauvoir and Arendt, neither of whom have (as far as I know) used the concept of empathy but whose philosophical work coheres precisely around the relation among self, other, and world.

ENGAGEMENT, LIMITS, AND TRANSCENDENCE

Let us first look at the question of engagement and moral concern. The young police student wants to do more, or something else, for the boy than is granted by the experienced instructor. The nurse crosses, as one could argue, a certain professional line when she calls the woman an "old crow."[6] What happens when we step into the life of a stranger? How involved should we become in other people's lives? Shall we do more or something other than what professional duty or everyday life routines prescribe? According to Beauvoir, a way of relating to these questions is to gain an insight in the fact that we always already *are involved* in the lives of others. The follow-up question is then how we should *relate* to our engagement. In her essay "Pyrrhus and Cineas," a text written during Nazi Germany's occupation of France and considered her first philosophical publication, Beauvoir introduces the image of Candide's garden from a satirical novel by Voltaire to show a basic moral philosophical problem. The novel's conclusion is that one should tend our own garden rather than speculate on abstract philosophical problems. Yet, Beauvoir does not accept this dichotomy. There are those, she writes, who see the whole world as their garden. For others, a small pot of flowers is too much to take care of (2014). We cannot so easily introduce an a priori distinction between what concerns us and what is "outside our garden." We are related in different ways to the world as "our garden," not in any abstract or predefined way, but as a particular field that concerns us, that is, part of our personal history and decisions based on our individual freedom. Whosoever "pops up" in our experiential field as an expressive subject who concerns me, as another (qua empathy in a phenomenological-epistemological sense), and not just as a thing-like object, is dependent on one's life-situation and history. In our example with the police, the young student, who has not met such misery previously, is touched by the boy's life situation whereas her experienced instructor considers him to be a "case for social services" among others.

To illustrate the different ways we can relate to others, Beauvoir uses another example of two parents responding to a child who cries because the concierge's son has died: "Why are you crying? He's not your brother. You do not know him" (Beauvoir 2004, p. 92). Another time, when a woman cries over her shoes leaking water, they ask her: "Why does that matter, think of the men dying of hunger in China" (p. 89). In the first case, the child is asked to care only about himself. In the other example, the woman should ignore her life; what causes her sadness is deemed not to be as important as other things (i.e., the fate of others). Beauvoir formulates a paradox, which has to do with our understanding of morality and objectivity: To be able to care for someone, we must be involved in the person's life. On the other hand, a moral attitude seems to require us to transcend the here and now, those with whom we are already involved: to care about what not only concerns us but also to acknowledge the needs of those to be taken care of. Looking at our examples, the police student cannot choose not to engage with the life of the boy. In being drawn into his life, she feels with him and engages in his life. She experiences the chaos; she is struck by the smells of the messy apartment, by the signs of aggression, and misery. But she does not act on her engagement. She dares not to. Even this is, if we follow Beauvoir, a way of relating to one's engagement; there is always a choice. The experienced nurse, in contrast to the inexperienced police student, takes a risk by calling the old woman an "old crow." One could describe this as breaking with the professional code. However, it also serves as a certain opening that leads to the old woman accepting her.

But, given that lines need to be drawn to define our actions, e.g., to define the difference between acting as a police officer and a nurse or between a police officer and a private person, how shall these lines be drawn? Beauvoir's answer is simple: We do not have to draw a line between what concerns us and what does not but between different modes of engagement. We feel sorry for or angry at someone because we are committed to the world. We constantly exceed our here and now through our projects in the world. Of course, we draw a line to define our projects and to formulate goals, but we are not only interested in achieving goals. We are interested in the possibility of exceeding them. Beauvoir further states in her essay that the reason why it is at all possible to care about something that happens outside of ourselves lies in our potential as a subject. If we were things, objects, then nothing would concern us: "The existence of things is 'solitude,' they are separated from other things. It is the essence of the thing that can be identified as separate from other things, which is not the case for a subject." (Beauvoir 2004, p. 92) As subjects and not things, we are always already involved in life with others through our commitment to the world: We love, we think, we desire. To be a subject means to reach out beyond oneself. This is what the term *transcendence* stands for:

> It is because my subjectivity is not inertia, folding in upon itself, separation, but, on the contrary, movement towards the other that the difference between me and the other is abolished, and I can call the other mine. Only I can create the tie that unites me to the other. I create it from the fact that I am not a thing, but a project of the self towards the other, a transcendence. (Ibid., p. 93)

The concierge's son, who died, as Beauvoir writes, is no longer a total stranger if I am engaged in his life (Ibid.). Yet, engagement is not enough. What counts is the way I relate to my engagement and what action follows this engagement. A stranger, whom I have never met before, can become a friend or a familiar person, if she or he enters my life as significant. But *my* subjectivity is something that is as much at stake as one of the others. I can decide to draw a line, for example as a professional, and define once and for all, what concerns me and what does not concern me—which might be the case with the instructor in the police example—but doing so has consequences for my subjectivity. I am not only drawing a line toward the other but also for myself because I am limiting my possibilities as a subject (my freedom).[7] In a way, one could say that the moment the nurse allowed herself to react on her being hurt by the old woman's anger she treated her no longer as an "object" one has to take care of but as a subject that transcends her being. This holds even true for her own subjectivity. She did not act as a "nurse" but as a subject.

Beauvoir's perspective on subjectivity as transcendence highlights another dimension of intersubjectivity, which is relevant for the question of empathy as self-other relation: I cannot fully grasp my own and others' perspectives. My engagement is embedded in my history, depending on my past actions and habits but also on my place in the world. I cannot completely choose with whom and in what I am involved. But even the perspective of the other is somewhat inaccessible to me. Because the other, whom one can address as woman with dementia, customer, patient, child is also a subject, he or she always escapes me in this regard (Beauvoir 2004, p. 94). As a subject, I am subjected to the other. My actions are for the other what they mean to either him or her. I cannot force the other into the role I intended.

Even if Beauvoir is not interested in the notion of empathy, I believe her understanding of human subjectivity as grounded in engagement and transcendence can help us understand the relation between ethics and empathy. That I can transcend my perspective is a prerequisite for being able to relate to something or someone I do not know about (yet) but with what or whom I am involved. In this endeavor, I am also dependent on the transcendence (and freedom) of the other. Yet, my engagement is not arbitrary. It is based on my personal history and on the collective practices I participate in. It is these practices that constitute habits—also habits of engagement and moral concern. If I have worked for a long time in a profession, I might not become engaged in the life of others as I would as a beginner. Having said this, I may also develop an instinct for distinguishing between those situations where action is required and others where engagement is exhausting and I am better off handing over the task to other people (e.g., another profession). I can also become aware that I am governed by different, possibly conflicting, interests. If we return now to the situation in the apartment with the boy, one can see that two different types of engagement are in conflict with each other: the police student's engagement in her own fledgling career, who must follow the orders of the police instructor, and a more concrete engagement with the boy based on her strong emotional experiences within the apartment. This goes back to the issues of understanding the world and understanding one's action. Who am I in the situation and what am I doing?

One can see here a quite simple point, namely that, from Beauvoir's perspective, to engage in the life of others turns out to be a complex and ambivalent task. An understanding of professional engagement, such as nursing or policing, is about a certain delimitation of one's field of action. It is also a matter of "acting as", that is, being a representative of a certain role. You are thereby also answerable to those who occupy the same (or similar) roles as you. This puts police students in training in a particularly difficult situation; they are confronted not only with questions such as what to do but also *who* am I in the situation and who do I want to be? The professional role is also associated with a certain ethos that, for example, defines the manner of being a good police officer or a good nurse. At the same time, with Beauvoir, we can establish an understanding of engagement and action as something defined in relation to a concrete situation, where we are confronted with boundaries that have been maintained in advance and boundaries that appear only in the interaction with others. A routine situation can prove to be something else, a situation of shame, which, in the example of the old woman sitting on the toilet, can turn into a transformative moment in which the relationship changes.

PLURALITY: THE WORLD OF OTHERS AND THE POSSIBILITY OF A COMMON WORLD

Let us now turn to the question of a shared or common world and objectivity. While Beauvoir takes her starting point from the situated freedom of an individual, Arendt's analysis of action, as developed in *The Human Condition*, starts from the idea of plurality and a possible common world. Arendt is not writing about empathy either, but her concept of action is interesting for a more pluralistic understanding of empathy as something that occurs together with others or as part of a group. For Arendt, plurality is "the basic precondition for human existence" (2018, p. 7). We are born in a world with and among others. Arendt calls this a "fact" (Ibid.) and the "basic condition" (p. 175) of action and speech. We are always already born into a world of and with others.

> Human plurality, the basic condition of both action and speech, has the twofold character of equality and distinction. If men were not equal, they could neither understand each other and those who will come after them. If men were not distinct, each human being distinguished from any other who is, was or will ever be, they would need neither speech nor action to make themselves understood, Sign and sounds to communicate immediate, identical needs and wants would be enough. (Arendt 2018, p. 175f.)

Plurality, however, as Sophie Loidolt argues in her phenomenological reading of Arendt (Loidolt 2016, 2018), should not be seen as something quantitative, for example, a crowd of people at a square or at a workplace, but as something experienced and expressed in relation to others and the world. Plurality is nothing that only exists there; it is something that potentially can be realized in our actions. Based on this potentiality it is up to us to shape a sense of togetherness with others. That is to say, plurality is one opportunity to be with others; it can either be realized or not. (Arendt 2018, p. 11) Here Arendt is close to Aristotle's notion of praxis. The activities that characterize a life among others and through which plurality can be realized are (in contrast to work and production, which is directed toward life and the world of things) political action as well as speech and judgment. Like virtue, plurality needs a sort of cultural vehicle to become actualized, it is not an individual endeavor but can only be realized with and in relation to others.

This is though not an unambiguous endeavor. By means of action and speech, we express both our uniqueness of who we are, but also establish relations to others, who in turn express who they are in their action:

> The manifestation of who the speaker and doer unexchangeably is, though it is plainly visible, retains a curious intangibility that confounds all efforts toward unequivocal verbal expression. The moment we want to say who somebody is, our very vocabulary leads us astray into saying what he is; we get entangled in a description of qualities he necessarily shares with others like him; we begin to describe a type or a 'character' in the old meaning of the word, with the result that his specific uniqueness escapes us. (Arendt 2018, p. 181)

The unique "who," cannot be captured via description. If we understood the other's expression and described them in terms of a what, we would end up confronting them like an object. Here we see similarities to Beauvoir's concept of transcendence. Subjectivity as well as plurality is an elusive phenomenon. My relatedness to the world always eludes full objectification, and thus, it cannot be treated like an object in the world. Our relatedness via action and speech constitutes our very subjective (*jemeiniger*) perspective toward the world, and does not allow for a reification without the subject negating what it is. It is, as Loidolt writes, exactly this dimension of "who" or "whoness," a first-person perspective, that Arendt is interested in in her phenomenological conception of plurality (Loidolt 2016). What does this mean for the question of empathy? It means that expressions are no equivocal phenomena. Even though I may directly and immediately encounter the other expressing something, I may not identify it as a *what* (e.g., as an anger or fear) but as an expression of *who* I am in a complex life-situation. This holds also true for my own experiential life. The nurse in our example, who expresses anger about the old woman calling her useless and using animal names, by leaving her in the toilet, ends up giving expression to who she is, namely a vulnerable subject.

Interesting for our discussion of empathy is also Arendt's reasoning around similarity and difference. Arendt believes that difference in the form of human distinctness (singularity) is one prerequisite for communication and action. It is by virtue of our differences and the fact that we see the world in different ways, that we can have a mutual understanding of a shared world at all. "Difference" is here not meant as a description of different cultures, age groups or professions, but as an expression of the unique and singular perspectives that constitute a plurality of subjects (see Loidolt 2016). In this sense, difference is epistemologically relevant and can with the help of Arendt's concept of plurality be seen as a presupposition for objectivity, for the idea of a common world. Only the different positions we take on about the world enable us to understand the world as a world (i.e., not only as the sum of objects and things but as a meaningful horizon for our actions). Just because I am unable to perceive the world from the same space as the person close to me, an understanding of its objectivity is secured; if everyone looked at the same thing from the same position at the same time (if ever this were possible), then only one side of the object would appear.[8]

What does that mean in relation to our examples and the question of empathy? Stepping into each other's lives, literally looking at things together, comparing our views, negotiating about what things mean to me or someone else—such as, for example, crushed glass for a psychotic, the pepper spray for a scared police cadet, a closed toilet door, a certain facial expression—a possible common world can unfold, in front of our very eyes. Not in terms of a perspective taken or with the use our imagination, but as the result of concrete acts: movements, touches, sayings. Yet, as much as plurality, the idea of a common world is a vulnerable phenomenon. It can easily be destroyed, corrupted, or deformed; for example, if individual actions are subordinate to an external goal, or if there is an enormous pressure placed on professionals to be efficient, as is the case in modern welfare societies. To exist with others, to be formed by others, runs the general risk of falling prey to what Arendt calls an "aligned gaze," meaning a certain alignment or sharing of perspectives as a leveling off of "ways of seeing." When we consider professional action, certain ways of seeing and doing things, are on the one hand necessary to define a professional role, but can also be destructive for an understanding of action, in the way Arendt develops it in contrast to other activities, such as work. We do as "we" always do. Instead of seeing things from several perspectives, this can lead to us seeing everything with "one eye," with the gaze of the police or a nurse. This leads potentially not only to the problem that the perspectives of others or other perspectives, are no longer taken into consideration (something that may be described as a lack of empathy[9]) but also to a loss of the ability to act. The "fact" that we find each other in the company of others can then take the shape of a uniform collective, something that Arendt sees as the first steps toward a totalitarian system, where actions are reduced to reacting to external conditions:

> Totalitarian domination, which seeks to organize the infinite diversity of human beings and the difference as if all mankind were just one individual, is only possible if each person can be reduced to an unchanging, identical unit of reactions, so that each such bundle of reactions can be arbitrarily exchanged for one another. (Arendt 2019, Swedish edition p. 552, my translation)

If we now link this back to Botvidsson's story, it can be said that the instructor only reacted to the problem with the boy instead of acting in relation to one specific and unique situation that requires a novel assessment. But moreover Botvidsson chose her role of being a "good" student, by refraining from criticizing her experienced colleague. She valued this to be more important than acting on her intuition about the boy. It is the difference between the student's and the experienced police officer's view of the situation that creates a potential precondition for communication and plurality. But there is also a similarity between the two perspectives, namely that they both have knowledge of the law and the police's space for agency (*Spielraum*), which would allow them to find the appropriate response. The problem is that it seems there is no space in their professional practice to face the situation in its own right (Schwarz & Lappalainen 2020). This depends on the student being in the situation of a "trial"; she wants to show herself to be cooperative, but also on a certain established culture of efficiency and "collectivism" that defines the police force. If demands on efficiency are so great that there is neither time nor resources to reason and look at a situation from different perspectives, and if the esprit the corps is so strong that one puts the interest of the group above the interest of "truth" and "objectivity" (Karp and Stenmark 2011), then the idea of a common world and (inter-)action in Arendt's understanding is corrupted. In a way, with Beauvoir, the question of plurality is in the hands of those agents engaged in a given situation. They can decide on how they act on their engagement. The police student can decide to say something to her instructor. As the nurse acted on her anger. Yet, it is also dependent on conditions and preestablished routines, for example the law, recruitment, or good education, which create the space for plurality in a professional community. Thus, empathy as a recognition of other perspectives, is both a presupposition and a threat for an understanding of a common world. Following Arendt, it is only when we relate to a world between us, not only to each other, that we can establish something between us which might count as something common.

ENGAGEMENT NOT EMPATHY?

Let us summarize shortly what has been said so far: In "Pyrrhus and Cineas," Beauvoir develops the ethical question of how to act in a way that is inseparable from the existential question of why to act at all and who we are as an acting subject. To her, the question of the structure and justification of ethical action cannot be separated from the question of the structure of action as such (Bergoffen 2004). For Arendt, action does take place in a social sphere, with others. It is in relation to other perspectives, as a realization of plurality, that an understanding of a common world can occur, reassured and negotiated via speech and interaction. From these perspectives, the moral sphere is not merely the sphere of "good action," but the sphere where our actions and interactions are at stake and where we show each other *who* we are. This is the meaning of praxis. If we put Arendt's and Beauvoir's perspectives together, ethics is not about the "ingredients" of morally good action, but (also) a reflection about what we mean by morally relevant situations and how we can detect and relate to them. In basic form, these two perspectives (also) provide a reflection on praxis, about what and how we do things together and who we are and show ourselves in our interactions with others. Proceeding from an understanding of praxis as the sphere of action (not of production or work) ethics is first and foremost related to concrete situations of (inter-)action that includes epistemological dimensions and vice versa (Schwarz & Lappalainen 2020).

How is this related to empathy? Empathy, as the experience of other subjects, as both experiencing and expressive, has an ethical significance if it takes place in morally relevant *situations*. But what are morally relevant situations? As Arendt writes in "Thinking and Moral Considerations" (2006), we never know which situations might end up tipping over into something other; it can happen in a routine situation "at work" or at an occasional meeting with a stranger on the street. With Arendt, I would characterize situations as morally relevant if they are characterized by the *possibility* of plurality. But are not all situations that way? Since plurality can be both realized and denied, empathy can be present in terms of a lack, as part of morally despicable situations and where the whoness of the other is reduced to a what and actions are reduced to reactions. Or in situations where subjects are interested in each other, in terms of an inter-esse, as a relatedness toward a world between them. Yet, the world "between us" is not a given. Following Beauvoir, as an individual I am separated by my freedom and my projects from others and their freedom and projects. This leads to conflicts and misunderstandings, something that is inevitable. But the fact that, through my freedom, I am separated from others leads necessarily also to relations to others, including engagement and caring. On first appearance, this sounds counterintuitive. But it depends on an understanding of our existence as ambiguous; we are both a subject who acts in the world and an object conditioned by the world and the freedom and projects of others. As such, the individual is dependent on others and is able to join in the project of others; we are constantly drawn into the lives and projects of others. This entails a certain responsibility toward the world and to others. Namely in maintaining and paying attention to our engagement in the form of relations with others and with the world. Debra Bergoffen frames this in her introduction to "Pyrrhus and Cineas" as a challenge:

> Given that others exist for me as objects in the world whose instrumentality is necessary for the success of my projects, how can I get them to support my cause without violating their status as human subjects who, like me, perpetually escape their objective giveness? (Bergoffen 2014, p. 84).

Theorists of empathy often work with suffering as a paradigm example, which has both urgency and immediacy built into it. But once we have acknowledged the suffering and have done what we can do to relieve it, we are still left with questions such as: Who am I, who are you, and what are we doing? Empathy is often described as a kind of discernment, "a way of seeing what is going on in a world that we share with other human beings" (Svenaeus 2014, p. 295).[10] I would agree that in my encounter with others there is an immediate experience of the other person's expressions; based on my own feelings, I do not need to interfere in the thoughts and actions of others (the theory of mind), nor do I need to have the same feelings or do other complex cognitive somersaults to understand that the other is in pain. But the meaning of such expressions is dependent on the broader situation in question. In some cases, we can say that it is because we experience the other as suffering without really knowing what exactly is going on (maybe the person herself does not know either); the situation calls for action. In other cases, as in the case of the boy in the apartment who does not show any signs of fear or suffering, it is the absence of expression in combination with the horrible situation that points to a problem (even if it is unclear what is to be done). I agree with what I call the epistemological perspective, that I can immediately experience the other person as joyful, sad and so on, and with the ethical perspective that this in some cases even leads to an immediate reaction of me wanting to act on my engagement and help (by relieving the suffering). However, to get a handle on the meaning of this expression, I have first to relate to different subjects (including my own) engagement in the situation as a whole. To say that empathy is not a special field of knowledge about others does not mean that I wish to formulate a skepticism in relation to other subjects but rather of the possibility of separating the understanding of others from an understanding of the situation as a whole.

CONCLUSION

In this chapter I have presented an alternative perspective on the relation between ethics and empathy, namely from the perspective of (professional) practice. I started out with two examples, one from the profession of policing and the other from elderly care, to show a certain ambivalence about the possibility of entering into the lives of others. Is empathy some sort of "tool" or "special knowledge" that enables us—whether a doctor, nurse, a teacher and so on—to gain access into the perspective of the other? Might empathy allow us to build a common world? With the help of Arendt's concept of plurality and Beauvoir's idea of engagement, we can state quite the opposite: It is on the basis of empathy (i.e., our experiences of and with others in concrete situations), that possible gaps occur. It is because we do not understand entirely the world of the other, who the other is and who I am in relation to them, that I can speak of a common world that engages and puzzles me. In this chapter, I have not sought to find a new concept of empathy or a new approach to it. My intention instead has been to offer a more realistic and persuasive account of empathy as an embedded phenomenon. Looking at real-life examples, it becomes obvious that empathy, or the questions of understanding others, is not a special domain of knowledge beset with special problems. The understanding of others always already takes place in terms of an understanding of the world in which we are both acting, trying to understand who we are, what we are, and what we are doing (or supposed to do).

ACKNOWLEDGEMENT

I want to thank Carl Cederberg and Stina Bäckström for their helpful comments on a previous version of this chapter.

NOTES

1. Thomas Fuchs offers, as it seems to me, a mediating perspective between epistemological and ethical approaches, by distinguishing between different layers or forms of empathy, from a more basic and bodily direct perception of another subject as experiencing and expressive, to other higher forms, including imaginative place taking and ethical reasoning (Fuchs 2017).

2. Here, I am inspired by the Norwegian philosopher Jakop Meløe, who in his work on fishermen in northern Norway has come to an understanding of the other via a joint praxis. To understand another is to "step into the other's world" (Meløe 1974).

3. In the case of interpersonal professional practices, the doing is also a joint doing with colleagues and is related to the life (worlds) of others, often (at least initially) strangers whose world the professional is drawn into and must relate to. This relation is asymmetrical but not only in relation to the different perspectives on experiential states but in relation to the positions with respect to the professional practice and responsibility for action where the one acts out of routine and the other can be considered in a state of a crisis (Overmann, 1996).

4. The essay is one of several texts collected within a research-project on collective judgment. Some of them, among others Botvidsson's text, are published in Swedish in Lappalainen 2021.

5. See Englander 2019.

6. Within professional ethics there is a discussion on the relation between professional action and ethics and where the line should be drawn (Slote 2007). There is also a discussion on moral distress (Jameton, 1993), and a feminist debate about (often female) healthcare professionals who work in care-professions (REF).

7. In *An Ethics of Ambiguity* (1976), Simone de Beauvoir describes several forms of an inauthentic existence, where one more or less voluntarily negates one's freedom. She does not explicitly mention the professional but the role of the "serious man" who shows similarities to the professional.

8. See Linda Zerilli's (2016) excellent discussion about perspective as something corrective and not distorting.

9. For a similar argumentation see Thomas Fuchs (2019) article on the mechanism of exclusion and the limits of empathy in the case of Nazi perpetrators.

10. Svenaeus (2014)relates this understanding to the idea of practical wisdom, Phronesis, as rooted in empathy: "Phronesis," Svenaeus writes, "must take its starting point in being able to feel and know the state and predicament of the other person in the situation in which we strive to seek the best solution for the people involved. This discernment is aiming to map out what I earlier referred to as a moral dilemma, or, perhaps better, a situation which calls for action, but in which it is hard to know what the best thing to do is."

REFERENCES

Arendt, H. (2006). Thinking and Moral Considerations. In *Between Past and Future: Eight Exercises in Political Thought*. Penguin.

———. (2018). *The Human Condition*, 2nd ed. University of Chicago.

Arendt, H., & Jakobsson, Jim. (2019). *Totalitarismens ursprung.* Göteborg: Daidalos.

Aristotle. (2011). *The Nicomachean Ethics*. University of Chicago.

Beauvoir, S. d. (1976). *The Ethics of Ambiguity*. Kensington Pub. Co.

———. (2004). Pyrrhus and Cineas. In: M. Simons, ed., *Simone the Beauvoir. Philosophical Writings* (pp. 98–150). Urbana: University of Illinois Press.

———. (2014). Pyrrhus and Cineas. In: M. Simons, ed., *Simone the Beauvoir. Philosophical Writings* (pp. 98–150). Urbana: University of Illinois Press.

Berger P. L. & Luckmann, T. (1966). *The Social Construction of Reality. A Treatise in the Sociology of Knowledge*. New York: Doubleday.

Bergoffen, D. (2004). Introduction. In: M. Simons, ed., (2014), *Simone the Beauvoir. Philosophical Writings*, 77–87. Urbana: University of Illinois Press.

———. (2014). Introduction. In: M. Simons, ed., *Simone the Beauvoir. Philosophical Writings*, 77–87. University of Illinois Press.

Botvidsson, T. (2021). Att möta ett barn i misär. In J. Lappalainen, ed., *Aspiranten och erfarenheten. Polisens praktiska kunskap*. Huddinge.

Darwall, S. (1998). Empathy, Sympathy, Care. *Philosophical Studies* 89(2/3), 261–82.

Decety, J., & Lamm, C. (2006). Human Empathy Through the Lens of Social Neuroscience. *The Scientific World* 6, 1146–63.

Englander, M. (2019). The Practice of Phenomenological Empathy Training. *Journal of Phenomenological Psychology* 50, 42–59.

Fuchs T. (2017). Levels of Empathy—Primary, Extended, and Reiterated Empathy. In V. Lux & S. Weigel, eds., *Empathy*, 27–47. Palgrave Macmillan.

———. (2019). Empathy, Group Identity, and the Mechanisms of Exclusion: An Investigation into the Limits of Empathy. *Topoi* 38(1), 239–50.

Hamington, M. (2017). Empathy and Care Ethics. In H. Maibom, ed., *The Routledge Handbook of Philosophy of Empathy*, 264–72. Routledge.

Husserl, E. (1982/1913, 1950, 1976). *Ideen zu einer reinen Phänomenologie und phänomenologischen Philosophie*. In Erstes Buch: Allgemeine Einführung in die reine Phänomenologie, edited by K. Schuhmann. Martinus Nijhoff.

———. 1982. *Ideas Pertaining to a Pure Phenomenology and to a Phenomenological Philosophy, First Book*. Trans. F. Kersten. Kluwer.

Jameton, A. (1993). Dilemmas of Moral Distress: Moral Responsibility and Nursing Practice. *AWHONN'S Clinical Issues*, 4(4), 542–51.

Karp, S., & Stenmark H. (2011). Learning to Be a Police Officer. Tradition and Change in the Training and Professional Lives of Police Officers. *Police Practice & Research* 12(1), 4–15

Krueger, J., & Overgaard, S. (2012). Seeing Subjectivity: Defending a Perceptual Account of Other Minds. *ProtoSociology: Consciousness and Subjectivity* 47, 239–62.

Lappalainen, J., ed. (2021). *Aspiranten och erfarenheten. Polisens praktiska kunskap*. Huddinge.

Loidolt, S. (2016) Phenomenology of Plurality. Discovering the We. In T. Szanto, *Phenomenology of Sociality: Discovering the We*. Routledge, Taylor & Francis Group.

———. (2018). *Phenomenology of Plurality: Hannah Arendt on Political Intersubjectivity*. Routledge.

Meloe, J. (1983). The Agent and His World. In G. Skirbekk, ed., Praxeology, 38–69. Bergen.

———. (1997). Om å forstå det andre gjør. In: Greve and Nesset, eds., *Filosofi i et nordlig landskap. Jakob Meløe 70 år* (pp. 337–45). Tromsø.

Morgan, A. (2017). Against Compassion: In Defence of a "Hybrid" Concept of Empathy. *Nursing Philosophy* 18(3).

Oevermann, U. (1996). Theoretische Skizze einer revidierten Theorie professionalisierten Handelns. In A. Combe & W. Helsper, eds., *Pädagogische Professionalität*, 49–69. Suhrkamp.

Olofsson, C. (2011). Att arbeta tillsammans med människor. In L. Alsterdal, ed., *Omtankar. Praktisk kunskap I äldreomsorg*. Huddinge.

Schwarz, E., & Lappalainen, J. (2020). Collective Phronesis? An Investigation of Collective Judgement and Professional Action. In R. Giovagnoli & R. Lowe, eds., *The Logic of Social Practices*, 20–35. Springer.

Slote, M. (2007). The Ethics of Care and Empathy. Routledge

Svenaeus, Fredrik. (2014). Empathy as a Necessary Condition of Phronesis: A Line of Thought for Medical Ethics. *Medicine, Health Care and Philosophy* 17(2), 293–99.

Zahavi, D. (2001). Beyond Empathy: Phenomenological Approaches to Intersubjectivity. *Journal of Consciousness Studies* 8(5–7), 151–67.

———. (2022). Empathy, Alterity, Morality. In M. Englander & S. Ferrarello, eds., *Empathy and Ethics*, chapter 22. Rowman & Littlefield.

Zerilli, L. (2016). *A Democratic Theory of Judgement*. University of Chicago Press.

Chapter 21

An Empathy-Based Phenomenological Ethic for Gaming

Michael Agostinelli Jr.

ABSTRACT

People are interacting with each other more and more through a myriad of digital spaces: social media, email, online dating sites, and so on. Social media has garnered the vast majority of the attention when it comes to these types of interactions. But there is another segment of the digital realm that is becoming a behemoth in its own right: online gaming. With the growing number of people flocking to online gaming, the interactions taking place in this digital space need to be more thoroughly studied, especially when it comes to acting ethically and empathically in these interactions. This chapter's goal is threefold: to explain the phenomenology of online gaming; to show the importance of acknowledging the lived experiences of those we interact with while playing these games; and to argue that an emphasis on empathy can help us establish a working ethic that will benefit all gaming participants.

Keywords: empathy, phenomenological ethics, games, videogames, toxicity, reality, emotions, embodied interaffectivity, bodily resonance.

> The human being is essentially a mortal being, essentially a worker, essentially a fighter, essentially a lover and—essentially a player"
>
> —Eugen Fink (2016, p. 18)

People are interacting with each other more and more through a myriad of digital spaces: social media, email, online dating sites, and so on. Social media has garnered the vast majority of the attention when it comes to these types of interactions. But there is another segment of the digital realm that is becoming a behemoth in its own right: online gaming. With the growing number of people flocking to online gaming, the interactions taking place in this digital space need to be more thoroughly studied, especially when trying to determine how we can and should act ethically and empathically in these interactions. There is a general argument—that is, within the gaming community—that one need not worry about being ethical within videogames and their inherent person-to-person interactions for a number of reasons, among them that play (of all types) is not meant to be taken seriously, that videogames and their digital worlds are not real, and that there is no interplay between the "real world" and the digital one (in other words, one has no bearing on the other). This chapter's goal is to show that these claims are not only false, but that accepting the realness of play—specifically the type of play found in videogames—will allow us to move toward a moral philosophy for digital play that will benefit all involved.

To counter the preceding claims I will use a threefold approach. First, I will explain the phenomenology of digital gaming by comparing "real-world" games with their digital counterparts, as well as explain how the interfaces and instruments we use to play these digital games do not inhibit our lived experiences. Second, I will discuss how online gaming is not merely an abstract, inanimate arena where lifeless, inhuman avatars/characters interact but instead a shared digital space that players (as their individual selves) inhabit and where the experiences of all involved are co-constituted, much like they are in the real world, and, by doing this, I will show the importance of acknowledging the lived experiences of those we interact with while playing these games. Lastly, I will argue that an emphasis on empathy can help us establish a working ethic that will benefit all gaming participants before giving suggestions for how to implement such an ethic.

THE PROBLEM

Internet bullying is a well-known problem. So far, the primary focus for research has concentrated on social media platforms like Facebook and Twitter, but the toxic behavior found within videogames and on videogame streaming services, such as Twitch and Facebook Gaming, needs to be part of the conversation as well. The playing of videogames has been gaining in popularity for some time and is now a multibillion-dollar industry on pace to surpass $200 billion in revenue by 2023 (Field Level Media, 2020). This means that the playing of videogames is quickly becoming one of the more common ways people interact with each other. The more popular videogames become, the greater the chance for unethical behavior to occur within them.

Bullying, a sadly all too common phenomenon in the real world, has been present in the videogame community from the beginning. But it appears to only be getting worse. In 2008, a "large scale online survey found that adolescents who reported bullying others in real life were more than 2.5 times as likely to report bullying others online" (Ang & Goh, 2010, p. 388). We can see the effects of this preponderance of cyberbullying play out in multiple studies with claims like "65% of German adolescents reported having observed cyberhate," that among "Finnish adolescents, 6% reported that they have had posted, forwarded, or shared online hate material," and that a "German study of 9,512 students found that 2.4% of the participants could be classified as cyberbullies" (Wachs et al., 2019, p. 180).[1] Studies such as these tell us what many have already assumed, "that the Internet platform may extenuate existing behaviors; traditional bullies can now tap on the ample opportunities afforded via cyberspace to torment victims" (Ang & Goh, 2010, p. 388). Add to this the phenomenon of online disinhibition—"defined as a lowering of behavioral inhibitions in the online environment" (Lapidot-Lefler & Barak, 2012, p. 434)—and we have a recipe for unethical interactions on an unprecedented scale. This toxic behavior manifests online in ways "that apparently would not be exhibited in a similar scenario in the 'real world'" (Lapidot-Lefler & Barak, 2012, p. 434). In other words, the digital worlds of videogames are seen as not real, as not requiring the same level of restraint of the self or concern for the other that would be expected in more serious arenas.

CLARIFICATIONS: GAMES AND GAMING BEHAVIOR

It is my hope that much of what I discuss here can eventually be applied more broadly to all sorts of games—both digital and not—but, for the purposes of this chapter, let us narrow down the topic of discussion. For those, like myself, who have a long, storied history with videogames, what follows will feel unnecessarily complex and commonsensical enough to not need explanation. But for those who have never played a videogame or who have only the most minimal of experience with them—Is there anyone in the West who has not played at least a couple of rounds of *Pac-Man* (1980), *Tetris* (1984), or *Candy Crush* (2012)?—some level of clarification is certainly in order. Here, I will specify both the type of videogames as well as the types of behavior that are the focus of this chapter. But first, I will clarify what I mean when I talk about the realness of videogames.

Terminology—Videogames, the "Real World," and Reality

Throughout this chapter I will frequently use the term *real world* in contrast to things like games, videogames, and digital worlds. I will argue that there is no true distinction between interactions with and within videogames and interactions in the "real world," so the use of these terms in opposition to each other might confuse some. What I mean by the term "real world"—specifically presented throughout in quotation marks—is what I believe most people would take it to signify: the world outside of the imaginary or the digital, the very *real* world of perception and experience we all share with each other outside of videogames. The use of "real world" in this way is to show how the general public—and, perhaps, some corners of philosophy—understands the term as opposed to what it is I am presenting here. This then means I must explain what I have in mind when I use terms like real, reality, or any derivation thereof. For this we need a basic understanding of phenomenology and phenomenological reality.

Jim McCrea (n.d.) provides simple definitions for both phenomenology and phenomenological reality. He writes, "Phenomenology is an analysis of our immediate and pure perceptions of reality, which puts aside all preconceptions about it" and that "Phenomenological reality is precisely that which is perceived by the mind, before any thinking about it takes place in the intellect." In other words, phenomenological reality is that which we immediately experience prior to rationalizing or intellectualizing these experiences—that is, the sense data that our bodies perceive. McCrea writes, "This involves all five senses: sight, hearing, touch, taste, and smell. It involves our entire body." Now I must admit, that as of writing this chapter videogames do not trigger all the senses to the same extent or in the same way as do experiences in the "real world"—one cannot currently smell the flowers in a videogame or taste any of the foods found within, for example—but videogames do, in fact, trigger all of our senses in some way[2] and the experience of playing videogames does involve the entire body (an idea I will discuss as it pertains to embodied interaffectivity and bodily resonance). It is often through the rationalizing of videogame experiences after the fact that it becomes possible for many players to claim that their actions are not real and therefore do not matter. By understanding videogames through the lens of phenomenological reality, we avoid this type of post hoc intellectualizing which then forces us to focus squarely on the immediate experiences of those involved.

Cooperative Videogames

The focus of this chapter is the idea of acting ethically while playing not all videogames but a specific type: online, cooperation-based games that may or may not have a competitive aspect, but which have a strong emphasis on teamwork and collaboration. The distinction made here is important.

There are many videogames that are known to novices and experts alike which focus primarily on individual play with little or no emphasis on cooperation between human players. Games like the original *Super Mario Bros.* (1985), *Sonic the Hedgehog* (1991), and *Crash Bandicoot* (1996) were all games that focused almost solely on the single-player experience. Even the multiplayer game mode found in *Super Mario Bros.* was nothing more than two individual players taking turns playing alone with no carryover between the game of "player one" and the game of "player two"—that is, how one player performed had no in-game impact on the other player. Alongside this we find games that might have had some level of solo play but were really built for head-to-head competition between two human players. Games like the *Street Fighter* (1987–) and *Mortal Kombat* (1992–) series do in fact have single player modes where the human player can fight computer-controlled opponents, but the primary draw of these types of games is found in direct competition between two human players. Of these two types of games mentioned so far—those focused almost entirely on solo play and those focused almost entirely on competitive play—there is no form of cooperation meant to be practiced by multiple human players.

To the two types of videogames detailed already let us add a third: games featuring multiple human-controlled characters who are meant to work cooperatively toward a shared goal or against a common opponent. Games that fall into this category tend to focus on player-vs-environment (PvE), player-vs-player (PvP), or a combination of the two.[3] Cooperative PvE generally takes the form of a team of human-controlled characters (though these games can usually be played individually as well) working toward a shared goal, often against computer-controlled enemies. For example, *Call of Duty: World at War* (2008), as well as several of its sequels, featured a game mode where human players worked together as a team to defeat wave after wave of computer-controlled zombies. Cooperative PvP, on the other hand, is focused on a team of human-controlled characters competing against other human-controlled characters (again, these types of games can usually be played individually, but the focus here is on those that emphasize teamwork). *Call of Duty: World at War* featured multiple game modes that focused entirely on PvP play in which the goal was either to eliminate your opponents or to complete certain in-game objectives.

For the purposes of this chapter, the focus is on online games that feature PvE or PvP play and require, or at least heavily encourage, cooperative play between human-controlled characters. Being online introduces the element of anonymity (why should someone act ethically when no one knows who they are?) while focusing on cooperation-based games allows us to examine why some choose to participate in a game focused on teamwork yet work against their teammates. The question I seek to answer is why in these types of games, where teamwork is either preferred or required, are there so many players who act in ways that are antithetical to this dynamic and how can we counter such behavior?

Toxic Videogame Behavior

> In the world of online gaming, undesirable behaviour is commonplace. Players will kill teammates, verbally abuse their peers, and misdirect new community members, spreading chaos and disorder.
>
> —Cook et al., 2018, p. 3323

I would imagine that when most people hear of "toxic behavior" in online videogames they immediately think of hostile verbal or written interactions featuring heavy use of profanities and slurs. Though they are certainly not incorrect in thinking this—this is definitely a long running issue in online gaming—it is far from the only problem gamers face and might not even be the most common. Familiar forms of toxic gaming behavior include:[4]

- Toxic communication—The aforementioned slinging of insults usually containing profanity and slurs.
- Trolling/griefing—Intentionally making another player's experience a negative one beyond simply beating them at the game. Examples include joining someone's game of *Minecraft* (2011) to destroy their progress or dragging out a game that is essentially over for the purposes of endlessly punishing the enemy team, as can be done in games like *Heroes of the Storm* (2015) or *League of Legends* (2009).
- "AFKing"—The act of being "Away From Keyboard," which means a player is not actively participating in the game.
- Disconnecting/quitting early—This one is mostly self-explanatory, though the benefits might not be. Quitting early is as simple as leaving the game, but the use of certain methods of "disconnecting" from a game can make it so that the player does not receive any negative repercussions for their actions.

- Cheating/hacking/glitching—There are countless ways for players to gain an unfair advantage in online videogames with the most common being the use of outside programs or applications to give a player the upper hand (cheating), altering the game's code to give a player an advantage (hacking), and the exploitation of broken in-game mechanics (glitching).
- Selfish play—This can take many forms. Often the most common is the stealing of in-game items or rewards from other players but can also involve players refusing to play toward the objective of the game, instead focusing on padding their in-game stats.
- Team killing—Many games make it possible to kill one's own teammates. This is often meant to be an unfortunate and unwanted occurrence, though some players choose to do this intentionally to anger their teammates. This could also fall under trolling/griefing.

All of the forms of toxic behavior can have a negative impact on both teammates and opponents alike (even the last two, selfish play and team killing, can negatively impact the game for opponents because they will not get the proper competitive experience they hoped for when they joined the game). But, again, my focus here is on the toxic behavior aimed specifically at teammates, at those players one is meant to work with to accomplish some explicit cooperative goal. Now that we have narrowed down what type of gaming experience is the focal point of this chapter, we can move on to my first major claim: that online gaming has a lived experience no different from "real world" games/sports and that the digital nature of online gaming and the use of gaming "instruments" does nothing to lessen this lived experience.

THE LIVED EXPERIENCE OF GAMING

It is easy to look at videogames and feel the need to bracket off the experiences one has in the digital realm from those in the "real world." Even if we were to strictly limit ourselves to comparing "real world" games with their digital counterparts, we see that there is certainly some level of difference between the two. But are these experiences so different as to be categorized as entirely separate and unique unto themselves? I do not believe so. In this section, I will compare interactions with and within digital games to interactions with and within "real world" games to show that the differences are not as large as we might initially believe them to be. The goal here is to acknowledge that one's lived experience transcends what we think of as the "real world" into the countless digital worlds available to us and to show that these lived experiences are, in fact, one in the same.

"Real" Games versus Videogames

When acknowledging the lived experience of videogames, one of the first hurdles we need to overcome is the idea that the interactions with and within videogames are somehow less "real" than interactions in the "real world." For example, at first glance, one might argue that there is an inherent difference between a videogame and a more traditional boardgame like *Monopoly* (1935) or *Sorry!* (1929). In a videogame, players inhabit a digital self—sometimes embodied within an imaginary, visible character/avatar and sometimes not[5]—whereas in *Monopoly* or *Sorry!* this is seemingly not the case. But this is merely a matter of perspective. Take *Monopoly*. When beginning a game of *Monopoly*, each player chooses a game piece, otherwise known as a token, that represents them on the game board. There have been countless tokens used throughout the game's history, from the battleship and race car to the dreaded thimble (did anyone actually want to be the thimble?), but their presence has always been a mainstay of the game. During the game, players roll dice that determines the number of spaces on the board their token is meant to move and wherever their token falls an option or consequence is the result. While the game is going on, I am the token, and the token is me. My actions, as it pertains to the game, are inextricably tied to my token and my possible choices within the game are determined by where my token has landed. In *Monopoly*, I roll the dice and, based on that roll, I move my token. Once my token has landed on a space on the board, I am met with either a choice or a consequence. Perhaps I have the option to buy a piece of property or maybe the space I have just landed on is already owned by another player and I must pay them rent. The game's rules, the game board, the token that represents me, and my personal actions and choices determine how the game plays out. They are all fundamental to the lived experience of the game. Now, I ask, how is this any different from a videogame?

A videogame has its own rules, its own "board" (the digital world in which we play), and a token (the character/avatar we use to interact with the game's world and other players), in addition to my personal actions and choices. Regardless of whether I am playing *Monopoly* or *Call of Duty: World at War*, I am inhabiting the game's world, inserting myself into a realm that is not partially real and partially imaginary (let's say 50 percent real + 50 percent imaginary) but a simultaneous combination of both (that is, 100 percent real + 100 percent imaginary). In fact, I argue that while playing any game, even one in which we inhabit a digital, imaginary self in a digital, imaginary world, that the happenings of that game—that is, the lived experience as it is constituted by the events, the choices, the interactions, and the ethical dilemmas within—are wholly and entirely real. That's nonsense, you say. There is a distinct separation between what happens in a game and what happens in real life! (This is a claim I will look at more in-depth.) To that I say: The next time you are playing either a boardgame or a videogame, either openly cheat or throw an absolute tantrum. Flip the game board, steal from the *Monopoly* bank, throw your videogame controller across the room right in front of your friends or family. Then answer this: Your actions, as they pertain to the game (and they are, in fact, related to or caused by the game), how will they be judged by those around you? Will they be seen as merely elements of the game and wholly separate from who you "really" are? Will your actions be judged only when you play another game—that is, is there a *game you* and a *real you* separate from each other—or will your actions (and the consequences thereof) transcend the game into the "real world"? Think of anyone you have ever had a bad experience with while playing a game. Did their actions, to some degree, negatively impact how you viewed them afterward even after you had finished with the game? It is hard to imagine they did not. Perhaps it is best to just accept that there was no separation to begin with.

Interacting with Videogames: Extensions of Our Bodies

Another barrier for understanding the lived experience of videogames has to do with the tools or instruments that we use to interact with the game. For example, one could point out that my analogous use of *Monopoly* and its tokens is flawed in that every time I take my turn it is my hand throwing the dice, my hand moving my token around the board, my eyes seeing this all unfold, and my mouth and ears being used to communicate with the other players. There is no technological impediment between myself and those with whom I am playing.[6] Any interaction—either with the game board, its pieces, or with the other players—is as simple as my hand → game piece or my mouth → another player's ears. With a videogame, there is a rather large technological barrier among myself, the game, and the other players. Assuming I am using a keyboard and mouse to play a game—let us use the example of playing *Call of Duty: World at War*—if I wish to move my in-game character forward I have to push down on the W key. This action is then translated into electrical impulses that are sent to my computer, which tells the game what I have done, which then translates it into movement within the game, which is then sent as more electrical impulses to my computer screen where I am finally able to observe the action begun by my pushing the W key. This (overly simplified) chain of events, from key press to onscreen consequence—an aspect of gaming, known as *input lag* or *input latency*, that is so problematic for some players that there is a constantly evolving stream of new technology meant to minimize the time from "real world" action to in-game action—does not take into account the online element of the game where this action then needs to be sent over even more wires (i.e., the internet) using even more electrical impulses to the computers of any number of other players participating in the same game.

How can one say to have a lived experience with so many layers to penetrate between their action and its result? How can the lived body (*Leib*) be said to interact with something it can never fully touch or feel? The solution is simple: The tools we use to interact with videogames (e.g., mice, keyboards, controllers, etc.) should not be seen as impediments to our experience but instead as extensions of our lived bodies that allow us to reach into the digital realm. This both means that we physically interact with the digital worlds in which we play—that is, my physical self moves my digital self and no amount of tools or instruments placed between these two selves changes this fundamental interaction or experience—and that these games then act on us—that is, what happens within the game, to my digital self, also happens to my physical self and, again, no amount of tools or instruments placed between these two selves changes this fundamental interaction or experience. In the end, the physical self and digital self are not separate, but, in fact, are intertwined into one physical/digital being.

To better explain this, let us turn to a quote from Thomas Fuchs and then compare our interaction with games with how we also interact with everything from musical instruments to the world in general. Fuchs writes,

> Incorporation is a pervasive characteristic of the 'lived' or subjective body (Leib) which always transcends itself and connects with the environment. This is the case for example in every skillful handling of instruments, as when playing piano and letting the fingers find their way by themselves; or when a blind man probes his environment with a stick and feels the surface at the top of it. In such cases, the instrument is integrated into the body motor schema like an extension of the body, subjectively felt as 'melting' or being at one with the instrument. (2016, p. 198)

Here, Fuchs acknowledges that the lived body is not separated from its environment or from its experiences by any tools or instruments it may use to create or live those experiences. A musician does not simply use or play an instrument, she becomes one with the instrument. The instrument becomes an extension of her own body with which she can mold sound. Without the instrument, the music in her head cannot escape. Without her, the instrument is merely an object with no purpose. They come together as one, not as a person merely wielding a tool but as an artist joining with an instrument to birth music into the world. The same can be said of the blind man and his walking stick. The walking stick becomes an extension of the blind man's body, and its presence should not be seen as anything less. Whereas the loss of his sight might have hindered his ability to interact with the world, the walking stick lessens this loss, even if only to a small degree. The walking stick is not simply a tool or instrument with which he interacts with the world, it becomes a part of his lived body and a fundamental piece of his lived experience.[7]

As with the musician and her instrument and the blind man and his walking stick, the use of technological devices to interact with videogames should not be seen as some form of impediment that prevents gamers from having a fully constituted lived experience with and within their games. When I am playing a game, the keyboard, mouse, or controller are not simply tools or instruments that I mindlessly wield. They are extensions of my body. In the heat of simulated battle, they are as much a part of me as any of the body parts I was born with. They allow me to transcend the physical and technological boundaries between me and the game—and between myself and other players—and make it possible to experience the imaginary in a fully real way (to the extent that there is no actual division between the two). Once we have accepted this idea—that these instruments are extensions of our bodies and that the physical and digital become one and contribute to our lived experience—we can then understand our interactions with and within these games and game worlds in more traditional phenomenological terms.

THE SHARED DIGITAL SPACE OF GAMING

The way the average person views videogames is that we, in the "real world," connect to a digital world but that these two spaces remain wholly separate. To enter one is to leave the other behind. This has one powerful and problematic effect: We allow ourselves to believe that our actions in videogames, specifically those aimed at other players, do not matter because we are in this seemingly imaginary nonworld and that these actions are not actually aimed at other people but are instead aimed at the game. One could argue that when I enter the digital realm of a videogame, I leave the morality of the "real world" behind and that morality only becomes real again once I have ceased playing the game. For example, when I play a game like *Tom Clancy's Rainbow Six Siege* (2015)—a team-based first-person shooter where two squads face off against each other—I can make the decision to kill my own teammates. If I choose to view this game and its world as something separate from the larger world around us—that is, the "real world"—I can allow myself to ignore traditional social mores and play counter to the intentions of the game. This would be analogous to stealing the ball from my own teammates or scoring against my own team in games like basketball or soccer. But these games, being both "real" and face-to-face, deter such interactions. The solution to this is to acknowledge the true reality of online videogames: that they are a shared, co-constituted space just like any other and that our actions shape the experiences of others as do their actions shape our own. We inhabit the digital world. We live in it, act in it, and, through the combination of our actions and of those with whom we are playing we transform, co-create, and co-constitute this digital world. In this way, the videogame realm is little different from the "real world." To show that these interactions are as real and as meaningful as any others, let us look at the interconnectedness of digital interactions, emotions, and physical/bodily responses.

Emotions

When playing cooperative videogames, we are not interacting solely with the game or with the digital characters within them. We are interacting with flesh and blood humans who are also sharing this world with us. To ignore this human element not only cheapens the gaming experience for others, but it also cheapens the experience for ourselves. Playing these types of games is not as simple as two players separately joining and separately experiencing the same game concurrently. It is not Player 1 + Game A and Player 2 + Game A. It is Player 1 + Player 2 + Game A (in a circular, not linear, relationship). The players and the game do not stand apart creating wholly detached and isolated experiences. Instead, the actions of Player 1 affect Player 2, the actions of Player 2 affect Player 1, the actions of both affect Game A, and the actions of Game A affect both players. Fuchs uses the terms "embodied interaffectivity" and "bodily resonance" to describe such interactions and the emotions they generate in the "real world." Better understanding these concepts will give us a greater appreciation for how digital interactions are very real. Bodily resonance is probably the simpler of the two concepts. Fuchs writes,

> Emotions are experienced through what I call bodily resonance (Fuchs 2000, 2013a). This includes all kinds of local or general bodily sensations: feelings of warmth or coldness, tickling or shivering, pain, tension or relaxation, constriction or expansion, sinking, tumbling or lifting, etc. There is no emotion without at least the slightest bodily sensations and movement tendencies. (2016, p. 196)

In other words, emotions are not simply internal feelings wholly detached from the human body. They are not products of the mind alone, seemingly trapped within one's brain. Instead, emotions can be, and usually are, exhibited through overt, real physical manifestations. Often, we are unaware of the physical reactions we have to our emotions even when trying our best to hide them. How often has our body language or facial expressions given away how we truly feel to others, possibly even before we knew the truth ourselves? To this idea of bodily resonance, we can add Fuchs's concept of "embodied interaffectivity." He writes, "According to this concept [embodied interaffectivity], emotions may not primarily be localized within a single individual, but should rather be conceived as phenomena of a shared intercorporeal space in which the interacting partners are involved" (2016, p. 196). In other words, emotions, which we often think of as belonging solely to individuals and inherently internalized, are actually created and shared by and through interactions between multiple people participating in a shared space. Fuchs is not speaking to the specific topic of this chapter and his concerns have to do with physical interactions in the "real world," but I do believe that the concepts can and do apply to the game world as well.

The emotions one feels when playing a cooperative videogame are not purely individualized. They are a product of the interactions occurring with and within that game—between the player and the game and between the player and other players. Though the interactions may appear disembodied due to the digital nature of the games, embodied interaffectivity is present. Expounding on the comment mentioned above, Fuchs writes,

> Of course, when I am moved by an emotion, I may not always be aware of my body; yet being afraid, for instance, is not possible without feeling a bodily tension or trembling, a beating of the heart or a shortness of breath, and a tendency to withdraw. It is through these sensations that we are anxiously directed towards a frightening situation, even if we do not notice them. (2016, p. 196)

When we feel an emotion, it is not merely an internal impression separate from our bodily sensations. There is an interplay between the two where an emotion causes physical effects. Anyone who has ever spent a decent amount of time playing videogames knows that the feelings and emotions caused by videogames are just as real as those caused by interactions and happenings in the "real world." The fear generated by a *Resident Evil* (1996–) game will be felt throughout the body, as will the regret over decisions made in a game like *Spec Ops: The Line* (2012), or the unmitigated joy felt when defeating an exceptionally difficult boss in any of the *Demon's Souls/Dark Souls* games (2009–). But, more importantly, the interactions experienced between players—that is, how the actions of one human affect another—creates emotions just as real and just as strong. This embodied interaffectivity within videogames both strengthens my previous argument concerning the interconnectedness of the physical and digital worlds and solidifies the idea that, much like in the "real world," these digital worlds are shared spaces co-constituted by the player, other players, and the game.

An objection to these claims of embodied interaffectivity and bodily resonance might be that we are incapable of seeing, hearing, feeling the other players in a truly personal, intimate way. We are again faced with a technological impediment that prevents us from experiencing the other. To some extent, this is true. I cannot claim to know the other player or their emotional state in the same way that I could make the same claim about someone sitting across from me in a restaurant. But there is a solution to this, and it comes from Alfred Schutz. He writes,

> The behavior and action of others are, however, revealed to me, not only through their bodily movements, but also in the results of these movements, e.g., sound waves, changes in other objects, and so on. And I can pose the question for myself of what produced these changes and by what process. Now, I find all these external events intelligible. They have meaning for me. But the meaning I find in them need not at all be identical with what the person who produced them had in mind. For these objectifications of meaning in the external world are mere "indications" (Anzeichen) of the intended meaning of the actor or the producer of the object in question. (1967, p. 21)

We not only experience the other person, but we also experience the consequences of their actions, the aftermath of their behavior. So yes, there is some level of impenetrability associated with interacting with another person digitally in the sense that I cannot see or hear them directly as they act. But I can see the ramifications of their actions and, through this, come to know their intentions, their goals, and, to some degree, who they are as a person. Do I need to be in the same room as a person cheating at a videogame to come to some conclusion about their character? If someone hurls profanities and racial epithets at me while playing together, does the technological barrier between us or the fact that we have never personally met mean that I cannot assume who they are as a person? By seeing how they act within a game, by seeing the consequences of their actions (e.g., playing selfishly, partaking in hostile communication, intentionally losing), I can still come to some understanding about that person. The physical distance between us matters not.

EMPATHY AS A GATEWAY TO ETHICAL GAMING

Up to this point, the primary focus of this chapter has been to defend the realness of interactions with and within videogames and to argue that accepting this realness has real repercussions, the most important of which is to point us in the direction of acting ethically when we play. But we are still left wondering how we can do that. One possible solution is to game empathically. In this section I will discuss the importance of empathic thinking and explain ways in which we can promote empathy in the videogames we play.

Empathy

Empathy is one of those terms where its use is so common that defining it seems unnecessary. Surely everyone knows what we mean by empathy. The truth is there is no perfectly agreed upon definition of empathy. In fact, an article by Dan Zahavi, which I will be leaning on heavily, begins with the sentence, "Although there in recent years has been something of an upsurge of interest in and work on empathy, there is still no clear consensus about what precisely it is" (2014, p. 129). Here I will discuss interpretations of empathy found in the social sciences and among several philosophers—namely, Lipps, Scheler, and Stein—before providing my own working definition of it. The debate over empathy—specifically how we define it—is not the focus of this chapter. The point here is to provide as simple of a working definition as possible and a technique for implementing it in our digital interactions.

Empathy in the Social Sciences

In the social sciences, empathy is often divided into two categories: cognitive empathy and emotional empathy. "Cognitive empathy refers to the experience of intentionally taking another person's point of view" (Belman & Flanagan, 2010, p. 12). Researchers further breakdown emotional empathy into two more categories: parallel and reactive. "Parallel empathy is roughly equivalent to the lay understanding of empathy as vicarious experience of another's emotional state," whereas "reactive empathy describes an emotional response that is unlike what the other person is experiencing" (Belman & Flanagan, 2010, p. 12). Parallel empathy is to feel either the same emotion or one similar to that being experienced by another, while reactive empathy is to feel an entirely different emotion altogether, though it is triggered by the empathic viewing of another. Although I do believe both forms of emotional empathy are possible even in the physically removed interactions of the digital world, I will be focusing primarily on cognitive empathy.

To practice cognitive empathy is to place yourself in the shoes of another, to attempt to feel what they are feeling and to understand what they are personally experiencing. One of the more common arguments against empathy—which I will discuss—is that it is nigh impossible to truly understand the emotions and experiences of other people. Even if we were to experience events that are almost identical, it would be impossible for us to say that we truly know what the other person is thinking or feeling. Imagine two people have recently broken up with their significant others. Although their overall experiences might have been similar and they might have gone through a similar range of emotions, neither could say they truly understand the experience of the other because, in the end, they are both different, unique individuals with distinct personal contexts. What is important here is not whether the use of cognitive empathy can allow someone to gain a perfect understanding of the emotions and experiences of another. Instead, what is important is the cognitive process—that is, the mental action of trying to understand a situation through the eyes of another. When we combine this process with what I will discuss next, we will be left with a simple technique for empathic, ethical gaming.

Phenomenological Empathy

In his chapter "Empathy and Other-Directed Intentionality," Zahavi discusses how several philosophers have tried to define and understand empathy. He begins by explaining the views of Theodor Lipps before contrasting them with those of Max Scheler, Edith Stein, and others. I will pull from the thoughts of these three philosophers and combine them with the understanding of cognitive empathy from the social sciences presented above to give us our working definition.

Lipps's Model

Theodor Lipps believed that "To feel empathy is to experience a part of one's own psychological life as belonging to or in an external object" (Zahavi, 2014, p. 130). In other words, when I feel empathy toward *some thing*, be it a person or an object, I am not observing the emotions of *that thing*. Instead, I am projecting my own emotions onto it. For example, "When we perceive the facial expressions of others, we immediately co-apprehend the expressed emotions, say, the anger or sadness" but not "that we actually perceive the anger or sadness" because "anger and sadness cannot be perceived, since they are not to be found in the external world. We only know directly of these emotions through self-experience" (Zahavi, 2014, p. 130). In the end, Lipps believed that "the only emotions we have experiential access to are our own" (Zahavi, 2014, p. 130).

If we look at the example of sadness here, we can see what is meant by Lipps's interpretation of empathy. Perhaps I see a gentleman on the street who looks downright dismal and melancholy. He has all the markings of one who is sad. His shoulders are slouched, his eyes look weary and tired, perhaps even puffy from crying. I look at him and my immediate reaction is "This man is sad!" According to Lipps, I am not actually observing *his* sadness. I am unable to know *his* sadness. Instead, I project my understanding of my own experiences with sadness onto him—this is how I walk when I am sad, how I look when I am sad, how I carry myself when I am sad—and, seeing these things in the man's appearance and demeanor, I conclude that he is sad.

I believe that many, if not most, people tend to think of empathy in this way. Perhaps I cannot say that I know, intimately and explicitly, the feelings of another but through my own experiences with my own emotions I can come to some conclusion about the emotions of another.

One of the problems with Lipps's model of empathy, at least for other philosophers, is that its emphasis on the projection of our emotions onto others "imprisons us within our own mind. It fails to do justice to the genuine and true self-transcendence that we find in empathy" (Zahavi, 2014, p. 133). But I believe that Lipps's model, when combined with the reflections of Scheler and Stein, and the definition of cognitive empathy discussed above, will leave us with an understanding of empathy we can use to game ethically.

Scheler and Stein

According to Zahavi, Scheler believed that although "empathy is what allows me to understand other experiencing subjects. It neither entails that the other's experience is literally transmitted to me, nor does it entail that I undergo the experience I observe in the other" (2014, p. 133) and "that the distinct cognitive activities of the other person, his or her thoughts, will remain concealed and hidden, until the other decides to reveal and communicate them" (2014, p. 134). For Stein, empathy is "the term of choice for the experience [*Erfahrung*] of foreign consciousness. It is the basic cognitive source for our comprehension of foreign subjects and their experiences, and it is what more complex kinds of social cognition rely on and presuppose" (Zahavi, 2014, p. 134). In other words, both Scheler and Stein acknowledge that empathy allows us to understand "other experiencing subjects" and to experience "foreign consciousness," but we are unable to claim to know exactly what it is that another being is feeling. Even if I were able to project my personal experiences of sadness onto another individual, I cannot claim that they are, in fact, feeling either the same type or level of sadness or if they are even feeling sadness at all. Whereas Lipps's model seemingly ignored this problem, Scheler and Stein make it explicit.

But Stein makes a claim that I believe works perfectly with the types of interactions we are discussing here. In response to the more traditional understanding of empathy through an argument from analogy, Stein did not deny "that we occasionally employ this kind of inferential reasoning, but on her view, it never provides us with an experience of other minds, but only with a more or less probable knowledge of others' mental states" (Zahavi, 2014, p. 135). The key here is "probable knowledge." I cannot definitively know the emotions or experiences of another, but I can have some level of probable knowledge about them. In other words, we do not need to know for a fact that another person—in this case, another videogame player—is sad, upset, or disgusted with my in-game actions. I just need to have probable knowledge of how they are most likely feeling and from that I can determine how I should act.

Working Definition of Empathy

We now have both a phenomenological understanding of empathy and one taken from the social sciences. Here I would like to combine them into a working definition of empathy that we can use to promote an empathic ethic for gaming.

As Scheler and Stein acknowledged, the existence of empathy does not mean that I have full knowledge of another person's mental state. As Scheler pointed out, unless this person decides to explicitly communicate their emotions to me, their emotions and mental states will always be, to some extent, hidden from me—and this is assuming they are honest in their communication. But Stein's idea of empathy giving us probable knowledge of another person's mental states, combined with the concept of cognitive empathy, means that even if we can never know to an absolute certainty what someone is feeling, by cognitively placing ourselves in another player's place we can know enough to determine how we should act. For example, let us say I am playing a game where teamwork is crucial for our team to complete our goal. To play selfishly or to ignore the game's objective would be to place my team at a massive disadvantage. Now I cannot know for certain that my teammates will be upset with me if I were to play selfishly, but, using cognitive empathy, I can ascertain a level of probable knowledge that tells me that they will more than likely not appreciate my actions. Would I like it if I were providing good, helpful teamwork and one of my teammates decided to do their own thing and caused us to lose? Probably not. Would I like it if I were trying to enjoy a calm, casual game and someone decided to verbally berate me with foul language and slurs? Again, probably not. Using this information, I can determine my best course of action when playing. This particular game requires solid teamwork and useful—though not necessarily friendly—communication and those deciding to play would probably prefer that all involved provided such teamwork and communication, therefore I should do my part and supply both. Here, we finally have both a working definition of empathy as well as a technique for implementing its use in a way that allows us to act ethically, even in a scenario where we can, at best, only have probable knowledge of what is the right thing to do.

IMPLEMENTING OUR EMPATHY-BASED ETHIC FOR GAMING

Assuming we accept the claims I have made so far—the realness of game-related lived experiences; that the tools of gaming are extensions of the lived body; that the digital worlds that we interact in are shared, co-constituted spaces; and that we can use empathy to guide us toward more ethical actions while playing—we are left asking: How can we promote empathic, ethical gaming and improve the types of interactions that occur within the games we play?

Accept the Realness of Play

Several times in this chapter, I have made arguments in favor of the realness of videogames and the human-to-human interactions within them. There is a reason for this: by discounting the possibility of these interactions being real—due to the supposed imaginary nature of videogames and everything attached to them, including our interactions within them—we allow ourselves to act in ways that are not only antithetical to common moral philosophies, but in ways that assume no possible moral code can exist. In other words, because videogames are not *real* then nothing I do within them can have a *real* effect and I am not bound by any *real* morality. I can be as selfish and toxic as I want because none of it is real, none of it matters. Perhaps play is not as serious or important as cultivating personal relationships or working to support a family—though play can surely be used to improve both—but this does not mean that play is somehow pointless, without meaning, and not real enough for us to act ethically while we do it. For us to take the first step toward ethical gaming, we need to acknowledge that the interactions we have with and within videogames are, in fact, very real.

Let Empathy Guide Us

As stated previously, there is no consensus on what empathy is. But although we cannot conclusively claim to know what it is, we can use some basic understandings of the concept to create a working definition that we can then implement to play ethically. To use cognitive empathy and to reach some level of probable knowledge about the feelings of others allows us to think through our own actions as we play. No, I cannot claim to know the emotions of another, I cannot state that my actions will necessarily result in certain emotional responses within other players, but I can place myself in their situation and come to some sort of understanding as to how my actions will affect those I am playing with. To disavow the usefulness of empathy—even if our understanding of it is limited—is to lock ourselves away from those we are interacting with. And since the digital world is a shared, co-constituted space, we will end up not only hurting others but ourselves as well. The experiences of others will suffer which means the game will suffer which means we will suffer. To be empathic in our play with others is to promote a healthier experience for all involved, ourselves included.

Promoting empathic thinking while playing online videogames is not merely some abstract good-for-its-own-sake. Instead, it serves a real purpose. Studies have shown that "it is generally found that empathic responsiveness is positively related to prosocial behaviors and negatively related to bullying" (Ang & Goh, 2010, p. 388) and that "empathy improves people's attitudes and behaviors towards other individuals or groups, while a lack of empathy is associated with more negative attitudes and behaviors" (Belman & Flanagan, 2010, p. 13). What I have proposed here, the use of empathic thinking to promote ethical playing, is both possible and necessary.

Promote Empathy through Our Games

Lastly, game designers, developers, and publishers can implement empathic teaching into their games. Although there have been games built with the explicit purpose of having players engage empathically with other in-game characters, sometimes meant as a stand-in for "real world" people and groups, I am thinking more along the lines of using empathy training in a more directed manner, one which would encourage empathic thinking within the game toward other players. As it stands, those found to be engaging in unethical actions within a game are given punishments like in-game sanctions (e.g., the loss of items or competitive rank), short-term suspensions (these can range from mere minutes to several months), and even a permanent ban of their account. Although I see nothing inherently wrong with these types of penalties, they do not necessarily encourage those being punished to become better, more ethical players. By implementing something like a game mode where a problematic player is encouraged to empathize with others, their behavior can be improved to prevent further abuses down the line. Of course, this would not be a perfect solution—as one will never exist—but it would be a step in the right direction. As Belman and Flanagan state in their article "Designing Games to Foster Empathy":

> Games are particularly well-suited to supporting educational or activist programs in which the fostering of empathy is a key method or goal. This is because they allow players to inhabit the roles and perspectives of other people or groups in a uniquely immersive way. (2010, p. 11)

Perhaps by promoting more empathic and ethical playing, we will reap the benefits in other areas of our lives. As it stands, videogames are becoming a bigger and bigger part of our economies, societies, and cultures. Instead of seeing them as imaginary wastes of time, we can see them as a real way to advocate for more empathic and more ethical thinking everywhere we interact with others.

CONCLUSION

This chapter's purpose was to provide a phenomenological perspective on the realness of videogames and the interactions found within and to show how the use of empathy can allow us to create an ethic to better moderate these interactions. Using the concepts of the lived experience of games, embodied interaffectivity, bodily resonance, and the shared, co-created space of games, I argued against the idea that videogames and our actions within them are not real. I then discussed several definitions of empathy found within the social sciences and phenomenology before introducing my own working definition and providing an empathy-based ethic for gaming. Lastly, I proposed several steps we can take to implement this ethic to improve the interactions we have with and within videogames.

I do not believe that the claims I have made in this chapter will convince all readers. In fact, I imagine a great many people will choose to cling to the notion that videogames are not real—and, therefore, neither are our interactions within them—but this is a field of study that needs more attention going forward. Online gaming is quickly becoming one of humanity's biggest recreational activities and people are interacting more and more through these games. A better understanding of these interactions and the laying down of an ethical framework that underscores them is not merely something that would be nice to have, it is rapidly becoming something that is absolutely necessary.

NOTES

1. The studies referenced here speak to specific research done in Finland and Germany, but the problem of cyberbullying transcends national borders and is pervasive worldwide. Ang and Goh (2010), for example, focused on adolescents in Singapore; Patchin and Hinduja (2010) focused on adolescents in the United States; and Beckman et al. (2014) focused on adolescents in Sweden. Needless to say, wherever the internet is widely available there seems to be a rising problem with cyberbullying and online toxicity.

2. Although we might not be able to smell or taste things within a videogame, these senses are not simply turned off while playing. Often the sensations we experience outside of the game while playing (e.g., the smell of the room we are in, the taste of snacks we might be enjoying, etc.) become inextricably entangled with the playing experience, triggering memories long after the event has happened. For example, the smell of my maternal grandmother's basement, the feeling of the thinly carpeted concrete floor under my feet, and the consistently cold temperature of the room all bring back memories of past gaming experiences whenever I return to that particular room.

3. Ultimately all videogames are PvE, PvP, or a combination of both, not just multiplayer ones. For example, I mentioned *Super Mario Bros.*, which is essentially entirely PvE, and *Street Fighter*, which can be PvE but is really meant for PvP play. Games like the *Demon's Souls/Dark Souls* series are generally meant for solo play but feature both PvE and PvP.

4. Cook et al. (2018, p. 3329) provide a handy chart explaining the various types of trolling and other forms of toxic in-game behavior.

5. There are games that feature a disembodied player-character. These games usually place the player in the role of some powerful hierarchical figure (e.g., general, king, etc.), but even in this seemingly disembodied role, the player is embodying an in-game character. The only difference is that we cannot see them.

6. For simplicity's sake I am ignoring the possibility that people might be using certain technological aids to assist with their sight or hearing (e.g., eyeglasses, hearing aids, etc.), though I doubt most people would believe those tools to be on the same level as the technological barriers found with videogames.

7. One possible argument against this claim is that the blind man does not feel through the stick but instead feels what is happening to the stick (e.g., it is bouncing along flat ground, now it has hit what can be assumed is a curb, now it is back to bouncing along flat ground). There is no sensation in the stick, only in the man's hands, and therefore, the idea that it is an extension of the body is flawed. The same could then be said for the instruments we use to play videogames. I counter this by asking, what if the blind man had nerve damage in both of his arms that meant his hands had no physical sensation? If his hands could not feel the difference between touching a granite countertop or a glass table, would we then claim that his hands are no longer a part of his lived body? Doubtful. The walking stick is less of an abstract tool and more of a nonfeeling extension of the man's arm. Capable of feeling sensations or not, it is a part of his body.

REFERENCES

Ang, R. P., & Goh, D. H. (2010, March). Cyberbullying among adolescents: The role of affective and cognitive empathy, and gender. *Child Psychiatry & Human Development*, 41(4), 387–97.

Beckman, L., Hagquist, C., & Hellström. (2014). Discrepant gender patterns for cyberbullying and traditional bullying—An analysis of Swedish adolescent data. *Computers in Human Behavior*, 29, 1896–903.

Belman, J., & Flanagan, M. (2010). Designing games to foster empathy. *Cognitive Technology*, 14(2) & 15(1), 11–21.

Cook, C., Schaafsma, J., & Antheunis, M. (2018). Under the bridge: An in-depth examination of online trolling in the gaming context. *New Media & Society*, 20(9), 3323–40.

Field Level Media. (2020). Report: Gaming revenue to top $159B in 2020. https://www.reuters.com/article/esports-business-gaming-revenues/report-gaming-revenue-to-top-159b-in-2020-idUSFLM8jkJMl

Fink, E. (2016). Play as symbol of the world (I. Alexander & C. Turner, Trans.). Indiana University Press.

Fuchs, T. (2016). Intercorporeality and interaffectivity. *Phenomenology and Mind*, 11, 194–209.

Lapidot-Lefler, N., & Barak, A. (2012). Effects of anonymity, invisibility, and lack of eye-contact on toxic online disinhibition. *Computers in Human Behavior*, 28(2), 434–43.

McCrea, J. J. (n.d.). Scientific vs. phenomenological reality. *Truth in Philosophy*. https://sites.google.com/site/truthinphilosophy/scientific-vs-phenomenological-reality

Patchin, J. W., & Hinduja, S. (2010). Cyberbullying and self-esteem. *The Journal of School Health*, 80(12), 614–21.

Schutz, A. (1967). The phenomenology of the social world (G. Hopkins & F. Lehnert, Trans.). Northwestern University Press.

Wachs, S., Wright, M. F., & Vazsonyi, A. T. (2019). Understanding the overlap between cyberbullying and cyberhate perpetration: Moderating effects of toxic online disinhibition. *Criminal Behaviour and Mental Health*, 29(3), 179–88.

Zahavi, D. (2014). Empathy and other-directed intentionality. *An International Review of Philosophy*, 33(1), 129–42.

Games Referenced

[If part of a series the citation given here is for the first game released. If referencing a specific game in the series, then the year for that release is used.]

Blizzard Entertainment. (2015). *Heroes of the Storm* (PC Version) [Videogame]. Irvine, CA: Blizzard Entertainment.

Capcom. (1987). *Street Fighter* series (Arcade) [Videogame]. Osaka: Capcom.

Capcom. (1996). *Resident Evil* series (PlayStation) [Videogame]. Osaka: Capcom.

FromSoftware. (2009). *Demon's Soul* series (PlayStation 3) [Videogame]. Tokyo: Sony Computer Entertainment/Irvine, CA: Atlus USA.

King. (2012). *Candy Crush* (Apple iOS/Android) [Videogame]. Malta: King.

Midway. (1992). *Mortal Kombat* series (Arcade) [Videogame]. Chicago: Midway.

Mojang. (2011). *Minecraft* (PC Version) [Videogame]. Stockholm: Mojang.

Namco. (1980). *Pac-Man* (Arcade) [Videogame]. Tokyo: Namco/Chicago: Midway.

Naughty Dog. (1996). *Crash Bandicoot* (PlayStation) [Videogame]. Tokyo: Sony Computer Entertainment.

Nintendo EAD. (1985). *Super Mario Bros.* (Famicom/Nintendo Entertainment System) [Videogame]. Kyoto: Nintendo.

Pajitnov, A. & Pokhilko, V. (1984). *Tetris* (Electronika 60/Nintendo Game Boy) [Videogame]. Multiple publishers.
Riot Games. (2009). *League of Legends* (PC Version) [Videogame]. Los Angeles: Riot Games.
Sonic Team. (1991). *Sonic the Hedgehog* (Sega Genesis) [Videogame]. Tokyo: Sega.
Treyarch. (2008). *Call of Duty: World at War* (PC Version) [Videogame]. Santa Monica, CA: Activision.
Ubisoft Montreal. (2015). *Tom Clancy's Rainbow Six Siege* (PC Version) [Videogame]. Montreuil, France: Ubisoft.
Yager Development. (2012). *Spec Ops: The Line* (PC Version) [Videogame]. Novato, CA: 2K Games.

Chapter 22

Empathy, Alterity, Morality

Dan Zahavi

ABSTRACT

On a widespread and common understanding, empathy is a force of good. It allows us to experience the world of others and is of crucial importance if we are to combat selfishness and indifference. The proposal that empathy might be the solution to many current social problems has not surprisingly triggered a sceptical pushback. In a number of publications, the Yale psychologist Bloom has spoken out "against empathy" and argued that empathy is one of the leading motivators of inequality and immorality in society, and that the attempt to restrain our empathy, might consequently be the most compassionate choice we can make. For Bloom, empathy is primarily defined as a form of affective sharing. To empathize with someone is to come to feel what the other is feeling.

The aim of the following chapter is to offer an alternative account of empathy, namely one rooted in the work of the early phenomenologists. The question eventually to be addressed is whether empathy on this alternative reading is similarly devoid of moral significance.

Keywords: empathy, ethics, Husserl, Stein, Scheler

INTRODUCTION

On a widespread and common understanding, empathy is a force of good. It allows us to experience the world of others and is of crucial importance if we are to combat selfishness and indifference. In his commencement address to the 2006 class of Northwestern graduates, Barack Obama urged them to cultivate empathy and insisted that the empathy deficit in the United States might be a more pressing problem than the federal deficit (Obama 2006). In a book published a few years later titled *The Empathic Civilization: The Race to Global Consciousness in a World in Crisis,* the social theorist Jeremy Rifkin went even further. He called for a new "age of empathy" and argued that we ought to expand our empathic consciousness and allow empathy to flourish on a global scale if we are to revitalize the biosphere (2009: 153, 593).

AGAINST EMPATHY

The prevalence of such high-profile endorsements of empathy along with the proposal that it might be the solution to many current social problems has not surprisingly triggered a skeptical pushback. In an article from 2015, the two Danish anthropologists Bubandt and Willerslev insisted that empathy is not always a moral virtue (Bubandt and Willerslev 2015: 6). They claimed that existing literature on empathy has failed to realize to what extent empathy—understood as a first-person imaginative projection of oneself into the perspective of another (2015: 5)—is also active in deception. Our ability to imagine how others see and experience the world is not simply at work in efforts to promote mutual understanding, compassion, and social cohesion but can also be used for deceptive, manipulative, and violent purposes. Indeed, empathy has a dark side to it and can be used for nefarious purposes, which according to Bubandt and Willerslev is something that has been "almost entirely overlooked" by existing accounts (2015: 6).

An even more critical assessment of empathy can be found in the work of Paul Bloom. In a short target article from 2014 and in a full-length book from 2016, Bloom has spoken out "against empathy" and argued that empathy is one of the leading motivators of inequality and immorality in society and that the attempt to restrain our empathy, might consequently be the most compassionate choice we can make. Bloom presents two different arguments in favor of this conclusion. He first points to research suggesting that empathy is biased. We tend to empathize with those whose needs are salient and who are close by and similar to ourselves. Furthermore, empathy concerns our relation to specific individuals. But if we want to make the world a better place and promote policies affecting larger groups of people, we should put empathy aside and instead promote a form of rational compassion because a keen sense of justice and moral obligation is far more relevant. In addition, Bloom also argues that empathy is overrated when it comes to its role in close interpersonal relationship. For Bloom, to empathize with another person in pain or distress is to feel what the other person is feeling. But if the empathizer suffers as a result of empathizing with your suffering, this will not be to your own advantage. If you seek medical or psychological help, you would like the physician or psychotherapist to be calm and confident, rather than to be overwhelmed by negative emotions (Bloom 2014: 16). After all, in the latter case, the empathizer might end up being more concerned with alleviating his or her own distress than with caring for you.

When comparing Bubandt and Willerslev's criticism with the one coming from Bloom it is noticeable that they all operate with conflicting definitions of empathy. For Bloom, empathy is primarily defined as a form of affective sharing. To empathize with someone is to come to feel what the other is feeling. It involves what is often called "matching" or "isomorphic" states in empathizer and target. For Bubandt and Willerslev, by contrast, empathy is primarily (but not exclusively) defined as imaginative perspective-taking (for a more extensive analysis, see Throop & Zahavi 2020). In the current literature on empathy, there has been a proliferation of distinctions, and it is, for instance, possible to encounter discussions of mirror empathy, motor empathy, affective empathy, reenactive empathy, and cognitive empathy. The most basic distinction, however, is the one between affective empathy and cognitive empathy, and to a large extent, it is precisely that distinction we find exemplified in the brief comparison of Bubandt and Willerslev with Bloom. If this is correct, and if Bubandt and Willerslev are indeed primarily addressing cognitive empathy in their critical article, one might raise doubts about the originality of their claim. The notion of cognitive empathy is often used interchangeably with notions such as perspective-taking or mindreading, but nobody would presumably dispute that mindreading can be used for manipulative purposes. More importantly, however, given how Bloom and Bubandt and Willerslev define empathy, one cannot really fault them for questioning the alleged link between empathy and morality.

PHENOMENOLOGY OF EMPATHY

My aim in what follows is to offer an alternative account of empathy, namely one rooted in the work of the early phenomenologists. The question I will eventually address is whether empathy on this alternative reading is similarly devoid of any moral significance. Is its link to morality equally tenuous?

To understand what the early phenomenologists (Husserl, Stein, Scheler) had to say on empathy, we need to start with the work of Theodor Lipps. In a number of publications from the first decade of the twentieth century, Lipps had defended the idea that *Einfühlung* (a notion originally coined in the field of aesthetics) was of relevance for social cognition, and it was Lipps's notion that the U.S. psychologist, Edward B. Titchener, subsequently rendered as empathy in his 1909 *Lectures on the Experimental Psychology of Thought-Processes*. According to Lipps, we can distinguish three different domains of knowledge and three different sources of knowledge: Perception enables knowledge of external objects, introspection enables knowledge of one's own mind, and finally there is empathy, which affords knowledge of other minds. Lipps consequently did not simply consider empathy a modality of knowledge *sui generis*, he also presented it as an epistemic notion, one that did not have any specific prosocial or moral connotations (Lipps 1907: 697–98, 710, 1909: 222).

Whereas the phenomenologists would be quite sympathetic to these latter claims, they had many issues with other aspects of Lipps's theory, in particular his idea that I can only understand those of the other's experiences that I have had myself, that I cannot recognize anything in the other, unless I put it there myself, and that empathy consequently relies heavily on projection. This reliance on projection is clearly articulated in the following quote from Lipps' book *Die ethischen Grundfragen* from 1905:

> The other psychological individual is consequently made by myself out of myself. His inner being is taken from mine. The other individual or ego is the product of a projection, a reflection, a radiation of myself—or of what I experience in myself, through the sense perception of an outside physical phenomenon—into this very sensory phenomenon, a peculiar kind of reduplication of myself. (Lipps 1905: 17)

If we now look at Husserl's *Zur Phänomenologie der Intersubjektivität I (1905–1920*) and *Ideen II* (*c. 1912–1928*), at Scheler's *Wesen und Formen der Sympathie (1913/1923)* and at Stein's *Zum Problem der Einfühlung (1917)*, we will find three different accounts of empathy, but three accounts that share so many central features that I think it is warranted to talk of a phenomenological account of empathy.[1] As Ingarden was later to observe, when he was working on his dissertation, which was submitted in 1918,

> extensive discussions took place regarding so-called "empathy," a notion that had been proposed by the psychologizing German aestheticians such as, for instance, Theodor Lipps. A number of phenomenologists such as M. Geiger, Max Scheler, Edith Stein and later also Husserl participated in this discussion and it became increasingly clear that the classical theory of "empathy" which considered it a kind of projection of one's own psychical states into foreign bodies had to be abandoned and replaced by a theory of a special kind of perception of the psychical states as they are manifest in bodily expression. (Ingarden 1994: 170–71)

Scheler, Stein, and Husserl all rejected Lipps's reference to projection, they all saw empathy as a form of *Ausdrucksverstehen*, as an experiential encounter with and disclosure of the other's embodied and embedded experiences, and for all three, empathy amounted to a basic form of other-understanding.

In her dissertation, Stein makes it clear that she considers empathy the name for a sui generis form of intentionality directed at other experiencing subjects. It is the basic cognitive source for our comprehension of foreign subjects and their experiences, and it is what more complex kinds of social cognition rely on and presuppose (1989: 6, 60).

Scheler frequently uses the term *Fremdwahrnehmung* (other-perception) and titled his own theory "a perceptual theory of other minds" (2008: 220). As he writes in a by now classical passage,

> we certainly believe ourselves to be directly acquainted with another person's joy in his laughter, with his sorrow and pain in his tears, with his shame in his blushing, with his entreaty in his outstretched hands, with his love in his look of affection, with his rage in the gnashing of his teeth, with his threats in the clenching of his fist, and with the tenor of his thoughts in the sound of his words. If anyone tells me that this is not "perception," for it cannot be so, in view of the fact that a perception is simply a "complex of physical sensations," and that there is certainly no sensation of another person's mind nor any stimulus from such a source, I would beg him to turn aside from such questionable theories and address himself to the phenomenological facts (Scheler 2008: 260)

As for Husserl, he claims that the mindedness of the other, his thinking, feeling, desiring, is intuitively present in the gestures, the intonation and in the facial expressions. The expressivity of the other is imbued with psychological meaning from the start, and it is empathy that allows us to understand and grasp this psychological meaning.

> Empathy is not a mediate experience in the sense that the other would be experienced as a psychophysical annex to his corporeal body but is instead an immediate experience of the other (Husserl 1989: 384–85; translation modified).

> It would be countersensical to say that it [foreign subjectivity] is inferred and not experienced when given in this original form of empathic presentation. For every hypothesis concerning a foreign subject already presupposes the 'perception' of this subject as foreign, and empathy is precisely this perception (Husserl 1973: 352).

> Just as something past *as* past can only be given originarily through recollection, and something in the future only through anticipation, *something alien as alien* can only be given originarily through empathy. Originary givenness in this sense and *experience* are identical (Husserl 2019: 376)

The phenomenological approach to empathy quickly found resonance outside the narrow philosophical scene. Consider, for instance, Paul Schilder's 1924 publication *Medizinische Psychologie für Ärzte und Psychologen*. Schilder is, of course, primarily known for his work as a psychiatrist and psychoanalyst. He introduced the notion of body image and is also considered one of the founding fathers of group psychotherapy. In the introduction to his book, however, he advocates an approach to psychology that combines phenomenology and psychoanalysis and repeatedly refers to the insights of Husserl and Scheler (1924: iii, v). And in the chapter on how we come to understand others, Schilder then offers the following concise presentation:

In Lipps, we find a convincing criticism of the argument from analogy. As an account of how we come to understand others, it is fallacious. Lipps then introduced empathy as an alternative explanation, but for him, empathy is primarily about projection. Not only do I project myself into the other, but I also place my feelings, desires etc. in the other. As Schilder then remarks, it is not really clear how this would allow us to grasp foreign experiences. It also does not seem to be true to experience. When I see somebody who is angry, that does not have anything to do with my own anger because I don't have to be angry as well. Even in a case, where, say, my friend is angry because something unjust has happened to him, and I become angry as well, my own anger will stand next to my perception of his anger, and will not have any essential relation to it. For Schilder, Lipps's notion of empathy consequently does not at all lead us out of our own subjectivity. Rather if everything were derived from ourselves, we would be caught in a hopeless game of mirrors, where we would only encounter ourselves. As Schilder then writes, just as we cannot reduce perception to sensation, we cannot reduce the perception of other subjects to a mere aggregation of our own experiences. Rather we ought to recognize that there is an immediate perception of foreign experiences, of foreign subjectivity, and that this type of other-perception (*Fremdwahrnehmung*) cannot be analyzed further but must be considered irreducible. What might serve as examples of this other-perception? We can grasp the other intuitively, when confronted with the expressivity of the other, her posture, tonality, mimicry and gesticulations (Schilder 1924: 276–79).

Let me try to make the main idea in the phenomenological proposal clearer by highlighting in turn its positive and negative claim.

Compare the following two situations:

- You enter your son's room, discover that he has smashed all his carefully constructed Lego sets and infer that he is upset about something.
- You are talking with your son, and suddenly he breaks down. You see and hear his anguish and distress in his countenance and voice.

Scheler, Stein, and Husserl would all insist that you in the empathic face-to-face encounter can obtain an acquaintance with the other's experiential life that has a directness and immediacy to it that is not possessed by whatever beliefs you might have about the other in his or her absence. To put it differently, empathy affords you with the here and now presence of an experience that is not your own.[2] Importantly, for the phenomenologists, empathy isn't restricted to affective states but concerns our general ability to access the life of the mind of others in their expressions, expressive behavior and meaningful actions.

What then about the negative part. First of all, the phenomenologists insist on the difference between empathy and imaginative perspective-taking. We are here dealing with two different phenomena, which can occur independently of each other. I can, for instance, try to imagine what it must have been like for Caesar to cross the Rubicon, but as valuable as this might be, it will not give me the kind of experiential understanding that empathy provides. Likewise, recognizing the sorrow in the face of my friend, does not require me to engage in any imaginative exercise. As Stein puts it, when I empathically grasp another's anger, the anger is not felt as my own anger nor as a remembered anger, let alone simply as an imagined anger. No, it is throughout given to me as the other's anger, as an anger lived through by the other (Stein 1989: 10–11).

Secondly, although it is a common view that empathy is a form of affective sharing (Darwall 1998; Decety & Lamm 2006), the phenomenologists would disagree. Most defenders of the affective sharing thesis never define what they actually mean by sharing—are we supposed to share affects in the same way we share (1) attention, (2) a bottle of wine, or (3) a toothbrush—and often all they mean by claiming that the empathizer come to feel what the other person is feeling is that the empathizer and target come to be in similar or isomorphic affective states—which strictly speaking doesn't amount to sharing at all. This is incidentally also why Scheler is quite explicit about the difference between empathy and emotional sharing (*Miteinanderfühlen*) (Scheler 2008: 8). But what then about the claim that the empathizer is in the same state as the target? Well, that claim is precisely being questioned by the phenomenologists. Consider the following three examples: You might empathically grasp your colleague's joy when he receives notice of his promotion even though you are personally angered by this piece of news. You might recognize the fury in the face of your assailant, even though you yourself are fearful rather than furious. You might empathically grasp that your friend loves his wife, without you loving her as well.

Whereas empathy in contemporary discussions has often been defined either as a matter of affective sharing (to empathize with someone is to come to feel what the other is feeling) or as a question of imaginative perspective-taking (to empathize with someone is to imagine what it would be like for the other to be in his or her shoes), the phenomenological account of empathy is quite different.

Empathy must be clearly distinguished from emotional contagion, emotional sharing, and imaginative perspective-taking. Empathy is not about me having the same mental state as the other but about me being experientially acquainted with an experience that is not my own. Empathy must consequently be appreciated as a particular experiential engagement with the other. It is not about creating similarity, let alone fusion, but about preserving difference. Indeed, empathy recognizes and preserves the difference between self and other, which is also why Husserl can write that consciousness in empathy transcends itself and is confronted with otherness of a completely new kind (Husserl 1973: 8–9, 442).

THE MORAL SIGNIFICANCE OF EMPATHY

Given the just outlined understanding of empathy, what should one then conclude vis-à-vis its moral significance? Are there reasons to question the verdict made by Bloom and Bubandt and Willerslev? One thing that ought to be immediately clear is that the classical conception of empathy that we find in the work of the phenomenologists differs markedly from the conception criticized by the three authors. None of the phenomenologists would argue that empathy is intrinsically prosocial, let alone sufficient for morality. Contrary to Bubandt and Willerslev's claim that the dark side of empathy has been overlooked, already Scheler (2008: 8, 14) insisted that cruelty presupposes empathy, and that the latter is consequently no hindrance for the former. However, it does not follow from the fact that empathy is not sufficient for morality, that it has no significant role to play. Deprived of empathy, we would lack a basic experiential grasp of others as co-subjects, and this would impede our ability to properly identify targets of moral action. This more modest position is not new. In an insightful article titled "Respect as a moral emotion: A phenomenological approach," Drummond (2006) made the same claim. It is basic empathy that allows us to experience the other as other, as an irreducible conscious agent, and thereby it is also that which opens the "moral space" in which respect is located (2006: 17, 20). Moreover, it is through empathy that I can experience the other as having "morally significant emotions, needs, or wants" which in turn can motivate me to prosocial action (2006: 16).

Let me expand a bit on this point, by returning to a clinical context that Bloom also used to demonstrate what he took to be the deleterious consequences of empathy. Social understanding comes in many different forms.

Let us assume that a patient has been paralyzed as a result of a traffic accident, and that healthcare practitioners (be it a physician, a nurse, or a psychotherapist) are confronted with the question of how the patient is feeling about his new life situation. How might the practitioners seek an answer? They might draw on theoretical knowledge. Being deprived of your mobility is likely to limit your ability to satisfy your wants and desires and will also force you to reassess your life goals, all of which is likely to decrease your quality of life and make you distressed if not depressed. Another possibility of course is to try to put oneself in the other's position. By imagining what it would be like for me to be paralyzed, I might come to appreciate what it must be like for you. But to seek to understand the other on the basis of prior theoretical knowledge or by imaginative perspective-taking risks violating or doing away with the other's perspective altogether. Imaginative perspective-taking, in particular, risks being nothing but an imposition of one's own view upon the other, might in the end be nothing but an attempt to constitute the other through projection and fantasy. This danger is well illustrated by what has become known as the *disability paradox* (Albrecht & Devlieger 1999). Although external observers often judge individuals with serious and persistent disabilities to live an undesirable or even miserable life, when asked themselves those individuals often report that they experience a good or excellent quality of life. Against this background, the clinical relevance of empathy, or what might be termed *empathic openness*, should be obvious. As a form of encounter that preserves and respects the other's otherness, empathy lets me approach the other with the requisite attitude of humility; there is still much that I do not understand. As Elizabeth Spelman puts in,

> While I am perceiving someone, I must be prepared to receive new information all the time, to adapt my actions accordingly, and to have my feelings develop in response to what the person is doing, whether I like what she is doing or not. When simply imagining her, I can escape from the demands her reality puts on me and instead construct her in my mind in such a way that I can possess her, make her into someone or something who never talks back (1988: 181).

Even though empathy does not in and of itself amount to or result in pro-social action, it might still serve an important preparatory role. What we shouldn't forget, however, is that the experience of the other as other by the same token also allows for immorality and abuse. To repeat Scheler's point, cruelty presupposes empathy. If one were insensitive to other people's suffering, as, say, might be the case in severe forms of autism; if one as a result of pathology were incapable of discriminating human beings from pieces of furniture or logs of wood (Bosch 1962/1970: 5) and treated them accordingly, one could hardly be accused of being cruel or brutal vis-à-vis them (Scheler 2008: 14).

So far, the moral significance of empathy remains somewhat ambiguous. We will reach a similar result if we consider a different line of argument that can also be found in the phenomenological literature. As mentioned earlier, it has become customary to distinguish different types of empathy. One distinction I have not touched on yet, is the one between unidirectional and bidirectional (or reciprocal) empathy. Whereas I in the former case is directed at the other as a minded experiencing subject, the unidirectional form of empathy remains third-personal. I am targeting the other as a he or a she. Bidirectional empathy, by contrast, is second-personal—at least in the typical case.[3] I am addressing the other as a you, that is, as somebody who is also addressing me. It so happens that Husserl in his work on community, very much emphasized the role played by reciprocal empathy for communication, dialogue, mutual understanding, and group identification, in short for the constitution of a common social world (1989: 202–5, see also Zahavi 2015, 2018, 2019). If this reasoning holds true, reciprocal empathy might be seen as a necessary precondition for the constitution of a community with all the normative entailments it brings along. But again, being part of a community is not simply a matter of living in harmony and friendship, it also allows for new forms of oppression, violence, ostracism etc.

Whereas empathy is clearly not sufficient for morality, it is also not irrelevant for morality. Without empathy, our moral life would look quite different.

CONCLUSION

Let me briefly return to Bloom's and Bubandt and Willerslev's criticism of empathy. As should be clear by now, I think their criticism lacks both novelty and pertinence. Not only do I think that they all mischaracterize empathy, but their main claim, that empathy is not sufficient for morality, has also been made many times before. In their discussion of empathy, they all three latch unto fairly widespread conceptions of empathy, and my intention is not to prohibit their divergent uses of the term, but at the very least, one might have expected their discussion of empathy to have been better informed about classical work on the topic.[4]

NOTES

1. It so happens that Scheler rarely uses the term *Einfühlung* himself, but prefers to speak of *Nachfühlen*. Does this amount to more than a different terminological choice (and a reluctance to use a term that Lipps had defined in a particular way)? Schloßberger has recently argued that Nachfühlen (which he translates as 'sensing') amounts

to an immediate experience of the (expressive) other as other, and that this is quite different from Einfühlung, which he defines as involving some (unconscious) inferential "putting oneself in another's shoes" (2016: 180–82). I can certainly see why it would be important not to ascribe such a position to Scheler, but I see no reason not to count Scheler as an empathy theorists, since other phenomenologists, in contrast to Lipps, precisely understood empathy very much in the same way as Scheler conceived of Nachfühlen. It is revealing that several of them, Husserl included, referred to Scheler's theory precisely as a theory of empathy (Husserl 1960: 147, Walther 1923: 17). For a more extensive discussion and comparison of Husserl's, Stein's and Scheler theories of interpersonal understanding, see Zahavi 2014.

2. For both Husserl and Stein empathy is both like and unlike perception. Empathy is unlike perception in that it does not give us its object, the empathized experience, originally. There will always, and by necessity, remain a difference in givenness between that which I am aware of when I empathize with the other and that which the other is experiencing. Empathy consequently cannot give us the empathized experience itself in its original presence. However, although empathy differs from perception by not giving us the object originally, it does resemble perception insofar as the empathically grasped experience is given directly and non-inferentially as present here and now (see Zahavi 2014: 125–32 for a more extensive discussion).

3. In a previous article, I distinguished between reciprocal empathy, where *A* and *B* are mutually aware of being attended to by the other, and a proper second-personal I-thou relation that also involves communicative engagement (Zahavi 2019: 254). Strictly speaking, one might envisage a situation of reciprocal empathy where *A* and *B* are merely in perceptual contact, without in any way reacting or responding to each other. But such a situation of say simply staring into each other's eyes is a limit case. Under normally circumstances, reciprocal empathy involves bidirectional responsiveness.

4. Thanks to Sophie Loidolt for helpful comments to an earlier version of this text.

REFERENCES

Albrecht, G. L., & Devlieger, P. J. 1999. The disability paradox: High quality of life against all odds. *Social Science & Medicine* 48: 977–88.

Bosch, G. 1962/1970. *Infantile Autism: A Clinical and Phenomenological-Anthropological Approach Taking Language as the Guide*. New York: Springer-Verlag.

Bloom, P. 2014. Against empathy. *Boston Review* 39(5): 14–19.

Bubandt, N., & Willerslev, R. 2015. The dark side of empathy: mimesis, deception, and the magic of alterity. *Comparative Studies in Society and History* 57(1): 5–34.

Darwall, S. 1998. Empathy, Sympathy, Care. *Philosophical Studies* 89(2–3): 261–82.

Decety, J., & Lamm, C. 2006. Human empathy through the lens of social neuroscience. *The Scientific World Journal* 6, 1146–63.

Drummond, J. J. 2006. Respect as a moral emotion: A phenomenological approach. *Husserl Studies* 22, 1–27.

Husserl, E. 1960. *Cartesian Meditations: An Introduction to Phenomenology*, trans. by D. Cairns. The Hague: Martinus Nijhoff.
———. 1973. *Zur phänomenologie der intersubjektivität II. Texte aus dem Nachlass. Zweiter Teil. 1921–28*, Husserliana 14, ed. by I. Kern. The Hague: Martinus Nijhoff.
———. 1989. *Ideas Pertaining to a Pure Phenomenology and to A Phenomenological Philosophy. Book 2: Studies in the Phenomenology of Constitution*, trans. by R. Rojcewicz and A. Schuwer. Dordrecht: Kluwer.
———. 2019. *First Philosophy: Lectures 1923/24 and Related Texts from the Manuscripts (1920–1925),* trans. by S. Luft & T. M. Naberhaus. Collected Works 14. Dordrecht: Springer.
Ingarden, R. 1994. *Frühe Schriften zur Erkenntnistheorie.* Tübingen: Max Niemeyer.
Lipps, T. 1905. *Die ethischen Grundfragen*. Hamburg: Voss.
———. 1907. Das Wissen von fremden Ichen. In T. Lipps, ed., *Psychologische Untersuchungen I*, 694–722. Leipzig: Engelmann.
———. 1909. *Leitfaden der psychologie*. Leipzig: Verlag von Wilhelm Engelmann.
Obama, B. 2006. Obama to Graduates: Cultivate Empathy [Online]. Available at https://www.northwestern.edu/newscenter/stories/2006/06/barack.html (accessed: 21 June 2020).
Rifkin, J. 2009. *The Empathic Civilization: The Race to Global Consciousness in a World of Crisis*. Cambridge: Polity.
Scheler, M. 2008. *The Nature of Sympathy*, trans. by P. Heath. London: Transaction.
Schilder, P. 1924. *Medizinische Psychologie für Ärzte und Psychologen.* Berlin: Verlag von Julius Springer.
Schloßberger, M. 2016. The varieties of togetherness: Scheler on collective affective intentionality. In A. Salice and H. B. Schmid, eds., *The Phenomenological Approach to Social Reality,* 173–95. Dordrecht: Springer.
Spelman, E. 1988. *Inessential woman*. Boston: Beacon Press.
Stein, E. 1989. *On the Problem of Empathy*, trans. W. Stein. Washington, DC: ICS.
Throop, C. J., & Zahavi, D. 2020. Dark and bright empathy: Phenomenological and anthropological reflections. Current Anthropology 61(3), 283–303.
Titchener, E. B. 1909. *Lectures on the Experimental Psychology of Thought-Processes*. New York: Macmillan
Walther, G. 1923. Zur Ontologie der sozialen Gemeinschaften. In E. Husserl ed., *Jahrbuch für Philosophie und phänomenologische Forschung* VI, 1–158. Halle: Max Niemeyer.
Zahavi, D. 2014. *Self and Other: Exploring Subjectivity, Empathy, and Shame*. Oxford: Oxford University Press.
———. 2015. You, me, and we: The sharing of emotional experiences. Journal of Consciousness Studies 22(12), 84–101.
———. 2018. Intersubjectivity, sociality, community: The contributions of the early phenomenologists. In D. Zahavi (ed.), *The Oxford Handbook of the History of Phenomenology*, 734–52. Oxford: Oxford University Press.
———. 2019. Second-person engagement, self-alienation, and group-identification. *Topoi* 38(1), 251–60.

Index

About the Editors and Contributors

ABOUT THE EDITORS

Magnus Englander is associate professor at Malmö University and associate editor for the *Journal of Phenomenological Psychology*. His phenomenological research is situated within the interdisciplinary research context of health and society, with an interest in topics such as psychopathology, empathy, and qualitative research methodology. He is the author of multiple articles on phenomenological psychology and the editor of *Phenomenology and the Social Context of Psychiatry* (Bloomsbury 2018).

Susi Ferrarello is assistant professor at California State University, East Bay. Among her books are *Husserl's Ethics and Practical Intentionality* (Bloomsbury 2015), *The Phenomenology of Sex, Love and Intimacy* (Routledge 2018), *Human Emotions and the Origin of Bioethics* (Routledge 2021), and *The Ethics of Love* (Routledge 2022). She writes for *Psychology Today* and works also as a philosophical counselor.

ABOUT THE CONTRIBUTORS

Michael Agostinelli Jr. graduated from California State University, East Bay with bachelor's degrees in philosophy and European history and a master's degree in philosophy from San Jose State University. His work in philosophy focuses primarily on applied ethics, specifically the implementation of ethical theory in the world of modern technology and the interactions that occur within.

Elodie Boublil is associate professor of philosophy at the University of Paris XII (France). Her areas of expertise include phenomenology, philosophy of health, clinical ethics and philosophical anthropology. Among her publications are *Vulnérabilité et Empathie: Approches Phénoménologiques* (Ed.) (Paris: Hermann, 2018); *Individuation et Vision du Monde* (Bucharest: Zeta, 2014); and *Nietzsche & Phenomenology: Power, Life and Subjectivity* (Bloomington: Indian University Press, 2013).

Francesca Brencio is associate researcher in philosophy at the University of Seville (Spain). She is also convener and instructor of the Pheno-Lab, A Theoretical Laboratory on Philosophy and Mental Health. Her research is in the areas of phenomenology, hermeneutics, and philosophy of psychiatry. She ahs published in many international journals of philosophy and psychiatry; most recently she was the editor of the volume *Phenomenology, Neuroscience and Clinical Practice. Transdisciplinary Experiences* (Springer, forthcoming).

Manuel Camassa (PhD) has studied philosophy and history at the University of Pisa in Italy and at the University of Lucerne in Switzerland. His four-year doctoral project was financed by the Swiss National Science Foundation (SNSF) and focuses on the moral role of empathy. Having achieved his PhD, he now works as a philosophy teacher in Lugano and continues his research. He deals especially with questions of ethics, phenomenology, and philosophy of emotions.

Scott D. Churchill is professor of psychology at the University of Dallas and editor of *The Humanistic Psychologist*; he has also served as president of the Society for Humanistic Psychology and the Society for Theoretical and Philosophical Psychology. His academic interests include phenomenological and hermeneutic methodologies, empathy studies, ecopsychology, and cinema studies. He has published more than eighty articles and chapters, and his book *Essentials of Existential Phenomenological Research* was published by the American Psychological Association in 2022.

Craig Derksen is associate professor of philosophy at California State University East Bay. He works primarily in epistemology, philosophy of science, and aesthetics. Much of his work revolves around integrating everyday experiences and popular culture with philosophical and empirical investigations. Among other topics, he has published on fear and zombies, ownership and audiences, fieldwork and teaching philosophy, cultural kinds and voices, and performances and technology.

Nicolas de Warren is professor of philosophy and Jewish studies at Penn State University. He is the author of *Husserl and the Promise of Time* (2010), *A Momentary Breathlessness in the Sadness of Time* (2018), *Original Forgiveness* (2020), and *German Philosophy and the First World War* (2023). He is currently writing a book on stupidity and cowriting a book on the philosophical implications of nuclear waste. .

John J. Drummond is the Robert Southwell, S. J. Distinguished Professor of Philosophy and the Humanities at Fordham University. He is the author of *Husserlian Intentionality and Non-Foundational Realism* (Kluwer) and *A Historical Dictionary of Husserl's Philosophy* (2nd ed., Rowman & Littlefield). He has edited or coedited seven collections of articles on phenomenology, including the recently published *Emotional Experiences: Ethical and Social Significance* (Rowman & Littlefield International), and more than one hundred articles.

Jannik M. Hansen is PhD from the Center for Phenomenological Psychology and Aesthetics situated at the department of psychology, University of Copenhagen. Jannik´s research centers on empathy, affect, and aesthetic experience. His research aims to clarify the constitutive role of empathy in aesthetic experience with visual art and to do so by establishing a dialogue between qualitative data and phenomenological analysis.

Simon Høffding is associate professor at the department of sports science and biomechanics at the University of Southern Denmark. He investigates all kinds of musical and artistic experiences from across qualitative and quantitative perspectives, always anchored in phenomenology, which guides his thinking on "phenomenological interviews" and "phenomenological mixed methods." He has authored papers in phenomenology, philosophy of mind, cognitive science, and music psychology as well as the monograph *A Phenomenology of Musical Absorption* (Palgrave 2019).

Joel Krueger is associate professor of philosophy at the University of Exeter. He works primarily in phenomenology, philosophy of mind, and philosophy of cognitive science, specifically, issues in embodied, embedded, enacted, extended (4E) cognition, including emotions, social cognition, and psychopathology. Sometimes he also writes about comparative philosophy and philosophy of music.

Carlos Lobo, Centre Gilles-Gaston Granger, Université d'Aix-Marseille. Phenomenologist and epistemologist, he published recently "Some Reasons to Reopen the Question of Foundations of Probability Theory Following the Rota Way," in *The Philosophers and Mathematicians* (Ed. H. Tahiri, Springer, 2018) and coedited *Weyl and the Problem of Space, From Mathematics to Philosophy* (Springer, 2019); *Écrire comme composer, le rôle des diagrammes en musique* (Delatour, 2021); and *When Form Becomes Substance, Diagrams, Power of Gesture and Phenomenology of Space* (Birkhäuser, 2022).

Esteban Marín-Ávila is professor of philosophy at *Un*iversidad Michoacana de San Nicolás de Hidalgo in Morelia, Mexico. He obtained his PhD at Universidad Nacional Autónoma de México and has been Fulbright Visiting Scholar at Penn State and undertaken research stays at Bergische Universität Wuppertal and Universidad Autónoma Metropolitana–Azcapotzalco, among other institutions. The topics of his publications include phenomenology, ethics, axiology, social ontology, violence, social emotions, and human rights.

Alexander Montes is a postdoctoral associate at the University of Rochester Medical Center. He recently completed his PhD in philosophy at Boston College. His research focuses on phenomenological ethics, especially phenomenological personalism, and ethical issues concerning freedom and informed consent in clinical research. His dissertation, "Freedom as Self-Donation: A Hildebrandian Account of the Cooperative Structure of Personal Freedom," focuses on Hildebrand's engagement with Kant and early phenomenology and argues, with Hildebrand, that freedom is inherently enhanced by freely willing what is morally good and lessened by willing what is morally wrong.

Dermot Moran is the inaugural holder of the Joseph Professorship in Catholic Philosophy at Boston College. He was previously professor of philosophy (metaphysics and logic) at University College Dublin. He is a member of the Royal Irish Academy and Institut International de Philosophie. Publications include *Introduction to Phenomenology* (2000), *Edmund Husserl: Founder of Phenomenology* (2005), and *Husserl's Crisis of the European Sciences and Transcendental Phenomenology* (2012), and he coauthored with Joseph Cohen *Husserl Dictionary* (2012). He is currently past president of the Fédération International des Sociétés de Philosophie (FISP).

Henning Nörenberg is postdoctoral researcher at the Department of Philosophy in Rostock, Germany. He has published on various topics in phenomenology, social ontology, political philosophy, and philosophy of religion. His current work focuses on shared normative background orientations and their affective dimension ("deontological feelings"). He is author of *Der Absolutismus des Anderen* (Alber 2014).

Tone Roald is an associate professor at the department of Psychology and the director of the Center for Phenomenological Psychology and Aesthetics at the University of Copenhagen. Her research interests center on aesthetics and phenomenological psychology, with the goal of clarifying how art creates meaning for us. Her most important publications include the *Subject of Aesthetics* (Brill, 2015), Why do we always generalize in qualitative methods? (Roald et al., *Qualitative Psychology*, 2021), *Art and Identity* (Roald and Lang, eds., Rodopi, 2013), and Sense and subjectivity (Roald and Køppe, 2015, *Journal of Theoretical and Philosophical Psychology*).

Eva Schwarz is a philosopher associate professor at the Center for Studies in Practical Knowledge at Södertörn University in Stockholm, Sweden. She is mainly working within the fields of phenomenology, subject theory, and social ontology. Her current research is concerned with collective action and judgment and the relation between ethics and epistemology in welfare professions.

Andrea Staiti is professor at the University of Parma and visiting professor at Boston College. Among his publications is *Husserl's Transcendental Phenomenology: Nature, Spirit, and Life* (Cambridge University Press, 2014).

Joona Taipale is a senior lecturer at the University of Jyväskylä. His areas of expertise include phenomenology, philosophy of psychology, and psychoanalysis. Most recently, his work has focused on human interaction and its early development. Taipale's international publications include *Phenomenology and Embodiment* (Northwestern, 2014), The Illusion of Contact (*International Journal of Psychoanalysis*, 2021), and Being Carried Away: Fink and Winnicott on the Locus of Playing (*Journal of Phenomenological Psychology*, 2021).

Íngrid Vendrell Ferran is professor of philosophy at the University of Marburg, Germany. Her research is in the areas of philosophy of mind (in particular, philosophy of emotion), epistemology, and aesthetics. Main book publications include *Die Emotionen. Gefühle in der realistischen Phänomenologie* (Akademie, 2008) and *Die Vielfalt der Erkenntnis* (mentis, 2018). Recent publications include "Feeling as Consciousness of Value" (*Ethical Theory and Moral Practice* 2021), "Hate: Towards a Four-Types Model" (*Review of Philosophy and Psychology* 2021), and "Empathy in Appreciation: An Axiological Account" (*Journal of Aesthetics and Art Criticism* 2021).

Stefano Vincini is postdoctoral fellow of the Humboldt Foundation at TU Dortmund, Germany. Formerly, he held postdoctoral positions at the University of Vienna, the National Autonomous University of Mexico, and was teaching affiliate at the University of Parma. He received his PhD in philosophy from the University of Memphis in 2016 under the supervision of Shaun Gallagher. He specializes in phenomenology, cognitive science, and the foundations of social ontology.

Maren Wehrle is assistant professor at Erasmus School of Philosophy, Erasmus University Rotterdam, The Netherlands. Her areas of expertise are phenomenology, feminist philosophy, and cognitive sciences. She published a monograph on the horizons of attention in *Philosophy and Cognitive Psychology* (Wilhelm Fink 2013), edited two volumes and a handbook in phenomenology, and published more than forty journal articles and book chapters on the topics of embodiment, habit, normality, normativity, and gender.

Dan Zahavi is professor of philosophy and director of the Center for Subjectivity Research at the University of Copenhagen. His most important publications include *Self-awareness and Alterity* (1999 and 2020), *Husserl's Phenomenology* (2003), *Subjectivity and Selfhood* (2005), *The Phenomenological Mind* (together with Shaun Gallagher, 2008, 2012, and 2021), *Self and Other* (2014), *Husserl's Legacy* (2017), and *Phenomenology: The Basics* (2019).